ORGANIZATIONAL
BEHAVIOR

FOURTH EDITION

ORGANIZATIONAL
BEHAVIOR

Dennis W. Organ
Indiana University

Thomas S. Bateman
The University of North Carolina at Chapel Hill

IRWIN
Homewood, IL 60430
Boston, MA 02116

Sponsoring editor: Karen L. Johnson
Developmental editor: Elizabeth J. Rubenstein
Project editor: Jean Lou Hess
Production manager: Bette K. Ittersagen
Interior designer: Tara L. Bazata
Cover designer: Jeanne M. Regan
Artist: Alice Thiede
Compositor: Graphic World Incorporated
Typeface: 10/12 Times Roman
Printer: R. R. Donnelley & Sons Company

Library of Congress Cataloging-in-Publication Data

Organ, Dennis W.
   Organizational behavior / Dennis W. Organ and Thomas S. Bateman.—
   4th ed.
      p.   cm.
   Includes bibliographical references and indexes.
   ISBN 0-256-06667-1
   1. Organizational behavior.   2. Psychology, Industrial.
   I. Bateman, Thomas S.   II. Title.
   HD58.7.0668   1991
   158.7—dc20   90–38348

Printed in the United States of America
2 3 4 5 6 7 8 9 0 DO 7 6 5 4 3 2 1

Preface

In previous editions of this textbook, we omitted what we considered passing fads and simplistic prescriptions for practice. We tried, instead, to make our case for a durable and viable conceptual approach to organizational behavior.

In this edition, our challenge was to maintain that tradition while providing a framework responsive to the needs of a different era—an era of turbulent changes in the business environment and one in which business education is accountable to its varied stakeholders. To this end, we have made the following changes in the fourth edition:

- We have, as before, updated the record to note important developments within organizational behavior and its sister disciplines. For example, one of the interesting developments in OB research and theory in the late 1980s concerned the reconceptualization and reappraisal of the role of individual differences in job satisfaction, job stress, and performance; we have traced the implications of this work for various issues in the workplace.

- We have noted the significant developments of the late 1980s surrounding the work experience. For example, we find an increasing emphasis on experimental approaches to employee compensation as a means by which organizations try to increase commitment and job motivation. We have tried to inform the reader of these approaches and to interpret them from an informed conceptual framework.

- In the previous edition, we used "boxes" to perform numerous functions: to provide specific examples, to work in relevant material from the mass media, to highlight the findings of a particularly interesting study, and sometimes merely to provide a visual break in the text. This time, we determined that the addition of "focus" (we no longer call them *boxes*) material would be more systematic, cumulative, and reinforcing. Thus, in every chapter we have added boxes that "Focus on" Management, International OB, and the Future. We Focus on Management in order to link the theoretical to the practical. We Focus on International OB in order to remind the reader of this ever-increasing dimension of organizations; we hope as well to prompt readers to reflect upon the possibility of American ethnocentrism. And we Focus on the Future—even when ideas may border on the fanciful—to reinforce a sense of the dynamism that now characterizes the work experience.

- We have made two changes in chapter structure that we think most users and readers will welcome. We now approach the motivation question by devoting Chapter 3 to the various motives that relate to work. We follow that with Chapter 4 on two heretofore competing models of "motivation process": the operant model and expectancy theory. Previously the operant model had gone under the heading of "learning," but most instructors really examine it from a motivational point of view. Chapter 5 attempts to show how operant and cognitive concepts have linked up in emergent models of work motivation. Previous users will find that we have thoroughly torn down and rebuilt the structure of this part of the text.

- The third edition had three "macro" chapters on structure, environment, and organization change and development. In rethinking the structure and environment chapters, we concluded that we had obscured some basic interrelationships that cut across those topics. We now have one chapter on organization design that features a more integrated treatment of formal structure, technology, environment, and strategy—all leading up to the concluding chapter on organization change.

We bear a heavy debt of appreciation to those who provided written reviews of the third edition—for calling our attention to anachronisms, redundancies, glaring omissions, excesses; for timely suggestions concerning content, format, and design; for making us aware of important sources of new materials; for telling us what strengths to build on and what faults were correctable. All of these reviews were of the highest level of professional workmanship. We trust that reviewers will see clear evidence of the improvements effected by their counsel. Our thanks go out to R. P. Beaulieu, Connie Briddell Fuller, Mary Ann Hazen, John Humpal, Raymond Hunt,

Glenn McEvoy, Steven McShane, Najmedin Meshkati, Lew Taylor, and Leland Wooten, as well as the many colleagues at Indiana University and the University of North Carolina whose thoughts in one way or another found expression in our writing.

Dennis W. Organ
Thomas S. Bateman

Contents

SECTION TWO
Foundations of Behavior in Organizations

SECTION THREE
The Individual and the Organization
Patterns of Conflict and Accommodation

SECTION FOUR
Groups and Their Leadership

ORGANIZATIONAL BEHAVIOR

Organizational Behavior

Scope and Method

1 Introduction to Organizational Behavior

What is organizational behavior (OB)?

What interest groups are involved in OB?

How did OB evolve?

What has OB accomplished?

What are the future directions of OB?

WHAT IS ORGANIZATIONAL BEHAVIOR?

Organizational behavior (OB) can describe a set of phenomena, an area of study, or a community of interest groups.

As a Set of Phenomena

OB refers to the behavior of individuals and groups in an organizational environment. In organizations, people perform their duties, pursue their interests, indulge in gossip and horseplay, make decisions, argue, and commit dastardly and heroic deeds. When these behaviors have organizational relevance—either because they affect organizational functioning or because they are shaped by organizational forces—they can be included in those phenomena labeled OB.

It is difficult to draw the line between what is organizational behavior and what is behavior but not organizational. Are family conflicts organizational behavior? Do social outings or a person's after-work exercise program qualify as OB?

Instead of providing arbitrary answers to these questions, we offer the following general rule: Behavior is organizational in character to the extent that *(1)* the organization, or some aspect of the organization, is the occasion that evokes the behavior, or *(2)* other members of the organization attribute organizational meaning or relevance to the behavior.

Most of us want to do more than put a label on events. When we observe a shooting star, a magician's sleight of hand, or changes in stock prices, we not only want to name these events, we hope to understand them. We ask "Why?" "How?", attempting to link these occurrences. We become more than observers; we become students searching to understand the phenomena. We seek out an area of study.

As an Area of Study

OB, as an area of study, is *the application of concepts, theories, methods, and empirical generalizations from the behavioral sciences to the analysis of behavior in organizations.* Let us examine some of the key terms in this definition.

Concepts, Theories   OB is not just a catalog of facts; it is a framework for thinking about behavior. Some of the concepts—the building blocks of this structure—will be familiar to you; many will not. The test of their power is their ability to "tie things together," to give coherence and meaning to a jumbled array of sense data and opinions, to enable you to see relationships and go beyond the unique event. The concepts and theories of OB give us the "big picture" for perceiving patterns and order in behavior.

Methods   OB is more than a storehouse of accumulated facts and opinions. It is a means of adding to that storehouse. The game is never over, the ledgers never closed. OB, like all disciplines, is a continual process of learning. But as we will see in the next chapter, each learning method has its respective shortcomings. We never "learn" with 100 percent certainty.

Empirical Generalization   We prefer this ungainly phrase to the simple word "facts," which implies bits of knowledge that are fixed and certain. While there are facts in OB, of much more interest are the tentative conclusions that extend the scope of a set of facts. It is a fact that, in XYZ corporation, most of the employees who quit last year reported less job satisfaction than those who stayed. Similar observations in other organizations would lead us to the empirical generalization that job dissatisfaction is related to turnover. Although this may not be true in every instance, it is useful and not unreasonable to assume such a relationship in the absence of contradictory information. In short, empirical generalizations trade off certainty or confidence for greater scope and breadth than contained in a fact. Fortunately, there are enough empirical data from OB and the supporting behavioral sciences to provide us with a useful set of empirical generalizations. With ongoing research using various methods of inquiry, we are optimistic that further empirical generalizations will emerge.

Behavioral Science   In organizations, people learn skills, express prejudices, become leaders, and develop ties to groups. People also do these things at home, with friends, and in the pursuit of hobbies. In other words, human behavior in organizations is similar to human behavior in other settings. We can therefore expect the behavioral sciences to help us understand behavior in organizations.

Table 1–1 shows how several disciplines from the behavioral sciences contribute to OB. Each of these disciplines addresses significant dimensions of human behavior; each is wedded to the scientific method of using theory and empirical observation to study behavior; and each boasts a large fund of knowledge from which to draw to enhance our understanding of behavior in organized settings. OB seeks to capitalize on this fund, at least as a foundation on which to build. For example, although work groups are not the same as friendship groups, if we understand what determines status in a friendship group, we will have some basis for exploring patterns of influence in a work group.

A fine line exists between what we call organizations and the many other social contexts characterized by some degree of organization. OB assumes that certain fundamental principles underlie behavior in any context and readily turns to those disciplines that have long studied such principles.

Behavior in Organizations   The formal organization creates a special kind of environment in two ways. First, organizations place more constraints on human behavior than do other settings. Official authority, job duties, and potential sanctions eliminate some of the natural variability and spontaneity implicit in behavior at home or on the playground. In a sense, then, formal organizations are unnatural because they require people to learn and adapt

TABLE 1–1

Related Disciplines Contributing to Organizational Behavior

Discipline	Relevant Topics
Experimental psychology	Learning; motivation; perception; effects of physical environment on psychomotor performance; stress
Social psychology	Group dynamics; attitudes and attitude change; impression formation; personality; leadership
Industrial psychology	Measurement of performance, abilities, job characteristics; employee compensation; applied motivation programs
Clinical psychology	Human adjustment; emotional stress; abnormal behavior; human development throughout the life cycle
Sociology	Socialization processes; social satisfaction; status systems; effects of major social institutions such as family, community, religion, organization structure
Political science	Interest groups; conflict; power, bargaining; coalitions, strategic planning; control
Anthropology	Comparative organizational structures; their functions in varying cultures; cultural influences on organizations; adaptation of organization to environment
Economics	Human resource planning; labor market changes; productivity analysis; cost/benefit analysis

to restrictions. This process is in itself intellectually interesting and pragmatically important.

Second, organizations have explicit purposes and goals to an extent not usually found in unorganized settings. Business corporations have to make a profit, which means they must produce goods or services with the efficient use of resources. In short, organizations must have a rationale, a reason for their existence. That rationale becomes the point of departure for evaluating the behavior that occurs in the organizational environment. For this reason, those who study OB—whether managers, students, or behavioral scientists—will seldom be indifferent toward the behavior observed in organizations. Instead, that behavior will be evaluated: Does it hinder or promote the unit's effectiveness in reaching its goal? Will it help to achieve some ends but not others? In sum, OB is "results oriented."

This ultimate quest for knowledge that will make organizations more effective does not in itself set OB apart from its sister sciences. Scholars in psychology, sociology, and political science share OB's concern with improving social policies and conditions; and those who study OB share with its sister sciences the value of knowledge as its own reward. But qualitatively the difference between OB and the other disciplines is OB's obvious concern with some "pay-off."

Two criteria provide the basis for evaluating behavior in organizations. One is performance—the ability of the organization to attain those ends or purposes that brought it into existence. Performance, of course, is usually complex. For a private corporation, performance may represent some weighted combination of return on stockholder investment, growth in sales, rate of introducing new products, and efficient use of resources. Maximizing the attainment of any one of these goals typically means a trade-off on the others. Some performance criteria—such as net contributions to the larger culture—may be so subjective as to preclude their routine use as a measure of effectiveness. To remain objective, researchers in OB generally avoid an evaluation of total performance by dealing empirically with one measurable facet of performance at a time. Supervisory styles may be compared in terms of their relationship with a measure of productivity or product quality (such as percent rejects); methods of organizing research and development activities are compared with respect to number of patents secured; personality traits of purchasing officers may be tested to determine how well they predict cost savings in procuring supplies. Weighting and combining various indexes to regulate policy requires a value judgment that must be made by a manager or public administrator, or sometimes by the public.

The second criterion used by OB to assess organizational practices is member welfare. Ultimately an organization is a "social contract" (Keely, 1988) among various groups of people who have a stake in the outcomes of organized effort. These stakeholders include owners, taxpayers, top-level managers, and all others who have committed themselves to the rights and obligations of the social contract. Thus, the collective interests of these various parties define a criterion. This often takes the form of some measure of satisfaction, especially when the members are full-time employees. Personal safety, psychological growth, and physical and emotional health are other aspects of member welfare. The phrase "quality of work life" captures the essence of our definition of member welfare. Figure 1–1 elaborates on these two criteria which underlie the evaluative judgments by OB.

We hasten to stress that performance and member welfare are separate criteria and that favorable judgments of organizations concerning either

FIGURE 1–1

Criterion Values in the Study of Organizational Behavior

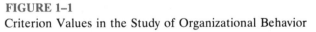

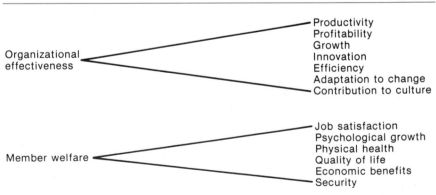

Organizational effectiveness
- Productivity
- Profitability
- Growth
- Innovation
- Efficiency
- Adaptation to change
- Contribution to culture

Member welfare
- Job satisfaction
- Psychological growth
- Physical health
- Quality of life
- Economic benefits
- Security

criterion do not automatically imply favorable views of the other. A company can have a long history of recording a high return on investment for stockholders and an industry reputation for making a good product at a fair price, yet its employees may feel unfairly treated. Conversely, there are organizations in which professional employees are well paid, supervised with respect and consideration, and given abundant opportunities for personal growth and development—yet these organizations do not render the amount or quality of services that would justify the resources allocated to them.

As OB continues to evolve as a field of study, we hope to develop theories and applications that will enable us to improve both the effectiveness of organizational performance and the benefits of organizational life. In the meantime, we must acknowledge that performance and member welfare stand as separate criteria, with no guarantee that improving one will improve the other.

OB as a Community of Interest Groups

OB can also describe a community of overlapping interest groups, as shown in Figure 1–2. The common bond among these groups is their vested interest in learning more about behavior in organizations.

FIGURE 1–2

Organizational Behavior as a Community of Interest Groups

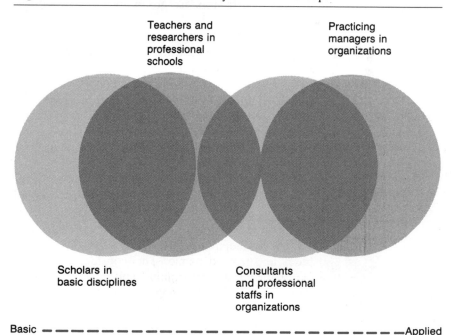

One OB interest group includes scholars in such basic behavioral sciences as social psychology and political science. As these scholars study and research human behavior, the trail of their intellectual interests often leads to behavior of considerable organizational relevance. For example, research into group dynamics has led to the study of cohesive work groups and the forces that affect group decision making.

Another interest group is composed of those who teach in professional schools of business and public administration, many of whom were trained in graduate programs in the basic behavioral sciences. Many others stay current by reading books and journals that report on new research and theoretical developments in those disciplines, while some do their own research in basic behavioral disciplines. Their special concern, however, is to teach new generations of managers and administrators how to improve their understanding of behavior in organizations. Because these future managers and administrators will be responsible for influencing organizational behavior toward constructive ends, the more they understand OB phenomena, the better they will be able to carry out that charge.

A third interest group is represented by professional consultants (some of whom also belong to one or both of the interest groups described above). Consultants draw upon the latest available findings, techniques, and technologies to validate employee selection tests, conduct attitude surveys, and plan programs to increase worker motivation and reduce absenteeism and turnover.

The fourth interest group includes practicing managers and other organization officials. This group is not a "full-time" OB interest group, but it has a vested interest in maintaining ties with the others. Through seminars, trade meetings, periodicals, and contacts with consultants, administrators keep abreast of new knowledge in OB and learn how to apply that knowledge to their own jobs.

As Figure 1–2 indicates, the four interest groups comprising the OB community fit roughly along a "basic"-to-"applied" continuum. This continuum is unbroken: the purely theoretical and genuinely pragmatic are securely intertwined and not easily disentangled. The basic-versus-applied emphasis is one of degree, not kind.

Influence in the OB community runs in both directions. The findings and insights of scholars in the basic disciplines ultimately find their way to the practicing manager, though sometimes disguised as commercial programs or copyrighted instruments. Teachers in professional schools monitor new conceptual developments in the basic disciplines concerning motivation, attitudes, and group dynamics. They consider the implications of these developments for job design, training, and managerial leadership and incorporate them into the curricula of professional schools, research their application in organizations, and communicate these developments to administrators.

In the history of science, the direction of influence also works in the opposite direction. Much of the 18th- and 19th-century revolution in the physical sciences resulted from confronting practical problems in industry, warfare, and medicine. The same can be said of OB. A good example is the study of group decision making. A graduate student in industrial management showed that—contrary to public opinion—groups make riskier decisions than individuals (Stoner, 1961). Social psychologists later explored this mystery and eventually came up with a vastly different view of how groups affect individuals.

THE EVOLUTION OF OB

As a set of phenomena, OB has been with us since the dawn of history. Yet as an area of study and as a community of interest groups, OB is of fairly recent vintage. Let us look at the historical development of these latter two aspects of OB.

Until the 1940s, the study of organizations was almost exclusively the province of an ill-defined quasi-discipline called "Management" (or as some called it, "Administration"). The primary focus of Management was on the formal structure of organizations—the lines of authority, the relationships of accountability, the component parts of the organization, and how they should be linked. Organizations were social machines, and management was the embryonic discipline devoted to answering the engineering questions of how best to design and maintain the machine. The design would determine how efficient the machine could be.

Students of Management were, by and large, managers. They drew from their experience and observations some ideas about fundamental, universally valid principles of organizing. Their contact with and exposure to academicians was minimal, largely because most academicians were not interested in studying management.

The principles of Management were, of course, implicitly grounded in some assumptions about human behavior. These assumptions, however, were derived from a casual, commonsense view of behavior. They included the beliefs that behavior in organizations would be rational, based on economic motives, and influenced by authority relationships between superior and subordinate. Beyond this, people were simply parts of the machine. Their behavior in organizations, then, could be made more efficient by properly applying engineering principles.

The Hawthorne Studies   The first serious challenge to prevailing Management doctrines came about unexpectedly as a result of the celebrated Hawthorne studies that began in the 1920s. Taking their name from the Hawthorne Works plant of the Western Electric Company in the Chicago area, these studies were initiated in an attempt to prevent late-morning and mid-afternoon drop-offs in productivity. Among the techniques studied were better illumination, different schedules of work hours and breaks, and even the effect of providing sandwiches to those operators who skipped breakfast.

Early results were inconsistent and disappointing. The researchers suspected that the experiments had failed because experimental work groups had not been physically separated from other groups engaged in their usual routines. Researchers also believed that neither the group supervisors nor the operators had completely cooperated with the researchers. Therefore, management decided to repeat the experiments, but this time separating the experimental group from other workers, and temporarily replacing the regular supervisor with a researcher. The researcher— ignorant of Management theory doctrines—enlisted the workers' full cooperation: he sought their advice and considered their preferences with regard to implementing the various experimental changes.

As the experiments proceeded, worker productivity showed fairly impressive gains. Unfortunately, the gains in output were not closely related to any particular change in lighting, work schedule, or rest periods. Frustrated and unable to interpret the data, the plant officials finally asked behavioral scientists Elton Mayo and Fritz Roethlisberger of Harvard University to come to Hawthorne to study the situation. Mayo and Roethlisberger concluded that the experiment that had taken place was not one of industrial engineering, but of change in the social organization. The change that had overshadowed everything else was the full development of the informal group as a result of the unorthodox supervisory methods that gave the group special treatment. Social as well as economic motives affected worker behavior and an informal organization developed to satisfy needs overlooked by the formal organization. The researcher had unwittingly capitalized on those motives and needs previously ignored by Management theory.

The ideas offered by the Mayo group were unprecedented in Management theory, and were so provocative that company officials began a massive program of in-depth interviews with the members of the work force. These interviews, conducted in a nondirective style that allowed workers to express their opinions, eventually included over 20,000 people. Subsequent to the interviewing program, a work group was studied in depth by an observer present throughout each day's entire shift.

The Hawthorne studies lasted over a decade. The results were reported and discussed in a book, *Management and the Worker,* published in 1939 and authored by Roethlisberger and Dickson. The concepts offered in this book went far beyond any existing body of Management thought. The authors proposed that behavior at work is due as much to a logic of "sentiment" as to the logic of fact or rationality. Sentiment had its own rules and its own manner of expression. Sentiments underlay the development of an informal organization, which could be seen most clearly in cohesive work groups with their own rules (some of which violated the official rules of the plant). Social needs sometimes overruled purely economic incentives.

The influence of the Hawthorne studies on management thinking and practice was not widespread until after World War II. But by the early 1950s, it was generally acknowledged that there was a "behavioral dimension of management." Unfortunately some writers interpreted the Hawthorne findings as proving that "a happy worker is a productive worker." This oversimplification may have made managers more sensitive to worker

CLOSE-UP

A Sampler of Observations from Gordon and Howell

There is a growing recognition that business administration is a respectable field of study for social scientists qua social scientists. . . . During the last few years, there has been a sharp upsurge of interest among the business schools in acquiring behavioral scientists, statisticians, and applied mathematicians . . . with the hope that they will contribute research findings important to business and indicate ways of enriching the teaching in business fields with more material gleaned from the underlying disciplines . . . applied social scientists — now a small minority in the business school — will grow significantly in the years ahead, as will their influence on curriculum and research. The reasons for this lie in the advances now being made in various of the social sciences. (pp. 347–48)

Thus, the business schools need to develop both more pure or fundamental research and, using the best tools now available, more applied research at a high analytical level. The former requires bringing the underlying disciplines directly into the business schools.

Research on organizational problems is still in its infancy. Here clearly the behavioral sciences have much to contribute. . . . There is need for more of a "behavioral" approach to the study of organizations. (pp. 382–83)

SOURCE: R. A. Gordon and J. E. Howell, *Higher Education for Business* (New York: Columbia University Press, 1959).

feelings and group morale, and thus had some positive effect on management practice. However, oversimplifying the findings also led to the development of a body of opinion now labeled the "Human Relations" school of management. Its theories fostered the ideas that satisfaction is a direct cause of productivity, that more cohesive groups are automatically more productive, and that worker participation is a panacea for problems in the work force. Research in OB has forced us to revise some of these appealing notions.

The Gordon and Howell Report   Behavioral science concepts infiltrated management in an unsystematic fashion through the 1940s and 1950s. In 1956, the Ford Foundation commissioned economists R. A. Gordon and J. E. Howell to investigate the quality of the curricula of the schools of business and commerce that had grown rapidly in number and enrollment since the 1920s (Gordon & Howell, 1959). Gordon and Howell visited many of these schools, talked to faculty, studied course outlines, and interviewed students. Their report, published in 1959, concluded that too many business school courses lacked rigor and substance and were weak in conceptual content. They urged business schools to incorporate more basic academic disciplines — mathematics, economics, and psychology. At about the same time, a similar study, with similar findings and recommendations, was conducted by F. C. Pierson (1959) for the Carnegie Foundation.

The Gordon-Howell report exerted enormous influence on the directions taken by schools of business and administration in the 1960s. A new breed of faculty was drawn into the study of management and new disciplines were spawned. Various academic specialties laid claim to particular provinces of management and imposed their respective philosophies, methods, and expertise on it. This created such distinctive areas of study as operations research, organization theory, and organizational behavior. (For a more complete account of the fractionation of management as a discipline, see Perrow, 1973).

The Gordon-Howell report shaped the curriculum and subject matter of today's academic programs in business. It has also guided the American Assembly of Collegiate Schools of Business (AACSB) in determining whether academic programs in business meet its certification standards of rigor, substantive content, and quality of instruction. By setting and enforcing these standards, the AACSB has helped provide the basis for academic respectability of business education programs.

Thus OB, like other emergent fields of study borne of the intermarriage of basic disciplines and management issues, has developed in the directions of rigor, objectivity, theoretical depth, and methodological sophistication.

WHAT HAS OB ACCOMPLISHED?

Because the OB community is still in its infancy compared to many other sciences it has not had time to develop the same structure and coherence that characterize other fields. It is therefore unrealistic to expect the same order of accomplishments as those that have occurred in medicine, physics, or biology.

Nonetheless, on a theoretical level, there have been notable strides toward developing OB's own conceptual language. We soon realized that the everyday concepts of practicing managers posed limitations for a scientific study of behavior in organizations because such concepts are often loaded with bias—for example, in popular thinking about the relative merits of autocratic and democratic leadership styles. Because commonly used terms (such as *morale*) were often conceived at a high level of ambiguity or had multiple meanings, statements concerning them could not be tested. In other cases, concepts took so narrow a focus around specific contexts that it was difficult to interrelate knowledge about those contexts to others, and vice versa. OB theorists and researchers have gradually developed their own concepts, defined for their own purposes.

OB has found instances where "facts" long seen as "obvious" were neither obvious nor facts. While not rejecting philosophies of generations of administrators, OB has found abundant evidence to challenge and reinterpret many commonsense views of work.

As Cummings (1978) pointed out, OB has generated an array of technologies, or practical techniques, that are increasingly used by organizations. Some techniques existed in crude forms long before OB was "born," but OB research has increased the power, validity, and precision of these methods. These management tools include the job attitude survey, techniques of performance appraisal, formats for group decision making, and methods of designing employee training and developmental programs.

THE STATE OF OB: SOME CRITICAL OBSERVATIONS

The Porter-McKibbin Report   The Gordon-Howell Report was not the last word in evaluating business school curricula. In 1984, two management scholars, Lyman Porter and Lawrence McKibbin, were commissioned by the AACSB to update the record concerning the quality and effectiveness of programs of business education. They conducted questionnaire surveys and interviews with a large sample of corporate executives, business school deans, and faculty.

Porter and McKibbin (1988) found that corporate respondents rated their recently hired MBAs as very strong in analytical skills and the ability to use quantitative tools in analysis. These graduates also had a considerable depth of knowledge in a specialized area, such as market research or management information systems.

But in certain respects, both the academic community and business leaders felt that business school curricula were deficient. Degree programs in business administration were rated as providing insufficient emphasis on:

Integration across functional areas of business.

Generating "vision" in students—the orientation toward taking bold, imaginative, risky courses of action, as opposed to solving structured problems in familiar contexts.

Communication skills, both oral and written.

Ethics in corporate conduct.

Entrepreneurism.

The international dimension of business.

Practical skills in managing people.

The Porter-McKibbin report posed the questions: Did we overshoot the mark in the quest for rigor and precision in business programs? Did Gordon-Howell lead us in some directions while blinding us to others? Was academic respectability attained at the sacrifice of preparation for the "real world"?

Of course, the "insufficiencies" reported by Porter-McKibbin did not single out OB. Their concern was the more general thrust of academic programs in business. But the implications for OB are rather obvious. Questions about ethics, creative vision, and communication and management skills would seem to be directed, at least in part, to OB.

Take note of the Focus on Management. The overwhelming sentiment among managers and administrators favored *more* emphasis on the study of behavior in schools of administration.

FOCUS ON MANAGEMENT

Education for Managers: More or Less Behavioral Emphasis?

Porter and McKibbin (1988), in conducting their recent survey and assessment of business education, posed the following question to business school deans and faculty, MBA alumni, chief executive officers (CEOs), senior corporate officers (SCOs), and vice presidents for human resources (VPHRs): "Is the amount of behavioral emphasis in the business school curriculum *too much, about right,* or *too little?* The responses:

	Deans	Faculty	MBA Alumni	CEOs	SCOs	VPHRs
Too much	11%	17%	8%	9%	4%	7%
About right	68	60	62	24	30	21
Too little	21	23	30	67	66	72

SOURCE: Porter and McKibbin (1988), p. 69.

TENSIONS IN OB

The Porter-McKibbin report will probably increase certain tensions within the OB community. Because of its subject matter, parentage, and diverse interest groups, OB has continually had to cope with certain dilemmas.

Rigor versus Relevance   Many members of the OB community believe that OB should strive to attain the highest standards of rigor in its research. At the extreme, this view would exclude from study any phenomena that cannot be quantified and manipulated under controlled conditions of observation. Other OB members oppose the elevation of rigor for its own sake; they argue that this position would reduce OB to only the most trivial problems, omitting the more interesting, relevant, and important issues that face organizations and managers. Both groups would preserve the links between behavioral scientists and managers, but the champions of rigor support the scientist while the advocates of relevance would give first allegiance to the manager.

Descriptive versus Prescriptive   Some OB camps feel that OB should stick to describing behavioral phenomena in organizations, and observing and reporting the relationships between variables. An opposing bias argues that OB must go beyond observation to recommend policy and practice. Should we merely note that various leadership styles have different effects or should we apply our own values to these effects and urge the adoption of one or the other style?

Objectivity versus Humanism   The humanistic camp of OB is characterized by a set of assumptions about human nature. These assumptions assert that with the proper environment, human nature is good. The goal of OB is to bring out the full flowering of human potential. Therefore, OB should find the means to construct such an environment and thus validate the assumption. The opposing view is that no such assumptions about human nature should be made a priori, and that speculation of this sort is best left to theologians and poets.

Theory versus Practice   Some quarters of OB stress the primacy of theory as the major concern. This point of view, while not hostile to practical applications, contends that theory is the most effective guide to research and that theory gives any discipline its continuity and coherence. The opposing view believes that theories of OB should emerge from a concern for, and assessments of, the techniques, policies, and practices that are used in organizations. Thus, OB should be an active party in the development of practical aids to management and should not wait until such applications can be thoroughly grounded in theoretical concepts and principles.

Our Position   We have tried here to strike a reasonable balance among the competing postures. Nonetheless, we have chosen to err in a particular direction, and the reader has a right to know our bias.

We lean toward rigor, description, objectivity, and theory. We recognize the value of relevance, but an overwhelming concern for relevance runs the risk of preoccupation with passing fads. We can prescribe a course of action to a friend or client, but to do this in a textbook might give a false, even arrogant, stamp of legitimacy to our personal preferences and values. We admire humanism in its intent but our institutions are imperfect and it seems a moot point whether human nature itself is perfectible. We agree that the ultimate value of a good theory is its ability to inform practice. We recognize that many useful practices need not rest on elegant theories. Still, we believe that theory has the unique ability to point the way beyond existing practice and to extract general principles that cut across the many forms and contexts of practice.

In essence, our position reflects the dominant viewpoints of OB as it has developed to this date. Still, the points of the Porter-McKibbin report are well taken. We suspect that in the future, people who teach and study OB will give somewhat more attention to the relevance and practicality of our ideas.

SOME PROBABLE DIRECTIONS OF FUTURE DEVELOPMENT IN OB

In the years ahead, OB will probably be influenced by certain deep, pervasive trends now underway in the business world. These trends, as they gather momentum, may call into question the validity and generalizability of what now passes for a cumulative fund of knowledge.

For example, in the 1960s and 1970s, OB reflected a considerable emphasis on worker satisfaction and individual fulfillment. The 1980s saw this orientation toward job satisfaction matched, if not eclipsed, by an urgent concern for productivity. This turnabout came in response to double-digit inflation in the late 1970s, deregulation in the 1980s, and declining American manufacturing competitiveness in world markets. OB in the 1990s will almost certainly undergo some revision in response to the following trends:

The continuing transformation of the U.S. economy from one based on industry to one based on information and services. Much of our "givens" concerning work were products of the industrial revolution. It is difficult to imagine work without considering the fixed time to start and end the workday, commuting to a central location to join throngs of fellow employees, and assuming a niche in a large bureaucratic organization. Yet, before the Industrial Revolution, such practices were the exception rather than the rule. The peculiarities of industrial manufacturing and technology brought certain customs and forms of organization that came to be accepted as permanent features of the landscape.

Now, a majority of the labor force works with information—gathering it, processing it, conveying it—rather than producing goods. The technology that supports information processing and transfer alters the way work is done in organizations. Even the phrase "in organizations" becomes a misnomer; many people now work at home with a personal computer. The process of managing no longer necessitates the physical presence of the manager with those managed. Increasingly, the real work will go on in temporary organizations of networks that cut across various functions, departments, corporations—even continents.

Naisbitt (1982) calls such developments a "megatrend." Toffler (1980) regards it as the "Third Wave," comparable to the Industrial Revolution. Since OB rests on concepts and assumptions of the industrial age, there will be a need to revise these concepts in the next decade.

The globalization of business. Anyone exposed to the media in the last 10 years knows there is increased foreign competition with U.S. firms in our own domestic market, and a growing importance of foreign markets to American firms. But the globalization of business is more than competition in international markets; more of our goods and services are themselves international in nature. Naisbitt provides two examples of this that foreshadow trends in the 1990s: 95 percent of baseball mitts are made from American cowhide, which is shipped to Brazil for tanning, then made into mitts in Japan; and when Japan first began making microprocessing chips, the electronic chips came from the United States, were assembled in Singapore, Indonesia, or Nigeria, with steel housing from India, and the "Made in Japan" label was added when the chip was put in a calculator in Yokohama.

Very simply, because more work will cut across nations, languages, and cultures, more of what we call organizational behavior will occur as interactions among people with vastly different traditions, values, and conceptions of the world. However, OB has serious limitations in the context of the globalized organization. It has developed almost entirely within the framework of North American and Western European cultural values, with the result that our conceptions of human nature, the individual, the group, time, space, ethics, authority, efficiency, and fairness are not shared by other cultures. New developments in OB will almost certainly arise from the awareness of cultural influences on behavior in organizations.

The maturing of the "baby boomers." In the United States unprecedented numbers of births occurred in the period 1946–1964. At each stage of development, the sheer size of this generation and its share of the total population has had far-reaching social, economic, and political effects. As children, the baby boomers caused a shortage of schools and teachers. As college students, they constituted a large voting bloc and were the vanguard of a "youth culture." When they entered the labor force, their expectations were different from those of their elders — and their influence has been felt on OB. Less interested in saving than in consumption, they rolled up high levels of personal debt.

Some of these baby boomers now hold significant positions of managerial and executive responsibility in organizations. Many others who aspired to such positions find themselves frustrated because of two interrelated trends: there are so many others like themselves to compete with; and there are fewer middle-to-upper-level managers due to the effects of information technology and global competition. With fewer opportunities, more bright people have plateaued earlier, at a lower level of responsibility. How will career success be redefined for these people as they reach their 40s?

The baby boomers are leaving in their wake a "baby bust." Younger workers — those born after 1965 — comprise a proportionately smaller percentage of the labor force, causing acute labor shortages in, for example, the fast food and retail businesses. Will these people be able to bargain for unprecedented considerations and dispensations as they enter their 20s and 30s? Will they bear oppressive burdens for doing the nation's work as their baby boomer seniors enter retirement?

The OB of the future will be conditioned by these forces. OB will address different questions, alter the priority of its variables, and reexamine its premises. To prepare the reader for a changing OB, we have noted in the chapters ahead the gathering forces of the future.

To fully appreciate changing trends in ideas and values, the future manager must appreciate the legacy of the immediate past and the present. We will provide the reader with an up-to-date account of behavior in organizations as OB now interprets it. The continuing intellectual growth and professional development of the administrator follow from a solid grounding in a set of conceptual and empirical frameworks. These frameworks do not substitute for common sense; they complement it. They do not replace judgment; they lead to informed judgment.

FOCUS ON THE FUTURE

Management in the Year 2010: Day in the Life of Tomorrow's Manager

6:10 A.M. The year is 2010 and another Monday morning has begun for Peter Smith. The marketing vice president for a home-appliance division of a major U.S. manufacturer is awakened by his computer alarm. He saunters to his terminal to check the weather outlook in Madrid, where he'll fly late tonight, and to send an electronic-voice message to a supplier in Thailand.

7:20 A.M. Mr. Smith and his wife, who heads her own architecture firm, organize the home front before darting to the supertrain. They leave instructions for their personal computer to call the home-cleaning service as well as a gourmet-carryout service that will prepare dinner for eight guests Saturday. And they quickly go over the day's schedules for their three- and six-year-old daughters with their nanny.

On the train during a speedy 20-minute commute from suburb to Manhattan, Mr. Smith checks his electronic mailbox and also reads his favorite trade magazine via his laptop computer.

8:15 A.M. In his high-tech office that doubles as a conference room, Mr. Smith reviews the day's schedule with his executive assistant (traditional secretaries vanished a decade earlier). Then it's on to his first meeting: a conference via video screen between his division's chief production manager in Cincinnati and a supplier near Munich.

10:30 A.M. At a staff meeting, Mr. Smith finds himself refereeing between two subordinates who disagree vehemently on how to promote a new appliance. One, an Asian manager, suggests that a fresh campaign begin much sooner than initially envisioned. The other, a European, wants to hold off until results of a test market are received later that week.

12:30 P.M. Lunch is in Mr. Smith's office today, giving him time to take a video lesson in conversational Chinese. . . After 20 minutes, he decides to go to his computer to check his company's latest political-risk assessment on Spain, where recent student unrest has erupted into riots. The report tells him that the disturbances aren't anti-American, but he decides to have a bodyguard meet him at the Madrid airport anyway.

2:30 P.M. Two of Mr. Smith's top lieutenants complain that they and others on his staff feel a recent bonus payment for a successful project wasn't divided equitably. Bluntly, they note that while Mr. Smith received a hefty $20,000 bonus, his 15-member staff had to split $5,000, and they threaten to defect.

6 P.M. Before heading to the airport, Mr. Smith uses his video phone to give his daughters a good night kiss and to talk about the next day's schedule with his wife. Learning that she must take an unexpected trip herself the next evening, he promises to catch the SuperConcorde home in time to put the kids to sleep himself.

SOURCE: *The Wall Street Journal,* March 20, 1989.

SUMMARY

Organizational behavior can be defined as a class of phenomena, as a discipline or area of study, and as an overlapping set of interest groups. The roots of OB are in the quasi discipline of Management, but its present character was largely shaped by the findings of the Hawthorne studies and the recommendations of Gordon and Howell for enhancing the academic stature of schools of business administration. OB, because of its diverse constituencies and the nature of its subject matter, must continually strive for a balance between the goals of rigor and relevance, description and prescription, objectivity and humanism, and theory versus practice. OB has leaned in the directions of rigor, description, objectivity, and theory, but the recent Porter-McKibbin report might well stimulate countervailing pressures. OB has made strides in the development of a body of theory, the empirical testing of conventional wisdom, and the application of various techniques for measuring and managing human resources. However, OB does not have a static character. The continuing conversion of our industrial economy into an information/services economy, the ongoing globalization of business, and the demographics of maturing baby boomers will further shape OB.

CONCEPTS TO REMEMBER

OB as a set of phenomena	Hawthorne studies	"Human Relations" school of management
OB as an area of study	Gordon-Howell report	
OB as a community of interest groups	Porter-McKibbin report	

QUESTIONS FOR DISCUSSION

1. Talk informally to one or more managers of a large or small business. What do they view as the major problems in an organization? How many of these are technical in nature? How many are primarily behavioral in nature?

2. Given our definition of OB, is it appropriate for OB to incorporate the study of ethics in organizations? If OB were to address itself seriously to ethical questions, how would this affect the nature and content of OB?

3. We identified three important trends that might influence future directions of OB. Given how we defined OB, can you think of other developments that would have such influence? Why? How? (Hint: Glance at the cover stories of news magazines in recent weeks, or look at feature articles in recent issues of *The Wall Street Journal.*)

REFERENCES

Cummings, L. L. (1978). Toward organizational behavior. *Academy of Management Review* 3, 90–98.

Gordon, R. A., & Howell, J. E. (1959). *Higher education for business.* New York: Columbia University Press.

Keeley, M. (1988). *A social-contract theory of organizations.* Notre Dame, IN: University of Notre Dame Press.

Naisbitt, J. (1982). *Megatrends.* New York: Warner Books.

Perrow, C. (1973, Summer) The short and glorious history of organization theory. *Organizational Dynamics,* 2–15.

Pierson, F. C. (1959). *The education of American businessmen.* New York: McGraw-Hill.

Porter, L. W., & McKibbin, L. E. (1988). *Management education and development: Drift or thrust into the 21st century?* New York: McGraw-Hill.

Roethlisberger, F. J., & Dickson, W. J. (1939). *Management and the worker.* Cambridge: Harvard University Press. New York: John Wiley & Sons, 1964, cited henceforth.

Stoner, J.A.F. (1961). *A comparison of individual and group decisions including risk.* Unpublished master's thesis, School of Industrial Management, MIT, Cambridge, MA.

Toffler, A. (1980). *The third wave.* New York: Bantam Books.

2 Theory and Research in Organizational Behavior

What is the nature of theory in organizational behavior?

What are the functions of theory?

How do we evaluate theories?

What are the different methods used to study behavior in organizations?

What are their advantages and disadvantages?

What kind of research is done by managers, and why? How can they do it better?

As a science matures, it develops a solid theoretical base and characteristic methods of research. Such is the case with organizational behavior (OB) as a social science. OB is increasingly characterized by the use of theory to explain and predict behavioral processes in organizations. To a similar extent, systematic methods of research are used to generate the data that inspire, test, and modify our theories.

This chapter will explain why theory is indispensable to increasing knowledge and understanding of behavior in organizations. The nature of theory must be appreciated as an extension of our basic thought processes. We will note the functions theory serves, and offer some criteria for assessing a theory's value.

THEORY

Students and management practitioners are impatient with theory. The student's ultimate put-down of a disliked course or reading assignment is, "It's too theoretical." The practitioner likes to say, "That's fine in theory, but it doesn't work in practice." Theory seems to stand totally apart from life and experience.

This attitude stems from a misunderstanding of what theory is and what a theory attempts to do. Students and practitioners are unaware that they are active users of theory.

A theory is a set of statements about how certain concepts are interrelated. The statements are based on certain assumptions that permit the logical deduction of further statements in the form of propositions or predictions. Neither esoteric jargon nor mathematical symbols are essential to a theory, although specialized language is often useful.

Percepts, Concepts, and Constructs

To understand how theory construction extends the natural thought processes, it is helpful to examine the distinctions between percept, concept, and construct. A *percept* is a single bit of sensation; it represents a unique, nonrepeatable event. You see a red stoplight at Fourth Street and Main at 5:33 P.M. on January 18, 1989; you hear an ambulance siren while walking to the drugstore; you feel the sting of the needle that gives you a flu shot. These are percepts: raw sense data. They are the stuff of human experience. Each day brings forth thousands of new percepts—most of them similar to previously experienced percepts, but each unique in some microscopic way.

Inasmuch as we experience multitudes of percepts each day, we seldom attend to them in terms of their uniqueness. Such a task would overwhelm us. Because we are unable to respond to each percept in a different way, we instinctively group them in terms of categories of thought, or concepts.

A *concept,* then, is the smallest unit of our conscious thought materials. It is a category of thought, or a way to group sense data together as if they were all the same. All percepts involving the stoplight at Fourth and Main become a category of thought, although a relatively narrow one. All stoplights, regardless of location, become a broader concept. The important thing to note is that a concept is an abstraction, a category of thought that can be as broad as our mental capabilities allow.

Conceptualizing is a powerful process. It enables us to simplify experiences by glossing over unimportant microscopic distinctions. It facilitates memory by allowing the use of fewer labels. It enables us to generalize from experience with some members of a category to others. Smaller categories can be grouped into larger ones (e.g., stoplights and stop signs may be grouped together); or larger ones can be broken down into smaller ones to highlight an important distinction (long stoplights and short stoplights, blinking ones and nonblinking ones).

In theory building, we continue this process, except that we relate categories of thought to one another. We use informal theories when we think of certain classes of behavior (such as "driving fast") in a class of environmental conditions ("slick roads"). This results in a class of outcomes ("loss of control of the vehicle's motion").

More formal theories extend this process, with an important distinction: the categories of thought become constructs. A *construct* is a concept intended purely for theoretical use. We use concepts in informal theory building and thinking; we use constructs in formal theories in science. The construct is more abstract than everyday concepts. The value of specific constructs depends on how useful they are in constructing a good theory, just as the value of everyday concepts depends on how much they assist in everyday affairs. In theories of OB, constructs will often be similar to familiar concepts, frequently having the same names, although somewhat different definitions.

There are rules for grouping things to form categories. We often define concepts that are similar in physical appearance or that have a common purpose (e.g., the concepts *skyscraper, hammer, underwear, vehicle*). To form constructs for theories, we are less likely to group according to observable physical characteristics and more likely to use function, effect, or patterns of covariation as defining characteristics. Leadership theorists, for example, often use the construct "consideration" to refer to all forms of supervisory behavior that lessen the psychological distance between the superior and subordinates. "Reinforcers" designate any consequences of behavior that make those behaviors more likely to occur. "Need for achievement" as a construct in motivation and personality theory denotes a characteristic mix of behaviors that tend to cluster together within and among persons.

Types of Constructs

Thus far, we have defined a theory as a set of concepts or constructs and statements describing how these constructs are related. The relationship between constructs provides a basis for discriminating among the types of constructs that may enter into a theory.

An *independent variable* is a construct that exerts a force on some other construct; it acts as a "cause" of something else. Changes in the independent variable precede predictable changes in something else. When we speak of various styles of supervision as having certain consequences, we are thinking of supervisory style as an independent variable.

Typically, the independent variables in theories of OB refer to some property of the organizational environment. Thus, independent variables frequently are concepts such as organizational structure, reward systems, leader behavior, organization climate, characteristics of the job, or characteristics of the work group. Furthermore, independent variables usually refer to entities that, at least in principle, can be changed or manipulated.

Dependent variables are the constructs that represent the effects or consequences of the independent variables. Dependent variables refer to the results of specific changes in the independent variables. A theory that states that supervisory styles affect employee absenteeism is placing supervisory style in the role of an independent variable and absenteeism in the role of dependent variable.

Dependent variables in OB usually refer to outcomes that we evaluate and are our criteria for evaluating the independent variables. If a certain supervisory style has positive effects (such as reducing absences), then that style is what we want—provided, of course, that it does not have undesirable effects that outweigh the effect on absenteeism. Dependent variables include productivity, attendance, grievances, innovativeness, employee satisfaction, safety records, and related outcomes that we care about.

Most students are by now familiar with the notions of independent and dependent variables. They have dealt with these terms in other courses in the physical, biological, and social sciences. The student may not, however, be acquainted with two other important types of constructs—intervening variables and moderating variables.

An *intervening variable* (also called *mediating variable*) transmits the effects of a prior variable to a subsequent variable. If a change in A causes a change in B, leading to a subsequent change in C, then B is an intervening variable. In other words, B is the link between A and C. When A affects C, it does so through, or because of, the effect it has on B. This makes B a dependent variable since it is affected by A; but B is also an independent variable because it, in turn, affects C. If a theory states that supervisory styles influence worker satisfaction, and worker satisfaction determines the level of absenteeism, we then have a theory in which the construct satisfaction plays the role of an intervening variable.

Intervening variables are important in theory development because they help us understand why or how one variable affects another. Furthermore, intervening variables have significant implications for practice.

Consider Figure 2–1. The fact that supervisory style affects absenteeism would lead us to put the burden for reducing absenteeism on supervi-

FIGURE 2–1

Construct B as an Intervening Variable

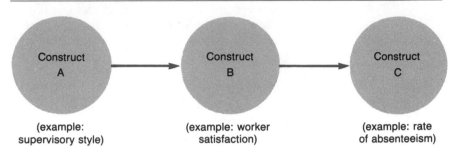

sion. But if we understand this relationship in terms of the mediating effect of satisfaction, we realize that other possibilities exist. Any other construct that affects satisfaction is likely to affect absenteeism. For example, if pay policies affect satisfaction, they will also affect absenteeism to some extent.

In OB, intervening variables often designate a person's psychological state. Job satisfaction, motivation, stress, organizational commitment, and group attachment illustrate constructs that are used as intervening variables in OB.

A *moderating variable* (often simply called a *moderator*) governs or limits the relationship between two other constructs. We may start with a simple theory asserting that A causes B. After further study, we qualify this theory to state that A causes B only under some conditions. Whether A affects B, or just how it affects B, depends on M. For example, our theory is that supervisory style affects absenteeism, but only for relatively routine or lower-level jobs; supervision has a negligible effect on the absence rate of people doing highly nonroutine jobs. The routineness of the job is a construct that serves as a moderating variable.

Unlike the intervening variable, the moderating variable does not have to affect, or be affected by, any of the other constructs of interest to us. Moderators regulate the relationships among the other constructs. Figure 2–2 illustrates an example of the moderator variable.

Moderating variables can determine *(a)* whether a cause-effect relationship between two other constructs exists, *(b)* whether the relationship is strong or weak, or *(c)* whether the effect is positive or negative. The following are examples of the three types of moderator effects:

1. If a theory states that job security causes satisfaction for older workers, but security has no effect on the satisfaction of younger workers, then age moderates the relationship between security and satisfaction.

FIGURE 2–2
Construct M as a Moderator Variable

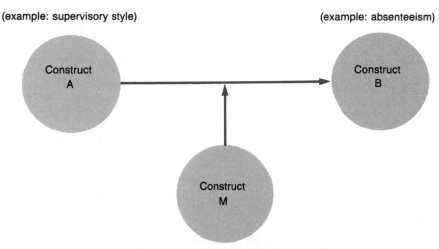

(example: routine versus nonroutine nature of job)

2. If we theorize that leader supportiveness has a significant effect on the morale of people working on routine jobs, but has a smaller effect on the morale of employees doing nonroutine jobs, we are saying that job routineness moderates the effect of leader supportiveness on morale.

3. Suppose we argue that time pressure improves the performance of low-anxiety persons but impairs the performance of high-anxiety individuals. This argument makes "anxiety proneness" a moderator of the relationship between time pressure and performance.

The most frequently used moderator variables in theories of OB involve some individual characteristic (i.e., age, gender, background, or personality) or some aspect of the job (i.e., job level, complexity, or the technology of the job). As interest in the international dimension of OB continues, we will find that culture also moderates many relationships. For example, certain supervisory practices might have effects in Pacific Rim countries different from those in Western Europe and North America.

Managers and Theory

In the examples of moderator variables, we have provided illustrations of simple, straightforward (but potentially useful) theories that a manager might have formulated without consciously acting as a theorist. All managers

FOCUS ON INTERNATIONAL OB

Theories made in the United States: Can They Be Exported?

Geert Hofstede (1980) analyzed survey data collected from 116,000 employees of a large U.S.-headquartered multinational corporation in 40 countries and identified four dimensions of national culture:

Power distance: The degree to which a society accepts the unequal distribution of power.

Uncertainty avoidance: The extent to which people feel threatened by ambiguous situations and value structure and security.

Individualism-collectivism: The tendency of a culture to emphasize individual autonomy, identity, and achievement versus emphasis on membership in, and loyalty to, the group or clan.

Masculinity-femininity: Cultural emphasis on those values (such as assertiveness, acquisition of money, productivity) more generally associated with men, as opposed to the "softer" values (such as quality of life, sympathy for the unfortunate, harmonious relationships) more characteristic of women.

Compared to other nations, the U.S. average ranked at the very top in individualism, well above the median on masculinity, below average on power distance, and near the bottom on uncertainty avoidance. In other words, our culture—what Hofstede calls "collective mental programming"—reflects values and modes of understanding not shared abroad. Hofstede argues that many of the U.S.-born theories of motivation, leadership, management, and organization structure are based on assumptions and facts quite peculiar to our own conception of social reality. Thus, many of our theories might have limited applicability in nations dissimilar to the United States in the four dimensions noted by Hofstede.

SOURCE: G. Hofstede, "Motivation, Leadership, and Organization: Do American Theories Apply Abroad?", *Organization Dynamics,* Summer 1980.

make decisions, and to do so, they must make some assumptions about how various concepts are related.

If managers and other action-oriented people use theories, why their discomfort with theories in behavioral science? The answer is found not in the intrinsic nature of theory, but in certain qualitative differences between theory-in-use or "informal theory" and the reconstructed or "formal theory" used by behavioral scientists.

First, the concepts and components of informal theory are usually couched at a low level of abstraction. The behavioral scientist, on the other hand, typically works with constructs at a more abstract level.

Second, and related to the first difference, informal theory usually addresses a very specific, sometimes unique, problem or set of problems, whereas formal theory in behavioral science encompasses a greater range of related problems. The manager theorizes about performance on a particular job; the behavioral scientist theorizes about performance in general or concerning a broad category of tasks.

Third, the manager uses ordinary, everyday language or labels in theory construction, while the behavioral scientist prefers abstract, general concepts with exotic or awkward labels. Why? Behavioral science uses abstractions so that knowledge accumulated about some aspects of behavior can be applied to seemingly unrelated behavioral phenomena.

Consider, for example, the job interview. The recruiter is trying to derive a maximum of information from a few minutes of observing and conversing with a candidate. The interviewer notes that the candidate has arrived promptly and has dressed neatly. The interviewer might leap to the "observation" that the candidate is well-organized and efficient. The interviewer has not actually made such an observation, but has taken evidence of certain traits and "extrapolated" this thinking to infer other traits that presumably go together with neatness and punctuality.

We could, if we wished, analyze this process narrowly in terms of the context of interviewing people. The psychologist is apt to see it in a broader context—something psychologists call "implicit personality theory." In this theory, people have preconceived notions about traits that go together, and they will often infer these traits in others without having the least bit of evidence. What happens in interviews also occurs in many other contexts—in our perceptions of leaders, in their evaluations of subordinates, and in the impressions that people in one group have of those in a different group. By conceptualizing this phenomenon at a more abstract and broader level, we can understand how impressions of people are formed without regard to context. When we learn how this process works in any one context, it tells us something of potential value about its occurrence in other situations.

The reader might agree, but ask why the language of everyday life is not used. One reason is that the more familiar concept labels have different shades of meaning for different people; by inventing a term with its own definition, the behavioral scientist avoids misinterpretations. Also, everyday concepts carry value-charged connotations that can get in the way of detached, logical analysis. To talk about democratic as opposed to autocratic leadership is to invite preexisting prejudices or emotions. Phrasing the issue in terms of directive versus participative supervision is less likely to trigger preconceived biases.

What Functions Does Theory Serve?

One of the functions served by theory has already been implied by the foregoing discussion. Theory helps organize our knowledge into a pattern whereby facts, data, and observed regularities are interconnected and take on a new meaning not evident when viewed in isolation. Theory brings to light similarities in seemingly dissimilar phenomena.

A theory is also useful to summarize a diverse body of knowledge in symbolic form. As Shaw and Costanzo (1970) state, a theory "permits us to handle large amounts of empirical data with relatively few propositions" (p. 9). Theory functions as a shorthand method of stating what we have learned or believe about a class of phenomena.

A third function of theory is to point the way to continued research, or to the pursuit of new facts. Theory prompts us to ask new questions about the phenomenon we are studying. Indeed, a good theory may raise more questions than it answers. Furthermore, theory helps us distinguish between trivial and important questions. Theories go beyond the data or experience that gave birth to them to suggest what new data or experiences will look like. Without a theory, it would be difficult to know what to study or how to study it.

The organizing, summarizing, and guiding functions are as important in informal theories as in formal theories. Practicing professionals store their accumulated observations in an organized and symbolic form. Tentative conclusions drawn from their experiences suggest new solutions to old problems or new problems to be addressed. The effective manager operates in a conceptual world of assumptions, logic, and tentative conclusions about relationships among variables, and the design of activities to test the truth-value or usefulness of those conclusions.

Alfred P. Sloan, Jr., in his autobiographical *My Years with General Motors* (1965), states that "every enterprise needs a concept of its industry" (p. 58). Sloan's ensuing account makes clear that he was very much a theorist — and self-consciously so — about the automobile industry. He attributed much of General Motor's success to the exercise of theory construction.

Former National Security Advisor to the President and Secretary of State Henry Kissinger also recognized the importance of theory. As Kissinger put it:

> Yet in foreign policy there is no escaping the need for an integrating conceptual framework. . . . A conceptual framework — which "links" events — is an essential tool. [Kissinger, 1979, p. 130]

What Are the Criteria for Evaluating a Theory?

Abraham Kaplan, in *The Conduct of Inquiry* (1964), discusses criteria by which the scientific community assesses the worth of a theory. The *norm of correspondence* is the most obvious one: How well does the theory fit the facts? How closely do predictions drawn from the theory match up with actual events? The layman thinks of this as the acid test of a theory. But suppose several theories all explain the data equally well — how do we decide which is best?

The *norm of coherence* requires that a theory should be internally consistent and straightforward in its logic. The connections should not be so loose or imprecise that totally opposite conclusions could be drawn from the theory.

The norm of coherence also includes the *principle of parsimony:* a theory should contain no more concepts or assumptions than are necessary to account for the data. A simple theory is preferable to a complex theory, unless the added complexity can explain significantly more than the simple theory.

The norm of coherence dictates that a new theory must fit with the preexisting theories in the field, assuming that these theories have validity. For example, a theory of leadership that assumes that subordinate satisfaction is a direct cause of performance does not mesh with fairly well-established theories about how attitudes and performance are related. No matter how well such a leadership theory fits the facts of a study or one's informal observations, it would not get high marks.

The *norm of pragmatism* does not refer to the practical applications of a theory, but rather to how a theory furthers the activities of scientists. This relates closely to the guidance function of theories. How much new research is suggested by the theory? What new puzzles or questions does the theory bring to light? To score well on the norm of pragmatism, a theory must be capable of being put to a test in which only certain results, and not just any conceivable result, could support the theory.

We would add to Kaplan's criteria another test that we inevitably apply to a theory: the *norm of intuitive appeal.* Some theories are appealing because they have the ring of plausibility; they sum up with an eloquent, convincing tone much of what we have felt or observed. Some theories appeal to us because they implicitly support our deeply ingrained views about human nature and its limitations or potentialities. Some theories simply have certain esthetic attractions because of the imagery or models they convey. Even in the hard sciences, like physics and astronomy, scientists' choices of competing theories are determined in part by the perceived beauty of a particular theory.

Pinder (1982), commenting about theories of work motivation, stated that we really cannot say just how valid some of our theories are. Some theories go beyond our presently available techniques of measurement and observation. Much of the research that tests established theories is based on some oversimplifications of what the theory really asserts. When the research evidence is mixed or inconclusive, we cannot say for sure whether the problem is in the theory itself or the way it has been researched. Often the final criterion of whether the theory still has influence is its intuitive appeal. Thus, Maslow's need hierarchy theory continues to occupy a niche among motivation theorists largely because of its intuitive appeal, even though it is not very well supported empirically and may not even be testable in its original form.

CLOSE-UP

Life Cycle of a Theory

Robert B. Zajonc (1960), noting the exceptional cases not consistent with current theories of attitude change, drew an analogy from the ancient theory that "nature abhors a vacuum." Centuries ago, that simplistic theory seemed to explain the action of pumps and suction. Then it was observed that pumps could not draw water to a height of over 34 feet. So, the theory was qualified to state "nature abhors a vacuum up to 34 feet." However, even this qualification could not handle the later finding that mercury could be drawn into a vacuum only up to 30 inches.

Eventually, Torricelli formulated a more inclusive theory: The pressure of air acting on the surface of a liquid forces it to rise into a pressureless vacuum. The height reached by the liquid depends on the weight of the liquid and the weight of the atmosphere at the surface of the earth.

The newer theory would not have been inspired without the old. As Zajonc notes, without the older theory, the exceptions would not have stimulated anyone to think about the phenomenon. The older theory was useful and was not discarded because of a few discrepancies. It yielded to a better theory.

THEORIES IN PROGRESS

In every field of study, theories come and go; they are born and eventually die. Their transitory nature bothers some students, who may feel that the time and effort taken to understand a theory is wasted if the theory is later discarded. But even when a theory falls by the wayside, it passes something along to the theories that succeed it.

A theory serves as a provisional statement, couched in conceptual language, of how various phenomena in nature or behavior are interrelated. A theory is a perspective on the state of knowledge as it then exists, coupled with some speculations about what additional knowledge may come to light.

As new knowledge develops, the theory undergoes revision; its constructs may be redefined, special conditions may be noted in which it does not seem to hold, qualifying statements are added, and exceptional cases are compiled. As these developments occur, the theory becomes cumbersome, less appealing esthetically, and less satisfying intellectually. Eventually a new theory emerges that shows how seeming contradictions and exceptional cases fall neatly into place. The new theory preserves the contribution of the old theory and passes it along, yet also provides a perspective that dissolves the nagging riddles.

Although some of the theories in the pages ahead will become historical curiosities, you have not studied them in vain. If they now serve the essential ends of any theory, their contributions will be well preserved by new theoretical developments.

TESTING AND APPLYING THEORIES

We test and apply our theories by descending from abstract concepts or constructs to observable events. In a sense, the various methods of doing this all do the same thing: they make use of *operational definitions* of the constructs to see if the relationships theorized to exist between the concepts are reflected in a sample of observed events. An operational definition of a construct is not the construct itself, but a means of illustrating the construct in a specific form. This operational definition often amounts to what we more commonly call a *measure* of the concept.

Suppose we theorize that the "heterogeneity" of a work group is related to its "creativity." Both of these concepts are abstract and incorporate many elements, and we cannot test this theory until we choose some specific indicators of heterogeneity and creativity. Perhaps we start by reasoning that a group of people who vary considerably in age is more heterogeneous than a group of people who are approximately the same age. Thus, one indicator of heterogeneity could be the range within the group of chronological age. Now we need an analagous indicator of creativity. It is reasonable to think that a creative work group will make numerous suggestions to management for ways to improve operations. Therefore, if the organization has a formal system for submitting suggestions, the number of suggestions submitted by the group over a given time period can serve as the index of "creativity." Our task is now straightforward: for a number of different work groups, we juxtapose the age range with number of suggestions (see Figure 2–3).

Suppose our data convince us that age range is related to number of suggestions submitted by the work groups. Have we proved our theory? Clearly we have not. "Heterogeneity" incorporates more than just variation in age, and "creativity" obviously involves more than tendering written suggestions. What we have is one finding consistent with our theory. We would have more confidence in the theory if alternative operational definitions of the constructs were also related. Perhaps we could conduct a new study in which we operationally define heterogeneity in the group by the number of different ethnic or religious affiliations represented (perhaps controlling for the size of the group). We might also use a different measure of group creativity, this time asking each supervisor to rate the group on a scale from one (meaning "not at all creative") to seven ("very creative"). Again, we see if there is any tendency for groups with more variation in ethnic or religious affiliation to be rated higher in creativity by their supervisor.

We would have maximum confidence in our theory if it continued to be supported with many different forms of defining the constructs. Inconsistent results would lead us to revise our theory, specifying a more circumscribed notion of heterogeneity and/or a more qualified conception of what we mean by "creativity."

FIGURE 2–3
Relationship between Theory and Research

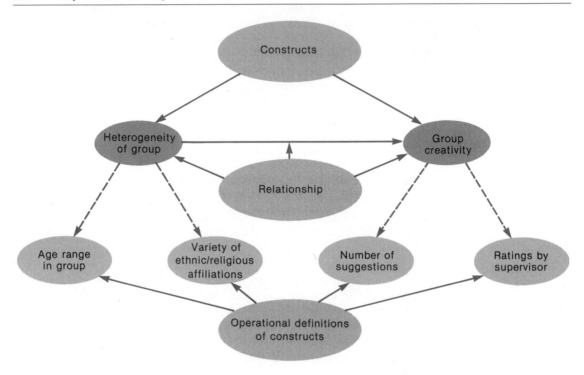

METHODS OF RESEARCH

A method of research is any means by which we observe or learn about nature — human or otherwise. Several types of research methods are used to learn about behavior in organizations — all useful, but each with its limitations. The user of knowledge about organizational behavior must be able to qualify that knowledge on the basis of the limitations of the method(s) used to produce it.

Naturalistic Observation

One method of research we all use is simply to observe human behavior in organized settings. We all have considerable experience in various organizations. From experience, observation, and recall we have some intuitive notions about the effects of leadership styles, incentives, and job stress. To the extent that we have described these beliefs, we may have discovered that others agree with us.

Thus each of us has a private fund of knowledge about behavior in organizations. Furthermore, this knowledge has been supplemented by the accounts of others who have offered their observations in the form of conversations, speeches, magazine articles, autobiographies (for example,

TABLE 2–1

Naturalistic Observation as a Method of Learning about Organizational Behavior

Forms	Personal experience; biographical statements; journalistic accounts; case study
Advantages	Contextual richness; sources of personal insights; generation of hypotheses; raw material for theory construction
Disadvantages	Selective observation and recall; biased focus toward the dramatic; difficult to separate the unique from the more generalizable; not subject to quantitative analysis

Sloan's *My Year at General Motors,* 1965), even fiction (in Cameron Hawley's novels, which drew from his own experience as a business executive).

A more systematic form of naturalistic observation is represented by the *case study.* In this method, one or more researchers enter an organization — sometimes as participants, otherwise as consultants or guests — to observe. Usually, the researchers have some particular focus for their observations. For example, Alvin Gouldner (1954) entered a gypsum plant to observe the result of sending in a new plant manager from corporate headquarters to tighten up bureaucratic rules and procedures (his observations are recorded in the book *Patterns of Industrial Bureaucracy*). Melvill Dalton (1959), a sociologist, became an employee of an industrial organization to examine the politics of management (his impressions formed the basis of his book *Men Who Manage*). While conducting the case study, researchers often keep diaries or journals of their daily experiences and supplement their own perceptions by examining company records and interviewing personnel.

Naturalistic observation is an attractive method of research because it confronts its subject head-on. It deals with raw, real-world behavior. Because its data are rich with the drama of human existence, it is easy to relate to accounts of these studies.

The shortcomings of naturalistic observation, however, as shown in Table 2–1, must be noted.* First, the "original data" are soon irretrievably lost, transformed, and mangled because of the limited information-processing capabilities of human beings. For instance, when we read, say, Sloan's account of his experiences at General Motors, we are not privy to the events as they actually occurred. We are totally dependent on Sloan's subjective frame of reference as it affected both his perceptions and his memories of events. We do not know if his account includes things he did not directly experience or observe. We do not know how much filtering has occurred, as it inevitably must, in the transmission of information. Finally, we do not know whether other observers would have drawn the same conclusions.

Experiments demonstrate that in naturalistic observation people make woefully inaccurate estimates of the degree of correlation among events. People often delude themselves into seeing systematic causal relationships

---

*The shortcomings discussed refer to the case study as a method of formal science. This is not to deny the obvious advantages of the case study as a method of instruction.

where such relationships do not exist. Thus, "conventional wisdom" is not supported by more rigorous study. For example, many people assume that greater job satisfaction leads to higher productivity, that groups make more conservative decisions than individuals acting alone, that extroverts make more effective leaders, and that high-level managers experience greater stress with a higher rate of heart attacks than blue-collar workers. As we shall see in the pages ahead, much research questions these beliefs.

Another shortcoming of informal observation or case studies is their tendency to have a biased focus on dramatic, unusual, or otherwise newsworthy phenomena (Weick, 1969). Mergers, strikes, changes in leadership, reorganizations, and the like are frequently the occasions for starting case studies. Such exciting events may not provide the best material for learning about organizational behavior.

As Karl Weick (1965) notes, much organizational behavior is routine and taken for granted. Dramatic and newsworthy events, almost by definition, are either nontypical occurrences or merely the end result of more subtle, day-to-day processes.

Finally, naturalistic observation of human behavior usually defies quantification. Statistics are not the be-all and end-all of any science, but comparative judgments are often useful, and quantification through measurement renders such judgments more reliable and communicable. Casual observation seldom gives us a basis from which to estimate the strength of relationships among variables or gauge the relative contribution of different factors to an end result.

These shortcomings make naturalistic observation more useful in the exploratory stage of studying a phenomenon. Case studies provide only a crude sketch of the terrain; more rigorous, sophisticated methods are essential to produce a workable map. Naturalistic observation can be a fruitful source of theory development, and can correct the mistake of studying only trivial issues rigorously. But by itself, naturalistic observation is a shaky foundation for a body of knowledge about organizational behavior.

Field Survey Research

An alternative to naturalistic observation in organizations is the design of systematic surveys of the opinions, perceptions, attitudes, or self-reported behavior of participants in organizations. Whereas naturalistic observation relies almost totally on the perceptions of the researcher, survey research taps the perceptions of others, at least as others report and describe these perceptions. After watching operators perform a repetitive task, the naturalistic observer might conclude that they are bored with or "alienated" from their jobs. Survey research would solicit the operators' own feelings about their work. The operators might, in fact, express considerable satisfaction with their jobs—possibly even rejoicing in their freedom from the paperwork and number crunching of a behavioral science researcher.

One form of survey research is the person-to-person interview. The researcher asks questions, to which the subject responds. The interview may

TABLE 2–2

Field Survey Research as a Method of Learning about Organizational Behavior

Forms	Face-to-face interviews, questionnaires
Advantages	Enables researcher to assess others' subjective frames of reference; allows a degree of quantitative analysis; formats can be standardized across studies
Disadvantages	Possible spurious relationships due to various forms of bias or distortion by subjects in responding; correlational data do not permit inferences about causal relationship

be unstructured in format with general questions which the interviewer could selectively probe in greater depth, depending on the respondent's answers. In a structured interview the questions would be formulated in advance so that the respondent could answer by choosing between a few response alternatives, such as "yes" or "no," "agree" or "disagree." The same questions would be used over and over again with subsequent interviewees.

Alfred Kinsey used the interview as his basic method of researching the sexual behavior of males and females (Kinsey, Pomeroy, & Martin, 1949). David Granick also utilized interviews with Soviet and European managers to assess the cross-cultural similarities and differences in the role of the executive (Granick, 1961).

People in different types of organizations can be interviewed to see whether they have correspondingly different experiences in their work, different levels of stress, or different types of problems. People can be interviewed about the leadership style of their superiors and about whether their work attitudes are related to leader style.

The chief advantage of the interview is that it offers observations independent of those of the researcher. There are limitations, however, with the interview as a method of research (see Table 2–2).

First, the person being interviewed might feel awed or threatened by the presence of the interviewer. Subjects might refrain from offering opinions or information that could place them in an embarrassing or vulnerable position. The interviewer must have a knack for putting subjects completely at ease and winning their confidence to reliably elicit candid responses. Kinsey apparently had this knack, even with very unusual subject populations, such as prison inmates (Christenson, 1971).

Second, the interviewer can unwittingly shape a certain pattern to the subjects' verbal responses by nods, grimaces, or other nonverbal cues. Considerable skill and training in interviewing are necessary to avoid such biases.

Finally, interviews are very expensive in terms of the researcher's time. For all these reasons, most contemporary research in organizational behavior uses the direct interview primarily in the preliminary phases of a more elaborate project using other methods.

The questionnaire represents a more efficient means of survey research that avoids some of the pitfalls of the interview. Questionnaires, like interviews, may be unstructured or highly structured in format. Increasingly, researchers attempt to use the more structured versions. By mailing questionnaires to potential subjects or distributing them to an assembled group, the anonymity of the respondent is guaranteed, and a vast amount of data in the form of written responses can be collected and computer-processed.

The increased use of questionnaires in survey research is due to the recent development of standardized instruments to measure subjects' perceptions of relevant organizational characteristics. Psychologists have designed scales to measure job satisfaction, supervisor's style, and beliefs about the kinds of rewards related to performance. Scales are scored by weighting the extremity of the answer in a given direction (for example, 5 for "strongly disagree" versus 1 for "strongly agree") summing across all items in the scale. The average scores of different groups can then be compared, as in the mean job satisfaction score for males versus females. Or scores on one scale can be compared with scores on another scale to see whether they are statistically related: Do higher scores by respondents on a scale measuring job satisfaction go along with higher scores on a scale measuring leader considerateness and vice versa? In short, the use of standardized scales in questionnaires facilitates quantification.

Despite the advantages of the written questionnaire over the interview, it does have its own problems. Its use presumes that respondents are both able and willing to describe their feelings or perceptions by circling a number or checking a blank space. Assured anonymity makes this assumption somewhat plausible, but even then respondents might consciously or unwittingly slant their responses in a direction more consistent with how they would like to see themselves rather than with their actual behavior. For example, in self-report studies of how people rank the various outcomes of their jobs (see, for example, Opsahl & Dunnette, 1966), money is not always ranked as the most important job consideration; to do so would be to view themselves as materialistic. Yet, as Opsahl and Dunnette note, people apparently behave as if money were quite important: professors move to institutions that pay them more; superstar athletes play out their contract options if they don't get the salary they want; and film stars go to court to recover commissions on the distribution of their films. The complicating factor of *social desirability* in response set must be considered when interpreting the results of questionnaire studies.

People also tend to structure their answers to different scales in a manner they perceive to be "consistent" or "logical," even if doing so inaccurately portrays life situations. One finding from questionnaire studies of supervisory styles is that people who describe their boss as autocratic report lower job satisfaction than those who view their boss as democratic or participative. It would be tempting to conclude that this type of supervisory style is a determinant of subordinate dissatisfaction. But an alternative explanation could simply be that dissatisfied workers describe everything else in their work environment to make it consistent with their

TABLE 2–3

Correlation between Style of Supervisor and Productivity of Supervisor's Section

	Job-Centered Supervisors	Employee-Centered Supervisors
High-producing sections	1	6
Low-producing sections	7	3

SOURCE: Adapted from P. Hersey and K. H. Blanchard, *Management of Organizational Behavior* (Englewood Cliffs, N.J.: Prentice Hall, 1969), p. 70.

dissatisfaction. This would be especially likely when they are describing something subjective and open to different interpretations, such as leadership style or "organizational climate." It is less of a problem when respondents are asked for reasonably straightforward, more objective, or emotionally neutral information, such as their hours of work.

One means of strengthening field survey studies is to ensure that some of the measures come from *different sources*. Again, suppose we want to test the theory that more considerate supervisors have more satisfied subordinates. When subordinates answer questions about both their own satisfaction and their supervisor's behavior, it can produce misleading results. To avoid that problem, use the subordinates' questionnaire responses to measure either their satisfaction or the supervisor's behavior, but not both. For example, we could have subordinates report their own satisfaction, but have the supervisor's boss provide responses to questions about the supervisor's level of considerateness. Or we could use subordinate responses to measure the supervisor's considerateness and use some other basis for estimating the group's satisfaction—for example, company records on absenteeism, quit rate, rate of requests for transfers to another work unit, or formally processed grievances.

The Causality Question

Most field survey studies provide evidence in answer to the following types of questions: Is there an *association* between X and Y? Do organizations or departments with more (or less) of A also have more (or less) of B?

Evidence of this sort is called *correlational*. It simply tells us that X *correlates* with Y, or A correlates with B. Where we find more or less of the one, we find more or less of the other. This evidence cannot tell us whether X causes Y, or Y causes X, or whether they correlate because they are both caused by something else.

Consider a study of supervisory styles reporting the results shown in Table 2–3. The study assessed the styles of supervisors by means of questionnaires distributed to workers in various departments. From responses to questions concerning the typical behavior of their bosses, the researchers could classify the styles of the supervisors as predominantly "employee-centered" (i.e., the major emphasis or concern of the supervisor was with employee relations) or "job-centered" (with primary emphasis on getting the work out). The researchers obtained measures of productivity by consulting company records of the volume of paperwork processed by the different groups.

The findings show that employee-centered supervisors tended to have more productive work units. One might conclude that the employee-centered style of supervision caused a higher level of group productivity than did the job-centered style. But is this the only tenable explanation for the results? No, because all correlational studies have a common limitation: they cannot show what is the cause and what is effect.

Anytime we have a correlation between two variables, say, A and B, it could be that A caused B or that B caused A. In the study described above, it seems logical to think that supervisory style caused the level of productivity. But it could be that the level of group productivity caused the supervisor to act in a certain way. Leaders of good groups do not need to be critical, punitive, or concerned about production; they have the luxury of attending primarily to personal relationships and promoting a comfortable work climate. The unfortunate manager who inherits a group of incompetent workers must set about improving the level of work. Thus, the productivity of the section could have been the cause and supervisory style a consequence or effect due to that cause.

Another explanation for the correlation between two variables is that they each may have been caused by some other unknown or unmeasured variable, C. A study conducted years ago, before polio vaccines were available, found a strikingly high correlation between consumption of a certain soft drink and the incidence of polio. The drink didn't make people more susceptible to polio, and polio didn't make people crave the pop. Both variables were caused by climate—polio occurred more often in the summer months and in warmer regions, and of course people drink more liquids in hot weather.

In order to infer that a correlation between A and B is due to A causing B, we must be able to manipulate A at our discretion, holding other possible causes of B constant, and then determine whether B changes as we manipulate A. Controlled manipulation does not occur in correlational studies. Instead, we have recorded observations of things "changing as they will."

Despite the absence of manipulation, field survey studies that are extended in time may give some basis for causal inference. If repeated measures of the important variables are taken over a period of weeks or months, presumably some of these variables will change—productivity will go up or down in some departments, supervisors in some units will be more or less considerate. If changes occurring in X consistently precede correlated changes in Y, but not vice versa, we can tentatively assume that X causes Y rather than the other way around. Of course, it is still

TABLE 2–4

Field Experiments as a Method of Learning about Organizational Behavior

Forms	Experimenter-induced change in one or more organizational units, with appropriate comparisons possible; natural experiments in which changes that occur in one or more units are not matched by comparable units
Advantages	Naturalistic environment; permits some degree of causal inference
Disadvantages	Occasions that permit such studies are not as frequent as desired and may not be representative; difficult to allow time for changes to take full effect while still controlling for other factors

possible that something else caused both the changes in X and the somewhat later changes in Y.

Suppose we are interested in the relationship between job performance and emotional stress. We find that, as of a given date, better performers report fewer problems with emotional stress than less effective performers. We have found a relationship. But does stress cause the poor performance? Does the poor performance itself create stress? Or does something else—conceivably poor diet or lack of sleep—affect both performance and stress?

Suppose we could keep tabs on the people in our study long enough that some people will experience some changes in both degree of stress experienced and quality of performance. If earlier changes in stress levels matched subsequent changes in performance, we have some basis for inferring that stress is the cause, performance level the effect. If earlier declines (improvements) in performance were correlated with later increases (decreases) in stress levels, it would appear that stress is the effect of poor performance rather than its cause. If we observed neither of these patterns, it is quite likely that some other variable accounted for their initial correlation.

Recently, longitudinal studies have been reported with increasing frequency in organizational behavior. Also, a variety of statistical tools suited to their analysis has come to light. Many of the causal inferences drawn from previous correlational studies have been reinvestigated using the longitudinal design. At this point, it appears that more and more researchers are adding this touch to their field studies and that it could soon become the dominant investigative tool in our discipline.

There remain some technical problems in the analysis of longitudinal data—problems we cannot appropriately address here. Basically these problems pertain to the researcher's ability to rule out spurious relationships. Even correlations between changes in variables can be influenced by unknown factors. Thus, even the longitudinal design is not a perfect substitute for direct manipulation of variables in the attempt to draw causal inferences (see Table 2–4).

Field Experiments

In a field experiment, we change an organizational variable in one setting, observe the consequences, and compare them to what happens in a similar setting where that variable was not altered. Or we compare them to the consequences in a similar setting where a different change was made.

For example, Morse and Reimer (1956) decentralized the level of decision making in some sections of a company by letting employees make more work-related decisions. In other sections, they centralized decision making by restricting the number of work-related decisions an employee could make. In both situations, the type of employee and the type of job were similar.

After 18 months, Morse and Reimer compared the two groups in terms of productivity. Both groups had increased productivity over previous levels, but the increase was slightly greater in the centralized sections. If the change had been made only in the decentralized sections, the increased productivity would have suggested that the decentralization was the cause of the increase. However, with the comparison (centralized) sections also showing an increase in productivity, we know that decentralization per se was not the causative factor.

In another field experiment, Muczyk (1976) conducted a study of the effects of a management-by-objectives (MBO) program on organizational performance. The MBO program was introduced in 13 branches of a multibranch bank. A comparable number of branches — matched by market areas, types and volumes of business, and personnel profiles similar to those in the experimental groups — served as controls, or baselines against which to assess the effects of the MBO program.

The branches using the MBO program did show positive changes in a number of banking performance criteria 6 months and 12 months later, but performance had also increased by comparable levels in the control branches. Without the control, the performance improvements might have been attributed to the MBO program rather than, for example, to changes in the national or state economic climates.

In the field experiment, then, the essential features include not only the ability to change something, but also the ability to control other relevant variables — either by using a comparison group or by holding all other factors constant. The latter is virtually impossible in a live organization, so comparison groups are usually necessary.

True field experiments are somewhat rare in the study of organizational behavior. In order to conduct them, researchers need permission to take the steps essential for proper controls. Organizational officials are understandably reluctant to permit changes they regard as risks to the reliability of normal operations. Those who do permit the changes may be so unusual — in either their philosophy or their tolerance for such risks — that the results obtained cannot be regarded as generally applicable to other settings.

TABLE 2–5

Laboratory Experiments as a Method of Learning about Organizational Behavior

Forms	Simulation of organizational variables
Advantages	Control; elimination of confounding factors; permits causal inference
Disadvantages	Reactivity of subjects; limitations posed by ethics; for some purposes, artificiality of environment; seldom suited to studying long-term effects

A particularly troublesome issue in field experiments concerns the time dimension. It may take months or years for the full effects of a change in an organizational variable to be felt (for example, Muczyk had reason to believe that the MBO program was just beginning to have an impact when his study was concluded). Yet the longer the experiment, the greater the opportunity for noncomparabilities between experimental and control groups to develop. In the Morse and Reimer field experiment, for example, one group (the centralized sections) experienced a higher rate of turnover in personnel than the other. This left a smaller group with the same amount of work to do, resulting in a higher rate of production per employee work hour.

When the researcher has reasonable control over important variables, organizational experiments form the ideal research method by combining rigor and realism. An increasing number of organization leaders welcome the chance to assess rigorously the effects of new programs, and there is a good reason for it. Managers, as well as scholars, have a vested interest in obtaining the most rigorous possible understanding of what is cause and what is effect. Lacking that understanding, they might waste incalculable resources changing the wrong things.

Laboratory Experiments

Undoubtedly the most misunderstood and least appreciated method of research in organizational behavior is the laboratory experiment. Since some of the knowledge base described in this volume rests on data generated by laboratory experiments, it is important that the reader comprehend the logic and rationale for studying behavior in the laboratory.

The term *laboratory* denotes only a setting that makes observation easier. A laboratory does not have to be on a college campus or in a psychology department, nor does it require exotic apparatus. An unused classroom, a vacant office, or a materials storeroom could constitute a laboratory. Nothing more awesome than tables, chairs, pencils, and paper need be used. As Weick (1965) points out, all you need for a laboratory is a setting, some subjects, and a task for the subjects. With these minimal requirements satisfied, the experimenter can proceed to study a vast range of behavior relevant to organizations (see Table 2–5).

The purpose of the laboratory setting is, first, to screen out distractions. Suppose you were interested in the effects of feedback on performance. You want to find out how the timeliness of feedback, the accuracy of feedback, or positive versus negative feedback affects people's work. You could spend a few hours or days in an actual organization watching how people perform without feedback, when it is delayed, or when it is erroneous. But if you honestly appraised the limits of your knowledge thus gained, you would be forced to hedge any conclusions drawn with numerous doubts and qualifications.

For example, supervisors who give quick feedback are likely to be different in a variety of ways from those who delay giving feedback to subordinates. They might also be more considerate, better planners, or simply more knowledgeable, and these differences obscure our observation of the effect of feedback per se. You would probably also find that positive feedback is given more quickly than negative feedback. If so, is any difference in the effect on worker performance due to the difference in timing or to the difference in positivity or negativity? There is no way to unscramble the separate effects of all these varying factors from the feedback itself.

The laboratory allows us to control those factors that are irrelevant to the question of theoretical interest. In so doing, the reader may argue, the laboratory makes the situation "unrealistic" or "artificial." That is precisely the purpose in taking the issue into the laboratory. We can see the phenomenon for what it actually is, not as we ordinarily find it camouflaged in its natural element. In the laboratory, the only reality that counts is the reality of the phenomenon we are investigating, and it is just as real there as it is anywhere else.

A second purpose of the laboratory setting is to allow the researcher to exert more control over the structure of events. Experimenters make things happen at their own convenience. The experimenter can also vary combinations of factors. For example, subjects can be given either positive or negative feedback, and the speed with which feedback is given after performance can also be varied. Thus, the experimenter can observe the separate as well as the additive or interacting effects of both timing and the positivity or negativity of feedback on subsequent performance.

In the "real world" we would not be likely to find proportionate representation of all four combinations, or we might have to wait an inordinately long time for a particular combination—say, quick negative feedback—to occur. The nature of the task, the time of day, and the personality of the feedback presenter can be kept constant across all of these combinations so that those factors can be excluded as alternative explanations of the results.

Third, the researcher knows and can state in unambiguous terms the conditions under which results were obtained. A certain task was used, subjects were drawn from a specified population of known attributes, and certain instructions were given. These statements are part and parcel of experimental findings; they serve as a baseline from which to assess the generalizability of the findings. Laboratory experiments thus engender a healthy caution in interpreting the limits of our knowledge.

Unfortunately, this virtue is often mistaken as a vice by the general public. The layman's typical response to a set of laboratory findings is "Yes, but you can't generalize from that set of conditions to the situation in the bank where I work." True enough, in one sense, but also true for the results of a field study at an oil refinery, a department store, or even some other banks. More important, in the latter settings we are hard-pressed to specify precisely the conditions under which the results were obtained. In the strict sense, we cannot generalize the *data* from one setting to another. Only theory can bridge the gap, and then only to the extent that unique features of any setting are known and can be interpreted within a theoretical overview.

Some critics argue that in laboratory experiments the subjects are not sufficiently involved in what happens. There are ways to increase subject involvement (Weick, 1965), but we should remember that much of everyday life is characterized by passive involvement. The frequent dependence on college freshmen and sophomores is also cited as a shortcoming of lab studies. However, only theory can guide us as to whether they are radically different from others in the general population in regard to the relevant attributes. If they are that different, there is no reason why laboratory experiments cannot use other kinds of people as subjects.

One limitation of laboratory experiments stems from professional ethics. Responsible investigators are prohibited, by conscience and professional guidelines, from subjecting persons to any conditions that might risk physical or emotional injury. In real organizations, participants are occasionally cheated, humiliated, or driven to nervous collapse. While a few psychologists have been accused of somewhat amoral conduct in the pursuit of science, all psychologists recognize that there are guidelines to follow in the treatment of subjects. Thus, the more brutal dimensions of organizational life lie beyond the pale of experimental methods.

A second problem in the use of the laboratory experiment concerns the reactivity of the method. When we say that a measurement device is reactive, we mean that the attempt to use it to measure something automatically alters the state of that which we would measure. For example, when you apply a tire pressure gauge to the valve stem, you release air, thus changing the pressure to a level other than that recorded on the gauge.

Laboratory experiments are often reactive because the subjects, being human, wonder what the experimenter's hypothesis is and try to adjust their behavior accordingly. They might try to help the experimenter by doing what they think is expected; they may try to do what looks good; or they may stubbornly act in a manner exactly opposite of the way they think the

FOCUS ON MANAGEMENT

Revolt against Rigor: More Relevance for Managers?

In recent years, a growing number of scholars in OB have expressed concern over misplaced emphasis on methodological rigor. These writers fear that too many researchers have elevated form above substance. To illustrate:

"We are conditioned by our scientific training to associate progress with greater rigor . . . but these indicators of progress are misleading . . . looser, nontestable, nongeneralizable descriptions (e.g., poems) of social facts are equally legitimate forms of representation and perhaps . . . even more appropriate forms of inquiry than the normal model of science" (Mitroff & Pondy, 1978, pp. 145–46).

"In many centers of behavioral science research, researchers are more concerned with proving a minor but neat conceptual point or resolving a measurement issue than with tackling issues that have clear practical application" (Lorsch, 1979, p. 178).

"The pursuit of reliable results leads some researchers to explore only trivial problems that have little importance to practitioners" (Webber, 1979, p. 17).

experimenter would predict. Experimenters, aware of this potential reactivity, may exert extreme efforts to disguise the true purpose of the experiment. Sometimes the entire enterprise is a theater of the absurd in which experimenter and subject try to outsmart each other.

MANAGERS AS RESEARCHERS

Murdick and Cooper (1982) argue that "although in the past businessmen have made vital decisions on the basis of untested hypotheses, the trend is toward more emphasis on research" (p. 49). This is because managers are increasingly better educated; research techniques have been streamlined and made more accessible to practitioners; the cost of failure has escalated enormously relative to the cost of some minimum research; and, perhaps most important, competitive pressures do not permit the luxury of muddling through with a series of seat-of-the-pants decisions based on guesswork.

We expect that future managers will involve themselves more actively in the research process at every step—identifying and defining important concepts, developing theoretical models, designing empirical tests of the models, collecting the data, and analyzing the results. Managers will turn to specialists and consultants for assistance but will assume a more active role in collaboration with the professional researcher.

We cannot provide an exhaustive account of the kinds of research that you, the future manager, might someday be doing, but we will note some forms of research that now engage considerable managerial energies.

Organizational Surveys Field survey research has been important in the development of the knowledge basis for organizational behavior as a discipline. More and more, organizations are using the survey as a method of research to enrich their own particular knowledge base for making decisions. For many firms, surveys provide periodic "audits" of the state of their human resources—analogous to an audit of their financial health by accountants.

The effective use of surveys is more than a clerical task. Indeed, some theoretical development should precede the administration of questionnaires. Managers first must identify the constructs—attitudinal, behavioral, demographic, motivational, or skill-related—that underlie the strategically significant characteristics of the work force. The administrator must have an embryonic conceptual framework articulating the factors—such as employee background, job design, relevant organizational environment dimensions—that affect important employee states. This theoretical work guides the process of selecting or designing the appropriate questionnaire measures and the later analysis of the data. Over time, trends can be noted for what they have to say about the internal dynamics of the organization.

The results are correlational in nature and thus preclude strong inference about cause and effect. Nonetheless, the data can provide some basis for many strategically important decisions concerning the management of human resources: What skills are available in abundant supply? What skills should be emphasized in future recruiting? What effects does the present compensation program have on employee attitudes? Is more training needed for lower-level supervisors? Are too many employees "underplaced" or "overplaced"? Do attitudes reflect the "culture" that top officials think is appropriate for corporate strategy?

Dunham and Smith (1979) provide an informative account of the many uses to which surveys may be put, as well as a set of principles for effective administration of surveys, with particular emphasis on surveys of employee attitudes. In one example, they show how researchers could arrive at rather precise estimates of the comparative importance of individual characteristics, job characteristics, and organization environment characteristics in accounting for employee job satisfaction.

Program Evaluation Huge sums of money are invested every year in ambitious programs aimed at improving corporate performance in product quality, customer satisfaction, employee commitment, inventory control, reduced absenteeism, and public relations. Do these programs work as intended? In the past, the answer has often been based on gut-feeling or, even worse, the tendency of program sponsors to justify the program by selective data. The trend, however, is to experiment with such programs on a small scale and evaluate the results before expanding the program and committing more resources. To do this, managers need some working knowledge of experimental design. Again, some theory development also comes into play: someone must define just what the "treatment" is, describe it operationally, relate it to an important construct, and explain what "effects" should be forthcoming. These effects have to be measured appropriately, and the theoretically correct comparisons made. Did the "treatment" improve the specific area of performance compared to the prior levels? Did the experimental group (or division) improve relative to a group (or division) in which no changes were made? What other factors have to be taken into account in interpreting the results? Can a monetary value be put on any improvements that occurred? Should the program be expanded to other areas of the organization? If so, what other areas should theoretically show similar effects of such programs?

Market Research   The development of a new product, the attempt to exploit a different market, or a major change in the method of advertising or delivering a product all involve substantial risk in immediate dollar costs and in corporate reputation. Thus, managers and professionals should covet sound research that minimizes the likelihood of a fiasco.

Successful marketing managers are inveterate theoretical model-builders. They develop and revise models of the target customers. Who are the intended customers? What are their self-concepts, motives, fantasies? From whom do they learn about products? Who actually makes the purchase decision, and what are the stages by which the decision is reached? What aspects of the product or service are they most sensitive to? Conceptual models answering these questions are tested against results from mailed questionnaires, returned warranty cards, archival industry information, census data, and interviews with dealers. Experiments are launched in the form of market tests in selected areas, distribution of free samples, or marketing the "concept" of the product at trade shows. Results are matched against predictions; some parts of the model may require alteration, or new concepts have to be defined.

Thus, whatever the functional area(s) in which your professional career unfolds, you will probably find yourself doing what the behavioral scientist does, and doing more at the level of sophistication and rigor of the behavioral scientist than was true a generation ago. The specific context of your research will obviously require context-specific knowledge — operations research, industrial marketing, employee compensation, and bond markets. But the fundamental principles of theoretical model development, research design, and data interpretation are much the same. Managers will always have to make decisions under conditions of uncertainty, using their intuition; theory and research will not solve all their problems. Nonetheless, the notion of manager as "lay scientist" has much to commend it as we approach the 21st century.

STRATEGIES FOR LEARNING ABOUT BEHAVIOR IN ORGANIZATIONS: CONCLUDING NOTE

In practice, methods of research in organizational behavior seldom fit neatly into any one class of the methods described. Any given study may actually germinate in the solitude of a researcher's reflection on past experiences in organizations, the insights that occur during a casual conversation, or a hunch that comes from reading accounts of current local or national events.

The researcher may or may not have a theory to work with at this point—perhaps there is only a vague sense of some forces that are interrelated. The person then becomes a bit more sensitive to future observations that seem to be drawn like a conceptual magnet to earlier ponderings. Eventually, the researcher develops a clearcut sense of what these ponderings are all about, and curiosity leads to an exploratory study. This may consist of a series of semistructured interviews with officials of an organization. The next step may be to distribute questionnaires to a sample of employees and tabulate the results.

All the while, the researcher's thinking becomes more structured. A more grandiose study is designed with more rigorous measures. Results are published and, if the results are of interest to others, similar studies with some variations in methods, research site, and instruments take place. Eventually every method we have described comes into service.

The optimal strategy of research, then, is one that combines various methods. Because each method has limitations, we remain skeptical about any findings produced by one method alone. When different methods produce similar findings, we have more confidence in the validity of the results. For example, naturalistic observation, field studies, and laboratory experiments all suggest that a specific, quantitative goal has more effect on performance than a general ("do your best") goal. On the other hand, while correlational field studies seem to show that certain leadership styles affect performance, laboratory experiments do not seem to confirm this effect. So we have to live with a degree of uncertainty about this relationship.

The reader may readily join in the use of optimal strategies of learning about organizational behavior. Learn from your experience, and learn what you can from others' experience. You might not conduct your own opinion surveys or controlled experiments, but you have access to results of such studies. Use such results to check your own conclusions. If the results agree, you may justifiably have a great deal of confidence in your knowledge. But if the results disagree, don't immediately scrap your accumulated observations or close your mind to what others have found in field studies or laboratory experiments. The latter may be suspect because of their inherent limitations as methods of research, and the same qualification should apply to the conclusions drawn from your own less rigorous methods. Adopt a flexible, tentative view of your knowledge in such a case. See if the discrepancy has any effect on how you perceive and interpret future experience, and revise your previous conclusions. That is what learning is all about.

SUMMARY

A theory is a set of statements describing the relationships among conceptual variables. Both behavioral scientists and administrators are active users of theory. Theory serves the functions of organizing and summarizing existing knowledge and guiding the search for new knowledge.

Theories are evaluated on the basis of conformity to empirical observations, internal consistency, parsimony, congruence with other well-established theories, utility in directing the search for new knowledge, and intuitive or aesthetic appeal. No theory ever occupies a permanent place in our knowledge. All theories are transient to varying degrees, surviving only until newer and better theories replace them, carrying forward the contributions of their predecessors.

In the study of organizational behavior, a variety of research methods contributes to the acquisition of knowledge from theory development and theory testing. These methods include naturalistic observation, field surveys, field experiments, and laboratory experiments. Each of these methods has its unique advantages and disadvantages, with the result that findings from studies using any single method must be qualified to take methodological imperfections into account. Our confidence in the validity of an assertion about organizational behavior is greatest when the assertion is supported by inquiries using a host of different methods.

All signs point toward future managers becoming more actively involved in the research process, from theory development to data analysis. Employee surveys, program evaluation, and marketing research are three representative forms of research that engage more and more practicing professionals.

CONCEPTS TO REMEMBER

Percept	Operational definition	Independent variable
Concept	Naturalistic observation	Dependent variable
Construct	Correlational evidence	Intervening variable
Norm of correspondence	Field experiment	Moderating variable
Norm of coherence	Laboratory experiment	Field survey research
Principle of parsimony	Reactivity	Social desirability in
Norm of pragmatism	Case study	response set

QUESTIONS FOR DISCUSSION

1. Consider a theory that states, "On simple tasks, background noise increases workers' alertness, which in turn increases productivity. On complex tasks, background noise has no overall effect." Identify the independent, dependent, intervening, and moderating variables.

2. Refer again to the results in Table 2–3. Suppose high-ranking officials concluded that "employee-centered supervision causes high productivity in subordinates." What do you think they would have proceeded to do? Why would this have been ill-advised, or at least premature?

3. *(a)* Which do you think is more effective in preparing for an exam: Using some of the available study time to study with a group, or using all available time to study alone? Try to couch your answer in terms of a theory.
(b) Suppose your instructor researched this question by having students report the number of hours they studied in a group, and found that this was related to higher exam scores. What do you conclude? Why? What if number of hours in group study were related to lower exam scores?

4. Discuss the appropriateness of using laboratory experiments to study: *(a)* the effects of noise on performing intellectual tasks; *(b)* the effects of group solidarity on group problem-solving; *(c)* the effects of early job challenge on a person's subsequent career.

REFERENCES

Christenson, C. B. (1971). *Kinsey: A biography.* Bloomington: Indiana University Press.

Dalton, M. (1959). *Men who manage.* New York: John Wiley & Sons.

Dunham, R. B., & Smith, F. J. (1979). *Organizational surveys: An internal assessment of organizational health.* Glenview, IL: Scott, Foresman & Co.

Gouldner, A. W. (1954). *Patterns of industrial bureaucracy.* New York: Free Press.

Granick, D. (1961). *The red executive.* New York: Anchor Books, Doubleday.

Hersey, P., & Blanchard, K. H. (1969). *Management of organizational behavior (p. 594).* Englewood Cliffs, NJ: Prentice Hall.

Hofstede, G. (Summer 1980). Motivation, leadership, and organization: Do American theories apply abroad? *Organization Dynamics.*

Kaplan, A. (1964). *The conduct of inquiry.* San Francisco: Chandler.

Kinsey, A. C., Pomeroy, W. B., & Martin, C. E. (1949). *Sexual behavior in the human male.* Philadelphia: Saunders.

Kissinger, H. (1979) *The White House years.* Boston: Little, Brown.

Lorsch, J. W. (March-April 1979) Making behavioral science more useful. *Harvard Business Review, 171-81.*

Mitroff, I. I., & Pondy, L. R. (1978). Afterthoughts on the leadership conference. In M. W. McCall, Jr., & M. M. Lombardo (eds.), *Leadership: Where else can we go?* (pp. 145-49). Durham, NC: Duke University Press.

Morse, N., & Reimer, E. (1956). The experimental change of a major organizational variable. *Journal of Abnormal and Social Psychology* 52, 120-29.

Muczyk, J. P. (1976). A controlled field experiment measuring the impact of MBO on performance data. Unpublished paper, Cleveland State University.

Murdick, R. G., & Cooper, D. R. (1982). *Business research: Concepts and guides.* Columbus, OH: Grid Publishing Inc.

Opsahl, R. L., & Dunnette, M. D. (1966). The role of financial compensation in industrial motivation. *Psychological Bulletin* 66(2), 94-118.

Pinder, C. C. (1984). *Work motivation.* Glenview, IL: Scott, Foresman & Co.

Schachter, S. (1951). Deviation, rejection, and communication. *Journal of Abnormal and Social Psychology* 46, 190-207.

Shaw, M. E., & Costanzo, P. R. (1970). *Theories of social psychology.* New York: McGraw-Hill.

Sloan, A. P., Jr., (1965). *My years with General Motors.* New York: MacFadden Books, Doubleday Publishing.

Webber, R. A. (1979). *Management: Basic elements of managing organizations.* Homewood, IL: Richard D. Irwin.

Weick, K. E. (1965). Laboratory experimentation with organizations. In J. G. March (ed.), *Handbook of organizations.* Skokie, IL: Rand McNally.

Weick, K. E. (1969). *The social psychology of organizing.* Reading, MA: Addison-Wesley Publishing.

Zajonc, R. B. (1960). The concepts of balance, congruity, and dissonance. *Public Opinion Quarterly* 24, 280-96.

Case

MAX RITTER

Max Ritter again leafed through the tables and charts which summarized the data from the company's opinion survey. Max, as assistant director of personnel and employee relations, felt a sense of personal identification with the survey. He had long been critical of the way his department made seat-of-the-pants decisions about employee programs. One of the convictions he carried away with his MBA degree was that corporations, and especially personnel departments, need to be a lot more systematic in the collection of data as a basis for formulating employee policies. More or less as a result of his persistent urging, the company had agreed to a comprehensive employee opinion audit, designed and conducted by two of Max's former professors from Midstate University's School of Business Administration.

As he got up from his desk to walk to the office of his boss, Jack Kelvin (head of the department), Max placed markers in the two sections he especially wanted to show Jack. One of the sections concerned comparisons of job satisfaction by different age groups, with the most satisfied groups in the 35-40- (a mean of 5.7 on a 7-point scale) and 41-50- (mean of 5.9) year-old groups. The least satisfied were those in their twenties (mean of 5.2).

"Jack, could you take a look at some of these analyses? I think they're pretty revealing about some of the things we do here," said Max as he handed Jack the report.

Jack looked over the figures for a few minutes, sat back in his chair, and reached for his pipe.

"Well, maybe. What exactly do you have in mind, Max?"

"Actually, the overall emphasis of our programs—pay, promotions, benefits, you name it—they all seem to be slanted toward seniority and tenure more than anything else. We do a good job for the older, maybe more experienced people, but I think we slight our younger employees. And you know very well that we've lost several of our good younger prospects in the last few months."

Jack—whom Max respected as an experienced personnel man, had no formal training in personnel but wound up there after several years in sales—puffed on his freshly lit pipe for a few minutes before answering.

"Well, sure we've lost some of the younger ones. But I don't recall them leaving with any real grievances. Either they had opportunities they couldn't pass up, or they felt they weren't cut out for this kind of business. You're always going to have more turnover among younger people. That's pretty much in the nature of things." Jack reached to point an index finger at the chart on the open page. "Anyway, is there really all that much difference in a 5.2 and 5.7? Both of those figures look pretty good to me."

Max reached over the corner of the desk to thumb back a few pages. "Look, it's the consistency of the difference that really tells the story. Not just overall attitudes, but feelings about supervision, working conditions, vacation policy, even the work itself. What it all seems to add up to is that we reward loyalty and experience more than we do qualifications, ability, and quality and quantity of work."

Jack leaned back and crossed his arms. "Well, I think loyalty's worth something, but aside from that I think you're making too much of some of these things. Maybe there's something in what you're saying, I just don't hear too much around here about any discontent among younger employees. They seem to produce as well as the others, so they can't be too upset."

Questions   Identify the assumptions made by Max and Jack about behavior in organizations. Assess the appropriateness of Max's conclusions and Jack's counterarguments. Should Max press further for changes in personnel policies? Why or why not? Suppose the consultants were asked to comment on what to do as a follow-up on the survey findings—what do you think their recommendations would be? In general, what can organizational officials do when different methods of observation suggest conflicting courses of action?

Foundations of Behavior in Organizations

3

Theories of Human Needs and Motives

What views of human nature have influenced the management of people at work?

What important needs and motives govern work behavior?

How are these needs and motives related to each other, and how do they change?

Managers frequently ask the question "Why?" about organizational behavior. Why do people choose one occupation over another? Why do some people work hard and others take it easy? Why do some leaders take one course of action and others proceed differently? Why do customers stop buying brand A in favor of brand B? Why does absenteeism soar in one division, but decline in a similar one just 35 miles away?

Theories of human motivation try to answer the "whys" of behavior. No theory can explain all behavior by all people all the time, but human motivation theories try to account for some behavior by some people some of the time. Here, we will focus on work-relevant behavior and on several different approaches to answering many of the "whys."

Some theories construe motivation as a matter of what is "in" people, an approach that assumes that behavior follows from certain needs, wants, desires, or drives. It has become fashionable to refer to these as *content* theories of motivation (Campbell, Dunnette, Lawler, & Weick, 1970). Content theories ask what it is that people seek from work. Some emphasize the needs or wants that we all have in common by virtue of our shared "human nature." Others emphasize the differences in our needs. Content theories will occupy us in this chapter.

In the next chapter, we will examine *process* models of motivation (Campbell et al., 1970), which are approaches that avoid making statements about what people want or need. These theories assume that at any time, any person wants *something,* and they ask what determines the connection between the need and a specific direction, intensity, and duration of behavior.

So, in a sense, the "why?" of behavior seems to break down analytically into two different questions: "What?"—what do people seek, what do they need? and "How?"—how does any particular need become connected to overt behavior?

CONTENT THEORIES OF WORK MOTIVATION

Theory X

Douglas McGregor (1960) coined the term "Theory X" as a convenient label for some assumptions about human nature in regard to work. These assumptions hold that the dominant needs people seek to satisfy through work are those pertaining to economics and security. People see work itself as a necessary evil, our lot to be endured (perhaps as a result of Adam's primordial fall from grace), tolerated only as a means to obtain groceries, keep debtors at bay, and perhaps provide a cushion for a comfortable old age. Given the available choices, people will seek work that minimizes labor and discomfort and maximizes material gain. Having made their choice, they will do what they must to keep a job, but no more than that; they will avoid hard work if they can. They will respond to external pressure, which is needed to overcome inherent tendencies to slothfulness, idleness, and inertia.

It is doubtful if any particular person ever voiced these assumptions, but McGregor's point in constructing this theory is well taken. Schools of management thought before the 1940s did seem to imply such a view of the rank-and-file of the nation's labor force. Elton Mayo (1933) called it the "rabble hypothesis."

This model of work motivation sounds outrageous today, but it probably had some validity in the times leading up to and well into the 20th century. Much of the work then—whether on the farm or in the factory—*was* unpleasant. And given the average standard of living at the time, most people probably did see economic necessity as the sole compulsion to work. For the professional, the manager, the prosperous entrepreneur, or the offspring of the wealthy propertied class, this was not the case, but they were in the minority.

McGregor was convinced that Theory X continues to influence the thinking of many of those who manage work organizations. Even though the conditions of work have changed and our existence is more secure, there are still administrators who might subscribe to some version of Theory X. They would argue that most people seek primarily the material rewards from work, that people will avoid work when external pressures (close supervision, monetary incentives, or threats) are weak, and otherwise seek a passive, "let well enough alone" accommodation to employment.

McGregor made another insightful observation: Those who manage organizations on the basis of Theory X assumptions cause people to re- spond in a fashion that seems to confirm those assumptions. In other words, acting on the basis of Theory X becomes an exercise in self-fulfilling prophecy. If managers try to regulate our behavior, limiting us to only the most physically and mentally onerous tasks, much of our work-relevant motivation *will* revolve around maximizing material gains, minimizing the discomfort of the work, and taking whatever advantage we can. In so doing, of course, we invite more stringent controls from those who organize us. The spiral continues.

McGregor took consolation in some evidence that, even by the 1950s, Theory X was gradually being supplanted in many quarters by a different view: Theory Y. We will defer for the moment what is contained in Theory Y, since it draws some support and inspiration from some of the "growth theories" examined below.

Human Relations Theory

You will recall that the Hawthorne studies had a major influence on management thought. In particular, results from these studies appeared to question the primacy of economic motives in governing work behavior. While no one could doubt the importance of having a job to obtain material comforts—and, indeed, some commentators have interpreted the Haw- thorne data as showing just this—the findings also pointed to the importance of *social* needs that influence work behavior. The arguments based on the

Hawthorne studies proposed that people, when given the opportunity, will spontaneously develop informal social structures that provide a satisfying sense of attachment or affiliation, and beyond that some sense of worth and personal identity. These structures give rise to emergent codes of what is acceptable behavior, whatever the official rules or policies state. Supervisors find it more convenient to accommodate these structures, or at least recognize them, than try to overcome them. This does not mean that informal organization is a "necessary evil" for managers, any more than work is a necessary evil for the work force. As often as otherwise, the informal organization complements the formal organization in serving constructive purposes — for example, promoting attendance, dealing with unforeseen problems at work, providing leadership, and passing on an accumulated store of knowledge and skills for working efficiently. Although economic need explained why people went to work, social needs accounted for what happened once people got there.

Maslow's Need Hierarchy

Abraham Maslow spent the early part of his career as a psychologist studying animal behavior. Later his professional interests turned to clinical psychology and counseling. He felt that existing psychological theories and research on motivation — almost completely based on the study of physiological drives in animals — were woefully inadequate for understanding most human behavior. In the early 1940s, he penned some preliminary notes as to what a complete theory of human motivation would involve. The two papers (Maslow, 1943a, 1943b) in which he reported these early observations had a profound influence on management thought and the conceptualization of work motivation in OB.

Maslow's underlying premise is that human needs can be arrayed in several distinctly different classes, which can be related to each other in terms of *prepotency*. The construct of prepotency implies something like "priority," in the sense that one class of needs, until satisfied, takes priority over certain others. As need satisfaction is realized, a different type of need becomes dominant in behavior until it, too, is satisfied, paving the way for still other needs to direct behavior. Thus, human motivation is a story of working from one set of concerns to "higher level" needs. The "hierarchy" metaphor captures this sequential arrangement of priorities in need categories.

Physiological Needs In human behavior, as in animals, physiologically based needs initially take top priority. People need oxygen, food, water, rest, shelter, protection from the elements, sex, avoidance of pain, waste elimination — what we might recognize as the "creature comforts." (We could probably include acquired needs based on addiction to drugs, since these urges are experienced by the nervous system much like the "real" physiological needs.) These needs govern our behavior until they are met.

To the extent that they have been taken care of, they will fade into the background of conscious behavior. Of course, they intermittently reappear—not even the most sumptuous meal banishes hunger forever, and occasional physical discomfort can arise in the most luxurious surroundings—and again become "urgent business" for a few minutes or hours.

Safety Needs   Having staved off his or her immediate physiological needs, a person next seeks to establish a safe, predictable, ordered environment. The motive theme here is security, and thus involves a conception of time and the future. The individual here reacts not to present pain, but to fear of and threat from ominous forces, looming natural calamities such as earthquakes and floods, violence, loss of possessions, breakdown of the social order. While Maslow reasoned that stable political and economic conditions largely satisfy this need for security in most adults, some people (perhaps because of early traumatic experiences) never feel completely secure and exhibit patterns of behavior that others consider "neurotic."

Love Needs   Reasonable gratification of physiological and safety needs prepares a person for the experience of wanting to give and receive affection in relationships with others—parents, siblings, friends, peers, spouse. (The love need here is distinguished from the sex drive, which is a physiological need, but satisfaction of sexual urges can become conditioned to the simultaneous gratification of the love need.) Individuals who have taken care of basic survival needs but who are lonely will be highly receptive to attention and consideration from others. Studies of prisoners of war have found that solitary confinement, even with adequate food and physical comfort, predisposes even the bravest and most patriotic soldiers to seek communication with their captors, even at the risk of revealing strategic military information or denouncing their government. We are all familiar with accounts of how a person comes to compromise supposedly higher moral values to gain acceptance by a group. The Hawthorne studies showed that informal social structures arise in work organizations to satisfy the needs that the formal structure often does not provide. Maslow noted that a prolonged thwarting of one's love needs characterizes the extreme cases of maladjustment and psychopathology: people who have given up even trying to get affection and whose behavior is utterly indifferent to the harm it may inflict on others.

Esteem Needs   As a person experiences some success in deriving affection in relationships, a set of needs centered around ego come to the fore. The term *ego* has a mixed connotation. On the one hand, we sometimes use it to describe people who seem preoccupied with their own status and self-confidence. On the other hand, as Maslow argued, it is a natural and healthy progression to reflect on one's worth, adequacy, and competence, once a reasonable degree of "inclusiveness" with others has developed. We seek attachments, but come to prefer those that provide a sense of respect from others, and which eventually form a basis for our own self-respect. Having gained acceptance, acceptance alone does not suffice; we must be able to regard ourselves as capable of independent thought and action, deserving of respect, and confident in confronting our problems. Intuitively, there seems to be a logical sequence here. First, we seek relationships that provide affection on any basis; then, secure on that basis, we strive for respect and affection. Once we have secured external respect, we have the foundation for deriving our own internal criteria for self-regard, even at the expense of or in opposition to attaining status in the eyes of others. Not everyone arrives at this last stage. Only a minority ever become so completely confident of respect from others that they venture more than precariously into their own sense of self-esteem.

Had Maslow studied other cultures, especially those of the Orient, he probably would have commented on the conditions that reinforce the individualistic versus the inclusive ego. The Western world—in its language, religions, family structure, political and social philosophies—values individual accomplishments and prestige. Conversely, Asian cultures and traditions, including those whose technological and economic development rivals if not surpasses the West's, continue to emphasize the kinship or community group. They would not regard it as "healthy psychological growth" for a person to elevate his or her need for self-respect or autonomy above the needs of the collective. For them, the ego has no value and no meaning when divorced from kinship and comrades.

The Need for Self-Actualization   For a few people—and Maslow regarded them as very few indeed—the satisfaction of basic survival and security needs, the attainment of love and affection, and both social and individualistic ego needs frees them to pursue something that even Maslow found difficult to describe. The ultimate need is what he called the quest for "self-actualization," a notion that includes the search for "fulfillment" or "realization of one's potential." Maslow observed it most clearly in creative people in the arts and sciences. As he put it, "a musician must make music, an artist must paint, a poet must write, if he is to be ultimately happy." Maslow did not mean to imply that only creative or artistic types or intellectuals experience this need—only that they probably articulate it better. People engaged in other pursuits could also get a sense of the biblical statement, "For this cause came I into the world." The suggestion is that of an overarching purpose, an all-consuming mission. In Maslow's later writings this need has quasi-mystical overtones, in which a person seeks a oneness with the universe.

Maslow found only a few people (himself not among them) in whom he could study the untrammeled drive of this need. Although these people had little concern for conventional codes of morality and behavior, they were not radical or rebellious. They had little concern for "self," since they were immersed in something larger than self. They were quite capable of what most people would regard as callousness, if not cruelty, toward those who loved them.

Nonetheless, Maslow was fascinated by this type of need and awarded it the special status of "growth" need. He regarded physiological, safety, love, and ego needs as "deficiency" needs. It is only when all of these deficiency needs have been completely satisfied that a person becomes psychologically healthy. Then, and only then, do the "growth" needs that define the search for self-actualization take control, but it is a tiny fraction of adults who ever reach this point.

Cognitive and Aesthetic Needs   Maslow discussed two other needs that did not fit into the sequence with the others. People experience a generalized "need to know," to explore and manipulate their environment. Infants will grasp for an unfamiliar object in the crib or the pens in Daddy's pocket. We want to know how the movie ends, what lies around the bend and across the river, what happens when we mix these two colors together.

We also have a need for beauty. In the bleakest work surroundings, people will introduce a little beauty—a flower, a picture, a souvenir of some kind. New versions of a product—a camera, computer, automobile, building—are evaluated in part on aesthetics, whatever their technical functions may be. Even scientists' preferences among competing theories is sometimes determined more by aesthetic appeal than pure rigor or precise empirical support. To overlook this need at work can invite all kinds of trouble.

Maslow would probably have placed these needs after the basic physiological and safety needs. As strong and universal as the inquisitive instinct and the need for beauty appear to be, history suggests that they do not flourish in times of famine, devastation, and social chaos.

It is odd that Maslow's taxonomy of human needs omits the notion of justice, especially since wars have been fought over it, emotions are aroused by blatant unfairness, and people often take risks to redress inequity. Perhaps his broader concept of safety needs envelops justice, inasmuch as an unjust world is one that is unpredictable and insecure. Or, it may fit better under ego needs, considering our sense of humiliation when we are treated unfairly.

Qualifications to the Need Hierarchy   Maslow made no pretense of offering a complete, exact theory. Quite reasonably, he offered some qualifying statements and caveats. For example, each need stage in the hierarchy did not have to be completely satisfied before the next set of needs appeared. Perhaps 80–90% satisfaction of physiological needs would allow safety needs to become important, and 60–70% satisfaction of safety needs would bring love needs to the fore. Also, any particular behavior might express multiple needs: for example, dining not only satisfies the hunger need, it also provides an occasion to pleasurably interact with others, even the opportunities for ego-striving (as when someone impresses us by ordering an unfamiliar wine, or uses the occasion to display rarefied knowledge on some topic). Finally, Maslow recognized the role of habit and custom in human affairs—the fact that some behavior is not need-directed at all, but is a matter of doing what we usually do, whatever the original reason for doing it.

Assessment of Maslow's Need Hierarchy   Much of what Maslow says is plausible and intuitively compelling. However, it has not been easy to test the theory with data. For one thing, his own qualifications and disclaimers make it difficult to assess whether discrepant findings contradict his theory or simply illustrate the exceptions or special cases he himself noted. Maslow did not take it upon himself to develop measures or "operational definitions" of the need categories, and some of them—particularly the self-actualization need—have presented major difficulties to researchers trying to give the theory an honest and fair test.

Certain ideas in the Need Hierarchy theory do lend themselves to empirical test. First, we can see if the clustering of specific desires that different people express in varying degrees conforms to the categories Maslow suggested. Second, we can test the notion that the more a given category of need is satisfied, the less important it becomes and the more important the next need in the hierarchy becomes.

A review of relevant research by Wahba and Bridwell (1976) provides mixed support for the Need Hierarchy. The data suggest that a more parsimonious two-level need system, rather than five distinct categories, is warranted. Studies suggest a clear separation between "lower-order" (physiological and safety) needs and various "higher-order" needs, including the love and esteem needs and possibly something like a need for self-realization.

Research supports the inverse relationship between degree of satisfying a need and its importance, but only for lower-order needs. The higher-order needs do not clearly show this dynamic; studies suggest that some degree of satisfying these needs actually renders them more important.

Survey data indicate that higher-order needs are somewhat more important to managers, entrepreneurs, and professionals than to hourly employees, who report lesser degrees of satisfaction with lower-order needs. Studies of careers suggest that safety needs appear most strongly in the early stages and that ego and self-fulfillment needs are more important in later career stages. These findings seem to support Maslow's logic.

Alderfer's ERG Theory

In response to some of the problems identified with Maslow's Need Hierarchy, Alderfer (1969, 1972) formulated a more parsimonious variation. Alderfer's version has three categories: *Existence* (E) needs, which correspond to Maslow's physiological needs and the material, nonpersonal aspects of security needs; *Relatedness* (R) needs, comprised of those safety needs that are satisfied only by protective relationships, the need for affection, and esteem needs that can be met only in a social context; and *Growth* (G) needs, or the desire for a sense of competence, autonomy, and achievement. Alderfer's Growth needs do not rule out, but also do not require, a pursuit of Maslow's mystical self-actualization.

Alderfer's framework has only a quasi-prepotency characterization. It allows an individual to experience simultaneously all three types of motives. Yet a hierarchical linkage is present, in that increased satisfaction of existence needs makes it more likely that relatedness needs become strong, and strong growth needs presuppose some degree of satisfaction of both existence and relatedness needs.

ERG theory also explicitly allows for something Maslow had noted only as the occasional exception to the rule: the likelihood that frustration in seeking gratification of some needs would eventually cause a person to emphasize, and seek greater satisfaction in, hierarchically lower needs. This notion, the *frustration-regression hypothesis,* is an important statement in all subsequent theories of psychological growth. To illustrate this concept, imagine a skilled technician who strives for greater challenge and self-expression in his or her work, but is repeatedly frustrated in this desire. The psychological pain of the frustration might lead the person to refocus attention on the material rewards to be derived from work, substituting the goal of increasing pay and benefits for psychological growth. Whether this happens and how soon it occurs would depend, among other things, on the person's tolerance for frustration and the perceived availability of alternatives for meeting the frustrated desires.

Alderfer's framework provides a better fit to the empirical measures of need satisfaction and lends itself to more precise predictions. And, perhaps because Alderfer's version is less ambitious than Maslow's, propositions based on the ERG version have fared somewhat better in tests against the data.

Argyris: A Theory of Psychological Growth

The Need Hierarchy theory and the ERG variation of it have in common the emphasis on a generalized growth dynamic. Argyris (1957) concentrated his attention on the very nature of psychological growth and human development. The developmental character of his model utilizes a different means of conceptualizing, but otherwise is quite consistent with, the idea of a hierarchical or sequential appearance of specific motives.

Argyris analyzed the distinct processes that occur as infants develop through childhood and adolescence to early adulthood. In the early stages we are *passive:* things happen to us; we are bound by the structure of the immediate situation. As we grow (not merely physically, but also psychologically), we become more *active:* we make things happen, we initiate a course of events, we construct situations of our own. We develop from total *dependence* on others—for food, hygiene, relief from physical discomfort, entertainment—to increasing *independence.* We change from creatures with virtually empty repertoires of capabilities to agents possessing complex, elaborate sets of skills and strategies. Our time horizon develops from one limited to the here and now to a sense of anticipating months and years into the future, a development that allows us to defer gratification of impulsive short-term desires for more significant later ends. Our interests gradually evolve from superficial, fleeting involvement (remember how quickly you became sated with Christmas toys?) to deep, enduring involvement. Correlated with all of these trends is the movement from an invariant subordinate status to an equal, collaborative status.

Argyris contended that, in the healthy adult, there is a strong need for these dimensions of growth to continue. However, when most young adults enter work organizations—where a significant portion of waking hours will be spent—they encounter obstacles to the path of continued psychological growth. Organizational structures, he argued, are predominantly founded on Theory X conceptions of human nature. Thus, external controls condition a sense of passivity and subordinate status. Narrowly defined jobs block the further development of one's repertoire of competence and inhibit deep involvement in tasks. Schedules programmed to the hour or even minute accentuate the short run in our conception of time. People still want to grow, as they have become accustomed to growing, but work organizations militate against it.

The result is frustration. One response to frustration is aggression—in some way, to fight, to struggle. Argyris interpreted much industrial conflict (e.g., labor-management strife, output restriction) as an expression of this underlying, pervasive frustration. But Argyris believed that the eventual response to frustration was *regression.* Given the pain of trying to grow and not being allowed to, and the only slight chance that aggression will actually change anything of significance, people simply stop trying to grow. Indeed, they revert to an earlier stage of psychological development. They focus on getting through the day, trying to minimize the physical discomforts, and looking for consolation in the "adult toys" their salaries can afford.

Argyris was doing more than sketching a theory of psychological growth; he was issuing a trenchant criticism of work organizations. We will not concern ourselves here with the question of whether this criticism was justified. In fact, his later writings in the 1960s and 1970s, while holding to his framework about psychological growth and the belief that work organization structures should reflect the need for growth, nevertheless became less shrill. Perhaps Argyris felt that some changes for the better had occurred during this time.

Herzberg's Two-Factor Theory

Herzberg's contributions to work motivation theory evolved from his efforts to explain confusing, inconsistent patterns in research findings concerning job satisfaction. After reviewing the massive literature reporting on factors associated with measures of job satisfaction, Herzberg and his associates conducted a new study. He asked 200 accountants and engineers to reconstruct, in their own words, job experiences they had associated with especially positive emotions about work and, conversely, episodes at work that they linked with very negative feelings about their jobs. Although this method, the "storytelling" or *critical incident technique,* later drew fire from Herzberg's critics, an analysis of the stories revealed some interesting patterns. Certain themes, when mentioned at all, were much more likely to figure in the positive work experiences; others showed up mainly when negative experiences were reconstructed. From these trends, Herzberg (1966) proposed that, contrary to intuition, satisfaction and dissatisfaction are separate and distinct phenomena, not opposites of each other, and they are caused by different things. Certain aspects of work — such as the physical environment, standard rules and procedures, pay, relationships with boss and coworkers — either *cause or prevent dissatisfaction.* In this sense, they are *hygiene factors:* we notice them only when there is a problem and we feel discomfort or irritation; when they are effective, we take them for granted and do not think about them. Other aspects of work — the stimulation of an interesting task, the sense of significant achievements, recognition for what we have accomplished, the notion of "agency" or responsibility for important outcomes — are what Herzberg considered the real *motivators.* Their absence does not cause dissatisfaction (although their absence might well make us more sensitive to irritants in the hygiene factors), but their presence provides both satisfaction and a renewable incentive to seek them further.

Herzberg elaborated on these two factors in a way that drew from, while contributing to, the work of Maslow and Argyris. Herzberg proposed that human beings have two types of needs or motives. One type we share with animals: the need to satisfy physical urges and avoid pain. These needs are important to us only when not provided by the hygiene factors of life and work. The hygiene factors do not bring "satisfaction" so much as temporary relief from "dissatisfaction." However, unlike animals, we have another type of need: Carnation's "contented cows" may require no more than ample food, shelter, gentle care, and protection from disease, but Homo sapiens requires *psychological growth.* Job *context* determines the extent and severity of dissatisfaction, while job *content* sets the limits for our capacity to experience positive satisfaction and the motivation for its renewal.

Herzberg's theory has generated more controversy than any other in OB and has exerted enormous influence on the business community. Herzberg, to an extent much greater than other work motivation theorists, actively pursued the implications of his theory for what he called "job enrichment." Moreover, he demonstrated a genuine knack for writing and speaking in terms that were persuasive to practicing managers.

Herzberg's influence probably compelled critics to carefully examine his work—both his theory and his method. The critics found much to criticize. Conceptually, his original theory seemed amenable to differing, even contradictory, interpretations and predictions. Methodologically, his story-telling technique is open to charges of bias due to the social-desirability effect: people tend to attribute negative events to what is around them (job context), but take credit for the positive events as things they did themselves (job content). In truth, tests of the Two Factor theory (or some version or interpretation of it) using different methods have usually led to results other than those Herzberg himself found.

Controversy aside, the development of work motivation theory has not been the same since Herzberg. Whether or not we accept his entire framework, OB theorists have been very influenced by certain themes he put into bold relief. Conceptualizing work motivation now takes as a given the important distinction between *extrinsic* and *intrinsic* attributes of work, the inclination to see them as serving different (though somewhat overlapping) sets of motives, and having different effects.

Convergence of the Growth Theorists: Theory Y

Douglas McGregor (1960) articulated a framework of managerial assumptions about human nature and work that captured the common thrust of Maslow, Alderfer, Argyris, and Herzberg. Calling this framework "Theory Y," in contrast to Theory X, he endorsed it as a valid and workable theory for administering work organizations, a way to get out of the trap of the self-fulfilling prophecies of Theory X. Theory Y does not deny the potency of the needs for creature comforts and security, but postulates that reasonable satisfaction of such needs—a level generally attained by most of the work force, at least in developed economies—sets the stage for a different orientation toward work. Theory Y assumes such an orientation to be active rather than passive, one that seeks and accepts greater responsibility, one that reflects self-control rather than the need for external control. If management suppresses these tendencies by continuing practices derived from Theory X assumptions, then—consistent with the frustration-regression hypothesis—people will revert to the more primitive stages of psychological development.

McGregor saw evidence that a trend toward a Theory Y conception of work motivation had begun among some of the younger, more sophisticated management people of his day. This trend probably owed something to greater awareness of the ideas of the Growth theorists, but to some extent occurred independent of their influence. McGregor did not see much evidence that this change extended from personal sentiments to changes in organizational governance at the institutional level—where it was most needed. As McGregor reasoned, work organizations compatible with the Theory Y framework would emphasize broad and substantive forms of participation by all employees in matters that significantly affected them, would redesign jobs to tap the ego needs for self-esteem and increased competence, and would encourage supervision that stressed teaching and coaching rather than controlling.

McGregor witnessed a bold effort by one particular company to convert to Theory Y management. Non-Linear Systems, in 1960 a small but growing electronics company in California, made a conscious attempt to put into practice what McGregor described as derivative of Theory Y. For a few years the firm continued to grow and showed improvements in productivity, customer relations, product quality, and reliability. In 1965, however, the company experienced financial troubles. Whether this resulted from Theory Y management, as the company president apparently believed, or simply from increased industry competition, senior officials backed off from some of the more radical attempts at decentralized, participative management. (For a more extensive account of the Non-Linear experience, see Miner, 1980, pp. 275–77.)

Non-Linear Systems's experience illustrates many of the attempts to reform organizational structures in the direction implied by the Growth theories of work motivation. First, the programs are started during periods of relative prosperity. Second, and understandably, they are not and do not purport to be controlled field experiments (as defined in the previous chapter). Instead, they are a loose collection of changes, some having little to do with Theory X–Theory Y. And the changes are not made in a coordinated, programmatic fashion, but on a piecemeal, trial-and-error, site-specific basis. Third, when some evidence of increased organizational effectiveness appears (and quite often this is the case), Theory Y advocates take this as support for their position. Skeptics argue that this confuses cause and effect, in that the initial prosperity and high productivity actually influenced the change in management. Finally, when operating and financial problems appear — as they inevitably must in business cycles — management decides it can no longer afford the luxury of experimental methods of management, and takes several steps backward toward more traditional management methods. Theory Y apostles sigh and say that it is in such crunch times that work organizations most need to consolidate institutional practices to foster participants' psychological growth needs. The abandonment of such practices indicates that management never really accepted Theory Y. The changes, without real confidence in positive human responses to work, were bound to lack real substance and doomed to be short-lived.

Where does this leave us with respect to the status of growth theories of work motivation and their application — bewitched, bothered, and bewildered? You could believe that these theories have substantial validity, but have never been given a fair test to prove themselves. Or you could argue that the recurrent cycle of reform-retrenchment speaks to the general inapplicability of these theories on a large scale in work organizations.

We hazard a couple of subjective observations here. Yes, the historical record does suggest a zigzag course in which radical reforms toward more humanistic conceptions of work motivation are succeeded by reversals, especially in times of financial hardship. But the pendulum seldom swings all the way back; there is a net residual effect toward Theory Y, as in a take-three-steps-forward, take-two-steps-back style. The long-term trend is roughly in line with growth theorists' hopes and expectations, with variations above and below the trend line. Also, it appears that managerial conceptions of work motivation are more tentative and flexible than suggested by either Theory X or Theory Y, tending toward one or the other depending on the context and the people in question.

Perhaps this is as it should be. Maslow himself (1965), while generally supportive of programs such as that attempted by Non-Linear Systems, reminded us of the tentative tone of his ideas and the fragility of the data documenting them. Remember, Maslow only expected a tiny proportion of people to become self-actualizers, and he did not claim that security and affiliation needs were so completely satisfied as to make other types of growth needs compelling in most people.

Strauss (1963) has distinguished between the *descriptive* validity of theories of psychological growth and the *prescriptive* applications to work organizations as advocated by some Theory Y adherents. We might agree that human development involves a progression toward more concern with ego and growth needs once lower-level needs abate. But such progression does not necessarily lead all people to pursue those needs in their vocation. Many persons will take the material benefits and economic security provided by their jobs and seek psychological growth in nonwork contexts—family, community activities, hobbies, or involvement in political or religious organizations. The idea that life's ultimate aspirations must be sought through work is, Strauss suggested, an academic's value judgment, not to be foisted on those who feel otherwise. The advantages provided by social organization in all of its institutional forms have a trade-off—individuals must yield some of their autonomy and curb the expression of some of their strongest urges.

Other Need Theories

Not all theories of human needs assume an inherent sequence of motives leading toward a concern for psychological growth. Murray, as early as 1938, had developed a taxonomy of *manifest needs* that, among others, included those recognizable from Maslow. In all, Murray distinguished some two dozen psychological needs, including Achievement, Affiliation, Power, Autonomy, Exhibition (to be the center of attention), Nurturance (to give comfort and sympathy), Succorance (seeking support from others), Order, and Understanding. The major points of difference between Murray and

FOCUS ON INTERNATIONAL OB

What Needs Does Work Meet? Differences among Nations

A research team headed by George England conducted a comparative study of the meaning of work (MOW) as perceived by employees in eight countries (the United States, the United Kingdom, Japan, Germany, Belgium, Yugoslavia, Israel, and the Netherlands). The researchers asked individual subjects to distribute 100 points across six objectives in such a way as to denote the importance of work for achieving that objective. In all eight countries, the objective considered most important was "providing the needed income." However, the importance of this objective *relative* to other needs varied considerably among the countries. Japanese respondents assigned 45 of the 100 points to the income objective, compared to 33 for the United States and 26 for the

Netherlands. Dutch subjects considered "interesting and satisfying work" (24 points) virtually as important as income, while the Japanese assigned only 13 points to the function of having interesting work. U.S. employees attached more significance to "prestige and status" (12 points) than did subjects in any of the other seven nations. The Netherlands group regarded the work objectives of "interesting contacts with other people" and "service to society" as more important than did other respondents.

SOURCE: MOW International Research Team, "The Meaning of Working: An International Perspective" (London: Academic Press, 1985). Cited in S. Ronen, *Comparative and Multinational Management* (New York: Wiley, 1986).

Maslow are as follows: *(1)* Murray did not arrange these needs in any order of priority. His framework allows for any number of needs to become aroused simultaneously, sometimes presenting the individual with a state of internal conflict. *(2)* In Murray's framework there is nothing inevitable in the appearance of all these needs; some are learned rather than inborn. *(3)* Murray drew a distinction between *latent* and *manifest* needs. Needs are latent (they do not influence thought and action) until evoked by relevant stimulus cues in the environment. In this sense, human needs are situational in nature. For example, the hunger drive is not completely a function of previous caloric intake and expenditure; it responds in part to visual and olfactory suggestions of food. Needs for achievement or power can lie dormant for long periods until a suitable occasion activates them.

Murray's taxonomy of human needs grew out of his attempt to account for *individual differences* rather than universal tendencies in human development. The current influence of his work lies in the contributions by Atkinson and McClelland concerning the needs for achievement, affiliation, and power. In that McClelland's study of these needs reflects more of an individual-differences orientation, his work is discussed in the chapter on personality.

Equity Theory: The Need for Justice

Ideas concerning the importance of fairness in the human condition go back as far as Aristotle, who offered the criterion of distributive justice that a person's share of community wealth should be proportionate to "merit." Many social philosophers and psychologists have elaborated on this, offering other criteria for the "just society." All of us know what it means to experience the emotion "righteous indignation" in response to what we regard as unfair treatment—by parents, teachers, employers, sweethearts, even God.

The issue of fairness arises in any exchange relationship between people, whether the exchange concerns tangible commodities (such as goods, money), services, gestures, or expressions of sentiment. Homans (1961) and Walster, Berscheid, and Walster (1973) have developed general theories of social behavior around this issue. Adams (1965) gave particular attention to the meaning of fairness in the employment relationship.

Three constructs form the core of Adams's model: Outcomes, Inputs, and Comparison Person. *Outcomes* include all that a person derives from, or attributes to, his or her participation in the work organization. Almost all of the research relevant to Adams's theory has zeroed in on pay, probably because it is such a salient outcome of work and can be precisely measured. But outcomes can also include status, intellectual stimulation, honors, or other nonmaterial rewards. Inputs represent all that a person regards as relevant contributions to the workplace. This would include effort expended on the job and job-relevant skills and knowledge, but could also include age, reputation, forgone opportunities, risks, positive influences on others at work, seniority, or experience.

Intuitively, we would expect fairness to have something to do with how our outcomes correspond to inputs. Adams argues that such comparisons are ambiguous without some sort of reference point to assess the correspondence of outcomes to inputs. This is where the concept of *comparison person* enters the picture. This construct does not signify a specific person (although it could conceivably represent a co–worker); it could be an average or composite for the work group, the organization, the industry, the local community, or other people deemed similar to oneself in a significant characteristic. Adams defines "equity" as the perception that one's own *ratio of outcomes to inputs* equals the corresponding ratio of the Comparison Person. If one's outcomes are only half the value of the Comparison Person's, equity reigns if one's inputs are also only half as great.

Adams does not indicate how an individual does this computing, except to suggest that a person subjectively weights various outcomes and inputs according to their perceived importance. Since his theory is one of equity as perceived by the individual, intuitive computational styles presumably vary from person to person. The significant assumption is that a person has some sense of overall outcomes and inputs and can array those against the Comparison Person in question.

Inequity can exist because one's own ratio of outcomes to inputs is either less or greater than those of the Comparison Person. Either way, the result is discomfort or disequilibrium, and the discomfort motivates the person to do something to restore equity. If one's own ratio is less than those of the comparison, the discomfort is felt emotionally as some sense of indignation—one has been shortchanged, abused, or exploited. If one's own ratio exceeds that of the comparison, the discomfort is more akin to guilt due to excessive outcomes relative to one's own and others' inputs.

An intriguing quality of Adams's theory—yet, its bedevilment—lies in the multiplicity of methods from which to choose to try to restore equity. The person might increase or decrease some inputs (e.g., effort; some inputs, such as age or experience, are not amenable to alteration), seek changes in outcomes (such as pay, benefits), or try to initiate changes in the outcomes or inputs of the comparison. Doing any of these would represent overt behavioral responses to inequity. If these options are not considered appropriate, a person might choose a perceptual means for establishing equity. This involves subjective reappraisal of any of the factors that enter into one's own or another's ratio. For example, a person feeling inequitably underpaid might revise the estimate of psychic benefits from the employment relationship or increase the subjective value of some of the comparison person's contributions. If neither behavioral nor perceptual methods of restoring equity are viable or acceptable, the individual can choose a different Comparison Person—for example, others in the profession rather than those in the same department. The ultimate means of righting an inequitable exchange relationship is to withdraw from the exchange. You break off the relationship with another person, resign your position, and look for another employer.

Adams's theory offers little guidance to predict which means of equity restoration a person will choose. This is unfortunate, because there is obviously a vast qualitative difference between saying to yourself, "Either I get my salary increased or I'm going to do as little as I can" versus thinking, "Well, perhaps my abilities and actual contributions are rather modest when compared to Robert's." Adams did offer these qualifying statements: people will probably make more use of perceptual modes of equity resolution when the inequity discomfort is in the form of implicit guilt due to overpayment; and people will resist perceptual changes in inputs that are psychologically costly. Some perceptual revisions, such as devaluing your talent, can take too great a toll on self-esteem; others can lead to reckless distortions of reality, with serious implications for subsequent coping with the world.

Adams's research has skirted the problem of multiple options for equity restoration by designing controlled but very realistic experiments in which effort or productivity were the only practicable factors the subject could alter. These experiments have featured a payment condition, a description of how this payment compares (favorably or unfavorably) to some "norm," and the dependent variable of the subject's work performance. Consistent with Equity theory predictions, people underpaid on an hourly basis produce less than equitably paid subjects, while those underpaid on a per-unit-of-output basis produce more but of less quality. The converse is true for those led to believe they are overpaid: greater production when paid per hour, lower production with higher quality when paid per unit.

Research by others yields similar effects due to underpayment, but effects of overpayment are not so consistent. Some critics of Adams's research contend that the way he defines overpayment in his experiments — telling the subject that "we're paying you $5 per hour, even though your experience and training really don't qualify for that rate" — challenges the person's sense of competence rather than producing a sense of inequitable overpayment. The ensuing performance of the subject really represents an "I'll show him how qualified I am" type of response, not a guilt-assuaging response.

Recently, other social justice theorists such as Leventhal (1976) have argued that Adams's theory is too narrowly couched in terms of only one equity principle, namely the *contributions* rule. Leventhal plausibly suggests that we sometimes define equity in terms of *equality* of outcomes, regardless of differences in inputs, and in some relationships outcomes are distributed according to *need* rather than contributions. Defining equity as equality becomes particularly attractive when contributions vary qualitatively among persons, are difficult to compare or measure, and a concern for harmony is paramount. The needs principle becomes salient when the specific outcomes in question affect survival or basic welfare of those closest to us and for whom we feel personally responsible.

In a more recent paper, Leventhal (1980) notes the situational importance of certain other criteria for defining what is equitable. In Japan, for example, age and tenure are given significant weighting for establishing what is fair pay; in the United States, labor unions have favored seniority as an equitable basis for allocating wages. True, Adams's model allows for age, tenure, and seniority, but to collapse these into a category that also includes productivity, level of responsibility, stress, leadership, and innovation seems to blur some critical differences involved in conflicts about what is fair or unfair.

Finally, attention has turned in recent years to *procedural* as well as distributive fairness (Folger & Greenberg, 1985). A person's indignation at inequitable underpayment will depend on the fairness of the methods used to distribute outcomes. In particular, abrupt departure from tradition in evaluating people's inputs will generally compound any perceived inequity concerning the final distribution of resources. Also, at least in North America and Western Europe, people expect to have some degree of "voice" or input in the decisions that determine their outcomes. Finally, there are many counterparts in the employment relationship to what we describe as "due process" and "civil liberties" in the legal and governmental sphere.

The need for fairness is not absolute. It sometimes yields to more immediately pressing motives. Some of the "overpaid" subjects in Adams's experiments who responded contrary to equity theory predictions were found, on subsequent analysis, to have urgent monetary needs. No doubt fear of rejection from peers could also take precedence over the desire to restore equity to self or others. What is remarkable is the extent to which resentment over felt inequity can lead a person to sacrifice much in material or even physical welfare; if you doubt this, you have not studied the history of labor unions. As Box 3–3 notes, many "irrational" behaviors seem otherwise when subsumed under a higher rationality concerning human dignity.

Lerner (1977) argues that a sense of a "just world" is essential to "taking the long view." Who would forgo immediate pleasures and indulgence without faith that a just order would provide repayment? This does not mean that inequities never occur, but that somehow the system will provide for correction over the long run. Such a view seems essential for allowing us to labor for any objective more worthy than the most narrowly selfish ends.

HOW USEFUL IS THE "NEED" CONSTRUCT?

What exactly is a "need"? If it is something essential to survival of the individual organism, we exhaust our list quickly when we mention food, water, oxygen, rest, and protection from the elements and predators. Such needs do not differentiate people from squirrels and do not go far in explaining much work behavior.

In what sense are affiliation, self-esteem, and fairness "needs"? Obviously a person can exist without them. Suppose then we define "need" as something not only essential to survival, but "without which the organism is worse off." This has a superficially reasonable tone, but introduces all the ambiguities and value judgments attendant to what we mean by "worse" or "better."

Skinner (1953) would argue that the use of the need concept invites circularity in thinking. We observe certain regularities in behavior, we infer that some need underlies such behavior, and then the need is used to explain the behavior from which it is inferred. Salancik and Pfeffer (1977) suggest something similar in proposing that various needs are self-attributions for our behavior derived from social feedback and comparison. That is, an individual who expends considerable energy trying to improve on previous performance often elicits comments from others such as, "You must have a strong need to achieve in your make-up." Repetition of such comments leads the person to infer such a need as the cause of his or her behavior.

Nonetheless, Landy and Becker (1987) argue that, even if needs do not have independent, autonomous status within the organism, the construct has value as a means to cognitively categorize the outcomes that give us satisfaction or pleasure. What is important is recognizing that individuals within the same culture will differ somewhat in their subjective groupings of satisfying outcomes. We can expect different cultures—in their varying linguistic structures and other conceptual modes of interpreting reality—to have different conceptualizations.

Furthermore, an aspect of Adam's Equity theory — the *social comparison* process — has potentially profound relevance for the "needs" postulated by other theories. Observation of what others have with respect to some need category powerfully conditions our notion of what is "sufficient" with respect to that category. It is easy to understand that the objective conditions that "satisfy" physiological needs in Bangladesh would not suffice in Pasadena, California. By the same token, the objective condition and outcomes that satisfy a need for self-esteem in one work setting would not do so in others. Needs are relative and dynamic, not absolute or fixed in degree. This may explain why people are never completely satisfied for long — and perhaps it is just as well, for then there would be no point in work.

SUMMARY

Content theories of work motivation attempt to identify the needs or motives that govern behavior at work. Early conceptions of human nature in regard to work emphasized economic and security needs and a disposition to avoid the discomforts of work. This Theory X model logically leads to the design of work structures that use material incentives and external controls to regulate work behavior.

The Hawthorne studies brought to light the importance of social needs and the social conditioning of human wants and desires. The need for affiliation does not so much override economic goals as it changes the context in which economic incentives are perceived and specifies what is acceptable conduct for pursuing them.

Maslow's Need Hierarchy theory offers a framework for prioritizing human needs and predicting the sequence in which they emerge. Maslow's theory predicts that after the material and security needs assumed in Theory X and the affiliation need are met, ego needs begin to affect behavior. Once these "deficiency" needs have been met, some people direct their attention to an ill-defined quest for self-realization or self-actualization, which is regarded as insatiable. Maslow also acknowledged the effects of apparent needs for cognition, or the need "to know," and a need for aesthetics, but did not give a clear indication of where they fit in the order of prepotency with respect to other needs. Alderfer's ERG theory offers a more parsimonious variation of Maslow's hierarchy and also made explicit a *frustration-regression* principle. The latter notion helps to explain why "lower order" needs continue to drive human behavior past their point of presumed satisfaction. Argyris elaborated on the nature of psychological growth and how most work organizations block the progress of continued growth in adults, generally leading to regression to a previous stage of human psychological development.

Herzberg's Two-Factor theory proposes that certain aspects of work satisfy lower-order needs and, in so doing, function as "hygiene factors" by reducing dissatisfaction. The more intrinsic content of work itself taps higher-order ego and growth needs and determines the level of positive feelings about work. Herzberg's model, while controversial, has had considerable influence on current developments in both theory and practice.

The convergence of Maslow, Alderfer, Argyris, Herzberg, and others in attributing to human nature a "growth dynamic" supports a Theory Y alternative to Theory X. Theory Y, articulated by McGregor, assumes that in the proper environment, people can be self-directed in work and in so doing yoke much more powerful motives to work than is possible with Theory X–inspired structures. The evidence for this proposition remains fragmentary and amenable to contradictory views. Even granting the importance and extent of growth motivation, there remains the issue of whether work is the natural, inevitable, or even desirable focus for such needs.

Some conceptions of human needs, such as Murray's, eschew any inherent ranking or sequential emergence of needs, but underscore human differences in which needs are felt most strongly. These differences correspond to differences in learning; their activation depends on appropriate situational cues. Adam's Equity theory proposes that a fundamental motive in the employment relationship is that of maintaining or restoring fairness. This motive finds expression through overt behavior or cognitive reappraisal. In the 1980s, other writers have built on Adam's ideas by noting the many competing principles of what constitutes fairness and by noting the importance attached to procedural as well as distributive justice. One notable feature of Adam's theory that has relevance for conceptions of other work motives is the effect of social comparison processes.

CONCEPTS TO REMEMBER

Theory X	Frustration-regression	Equity theory
Theory Y	hypothesis	Distributive versus
Need hierarchy theory	Two-factor theory	procedural justice
Self-actualization	Hygiene factors	Social comparison process
ERG theory	Latent versus manifest needs	

QUESTIONS FOR DISCUSSION

1. The need hierarchy model of Maslow continues to influence managers' thinking about both conceptual and applied issues of job motivation—despite the general lack of strong empirical support for this model. How would you account for this? (You might want to review the portions of Chapter 2 concerning the criteria for evaluating theories.)

2. Where would you place the need for justice or fairness in Maslow's Need Hierarchy? In ERG theory? Does it fit Theory X or Theory Y better? How could Herzberg's Two-Factor theory accommodate the need for fairness?

3. How well does the construct "need" describe or explain the reasons for the following activities: watching television, playing a video game, water skiing, praying, window shopping, donating blood. Do one or more of these activities suggest a type of need not identified in the theories discussed in the chapter? If so, how would you define the need in question?

REFERENCES

Adams, J. S. (1965). Inequity in social exchange. In L. Berkowitz (ed.), *Advances in experimental social psychology,* vol. 2, 267-99. New York: Academic Press.

Alderfer, C. P. (1969). An empirical test of a new theory of human needs. *Organizational Behavior and Human Performance* 4, 142–75.

Alderfer, C. P. (1972). *Existence, relatedness, and growth: Human needs in organizational settings.* New York: Free Press.

Argyris, C. (1957). *Personality and organization.* New York: Harper.

Campbell, J. P., Dunnette, M. D., Lawler, E. E., III, Weick, K. E., Jr. (1970). *Managerial behavior, performance, and effectiveness.* New York: McGraw-Hill.

Folger, R., & Greenberg, J. (1985). Procedural justice: An interpretive analysis of personnel systems. In K. M. Rowland & G. R. Ferris (eds.), *Research in personnel and human resources management,* vol. 3., 141–83. Greenwich CT: JAI Press.

Herzberg, F. (1966). *Work and the nature of man.* Cleveland: World.

Homans, G. C. (1961). *Social behavior: Its elementary forms.* New York: Harcourt, Brace, and World.

Landy, F. J., & Becker, W. S. (1987). Motivation theory reconsidered. In L. L. Cummings & B. Staw (eds.), *Research in organizational behavior,* vol. 9, 1–38. Greenwich CT: JAI Press.

Lerner, M. J. (1977). The justice motive: Some hypotheses as to its origins and forms. *Journal of Personality* 45, 1–52.

Leventhal, G. S. (1976). Fairness in social relationships. In J. W. Thibaut, J. T. Spence, & R. C. Carson (eds.), *Contemporary topics in social psychology.* Morristown NJ: General Learning Press.

Leventhal, G. S. (1980). What should be done with equity theory? New approaches to the study of fairness in social relationships. In K. G. Gergen, M. S. Greenberg, & R. H. Willis (eds.), *Social exchange: Advances in theory and research.* New York: Plenum Press, 27–55.

McGregor, D. (1960). *The human side of enterprise.* New York: McGraw-Hill.

Maslow, A. H. (1943a). Preface to motivation theory. *Psychosomatic Medicine* 5, 85–92.

Maslow, A. H. (1943b). A theory in human motivation. *Psychological Review* 50, 370–96.

Mayo, E. (1933). *The human problems of an industrial civilization.* New York: Macmillan.

Miner, J. B. (1980). *Theories of organizational behavior.* Hinsdale IL: Dryden Press.

Murray, H. (1938). *Explorations in personality.* New York: Oxford University Press.

Ronen, S. (1986). *Comparative and multi-national management.* New York: John Wiley & Sons.

Salancik, G. R., & Pfeffer, J. (1977). An examination of need satisfaction models of job attitudes. *Administrative Science Quarterly* 22, 427–56.

Skinner, B. F. (1953). *Science and human behavior.* New York: Macmillan.

Strauss, G. (1963). The personality vs. organization theory. In L. R. Sayles, *Individualism and big business,* 67–80. New York: McGraw-Hill.

Wahba, M. A., & Bridwell, L. G. (1976). Maslow reconsidered: A review of research on the need hierarchy theory. *Organizational behavior and human performance* 15, 212–40.

Walster, E., Berscheid, E., & Walster, G. W. (1973). New directions in equity research. *Journal of Personality and Social Psychology* 25, 151–76.

4 Process Models of Work Motivation
Operant and Expectancy Models

What determines the direction, intensity, and duration of work behavior?

How does Learning Theory explain the acquisition, maintenance, and change of work-related behavior?

How does Expectancy Theory explain differences in job effort?

How do the operant and expectancy models differ in their interpretations of job motivation issues?

In the play *The Odd Couple,* circumstances bring Felix and Oscar together as apartment-mates. Felix is compulsively neat and fastidious and his possessions and personal agenda are ultra-organized. Oscar is incorrigibly sloppy and unkempt and his belongings and affairs are always in disarray. Neither seems able to change the other and the amusement of the story derives from the continuing clash between such apparently incompatible lifestyles.

How would you account for the origins and persistence of such polar opposite behavior patterns? A need theorist might say that Felix has a strong need for structure and order and Oscar lacks such a need. Others would contend that this is merely another way to describe different behavior patterns or, at worst, a tautology: an inference drawn from one set of observations and then turned around to explain that from which it was inferred. Also, it is difficult to attach this difference in need to any recognizable form of need theories previously discussed. Felix and Oscar both earn comfortable incomes, both do work that requires a mix of professional skill and creativity (Felix is a studio photographer, Oscar a sports writer), and both feel the pangs of separation from their families. Because their position in respect to some hierarchy of needs is similar, we have to go beyond those needs to provide an explanation.

One perspective on the Felix-Oscar contrast looks to the *past.* Felix has *learned* one pattern of behavior and Oscar a very different one because of previous consequences of that behavior. A different perspective looks to conceptions of the *future.* Felix construes his relentless neatness as instrumental toward some distant goal, while Oscar has a different notion of the path that leads to his eventual valued outcomes.

In this chapter, we will examine two conceptual frameworks that make no assumptions about motive content or underlying needs, but focus on the process in which valued outcomes influence behavior.

LEARNING THEORY

We not only learn French, geometry, cost accounting, and ballroom dancing, we also learn absenteeism, courtesy, attitudes about product quality and customer service, and leadership. In other words, "motivation" is not some mysterious quality or cause of behavior; it is behavior itself and, like any other behavior, must be learned. Learning theory conceptualizes behavior as an ongoing process of *conditioning* that occurs in the context of some environment.

Classical (Respondent) Conditioning

If you have ever spent time in the kitchen, you have probably accidentally brushed your hand against a hot burner. When you jerked your hand away, you did not have to learn that behavior; it was an unconditioned reflex. But have you noticed that, perhaps while sponging off the top of the stove, you might jerk your hand away from a cold burner you accidentally touch? Or that you pull your hand away if, out of the corner of your eye, you notice a small red light glowing on the display panel of the stove? When you abruptly remove your hand not in response to the heat but to something *associated* with the heat, you have learned through a process of classical conditioning.

Classical or respondent conditioning is a *process in which a reflex or emotional response comes under the control of a new stimulus.* The Russian physiologist Pavlov studied this form of conditioning and found that his dogs would salivate not only when chewing their food, but when any characteristic cue — the appearance of the food bowl, or a bell — immediately preceded the feeding. The salivation was an unconditioned (i.e., unlearned) response to the food in the mouth, but a conditioned (learned) response to anything closely associated with, or immediately preceding, the original stimulus.

Early in this century, psychologists attempted to make the classically conditioned response the cornerstone of a general model of human behavior. This attempt failed because most human behavior has no basis in unconditioned reflexes. Classical conditioning appears limited to what we generally regard as involuntary behavior.

This is not to say that classical conditioning is irrelevant to students of organization. Although reflexes such as the eye blink and the knee jerk do not command our interest, those involuntary responses we call emotions are important if we are to understand organizational behavior.

Recall your first visit to the dentist. You sat in the waiting room, heard a high-pitched sound, were ushered into a room by someone in a starchy white uniform, detected certain odors, climbed into the strange barber's-type chair, saw the dentist approach you with an implement that had a little mirror on the end of it, felt the dentist rub something spicy on your gum, and then came the needle. Your emotional response to the needle contained something like fear, if not terror. Eventually you recovered, but on the next visit you probably felt fear building up in advance — as soon as those characteristic sights, sounds, and tastes succeeded each other. Originally those sensations were innocuous and posed no danger, but because of their association in time and place with the needle, they elicited a conditioned emotional response on your part. They did not produce exactly the same reaction as the needle in the gum, but some component of that reaction — an "anticipatory" response.

There is no established list of all objects or events that can trigger unconditioned emotional responses such as pleasure, fear, anger, disgust, or happiness. Whatever they might be — and they are probably few — our emotional responses to these objects or events become conditioned to other objects (including persons) and events associated with them. Moreover, any object or event that evokes a conditioned emotional response can then become the basis for still other objects or events to evoke a similar response — in other words, *second-order classical conditioning.* We come to like certain people, not because of what they themselves have done for us, but because they were present when other things evoked positive emotions. The converse is true for some people we associate with negative emotions. We come to have distinctive emotional responses to certain words, because of their characteristic covariation with events that aroused positive or negative emotions. Much of what we call attitudes develops around conditioned emotional responses.

There are some generalizations that can be made about classical conditioning. First, it is a nonlogical, nonrational form of learning; the "higher order" intellectual processes have little or nothing to do with it. Thus, it is irrational to dislike or fear people just because we associate them with something else that frightened us, particularly if they played no functional part in causing what frightened us. Second, it is a passive form of learning; we learn without doing anything ourselves. In fact, this learning occurs most intensively when we are restrained, helpless, or confronting new situations in which we are not prepared to take effective action. Perhaps this explains why some of our strongest conditioned emotional responses occur in the early stages of new experiences—the first week of college, the first month of a new job, or the day of arrival on your first trip overseas. The strength of those responses may account for why we can recall them so vividly in comparison to later stages of those experiences. This observation has obvious and profound implications for the significance of the socialization process in work organizations. Finally, since many emotional responses are learned, they can be "unlearned" to one degree or another. Fear of a boss associated with negative experiences can be *extinguished* if continued exposure to that boss no longer is accompanied by unpleasant events. In fact, the conditioned emotional response can eventually become positive if the presence of that person precedes events that arouse positive emotions.

Operant Conditioning

More significant to what we *do* at work, as opposed to what we feel, is the form of learning called *operant* (sometimes *instrumental*) *conditioning.* This is the *process in which instrumental behavior is shaped by its consequences* (Skinner, 1953). *Instrumental* denotes voluntary or purposive behavior. The term *operant* is derived from the same root as "operate," signifying behavior that operates on the environment to produce some consequence. Motor skills, job routines, work habits, and much verbal behavior qualify as operants.

The core concepts of the operant framework are the ABCs: Antecedents, Behavior, Consequences (Miller, 1978).

Antecedents   No operants occur in a vacuum; some context or occasion always sets the stage for any particular behavior. An antecedent (also called *discriminative stimulus*) is any cue that comes to exercise some control over behavior, in the sense that the behavior in question is more likely to occur given the presence of that antecedent. The degree of control that the antecedent has, precisely what is represented by the antecedent, and just what behavior it controls, all depend on what follows.

A useful, nontechnical classification of various types of antecedents includes the following: *(1) The presence of other people.* For example, most verbal behavior does not occur unless someone is within earshot. *(2) The presence of a particular person or type of person.* Your verbal behavior differs according to whether your parents, younger brother, roommate, or academic advisor is the person present. In a sense, each person we know controls a certain limited portion of our verbal (or more generally, behavioral) repertoire. When certain combinations of these individuals are present simultaneously, we feel reduced to a very small class of utterances to meet the conditions of all of these antecedents. *(3) Prior responses by others.* Other people's behavior can act as antecedents for your behavior, and vice-versa. Someone gives you something. That sets the stage for you to say "Thank you," which prompts the other person to say "You're quite welcome." Accomplished actors and negotiators cultivate a sensitivity to the nuances of other people's behavior that provide the cues for effective behavior on their own part. *(4) A prior response of your own.* You press the button for a soft drink only after you drop the coin in the machine; you strike the typewriter keys only after you have inserted the paper. *(5) The physical environment.* A couple of hours ago, I took a letter out to the mailbox and raised the red flag. I see the flag is still up, so I won't go see if *Sports Illustrated* has come. Later, the flag is down — I slip my loafers on, and I go look in the mailbox. All I got was three bills and four catalogs displaying wares I do not want to buy. My trip to the mailbox was not encouraged by the mail that was received, but the red flag had some control over whether I went out there to start with.

Behavior   In the operant ABCs, the B refers to *observable* behavior or combinations of responses; we have already restricted this to voluntary or instrumental behavior. The behavior must be describable in specific terms to qualify for analysis in operant terms. To say that someone "did a good job" or "has a poor work attitude" or "provided excellent service" does not lend itself to an operant interpretation. We must specify what responses constituted the good job, what overt actions reflect a poor work attitude, what visible behaviors produced the excellent service.

Consequences   The emphasis here is on the *immediate* consequences following behavior. How fast is immediate? With laboratory animals, immediate is measured in seconds. The conditioning of human operant behavior has more latitude (how much is not known) but often the important consequences follow within a few minutes. Long-delayed consequences are eventually important for other reasons, but specific operant behaviors are disproportionately influenced by their immediate consequences. Thus, many programs based on application of operant concepts do not emphasize monetary rewards, because seldom can those immediately follow specific

TABLE 4–1

Basic Contingencies of Reinforcement

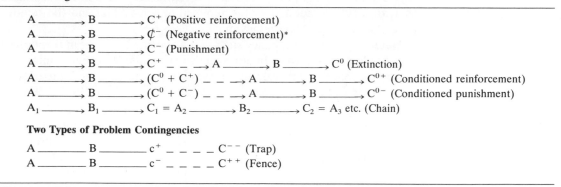

A $\longrightarrow$ B $\longrightarrow$ C^+ (Positive reinforcement)

A $\longrightarrow$ B $\longrightarrow$ $\cancel{C}^-$ (Negative reinforcement)*

A $\longrightarrow$ B $\longrightarrow$ C^- (Punishment)

A $\longrightarrow$ B $\longrightarrow$ C^+ _ _ $\longrightarrow$ A $\longrightarrow$ B $\longrightarrow$ C^0 (Extinction)

A $\longrightarrow$ B $\longrightarrow$ $(C^0 + C^+)$ _ _ $\longrightarrow$ A $\longrightarrow$ B $\longrightarrow$ C^{0+} (Conditioned reinforcement)

A $\longrightarrow$ B $\longrightarrow$ $(C^0 + C^-)$ _ _ $\longrightarrow$ A $\longrightarrow$ B $\longrightarrow$ C^{0-} (Conditioned punishment)

A_1 $\longrightarrow$ B_1 $\longrightarrow$ $C_1 = A_2$ $\longrightarrow$ B_2 $\longrightarrow$ $C_2 = A_3$ etc. (Chain)

Two Types of Problem Contingencies

A $\longrightarrow$ B $\longrightarrow$ c^+ _ _ _ _ C^{--} (Trap)

A $\longrightarrow$ B $\longrightarrow$ c^- _ _ _ _ C^{++} (Fence)

*Negative reinforcement occurs when a behavior (B) is followed by *removal* of a negative (aversive) stimulus.

work behavior. However, we have reason to believe that a response that is already strong can be *maintained* by consequences that are delayed (Brown & Herrnstein, 1975).

Contingencies of reinforcement describe various interrelationships among specific antecedents, behavior, and consequences. A *functional analysis of behavior* examines behavior as a function of these contingencies.

Table 4–1 illustrates some of the basic contingencies found useful in a functional analysis. *Positive reinforcement* increases the likelihood of reoccurrence of prior behavior in the presence of particular antecedents. A positive reinforcer is defined technically as a consequence that strengthens the response preceding it. Note that the definition of positive reinforcer says nothing about the type of need (if any) that is met and does not hinge on whether we would ordinarily think of the consequence as a reward.

Extinction is the weakening of a behavior in a specific context due to the absence of positive reinforcement. Extinction is not "forgetting"—we forget something because we do not use it or do it over some interval of time. In extinction, the behavior does occur, but has no reinforcing consequences. Extinction, however, may occur more or less rapidly depending on the strength of the behavior, which in turn depends on the extent and previous conditions of its positive reinforcement. Extinction is not punishment, but a "null consequence." Specific behaviors extinguish when they have no positively reinforcing consequences.

Negative reinforcement describes a contingency in which a behavior is strengthened by the *removal of an aversive consequence*. Here again, the definition of what constitutes an aversive stimulus is empirical, not subjective or qualitative: it is one whose removal is reinforcing. We are familiar with such stimuli: direct eye contact with a stranger in cramped quarters, such as an elevator, bothers us. This direct eye contact is an aversive stimulus not because subjectively it produces "discomfort," but because some behaviors—such as looking at the floor numbers above the elevator doors, or looking down at your shoes — are reinforced by the removal or avoidance of eye contact. Again, note that negative reinforcement is not punishment; it is a consequence defined by the removal of something, and the removal strengthens the preceding behavior.

Punishment is a contingency such that a specific behavior in response to an antecedent is following by an aversive stimulus. Whether punishment weakens a behavior or merely suppresses it temporarily is an issue of some debate among operant theorists (cf. Scott & Podsakoff, 1982). What is agreed is that punishment is a more complex process than positive reinforcement. Whatever its effects on the prior behavior, punishment has side effects as well, such as classically conditioned emotional responses to other aspects of the situation. Those who apply operant concepts to work behavior prefer to "accentuate the positive." If it is not practicable to eliminate undesired behavior by positively reinforcing different, constructive responses, then the preferred alternative is either to change the antecedent conditions that trigger the undesired behavior or use extinction — that is, allow the behavior to occur, but see to it that the behavior does not have a reinforcing consequence.

When behavior has a positive consequence, it often has other predictable consequences as well. Only a positive reinforcer can strengthen the prior behavior, but other consequences can acquire this power when they regularly and immediately precede a positive reinforcer. Thus we have *conditioned positive reinforcement*. McDonald's golden arch functions as a positive reinforcer to millions of people because its appearance reliably precedes more basic positive reinforcers. *Conditioned punishment* can also occur. Here an aversive consequence to behavior makes any correlated consequences conditioned aversive stimuli.

One explanation for conditioned positive reinforcement and conditioned punishment assumes that any positive reinforcer or aversive stimulus elicits an involuntary psychoneural response. Whether we think of this as an emotion or more like a reflex, it is a response susceptible to classical conditioning. Thus, when any positive reinforcer triggers this response in the central nervous system, the response also comes under the control of other stimuli present at the time.

What this means, in practice, is that a diverse array of otherwise neutral events or objects can come to act as reinforcers or punishers because of what they have been associated with, or what they signify. For the administrator, this is both good news and bad. The good news is that it multiplies the number of possible consequences that can be used to shape constructive behavior. The bad news is that, by the time people enter work organizations, they already have experienced much of this conditioning process, and it is not the same for any two persons. Thus, what acts as a conditioned positive reinforcer for some people is a null consequence or possibly even a conditioned punisher for others. Fortunately, by virtue of the fact that the larger culture has provided for some commonality in reinforcement histories, we can often predict what the general effects of some consequences on behavior are likely to be.

The *chain* is a sequence of behaviors linked by the fact that the reinforcing consequence of a prior behavior "doubles up" as the antecedent for a subsequent response. You flick the switch on your personal computer and the consequence is the satisfying whir leading up to the appearance of the cursor. Your first response has been positively reinforced. The consequence—the cursor on the screen—now provides the antecedent for pressing the keys that load the software. This response is reinforced by the consequence that the main menu appears. And so on, until some ultimate consequence (a printed document) completes the chain or some unrelated antecedent stimulus intrudes (the telephone rings) and initiates a different chain.

When we first undertake to learn a new, complex set of responses, we do so under conditions that enable the consequences of initial actions to become conditioned positive reinforcers. Instructors first concentrate on basics or preliminaries and voice warm, enthusiastic approval when we get them right. We have not yet accomplished anything of value, but the verbal reinforcement of the instructor conditions these early consequences—the proper alignment of the paper in the typewriter, the simmer of the water in the saucepan, the click of the turn signal on the car—to have some middling but functional positive reinforcement. By not allowing the student to proceed until these early consequences are experienced, the instructor also guarantees that they will act as antecedents for subsequent responses.

Let us examine two types of "problem contingencies." In the *trap* contingency, an antecedent condition evokes a behavior that leads to immediate (though sometimes trivial) reinforcing consequences. Thus the behavior is strengthened and recurs in numerous situations. Eventually, repeated occurrences cause a serious, significant negative outcome. Common traps are cigarette smoking, eating candy, gambling, the use of credit cards, and sunbathing. Even watching televised sports programs is a trap; you sit down and follow the action for a few minutes, the reinforcement for doing so leads to another few minutes, and without having intended it, you wind up watching a four-hour, extra-inning ball game. Your team has lost, you're tired, you haven't done your chores—in general you find yourself in a much worse situation than you had earlier.

In a *fence* contingency, a specific behavior has either a null (nonreinforcing) consequence, or more commonly, minor aversive consequences. However, the long-term repetition of the behavior has significant positive outcomes (even if the outcome is positive only in the sense of *avoiding* a serious negative outcome). The practice of wearing a seat belt in a car is a most vexing sort of fence. Most people believe statistics that affirm that using a seat belt is almost certain to be to the driver's advantage in the event of a crash. The problem is that many people are more influenced by the immediate nuisance value of this practice. Another fence is flossing one's teeth. Most people brush their teeth, not so much for its effect on the health of teeth and gums, but for the immediate reinforcement of an improved taste in the mouth. Even though some experts believe that flossing is actually more critical than brushing in preventing gum disease, comparatively few people floss. The reason: there is no immediate positive consequence, only such aversive consequences as when the floss gets snagged around a tooth or hurts the gums.

Schedules of Positive Reinforcement

The long-term effects of a positive reinforcement contingency depend on the *schedule of reinforcement.* A *continuous* schedule of reinforcement provides positive reinforcement for every instance of a specific behavior in the context of a specific antecedent. Positive reinforcement on such a consistent basis promotes rapid acquisition of a new behavior or marked increase of frequency of a weak response. However, a contingency that exists only on this schedule produces a behavior that is quick to extinguish when positive reinforcement no longer follows the response.

Behaviors shaped by contingencies with *intermittent* schedules of reinforcement are more resistant to extinction. *Fixed-interval* schedules provide positive reinforcement according to some constant interval of time, contingent on occurrence of the behavior near the end of the interval. Although this schedule promotes resistance to extinction, it also leads to uneven rates of the behavior over the interval: a scallop effect with low rates of response throughout most of the interval after reinforcement, and a high rate of behavior as the end of the interval approaches. Professors have commented that the behavior of studying follows this scallop pattern—perhaps attributable to the fixed interval schedule on which feedback from exams is given. Such schedules are also common in work organizations—the distribution of pay checks, coffee breaks, much of the feedback people receive about their work. Whenever reinforcers are dispensed at fixed periods of time, the predominant effect is to strengthen whatever behavior occurred near the end of the interval, whether that be clock-watching, attendance, or clean-up.

Fixed ratio schedules dispense reinforcement according to some constant quantity of specific behaviors. Rest periods contingent on processing 30 customer orders or quality inspection of 50 microwave ovens would constitute such a schedule. You use it on yourself when you take a study break after reading 15 pages of text or stop for a soft drink after 100 miles of driving.

The effects of fixed ratio schedules on behavior depend less on the ratio itself than on the number of responses between occasions of some reinforcement. One unit of reinforcement for every 10 responses is the same ratio as 10 units of reinforcement following 100 responses, but qualitatively they are different. The longer the stretch of behavior between episodes of some reinforcement, the more likely that the behavior will be weak following reinforcement. The behavior may pick up in frequency and intensity as the end of the block of responses nears. You may have experienced this "goal gradient" effect when you turned the pages faster near the end of a book or drove faster near the end of a long trip. This effect can lead to excessive haste, at the expense of quality, as you approach the end of a long batch of work. When the quantities of behavior required for reinforcement reach particularly large dimensions, a more serious effect occurs. The slowdown in behavior postpones the reinforcement that much more. Temporary extinction may occur. The rough rule of thumb for fixed ratio schedules, whether applied to others or to oneself, is that a modest amount of reinforcement for a smaller quantity of behavior works better than requiring large quantities of behavior for a large amount of positive reinforcer.

Variable interval and *variable ratio* schedules are similar in principle to their fixed counterparts, except that while the interval or ratio has some average value over the long run, it varies considerably in the short run. Consider your habit of checking the mail. On average, you may get one "good" piece of mail every three days. But you might get something nice several days in a row, or go for two weeks without good mail. This represents a variable interval schedule. Games of chance feature a variable ratio schedule—you win on average every nth play (over the long run, guaranteed to favor the gambling establishment), but you might win several times in a row or play a hundred times for nothing.

Behavior shaped on a variable schedule of reinforcement is resistant to extinction. You still check the mail—even when a month has gone by since you got anything you wanted. You still want to go to the plate even when you've gone 0 for your last 22 at bats.

Sometimes this resistance-to-extinction effect of variable schedules presents problems—particularly in the "unlearning" of incorrect behavior. A person who uses the wrong technique for serving a tennis ball will nonetheless score an occasional ace; someone who holds a rifle improperly will hit the bull's-eye on some variable basis. When the individual tries to shift to the correct but unaccustomed method, at first little success is experienced, so the lapse to the old but wrong technique occurs. This has prompted legions of instructors to argue that "it's easier to teach effective skills in this area to someone who has never had any experience with it at all."

Operant experts have studied more complex schedules of reinforcement, but from the basic types we have noted, we can describe an "optimal" combination of schedules. Continuous schedules of reinforcement—or at least very frequent reinforcement—facilitate the rapid acquisition of a behavior in a particular context of antecedent stimuli. Once behavior has attained some strength, a gradual shift to variable ratio or variable interval schedule of reinforcement helps maintain the behavior in the face of eventual interludes of nonreinforcement.

Types of Positive Reinforcers

Operant theorists contend that, once a consequence demonstrates its power to act as a positive reinforcer, the timing and scheduling of the consequence matter much more than the *type* of reinforcer. Their position is that even if we could sort out reinforcers according to what needs they satisfy—an exercise that would not interest them very much—we still could not predict the effectiveness of the reinforcer in shaping behavior on that basis.

For certain purposes, we find it useful to distinguish between *contrived* and *noncontrived* reinforcers. Noncontrived reinforcers are naturally occurring consequences created or produced by the behavior itself. Certain pleasing sounds are the natural consequence of specific (and subtle) behaviors used in playing a guitar or violin—those behaviors directly caused those consequences. A neat bedroom or office is the naturally occurring consequence of the behaviors that preceded it—making the bed, arranging books, hanging up clothes, sweeping up debris.

A contrived reinforcer, on the other hand, is artificial. It only happens because someone contrived or arranged for the consequence to follow the behavior. Someone who gives a child candy for cleaning his or her room, or gives a student an A+ for correctly reciting a poem, uses a contrived reinforcer. In the natural order of things, cleaning a room does not produce candy and reciting a poem does not generate an A+.

The distinction can blur when the consequence of your behavior takes the form of another person's behavior. When you recite a poem and those present applaud, is the applause contrived or noncontrived? It could be contrived in character if the people applauded to encourage further recital. On the other hand, many competent behaviors performed in the presence of others often do have an arguably natural effect in leading others to express their admiration.

There are those who would make this distinction a moral issue. One school of opinion takes a dim view of the use of clearly contrived reinforcers (such as grades, gold stars, points, tangible products), arguing that the appropriate motivation for learning a particular skill is the constructive purpose to which the skill or habit will be put. In other words, the incentive for learning new words should be the enhanced powers of self-expression and appreciation of language, not to get good marks or gold stars. Otherwise, without the continued support of artificial rewards, you wouldn't have any interest in continuing to learn new words.

A variation of this argument is that behavior shaped by contrived reinforcers causes a sense of external control, which militates against psychological growth. On the other hand, behavior sustained by noncontrived consequences of the behavior itself promotes a self-concept of internal control and feelings of competence. Such feelings whet the appetite for continued psychological growth, a much more powerful motive than the desire for artificial incentives.

Afficionados of operant concepts prefer to treat the contrived-noncontrived issue in empirical and pragmatic rather than moral terms. They would argue that, empirically, contrived reinforcers are just as effective as noncontrived reinforcers *if* the criterion is rate of acquisition of behavior or consistency and strength of the behavior, and *if* the contrived reinforcer is optimally scheduled. When contrived reinforcers lack effectiveness, usually it is because they are delayed consequences or because they occur on a fixed interval schedule.

The pragmatic case for contrived reinforcers rests on two considerations. First, they play an important role in the early stages of learning a skill—because at that stage, the behavior does not have the means of generating natural or noncontrived reinforcers. A person learning to play a musical instrument or speak German might eventually attain a proficiency that creates naturally occurring positive consequences of such behaviors. But initially such naturally occurring positive consequences are not forthcoming, and contrived reinforcers may be needed to sustain the effort, the practice, until the requisite skill levels are attained. This applies not only to skill, but also to many habits and routines that require considerable practice before they yield consequences that offset the costs of the routine itself. Most people derive some reinforcement from neat living spaces and work areas, but only with practice do the housekeeping routines become so efficient that the costs (in time and effort) become affordable in proportion to the benefits.

Second, the noncontrived benefits of some constructive behaviors do not occur on a schedule that would sustain the behavior. Recall the fence—a contingency in which the benefits accrue only long after the initiation of the designated behavior. Contrived reinforcers are then needed to bridge the gap between behavior and the ultimate benefits produced by the behavior. In some of these contingencies, the noncontrived payoff, while substantial, rarely occurs and thus could not by itself sustain the behavior. In baseball, a batter who pops up to the infield should run hard to first base, because the infielder might misplay the ball. This happens so seldom that reaching base safely could hardly sustain the effort, but verbal encouragement from teammates and coach provide the contrived reinforcement for hustle.

The operant view is that contrived and noncontrived reinforcers play complementary rather than contradictory roles in shaping constructive behavior.

The Law of Relative Effect: How We Distribute Behavior

In 1911, E. L. Thorndike anticipated the core premise of operant concepts with his Law of Effect, which stated that a behavior in a particular situation that was followed by a positive consequence tends to be repeated in that situation. The Law of Effect essentially describes what we have called a positive reinforcement contingency. What the Law of Effect does not tell us is what happens when *two different* behaviors in the same situation are both followed by positive consequences. In the real world, it often happens that for any given antecedent condition, various behaviors can be performed, all with some degree of positive reinforcement. They cannot all be repeated simultaneously, of course, and sheer limits of time and opportunity ensure that the strengthening of some behaviors must occur at the expense of others. The *Law of Relative Effect* (sometimes called the *Matching Law*) provides a basis for predicting the distribution of behavior in a situation that reinforces competing responses.

Consider Beth, a college student who spends her freshman and sophomore years at a small, all-female school in a rural part of the state. The school has no big-time sports program, few structured noncurricular activities, and infrequent social events. Beth takes mostly required courses, which do not interest her very much. She averages about three hours of study per day outside of class.

For her junior and senior years, Beth transfers to the large state university to pursue her major field of interest, journalism. The university has a large student body, many student activities, a dizzying schedule of concerts and shows, all in a metropolitan setting. Beth finds her journalism courses much more interesting than the required courses, but studies only two hours a day, compared to the three she averaged before. Why? *Competing behaviors are reinforced at an even greater rate of increase.*

According to the Law of Relative Effect (Brown & Herrnstein, 1975), it is the *relative* or *comparative* rate of reinforcement that determines the frequency of behavior in a particular situation over a period of time. If behavior B1 generates twice as much positive reinforcement as behavior B2, then—other things equal—over time, B1 will occur twice as often as B2. If the reinforcement for B1 suddenly decreased, the rate of occurrence of B2 would increase. Even though no greater reinforcement for B2 was provided, its comparative rate of reinforcement has increased because of the decrease in reinforcement for B1. In other words, "each separate form of behavior is controlled by all the rewards and punishments operating at a given time" (Brown & Hernnstein, 1975, p. 84). Whenever we change the rate of positive reinforcement of some behavior in a situation, we automatically alter the *relative* rate of reinforcement for any competing behavior. Thus, the distribution of the entire set of behaviors is altered.

"Motivation Problems": Operant Interpretations

"Motivation problem" exists when, in our judgment, a necessary or desired behavior occurs too infrequently in some designated antecedent situation. For example, machine operators do not wear safety helmets and goggles as often as they should; telephone receptionists do not return customer calls within five minutes; sales staff do not turn in complete expense reports promptly; team project members miss too many meetings or show up late.

Managers with an operant twist to their thinking do not analyze these problems with reference to "what's missing inside the person." They look at the contingencies surrounding the behavior in question. Their analysis leads to one or more of the following conclusions.

1. *The behavior too seldom has positive consequences.* Because we tend to take many constructive behaviors for granted, we do not arrange positive consequences. Add to this the tendency to avoid repeating behaviors that are not reinforced. The doctrine of "management by exception" (the idea that managers should concentrate attention on deviations from the standard) militates against monitoring and reinforcing high rates of expected behaviors.

2. *The positive consequence follows too late.* The operant perspective emphasizes the immediate consequence of behavior. A kind word from the supervisor following an exemplary action will do more to strengthen that action than a formal letter of commendation four days later. Delayed positive consequences actually may strengthen a different response altogether.

3. *The desired behavior actually has aversive consequences.* Managers profess to encourage abundant feedback and upward communication from their groups. Certainly the well-being of the system demands a steady flow of negative feedback about flawed products, breakdowns in service, and errant processes. Yet often the ire of the manager is directed at the messenger with the bad news, unintentionally punishing such behavior.

4. *Competing behaviors are reinforced at a greater rate.* Managers, especially those at lower levels of supervision, feel pressure for short-term results, especially in meeting quantitative goals for production, revenue, sales, and the like. Quite naturally, they often give disproportionate reinforcement for behavior that directly meets these pressures, and recognition of qualitative contributions that provide longer-run value is lost in the shuffle. This raises a related point: leader behavior that provides positive reinforcement is itself behavior that must be sustained by its consequences. Thus, patterns of positive reinforcement are interlocked throughout the system. The results that top-level managers strive for will determine how their subordinate managers use positive reinforcement.

A different form of motivation problem concerns work-related behaviors that are dysfunctional for the organization or even not in the long-run best interests of the person doing the behavior. Violation of safety rules, absenteeism, excessive socializing on company time, littering the workplace, "juggling the figures," are all familiar problems. The operant theorist addresses these issues by asking: What situational antecedent cues trigger the undesired behavior? What immediate consequences reinforce and sustain the behavior? The shrill cry from officials demanding effort to meet short-run quantitative goals might encourage production people to take questionable risks with hazardous machinery. Staff members might "play with the

FOCUS ON MANAGEMENT

What Do Effective and Ineffective Managers Do Differently?

Judith Komaki assembled a team of six researchers to observe the behavior of 24 managers, half of whom had been independently rated in the top quartile of effectiveness within a large medical insurance firm, and half of whom had been rated in the bottom quartile. The researchers, unaware which managers had been rated effective, observed the managers for 30-minute intervals and repeated the observations for up to 20 periods per manager. Managerial behavior was coded in one of seven categories: *(1)* performance antecedents (instructions or reminders to subordinates), *(2)* performance monitoring (collecting information about a subordinate's performance), *(3)* providing positive or negative consequences, *(4)* solitary (not interacting with subordinates), *(5)* nonwork related, *(6)* work related (referring to work but not performance as such), and *(7)* own (i.e., the manager's) performance.

The effective and ineffective managers did not differ in how much time they devoted to providing antecedents, providing negative consequences, or dispensing positive consequences. The *only* difference in the behavior categories was *performance monitoring,* in particular, the actual sampling of subordinates' work as the major form of monitoring. Komaki interprets the results as suggesting that effective managers, by spending more time monitoring subordinates' performance, are much more likely to make both positive and negative consequences *contingent* on specific behaviors.

SOURCE: J. L. Komaki, "Toward Effective Supervision: An Operant Analysis and Comparison of Managers at Work, *Journal of Applied Psychology* 71 (1986), pp. 270–79.

---

numbers" to meet quotas. Officials might unwittingly reinforce such actions by making approval contingent on presenting the right numbers, regardless of the substance that lies beneath the numbers. Colleagues might also provide that kind of reinforcement for behavior that keeps the pressure off the group, even if the behavior has later dysfunctional effects on group performance.

The Operant Perspective: Concluding Note

The well-worn adage that "a thousand-mile journey begins with the first step" must have come from an intuitive operant thinker. Fundamental to that cast of mind is the appreciation that all manner of grand and glorious accomplishments arise from small, specific behaviors. The equally small—but timely—positive consequences of those behaviors keep the process going. Neglect the here-and-now importance of the little steps and no amount of promised riches will sustain the striving.

In the operant view, there are two types of ineffective administrators. One simply denies the need for positive reinforcement and works on the

CLOSE-UP

Profits and Injuries

Health economist James Robinson used Bureau of Labor Statistics to track accident rates in various industries back to 1926. He found a strong positive correlation between injury rates and the business cycle: in times of expansion and increased sales and production, there are higher accident rates.

Robinson attributes this correlation in part to the hiring of more inexperienced workers when plants increase production, but he notes that this does not statistically account for the effect. It appears that the push to meet higher production levels causes a decline in attention to safety standards and violations of safety rules.

SOURCE: "Boom Time Injuries," *Psychology Today,* December 1988, p. 18.

assumption that people should do what they are expected to do, regardless of consequence. Another type provides positive consequences in abundance, but not contingent on any particular behavior—in other words, all behavior is treated the same. The operant definition of an effective administrator is one who arranges for positive consequences contingent on behavior that contributes constructively to the larger system.

EXPECTANCY (VIE) THEORY

Since early this century, psychologists have followed one of two strikingly different approaches. The *behaviorist* tradition limits its subject matter to observable behavior, accounting for that behavior in terms of environmental causes. The *cognitive* tradition believes that mental processes—"cognitions"—mediate the effect of the environment in producing behavior. To explain and predict behavior, cognitivists maintain that we must model the logic and organization of those thought processes. The operant framework of work motivation represents the behaviorist influence in OB, whereas the major cognitive alternative is expectancy theory.

Vroom (1964) offered the first systematic version of expectancy theory, drawing largely from the work of the cognitive psychologist E. C. Tolman (1932). The key constructs to Vroom's model are *action, outcome, expectancy, instrumentality,* and *valence.*

An *action* is a behavior or set of behaviors over which a person has control and can choose to perform or not perform. You can choose to apply for a position at IBM, to seek an MBA, to put much or little effort into customer service, to ask an attractive person of the opposite sex to dinner.

An *outcome* is the actual result of an action, a result over which you do not have complete control. One possible outcome of your job application is that you receive an offer; another outcome is that you are rejected. You can choose whether to exert a high level of effort in sales, but the outcome — sales volume — cannot be known at the moment of your choice.

Expectancy is your subjective probability that a particular outcome will result from an action you take. Many students apply to several MBA programs because their expectancy that they will be admitted to the program of their first choice is .5 or less, while they feel confident (i.e., a subjective probability of about .9) that their applications will be successful at their second or third choices. Of course, we seldom think of these expectancies in precise, quantitative form. We do, however, distinguish several levels of likelihood about the various outcomes of our actions, as reflected in phrases such as "sure thing," "I'm fairly optimistic," "it could go either way," "a long shot, but it's worth taking," and "ain't no way."

Instrumentality describes the link between a "first-level" outcome and a "second-level" outcome. Outcome A is positively instrumental to outcome B if the occurrence of A makes it more likely that B would subsequently occur. Thus, admission to certain graduate programs is ultimately instrumental to securing a job in investment banking in the Northeast. Instrumentality can also be negative, i.e., one outcome can reduce the chances of others happening — for example, enrollment at certain schools might eliminate frequent trips home.

The concept of instrumentality has much in common with the notion of expectancy. The main difference is that expectancy is a subjective probability concerning an outcome resulting from an action, whereas instrumentality is a subjective belief about how one outcome makes others more or less likely.

People acquire these subjective beliefs in many ways. They can be based on experience or arrived at from observation of others' actions and outcomes. We might rely on what others tell us; a friend might counsel, "Don't apply to Harvard because you haven't got one chance in a hundred of being accepted." Sometimes our ideas of expectancy and instrumentality are just wild guesses if they pertain to matters in which we are inexperienced and have no means of gathering information that would apply to our own circumstances. What is important in Expectancy Theory is not the accuracy or validity of these beliefs, but simply what these beliefs are, because the assumption is that such private assessments determine behavior. The objective fact that two out of every three new businesses fail within five years of start-up obviously does not deter some entrepreneurs who think (rightly or wrongly) *their* chances of success are much better than that.

The *valence* of an outcome concerns its desirability or incentive value to the person. Valence signifies nothing about the satisfaction that might be achieved when the outcome is attained, only how much the person presently wants that outcome. Valence, like expectancy or instrumentality, is subjective and can be misguided — someone has commented that "answered prayers" occasion more grief than prayers unanswered. Nonetheless, the outcomes to which we attach present value will potentially dictate our course of action. Like instrumentality, valence can be positive (we prefer the occurrence of an outcome over its nonoccurrence) or negative (we prefer nonoccurrence).

One proposition of Expectancy Theory is that the valence of any focal outcome is determined by *(1)* the subsequent outcomes for which the focal outcome is positively or negatively instrumental, and *(2)* the valence of those subsequent outcomes. In other words, an outcome is subjectively good or desirable because its predominant effect is to make other good outcomes more likely and/or to make unattractive outcomes less likely. For example, outstanding job performance is positively valent to the extent that a person sees it as instrumental to other desired outcomes—such as wealth, recognition, status.

That raises the question, If this outcome is positively valent because it leads to other outcomes that are positively valent, what determines the valence of those other outcomes? The logic of Expectancy Theory says that, once again, the valence of second-level outcomes is determined by their implications of still more distant outcomes. We have, then, a potentially infinite regress of outcomes to further outcomes—nothing is good in itself, but good only for what it leads to. However, an expectancy theory of work motivation skirts this problem by allowing for some outcomes to have "intrinsic valence" and thus do not require linkages to other outcomes.

A second proposition of Expectancy Theory states that, of several mutually exclusive actions, a person will opt for the action that maximizes the summed products of expectancy X valence for the various foreseeable outcomes of the action.

Let us work through a very simple illustration. Consider the action of asking a particular attractive person of the opposite sex to join you for dinner. Also, consider an alternative action—dining alone or with another acquaintance. For convenience, assume that the outcome of this alternative action can be foreseen with certainty and that its valence represents a baseline value arbitrarily set to zero (i.e., indifference). What factors determine whether you will take the first action of asking the attractive person to dine with you? Two possible outcomes probably loom uppermost in your thinking. One is acceptance. Such an outcome presumably holds considerable positive valence to you. You might or might not think through a long string of subsequent outcomes, but in any case your present assessment of this outcome would on balance register as strongly positive. Another possible outcome is refusal. Actually, there are several other possible outcomes representing various forms of refusal, ranging from "I really wish I could join you, I'm tied up with something I can't get out of, but thanks, maybe another time," to decidedly unequivocal rejection. Somewhere in there lies an outcome with strong negative valence—just how negative depends on how sensitive you are. Finally, you assess the expectancies. What is your subjective probability that the attractive person will accept? Reject? Your eventual action of *not* extending the invitation to this attractive person could be explained after the fact in essentially two ways by Expectancy Theory. You might have thought there was little chance that the person would have accepted. Alternatively, you might have estimated the chances of acceptance as much better than 50–50, but you felt that a rejection would have been so devastating that it outweighed the positive value of the more likely acceptance. The same logic could explain why you did in fact extend the invitation. Either you felt supremely confident that the person would accept, or the positive value of acceptance seemed so overwhelming in comparison to the trivial negative value of any form of refusal that even one chance in 20 of acceptance justified the action. The product of Expectancy X Valence, not the absolute value of either alone, determines the force on behavior.

Some critics have argued that Expectancy Theory vastly overstates the rationality underlying human behavior. That depends on what you mean by rationality. If it means knowing all possible consequences of our actions and their exact probabilities of occurring, coupled with the ability to order our preferences on the basis of what is good for us or what will bring us happiness, then Expectancy Theory does not demand rationality. If rationality requires accurate, undistorted processing of the information available to us, then again the theory does not presume rationality. If by rationality, we mean acting on the basis of what we value (for whatever reason) and what we anticipate (on whatever basis) will result from our actions, then Expectancy Theory does indeed assume rationality.

An Expectancy Model of Work Effort   Staw (1977) has provided a useful version of an expectancy theory framework of job motivation (see Figure 4–1). This framework applies equally well to explaining the level of effort expended on the job in total or the effort directed to some portion of the job (e.g., allocation of time and energy to customer service). Level of effort corresponds to the concept "action"—a person chooses how hard to work from some intuitive sense of several alternative levels of effort. To make this choice, the person must have some notion (P1) of the likelihood that each level of effort would result in good performance. Performance is a first-level outcome; the person does not usually have complete control over this, although it depends in greater or lesser degree on effort. The value a person places on performance depends on how instrumental it is to further outcomes—in other words P2 denotes the extent to which performance leads to *extrinsic* rewards such as significant pay raise.

The Staw version also includes another type of outcomes for which performance might be instrumental: *intrinsic* rewards, such as pride in accomplishments. A person who is ego-involved in a skilled task or professional work might anticipate that outstanding performance would bring a highly satisfying sense of achievement and self-esteem, even if

FIGURE 4–1

An Expectancy Theory Framework

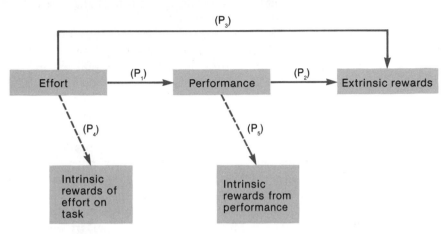

SOURCE: Adapted from Staw, 1977.

performance had no effect on pay. Conceivably, even effort itself—aside from its effect on performance or achievement—might lead to intrinsic rewards. Some tasks are more stimulating or interesting to be involved with; for example, some people enjoy the very process of conducting statistical analysis on a microcomputer, regardless of how much effect this has on actual performance. Finally, we note the plausibility of a person attaching some probability (P3) to increased extrinsic rewards purely on the basis of effort. Certainly we have known of some leaders who show their appreciation of effort itself, even when the effort fails to accomplish anything of substance in the short run.

A complete analysis would also include *negative* outcomes. Increased effort leads to greater fatigue, loss of leisure time, perhaps some psychological stress, and possibly the disapproval of some co–workers. Too little effort invites supervisory reprimands and possible feelings of guilt. For simplicity of illustration these negative outcomes are not explicit in the model, but the individual would take these into account.

The model predicts that the individual assesses each discriminable level of job effort according to the subjective probabilities (the Ps) of the various outcomes occurring, and arrives at that level of effort that maximizes the total "payoff" (when negative as well as positive outcomes are considered). Let us now examine, using the model, why a person might rationally choose a relatively low level of job effort.

Low P1   Why would a person see little chance of greater effort leading to better performance? The individual may lack the relevant ability to be a high performer. The motivational problem here is low ability; the remedy is either training or reassignment to a position more appropriate to the person's skills. If the person has the requisite abilities but lacks confidence, someone (probably the supervisor) needs to change the person's estimation of his or her talents.

There are other reasons that can explain why a person sees little relationship between personal effort and actual performance. Sometimes one's own performance depends to some extent on others' efforts, just as a running back's yardage depends on the center snap, the quarterback's handoff, and especially the blocking of the line. Ability aside, if you feel you can't count on others to put forth more effort on their assignments, you might rationally conclude that more effort on your part will make little difference. Thus, whenever individual performances are interdependent, the confidence a person has in co-workers' efforts will determine the person's own P1. If good performance requires certain resources — in terms of information, budget, staff, quality materials, physical facilities — and the individual lacks those resources, then even a person with considerable ability would see little chance that more effort would lead to improved performance. No matter how much the person values good performance, if P1 is low, then little increase in effort is likely to be forthcoming.

Low P2   The individual might *not* value good performance. The valence of good performance, as an outcome, depends on the subsequent outcomes to which good performance is instrumental. And, a person might not see that performance has much effect on outcomes in the form of extrinsic rewards. Why? If past experience proved that the organization had no reliable procedures for assessing or even noticing the level of individuals' performance, or if pay increases depended on factors other than performance (e.g., seniority or "politics"), there would be no incentive for good performance. Even if the formal reward system discriminates among levels of performance and pays its staff accordingly, people sometimes have little basis for recognizing this difference. For example, Lawler (1973) reported that employees underestimate the differentials in pay when they lack information about how their pay compares to others' salaries. The "common knowledge" erroneously convinces them that high and low performers are paid the same.

Some people still highly value good performance even if they gauge P2 at virtually zero. These are the individuals who attach considerable intrinsic rewards to job performance.

THE OPERANT AND EXPECTANCY MODELS COMPARED

There are important differences between the way operant frameworks and expectancy models explain job behavior. These differences can have managerial implications.

The most obvious difference between the two models is the importance of *thought* as determining behavior. The operant framework makes no explicit recourse to mental processes as causes of action. The causal factors are the contingencies of reinforcement, regardless of the extent to which people think about them or are even aware of them. In the expectancy view, how people think about their environment is much more important than what the environment really represents. Your preference for one or the other will depend on your estimation of the role of conscious thought processes in directing human behavior. Some students and managers object philosophically to a scheme that downgrades the importance of reason in human affairs. But we can note a practical as well as a philosophical distinction. If, as an administrator, you think in operant terms, your major concern rests on designing the contingencies of reinforcement. If you take the expectancy view, it is equally important to communicate and explain the contingencies to personnel. Furthermore, you would put considerable importance on the credibility of your communications.

The operant model accounts for present behavior in terms of the *past,* that is, exposure to previous contingencies and schedules of reinforcement have molded current behavior. Expectancy theory contends that present behavior arises from people's conceptions of the *future.* This can amount to mostly a stylistic difference; after all, previous experience has much to do with conceptions of the future. But expectancy theory, in principle, allows for the possibility that a person could ignore the past and anticipate a vastly different future. Does this difference in the models have any pragmatic implications? Assume that you, as a newly arrived administrator, inherit a situation characterized by faulty reward systems and marked by low performance. You try to make changes to reward improved performance. Should you expect immediate, radical improvement? Yes, if you were an expectancy theorist—assuming you had clearly explained the changes you would make and people believed you. But if you analyze behavior in operant terms, you would allow for the effect of past conditions to continue to influence present behavior, until people had sufficient exposure to the new contingencies. Therefore, you would expect more gradual improvement over a longer time period. You would not change your methods just because the initial effects on performance were slight.

Another important difference is the *timing* of outcomes. The operant framework emphasizes *immediate* consequences of behavior. Expectancy theory does not limit when future outcomes may occur—so long as the individual places a high subjective probability on their actual and eventual occurrence. Our discussion of expectancy theory made frequent mention of such outcomes as salary increases (which might not be realized until months after a person has chosen a level of job effort), while the discussion of the operant model avoided references to pay. Obviously your beliefs about how much pay influences work motivation could predispose you to one or the other of these models.

If we could give you authoritative, definitive answers to questions surrounding these issues, we would have picked one model and dispensed with the other. Unfortunately, we have no final answer to the question of how much behavior is caused by conscious thought processes. We cannot estimate how much people will allow conceptions of the future to override past experience. There is no way to break down the immediate consequences and more distantly imagined outcomes. These questions have been addressed in psychological experiments and in field studies of organizational behavior, but the evidence is far from conclusive. Your own bias and your own experience will dictate your conclusions.

A reasonable approach might be to regard each model as valid, but *with respect to different classes of work behavior.* This interpretation is offered by Landy and Becker (1987), who view the operant model as especially applicable to specific behaviors that recur in the day-to-day routines of the work environment. Thus, job performance related to work habits—use of safety equipment, equipment maintenance, prompt communications, attendance and punctuality—lends itself most readily to operant explanations. Habits and routines neither require nor permit conscious reflection on what one is doing or the alternative courses of action. Expectancy theory seems better suited to explaining instances of conscious decisions about behavior. Periodically, we engage in acts of commitment at work—to emphasize a particular dimension of our work, to seek training in a specialized area, to change our career goals. This occasions a process of contemplating the alternatives and trying to assess their consequences well into the future. Expectancy theory offers a plausible account of how we go about making these commitments.

Work behavior involves much that is routine and recurring as well as the less frequent, but equally important, acts of commitment. And, more important, routines and commitments are complementary. You might decide that you need to alter your diet to lose a few cosmetic pounds. Making the commitment to do this is a conscious decision, arrived at by assessing the incentive value of a slimmer you and estimating your chances of achieving that goal. The initial commitment is not the end of the story—that commitment is enacted over time by routines of behavior, day in and day out. Whether those routines are maintained and at what level probably will be explained by the near-term consequences of the specific behaviors comprising those routines.

SUMMARY

Learning Theory defines motivation as behavior acquired and maintained through conditioning processes. Classical conditioning accounts for the process in which reflexes and emotional responses come under the control of new stimuli. Operant conditioning explains instrumental behavior in terms of its immediate antecedents and consequences, which define various contingencies of reinforcement. The speed with which behavior is shaped and its strength and durability depend, in part, on the schedules of reinforcement. The Law of Relative Effect states that, over time, we distribute our behaviors according to their relative rates of positive reinforcement. Thus, an operant theorist's analysis of motivation problems defines the behavior in specific terms and examines the antecedents and consequences of those specific behaviors.

Expectancy theory defines motivation as the choices a person makes as to the direction of behavior and the level of effort expended on that behavior. These choices follow from the individual's conception of the probabilities that various outcomes will follow from behavior and the valence or incentive value associated with those outcomes. The Expectancy theorist analyzes motivation problems in terms of the factors that influence a person's anticipation of future outcomes—the outcomes of the behavior itself and the subsequent outcomes rendered more or less likely.

The Operant and Expectancy models differ most obviously with respect to the importance of immediate consequences of behavior, the relative importance of the learned past versus the anticipated future, and the extent that conscious thought and intentions mediate environmental influences. The Operant model accounts best for recurring work behaviors in the form of routines and habits; the Expectancy model gives a more plausible explanation of conscious decisions and commitments. Thus, both frameworks appear to have considerable relevance to work behavior.

CONCEPTS TO REMEMBER

Classical conditioning	Positive reinforcement	Contrived versus
Operant conditioning	Negative reinforcement	noncontrived reinforcers
Antecedents-Behavior-	Chain	Law of Relative Effect
Consequences	Trap	Expectancy
Contingencies of reinforcement	Fence	Instrumentality
Functional analysis of behavior	Schedules of reinforcement	Valence
Extinction		

QUESTIONS FOR DISCUSSION

1. Identify some habit—good or bad, work-related or personal—that is characteristic of your daily behavior. Do a functional analysis of this habit: Define the behavior in specific terms, describe the antecedents and consequences, and describe the schedule of reinforcement.

2. We have all experienced reinforcement contingencies that don't work—either for ourselves or others. Identify the major reasons for such faulty or ineffective contingencies.

3. Review the definitions of *trap* and *fence* as reinforcement contingencies. What types of strategies would an operant theorist pursue or recommend to deal with these problem contingencies?

4. Identify the sources of the "expectancies" and "instrumentalities" that influence your choices concerning how hard you study in a particular course.

5. How do the Operant and Expectancy models compare in explaining: *(a)* what clothing you wore today, *(b)* attendance at class today, *(c)* the extent to which you participated in class discussion today, *(d)* the amount of physical exercise you had today (or the day before), and *(e)* items you purchased today (or the day before).

REFERENCES

Brown, R., & Herrnstein, R. J. (1975). *Psychology.* Boston: Little, Brown.

Komaki, J. L. (1986). Toward effective supervision: An operant analysis and comparison of managers at work. *Journal of Applied Psychology* 71, 270–79.

Landy, F. J., & Becker, W. S. (1987). Motivation theory reconsidered. In L. L. Cummings & B. Staw (eds.), *Research in organizational behavior,* vol. 9, 1–38. Greenwich, CT: JAI Press, Inc.

Lawler, E. E., III. (1973). *Motivation in work organizations.* Monterey, CA: Brooks/Cole Publishing.

Miller, L. M. (1978). *Behavior management.* New York: Wiley-Interscience.

Scott, W. E., Jr., & Podsakoff, P. M. (1982). Leadership, supervision, and behavioral control: Perspectives from an experimental analysis. In L. W. Frederiksen (ed.), *Handbook of organizational behavior management.* New York: John Wiley & Sons.

Skinner, B. F. (1953). *Science and human behavior.* New York: Free Press.

Staw, B. M. (1977). Motivation in organizations: Toward synthesis and redirection. In B. M. Staw & G. R. Salancik (eds.), *New directions in organizational behavior.* Chicago: St. Clair Press.

Tolman, E. C. (1932). *Purposive behavior in animals and men.* New York: Century.

Vroom, V. H. (1964). *Work and motivation.* New York: John Wiley & Sons.

5

Emergent Process Models of Work Motivation

Linking the Operant and Cognitive Frameworks

What concepts provide the links between the operant and cognitive approaches?

How do we conceptualize self-control and self-management in a process model of motivation?

How do goals figure into a process model of work motivation?

What is the effect of combining extrinsic with intrinsic motivators?

In recent years we have seen indications that operant and cognitive conceptions of human behavior are inching toward each other, resulting in a more unified framework that possesses the strengths of each approach. The bridge linking these two paradigms rests on essentially two observations. The first observation is that the most important dimension of the environment of any particular person is that represented by other persons and the behavior of those other persons. One person's behavior can be analyzed in terms of the antecedents and consequences of that behavior, but the important antecedents and consequences are social in nature. These antecedents and consequences are not "givens," but are behavior in their own right; they remain to be accounted for and are often altered by the very behavior they control. Thus, the behavior of managers influences subordinates, but in so doing the resultant behavior of subordinates has some effect on what managers will do in the future. The second observation notes the ability of humans to construct and use *symbols* to simplify and denote complex environments, to describe or prescribe behavior, and to clarify contingencies among antecedents and consequences of behavior. Most of these symbols are socially transmitted and shared as we participate in a verbal community, and they allow us to transcend our immediate physical environments. For the operant theorist, symbols (or, more accurately, particular combinations of symbols) can be taken as a special —perhaps higher-order—form of antecedent of behavior, an antecedent that can usually be observed and recorded. For the cognitive theorist, symbols are overt manifestations of covert thought, since arguably symbols are the very stuff with which we think.

Social learning theory is a loose descriptive term for a number of approaches to motivation that emphasize the importance of social and symbolic controls of individual behavior. Two approaches noteworthy for their influence on efforts to develop comprehensive accounts of human action are Skinner's treatment of rule-governed behavior and Bandura's social cognitive theory.

Skinner: Rule-Governed Behavior　　B. F. Skinner, the foremost exponent of the operant paradigm and a resolute opponent of explaining behavior by recourse to "inner processes," has offered an analysis of rule-governed behavior that even many cognitivists could appreciate. Skinner (1969) noted that the verbal (social) community often requires us to report on our behavior and the variables of which it is a function. We are asked, "What did you do?" and "Why did you do that?" The verbal community reinforces us for giving informative and accurate accounts of our behavior. This leads us to cultivate *awareness,* a tendency to observe our own behavior and to summarize in symbolic form the contingencies surrounding it. This ability, aside from securing the approval of others, turns out to have other uses. We develop a means of extracting rules to guide future behavior. It is useful to communicate these rules to others and to learn such rules from those with relevant experience.

Much of our behavior comes under the control of verbal descriptions of the contingencies of behavior—some extracted from analyses of our own behavior, most provided by the verbal community. Someone who advises you to "begin your speech with a joke so you'll get the audience on your side," or instructs you to "drop your racquet down, then swing up through the ball to make a strong, low shot," is giving you a verbal description of a reinforcement contingency. Some such descriptions are *tacts,* in which the consequences are known but not controlled by the source providing the description. Others are *mands* (commands, demands), verbal descriptions of reinforcement contingencies in which the source controls the consequences (often aversive ones).

Skinner observes that "even fragmentary descriptions of contingencies speed the acquisition of effective terminal behavior, help to maintain the behavior over a period of time, and reinstate it when forgotten" (1969:143). A rule functions much like other antecedents of behavior; it becomes an occasion on which certain behaviors will provide reinforcing consequences. We follow such rules because previous behavior in accord with such rules has been reinforced.

Skinner notes the special advantages of behavior that comes under the control of rules: "Long-deferred consequences, ineffective in shaping behavior, may also lead to useful rules . . . rules may enable the long-term consequences to offset the immediate. . . . Rule-governed behavior is particularly effective when the contingencies would otherwise shape unwanted or wasteful behavior" (1969:168).

Bandura: Social Cognitive Theory   Albert Bandura (1986) has offered a framework that, like Skinner's, emphasizes the predominance of socially mediated antecedents and consequences of behavior and the importance of symbols as media of these antecedents and consequences. However, Bandura has gone much further, recognizing the covert (as well as overt) repertoire and manipulation of symbols involved in the *self,* or person. In Bandura's social cognitive model, "persons are neither autonomous agents nor mechanical conveyors of animating environmental forces. Rather, they serve as a reciprocally contributing influence to their own motivation and behavior within a system of reciprocal causation involving personal determinants, action, and environmental factors" (1986:12).

Figure 5–1 summarizes the essential points of Bandura's perspective. It considers the reciprocal relationships among behavior, environment, and the person. The portion included within the dotted line represents the traditional subject matter of the operant theorist—recognizing the effect of environment on behavior and the way in which behavior operates on the environment to produce reinforcing consequences. Bandura's position is that the dotted portion is an incomplete and, by itself, inaccurate rendering of human behavior. He contends that elements of the person—conceptions of the self, conceptions of future goals, and conceptions of means-ends

FIGURE 5–1

Bandura's conception of triadic reciprocality of the interaction among person, environment, and behavior. Dotted portion represents traditional subject matter of operant framework of behavior.

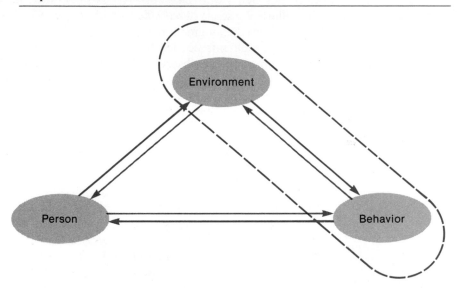

relationships—can override the immediate consequences of behavior. Immediate consequences matter only to the extent that they are integrated into more complex, symbolic rules to guide behavior. Rules and conceptions of future consequences can, in fact, enable a person to resist the effects of short-term consequences. People will persist in courses of action despite lack of reinforcement—even despite immediate aversive consequences.

Bandura also notes how the environment affects the person independently of its effect on behavior per se. *Vicarious processes,* in which we learn from attending to others' behavior, are important here. As Yogi Berra is supposed to have said, "we can observe a lot by just watching." We can observe how others assemble various elements of behavior into a distinctive performance, and we can observe the consequences to others of their performances. Given our symbolic capabilities, we can *extract rules* for how these performances were generated and the kinds of consequences they produce in various settings. These rules are *encoded* in memory as part of the person without the need for that person to attempt the performance or experience the consequences at that time. The person may occasionally engage in *covert rehearsal* of the performance, using symbols to think through the sequence of steps in an intricate ballroom dance or presentation to a sales group. Later, given the appropriate *incentive structure* of the situation, the person retrieves the rules to guide the production of the performance in order to attain valued consequences or make progress toward some goal.

Not only do elements (rules, memory structures, goals) of the person influence behavior, but behavior itself can alter the person. The fact of generating performances—that is, the competence or *efficacy* with which one assembles behavioral elements—feeds back into the conception of self, particularly the sense of *self-efficacy* with respect to an area of performance. Self-efficacy (the judgment of one's capabilities to organize and execute the behavioral elements needed to attain a specific type of performance) can also be influenced by observing others' behavior in similar situations. Once formed, self-efficacy becomes a major factor determining what courses of action a person will attempt (irrespective of the anticipated outcomes) and how long one will persevere in a course of action when initial efforts are unsuccessful.

Bandura gives due recognition to the importance of external consequences—those experienced as well as observed, immediate as well as delayed—and also accords a significant role to *self-regulatory mechanisms*. Skinner has commented that our verbal community induces us to observe our own behavior and to report it. Bandura agrees, but suggests that we do more than observe our behavior (that is, the type of behavior, its quality, quantity, consistency). He argues that we also *evaluate* our own behavior according to a personal standard. Evaluation may, for example, take the form of comparing our performance according to a standard we have internalized from observing models (such as parents, respected co-workers, leaders) or according to some subgoal marking progress toward an eventual objective. We then administer our own consequences in the form of *self-reaction*. For example, I can look back at the writing I have done for the last couple of hours. Does it meet my own standards (perhaps more or less demanding than those of other writers) of clarity of exposition? Have I fulfilled my quota set for each day to meet an eventual deadline? If I judge my behavior favorably, I might reward myself with a bike ride, or I might simply add something to my self-esteem or self-respect. If I judge my behavior unfavorably, I will rewrite and revise, even if that means missing the bike ride, and I probably lower my self-respect a notch or two until I can execute behavior that does meet with a positive self-evaluation.

Self-Management   Nowhere else do the operant and cognitive perspectives converge so fruitfully for OB as in their treatment of self-control or self-management (Kanfer, 1975; Luthans & Davis, 1979; Manz & Sims, 1980; Scott & Podsakoff, 1982). Self-management is arguably a critical component of job motivation. Luthans and Davis (1979) consider self-management a "prerequisite for the effective management of organizations, groups, and individual subordinates," implying that one cannot manage others unless one can manage oneself. Manz and Sims (1980) regard self-management by subordinates as an important substitute for, or complement to, leadership.

An operant rendering of self-management would focus, as before, on the ABCs (antecedents, behavior, and consequences). People manage their own behavior by manipulating the antecedents that make certain behaviors more or less difficult to perform, executing the behaviors, and providing their own consequences contingent on the behaviors. Consider the man who feels he wastes too much time watching television. He believes the time spent is disproportionate to the real benefits derived and the lost opportunities for doing more constructive chores or making more enriching use of leisure time. Part of the problem is the fact that the television is conveniently located near his favorite easy chair with remote control within comfortable reach. He turns on the set just "to see what's on." Some channel-switching finds a mildly entertaining program—in other words, some weak positive consequences that occur just soon enough to reinforce the passive behavior of watching the program. Eventually, "just a chance to rest a few minutes" has turned into an hour and a half of idle, unproductive behavior. One means of controlling this behavior is to move the TV to an inconvenient place (we have heard of one individual who put the instrument on a high shelf in the hallway where there were no chairs). This should ensure more selective viewing behavior. Other forms of manipulating the antecedents of one's behavior include putting Post-it® reminders on the desk, the dashboard of the car, the refrigerator; or, remembering that so many of the cues for our behavior are socially mediated, avoiding or shortening our encounters with certain individuals while seeking more contact with certain others.

Self-reinforcement (or, on occasions, self-punishment) is the other end of self-management. This includes not only the form of the consequences we make contingent on our own behavior, but also the scheduling of them—whether we schedule the consequences according to a fixed behavior or a fixed amount of time engaged in the behavior or on a more variable (but "averaged") basis. Implicit in the idea of self-reinforcement are the processes of observing our own behavior and evaluating it according to some standard—improving on some measure of past instances of the behavior, matching some self-set criterion, or meeting some goal; contingency of self-reinforcement means that some standard should be met.

Self-control per se does not, by itself, ensure that one is successful, productive, or in any way able to improve on alternative *external* control of our behavior. People may construct their antecedent stimulus environment to maximize "good feelings" rather than productive behavior. How many times have you put your textbook, tax forms, or unanswered correspondence in an unobtrusive place "so I won't feel guilty about it"? People construct self-reinforcement contingencies that are either too permissive to lead to more productive behavior, or so unrealistically strict that prolonged nonreinforcement leads to despair and depression (extinction). (See Close-Up for an example of the dysfunctional effects of perfectionism.)

CLOSE-UP

The Perfectionism Syndrome

The ultimate in self-management methods would involve perfection as a self-set criterion for self-reward, right? Not according to psychiatrist David D. Burns. He finds a recurring syndrome of perfectionism in the patients he treats for depression. Contrary to the notion that perfectionism results in the highest levels of performance (a notion endorsed by the perfectionists themselves), it often militates against personal productivity. The perfectionism syndrome includes the following:

A fear and anticipation of rejection when judged as imperfect, with subsequent defensive reaction to any criticism.

Dichotomous thinking: performance of an activity is either completely successful (perfect) or a failure; nothing in between.

The fantasy that successful people achieve their goals with minimal effort, few errors, total self-confidence, and no emotional stress. Because of this fantasy, perfectionists see their own coping as inadequate and unacceptable.

An unwillingness to risk mistakes that are necessary to realize creative work.

Inhibitions from trying new activities because of fear of mistakes.

Lack of joy in many activities because of self-critical attitudes.

Procrastination on many projects because of fear of imperfection.

By "perfectionism" Burns does not mean the "healthy pursuit of excellence by men and women who take genuine pleasure in striving to meet high standards," or of the *selective* use of very demanding goals. Rather, perfectionism is the ultimately self-defeating tendency to see mistakes as failure.

Burns finds that a therapeutic program for perfectionists is to keep a diary of their activities in which they predict how satisfying an activity will be, record afterward the satisfaction actually derived, and rate their effectiveness. Much to their surprise, perfectionists realize that satisfaction and effectiveness are far from perfectly correlated. Also, a running account of self-critical cognitions reveals to these people some of the distortions in their assumptions that a mistake means failure, rejection, and less worth as a person.

SOURCE: David D. Burns, "The Perfectionists's Script for Self-Defeat," *Psychology Today,* November 1980, pp. 34ff.

More to the point, however, according to operant theorists (Skinner, 1969; Scott & Podsakoff, 1982), *self-control or self-management itself is behavior and is learned and maintained much like other behavior.* Consider the following symbolic representation of self-management:

$$A^{sm} \longrightarrow (A \dashrightarrow B \dashrightarrow C) = B^{sm} \longrightarrow C^{sm+}$$

The part in parentheses denotes the self-management: manipulating the immediate antecedents of one's responses, evaluating the responses, and arranging the immediate consequences of them. All of this is behavior, a higher-order response if you will. But it is not autonomous behavior that materializes from nowhere. It is behavior that is, in turn, evoked by a significant prompt. The prompt may come from a manager or leader who specifies a standard for long-run professional performance, or the observation that prestigious models who persevere in training and practice eventually attain valued outcomes. Furthermore, unless the self-management (as a program of behavior in itself) leads to positive outcomes—recognition, status, promotion, at the very least support from others—self-management as a class of behavior will weaken.

A cognitive theorist would find little to argue with in this formulation. The only point of dispute would concern the degree to which it is useful to distinguish a variety of covert mental processes as causal factors in themselves. Both approaches require short-run consequences to mediate the effect of long-run outcomes. Both approaches concede that much behavior (such as habits and routines) will proceed in "automatic pilot" fashion, responding largely to chance, fortuitous consequences of the external environment. Both allow for the possibility that this behavioral inertia can be disrupted by interventions that lead people to take a more active role in regulating their own behavior.

GOAL-SETTING THEORY

The discerning reader will note that the notion of a *goal* has considerable relevance. The contingencies described to us by others often take the form of an implicit goal—for example, "those staff members with perfect attendance for the whole month will receive coupons for free dinner for two at Beaumont's." We also set goals for ourselves, goals that become a basis for observing and evaluating our behavior and administering self-reinforcement. Indeed, the concept of self-management seems empty without a goal. More significantly, the setting of a goal often acts as the switch to turn on the more serious forms of self-management in general.

We noted previously that work effort can be shaped in an "automatic" fashion as habits and routines under the control of immediate consequences, or on occasion by conscious choices of commitments or decisions. *Goal-setting theory* (Locke, Shaw, Saari, & Latham, 1981; Locke & Latham, 1984) amounts more or less to an explanation of the degree to which "interventions" can break the hold of routines and habits and bring behavior under more conscious control.

Goal-setting theory is not so much a theory as it is a critical conceptual linkage between the theory of intentional behavior (Ryan, 1970) and a useful model of individual performance. Locke (1968), drawing from the work of Ryan as well as objectivist philosophy (Rand, 1964; Branden, 1966), holds that *intentions* are the immediate determinants of behavior. Intentions do not arise out of a vacuum. They culminate from the stored products of a person's background—the individual's *values* (which govern the feelings one has about future outcomes), the person's *repertoire* of behavior plans, and

---

CLOSE-UP

Self-Management, Self-Efficacy, and Job Attendance

Gary P. Latham and Collette A. Frayne theorized that many high absence rates are caused by an individual's lack of confidence in coping with such work problems as conflict with the boss, disagreements with coworkers, family obligations, and transportation difficulties. Latham and Frayne worked with a group of 40 unionized carpenters, electricians, and painters employed by a state government. They picked 20 of these people at random and spent one hour per week teaching them to set short- and long-term goals for job attendance, to "contract" contingencies with themselves, monitor attendance, and administer self-reinforcement for meeting goals. The results, in average number of hours on the job per week (with 40 hours representing perfect attendance) for the treatment (T) as compared to the control (C) group, were as follows:

	Before	Three Months Later	Six Months Later	Nine Months Later
T	33.1	35.7	38.6	38.2
C	32.3	30.0	31.6	30.9
Self-Efficacy Scores				
T	45.0	60.2	86.6	87.5
C	46.4	45.8	46.0	44.9

The results indicate not only improved work attendance in the treatment group, but also suggest a positive feedback loop in which increased self-efficacy contributed to better attendance, which in turn further increased self-efficacy. When the treatment was extended to those originally in the control group, the results replicated the original program: average work hours per week increased from 30.9 to 34.9 and self-efficacy scores increased from 44.9 to 63.6. Interestingly, anecdotal evidence suggested that several individuals had spontaneously begun applying these self-management methods to diet, smoking, exercise, and personal finances.

SOURCE: G. P. Latham and C. A. Frayne,"Self-Management Training for Increasing Job Attendance: A Follow-Up and a Replication," *Journal of Applied Psychology* 74, (1989), pp. 411–16.

---

predispositions to perceive or interpret the external world within certain mental structures. These stored products of the past bear on the individual's sense of the immediate situation. From this sense of the *means-end* relationships between alternative behavior sequences and valued outcomes, the individual forms an intention to behave in one way or another. Anything that influences the person's behavior must affect the person's conscious intentions.

To set or accept a goal obviously represents a form of intention. How do these intentions vary as a function of the characteristics of the goal? Locke's answer is that the more *specific* the goal, the stronger the intention. Thus, a quantitative goal (lose 10 pounds in the next two months, write 10 pages this week, increase total sales by 15 percent in the next quarter) evokes stronger intentions (hence greater effort) than a general or nonspecific goal (try to lose some weight, get as much writing done as I can, improve my sales performance). Laboratory and field research support this assertion (Mento, Steel, & Karren, 1987). More *difficult* goals should also evoke stronger intentions and more intense effort than easy goals, provided the individual accepts and continues to accept a difficult goal. Research generally supports, with some exceptions, this proposition (Mento et al., 1987). However, it is difficult to test this proposition since it is necessary to identify what acceptance means, how it is measured, and know when or if acceptance is revoked.

In Locke's framework, incentives influence effort only to the extent that they induce the person to set specific, difficult goals or lead the person to accept the specific, difficult goals urged by others. Similarly, feedback about one's performance has no effect on effort unless it leads the person to set specific difficult goals, or uses it to guide effort toward a specific, difficult goal. The individual's personal role in formulating the goal is only relevant to the extent that such participation renders one more accepting of the goal or results in more specific, difficult goals. Research supports the notion that incentives, feedback, and participation have the postulated effects on goal-setting. However, the data also suggest that their effects on performance (and, presumably, effort) are to some extent independent of goals (Pritchard & Curtis, 1973; Anderson, Crowell, Dorman, & Howard, 1988; Mento et al., 1987). In other words, incentives and feedback do not appear to function, as Locke suggested, solely through conscious goals and intentions.

Ajzen and Fishbein (1977), like Locke, regard behavioral intentions as determinants of behavior itself. Unlike Locke, however, their theory and research do not see the link between intentions and behavior as perfect or absolute. Often one's intentions give way to different behaviors evoked and sustained by cues and consequences in the situation. Ajzen and Fishbein suggest that the relationship between intentions and actual behavior is *moderated by the specificity of the intention.* A behavioral intention is specific to the extent that the intended behavior itself, the object of the behavior, the situational context of the behavior, and the time of the behavior are precisely formulated.

If we modified Locke's framework to incorporate Ajzen and Fishbein's observations, we would essentially allow for intentions to play only a partial role in determining work effort and behavior. Then we would consider setting specific, difficult goals a method for actualizing intentions so that they have a greater effect on effort. This would maintain consistency with the more general assertion that a cognitive framework better explains those behaviors that represent decisions and acts of commitment, while operant concepts explain recurring routines of behavior. When our intentions lack specificity, we may be characterized as lacking in commitment and withholding conscious decisions. Thus, our behavior will be carried along by the moment-to-moment consequences of what we do. This flux of behavior can be halted by an episode that evokes the decision-making process. One such episode is commitment to a specific goal.

Recent evidence suggests that *publicly set goals* enhance and maintain commitment to a *specific, difficult* goal more than privately set goals (Hollenbeck, Williams, & Klein, 1989). Personality factors appear to determine whether self-set or externally imposed goals arouse the greater commitment (Hollenbeck et al., 1989).

COGNITIVE EVALUATION THEORY

We have seen that the operant model of the motivational process allows for behavior to be maintained by either noncontrived or contrived reinforcers. Recall that noncontrived reinforcers are "response-produced consequences," that is, consequences that have a natural and inherent relationship to the responses that produced them. This type of reinforcer often takes the form of some kind of immediate change in the stimulus situation. Thus, working on a crossword puzzle, refinishing old furniture, or testing out new software involves behavior that is reinforced by a particular observable effect on the puzzle, the furniture, or the computer screen. *Why* such effects act as reinforcers is not clear. Some, such as Skinner (1953), argue that an organism positively reinforced in this way would have a survival advantage in the evolutionary process, because this species would learn more about its environment. Others, such as White (1959) or deCharmes (1968), contend that such effects act as reinforcers because—and to the extent that—they satisfy an intrinsic need to feel competent as an "Origin" acting on the environment, as opposed to a "Pawn" that is controlled by the environment. This view is reminiscent of the concept of need for psychological growth. In any case, performance on many tasks can be sustained by noncontrived reinforcers, without need for any other sources of reward provided.

Contrived reinforcers, on the other hand, are arranged and distributed by an external agent or system, such as the organization's formal reward system or the officials who administer it, or other agents of external control (parents, teachers, coaches). Organizations make considerable use of this type of reinforcer.

Either type of reinforcer can sustain high rates of behavior when it occurs at the appropriate time and on a judicious schedule. Contrived reinforcers may be needed initially to sustain practice on a task. Once behavior is sufficiently competent to generate its own reinforcers, contrived or artificial reinforcers can be gradually phased out—they are no longer necessary. If noncontrived reinforcers are weak or infrequent (the task is boring or tedious), contrived reinforcers (possibly contrived by the individual in the form of self-reinforcement) might always be necessary.

We describe *intrinsic motivation* as that behavior governed by noncontrived reinforcement, and *extrinsic motivation* as that behavior controlled by contrived reinforcement. There is some vagueness and inconsistency in the way these terms (especially intrinsic motivation) are used (Dyer & Parker, 1975). The confusion arises because some use the term *intrinsic motivation* merely to describe a type of behavior (one not under control of extrinsic incentives), while others use it to imply certain internal states (pride, feelings of psychological growth) that account for the behavior. Notwithstanding the confusion, the general distinction between the two forms of motivation seems useful.

A controversy that arose in the early 1970s and still has not been resolved involves the question: What happens when extrinsic motivation is added to intrinsic motivation? Previously, this question had not posed a problem. Few would have raised the question: If either intrinsic or extrinsic motivation by itself can sustain high rates of effort, why would one need both? But either the operant framework or expectancy theory would probably have answered that adding sources of extrinsic motivation (or contrived reinforcers) to intrinsic motivation (noncontrived reinforcers) can only help increase the total motivation.

Deci (1971, 1975) presented the case for why, paradoxically, extrinsic motivation would displace intrinsic motivation rather than add to it. He argues that fundamental to intrinsic motivation is a self-perception or *attribution* that one's behavior is internally caused. Drawing from Bem's self-attribution theory (1972), Deci suggests that one can infer internal causation only when causation cannot be attributed to other obvious, external forces. Thus, if a person initially engages in a task because of intrinsic motivation, and then extrinsic inducements for task effort are introduced, eventually this person will look at his or her own behavior and see that "it could be accounted for" by the extrinsic inducements. The person sees himself or herself as a Pawn, one who is externally controlled. Effort on the task will continue, of course, as long as strong external incentives are in effect. When these are withdrawn, the evidence of diminished intrinsic motivation will appear in a significantly lower level of involvement in the task.

Deci and others have tested this paradoxical hypothesis with variations on a standard procedure. First, subjects are presented with a task (such as a puzzle) already known to arouse interest. The researcher notes the amount of discretionary time (T1) subjects devote to the task (in some instances the researcher uses a different measure, such as task performance). Second, the researcher introduces to an experimental group an incentive such as cash, contingent on how well subjects perform the task. The control group does not hear of any such incentive. Again, the researcher notes the amount of discretionary time (T2) subjects devote to the task. In virtually every instance, T2 significantly exceeds T1 for the experimental group, while T2 and T1 are about equal for the control group.

In other words, the monetary contingency *does have an effect* over the baseline condition. In the third phase, the cash incentive is withdrawn from the experimental group and the researcher notes the amount of free time (T3) subjects spend on the task. In most of the studies, T3 for the experimental group is not only less than T2 (when the incentive was in effect), T3 is significantly less than T1—*before* the incentive was introduced. The control group shows no such decline from T1 to T3. This finding appears to support Deci's suggestion that the extrinsic motivation introduced by the promise of contingent monetary reward displaces, rather than complements, the original intrinsic motivation.

According to Deci, it is not the mention of money as such that displaces intrinsic motivation; it is the *controlling aspect* of the money that has the effect. Thus, paying people a flat hourly rate for their time in the study should not alter their attributions of causality. Only when the money is *contingent* on performance would intrinsic motivation be reduced.

What about other extrinsic consequences? Interestingly, positive feedback from the researcher about the person's performance does not have the effect described above. Or, at least it does not have the effect for males. Deci accounts for this by distinguishing between the *controlling versus competence information* effects of extrinsic consequences. Arguably, the controlling aspect of contingent monetary consequences swamps its aspect of providing information about one's competence. Males interpret positive performance feedback almost entirely in terms of what it says about their competence. Females receiving positive feedback from a "higher-status" male tend to focus more on its controlling aspect.

At face value, these results and their explanation in the form of Deci's Cognitive Evaluation theory have profound implications for organizational reward systems. The suggestion is that monetary rewards contingent on quantity or quality of performance would undermine the intrinsic interest people have in their work. Presumably no damage is done when people perform work that lacks intrinsic appeal; extrinsic incentives would be needed to sustain effort and they would not displace intrinsic motivation because there was none to begin with. People engaged in professional, creative, or craft work—where one would expect significant intrinsic motivation—would, by the logic of Cognitive Evaluation theory, have lessened involvement in the job after exposure to controlling monetary incentives.

The damage, in terms of level of actual effort, occurs only when the incentive is withdrawn. Effort actually increased when the incentive was introduced and while it was still in effect. If performance is the concern, and the incentive has positive effects while in effect, why would any manager in his right mind want to withdraw it? Perhaps Deci would answer that even if the incentive continues to operate officially, inevitably there are times and occasions when it is inoperative. For example, some aspects of performance might not be covered by the incentive plan, or people will reach the limits of the available incentives. In such cases, the effect is that the incentive is temporarily withdrawn and, if intrinsic motivation has suffered, effort will be less than if the incentive had never existed.

Other Explanations   If we concede the reliability of the data reported by Deci and others, can we account for the reduced effort following removal of monetary incentive without concluding that intrinsic motivation was reduced?

An alternative explanation would point to the *frustration* or resentment experienced when a bonus, once having been offered, is withdrawn. Yet another explanation takes into account the increased effort on the task when the bonus was in effect; perhaps the increased intensity of involvement led to a temporary *satiation* (overkill) with the task. Either explanation would imply that the reduction of interest in the task would be temporary. However, studies that measured intrinsic interest several days or weeks after exposure to the monetary incentive indicate that intrinsic motivation continues to remain lower than its original value.

We might interpret the results in terms of Equity theory. A person might feel a trifle guilty for receiving increased extrinsic rewards for performing an enjoyable task. If so, the guilt may be reduced by revising downward one's estimate of the joy in doing the task.

Finally, consider the possibility that making money contingent on your performance of a task introduces a certain form of pressure into the situation by arousing *evaluation anxiety*. You might work harder on the task so as not to fail and thereby embarrass yourself, but you would feel discomfort. Conceivably the emotional response of anxiety would generalize to the task, making it less attractive.

Either the equity or the anxiety-conditioning explanation would still suggest lessened intrinsic motivation, although for reasons somewhat different from those advanced by Deci.

Generality of the Effect   The inhibiting effect of contingent extrinsic incentives does not invariably occur. Reviews (Staw, 1976; Boal & Cummings, 1981) suggest that the effect ocurs only when *(1)* the contingent extrinsic incentive is salient and dominates the person's conscious awareness of the task situation, and *(2)* when the provision of a pay incentive violates one's sense of what is appropriate in the task situation. One could argue that many extrinsic reward systems could make outcomes contingent on performance without necessarily creating these conditions. If those outcomes were received at infrequent intervals, or if they constituted only a small portion of total outcomes, their contingency might not be particularly salient most of the time. Of course, their effect as an incentive for immediate performance might also be lessened. And certainly many work settings do have a tradition of basing some part of a person's pay on some aspects of performance.

We need not interpret Cognitive Evaluation Theory as a basis for utterly rejecting all forms of performance-contingent reward systems, even for intrinsically rewarding jobs. But the theory and the research supporting it give us ample reason to think carefully about whether certain pay systems will work as intended. The evidence—with few exceptions (e.g., Jordan, 1986) based on either laboratory experiments with students or studies of school children—does indicate that the controlling effects of pay, in particular, are not an unmixed blessing.

SUMMARY

The operant and cognitive frameworks of motivation theory have recently drawn closer to each other by recognizing the importance of the social and symbolic dimensions of human behavior. Skinner has extended the generality of an operant framework with his analysis of rule-governed behavior. Bandura's social cognition theory incorporates explicit analysis of the self-system and its reciprocal relationship to both behavior and the environment. The concepts of self-efficacy and self-regulation emerge as critical components of Bandura's framework. Self-management can be analyzed in operant terms as behavior itself or addressed via other self-referent processes. In either analysis, goals figure importantly, and a large body of research findings attests to the influence of specific, difficult goals on work effort. Goals constitute the basis for self-regulation of behavior as well as providing the occasion to elicit self-regulation as a form of behavior itself.

Cognitive evaluation theory addresses the question of what happens when extrinsic incentives, such as money, are made contingent on performance of intrinsically motivating tasks. In apparent contradiction to traditional forms of both operant and cognitive frameworks, cognitive evaluation theory and the supporting research suggests that performance-contingent extrinsic rewards displace, rather than supplement, intrinsic motivation. This effect appears to be limited to situations in which the extrinsic incentive is both psychologically salient and by tradition inappropriate.

CONCEPTS TO REMEMBER

Social learning theory	Social cognitive theory	Self-management
Rule-governed behavior	Various processes	Goal-setting theory
Tacts	Self-efficacy	Cognitive evaluation theory

QUESTIONS FOR DISCUSSION

1. Why do some people consistently meet deadlines (completing and turning in a term paper, or finishing a work project) while others consistently fail to do so? Formulate your answer in terms of social learning theory.

2. In a televised interview, best-selling author John Updike said he sets a goal of writing three pages per day. If more difficult—as well as specific—goals enhance effort and performance, why shouldn't Updike set a goal of 5 or 10 pages per day?

3. We know that today's professional baseball, football, and basketball players—especially the star players—make much more money (even after adjusted for inflation) than did the pro athletes of generations ago. We also hear more from today's stars about the stress and pressure and gruelling schedule than was the case decades ago—in spite of the fact that players today travel by air rather than train or bus, lodge in air-conditioned hotels, and are constantly attended to by trainers and physicians specializing in sports medicine. How might cognitive evaluation theory interpret these developments?

4. What are the advantages to a manager when subordinates practice a high degree of self-management? How would a manager cultivate self-management among subordinates?

5. One writer has suggested that developing leaders in business is like "breeding rabbits. . . . If you assign your best junior talent to work with your best unit leader, in 18 to 36 months you will have another potential top unit leader. Identify your best leaders. Match them with your best upcoming talent. Give nature and 18 to 36 months of real business operations time to work, and that's all there is to it." (Jack Falvey, "Manager's Journal," *The Wall Street Journal,* October 3, 1988.) What forms of social learning theory might be involved in this strategy?

REFERENCES

Ajzen, I., & Fishbein, M. (1977). Attitude-behavior relations: A theoretical analysis and review of empirical research. *Psychological Bulletin* 84, 888–918.

Anderson, D. C., Crowell, C. R., Doman, M., & Howard, G. S. (1988). Performance posting, goal setting, and activity-contingent praise as applied to a university hockey team. *Journal of Applied Psychology* 73, 87–95.

Bandura, A. (1986). *Social foundations of thought and action: A social cognitive theory.* Englewood Cliffs, NJ: Prentice Hall.

Bem, D. J. (1972). Self-perception theory. In L. Berkowitz (ed.), *Advances in experimental social psychology,* vol. 6. New York: Academic Press.

Boal, K., & Cummings, L. (1981). Cognitive evaluation theory: An experimental test of processes and outcomes. *Organizational Behavior and Human Performance* 28, 289–310.

Branden, N. (1966). Emotions and values. *Objectivist* 5, 1–9.

deCharmes, R. (1968). *Personal causation: The internal affective determinants of behavior.* New York: Academic Press.

Deci, E. L. (1971). Effects of externally mediated rewards on intrinsic motivation. *Journal of Personality and Social Psychology* 18, 105–15.

Deci, E. L. (1975). *Intrinsic motivation.* New York: Plenum Press.

Dyer, L., & Parker, D. F. (1975). Classifying outcomes in work motivation research: An examination of the intrinsic-extrinsic dichotomy. *Journal of Applied Psychology* 60, 455–58.

Hollenbeck, J. R., Williams, C. R., & Klein, H. J. (1989). An empirical examination of the antecedents of commitment to difficult goals. *Journal of Applied Psychology* 74, 18–23.

Jordan, P. C. (1986). Effects of an extrinsic reward on intrinsic motivation: A field experiment. *Academy of Management Journal* 29, 405–12.

Kanfer, F. H. (1975). Self-management methods. In F. H. Kanfer & A. P. Goldstein (eds.), *Helping people change,* 309–55. New York: Pergamon Press.

Latham, G. P., & Frayne, C. A. (1989). Self-management training for increasing job attendance: A follow-up and a replication. *Journal of Applied Psychology* 74, 411–16.

Locke, E. A. (1968). Toward a theory of task motivation and incentives. *Organizational Behavior and Human Performance* 3, 157–89.

Locke, E. A., & Latham, G. P. (1984). *Goal setting: A motivational technique that works.* Englewood Cliffs, NJ: Prentice Hall.

Locke, E. A., Shaw, K., Saari, L., & Latham, G. P (1981). Goal setting and task performance: 1969–1980. *Psychological Bulletin* 90, 125–52.

Luthans, F., & Davis, T. R. (Summer 1979). Behavioral self-management — the missing link in managerial effectiveness. *Organizational Dynamics,* 42–60.

Manz, C. C., & Sims, H. P., Jr. (1980). Self-management as a substitute for leadership: A social learning theory perspective. *Academy of Management Review* 5, 361–67.

Mento, A. J., Steel, R. P., & Karren, R. J. (1987). A meta-analytic study of the effects of goal-setting on task performance: 1966–1984. *Organizational Behavior and Human Decision Processes* 39, 52-83.

Pritchard, R. D., & Curtis, M. I. (1973). The influence of goal setting and financial incentives on task performance. *Organizational Behavior and Human Performance* 10, 175–83.

Rand, A. (1964). The objectivist ethics. In A. Rand (ed.), *The virtue of selfishness.* New York: Signet.

Ryan, T. A. (1970). *Intentional behavior: An approach to human motivation.* New York: Ronald Press.

Scott, W. E., Jr., & Podsakoff, P. M. (1982). Leadership, supervision, and behavioral control: Perspectives from an experimental analysis. In L. W. Frederiksen (ed.), *Handbook of organizational behavior management.* New York: John Wiley & Sons.

Skinner, B. F. (1953). *Science and human behavior.* New York: Macmillan.

Skinner, B. F. (1969). *Contingencies of reinforcement: A theoretical analysis.* Englewood Cliffs, NJ: Prentice Hall.

Staw, B. M. (1976). *Intrinsic and extrinsic motivation.* Morristown, NJ: General Learning Press.

White, R. W. (1959). Motivation reconsidered: The concept of competene. *Psychological Review* 66, 297–333.

6 Perception

How do we process information from the environment?

How do we reduce the complexity of the stimulus world to a simpler basis for action?

How do we form impressions of people?

How does our own behavior affect our perception of others?

What are the implications for job performance assessment and interviews?

Are you a perceptive person? Are you more observant than most people? Test your powers of observation and recall with the questions below:

1. Which way does Abe Lincoln face on a penny?
2. In which hand does the Statue of Liberty hold her torch?
3. What is the highest number on an AM radio dial?
4. How many tines are on a standard dinner fork?
5. What two letters do not appear on a standard telephone dial?
6. Most U.S. postage stamps give their denominations with a number plus:
   a. cents
   b. c
   c. ¢
7. On the back of a $5 bill is the Lincoln Memorial; on a $10 bill it's the Treasury building; on a $20 bill the White House. What's in the center of the back of a $1 bill?
8. If a common pencil isn't cylindrical, how many sides does it have?
9. Does "Coke" or "Coca-Cola" appear on every can of the soft drink?
10. How many geometric shapes are in the CBS "eye" logo?

Chances are you have seen these objects (or pictures of them) hundreds of times, yet few readers will have much confidence in their answers. This lack of confidence tells us something very basic to an understanding of the perceptual process: We do not use all the information in the environment surrounding us.

Perception is the process by which individuals select, organize, store, and interpret sensory stimulation into a meaningful and coherent picture of the world around us. Our brain does not passively register all available stimuli. We actively select what we perceive.

Human beings have a *limited span of perception.* Some persons can attend to more stimuli than others, and certain conditions affect the breadth of attention span over time for any one individual. But there is a definite upper limit to the amount of sensory stimulation a person can process. The immediate effect of this limitation is that we have to be selective.

Also, even that limited sample of stimuli must undergo some *transformation.* The sense organs can discriminate and differentiate more than our information-processing center can interpret. We have to recode the raw data into a simpler form of organization. The human ear, for example, can distinguish 11,000 separate tones, and the eye can discriminate 35,000 different hues, but in the immediate act of perceiving, we cannot possibly make use of this potential. George A. Miller, an expert in the study of human information processing, argues convincingly from his findings (Miller, 1956) that we generally can deal with only about seven bits of information at one time. The result of this disparity between what the sense organs can register and what the mind can process is that we have to organize raw data into categories of thought. Call these categories words, labels, concepts, constructs, or whatever; the important point is that we use these categories to summarize and record what seem to us the most "important" aspects of an otherwise overwhelming amount of sensory stimulation.

At this point we irretrievably lose some information. Having used the category "15-cent stamp" for collapsing the voluminous data contained in a small rectangular piece of paper (and if you doubt that such a volume of data exists, you have never talked to a serious stamp-collector), you cannot retrieve the information about whether there is a cents, c, or ¢ on it. That information was not important and was "processed out." (Oh, yes—the answers to the quiz: (1) he's looking left, which means to us his nose points right; (2) right hand; (3) 1600 (or 160); (4) usually four; (5) Q and Z; (6) c; (7) no picture, just the word ONE in large letters; (8) six; (9) both; (10) three—a circle inside a football inside a circle. If you answered more than five or six correctly, you did better than the average person. (Source: *Indianapolis Star Magazine,* Jan. 6, 1960.)

The perceiver's category system will determine how much and what kinds of stimulus information will be accessible in short-term memory. The category scheme also affects the perceiver's sensitivity to subtle differences between similar stimuli. The Hanunuo natives of the Philippines have names for 92 different varieties of rice and consequently are able to note the differences among those varieties. English-speaking persons have one word—rice—and would have trouble noting distinctions between varieties (Brown, 1965).

Generally, we develop rather complex, highly discriminating category schemes for objects that are important to us. A skier will develop a richer vocabulary for snow because different textures of snow affect skiing techniques. We develop concept names as internal cues because distinctions between them are important.

A person's total category scheme largely determines that person's powers of observation, recall, problem solving, and creativity. In fact, the most consistent predictor of a manager's income and career mobility is vocabulary (Campbell, Dunnette, Hawler, & Weick, 1970). This is not because successful managers impress others with big words, but because they have better equipment for observing, interpreting, storing, and recalling subtle distinctions.

Having categorized a portion of the sense data, the perceiver can proceed on the basis of certain built-in *assumptions* to make *inferences* about the perceived object. Having categorized an object as a desk, I can infer that it is solid, would support my weight, would hurt me if I fell against it, and would provide a level surface for writing. Perception invariably entails numerous leaps of faith; we always infer beyond the given data. It would be too time-consuming to examine every desk encountered. We capitalize on the economizing process in perception by proceeding from categorization to inference.

Not all such inferences are correct—the desk may be made of papier-mache, and if I leaned against it I would tumble to the floor. If this happened, I would recode the object based on new information generated by my own behavior—the object is now defined as a paper desk, and different inferences (it will tear, burn) result. But the inference-generating process never stops; it is so instinctive that we often mistake our inference for direct observation, especially when conditions for perceiving are not optimal.

Laboratory experiments have demonstrated this confusion between inferences and direct observation. Such studies use the tachistoscope, a device for studying characteristics of human visual perception under less-than-optimal conditions. It projects images on a screen for tiny fractions of a second. The experimenter can manipulate the characteristics of the image to find out what subjects "see." In one study (Bruner & Postman, 1949), the experimenter projected ordinary playing cards, but reversed the conventional association between suit and color for some of the cards—spades and clubs were red, hearts and diamonds black. Most subjects reported seeing the cards as they had always seen them. They had inferred that a three of diamonds would be red, because that inference follows from that category. They were not aware that they had made such inference; the inference was experienced as direct observation.

To summarize, we attend to a selected sample of available stimuli; we recode the raw sense-data into a category system; we use the rules of the category system to make predictions; we act on the basis of such predictions; and the results of our actions may alter our original perceptions. See Figure 6–1 for a diagram of the perceptual process.

THE PERVASIVENESS OF THE PERCEPTUAL PROCESS

Arguably, perception is at the crux of virtually all significant behavior. Much behavior comes under the control of stimulus cues in the environment, but if one cannot attend to all possible stimuli, we must account for *which* stimuli engage a person's attention. Even more important, we must recognize that the active role played by the perceiver means that different perceivers will respond quite differently to any given stimulus.

We will not take the position that there is no objective reality, and that the only reality is what people subjectively make of it. However, we will argue that many important issues in organizations cannot be reduced to objective confirmation. When such is the case, differences in attitudes will arise as a consequence of differences in processing selective information. The assessment of problem situations and decision alternatives will depend very much on differences in perceptual frames.

Consider such basic matters of organization as selecting personnel, evaluating an individual's performance, describing a style of leadership, determining the effectiveness of programs, defining the quality of a product,

FIGURE 6–1
Model of the Perceptual Process

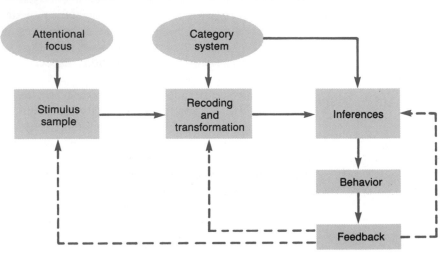

or assessing one's career options. These questions do not lend themselves to objectively verifiable measurement, but rest on inherently subjective processes involving the sampling, weighting, and integrating of sense data.

It is also important to recognize the feedback loops between perception and behavior. Differences in perception underlie differences in attitudes and behavior; also, attitudes and behavior often have the effect of locking in the original perceptions. To see someone as hostile often leads to the very actions that provoke hostility; to sense job pressures might well prompt a chain of panicky, compulsive responses that have pressure-generating consequences.

STIMULUS SELECTIVITY

The sample of available stimuli to which we attend is not random. Characteristics of the stimulus setting interact with characteristics of the perceiver to determine the focus of attention.

Stimulus Characteristics   In a crowd of people of average height, we will notice the one tall person; in a living room filled with people wearing white dinner jackets, we immediately see the one person in a blue sweater; on a printed page, a word in all capital letters or italics will quickly catch our eye. A noise that has been screened out of awareness will be noticed if its pitch, rhythm, or volume changes. In short, *differential stimulus intensity* of an object in relation to other objects tends to bias the sample of stimuli selected. Similar stimuli fade into the background, while a few dissimilar stimuli stand out.

Motion against a static background also draws attention. Long ago, merchants realized that drivers will readily notice a neon sign in which sequential lighting of adjacent bulbs creates the illusion of motion. Magicians keep their hands moving in flourishing gestures to distract the audience from any clues that might give the trick away.

Novelty also draws the perceiver's attention. Advertisers continually seek unusual and unexpected images to command the attention of the jaded TV watcher or magazine reader.

Characteristics of the Perceiver   To some extent, hereditary or physiological differences lead to characteristic tendencies to more readily perceive certain stimuli. Left-handed instructors, for example, tend to focus more on that part of the classroom to their left; people vary in the kinds of sounds to which they are most sensitive.

But *motivational state* undoubtedly represents the most important perceiver characteristic in influencing the focus of perception. A hungry person entering a hotel dining room will tend to ignore the finer points of the tapestries or the chandeliers, seeking only the standing rump roast or the dessert trolley. A troubled, insecure staff official will read or hear of a corporate reorganization and focus only on the details that might affect his or her job tenure, while someone driven by a desire for higher status will focus on the possibilities for promotion. Thus, one effect of motivational state is the *direction* of perceptual focus.

Motivational arousal has another effect on perception: the *more intense* the state of motive arousal, the *more narrow* the focus of perception, on stimuli relevant to that particular motive and the greater the tendency to ignore irrelevant stimuli. In one study (Organ, 1977), the experimenter gave subjects typewritten copies of an essay strewn with grammatical and typographical errors. He asked the subjects to identify and correct as many errors as they could. Half the subjects were given additional bonus points contingent on the number of errors found; the other subjects were not given this incentive. After collecting the essays, the experimenter administered a multiple-choice test of the essay's contents (facts, names, and numbers). Those who proofread for the bonus scored significantly lower on this test. Their stronger motivation to accomplish the assigned task made them oblivious to details unrelated to that task.

Ironically, intense motivation can impair performance if performance requires sensitivity to subtle stimuli. Strong motivational states activate the category systems most relevant to dealing with those motives and simultaneously suppress those coding schemes irrelevant to the motive. This finding suggests that powerful extrinsic incentives, while boosting performance on simple jobs or familiar tasks, sometimes have the effect of impairing performance on tasks requiring creative responses. The more intense motivational state leads us to screen out all but the most obvious cues for performance.

PERCEIVING PEOPLE: FORMING IMPRESSIONS OF OTHERS

Our real interest in others goes beyond their immediate behavior and their physical characteristics and concerns their traits, motives, abilities, and other stable attributes. If we assess someone in terms of a future relationship — as friend, client, employee, or partner — we have to get past the immediately available information and infer something about that person's abiding dispositions.

The Attribution Process   In piecing together an impression, we first assign some cause to the person's immediate behavior, and then go beyond that behavior to make inferences about underlying traits. Trait names are our important constructs in perceiving people. As Brown (1965) notes, it is easier to recall a few trait names than the myriad of behavior data we actually observe. Therefore our information processing concerning other people quickly recodes observations of behavior into trait names. If you think of someone you now know very well, you think of that person in terms of adjectives (warm, sociable, easygoing) rather than specific actions.

Before you can move from the observation of behavior data to trait inferences, you have to *attribute* the various behaviors either to external causes (such as situational factors) or to internal causes (such as traits, motives, or abilities). The *basic rule of attribution* is that behavior judged to be externally caused is not informative about the traits of the person (Heider, 1958; Jones & Davis, 1965). Put another way, behavior that can be explained by external factors tells us little about a person's underlying dispositions. This is also called the *discounting principle* in person perception. We discount the information value of a person's behavior if we can easily explain the behavior by reference to external forces.

Suppose you enter a restaurant and the host greets you with a bow, a wide smile, and expansive gestures of concern for your comfort. Do you infer that this host is a warm, kind person? Hardly. He is supposed to act that way — external influences dictate this behavior. The expectations of his boss, the desire for satisfied customers, the hope for a generous tip, all could cause such deferential behavior.

Consider another example, this one from work: you supervise someone very closely, taking special effort to monitor how hard she is working, and also making sure she knows you are keeping a close check on her. As you monitor her work, she keeps at the task, not goofing off. What inference can you draw about her diligence? She is working diligently, but is it because she knows you are watching her? You cannot assume with confidence that diligence is one of her stable attributes. In fact, a study by Strickland (1958) shows that close supervision by a superior over a subordinate does foster a lack of confidence that the subordinate would work as hard if not closely supervised. This finding echoes what McGregor said about managing on the basis of Theory X assumptions about work motivation: close, controlling supervision will generate the "evidence" on which it was assumed.

We can assign internal causes to a person's behavior only under certain conditions: when no obvious external forces could explain the behavior; when the person's behavior actually runs counter to the direction of any such situational forces; or when two or more strong external forces would exert roughly equal but opposite effects on behavior so that the balance is determined by internal dispositions. If the restaurant's host greeted us in a surly, insulting fashion, we might assume that his behavior reflected a cold or uncaring disposition, since the situational forces would have had the opposite influence. On the other hand, if you passed this person on the street when he was wearing his street clothes, not his tux, and he stopped to pick up a dropped parcel for you, you would feel that his behavior originated from a kind nature, since no overpowering forces in the situation demanded such behavior.

Criteria for Attributing Behavior   Kelley (1967, 1971) has developed a model that predicts how we use multiple observations of a person's behavior, over time and varied situations, to make inferences about that person's dispositions. In Kelley's model, we attribute the cause of behavior to either the *person,* an *entity* (which could be either an object or another person to whom the behavior is directed), or the *context.* Our inference as to which of these factors causes the behavior is determined by the criteria of *consensus, consistency, and distinctiveness* (see Figure 6–2).

Consensus is the extent to which other persons show the same kind of behavior toward a particular entity or in a particular context. In the above example, the restaurant host who greets us congenially is doing what anyone else in that situation would do, so consensus is high, and we discount the idea that the behavior reflects the person's actual traits.

Consistency is the degree to which the person behaves the same way toward the entity in other settings or on other occasions. The headwaiter who is congenial toward us in the laundromat or public library is one we judge to be a warm, outgoing person. Thus, a highly consistent mode of behavior is more apt to be taken as caused by stable internal characteristics of the person.

Distinctiveness is the extent to which the person behaves in this fashion only toward the particular entity. If the headwaiter treats everyone in a congenial fashion, but acts brusquely toward one particular customer, we as onlookers probably attribute the brusqueness to something peculiar about the customer. High distinctiveness of behavior toward a specific entity suggests the entity as external cause.

Consider Herbert, a retail clerk whom we have seen act rather curtly toward a certain customer, Mrs. Smith. If other clerks act the same way toward her, consensus is high, and we probably conclude that Herbert's

FIGURE 6–2
Kelley's Criteria for Inferring the Causes of Behavior

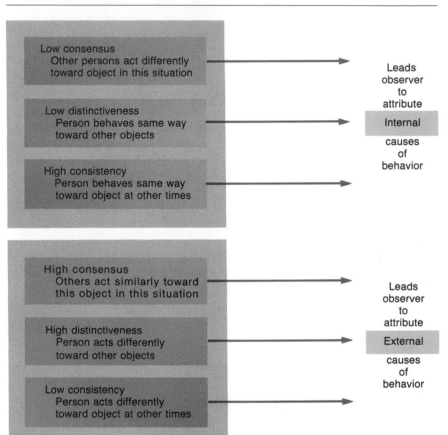

behavior is due more to something in Mrs. Smith than to his own make-up. If Herbert acts that way toward numerous other customers, distinctiveness (of the entity, Mrs. Smith) is low, and we tend to see Herbert's behavior as indicative of some internal trait (for example, impatience, tactlessness). If however, Herbert behaves quite differently toward Mrs. Smith or anyone else in other contexts (for example, when the store is not so crowded or when closing hour is not imminent), consistency is low, and we perceive the context — rather than Herbert or Mrs. Smith — as the cause of the behavior.

Even with multiple observations of a person's behavior, ambiguities may arise. Our logic might not operate as precisely as Kelley's model suggests. Suppose that two of the three factors (person, entity, and con-text) are "confounded" or bound together in our observations. For example, we might notice Herbert's behavior only toward a particular customer or in a particular context (such as a busy time). Do we reserve judgment, or do we hazard an inference about the cause of Herbert's behavior?

Evidence suggests that we tend to perceive the person as the cause of his or her behavior and thus infer some personal trait. Without evidence of external causes of the behavior, and without the opportunity to compare the behavior with that of other people in that situation, we err strongly in the direction of seeing the person as cause. This *fundamental attribution error* (Ross, 1977), the tendency to overattribute internal causes of behavior, has profound implications for management. It means that managers, if they do not restrain this tendency, will too often try to change people when they should worry about changing the situation.

The fundamental attribution error is aggravated when someone's behavior affects us. The behavior then has *hedonic relevance* (i.e., it causes positive or negative consequences for us personally), and makes us more likely to overattribute the behavior to the person's characteristics (Jones & Davis, 1965).

Recall that strong motivational or emotional arousal narrows our perceptual focus, rendering our perception less sensitive to subtle cues. If a person's behavior directly affects your emotions, you will probably focus on the salient stimulus (the other person), oblivious to less glaring cues in the situation surrounding the person. For example, when you see a policeman directing traffic, occasionally speaking sharply to pedestrians and motorists, you probably infer nothing about the cop's personal traits. He simply does what his job and situation require. But should you cross the street prematurely, and be reprimanded by him, his behavior has hedonic relevance — it affects you, possibly causing you embarrassment. Suddenly you see his behavior not as a job requirement, but as evidence of an arrogant and bullying nature. As Roethlisberger and Dickson (1939) noted five decades ago in their analysis of worker attitudes, strong emotions reduce our ability to decipher subtle perceptual distinctions.

Research evidence (Walster, 1966) also suggests that the *seriousness of the consequences* of a person's behavior also affects our weighting of internal versus external causes. The more serious the consequences, the more we indict the person as a cause. If a car is parked on a hill without the emergency brake applied and rolls a few yards to stop against a curb, we dismiss it — it could happen to anybody. But if the car crashes into someone's living room or injures a child, we assign blame to a careless, criminally negligent, and inconsiderate driver.

To summarize, we intuitively follow certain lines of logic (consensus, consistency, distinctiveness) to determine whether observed behavior should influence our perception of a person's traits or whether the behavior should be attributed to external factors (the entity or the context). But incomplete or ambiguous information regarding those lines of logic leaves us much more prone to attribute the behavior to the person as cause. This tendency becomes even more pronounced when the behavior personally affects us or when the behavior is viewed retroactively in light of serious consequences that occurred.

Actor versus Observer: Divergence of Perspective   There is one important exception to the rule that we overattribute causality to internal traits. That exception concerns how we perceive our own behavior. We generally account for our own actions in terms of the situation. This *actor-observer* effect (Jones & Nisbett, 1971) has been documented in numerous studies. Others behave because that is the way they are; we behave in a selective, deliberate fashion dictated by the situation. We don't see our own traits as controlling specific behavior. When you rush, you explain your behavior (if asked to do so) by reference to external time pressures. When you see someone else rush, you're more apt to think the reason is innate impatience.

This divergence of actor versus observer perspective contains the seeds for many a heated argument between manager and subordinate or between co-workers. Subordinates ascribe their behavior to the constraints of resources, eccentric clients, dependence on co-workers, time pressures, or the task environment. Managers, conversely, interpret subordinate behavior or performance as the product of that person's character, style, or competence. Subordinates are also likely to perceive the manager's behavior as due to to the manager's temperament, managerial ability, personality, or innate leadership style. Managers feel their behavior is dictated by organizational pressures, top management directives, and limitations of the work group.

Physical Cues   Our inferences about others' traits derive not only from observations of behavior, but also from observations of their physical characteristics. Such inferences often rest on prevailing stereotypes of questionable validity—red-haired people are temperamental, blue-eyed people are cold and restrained, tall people have more self-confidence, chubby people are easygoing and self-indulgent. Physical cues that reflect gender or ethnic group membership may also suggest stereotypic traits (see Focus on International OB, page 142).

The most pervasive influence of physical cues on trait inferences is the general perception of another's physical attractiveness. Physical attractiveness has a *halo effect* on our impressions of others. A halo effect occurs when an obvious characteristic about a person colors our impressions about the person's other characteristics. Halo effects are particularly strong when the characteristic is one we consider positive or negative. In our culture, physical attractiveness (or its opposite) is a value-tinged characteristic. This is not just attractiveness of the opposite sex; our first evaluative judgment of a man or a woman tends to involve physical attractiveness in virtually any context.

Social psychological studies provide evidence that we attribute more desirable traits to attractive people. Good-looking children are assumed to have better personalities, to be better behaved, to be more honest (Dion, 1972). Physical attractiveness also has an effect on interviewers' judgments when they assess résumés of applicants for a managerial position (Dipboye, Fromkin, & Willback, 1975).

A journalist interviewed a cosmetic surgeon who could project someone's face on a video screen and demonstrate, by using a stylus to draw on a control pad, how the person's appearance would change with various types of cosmetic surgery—erasing deep laugh lines, tucking in the chin, taking off some pouch from the cheek. The model used in this demonstration was an older man with droopy jowls, a beaked nose, and several chins. As the surgeon sketched on the video pad what the effect of an operation would be, the reporter noted that the model began to look less like "an unsuccessful door-to-door salesman of tacky aluminum siding" and more like "the British ambassador to someplace important"; "the scary thing was that . . . I found myself liking him more as the videosurgery proceeded . . . the surgery didn't just make him look better, it made him look smarter, richer, better-educated, and like a generally nicer person" ("After a Fashion," Patricia McLaughlin, *Indianapolis Star,* May 22, 1988).

In a study conducted at the University of Pittsburgh, judges rated, on a scale of 1 to 5, the physical attractiveness of 750 MBA graduates. The men and women who were judged better-looking received higher starting salaries. Overall, each unit on the five-point scale of attractiveness translated into about $2,000 more salary (Frieze, Olson, & Russell, 1989). Attractive people are presumed to have other positive qualities—intelligence, poise, confidence, emotional adjustment, perhaps luck.

Height also appears to exert a halo effect on our impressions of others—especially men, but perhaps increasingly so of women as well. Another study (cited in Keyes, 1980) by the Pittsburgh researchers cited above found that male graduates who stood 6 feet, 2 inches tall averaged 12 percent more in pay than those shorter than 5 feet, 11 inches (the pay advantage for above-average academic standing, by contrast, was only 4 percent!). In this century, the taller of the two major political party presidential candidates has won 18 of 22 elections. The chances of this occurring randomly are less than two out of a thousand. All of our presidents except James Madison and Benjamin Harrison have been taller than the average men of their times.

Another study (also cited in Keyes, 1980) showed that when given a choice among two equally qualified candidates, one over 6 feet tall and the other only 5 feet, 5 inches, sales recruiters chose the taller candidate. Seventy-two percent of the recruiters chose the six-footer, 27 percent expressed no preference one way or the other, and only one percent picked the shorter applicant.

Trait Configurations   We have discussed how perceivers attribute a trait to the perceived on the basis of inferences drawn either from observed behavior, physical cues, or halo effects. Our inference processes seldom stop with a single trait, but use clusters of traits that go together. As Bruner, Shapiro, and Tagiuri (1958) described it, people have *implicit personality theories* about the relationships between one trait and another. You may believe that generous people are also honest and happy; that a neat person is likely to be punctual and efficient. Some implicit personality theories appear to be widely shared; others are more idiosyncratic.

The effect of such theories is that, correctly or not, we use evidence of one trait to infer the existence of others. More important, we often do not realize that such second-order inferences (first-order inferences being those drawn from observed behavior or physical cues) were actually made without directly observed data. If you observe that Walter keeps his desk and work area very tidy and uncluttered, your impression may move quickly from "he is a neat person" to "he is also efficient and punctual." You do not realize that you have no evidence of his efficiency or punctuality.

Implicit personality theory enables us to take a little information about someone a long way. This eases interaction with others and the making of judgments on which such interaction proceeds. However, the more we go beyond the information given to us, the greater the probability of error. But so what? Can we not revise our impressions of others in the light of new information?

First Impressions   The bulk of experimental evidence argues for a *primacy effect* in our impressions of others. Impressions formed from the initial encounter with a person exert a disproportionate influence on our continued perception of them. Experiments (such as Luchins, 1957) with this phenomenon show that, when subjects receive contradictory information about a person, the earlier information dominates the overall impression that they form. For example, if your first exposure to someone suggests an outgoing nature and subsequent observation indicates an aloof quality, you will think of the person more as outgoing. As Brown (1965) comments, "first impressions appear to be as critical as secretarial schools have always said they were."

This does not mean that first impressions are permanent, or that we ignore subsequent data about people. Rather, the initial trait inferences act as a baseline with which subsequent observations must be assimilated. Suppose that your first encounter with a newly hired employee leads you to think that he has limited abilities. Then in the next few days you see that his work looks pretty good. Rather than discard your initial impression altogether, you find a way to reconcile these subsequent observations with that impression. You might see the new worker possessing modest ability, but working hard to realize his potential. Or, you might regard the work as requiring thoroughness and neatness rather than mental ability. Or, you could hold to your impression of generally limited abilities, but with a narrow, specific sort of aptitude for this specialized task. Eventually, if he shows high-caliber work on an array of important jobs, you may alter your impression quite a bit. But the point is this: the first impression filters subsequent observations.

The Self-Fulfilling Prophecy

Our perception of an object does not affect the object itself, but our impressions of people can, at least indirectly, affect their behavior. Moreover, initially erroneous impressions by a perceiver can lead the perceiver to shape the behavior of the target person in a fashion that seems to validate the original impression.

Psychologists Robert Rosenthal and Lenore Jacobsen (1968) selected an elementary school in a lower-class neighborhood and gave all the children a nonverbal intelligence test. They explained to the teachers that the test could identify intellectual bloomers—children whose intelligence would show a sudden surge in development. Rosenthal and Jacobsen then randomly picked 20 percent of the children in each room and gave their names to the teachers. The teachers were told these pupils would become intellectual bloomers. In fact, there was no real basis, from the test or otherwise, for expecting any greater intellectual development in these children. They had been chosen randomly and any difference between these children and the others (controls) resided solely in the teachers' impressions. Eight months later, the researchers retested the pupils. Those the teachers had thought would "bloom" showed an overall IQ gain of four points, while the control children, on average, did not increase their IQ.

This study sparked an intense controversy, and some critics pointed to possible flaws in the research procedures. A number of subsequent studies, however, have largely supported the generalization that teacher expectations affect student achievement.

Impressions and expectations per se do not actually affect the targets of the impressions. Rather, the impression of someone influences how we behave toward that person. Our behavior provides cues toward which the person responds, and following such response, our behavior reinforces, fails to reinforce, or possibly punishes the response. The point is that our initial impression may well determine the cycle of responses and counterresponses that follows. The original perception, even if unfounded, triggers a sequence that makes the perception a self-fulfilling prophecy (see Figure 6–3).

Later studies by Rosenthal and others have explored the behavioral mechanisms that mediate the effect of teacher expectancies on student achievement. First of all, teachers enact a warmer interpersonal climate with those they expect to excel scholastically. Second, the warmth they provide to such pupils is given for different reasons than the warmth given to others.

FIGURE 6–3
Model of the Self-Fulfilling Prophecy in Person Perception

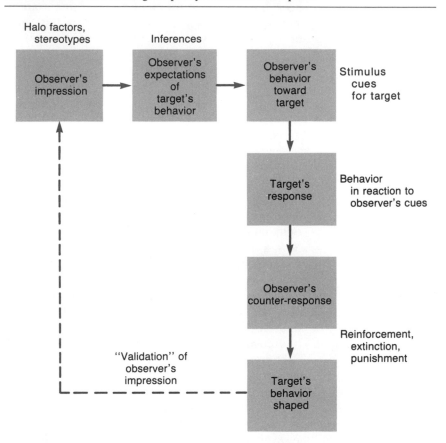

The teacher smiles fondly at the expected bloomer who asks a profound question or offers an insightful comment. The student already labeled as slow receives warmth for being slow; if he or she makes a perceptive comment, the teacher reacts with veiled defensiveness. Third, teachers actually spend more time with those already considered "fast"—that is, the teachers teach them more. Finally, teachers give such children more opportunities for practicing and displaying their learning—they call on them more, give them more time to answer, and assign them to important roles in class projects.

In the Rosenthal-Jacobsen study, the researchers planted seeds of expectations that later bore fruit. Would such impressions have formed without the intervention of psychologists? If so, would "naturally occurring" expectations have been more valid? Evidence suggests that the answers are: Yes, teachers do form such impressions very early, and no, the impressions

---

CLOSE-UP

Pygmalion Goes to Boot Camp

To assess the generalizability of the self-fulfilling prophecy, researchers Dov Eden and Abraham Shani conducted a field experiment at a military training base in Israel. One hundred and five trainees were selected for a 15-week combat command course on the basis of prior records and test scores. Four days before the trainees arrived at camp, their four prospective instructors were given information about the "command potential" of the trainees. One third of the soldiers were singled out as showing high potential, one third were described as regular in potential, and one third as "unknown" in this respect due to insufficient data. Actually, the assignment of individuals to these categories was random, and the three groups were actually matched on all relevant criteria.

Those soldiers who were expected to do better due to their high potential scored higher at the end of the course on both written exams and field demonstrations—even though the exams were administered by officers who had not been their instructors. The high expectance trainees also scored higher in attitudes toward the course and toward instructor leadership.

"Boosting expectations among superiors evoked more positive perceptions of leadership behavior on the part of supposedly high potential subordinates. If these reported perceptions reflect actual leadership behavior, then leadership may be a means by which superiors unwittingly fulfill their own prophecies" (Eden & Shani, p. 198).

SOURCE: D. Eden and A. B. Shani, "Pygmalion Goes to Boot Camp: Expectancy, Leadership, and Trainee Performance," *Journal of Applied Psychology* 67 (1982), pp. 194–99.

---

are not formed on any particularly objective or valid basis. Teachers tend to expect more rapid development from physically attractive children, from children of parents with higher socioeconomic status, and from children whose older siblings were "fast."

Such expectations actually generate a course of events that transforms them into reality.

You should have no difficulty imagining how self-fulfilling prophecies operate in other kinds of organizations. Given a group of subordinates, a manager can form initial impressions of their potential as employees on the basis of physical attractiveness, the reputation of the school or college they attended, their gender, the timbre of their voices, or the impressions described on their personnel file by the one who interviewed them. The manager spends more time with the "best and brightest," teaching them more, introducing them to other key figures, providing more feedback, and giving them a closer look at the inner face of organization operations. Finally, the manager will provide more "response opportunity" to those seen as bloomers—giving them more nonroutine assignments, more visible roles to play, and more time at center stage.

FOCUS ON INTERNATIONAL OB

Asian-Americans: "High-Tech Coolies"?

Asian-Americans, who often graduate at the top of their college classes, are highly valued for technical positions (e.g., quantitative analysis and computer programming) and usually earn high marks as diligent workers. However, they apparently have little success penetrating the ranks of management. Government statistics show that this group accounts for 8 percent of all professionals and technicians, but only 1.3 percent of managers.

Many Asian-Americans believe the obstacle preventing their entrance into management is a racial stereotype of passivity. They are seen as analytical and quiet, retiring and unassertive, modest and unaggressive. They fail to plug into the social networks revolving around cocktail parties and golf. But which is cause and which is effect? Are they excluded from the network because they are viewed as passive, and then reconfirmed as passive because they are not active networkers?

SOURCE: Winifred Yu, "Asian-Americans Charge Prejudice Slows Climb to Management Ranks," *The Wall Street Journal,* September 11, 1985.

PERCEIVING PERFORMANCE

In some instances, perceiving a person's overall or characteristic performance is a straightforward process. Consider, for example, the case of Ricky Henderson, the Oakland Athletics outfielder, in the 1989 American League playoffs. While not every observer would condone his selection as the playoffs' Most Valuable Player, anyone familiar with his hitting, scoring, base stealing, and defensive play would agree that his performance in those five games was very good.

Unfortunately, job performance is seldom clearcut in definition, interpretation, and assessment, and perception of job performance is usually influenced by many extraneous variables. Furthermore, managers' workdays are often fragmented and filled with unexpected interruptions (Mintzberg, 1973) making it unlikely that many managers can systematically observe the work behavior of each and every subordinate. Often a manager's conception of an employee's typical performance rests on snippets of observations.

Nonetheless, managers do form perceptions of people's performance, as indeed they must. Most administrators are charged with rendering some periodic formal appraisal of subordinates' performance. (For a succinct discussion of the various formats and techniques of formal appraisal, and their respective merits and shortcomings, the reader may consult Schuler &

Youngblood, 1986.) The manager's evaluation of a subordinate's performance, whether official or not, has important consequences. Many of the manager's actions toward the employee depend on it: rewards, salary recommendations, disciplinary actions, and task assignments. The employee's reputation and career are at stake. Therefore, the process by which managers perceive subordinate performance deserves serious study.

Feldman (1981), drawing from social psychological theory and research, has shown how perception of performance begins with categorizing the subordinate according to *prototypes*. Managers have rough prototypes for workers just as we have ready-made categories for persons we encounter socially. These prototypes represent combinations of various attributes. Different managers think in terms of different sets of prototypes: we would all recognize the Fraternity Type (gregarious, physically attractive, conventional in behavior, perhaps not a very profound thinker); the Yuppie (very ambitious, hard-working, striving for material outcomes in order to indulge expensive tastes); the Girl Next Door (deferential to males, nonthreatening, reliable, sweet disposition); the Flake (high in potential, unconventional in dress and manner, unpredictable); the Wimp (small in stature, meek in voice, anxiety prone, unassertive); and the Rocket Scientist (strong in theory and application of quantitative analysis, but weak on pragmatics and oblivious of politics). The point is not that any particular manager uses these particular prototypes, but that managers generally use categories in some such fashion. The manager does not have to see in a person all of the traits that define a particular prototype to assign the person to that category. Prototypes are usually somewhat fuzzy to begin with. Furthermore, as Feldman notes, "people's impressions of . . . others are unwittingly influenced by factors that make certain kinds of information more salient or prominent in the perceptual field" (p. 129). In other words, an administrator may be unaware that her categorization of John as a wimp is unduly influenced by John's squeaky, high-pitched voice. In fact, the manager may not even be aware of having categorized John at all.

Having consciously or unwittingly categorized John in terms of some prototype, the manager's recall of John's behavior will be biased toward the general characteristics consistent with that prototype. The manager easily recalls instances in which John acted indecisively, glossing over those where John dealt resolutely with job matters. Moreover, the manager will tend to attribute John's indecisiveness to internal causes (i.e., traits), while attributing any acts of resoluteness to external causes (i.e., "It was a routine matter he was acting on"). Thus, "categorization not only selectively influences and biases recall, it prevents contradictory evidence from appearing" (Feldman, 1981, p. 135).

Feldman's explanation for these phenomena involves information processing. He argues, based on previous research, that our information about people's actual behavior is often stored only temporarily, in a "workspace." Because our capacities for short-term information storage are limited, periodically this workspace is cleared. When this happens, the prototype is used to aid long-term storage of information. In the process, points of noncorrespondence between the person's behavior and the prototype are suppressed.

Managers can still change their impressions of a person's performance if the target person's performance clearly deviates from the prototype and there are no easy explanations for this. The wimp who shuts down a boisterous co-worker in a committee meeting and repeatedly urges bold, risky courses of action will probably force his manager to reexamine her impression. This reflection is more likely to trigger a *controlled,* as opposed to *automatic,* process of categorization. The manager will think more deliberately about John's characteristic behavior and performance. And, more interestingly, "recategorization of a person may cause a reconstruction of memories about that individual such that memories consistent with the new categorization become more accessible" (Feldman, 1981, p. 136).

However, the nature of the typical manager's workday almost forces the manager to rely heavily on quickly formed impressions of subordinates. We could urge that current and prospective administrators be more cautious and hesitant in forming impressions and/or plan systematic occasions for deliberate, controlled observation of employees' performance, but it is doubtful this caveat would or could be heeded by many. Nonetheless, it is instructive to recognize the ubiquity of these phenomena in perceiving performance. Having come to that recognition, managers should provide as many objective criteria as possible for judging performance, and include other sources of evaluation (co-workers or clients) in addition to themselves. Beyond that, administrators might also make it a rule generally to attach a degree of tentativeness to whatever impressions they have about subordinate performance.

Perceiving Poor Performance: Attributions and Actions

Feldman's work has focused mainly on factors that distort the impression of a subordinate's performance, but Mitchell, Green, and Wood (1981) have addressed the question of how leaders respond to obviously poor performance by a subordinate. In particular, Mitchell and his colleagues examine how a manager assigns causes to poor performance and what the manager does after the causes are assigned.

Mitchell et al. (1981) begin with the criteria of consistency, consensus, and distinctiveness suggested by Kelley's (1967) attribution model. That is, the more consistent the poor performance by that worker, the more likely that poor performance is attributed to some internal characteristic. Internal causes include low ability and low effort. Similarly, the fewer the other workers who have performed poorly (low consensus) on this task, the more likely that the manager will ascribe the causes of poor performance to internal factors. The attribution of internal causes will likewise be more probable if the subordinate tends to exhibit poor performance on a variety of tasks (low distinctiveness). On the other hand, if poor performance is inconsistent with the subordinate, if most other workers would have performed poorly, or if this worker shows satisfactory performance on other tasks, then the leader is more likely to ascribe the poor performance to external factors. External causes of poor performance could include the work environment (e.g., noise, distractions, or overload), the difficulty of the task, or simply bad luck in this particular instance — "The cards just didn't break his way this time."

Logically, one would think that the manager would have every reason to be careful and objective in assigning the causes of poor performance. After all, the appropriate action to be taken by the leader depends on the presumed cause of the poor performance. If the cause is internal, the manager must discipline the worker (if the cause is lack of effort) or arrange training or reassignment for the person (if the problem is insufficient ability). If the cause is external, the manager needs to redesign the task or improve the work environment.

However, pyschological forces distort the leader's otherwise logical application of Kelley's criteria for assessing the causes of poor performance. Mitchell et al. (1981) hypothesize that a "self-serving bias" on the part of the leader enters into the equation. To perceive subordinates as the cause of unsatisfactory work, either because of poor effort or low skill, shifts blame away from the leaders themselves. On the other hand, to see the cause in the task itself or in the job environment implicates the leader. This bias is added to the more general tendency to overestimate persons and underestimate situations as causes of behavior. Thus, managers are more likely to attribute the causes of poor performance to internal rather than external factors. The empirical findings of Mitchell support this.

The relationship between leader and subordinate also influences the leader's attribution. If the manager likes the subordinate, he is apt to attribute unsatisfactory performance to external causes. Conversely, internal causes of work are attached to a worker who is not particularly liked.

The severity of the effects of poor performance also can determine the nature of the manager's attributions. The more serious (the more costly, tragic, or disastrous) the effects, the more likely the supervisor will ascribe the behavior to intentional carelessness or congenital stupidity. For example, if a nurse's deviation from standard procedure causes cardiac arrest in a patient, the nursing supervisor will likely blame the nurse. The very same infraction causing only mild discomfort to the patient would likely be explained by external causes.

Interestingly, Mitchell and Kalb (1982) found that a supervisor with considerable experience in the tasks performed by subordinates is more likely to point to external causes (task difficulty, the environment) of poor performance than would a supervisor who is inexperienced in those tasks. Apparently, a supervisor who has actually done the subordinate's job has more empathy and can see the situation from the subordinate's perspective.

PERCEPTION IN THE JOB INTERVIEW

Perhaps no other work situation taxes our fragile perceptual ability as much as the job interview. The results are critically important to both the interviewer and the applicant; the costs of error are serious. As we have already noted, the accompanying motivational and emotional arousal narrows our perceptual span and reduces our abilities to process complex or novel stimuli. Also, both parties have a vested interest in contriving or manipulating the impressions they put forward. The typical interview lasts for 30 minutes or less, and the interviewer may have a dozen or more applicants in succession. How do these conditions affect the perceptual process?

There is evidence (Webster, 1982) that the interviewer reaches an accept-or-reject decision very early in the interview, frequently in the first four or five minutes. This is especially likely if the interviewer had access to preinterview information (e.g., from a written application form) that caused a negative impression. Furthermore, if the initial impression is at all negative, it is much less likely that the impression will be subsequently changed. The interviewer is influenced more by negative than by positive information (Kanouse & Hanson, 1972). Webster (1982) accounts for the negative bias of the interviewer as follows: The error of selecting an unsatisfactory employee is much more obvious and visible than that of rejecting what would have been an outstanding performer. The result is that the somewhat bland, weakly positive candidate has an edge over a potentially much better prospect who presents some glaring (though possibly trivial) shortcoming.

Dipboye (1982), after a literature review, concludes that all but the first few minutes of the interview are likely to be an exercise in the self-fulfilling prophecy. An initial impression is formed, based on pre-interview information or some halo factor such as physical attraction. The interviewer either likes or dislikes the applicant (although the interviewer may have no inkling of why or may misattribute the impression). Thereafter, the interviewer reacts to the applicant quite differently, depending on whether the early impression is favorable or unfavorable. The studies Dipboye reviewed suggest that interviewers will sit closer to, maintain more eye contact with, provide more information to, and smile more at those prospects of whom a favorable early impression was formed. This posture helps the prospect relax somewhat, feel more confident, and in general, perform better in the situation. If the early impression is negative, the interviewer will keep the exchange on a formal footing to test the candidate, and otherwise do those things that maintain tension. This makes it difficult for the candidate to relax, and makes some *faux pas* more likely. Quite unintentionally, the interviewer acts on his or her impression in such a way as to evoke the behavior from the applicant that matches the prior expectation.

FOCUS ON MANAGEMENT

Haloes and the CEO

When corporate boards of directors get down to the "short list" of candidates for Chief Executive Officer, how do they make the final choice? According to O. William Battalia, chairman of an executive search firm, here are some of the details that have knocked technically qualified candidates out of contention:

Flabby handshakes

Poor posture

Scratching

Short socks

Baldness

Pipe smoking ("too academic")

Wearing lots of rings and jewelry

Bow ties

What clinches the decision in a candidate's favor? "Intellectual gymnastics, a compelling ability to communicate, physical attractiveness, and personal charm."

SOURCE: *The Wall Street Journal,* November 15, 1988.

Even if the interviewer scrupulously weighs only the most relevant information, impressions of a candidate can be strongly influenced by *contrast effects.* The recruiter usually has no trouble assessing clearly outstanding or obviously weak prospects on their own merits. But a study (Wexley, Yukl, Kovacs, & Sanders, 1972) in which college students rated applicants in videotaped interviews showed that assessments of average candidates were strongly influenced by the caliber of those who immediately preceded them. Those who followed weak applicants received much higher ratings than those who followed outstanding prospects. In fact, the differences were nearly as great as the difference between ratings given to high- and low-suitability applicants themselves.

It is not surprising that experts in personnel and industrial relations regard the interview as a poor diagnostic tool, of just about zero validity beyond preinterview information. Furthermore, the studies reviewed by Webster (1982) suggest that sophisticated personnel recruiters are prone to the same distortions, biases, and premature inferences as college students.

In one respect, however, Webster is more optimistic. He concludes that two different models are appropriate for the perceptual process that occurs in the interview. The "conflict" model fits the case in which the interviewer is responsible for making a reject-or-accept decision. The stress of such responsibility evokes the defensive coping mechanisms that are most likely

CLOSE-UP

Tie-Breakers in the Employment Interview

Bill Bohnert, vice president for corporate development for the Louisville catalog production firm Paul Schultz Cos. Inc., has developed a list of tie-breakers when he has to choose among several technically good applicants:

Being late for the interview without calling or explaining.

Sloppy appearance. ("Don't let me guess at the professionalism underneath, let me see it when I first see you.")

Misspellings on the application form and poor grammar in either written or oral communication.

Talking about past rotten jobs and poor supervisors. ("When I hear this I develop the distinct impression that you'll soon be talking about our company the same way.")

Failing to maintain eye contact and appearing obviously ill at ease. ("A job interview is a test of interpersonal skills.")

Inaccuracies, exaggerations, and untruths. ("If you distort the truth to get the job, you'll distort the truth to keep the job.")

SOURCE: Frank Kuzmits and Lyle Sussman, "Managing People," *Louisville Courier-Journal,* January 18, 1988.

to warp perceptions. On the other hand, when the task of the interviewer is simply to describe, without the burden of making the hiring decision, then a more straightforward "cognitive information processing" model applies. When the interviewer's task is merely to describe the applicant, perceptions formed are more accurate and informative. Perhaps, then, the proper role of the interview is to collect information that can be passed along to others who have the responsibility for making selection decisions.

Finally, those who contend that the interview has little value in predicting individual performance of a technical sort might well be missing the point of what the interview is all about. The interview will not add much to the already available information about the interviewee's technical ability, competence, intelligence, training, creativity, or relevant experience. But the interviewer often is not looking for that kind of information anyway. The purpose of the interview is often to find out something about other work-relevant traits—Is this person likely to be a team player? Would she display the kind of sportsmanship, neighborliness, and consideration that typify the good citizen in work relationships with others? Such characteristics do not predict an individual's technical, in-role performance, but do have much to do with the efficient functioning of the group (Organ, 1988). Perhaps the interview does provide a basis for some reasonably accurate (even though subjective) assessment of the applicant's characteristics that pertain to working with others. (See Close-Up for cues used by recruiters as "tie-breakers.")

CONCLUSION

The more complex, ambiguous, and dynamic our environment becomes, the more we rely on our own devices to support the perceptual process. Behavior in organizations typically scores high in complexity, ambiguity, and dynamism; therefore, those who observe behavior in organized settings resort to shortcuts in perception, even at the risk of error. It would be unrealistic for us to tell you to base your impressions only on valid data. It is more appropriate to counsel a tentative, flexible style in forming impressions of the physical and social reality around you. Most of our "knowledge" derives from economizing processes—which aid perception but also lead to errors—and we should be more sensitive to cues that contradict such knowledge. We also become more likely to qualify any knowledge conveyed by others, even if ostensibly based on direct observation, for we realize the frailty of their perceptual systems, too. In short, we realize that we may know a great deal, but we know very little for sure.

SUMMARY

In perceiving the world around us, we do not take account of all potential stimuli. Our sense organs focus selectively, determined in part by the characteristics of stimulus objects and in part by our own characteristics, such as motivational state. We actively use category systems to transform and simplify sensory stimulation. Using such category schemes, we make inferences and predictions that guide behavior.

Perception is a process in which we use observations of behavior and physical cues to infer traits. We work through the attribution process of assigning internal or external causes to behavior. Typically, we tend to overestimate the person (as opposed to the situation) as a causal force. We draw on physical cues—such as personal attractiveness or ethnic group membership—or use halo factors or stereotypes in forming an impression of certain traits. Furthermore, our conceptions lead us to infer some traits from evidence concerning other traits.

Our impressions of people, unlike those of objects, can indirectly shape their behavior through the manner in which we act on our impressions. This effect forms the basis of the self-fulfilling prophecy, in which originally erroneous impressions lead to response/counter-response sequences that seem to confirm the original impression.

The dynamics of social perception have direct implications for the assessment of subordinate performance, especially if that performance is unsatisfactory. Also, the effects of halo factors and the self-fulfilling prophecy combine to threaten the validity of the job interview.

CONCEPTS TO REMEMBER

Motivational effects on perception	Fundamental attribution error	Negative evaluative set in interviews
Span of perception	Hedonic relevance	Prototypes
Attribution process	Actor versus observer perspective	Consensus
Stereotypes	Primacy effect	Consistency
Halo effect	Self-fulfilling prophecy	Distinctiveness
Implicit personality theory	Contrast effects in interviews	

QUESTIONS FOR DISCUSSION

1. Discuss the pros and cons of making personnel decisions on the basis of such observations as those noted in the Focus on Management and the Close-Up, "Tie Breakers in the Employment Interview."

2. How do you account for the persistence of stereotypes and implicit personality theories? Choose an example of each to illustrate your reasoning.

3. Physical attractiveness and height were noted as two frequently occurring halo effects in forming impressions and evaluations of others. What others come to your mind? Try to think of halo effects that might significantly influence the perceptions of a corporate recruiter in an interview or a manager appraising a subordinate's performance.

4. Try to identify several prototypes (other than those mentioned in this chapter) used to categorize employees in a manager's perception. Make explicit the defining attributes of the prototypes.

5. Can you think of an instance when the self-fulfilling prophecy has worked to your disadvantage? In your favor? Describe as precisely as you can the mediating behavioral linkages—your own behavior as well as that of others.

REFERENCES

Brown, R. (1965). *Social psychology.* New York: Free Press.

Bruner, J. A., & Postman, L. (1949). On the perception of incongruity: A paradigm. *Journal of Personality* 18, 206–23.

Bruner, J. A., Shapiro, D., & Tagiuri, R. (1958). The meaning of traits in isolation and in combination. In R. Tagiuri & L. Petrullo (eds.), *Person perception and interpersonal behavior.* Stanford: Stanford University Press.

Campbell, J. P., Dunnette, M. D., Lawler, E. E. III, & Weick, K. R., Jr. (1970). *Managerial behavior, performance, and effectiveness.* New York: McGraw-Hill.

Dion, K. (1972). Physical attractiveness and evaluation of children's transgressions. *Journal of Personality and Social Psychology* 24, 207–13.

Dipboye, R. L. (1982). Self-fulfilling prophecies in the selection-recruitment interview. *Academy of Management Review* 7, 579–86.

Dipboye, R. L., Fromkin, H. L., & Willback, K. (1975). Relative importance of applicant sex, attractiveness, and scholastic standing in evaluation of job applicant resumes. *Journal of Applied Psychology* 60, 39–43.

Eden, D., & Shani, A. B. (1982). Pygmalion goes to boot camp: Expectancy, leadership, and trainee performance. *Journal of Applied Psychology* 67, 194–99.

Feldman, J. M. (1981). Beyond attribution theory: Cognitive processes in performance appraisal. *Journal of Applied Psychology* 66, 127–48.

Heider, F. (1958). *The psychology of interpersonal relations.* New York: John Wiley & Sons.

Jones, E. E., & Davis, K. E. (1965). From acts to dispositions: The attribution process in person perception. In L. Berkowitz (ed.), *Advances in experimental social psychology,* vol. 2. New York: Academic Press.

Jones, E. E., & Nisbett, R. E. (1971). *The actor and observer: Perceptions of the causes of behavior.* New York: General Learning Press.

Kanouse, D. E., & Hanson, L. R., Jr. (1972). Negativity in evaluations. New York: General Learning Press.

Kelley, H. H. (1967). Attribution theory in social psychology. In D. Levine (ed.), *Nebraska Symposium of Motivation,* vol. 15, 192–238. Lincoln, NE: University of Nebraska Press.

Kelley, H. H. (1971). *Attribution in social interaction.* New York: General Learning Press.

Landy, D., & Sigall, H. (1974). Beauty is talent: Task evaluation as a function of the performer's physical attractiveness. *Journal of Personality and Social Psychology* 29, 299–304.

Luchins, A. S. (1957). Primacy-recency in impression formation. In C. I. Hovland (ed.), *The order of presentation in persuasion.* New Haven: Yale University Press.

Miller, G. A. (1956). The magical number seven, plus or minus two: Some limits on our capacity for processing information. *Psychological Review* 63, 81–97.

Mintzberg, H. (1973). *The nature of managerial work.* New York: Harper & Row.

Mitchell, T. R., Green, S. G., & Wood, R. (1981). An attributional model of leadership and the poor performing subordinate. In L. L. Cummings & B. M. Staw (eds.), *Research in organizational behavior,* vol. 3, 197–234. Greenwich, CT: JAI Press, Inc.

Mitchell, T. R., & Kalb, L. S. (1982). Effects of job experience on supervisor attributions for a subordinate's poor performance. *Journal of Applied Psychology* 67, 181–88.

Organ, D. W. (1977). Intentional versus arousal effects of goal-setting. *Organizational Behavior and Human Performance* 18, 378–89.

Organ, D. W. (1988). *Organizational citizenship behavior: The good soldier syndrome.* Lexington, MA: Lexington Books.

Roethlisberger, F. J., & Dickson, W. J. (1939). *Management and the worker.* Cambridge, MA: Harvard University Press.

Rosenthal, R., & Jacobsen, L. (1968). *Pygmalion in the classroom.* New York: Holt, Rinehart & Winston.

Ross, L. (1977). The intuitive psychologist and his shortcomings: Distortions in the attribution process. In L. Berkowitz (ed.), *Advances in experimental social psychology.* New York: Academic Press.

Schuler, R. S., & Youngblood, S. A. (1986). *Effective personnel management.* St. Paul, MN: West Publishing Co.

Stogdill, R. M. (1948). Personal factors associated with leadership: A survey of the literature. *Journal of Psychology* 25, 35–71.

Strickland, L. H. (1958). Surveillance and trust. *Journal of personality* 26, 200–215.

Walster, E. (1966). The assignment of responsibility for an accident. *Journal of Personality and Social Psychology* 5, 508–16.

Webster, E. C. (1982). *The employment interview: A social judgment process.* Schomberg, Ontario, Canada: S.I.P. Publications.

Wexley, K., Yukl, G., Kovacs, A., & Sanders, R. (1972). Importance of contrast effects in employment interviews. *Journal of Applied Psychology* 56, 45–48.

Yu, W. (1985). Asian-Americans charge prejudice slows climb to management ranks. *The Wall Street Journal,* September 11, 1985.

7 Attitudes

What is the structure of attitudes?
How are attitudes and behavior related?
How are attitudes acquired?
How are attitudes changed?
What determines the effectiveness of persuasion?

Over half a century ago, Gordon Allport (1935) suggested that the "concept of attitude is probably the most distinctive and indispensable concept in contemporary American social psychology" (p. 798). Allport may have been too modest; he did not foresee the extent of the *business* that thrives on our preoccupation with attitudes. Corporations spend hundreds of millions of dollars attempting to divine the attitudes of consumers toward their products, packages, and institutions. Companies devote millions of man-hours conducting interviews to discover work-relevant attitudes of potential hirees. Consulting companies generate six-figure revenues from conducting surveys of employee attitudes. Mayors follow the latest studies ranking their communities on the "quality of life," knowing such data immeasurably influence public attitudes toward their cities. A key player on any big-time politician's team is the pollster who tracks voters' sentiments about the candidates. You can scarcely depart any restaurant or hotel without encountering some attempt to record your feelings.

The concept of attitude is more than just a central concept in social psychology. It holds an equally important status in the economics and politics of the late 20th century.

Why are so many resources allocated to the measurement and interpretation of attitudes? Undoubtedly, the major reason is the assumption that attitudes, in some fashion, *mediate* the influence of the "real world" on behavior. People actively perceive their environment and attach *meaning* to what they perceive. Objects are not merely perceived; they are related to other objects, they are interpreted, and they are evaluated. Ultimately, we respond as much to this internal construction of meaning as we do to the object itself. We cannot understand behavior in organizations without reference to this covert process by which meaning is constructed. Therefore, we must examine how attitudes mediate overt responses to external stimuli. Figure 7–1 diagrams this mediating role.

WHAT IS AN ATTITUDE?

Interestingly, while social psychologists agree on the indispensability of attitude as a construct, they have not agreed on just how we should conceptualize what an attitude is (McGuire, 1985).

Attitude as Affect Some theorists (Berkowitz, 1980) favor the simplest possible rendering, which is a conception of attitude as a feeling or emotional response to a person, object, or idea. In this approach, your attitude toward your supervisor is the degree of positive or negative *affect* (feeling) you have toward that individual. What you *think* about the person and how you *act* toward the person would go beyond the attitude itself.

The rationale for this simple, bare-bones conception of attitude is that feeling, thinking, and behaving are semi-independent processes (Zajonc, 1980). For example, emotional responses (such as liking or disliking)

FIGURE 7–1

Mediating Role of Cognitive Processes

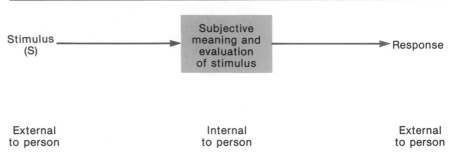

toward persons or things can be *conditioned* by the mere presence or contiguity of those persons or things with other objects that already evoke an emotional response. Studies reviewed by Zajonc (1980) strongly suggest that we can have positive or negative feelings about objects even before we have had the opportunity to process any information about them. These feelings do not invariably forecast our behavior in any precise way. I have positive feelings about products that I have never purchased and I have negative feelings about people toward whom I nevertheless act quite congenially. In principle, feelings can be measured in terms of certain predictable physiological processes without reference to either knowledge or voluntary behavior. For example, the electrical conductivity of the skin increases when a person experiences an emotional response, and this galvanic skin response (GSR) can be calibrated fairly precisely when the individual is presented with a potential attitude object (Dickson & McGinnies, 1966).

Attitude as Affect Plus Cognition   An alternative conception would define attitude as an assemblage of affect (feeling) with *cognition* (belief). In this approach, not all beliefs or opinions are attitudes, since some beliefs (for example, the belief that a tomato is a fruit rather than a vegetable) do not engage our feelings. But neither would all feelings qualify as attitudes—a loud noise can trigger an emotional response regardless of whether we have any beliefs about the cause or significance of the noise. This approach is preferred by Jones and Gerard (1967), who treat an attitude as the "implication of combining a belief with a relevant value" (p. 159) and regard the underlying structure of an attitude as a sort of "syllogism." For example:

> Invasion of privacy is bad,
> Random drug testing invades privacy,
> Therefore, random drug testing is bad.

This conception of attitude requires some preexisting or higher-order value, along with one or more beliefs about how some object or person relates to that value, and results in a derived feeling toward that object or person. Thus, according to Leavitt, Pondy, and Boje (1989), "attitudes provide the meeting place of the emotional and reasoning sides of people" (p. 133).

One implication of this approach is that a person's *values* provide the anchor for attitudes, which develop through beliefs about how various objects and persons relate to those values. A person's value system is presumed stable and resistant to change, but attitudes toward specific objects can change if the person has cause to alter beliefs about how those objects promote or militate against basic values.

Rokeach (1982) has suggested that we distinguish between *terminal* and *instrumental* values. Terminal values, while quite abstract, represent the ultimate qualities of life—harmony, personal success, wisdom, happiness, beauty, physical pleasure. Theoretically, the terminal values that a person holds most dear should enable us to predict with some success that person's attitudes, provided of course we know something about the person's beliefs. Instrumental values, on the other hand—feelings about efficiency, hard work, honesty, obedience, self-reliance—are derived values representing an abstract belief about the qualities that would promote terminal values. Attitudes toward more specific objects then form around beliefs about the relationship between those objects and instrumental values.

Fishbein and Ajzen (1975) offer a plausible and intuitively appealing model to account for attitudes, taking an attitude as the weighted sum of a person's beliefs about something. Each belief links to a value; each value has a greater or lesser, positive or negative, quality; and each belief linkage is weighted by the degree of confidence a person has in that belief. In Figure 7–2 we represent three different attitudes toward random drug testing in the workplace. Different individuals interpret random drug testing in the context of different sets of values—a safe workplace, invasion of privacy, healthier employees, violation of due process, greater efficiency—and differing beliefs about the efficacy of random drug-testing in promoting those values. Double pluses or minuses indicate stronger values, single plus or minus a weaker value, solid lines represent strong confidence of beliefs, dashed lines denote less confidence of belief. How would you characterize the overall attitude toward random drug testing in the three different cases?

Values are more stable than attitudes, but values can and do change over longer intervals, especially the attitudes of successive generations. Focus on the Future summarizes how some writers have characterized the changing values of the work force since the 1950s and how they project these changes into the 1990s.

FIGURE 7–2
Three Attitudes toward Random Drug Testing in the Workplace

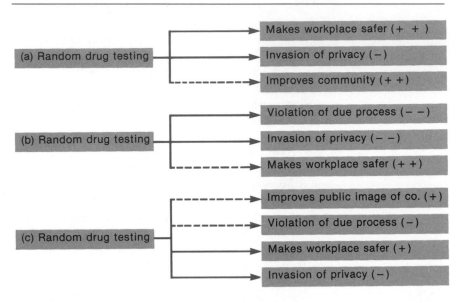

Attitudes as Affect, Cognition, and Response Tendencies Finally, some attitude theorists prefer to think of an attitude as a hypothetical construct containing affective, cognitive, and behavioral components (Rosenberg & Hovland, 1960). Thus, your attitude toward your boss includes your feelings toward that person, your beliefs (or knowledge, however gained) about the person, and also your *inclinations* to behave in certain ways toward that person. If you held a positive attitude toward your immediate superior, there are all sorts of things you *might* do—such as voluntarily spend more time in casual conversation with this individual, or defend this person against the disparaging comments of a co-worker or outsider—whether you actually do them or not.

The major argument against defining an attitude so as to include a behavioral component is the fact that questionnaire measures of people's feelings and beliefs seldom predict subsequent behaviors very well (Wicker, 1969). We can behave politely, even warmly, toward people we privately dislike, and we can have positive feelings about many products we have never purchased.

Behavioral components are included as part of an attitude because attitudes are usually measured by reference to a behavior—for example, the behavior of answering some questions either orally or in writing. Persons who favor random drug testing in the workplace will answer certain questions differently than those opposed to such testing. Thus, one has to assume that at least *verbal* behavior represents some part of the individual's attitude.

Also, by qualifying the behavioral component as response *tendencies,* we are not requiring that any particular overt behavior (other than verbal behavior) actually be demonstrated, only that *given the appropriate circumstances, such behavior would be observed.* Appropriate circumstances would include a situation in which the attitude was activated (made consciously relevant; Calder & Schurr, 1981), the means and opportunity of emitting the behavior were at hand, and no countervailing attitudes were engaged.

A very sizable literature has accumulated concerning the predictability of behavior from measures of attitudes. The findings are not wholly consistent, but the following conclusions have support:

1. *Measures of general attitudes seldom predict specific behaviors well.* Your attitude toward labor unions in general might not affect your behavior toward a particular union local president in your community. On the other hand, when the attitude about a specific object is measured, the correlation between attitude and a specific behavior improves. Measures of attitudes about specific political candidates have successfully predicted whether or not people vote for those candidates.

On the other hand, measures of more general attitudes predict behavior better to the extent that we observe people's behavior across a wide spectrum of possible behaviors in varied settings over time. Your general attitude toward unions might not predict anything you or I would do today; tomorrow it might predict whether you buy a raincoat with a union label, and next month it might predict whether I cross a picket line at the neighborhood grocery store.

2. *Attitude measures predict behavior only to the extent that the situation does not limit the freedom of behaving in the manner suggested by the attitude.* If you have an unfavorable view of unions, but your job requires membership, and supporting the union is a precondition for maintaining good relations with co-workers, then your behavior will not likely reflect an antiunion attitude. If you moved to a different area and obtained a job in a nonunionized plant, there would be more freedom to express the attitude in overt behavior.

3. *Attitudes may remain latent until something activates them.* You may have a strong attitude about unions, but your day-to-day environment may contain nothing to trigger that attitude—you do not encounter union members, you do not discuss politics or the national economy, you purchase products that do not identify whether they come from unionized plants, your life is not disrupted by strikes or other work stoppages. Clearly there is no basis for predicting any important aspects of your behavior from a pencil-and-paper measure of your attitude.

4. *Attitudes predict behavioral intentions better than they predict behavior.* Research generally supports the model proposed by Ajzen and Fishbein (1977): Attitudes determine behavioral intentions, but the relationship between intentions and actual behavior depends on the *specificity* of those intentions. Specificity pertains to the intended action itself, the target of the action, and the time and circumstance of the action. The more specific an

FOCUS ON THE FUTURE

What Will Work Values Be in the 90s?

Myers and Myers (1974) suggested that many supervisory problems are symptoms of "clashing or poorly understood value systems" (p. 7). Clashing values are likely when different levels of management represent values formed in different eras.

People who came of age in the 1940s and 1950s (most of whom would now approach retirement) formed values influenced by the Depression of the 1930s and World War II. They valued security, hard work, loyalty to the organization, self-discipline, efficiency, frugality, and respect for authority. Their heroes were military leaders (Douglas MacArthur), disciplinarians (Oklahoma football coach Bud Wilkinson), and captains of industry and manufacturing (GM President Charles E. Wilson, IBM leader Thomas Watson).

The generation of the 60s and 70s matured in an era of affluence, which they took for granted; the Depression was ancient history and World War II a background for B movies with John Wayne. Compared to their forebears, they placed stronger values on personal freedom, self-development, egalitarianism, and defiance of authority structures and authority figures—while disdaining efficiency and material wealth. Their heroes were the activists who took on the Establishment: Cesar Chavez, Martin Luther King, Jr., Robert Kennedy, Ralph Nader.

The 1980s, according to *Newsweek*'s first issue of 1988, were symbolized by the "Yuppie" (Young Urban Professional) profile of values. "Material success became a kind of free-floating standard of excellence," all the more so if accompanied by conspicuous, tasteful, elegant (and nonpolluting) consumption—no U. S. generation in this century saved so little of its considerable income. Hard work was valued to the extent it quickly led to status and fortune—not as a developer of character, a means of production of

intention with respect to those four dimensions, the more likely that the intention will be translated into actual behavior. Most people intend to "pursue a more healthful lifestyle," but how many ever do it? On the other hand, someone who intends to go for a two-mile walk by the river this afternoon, or eat red meat no more than three times a week, is more apt to carry through.

Our own inclination is to go with the definition of attitude as a tripartite system of affect (feeling or emotion), cognition (belief or knowledge), and behavior (response tendencies). Empirical support for this position comes from Breckler (1984). However, the distinctions among the three positions we have described are perhaps more apparent than real, at least for our purposes. The work-related attitudes in which we are interested—attitudes tangible goods, or long-run security. Loyalty to an organization seemed outmoded in the light of overnight corporate takeovers and divestitures. Heroes were the young wheeler-dealers on Wall Street, venture capitalists, and the envied line-up on Robin Leach's "Lifestyles of the Rich and Famous."

But, says *Newsweek,* "decades are not a function of a calendar time. They are trends, values, and associations, bundled up and tied together in the national memory." Symbolically, the 1980s ended with the 500-point plunge of the Dow on Oct. 19, 1987. Greedy moneychangers went out of fashion and Yuppie-bashing was in.

What values will take on new strength in the 90s? *Newsweek* discerned some prophetic overtones in: a trend of rising applications to academic programs in social work and education; an increase from 29 percent in 1982 to 49 percent in 1987 of polled adults who reported involvement in "any charity or social-service activity, such as helping the poor, the sick, or the elderly"; a turning away from marathoning and aerobicise to plain old walking; rejection of the anorexic or sculpted body and new tolerance for plumpness; increased fondness for quiet evenings at home

rather than going out. In other words, more appreciation for the values of altruism, public service, kinship, and clanship, with a rejection of narcissism and egocentrism.

But we should heed the findings of James A. Lee (1988). He notes that "near the end of each decade, there is inevitably an increase in the number of articles predicting vast changes in the way managers will manage, the way they will view their authority and their subordinates . . . ." His research, however, indicates very little change from 1965 to 1986 in the rankings managers gave to 15 characteristics of the ideal manager. The only shifts that were statistically detectable were a slight decline (on average, from seventh to ninth) of "respect for authority" and a marginal increase (from eleven to nine) on the ranking of "willingness to take risks."

SOURCES: S. P. Robbins (1989), *Organizational Behavior* (Englewood Cliffs, NJ: Prentice Hall); M. S. Myers and S. S. Myers (1974), "Toward Understanding the Changing Work Ethic," *California Management Review* 16, 7-19; "The Eighties Are Over," *Newsweek,* January 4, 1988; and J. A. Lee (1988), "Changes in Managerial Values," *Business Horizons* 31, 29-37.

toward supervision, various forms of pay systems, imminent changes in the organization, people in other departments, prejudices for or against certain groups of individuals—would almost certainly involve some mixtures of feelings, opinions, and action tendencies.

DIMENSIONS OF ATTITUDES

Attitudes that seem similar can be quite different. To understand the meaning of an attitude, it is necessary to know more than just whether the person favors or opposes some object, or what beliefs the person associates with the attitude.

Attitudes vary in *intensity,* that is, the strength of the emotional response (Katz, 1960). Two bus drivers may both have negative attitudes toward random drug testing and have similar beliefs about what the effects of drug testing would be. Yet one has very strong feelings on the matter, while the other is less emotionally involved. We would expect, then, that the two drivers might differ in their response to a proposal by the urban transportation director that bus drivers actually be tested periodically on a random basis for substance abuse. Also they are likely to differ in their susceptibility to persuasive arguments about the benefits of such a program. And we would expect individuals who are more emotional in general to display more intensity in any attitude.

Attitudes also vary in *centrality,* or the relevance of the attitude to a person's self-concept. To someone whose father and grandfather were pioneering unionists, whose upbringing was suffused with a working-class consciousness, a prounion attitude is part and parcel of that person's sense of identity. A worker whose union sentiments relate only to economic self-interest is less likely to make the attitude a central self-concept component.

The *interconnectedness* of an attitude refers to the connections of that attitude to other attitudes. For some employees, their attitude concerning preferential hiring practices for certain minority groups is a question of pragmatism—will it "do some good" as far as the company is concerned. For others, this attitude is intricately bound up with many other attitudes of a political, philosophical, or social nature.

Attitudes, even when indistinguishable from each other as measured by questionnaire or survey, can have either an *active or passive* character. An active attitude is at the forefront of a person's consciousness and is easily evoked by a large class of environmental stimuli (Calder & Schurr, 1981). A passive attitude stays in the background of a person's thoughts, only coming to the surface when a person is asked to express feelings about the object of the attitude. Survey after survey shows that a huge majority of American workers report generally positive attitudes about their jobs. But for many respondents these attitudes are almost certainly passive in nature; most of the time they are scarcely aware of their job attitudes.

The *specificity versus generality* of an attitude is another important dimension. You may have a very positive disposition toward unions in general, yet despise a particular union official. You could think little of the French in general, yet hold in high regard the writings of Sartre. You might feel good about your job in general, but complain about the low pay.

Why do we note these various dimensions of attitudes? The characteristics of the attitude can determine how resistant it is to change—especially how resistant it is to persuasive arguments. You would expect attitudes that are intense, interconnected, and central to persevere longer than others. Also, these characteristics moderate the relationships between measured attitudes and overt behaviors. Active and specific attitudes are more likely to direct a person's behavior than passive or general attitudes.

Keep in mind the rather complex, precarious relationship between attitudes and recurrent behavior patterns. Administrators may have good reasons for wanting to survey work-related attitudes at regular intervals and to take reasonable steps to promote positive attitudes, but they should not assume that proper attitudes constitute a sufficient basis for productive behavior. Attitudes have weak effects on behavior unless the situation facilitates and supports the behavior. You might be strongly in favor of a clean, tidy workplace, but you are not likely to engage in regular tidying up if competing behaviors provide more immediate reinforcement.

THE CONSISTENCY PRINCIPLE

People seek to maintain consistency or "fit" between the affective, cognitive, and behavioral components of an attitude. We try to maintain a semblance of harmony regarding our feelings, beliefs, and actions with respect to some object or person. Heider's Balance Theory (1946), Osgood and Tannenbaum's Congruity Theory (1955), and Festinger's Theory of Cognitive Dissonance (1957) all underscore our concern with minimizing any inconsistency between the components of an attitude.

Perfect consistency is seldom attained for long; at times, we all act contrary to our beliefs and feelings, or feel one way while our beliefs point in the other direction. Perhaps a more appropriate version of the consistency principle would be: Within the limits of our freedom of action and a reasonably sane perception of reality, we seek to maintain a consistent thrust in our emotions, beliefs, and observable behavior.

What is particularly instructive is to note how either of the three components, once activated, generates forces to bring the other two components into alignment.

Beliefs → Feelings, Behavior

The consistency principle seems quite plausible and familiar if we start with the belief component. Given a set of beliefs about some object, it seems obvious that our feelings and behavior toward the object would follow quite naturally. If you believe that a union would maximize your wages and benefits, improve your working conditions, and protect you from unfair management practices, you would feel very positive about the union and would probably contribute time, effort, and money to support it. To this extent, you would illustrate what Katz (1960) terms the "rational model" of attitudes. This model of social attitudes was emphasized by the Greeks, the Renaissance scholars, and the 19th-century exponents of the inevitability of human progress. It also forms the basis for the institutions of a democratic society. The rational model assumes that knowledge and understanding precede actions and emotions; that our minds control our impulses and our passions.

Behavior → Beliefs, Feelings

The consistency principle is not limited to the case in which feelings and behavior follow from beliefs. The principle's power lies in the less obvious predictions that belief may *follow* from either feelings or behavior.

CLOSE-UP

Attitudes in the Workplace: Discoveries by the Hawthorne Researchers

The studies conducted in the 1920s at the Hawthorne plant of the Western Electric Company produced the first serious analysis of attitudes in the workplace. In particular, the massive interviewing program, in which over 20,000 workers and supervisors participated during 1928–30, stimulated the development of a rather sophisticated conceptual framework for understanding work attitudes. Though working without the benefit of social psychological theories, which were as yet ill-formed, the Hawthorne researchers anticipated much of the later development of attitude theory (Roethlisberger & Dickson, 1964):

1. Attitudes are mixtures of fact and sentiment. In some instances the fact could be unambiguously confirmed or refuted. But in many cases "fact and sentiment are inextricably mixed so that verification in most cases is impossible" (p. 265).
2. A "logic of sentiments" (p. 263) exists quite distinctly from the logic of facts. For example, a negative feeling toward A may generate a similar feeling about B, even though there is no factual connection between A and B. Attitudinal consistency is not synonymous with logical consistency.

3. Attitudes have both a manifest content and a latent content (pp. 266–67). Manifest content refers to a person's conscious and verbally reported associations with his or her feelings. Latent content is the underlying, more subtle origin or cause of the person's mood. Thus, workers may complain about the physical conditions of work, taking this to be the cause of their discontent, when the real source of the problem is a vague sense of diminished status.
4. Intense attitudes distort a person's perception of the environment. "Certain events grew to have such a distorted emotional significance for the employee that his capacity for effective discrimination was greatly reduced" (p. 292).

And, perhaps, most important:

5. Job attitudes are not shaped solely by the work environment, but often derive from a person's nonwork experiences. "Apart from such a [broader] context they [sentiments] are meaningless. They cannot be assessed apart from the situation of the individual" (p. 265).

Aronson (1973) reports several experiments in which subjects were induced to take actions they assumed would hurt another person (although the injury was actually faked). The subjects were later asked their opinions of the victim. Subjects described the victim in unfavorable terms (stupid, dull, mean, unattractive). Apparently, the subjects needed to derogate their victims, to attribute unfavorable traits to them, in order to justify their actions. Furthermore, those subjects with the highest self-esteem—in other words, those who regarded themselves as kind and fair—apparently had the greatest need to justify their cruelty. Accordingly, they assessed the injured party most negatively. The point is that the behavior came first, and both feelings (dislike of the victim) and beliefs (about the victim's traits) had to fall into place consistent with the behavior.

The need to keep beliefs consistent with behavior can even override objective feedback contrary to those beliefs. In a study by Staw (1976), subjects played a management game in which they had to allocate capital funds to one of two projects. Whichever project was chosen, the game was rigged to show later that the project was not succeeding; at that point subjects had the option of putting the remainder of their funds to a different use. Instead, the subjects seemed to be strengthened in their beliefs that more money should be allocated to the failing project. And, the worse the venture seemed to be doing, the more money they allocated to it.

This phenomenon of "escalation of commitment" appears to have broad relevance to organizations. Supervisors who voted for hiring specific individuals later gave more positive performance ratings to those persons than did supervisors who rated personnel on whom they had not previously voted. Conversely, supervisors who voted against candidates who were hired anyway later rated their performance lower than the performance ratings given by supervisors to personnel on whom they had not voted (Schoorman, 1988).

In his autobiography (1764), Benjamin Franklin told of a political figure who was antagonistic to Franklin and constantly fought against Franklin's programs. As it happened, Franklin wanted a copy of a certain book, which no one in Philadelphia had except his opponent. Franklin called on the man and asked if he might borrow the book. The man lent him the book, and thereafter he and Franklin got along famously, both personally and professionally. Franklin derived a rule from the experience: If you want to convert an enemy into a friend, ask a favor of him. If he does the favor, he is behaving favorably toward you, and thus will be disposed to like you and entertain positive beliefs about you.

A classic study capitalizing on a natural experiment demonstrated how attitudes changed as a consequence of the organizational role enacted by an individual (Lieberman, 1956). During a three-year period, the researcher measured the attitudes of employees in two appliance plants on three different occasions. Between the first and second measurements, 23 of the original employees became foremen and 35 were elected by their peers to be union stewards. Initially, there was no difference between these two subgroups in attitudes toward the company, its management, the union, or on seniority versus ability as the determinant of pay increases. The second round of attitude measurement revealed that those promoted to foreman entertained a more favorable attitude toward the company and generally supported merit-based pay; those who became union stewards shifted attitudes toward increased support for the union and for seniority as pay criterion. About two years later, half of these subgroups had returned to their original roles; the data showed that their attitudes shifted back toward their original levels.

There are limits to the effect of behavior in generating consistent feelings and beliefs (just as there are limits to the effect of beliefs in generating correspondent behavior). Our behavior impels our beliefs only to the extent that the behavior *cannot be justified independently of our beliefs.*

You are required by law, and by the possibility of imprisonment, to pay taxes, so paying your taxes does not generate any need to have positive beliefs about taxes or the government. Your job may require you to gush with praise and kindness toward a client, your boss, or work associates, but that doesn't mean your opinions of these people match your behavior. But, to the extent that our behavior is not explainable by external incentives, our beliefs and feelings tend to be consistent with it.

Feelings → Beliefs

The "rational" model of attitudes gives cognition the causal priority over affect. That is, our interpretation and appraisal of objects or people determines how we feel about them (Lazarus, 1968). There is also growing evidence to support the contrary position: our feelings about something may precede our understanding, appraisal, or even recognition of the object (Zajonc, 1980). Most of us have had this experience when meeting a stranger, or seeing a picture of a person, or even hearing the name of a stranger. Instantly, and unaccountably, we have some sense of liking or disliking the person. After we become aware of this emotional response, we begin to analyze what causes it. If the emotional response persists, we usually search for beliefs about the person—that is, inferences about the person's traits or dispositions—that would justify our feelings. Hollywood producers test-marketed movie titles in the 1950s to ascertain the theater-going public's affective response (Spoto, 1983, pp. 244-45). They realized that people can react positively or negatively to a movie from the title alone, without knowing who or what is in the movie. Certainly much of the advertising of commercial products is aimed at generating emotional response rather than substantive beliefs.

Rosenberg (1960) conducted a study in which 11 white subjects who opposed integrated housing were hypnotized and induced to feel positively about blacks moving into white neighborhoods. No reasons were given as to why they should feel this way. Rosenberg predicted that, after awaking from the hypnotic trance, the subjects would not only feel as they had been instructed, but would also spontaneously shift their beliefs about the consequences of a racially mixed neighborhood. The findings supported his prediction. A change in feelings or affect necessitated a change in belief or cognition.

Because emotional responses are more or less involuntary, they can be classically conditioned to objects or persons purely on the basis of temporal and situational associations. Such responses are not necessarily rational or logical, or even conscious. We may like, dislike, or fear objects, not because of their own intrinsic merits or properties, but because they were present when emotional responses were triggered by something else, or because they resemble what triggered the response. Because we like to think of ourselves as rational, and like to present ourselves to others as rational and consistent, we tend to select or generate cognitions (beliefs) that match the emotional response.

Not all social attitudes are irrational, impulsive, or illogical; frequently our emotional responses follow from what we know or perceive. We have some capacity to suppress affect until our search for information allows a more reasoned response. Even when affect precedes cognition, the process can be quite rational, as we seek to explain why we experience a certain emotional response. The important point is that attitudes can originate from any of the three components and that the striving for consistency occurs throughout the attitude structure. Beliefs may "cause" corresponding feelings and behavior. But our behavior may also cause our beliefs and feelings, and our feelings may determine our beliefs.

SOURCES OF ATTITUDES

Direct Experience   Some attitudes are formed from our experience. Experience with an object or person provides the most straightforward cognitions we can acquire about that object or person, as well as the reinforcing or punishing consequences of behaviors with respect to that object or person. Attitudes developed in this manner—even on the basis of the most limited, unrepresentative, and fragmentary experience with a person or object—will persevere despite more "objective" information. For example, if your rental car on a vacation happens to be a Buick LeSabre (your first experience with this make of car) and the transmission goes on the fritz—leaving you stranded at a motel in a small town for three days—chances are you will have a negative attitude toward this product for a long time. No matter what friends, *Consumer Reports,* or *Car and Driver* say about how good this automobile is, based on extensive tests and rigorous surveys of user opinions, you most likely will hold to the attitude based on your experience. Studies by Regan and Fazio (1977) and Fazio and Zanna (1978) indicate that people have more *confidence* in opinions based on direct experience and that attitudes formed in this manner better predict subsequent behavior than attitudes based on second-hand information. Thus, someone who has experienced frustrations working for a particular woman may develop an attitude resistant to women in management.

Direct experience has a powerful effect on general attitudes because personal experience is more vivid and graphic, and as a consequence is more "available" at any moment to our thinking processes (Tversky & Kahneman, 1974). Phrased differently, the attitude based on a single direct encounter probably is more active than one derived from more abstract information.

Mere Exposure   In general, people tend to be more favorably disposed toward those objects and persons with which they are most familiar. In fact, repeated exposure to a specific stimulus may breed positive sentiments toward that stimulus even in the absence of conscious awareness of such exposure (Moreland & Zajonc, 1977). This is why political candidates spend so much money on bumper stickers, posters, and media ads: Mere repetition of the candidate's name will lead citizens to vote for a familiar name regardless of whether the voter knows anything more about the candidate. This effect is particularly noticeable in the presidential primaries (before candidates have been strongly linked to stands on specific issues) and political races for less visible offices, such as state assemblyman or county council. Advertisements for many products—such as aspirin, beer, shampoo—aim more for brand recognition among buyers than the dissemination of any substantive knowledge about the product. Frequent exposure induces a low-grade positive emotion, which—in accord with the consistency principle—may also spread to beliefs and to response tendencies.

Exposure and repetition can, at some level, cause irritation, especially if repetition is concentrated in too brief an interval. You have probably heard a commercial jingle on television so frequently within one evening's viewing that you actually detested the ad and the product as well. But for the most part, the idea that "familiarity breeds contempt" has less empirical basis than the fact that "familiarity breeds content." Put simply, people come to like what they can recognize.

Those who propose significant changes in the operations and structure of organizations almost invariably provoke fierce resistance among a significant proportion of the people affected. Some of this resistance occurs because of threats to the material interests or status of some parties, but part of this phenomenon is due to our more positive attitudes toward the familiar as opposed to the strange. If changes are introduced gradually and in a more or less benign fashion, the same principle means that what people initially dislike will take on a more positive aura with increased exposure.

Socialization   Only a small portion of our attitudes are based on direct experience or exposure to the objects or ideas in question. Our beliefs, feelings, and general action tendencies evolve in a more roundabout, derivative fashion.

First the family, then increasingly other agents of socialization (the school, the church, and the peer group) shape attitudes through a variety of methods. Through the process of *operant conditioning,* these agents provide approval, status, and other rewards for voicing correct attitudes, while sometimes punishing incorrect sentiments. In light of the consistency principle, the more subtle and tenuous such reward and punishment processes are, the more likely the behavior thus shaped will exert forces toward correspondent feelings and beliefs.

Socializing agents also inculcate the fundamental values, often through the process of *classical conditioning.* In some traditional Jewish families, when a child first begins to read, a drop of honey is placed on a printed page and the child tastes the sweetness of the honey to associate pleasure with reading the book. Such practices shape the legendary strong values placed by the Jewish community on education and learning.

Much of what we know—as belief or fact—comes to us filtered by authority figures and the groups with whom we interact. Few of us learn by direct experience that smoking causes pulmonary disease, that merit pay for teachers improves or worsens the education of children, or that new technology will eliminate jobs. We learn such things from "expert opinion," "war stories" told by others, and to considerable extent from "opinion leaders" in our circles of friends and work associates.

Finally, *models* are important in the acquisition of attitudes, as with so many other forms of learning. We attend to models characterized by attractiveness, status, and competence. Whether the model in question is Daddy, the Eagle Scout in the troop, Michael Jordan, or a successful woman executive, emulating that individual often involves incorporating his or her expressed attitudes.

Ego-Defensive Attitudes   Katz (1960) has argued that some attitudes evolve to protect the self-image from the otherwise logical but disturbing implications of certain information.

Our attitudes often emerge or change to be consistent with our actions. If our actions harm people, and we have no prior basis for justifying such acts, we have a dilemma. How can we think well of ourselves yet know that we have without good reason hurt others? The tension created by such dissonance may prompt us to derogate those we hurt. We impute crass motives, inferior qualities, or undesirable traits to such persons—"they deserved it." Such beliefs allow us to defend our own egos from the damaging implications of our actions.

Undoubtedly many decent middle-class citizens who acquiesced in the Nazi treatment of Jews felt pressed to defend their self-images by groping for beliefs that Jews were Communist sympathizers, enemies of the Reich, or at least mercenary parasites. In our own country, those who supported the quarantining of Japanese-Americans in the panic on the West Coast that followed Pearl Harbor felt similar needs to rationalize their treatment of innocent people. Those who have actively or passively discriminated against women, blacks, or ethnic groups may defend their self-images by belief systems that ascribe inferior traits or abilities to them.

Ego-defensive attitudes may arise when we feel threatened by others. Older managers are often intimidated by brash young graduates with awesome technical skills—especially if the Young Turks make a point of emphasizing these differences. The older manager, to fend off the painful implication that he has become inferior, in defense may impute to these junior officials lack of judgment and common sense, arrogance, or narrow focus.

Unfavorable attitudes held by people in one group often cause the self-fulfilling prophecy to occur in the behavior of the stereotyped group. The self-fulfilling prophecy, in turn, provides a justification for actions toward the stereotyped group. If you, as a male, say that women are unqualified for top management positions and that therefore you won't train them for such positions, sure enough, women remain unqualified for the positions, and they know it as well as you do. Women thus may come to believe that they are unqualified only because they have been discriminated against, and both men and women are then justified in their attitudes—the men for believing that women are inferior at certain tasks and the women for feeling that men are biased and prejudiced. The research of Rosen and Jerdee (1976) has shown that older people are perceived to be significantly less capable of meeting creative, motivational, and productive job demands, even though the actual performance of older people does not support this belief.

Value-Expressive Attitudes   Many attitudes prevent individuals from revealing their true nature to themselves and others, but other attitudes give positive expression to one's central values and to the type of person one conceives oneself to be. Katz (1960) says, "Value-expressive attitudes not only give clarity to the self-image but also mold that self-image closer to the heart's desire" (p. 170).

Many of the attitudes espoused by professional groups (scientists, physicians, writers, accountants) serve to articulate the fundamental values to which their vocation subscribes. Scientists, for example, place a premium on the free and unencumbered pursuit of knowledge. This value becomes the point of departure for assessing many dimensions of work, organizations, and relationships. Similarly, a person who strongly endorses the Protestant work ethic's values of hard work and self-denial will tend to voice attitudes toward specific persons or practices as a means of reflecting this value. Values deeply embedded in a person's self-image remain somewhat ill-formed until expressed in some fashion. Expression is easier when values are attached to specific objects in the form of attitudes. The consistency and interconnectedness of these attitudes define the value and enable the person to communicate his or her self-image.

ATTITUDE CHANGE

In general, attitudes change for much the same reasons they arose in the first place. For example, consider the attitude that many of our colleagues in academe and business initially held toward the personal computer. In the early 1980s, when PCs first appeared in offices, homes, and show windows, many professional people responded with either cool indifference, detached amusement, or outright hostility. They argued that PCs were just expensive

Yuppie toys and that they wasted time rather than saved it. These sentiments probably functioned as a cover for the more basic impulse to resist what was new or to rationalize the unwillingness to take the time to learn how to use these newfangled gadgets.

Less than a decade later, while we might still find a few stalwart defenders raging against the PC invasion, multitudes of professionals have done an about-face in their attitudes. The reasons? What initially seemed so new and foreign is about as familiar as the old Remington typewriter or the Bic pen. No office or study even looks right without a monitor perched atop the desk. Also, direct experience with PCs perhaps initially with video games, or using a PC to look up a book in the library—yielded a bit of positive reinforcement. Models (colleagues, work associates) demonstrated how convenient these instruments could be for a multitude of tasks.

Those who railed against PCs for ego-defensive reasons (those who felt threatened by something they may be unable to learn how to use, and thus feared a loss of status or damage to self-esteem) gradually realized there was no cause to feel threatened. Computers and software became increasingly user-friendly and no longer intimidating. Furthermore, people began to link personal computing to such values as efficiency, neatness, order, independence, and self-sufficiency—even aesthetics.

The more general view concerning attitude change derives from the Consistency Principle. If one of the three components—affective, cognitive, behavioral—undergoes sufficient change to arouse the sense of inconsistency in the attitude system, the other components will follow suit. Furthermore, if change occurs in an attitude that is central to a larger system of attitudes, the same desire for consistency will exert a force for change in related attitudes.

A change in behavior that cannot be justified by strong external pressures often leads the individual to express beliefs and feelings consonant with the new behavior. To use this principle to change someone's attitude means that you must induce that person to act overtly in a fashion at odds with the person's original attitude. Yet you must do so in a way that does not present the person with "an offer he cannot refuse." That is, to use coercion or bribery might change the behavior, but your target would then feel justified in acting contrary to the attitude, and thus provide no compelling cause for changing originally held beliefs and feelings.

The "foot in the door" technique (De Jong, 1979) represents one means of inducing attitude change via behavior. The essence of this method—perhaps best known to us as a sales technique—is initially to request, in the most low-key manner, a more or less token response in the general direction toward which you hope to move an attitude. For example, someone trying to overcome your resistance to drug testing in the workplace might begin by asking you to sign a petition endorsing the "obligation of management to support the war on drugs." No harm in that, is there? Maybe you wouldn't agree to do even this, but maybe you would, since it would not seem to commit you to anything specific. Subsequently, you might be asked to secure the signed names of three other persons to this statement—thus escalating, however modestly, your active involvement. Or you might be asked to distribute to friends a few pamphlets describing the costs to industry of substance abuse. At some point your level of active involvement induces a reappraisal and perhaps revision of some of your earlier beliefs concerning the pros and cons of drug testing of employees, in your need to present a consistent line to yourself as well as to others.

No doubt the most frequent method of attempting attitude change, however, is through persuasion.

FACTORS DETERMINING THE EFFECTIVENESS OF PERSUASION

Persuasion is a process in which a source effects change in a target's attitude by changing key beliefs relevant to that attitude. Public officials and commentators have been interested in this process for many years, since they are so concerned with public opinion. Social psychologists have perhaps invested more of their resources into researching persuasion than any other single topic. The research has focused mainly on characteristics of three factors: the source, the message, and the target.

The Source   Highly credible sources are more effective in changing beliefs than less credible sources. A respected professional such as Dr. Kenneth Cooper has a better chance of changing your thinking about exercise than would a disc jockey or a garage mechanic.

The effect of source credibility appears to be greatest when the target actually receives the message. Some studies offer disturbing evidence of a "sleeper effect" in persuasion: as time passes after initial receipt of the message, highly credible sources lose some of their impact, while less credible sources exert greater effect on attitude change. The sleeper effect is shown graphically in Figure 7–3. After a few weeks, the target may be affected almost equally by messages from more or less credible sources. One possible explanation for this is that, with the passage of time, targets disassociate the content of the message from its origin. This phenomenon gives cause for some concern, since it suggests that rumormongers and charlatans, in the long run, may influence opinion nearly as much as experts.

Some recent studies and reanalysis of earlier ones raise some question about the genuineness of the "sleeper effect": Gillig and Greenwald (1974) suggest that the drop in effectiveness over time of a high-credibility source is not matched by a corresponding increase in the effectiveness of the low-credibility source.

FIGURE 7–3

The "Sleeper Effect" of Source Credibility on Persuasion

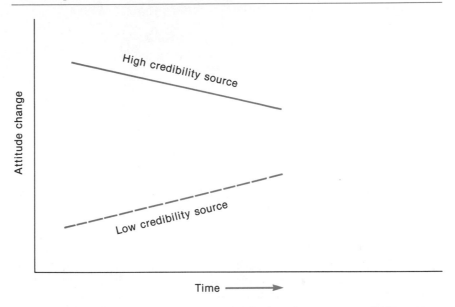

Qualifications and reputed competence, of course, bear very strongly on the credibility we impute to a source. There is also the question whether the source stands to benefit from the target's change in attitude. Even granting Dr. Kenneth Cooper's expertise in exercise physiology, his credibility might suffer if he were known to have financial interests in jogging shoes that he publicly endorsed. A manager's lack of persuasiveness may be due to subordinates questioning not the superior's expertise but his or her motives.

The source can increase the chance of effective persuasion by doing or saying something at the outset that suggests a kinship with the target. This is a time-honored technique among politicians, public officials, commencement speakers, and probably effective managers. The political candidate visiting a rural hamlet almost invariably remarks on his or her own small-town roots and usually opens the speech with some kind words about the community.

Such warming up to the recipient or audience presumably lowers the defenses of the latter. It increases the probability that the target will actually try to comprehend the source's arguments and softens any initial resistance on the part of the target. Of course, if the warming-up technique comes across as blatant, insincere ingratiation, the effect may be just the opposite.

According to the Focus on Management, one reason for the diminished credibility of top-level executives among the rank and file in many large organizations is the gulf that separates them in terms of working conditions, experience, and their respective shares of the spoils of victory. Lower-level

FOCUS ON MANAGEMENT

The Credibility Gap

According to a recent *Fortune* article, "Missives from the boardroom are met increasingly with disbelief, not just by the 'little people' but by everyone below VP. The Hay Group calls these doubters 'the fraternity of skeptics.' " A poll that asked middle managers, professionals, and hourly workers "When top management puts out information, how do you feel about it?" found that all three groups were less likely to have a positive response in 1988, compared to five years earlier. The Hay Group concludes that the attitudes of middle managers and professionals are becoming more like those of the hourly manager.

The apparent causes of the credibility (or trust) gap stem from the disproportionate share that top level managers take from the fruits of either success or failure. Average CEO compensation tripled from 1979 to 1988, while hourly production pay increased a much more modest 50 percent (barely exceeding the cumulative inflation of the

decade). Corporate-level managers are viewed as inhabiting their own separate world of luxury and perks, having never worked in the trenches and having no sense of either the problems or the sentiments of the rank-and-file.

What would close the credibility gap? According to *Fortune,* a sharing of the risks, such as the 60 percent cut in pay that President Ken Iverson of Nucor Steel took when his company went through hard times; more frequent appearance by company officers in face-to-face briefings, "drinking coffee from styrofoam cups and sitting in plastic molded chairs"; softening the distinctions between ranks in such things as office size, parking lots, and luncheon places; and perhaps mandatory tours of duty by all, including those with MBAs from elite schools, in hourly level jobs.

SOURCE: "The Trust Gap," *Fortune,* December 4, 1989.

employees (including some professionals and managers) almost automatically discount the relevance of messages from top officials because they are unable to see any common interests or shared perspective.

The Message   Should an advocate present only one side of the issue or acknowledge the contrary view as well? The research record suggests that a two-sided message is usually more effective at changing the target's beliefs. This is probably because a two-sided message has more credibility. Furthermore, the two-sided approach has a particular advantage over the one-sided attempt when the target is (1) intelligent, (2) familiar with the issue, or (3) clearly in initial opposition to the source's position. Any advantage of the one-sided approach seems to be limited to an audience not familiar with the issue (and therefore having few strong existing beliefs to begin with) or already in agreement with the source. Even in these situations, the effectiveness of a one-sided message may be short-lived. A series of

CLOSE-UP

The Two-Sided Sales Pitch

Two-sided messages in advertising were virtually nonexistent until recently. But Swinyard (1982) suggests that consumers may be more receptive to such ads than to the traditional "our product is best in every respect" theme.

William Swinyard took advantage of the opening of a new grocery store to conduct a field experiment in the design of advertising fliers. Half of the fliers mentioned only those store characteristics (lower prices) in which the new grocery outlet compared favorably to competitors. The other fliers, in addition to describing the store's good points, admitted that "We don't bag, we have no magazine rack, and there is no in-store bakery." Telephone interviews with housewives who received the two-sided fliers revealed that they were more likely to believe the claims about its good features.

Swinyard argues that the two-sided sales pitch may be particularly appropriate for complex products (cars, personal computers, appliances) that consumers appraise on many separate, independent dimensions.

studies by McGuire (1964) strongly suggests that exposing the target to contrary views and simultaneously refuting them makes the target less vulnerable to future persuasive arguments.

Will a message's persuasiveness be enhanced by playing on the fears of a target? Political candidates have sketched grim pictures of nuclear holocausts and starvation among elderly citizens that will come about if their opponents attain office; managers and owners have on occasion predicted that their pleasant environs would turn into vacant, rusted-out factories and windswept ghost towns if workers voted in a union; voluntary healthcare organizations have shown smokers the charred lungs of a deceased, two-pack-a-day addict. What is the effect of such appeals to emotion?

Janis and Feshback (1953) lectured to three groups of high school students on the importance of good dental hygiene. The first group heard a presentation with minimal use of fear-arousing tactics; the second heard a talk with a moderate appeal to fear; and the third group was exposed to rather scary pictures of the consequences of neglecting dental hygiene (bleeding gums, rotten teeth). A fourth group served as control subjects. The results, as measured by students' responses to a questionnaire one week later about their conformity to good dental hygiene habits, showed the minimum-fear appeal to be most effective (36 percent net change in conformity with prescribed practice), followed by the moderate-fear appeal (22 percent); the strong-fear message was least effective (only 8 percent net change).

The authors reasoned that arousal of strong emotion in the form of fear arouses the target's defenses; it interferes with the covert rehearsal of the arguments presented. The target, in a sense, "blocks out" the threatening stimuli. One suspects this would happen most frequently among those people predisposed to emotional upset. Recently one of the authors asked an acquaintance if she had seen pictures shown by animal protection groups of dogs caught in leg-traps or of commercial hunters bludgeoning baby harp seals in the Arctic. She replied that she avoided looking at such ads because they upset her. Therefore the ads never had the intended effect of inducing her to mail a contribution to the animal protection group or otherwise become active in their cause.

Yet in some instances, research has demonstrated the effectiveness of a strong fear-arousing approach. These are situations in which the source can somehow prevent the target from screening out the threatening stimuli and can specify immediate constructive steps to alleviate the fear. Such situations would require an unusually high level of control by the source (one-on-one doctor/patient interaction) and are not representative of most environments in work organizations. Managers who use such appeals may either tarnish their credibility or acquire a generally threatening aura that leads to avoidance behavior by subordinates.

The Target   With source and message characteristics equated, what kinds of people are most likely to bend to persuasive arguments?

The research on personality factors that might correlate with persuasibility has produced few consistent findings. The evidence suggests that persons with low self-esteem yield to persuasive messages more often and to a greater extent than high-self-esteem individuals; also, high-self-esteem people characteristically attempt to exert more influence via persuasion than do their low-self-esteem counterparts. McGinnies (1970) suggests that low self-esteem and high persuasibility "stem from the same type of previous experience, namely negatively reinforced instances of argument with others. That is, individuals who have systematically been punished for disagreeing with . . . others may come to agree . . . with greater frequency" (pp. 393–94).

Research through the mid-1960s also suggested that females were more persuasible than males. Females were more apt to have been reinforced for acquiescence (especially to male authority figures) than for assertiveness. Changing cultural demands and expectations in this respect suggests that sex differences in persuasibility have diminished in the last decade or two.

Studies reviewed by McGinnies (1970) show that the initial attitude of the target determines to some extent how successful a persuasive message will be. Those who previously hold extreme attitude positions tend to show more resistance to a persuasive message. Moreover, the discrepancy between the position advocated in the message and the position of the target is important. If the discrepancy is minor, little change in attitude results. This is apparently because the target, to fend off pressures to change beliefs, displaces the perceived position of the source in the direction of his or her own presently held attitude. In other words, the target interprets the message as supporting his or her own position. On the other hand, if the position advocated is extremely different from the target's, the recipient may exaggerate the discrepancy to reduce the credibility of the source. Therefore, the source must take some account of the present attitude extremity of the audience in order to fashion a message that has an optimal degree of discrepancy — not too little, not too great — with the attitude of the audience.

Alternative Routes to Persuasion   Under some conditions an army can succeed by a frontal assault on the enemy's forts; under other conditions it may be more effective to do an end-run around fortifications. According to the *elaboration likelihood model* (ELM) of cognitive response to persuasive messages (Petty & Cacioppo, 1985), a similar distinction can be drawn between two routes of persuasion: *central* and *peripheral.*

The central route to persuasion directly counters a person's beliefs and invites careful and intensive analysis of the issues. This approach attempts to engage the target's full attention to consider the relevant facts and the logic and implications of the arguments, and then extrapolate from them.

Obviously, for a message to do this and successfully change any opinions, the arguments have to to be sound, the documentation impressive, and the information overpowering. Also, the target must be sufficiently *involved* in the issue to follow through the intricacies of the information and argument, and the target must not be distracted by irrelevant demands on his or her attention.

The *peripheral* route to persuasion does not depend so much on the actual substance of the message, because the target is not induced to give the message careful scrutiny anyway. Instead, the real emphasis is on the characteristics of the source (such as status, expertise, or attractiveness) or some nonsubstantive property of the message (such as the sheer number of arguments, statistics, graphics). The content of the message might actually be weak in logic or authenticity of the data. Clearly, weak arguments would not change a person's beliefs, *if* the person attended carefully to them and covertly rebutted them. But if the individual were distracted and had little opportunity or inclination to "shore up defenses," even weak arguments might lead to effective persuasion.

The ELM provides a convenient larger framework for sorting out the otherwise inconsistent empirical findings in the literature on persuasion, as well as pointing to the comparative advantages of various media of persuasion. For example, the finding that source credibility and attractiveness determine the persuasiveness of a message holds true only for attitude change via the peripheral route — when the intended recipient is likely to be distracted or is not sufficiently involved in the issue to give the message careful scrutiny. Under conditions of low distraction (the central route to persuasion), the quality of the arguments determines attitude change and the characteristics of the source add nothing to the effectiveness of the message (Petty, Wells, & Brock, 1976). Thus, the ELM also provides a plausible explanation for the sleeper effect. Also, the ELM suggests that simplistic, repetitive messages work best for some media (television, radio, placards) while carefully constructed, rigorous arguments work best in other formats (printed media, intensive one-on-one encounters). Finally, the ELM would seem to support the case for certain media and message formats adapted to the peripheral route when the "shotgun" effect for a large, heterogenous audience is the target. Alternative formats fashioned for the central route make more sense for a "rifle"-type focus on a small, specialized audience strongly involved in the issue.

THE BOOMERANG EFFECT

Sometimes, the attempt to change someone's attitude will result in a change in attitude in the opposite direction. Daddy tries to persuade little Tommy to like asparagus, and instead Tommy hates it more than before. A manager tries to persuade subordinates to accept a new work procedure, and they resist the procedure even more fiercely.

Brehm (1972) explains that a person is aroused when he or she senses that a personal freedom is threatened. This arousal, which Brehm calls psychological reactance, leads the person to assert or restore that freedom. The more important the freedom is felt to be, the greater the reactance. When the magnitude of reactance is large relative to the persuasiveness of the message, there is the possibility of the boomerang effect. In other words, the person is likely to assert the freedom by a change in attitude opposite to that intended by the source.

What conditions are likely to trigger reactance and a corresponding boomerang effect? Heller, Pallak, and Picek (1973) demonstrated that a clear perception of someone's intent to change our attitude may be sufficient to arouse reactance. However, the greatest reactance is generated when evidence of intent is coupled with strong pressure exerted by the source. This pressure may be perceived because of the content of the communication (a one-sided, unfair, or distorted presentation of the evidence) or its tone (shrill rhetoric, appeals to fear, or implicit coercion). In general, our resistance hardens when someone is trying too hard to make us change our minds. Perhaps this is why so many efforts to enact sweeping changes in organizations meet with stubborn opposition.

Brehm (1972) notes that not all attempts to persuade arouse reactance. Reactance is most likely to occur when there is a perceived threat to those freedoms one considers most important. What kinds of attitude freedom do most people seek to preserve?

People are jealous of their freedom with respect to attitudes that are central to their self-concepts. Attempts to change such attitudes represent attempts to change their identities. Consider workers who like to use certain materials and procedures because they are closely linked to their self-images as meticulous artisans. A supervisor trying to alter their sentiments toward those methods is, perhaps unwittingly, striking at the core of their vocational self-images. It would not be surprising if, in response to influence attempts, they defended their freedom to hold such attitudes by valuing their procedures and materials all the more.

Also likely to arouse assertions of freedom are challenges to attitudes that are tightly connected to other attitudes comprising an ideology. For example, trying to change a client's attitude about some political issue could represent a challenge to a broad array of liberal or conservative values. The target of this attempt might well demonstrate reactance and a boomerang effect in order to preserve the integrity of his or her ideology.

Given the risk of a boomerang effect—which may include alienation from the source—should we avoid any attempt to change someone's attitudes? If the attitude has little relevance to job duties and job performance, the possible gains are not worth the risks. If the attitude is central to a person's self-concept, ideology, or ego-defense, the attempt to change the attitude could do more harm than good.

An attempt to change behavior by way of changing attitudes is not automatically less coercive—and less reactance-provoking—than simply dealing with the behavior per se. Oddly enough, we invite less resistance when our actions say, "You've got to do it, even though you don't like it," rather than "You'll do it this way, and you'll like it!" Ultimately, it is people themselves who change their own attitudes. Persuasive messages and alterations in the stimulus environment might initiate the sequence that results in attitude change, but in the final analysis, people change their attitudes when they are good and ready to do so.

We emphasize this point as a precaution to the reader against viewing attitude change as a matter of artful manipulation or a quick and easy exercise in propaganda. To be sure, some individuals have more talent than others at selling a point of view, at least in a series of hit-and-run encounters. But when you live with people in a sustained relationship, influencing attitudes does not lend itself to machinelike simplicity. In a democratic culture, people are conditioned to think of their attitudes and opinions as matters of rights, and attacks on them are not taken lightly.

Also, many persons regard attitude change as an instance of the broader pattern of reciprocity in social exchange between individuals. This suggests, as Costello and Zalkind (1963) have noted, that managers should stand ready to amend their own attitudes when it is timely and appropriate to do so. Such a posture increases the chances that they will find their subordinates receptive to persuasion. Attitude change is a two-way street; subordinates expect reciprocity.

SUMMARY

Attitudes—whether defined simply as the evaluative feelings a person holds with respect to an object, person, or idea, or generalized to include relevant beliefs and response tendencies—mediate the effect of the external stimulus world on overt behavior. Attitudes predict behavioral intentions better than they predict actual behavior, but the extent to which they predict either can depend on certain characteristics of the attitude (its centrality to the person's self-system, its active-passive dimension, its generality versus specificity) and certain characteristics of the situation (the presence or absence of attitude-relevant stimuli and the practicability with which attitude-related behaviors could occur). A large volume of research supports the general idea of a Consistency Principle, according to which people strive for a psychological congruence among the feeling, belief, and behavioral components of an attitude. Attitudes are both learned and changed directly through experience and indirectly through varied agencies of socialization. Both operant and classical conditioning, as well as modeling, account for much of the process in which such learning occurs. The functions of ego-protection and value-expression also enter into attitude formation and change. The more general principle underlying the dynamics of attitude change is the notion of introducing inconsistency into one of the components of the attitude system, prompting additional changes in other components to restore consistency. One strategy based on the Consistency Principle is to induce counter-attitudinal behavior; another is the attempt to use persuasion to alter beliefs. The effectiveness of persuasion depends on certain characteristics of the source, the message, and the target; the elaboration likelihood model explains why the effects of these characteristics vary from one instance to another. Under certain conditions, the attempt to change attitudes produces a boomerang effect, or change in the direction opposite to that intended.

CONCEPTS TO REMEMBER

Specificity of attitude	Attitude centrality	Value-expressive function
Affective component	Interconnectedness	Knowledge function
Cognitive component	Elaboration likelihood model	Persuasion
Behavioral component	Psychological reactance	"Sleeper effect"
Consistency principle	Ego-defensive function	Boomerang effect
Attitude intensity		

QUESTIONS FOR DISCUSSION

1. Sears, Roebuck and Company has had a department for surveying employee attitudes since 1939. This unit surveys the attitudes and opinions of all stores and their employees every three years, an un-

dertaking costly in time and money. Why do you think Sears would spend millions of dollars to do this? How do you think Sears uses this information?

2. How do advertisements for consumables (such as cigarettes, soft drinks, beer, and paper towels) differ from those for durables (such as automobiles, cameras, and lawn mowers)? Why do you think these differences exist? Try to account for these differences in terms of the components of attitudes, the functions attitudes serve, and the appropriate strategies for influencing different types of attitudes.

3. Why do political campaign managers concentrate their resources on the uncommitted voters?

4. Are attitudes rational or irrational? Explain.

5. In what instances should a manager avoid even trying to change a subordinate's attitude?

6. Are opinions the same as attitudes? If so, why? If not, what is the difference?

REFERENCES

Ajzen, I., & Fishbein, M. (1977). Attitude-behavior relations: A theoretical analysis and review of empirical research. *Psychological Bulletin* 84, 888–918.

Allport, G. W. (1935). Attitudes. In C. Murchison (ed.), *Handbook of social psychology.* Worcester, MA: Clark University Press, 798–844.

Aronson, E. (1973). The rationalizing animal. *Psychology Today,* May, pp. 46–52.

Berkowitz, L. (1980). *A survey of social psychology,* 2nd ed. New York: Holt, Rinehart & Winston.

Breckler, S. J. (1984). Empirical validation of affect, behavior, and cognition as distinct components of attitude. *Journal of Personality and Social Psychology* 47, 1191–205.

Brehm, J. W. (1972). *Responses to loss of freedom: A theory of psychological reactance.* New York: General Learning Press.

Calder, B. J., & Schurr, P. (1981). Attitudinal processes in organizations. In L. L. Cummings & B. M. Staw (eds.), *Research in organizational behavior,* vol. 3. Greenwich, CT: JAI Press, 283–302.

Costello, T. W., & Zalkind, S. S. (1960). *Psychology in administration.* Englewood Cliffs, NJ: Prentice Hall.

De Jong, W. (1979). An examination of self-perception mediation of the foot-in-the-door effect. *Journal of Personality and Social Psychology* 37, 2221–39.

Dickson, H. W., & McGinnies, E. (1966). Affectivity and arousal of attitudes as measured by galvanic skin responses. *American Journal of Psychology* 79, 584–89.

The eighties are over. (1988). *Newsweek,* January 4, 40–48.

Fazio, R. H., & Zanna, M. P. (1978). On the predictive validity of attitudes: The roles of direct experience and confidence. *Journal of Personality* 46, 228–43.

Festinger, L. (1957). *A theory of cognitive dissonance.* Evanston, IL: Row-Peterson.

Fishbein, M., & Ajzen, I. (1975). *Belief, attitude, intention and behavior: An introduction to theory and research.* Reading, MA: Addison-Wesley.

Franklin, B. (1964). *The autobiography of Benjamin Franklin.* New Haven: Yale University Press.

Gillig, P. M., & Greenwald, A. G. (1974). Is it time to lay the sleeper effect to rest? *Journal of Personality and Social Psychology* 29, 132–39.

Heider, F. (1946). Attitudes and cognitive organization. *Journal of Psychology* 21, 107–12.

Heller, J. F., Pallak, M. S., & Picek, J. M. (1973). The interactive effects of intent and threat on boomerang attitude change. *Journal of Personality and Social Psychology* 26, 273–79.

Janis, I. L., & Feshback, S. (1953). Effects of fear-arousing communications. *Journal of Abnormal and Social Psychology* 48, 78–92.

Jones, E. E., & Gerard, H. B. (1967). *Foundations of social psychology.* New York: John Wiley & Sons.

Katz, D. (1960). The functional approach to the study of attitudes. *Public Opinion Quarterly* 24, 163–204.

Lazarus, R. S. (1982). Thoughts on the relations between emotion and cognition. *American Psychologist,* 1019–24.

Leavitt, H. J., Pondy, L. R., & Boje, D. M. (1989). *Readings in managerial psychology,* 4th ed. Chicago: U. of Chicago Press.

Lee, J. A. (1988). Changes in managerial values. *Business Horizons* 31, 29–37.

Lieberman, S. (1956). The effects of changes in roles on the attitudes of role occupants. *Human Relations* 9, 385–402.

McGinnies, E. (1970). *Social behavior: A functional analysis.* Boston: Houghton Mifflin.

McGuire, W. J. (1964). Inducing resistance to persuasion. In L. Berkowitz (ed.), *Advances in experimental social psychology.* New York: Academic Press.

McGuire, W. J. (1985). Attitudes and attitude change. In G. Lindzey & E. Aronson (eds.), *The handbook of social psychology,* 3rd ed., vol. 2, 233–346. New York: Random House.

Moreland, R. L., & Zajonc, R. B. (1979). Exposure effects may not depend on stimulus recognition. *Journal of Personality and Social Psychology* 37, 1085–89.

Myers, M. S., & Myers, S. S. (1974). Toward understanding the changing work ethic. *California Management Review* 16, 7–19.

Osgood, C. E., & Tannenbaum, P. H. (1955). *The principle of congruity in the prediction of attitude change. Psychological Review* 62, 42–55.

Petty, R. E., & Cacioppo, J. T. (1985). The elaboration likelihood model of persuasion. In L. Berkowitz (ed.), *Advances in experimental social psychology,* vol. 19. New York: Academic Press.

Petty, R. E., Wells, G. L., & Brock, T. C. (1976). Distraction can enhance or reduce yielding to propaganda: Thought disruption versus effort justification. *Journal of Personality and Social Psychology* 34, 874–84.

Regan, D. T., & Fazio, R. (1977). On the consistency between attitudes and behavior: Look to the method of attitude formation. *Journal of Experimental Social Psychology* 13, 28–45.

Robbins, S. P. (1989). *Organizational behavior.* Englewood Cliffs, NJ: Prentice Hall, 120–21.

Roethlisberger, F. J., & Dickson, W. J. (1964). *Management and the worker.* New York: John Wiley & Sons.

Rokeach, M. (1973). *The nature of human values.* New York: Free Press.

Rosen, B., & Jerdee, T. H. (1976). The nature of job-related age stereotypes. *Journal of Applied Psychology* 61, 180–83.

Rosenberg, M. J. (1960). Cognitive reorganization in response to the hypnotic reversal of attitudinal affect. *Journal of Personality* 28, 39–63.

Rosenberg, M. J., & Hovland, C. I. (1960). Cognitive, affective, and behavioral components of attitude. In M. J. Rosenberg, C. I. Hovland, W. J. McGuire, R. P. Abelson, & J. H. Brehm (eds.), *Attitude organization and change.* New Haven: Yale University.

Schoorman, F. D. (1988). Escalation bias in performance appraisals: An unintended consequence of supervisor participation in hiring decisions. *Journal of Applied Psychology* 73, 58–62.

Spoto, D. (1983). *The dark side of genius: The life of Alfred Hitchcock.* Boston: Little, Brown.

Staw, B. (1976). Knee-deep in the big muddy: A study of escalating commitment to a chosen course of action. *Organizational Behavior and Human Performance* 16, 27–44.

Swinyard, W. (1982). The interaction between comparative advertising and copy-claim variation. *Journal of Marketing Research* 18, 173–86.

The Trust gap. (1989). *Fortune,* Dec. 4, 56–78.

Tversky, A., & Kahneman, D. (1974). Judgment under uncertainty: Heuristic and bias. *Science* 185, 1124–132.

Wicker, A. W. (1969). Attitudes versus actions: The relationship of verbal and overt behavioral responses to attitude objects. *Journal of Social Issues* 25, 41–78.

Zajonc, R. B. (1980). Feeling and thinking: Preferences need no inferences. *American Psychologist* 35, 151–75.

8 Dimensions of Individual Differences

How are personality concepts formulated and measured?

How do personality concepts figure in theories of OB?

How valid are personality concepts?

What are the important dimensions of personality?

How can the organization effectively accommodate diverse personalities?

"You have to be cut out for this job. Some people can get along in it, others couldn't. It depends on what you're cut out for."

These words did not come from a stockbroker, air traffic controller, or other highly specialized professional, but from a janitor who worked in a residence hall where the first author lived during graduate school. In utter simplicity, they express something we all intuitively know is important: individuals differ, and these differences must somehow be addressed by models of organizational behavior.

What accounts for the individual's uniqueness? To begin with, every individual — except pairs of identical twins — has a unique set of genes. Heredity sets the boundaries within which later states of development occur. To the extent that the central nervous system, hormones, and sense organs govern behavior, the individual's unique genetic base will account for some difference among people. To what extent nature or heredity determines individual differences is a matter of considerable controversy. Recent evidence (see the following Close-Up) adds weight to the view that a significant portion of what we call personality has an underlying genetic origin.

Each person also has a unique history of reinforcement, or background. It has long been recognized that parents respond differently to later-born children than to the firstborn. They are really different parents the second time around, having been changed by the experience of parenting the first child. As individuals are drawn into the expanding circles of different peer groups, subcultures, and institutions, these differences in reinforcement history accumulate. Some of these early effects will wash away; others will leave imprints that endure.

The ultimate effect of both heredity and reinforcement history, as far as organizations are concerned, is that organizational environments do not write on a blank slate. Such environments will have their effects, but the effects will be stronger on some than others, and will sometimes run in opposite directions for different people. Differences in organizational environments — in reward systems, job design, supervisory styles — will account for some observed behavior, but neither research nor informal observation has shown that such factors account for all of the behavior in organizations. The remaining variance must be chalked up to differences in characteristics of people. There is no way to argue with the oft-cited dictum of Kurt Lewin that $B = f (P, E)$: behavior (at a given time) is a function of both the individual personality and the environment. A current (and preferred) rendering of this statement asserts that behavior, the person, and the environment all reciprocally affect each other.

The Role of Personality in OB

Weiss and Adler (1984) have noted the following four ways in which personality constructs enter into theories, research, and application of OB.

CLOSE-UP

Personality: How Much Is Due to Genetic Differences?

To address the question of nature versus nurture as determinant of personality, psychologists have often compared the similarity in personality of monozygotic (identical) twins with that of dizygotic (fraternal) twins. Identical twins have identical genetic structure, while fraternal twins are no more similar in genes than nontwin siblings. Such studies, dating back to over a century ago, have always found much greater similarity in personality in identical twins. This evidence was never as conclusive as it might be, because most identical twins share the same environment as well as the same genetic package, and one could reasonably argue that identical twins are apt to be treated more similarly by parents, friends, other siblings, and teachers.

An ambitious study conducted by psychologists at the University of Minnesota has succeeded in bringing together 44 pairs of identical twins who were separated at birth or soon thereafter. These twins were mature adults when reunited and were tested on numerous measures of personality,

mental abilities, occupational interests, aesthetic preferences, physical characteristics, and sexual and medical histories.

The findings from this study published to date generally confirm—indeed, virtually duplicate—results of previous studies of twins reared together. The evidence from twins reared apart suggests that roughly *half* of the variation in such traits as extroversion, dominance, masculinity-femininity, conformity, flexibility, impulsiveness, emotionality, and need for achievement is genetically determined; and that more than a *third* of the variation in occupational interests is also due to heritability.

SOURCE: T. J. Bouchard, Jr., "Twins Reared Together and Apart: What They Tell Us About Human Diversity," in *Individuality and Determinism,* ed. S. W. Fox (New York: Plenum Press, 1984); and T. J. Bouchard, Jr., D. T. Lykken, N. L. Segal, and K. J. Wilcox, "Development in Twins Reared Apart: A Test of the Chronogenetic Hypothesis," in *Human Growth: A Multidisciplinary Review,* ed. A. Demirjian (London: Taylor & Francis, 1986).

1. *As a direct, independent variable.* Some personality concepts add to the explanatory power of environmental variables in accounting for behaviors of interest. We know that people will be absent from work less often if the organization has a program that rewards good attendance. But even without such a program, individuals with certain strongly held values are more likely to demonstrate good attendance records, and probably did so in previous jobs or in school.

2. *As moderator variables.* A moderator variable alters the strength or direction of effect that an independent variable has on a dependent variable. Thus, the overall effect of a close, structured, supervisory style on subordinate productivity may be practically nil when compared to a more loose, unstructured approach. But this result could be a "washout": favorable effects of close supervision on those with low self-esteem or self-confidence can be cancelled out by unfavorable effects on confident individuals who react negatively to what they see as heavy-handed bossism.

3. *As dependent variables.* In the short-run, personality is a given. But prolonged exposure to certain strong organizational forces will gradually have an effect in changing people. The bureaucratic personality is familiar as an exaggerated stereotype, but the idea probably contains a germ of truth—years of conditioning to abide by strict rules of procedure will eventually cause "rules-mindedness."

4. *As part of a dynamic system of reciprocal effects.* More realistic—and more complex—models of OB recognize the dynamic interplay between traits and environments over time. Traits can determine the environments people choose, and traits can underlie behavior that alters the environment. Environmental effects can subsequently feed back on the behavior (reinforcing it, punishing it, extinguishing it), thus either strengthening or weakening certain tendencies. In a longitudinal study, Kohn and Schooler (1982) found that people who were more self-directed and intellectually flexible were more likely to seek and attain positions that allowed or required responsibility and latitude. But by the same token, experience in positions that provided responsibility and autonomy increased the individual's flexibility and self-direction.

The Concept of Personality

The concept of personality is indispensable to everyday thinking. It is difficult to imagine in what other way you could think about the people you know. Like most instinctive concepts, personality is difficult to define. But we must be explicit and self-conscious about this construct if we are to bring it into a conceptual approach to organizational behavior.

The concept of personality, as we ordinarily use it, seems to imply something about the characteristic internal states of persons. As Brown and Herrnstein (1975) note:

> We seek to explain the fact that a given constant stimulus has varying effects on the same organism at different times, which leads one to believe that the effect is mediated by changing internal states . . . people differ in the readiness with which they fall into one state or another, and these readinesses are summarized as abiding properties of the organism—traits, temperaments, dominant needs, skills, and so on. [p. 529]

These internal states are inferred from consistency in behavior across different situations. Obviously no one always behaves the same way. We pray in church, whistle in the shower, yell at football games, and argue over the dinner table. But characteristic differences do seem to carry over across a variety of situations. The individual who is quieter than most in church tends to be more reserved at dinner. It is the comparative, not absolute, qualities of behavior that seem to be consistent.

Our native concept of personality includes the quality of stability. Personality is, by our definition, something that endures in its basic elements.

This is not an absolute characteristic—some aspects of personality undergo change under the force of chronically strong situations.

Personality—a person's self—consists of layers of habits and predispositions. The surface layers may change considerably over short periods, as reflected in changing preferences for clothes, entertainment, hobbies, or foods. Other predispositions, such as political leanings or job interests, change only gradually over longer periods, perhaps measured in years. Still more fundamental constituents of the self—temperament, moral values, ultimate purposes—typically change very little except over an appreciable portion of one's life span. We can all point to exceptions, to those occasional individuals who seem to undergo total conversions as a result of some extraordinary experience. Yet, we refer to such rare instances with astonishment, "like a sudden but total personality change." These radical changes occur so seldom that we assume considerable stability in the structure of personality.

Finally, our concept of personality involves the notion of uniqueness. Whatever the "readiness toward internal states," whatever the consistencies in behavior across situations, whatever the underlying characteristics that may persist, they are different for each individual.

Personality Measurement and Research

The empirical study of personality begins with some concept or construct thought to be useful in describing individual differences. Take "persistence," for example. This concept describes some important differences between people and refers to a stable, consistent trait. Some persons are more persistent than others. How do we measure this trait?

The most frequently used method for assessing personality traits is the *self-report* method. A questionnaire is devised and administered to subjects. The list of questions might include such items as:

Do you feel compelled to finish any book once you begin reading it?

If you are interrupted while doing some task, do you return to it as soon as possible?

Does it bother you to leave a crossword puzzle unfinished?

Do you refuse to take no for an answer?

Preferably there would be a dozen or more such questions. The number of questions a given individual answers affirmatively would comprise that person's persistence score.

Self-report measures present a number of problems. We cannot always be sure that people have the ability or the intention to describe their behavior accurately. However, the individual does have access to more information about his or her own behavior than anyone else. Furthermore, sophisticated, professionally developed personality inventories often include some device (such as a subscale of questions) that permits researchers to assess the plausibility of a respondent's set of answers.

Rating scales are also used in personality measurement. With this approach, an observer describes some other person's behavior with respect to some characteristic, such as persistence. Obviously, the observer should be someone who has observed much of the person's behavior. Thus, for a rating scale measure of Joe's persistence, I would turn to people who know Joe rather well—his friends, co-workers, boss, or wife. I would ask them a series of questions such as, "Does he almost always try to finish one task before starting another?"

The presumed advantage of the rating scale over the self-report is that observers are more objective and can better assess and report a person's characteristic behavior. But this advantage is far from absolute. People who know Joe may either like or dislike him, and these feelings could affect their ratings of Joe on some personality dimensions. Also, many who know Joe interact with him only in the context of a specific role, and thus aren't familiar with his total behavior. If Joe is a project manager, his co-workers may witness a lot of persistence on his part, but that is a role requirement. Those who interact with him away from work, or even in previous work roles, might not rate Joe as so persistent.

A *projective* measure of personality requires that a person respond to some ambiguous, unstructured stimulus, such as an inkblot, a cartoon, or a photograph. The person is asked what he or she "sees" in the stimulus, to make up a story about it, or describe feelings about it. The idea here is that the person will reveal much about his or her modes of thought, since the stimulus itself is too ambiguous to elicit standard, predetermined responses. The person's answers comprise a protocol, which is analyzed and scored by a trained clinical or research psychologist. Projective measures are usually less reliable than self-reports or observer ratings, since responses to projective measures require a subjective interpretation of their meaning. However, they may at times reveal more of certain areas of personality because the subject has less chance for artificially structuring responses.

The *behavioral* measure of personality places the individual in a controlled situation to which he or she must react. Some index of the person's overt behavior is used as a score. For example, we might give Joe a problem to solve. Unknown to him, there is no real solution. We observe how long Joe works on the puzzle until conceding failure. The ratio of this time period to the average spent by others could be taken as a measure of Joe's persistence. The advantages of this kind of measure are objectivity and the observation of actual behavior. The disadvantage is that it depends on a small, possibly unrepresentative sample of the person's behavior.

ARE PERSONALITY CONCEPTS VALID?

Is it meaningful to describe individuals in terms of stable, enduring personality traits? Your first impulse probably is to say yes, but some behavioral scientists have engaged in a spirited debate over the answer to that question.

Let us consider what is required for a personality concept, such as honesty, to have meaning and validity. First, there must be a considerable range of variation among people in the extent to which they exhibit honesty. If all people were equally honest, the concept would not be of much use. Second, the people who are more honest in one respect should generally be more honest in other respects. The person who displays more honesty in preparing income tax returns should generally also be more honest when taking examinations, filling out job applications, or playing poker. Otherwise, the concept has no generality. Third, if we have some measure of a person's presumed honesty, whatever the form of that measure, it should help us predict whether that person will be more honest than others in various situations.

Considering the second requirement — generality or consistency across situations — a study by Hartshorne and May (1928) is instructive. They found that school children were markedly inconsistent across situations in their degree of honesty. A child would steal money from a brother or sister but refrain from cheating on a test. The student who would neither cheat on an exam nor steal money might tell a lie to prevent embarrassment. Hartshorne and May's study, taken at face value, suggests that personality trait concepts overstate the consistency of behavior.

Can measures of personality predict behavior? Not very well, concludes Mischel (1968), after reviewing many studies. According to Mischel, even the best questionnaire measures of traits seldom correlate very closely with actual behavior in a controlled laboratory situation. Mischel interprets the evidence as support for the view that situations, not dispositions, account for most of our behavior (he excludes from this statement those individual differences that have to do with intelligence or aptitude).

Mischel's case against the consistency or predictive power of personality is reminiscent of our earlier discussion about attitudes. This is not surprising because traits and attitudes are somewhat alike: they are assumed to represent enduring characteristics of the person, and both are usually measured by self-report. You may recall that measures of attitudes often have low correlations with subsequently observed behavior. However, attitudes will predict behavior better if the behavior is sampled across numerous situations (as opposed to just one specific situation) or in those situations that do not exert strong external forces on behavior.

The same principles hold for the predictive power of personality measures. Epstein (1980) found that a subject's score on a measure of extraversion* seldom predicted any one behavior. However, the score often predicted the person's average behavior over a two-week period covering numerous situations. This point is important to remember as we assess the usefulness of personality concepts in explaining organizational behavior.

---

*Although "extraversion" and "extravert" are the spellings used in many technical contexts, "extroversion" and "extrovert" are more acceptable in standard usage and will be used consistently in this text.

While managers rarely need to predict a person's behavior at a given moment, they do need to project trend lines in behavior over time. Will Joe generally incline toward risk or caution? Does criticism adversely affect his performance or will it usually spur him ahead?

Another principle to keep in mind in assessing the empirical validity of personality traits concerns the strength of situational forces. Mischel (1977) characterizes *strong* situations as those which:

1. Are construed the same by different people.
2. Evoke similar notions among persons as to what responses are appropriate or effective.
3. Provide unambiguous incentives for appropriate behavior.
4. Require skills generally shared among people.

Conversely, *weak* situations are those which:

1. Permit differing conceptions or interpretations.
2. Provide few clues for appropriate behavior.
3. Hold no obvious incentives for one response over another.
4. Do not draw on previously learned stimulus-response connections.

Strong situations swamp the effect of personality differences and leave little room for personality to operate. Weak situations provide little control, leaving the field free for individual differences to manifest themselves.

Monson, Hesley, and Chernick (1982) conducted a study that illustrates this principle. They administered to student subjects a questionnaire measuring extroversion. Then they assigned the subjects to one of three conditions: forced-extroversion, forced-introversion, or neutral. In the forced conditions, confederates (pseudo-subjects who were really aides to the experimenter) were given instructions either to engage the subject in a lively conversation or to keep the other person from becoming involved in interaction. In the neutral condition, confederates neither prompted nor discouraged any form of interaction. Only in the latter condition did the subjects' scores on the extroversion scale correlate substantially with their subsequent behavior. Of additional and related interest, the variability of behavior across subjects was much higher in the neutral condition.

Some organizations have "strong cultures," with traditions, leadership, and peer pressures so consistent and intense that personality differences would have little effect on most work-relevant aspects of behavior. Such cultures deliberately attempt to select those people whose temperament, disposition, and values match those of the culture, and there would be less variance in either personality or in behavior compared to other organizations.

More generally, organizations present varying mixes of strong and weak situations, just as school features some courses with all of the requirements spelled out and others that lend themselves to varying interests, styles of study, and ways to demonstrate learning. Traditionally, administrators have hoped for and attempted strong interventions that would affect everyone the same. But some forecasts of the workplace in the 1990s see trends toward the flex principle: arrangements of work schedules, benefit programs, and participation in governance that cater to different tastes and temperaments. Arguably, personality concepts would have increased theoretical and practical relevance in such a flex-style organization of the future.

Personality Theory and the Manager

Within our constraints in this book, we cannot hope to do justice to the full scope of personality theory and research. We will try to sample some schools of thought that contribute most to an understanding of work behavior and also illustrate various approaches to understanding individual differences.

Approaches that postulate what the healthy or mature personality should be are excluded. We do not reject these clinical points of view, quite to the contrary, we applaud the humanitarian values and concern by which they are inspired. However, we fear that the adage, "A little knowledge is a dangerous thing," applies. We do not want to encourage simplistic judgments as to who is "sick" and needs "mending."

Furthermore, we have not drawn from the ample and extensive psychoanalytic tradition of personality theory. We will make no references to such constructs as the id, ego, superego, oral fixation, anal-retentiveness, or oedipal complex. Our training and expertise in the psychoanalytic or psychodynamic field is much too meager to provide an adequate account of the relevant theories, let alone to apply such models to OB. However, some theorists have drawn freely and with profit from this area to inform their concepts of organization (see, for example, Kets de Vries & Miller, 1984).

The sampling below is quite selective. However, each of the approaches reviewed has shown some utility for organizational behavior in both theory and practice.

APPROACHES TO STUDYING PERSONALITY

A Motive-Based Approach

Some motives or needs — such as those for food, water, sleep, and shelter — are temporary in nature. Our need for food persists only until we are satiated. Then our behavior is directed toward other goals until hunger pangs strike again or until some delicacy (for example, chocolate cream pie) appears in our perceptual field. Other motives are more enduring, more chronic, and less likely to be quickly satiated. The persistence and stability of such motives suggest one approach to studying personality. A stable motive is by definition a preoccupation with certain types of goal objects and thus a predisposition to respond in certain directions.

Atkinson (1958) and McClelland (1961) have discovered a technique for identifying such motives in human subjects. Their technique, called the Thematic Apperception Test (TAT), consists of presenting the subject with a still picture and asking the subject to make up a story about that picture. The picture might show an architect seated at a desk, with blueprints, drafting materials, and a photograph of the architect's family on the desk. The subject is asked to make up a story explaining what has led up to that scene, what the architect is thinking, and what will happen later.

The use of this projective technique is based on the assumption that, given such an ambiguous stimulus, people will project into it their own longings, desires, and goals. Motives are identified by the kinds of imagery or themes that emerge strongly in the subject's story.

Need for Achievement A strong achievement motive is identified by themes in the subject's story that relate to striving for excellence in task accomplishment. Need for achievement (or *n Ach,* as abbreviated by McClelland) reflects a strong goal orientation, an obsession with a job or task. Someone with strong *n Ach,* making up a story about the picture mentioned above, would talk about a challenging assignment that the architect is working on, such as the need to design a bridge that would withstand strong winds, yet also meet the criterion of cost or feasibility.

McClelland (1961) has identified a number of reliable behavioral manifestations of this need. People with high *n Ach* are attracted to tasks that challenge their skills and their problem-solving abilities; they have little interest in games where luck determines success. These persons set difficult but realistic goals that present a success probability of about .3 to .5. They avoid setting goals they think would be almost impossible to achieve or that guarantee success, but prefer tasks whose outcomes depend on individual efforts. If help is needed, they will select competent rather than congenial people. They have a compulsive need for quick, concrete feedback on their performance — especially feedback in precise quantitative terms. Achievement has a special meaning in this context. Scientists, teachers, and artists do not score high in *n Ach,* even though they may realize substantial achievement in a more general sense. They neither need nor obtain quick, unambiguous feedback about their efforts.

McClelland finds that entrepreneurs and managers are likely to have high *n Ach*. Whether in a socialist or a capitalist country, in private business or government, the more effective managers have a sharply focused goal orientation and a drive to compete. They make moderately risky decisions in settings in which they believe they have some control, and they constantly gauge the effectiveness of their decisions and effort by the numbers. McClelland suggests it is no accident that most cartoons set in a business office show in the background a chart with a curve depicting sales, profits, or production.

McClelland believes that the need for achievement is shaped early in life — in part by the culture (through such media as children's readers) and in part by parental styles that encourage children to take responsibility, promote independence, and reinforce achievement. He further asserts that the economies of entire nations rise or fall as a consequence of the culture's influence on the need for achievement, reflected in the development of the entrepreneurial instinct.

Need for Affiliation   A second motive identified in subjects' stories is the need to establish, maintain, or restore pleasant emotional relationships with other people. Persons with strong needs for affiliation *(n Aff)* want primarily to be liked by others; getting along with co-workers is more important than the group's accomplishments. In response to the picture of the architect, such persons emphasize the architect's thoughts about the family in the portrait on the desk: the good times they have had together, how much they mean to one another. Persons with high *n Aff* are more sensitive to other people's feelings than persons with high *n Ach*. They are attracted to tasks involving groups, while high *n Ach* persons prefer jobs that depend only on themselves. As managers, high *n Aff* persons might avoid task decisions that would engender emotional or social conflict.

It is tempting to infer that high *n Ach* persons make better managers than high *n Aff* individuals. However, some concern for affiliation is important if the manager is to develop the group structure and climate necessary for long-run effectiveness.

Need for Power   A third motive is the desire to exert control or influence over people. Unfortunately, this need can suggest something sinister. A strong need for power does not necessarily result in an autocratic or tyrannical leadership style. Winter (1967) found that this need *(n Pow)* could assume either an unsocialized or a socialized expression in college students. In the former case, it was reflected in a desire for sexual conquest or physical aggression. In its socialized form it was manifested by active membership in, or leadership of, student and community groups or organizations that sought constructive ends, such as civil rights, campus reform, and student government.

Managers should have at least moderate levels of *n Pow* to be effective. Otherwise, they would shrink from making decisions and would allow their groups to develop in aimless, uncharted directions. A manager's need for power is quite compatible with a leadership style that stresses the development and participation of subordinates; it does not imply a dictatorship.

The actual expression in behavior of these various motives depends to a large extent on the stimulus cues in the environment. Even a very strong need for achievement will not be manifested in an environment in which there is little opportunity for achievement (as we have defined it). Motives are latent or dormant unless aroused by salient stimulus cues.

A Trait-Based Approach

Allport and Odbert (1936) searched the dictionary and found over 3,000 words to describe personal characteristics. A trait-based approach to personality assumes that these surface traits can be accounted for by a much smaller number of factors (see Figure 8–1). This assumption draws support from repeated observation that many surface traits correlate to some degree with each other within clusters. For example, people who are impulsive also tend to be outgoing, active, prone to take risks, and talkative. Thus, underlying these traits is the construct of some personality factor, whatever we choose to call it.

The personality researcher using this approach typically starts with a questionnaire. Each item or question in the inventory asks the respondent how accurately a statement characterizes his or her behavior. Each item is, in a sense, a question about a trait as expressed in one's behavior or likes and dislikes. The total number of questions may range from 20 to several hundred. When a large sample of subjects responds to the questions, the results are submitted to a statistical treatment known as factor analysis. Factor analysis, taking account of the patterns of correlations between answers, identifies a small number of factors, each of which underlies a cluster of traits. However, the exact number of factors that emerges depends somewhat on judgment; it is not wholly determined by the data. Because of this, advocates of a trait-based approach have

FIGURE 8–1

The Trait-Based Approach to Personality

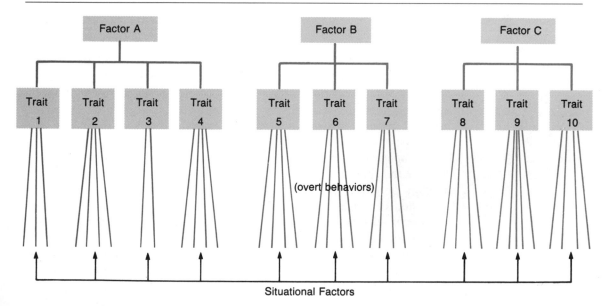

differed among themselves as to the number of factors that should be regarded as separate and distinct.

Hans J. Eysenck (1967) believes that two factors capture much of the important variance in measured personality traits. He has called these factors neuroticism and extroversion-introversion.

Neuroticism   Eysenck has interpreted this factor as degree of emotional stability. One might also think of it as predisposition to *negative affect* — the tendency to experience anxiety, guilt, tension, irritation, and other forms of emotional discomfort. Other researchers besides Eysenck have also found this construct useful in tying together correlated traits.

The person who scores high in neuroticism is quite sensitive to conditions of threat — real or imagined. Such a person, the High N, has a lower threshold than the Low N for the stimulus events that trigger emotional arousal in the forms of fear, guilt, or worry. In the work environment, the High N syndrome often manifests itself in the following ways:

1.   *Low tolerance for job ambiguity.* The High N prefers a work situation with explicit supervisory expectations, clear ground rules, and a well-structured task. This need for structure increases as pressure — in the form of serious consequences contingent on success or failure — also increases. We all desire some degree of clarity in our jobs, and we all fret when we are not clear about our responsibilities. But the High N is more apt to experience acute anxiety when confronting an unstructured job situation.

2.   *Need for reassurance.* The High N's discomfort with unstructured work situations arises partly because such situations do not provide reassuring feedback about the appropriateness of one's activities or efforts. The High N needs such feedback, even if only to know that he or she is not royally screwing things up. In the absence of such reassurance, High Ns worry about possible mistakes and tend to undervalue their progress. The High N is motivated by the need to avoid failure and its consequent embarrassment, self-reproach, and guilt feelings. While the Low N adheres to the motto, "In the absence of information to the contrary, I can assume I'm doing just fine," the High N tends to fear the very worst until reassured that this is not the case. Often such a person will fish for such consoling words from the supervisor or colleagues.

3.   *Unstable, job-related self-esteem.* All of us sustain bruises to our egos when we fail (in either an absolute sense, or relative to our own standards or others' progress), just as our egos inflate after success. For the Low N, this fluctuation of self-esteem occurs only moderately, around a fairly stable estimate of self-worth. For the High N, self-esteem is much more sensitive to episodes of success or failure, especially failure. Also, the High N's self-esteem is likely to be less compartmentalized; disappointments in job performance affect not only vocational self-esteem but also feelings of adequacy in other aspects of the self.

4. *Sensitivity to threat.* Sooner or later, every administrator has cause to threaten subordinates. The threat may be implicit, such as presenting negative feedback about someone's performance; it may take the form of an honest warning; or it may become an angrily delivered ultimatum. Mild threat is likely to arouse little anxiety for the Low N; in fact, it may hardly even register. The High N, on the other hand, is likely to be very concerned, even reading into the message something more serious than was intended. Strong threat may be necessary to get the Low N's full attention so that he or she can respond constructively. It could absolutely cripple the High N who may become so anxious that he or she cannot concentrate adequately on a complex task.

Have you ever noticed that some people, after being strongly rebuked for committing some error, work so hard at avoiding that same mistake that they proceed to make five other mistakes? Such people fit our description of the High N. Their easily aroused anxiety causes tunnel vision, a reduced span of perceptual attention. In such a state, a person loses the ability to detect nonobvious cues. On simple tasks, this effect may actually help performance, because it helps block out irrelevant distractions. But on tasks that require a wide attention span—which require a person to attend to a variety of quickly changing events in different parts of the perceptual field—this arousal usually impairs performance.

Ironically, the High N can be said to be overmotivated at times, especially by the concern for avoiding real or imagined aversive stimuli. The adverse consequences of overmotivation take such familiar forms as forgetting one's lines because of stage fright, or drawing a blank on the final exam even though one "knows" the material.

High neuroticism bears no relationship to intelligence or any kind of general aptitude we know of. In and of itself, this trait is neither good nor bad (nor, for that matter, is its opposite at the other end of the dimension). High Ns are in no general sense better or worse prospects for any responsible position of employment. The consensus of expert opinion is that tendencies toward high or low neuroticism are in considerable measure due to genetic factors. Eysenck's hypothesis, which seems to fit a number of findings but has not been demonstrated by direct test, is that differences in neuroticism are related to differential thresholds of arousal in the visceral brain, which integrates the autonomic functions of the sympathetic nervous system (Eysenck, 1967).

If neuroticism in behavior is a product of physiologically based factors, then organizational environments could not appreciably change this personality dimension. However, Kahn and his colleagues argue that the "presence of environmental stress seems to produce 'neurotic' emotional reactions in those who score low on the neurotic anxiety scale" (Kahn, Wolfe, Quinn, Snoek, & Rosenthal, 1964, p. 260). Such symptoms, they admit, may be temporary rather than chronic. Nevertheless, they regard it as plausible that persistent job stress may amplify the individual's tendencies toward the generalized trait of neuroticism.

The perceptive manager can recognize the patterning of symptoms that indicates which individuals might lie at one extreme end or the other of this dimension of personality. From such observations, the manager could make some reasonable predictions about how such persons would react to various forms of supervision, motivational pressures, and job stressors.

Extroversion-Introversion   The dimension of extroversion-introversion is a second broad, underlying trait that historically has figured prominently in the theoretical and empirical work on personality. However, there has been more disagreement about the meaning and interpretation of this dimension than with neuroticism.

We typically use the terms *extrovert* and *introvert* to relate to sociability: extroverts are more outgoing and gregarious, introverts more aloof. The meaning of extroversion in the psychological literature has been broader than this, although sociability may be one of a cluster of surface traits related to extroversion. Jung used the concept extroversion to refer to "the kind of outward orientation that makes a person highly aware of what is going on around him and causes him to direct his energy toward objects and people outside himself" (Tyler, 1965). Introversion referred to the opposite tendency—sensitivity to one's own feelings, memories, consciousness, and inner life.

A contemporary interpretation of extroversion as a personality dimension, as typified in the writings of Hans J. Eysenck (1967), is that extroversion relates to individual differences in the need for external sensory stimulation. In general, extroverts have a greater need for stimulation—in the form of social activities, crowds, adventures, frequent change in the environment, intensity of colors or noises, or drugs. Introverts need less stimulation, and are more often concerned with reducing stimulation from the environment than increasing it. Eysenck also believes that this dimension of personality, like neuroticism, has an underlying physiological basis.

This dimension is a continuous one, and the terms *introvert* and *extrovert* are used only in a relative or comparative sense. Most of us experience both needs at different times or in different proportions. There are occasions when we need to shut out stimulation and other times when we feel starved for stimulation. We try to regulate the flow of stimulation to maintain some comfortable level of subjective excitement. Given Eysenck's interpretation of this personality factor, we would expect extroverts and introverts to differ in those forms of behavior that aim to enhance or reduce stimulation. The extrovert, for example, is attracted to risk taking, especially physical risks. He or she is more likely to be drawn toward such endeavors as skydiving, downhill skiing, motorcycle racing, fast driving, and contact sports. Living close to physical danger, even death itself, is terribly stimulating. The extreme extrovert would probably agree with the words of the poet Robinson Jeffers, "Life and death upon one tether, running beautifully together." The introvert scarcely needs such stimulation.

Extroverts prefer job environments that provide novelty, variety, intermittent bursts of intensity, unpredictability, and spontaneity. Even occasional crises have their appeal. If their jobs or the surrounding context are bland, extroverts will soon look around for other sources of stimulation — practical joking, petty gambling, or making up little games to play. Such distractions help pull the extrovert through the day, but they may occasion some irritation for introverts.

Extroverts sometimes satisfy their need for stimulation from interpersonal and intergroup conflicts. The extrovert may, in dull times, make the most of incidents that provide a pretext for feuding, grievance, and in-house intrigue. The introvert would tend toward emotional exhaustion if such conflict became frequent or intense.

The major job-related problem for the introvert is sensory overload — for example, introverts are much more likely to be bothered by excessive noise (Weinstein, 1978). Introverts prefer predictability, orderliness, and stability in the job environment.

How is the extroversion-introversion dimension important to the study of behavior in organizations? Some implications are obvious. The introvert will usually do better on repetitive tasks or on tasks performed in environments that offer very little sensory stimulation. The extrovert will spontaneously engage in task-irrelevant behaviors to increase stimulation. On tasks performed in environments in which sensory overload threatens (for example, variable noise, random stimulus changes, or distractions), the extrovert will get along better. In short, extroverts are more apt to suffer — either in terms of lower satisfaction or deterioration in performance — from sensory deprivation or understimulation. Introverts more often fall prey to overstimulation, sensory overload, and excitation. As with other dimensions of personality, the differences are most striking at the opposite ends of the distribution.

To date, extroversion has received little attention in studies investigating motivation, performance, and leadership in ongoing organizations. Future research integrating this variable into theories of organizational behavior may increase their explanatory power.

Eaves and Eysenck (1975) report findings from a study of 837 adult pairs of twins that they interpret as strongly supporting the hypothesis of a genetic link to extroversion. Roughly half of the variance in extroversion scores could be attributed to heredity. Moreover, their data also supported the position that both sociability and impulsiveness are traits that derive from the broader dimension of extroversion.

If neuroticism and extroversion are basic yet separate and independent dimensions of personality, one might wonder what sorts of surface-trait

FIGURE 8–2

Trait Patterns Related to Combinations of Levels of Neuroticism and Extroversion

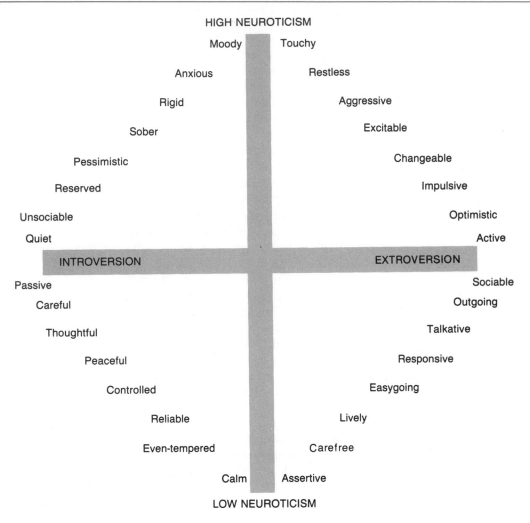

SOURCE: Adapted from H. J. Eysenck, *Eysenck on Extraversion* (New York: John Wiley & Sons, 1973), p. 27.

personality profiles result from a combination of high neuroticism and extroversion, low neuroticism and extroversion, high neuroticism and introversion, and low neuroticism and introversion. Eysenck (1973) suggests that Figure 8–2 presents a plausible classification of traits that emerge. For example, persons high in neuroticism will display different patterns of behavior, depending on whether they are introverts or extroverts. The highly emotional introvert copes with psychic turbulence by turning inward on it—withdrawing from social relationships and dwelling on fears and anxieties. The unstable extrovert copes by expressing his or her emotions, interpersonal aggressiveness, or hyperactivity.

Other Trait Approaches

R. B. Cattell and J. P. Guilford, two of the more prominent theorists of the trait-factor school of personality, believe that Eysenck has gone too far in reducing data from trait inventories to only two major factors. Cattell (1972) argues that, after identifying 16 major dimensions of personality from a very long inventory of questions, no further reduction is possible without distortion of the available data. Guilford (1975) proposes a scheme of 13 first-order factors and four second-level factors: social activity, introversion-extroversion, emotional stability, and paranoid disposition. Guilford also takes exception to Eysenck's formulation of the extroversion dimension, which Guilford calls a shotgun wedding of the traits of sociability and impulsivity—which he (Guilford) believes do not belong together as a factor.

Most of the other eminent trait theorists also believe that Eysenck is premature in pressing for a genetic explanation of these traits and factors, especially in the case of extroversion. They do not rule out heredity as a factor in some predispositions toward certain behavior patterns. But, given the present uncertainty over the number and identification of the underlying dimensions of behavior, they regard any hypothesis about precise physiological origins of these dimensions as speculative at best.

See the Focus on Management for trait-based typology that is currently in vogue in business, particularly in management education and development programs.

A Belief-Based Approach

Weiss and Adler (1984) contend that OB theory, research, and application have overemphasized those individual differences that have to do with motivational dynamics and neglected those dimensions of personality that involve cognitive processes—characteristic belief systems, information-processing styles, and stable differences in modes of perceiving. One definite exception is the work on *locus of control,* a person's generalized belief about the extent of internal (personal) versus external control of important individual outcomes in life.

Julian B. Rotter (1966) developed the theory and original measures of internal-external locus of control. Internals believe their behavior to be relatively decisive in determining their fate. Externals believe their behavior to be less decisive in this respect; they believe that chance, luck, or powerful agencies (persons or institutions) exert strong influence on their fortunes. The issue here is *not* differences in the *amount* of reinforcements, success,

FOCUS ON MANAGEMENT

The Myers-Briggs Type Indicator and Management Development

The Myers-Briggs Type Indicator (MBTI) uses responses to over 100 questions to classify people according to four categories: Extrovert (E) or Introvert (I); Sensing (S: orientation to details) or Intuitive (N: orientation to the "big picture"); Thinker (T: takes a logical, objective approach) versus Feeling (F: more subjective approach); and Perceiving (P: flexible opinions and openness to new information) versus Judging (J: driven to make final decisions and reach closure).

Combinations of the four categories result in 16 possible types. The INTJ (introverted, intuitive, thinking, and judging) type is said to be a Visionary—this type comprises only small proportion of the general population, but a disproportionate number reach the chief executive officer level. A more common type, often found among middle managers, is the ESTJ—extroverted, sensing, thinking, and judging. The Traditionalist is an ISTJ, or introverted, sensing, thinking and judging, and tends to be a stickler for rules and details, and is often found among accountants and finan-

cial executives. The entrepreneur, on the other hand, is usually an ENTP, who hates routine and looks for new possibilities.

Corporations account for 40 percent of the sales of the MBTI measure; prominent users include Apple, AT&T, Exxon, GE, 3M, and Citicorp. Its use is not for hiring or placement purposes but rather for management development programs. Participants learn that differences in types account for some of the perennial problems in communication between people.

While both managers and psychologists remain divided over the question of the underlying validity of either the theory or the measurement of the MBTI, the informal evidence suggests that at a minimum it represents a useful exercise for highlighting differences among people in thinking and problem-solving styles and stimulates efforts within groups to bridge these differences.

SOURCE: T. Moore, "Personality Tests Are Back," *Fortune,* March 30, 1987.

or rewards experienced. Externals may consider themselves very well off. Nor do the differences refer to the amount of power possessed by other entities in the environment. Rather, the differences refer to beliefs about whether outcomes (good or bad) are contingent on behavior.

Rotter's locus of control construct derives from his theory of social learning. Rotter asserts that reinforcers and incentives shape our behavior only to the extent that we believe our behavior actually causes—not merely precedes—such reinforcers. Many *specific* beliefs about personal control are based on either well-confirmed facts or confirming experience. Few individuals really believe they can, by their own behavior, control the weather. But most people know, from repeated experience, that they usually can control whether the lights come on or off. And most of us have our own specialized spheres of experience in work or hobbies in which we have learned how much of what happens is under our control. Rotter believes that in addition to specific beliefs (based on experience) about personal control over success and failure, there is a *generalized expectancy* of internal versus external locus of control. These generalized beliefs exert their greatest effects when we face situations in which the causal structure of events is unclear or when eventual outcomes are far removed in time from present behavior. For example, the generalized internal and the generalized external who are seniors in college will tend to have similar notions (other things being equal) about their degree of personal control over the grades they receive. But when they begin their careers as industrial sales representatives, internals tend to assume that their own behavior will largely determine how things work out. Externals, by contrast, will believe that forces beyond their control will determine their effectiveness. As time goes by, these generalized beliefs about personal control might become less important as repeated specific experiences shape their beliefs. In sum, our beliefs about personal control are a mix of specific beliefs based on experience and a generalized tendency to view one's own behavior as either a strong or weak force in determining one's fate. That tendency is stable, while the specific beliefs change.

An early study (Seeman & Evans, 1962) found that hospitalized internals made more persistent inquiries to the medical staff about the nature, origins, and treatment of their illness than did the externals. Since then, a number of studies have found that internals are more informed about their respective occupations and experience less ambiguity about their jobs. This difference makes sense—if you believe you can affect your own outcomes, it is likely that you will seek information concerning the type of behavior that is appropriate. On the other hand, the greater the weight you attach to forces beyond your control, the less likely you will bother to seek further information. Note that these differences in information-seeking habits could act to strengthen the original beliefs about locus of control. The more you use strategic bits of information to your own advantage, the more you confirm the assumption that you can take charge of your life.

A study by Anderson, Hellriegel, and Slocum (1977) demonstrated how internals and externals differ in response to an unfamiliar situation. The authors interviewed the owners and managers of 102 businesses seriously affected by flooding during Hurricane Agnes in 1972. In general, externals experienced greater emotional stress. Moreover, externals were more concerned about coping with their own tension and frustration, tending to withdraw from the task of rebuilding and to express resentment or woe about the "rotten hand they had been dealt." Internals went immediately to work to acquire new loans, resources, and personnel; to maintain their clientele; and to restore previous levels of production. Obviously, no one could have prevented the storm itself, but the internals had faith that a proactive, problem-solving stance could determine whether the flooding was a conclusive tragedy or only a temporary setback.

Internals, in general, perceive more order and predictability in their job-related outcomes. They have more confidence that their own effort determines how well they perform, and they believe that performance level determines how well they are rewarded (Mitchell, Smyser, & Weed, 1975). Internals usually report greater overall job satisfaction. While internals and externals both prefer to be supervised in a participative fashion, it matters more to internals. Again, this seems logical: the more importance you assign to your own behavior, the more latitude you would seek for doing things your way.

However, a person's locus-of-control beliefs could be so internal as to constitute, in effect, a denial of very real forces beyond control. A failure to heed such forces could lead to an inefficient, fruitless expenditure of time and energy. A study by Behrman, Bigoness, and Perreault (1981) of industrial sales personnel found that the best performers were neither the most internal nor the most external, but intermediate in generalized expectancies for locus of control. Thus, we cannot assume that "the more internal, the better."

Determinants of Internal-External Locus-of-Control Beliefs   In all probability, there are various causes of locus of control. The simplest explanation would be that internals and externals are rather accurate in their perceptions; that internals are simply products of an environment in which their behavior has actually determined their fates; and that externals have experienced futility in trying to determine their own lots. Some support for this argument comes from studies showing that minority groups and disadvantaged socioeconomic classes score more external on the Rotter questionnaire than do white middle-class groups. It seems plausible that disadvantaged groups exert less control over their fates. Nevertheless, economic, social, and political disadvantages do not seem to tell the whole story, for even relatively homogeneous groups vary considerably in locus of control, from extreme internal to extreme external.

Wolk and DuCette (1974) presented an intriguing explanation of the origins of locus of control. Their studies indicate that internals display a significant superiority over externals in amount of *incidental learning*—that is, in the ability to pick up incidental, apparently unrelated cues and relationships while concentrating on material relevant to some other task for which they have been given instructions. Internals seem to be blessed with a cognitive style that organizes stimuli into structures or chunks preserving maximal amounts of the originally embedded information.

This explanation fits well with operant concepts. Recall that the three important components of a contingency are the antecedent stimulus, the response, and the consequence. In real-life situations, a given response is rewarded only when certain stimuli are present. Furthermore, the elements of the stimulus that differentiate it from stimulus situations in which the response is not rewarded can be very subtle and elusive. It could be that externals habitually use a cognitive style that often fails to capture subtle differences in stimuli. As a result, an external sees only that he or she is sometimes rewarded and sometimes unrewarded for certain behavior, seemingly at random. If this is true for many classes of behavior, the person concludes that his or her behavior does not greatly influence his or her outcomes. On the other hand, the internal—due to different methods of processing information—picks out the subtleties of stimuli and concludes that, under certain conditions, a systematic relationship does exist between behavior and rewards.

In any case, much work remains to be done before we will know whether the organization can alter the locus of control of its participants, and if so, which of the correlates of locus of control also change. However, suggestive evidence comes from a study by Eitzen (1974) in which 21 delinquent boys were assigned in groups to foster homes. Their foster parents had been trained to use a comprehensive, systematic program of behavior modification using positive reinforcement. The foster parents shaped socially constructive behaviors by reinforcing the boys with points that could be exchanged for privileges and desirable objects. Over a three-year period, the average locus-of-control score of the group became steadily more internal, while a control group of high school students showed no such change. We may tentatively conclude, then, that organizations can foster a somewhat internalized sense of control by systematically administered reinforcement. We suspect that, by giving the individuals affected by reinforcement contingencies a chance to help design them, one might compound the effect on locus of control.

Value-Based Approaches

Among the more enduring characteristics of adults are the values they hold. Values have been defined as "conceptions of the desirable that are relevant to selection behavior. . . a special kind of attitude functioning as standards by which choices are evaluated" (Smith, 1963). Values are ideals, the reference points by which we measure the goodness of our actions, aims, and experiences.

A number of theorists have offered taxonomies of values. Allport, Vernon, and Lindzey (1951) drew from the writing of the German philosopher Spranger, who identified six basic values:

Theoretical: interest in the abstract truths that unify knowledge.

Economic: an orientation to pragmatic, workable, useful things.

Esthetic: interest in beauty.

Social: an orientation toward and concern for people.

Political: the pursuit of power and influence.

Religious: interest in spiritual and moral realms.

Allport, Vernon, and Lindzey devised a questionnaire that measures the relative strength of these values for the respondent. This measure, called the Study of Values, has been used extensively in research on differences among occupational, ethnic, and religious groups. For example, people who enjoy sales and related work tend to have stronger economic, political, and social values. According to Tyler (1965), the Study of Values "has been a useful instrument for identifying aspects of personality not readily measurable in other ways."

Donald Super (1962), in his research on vocational counseling, has developed a scheme for the analysis of job-related values. At the broadest level, a person's work values can be characterized largely as intrinsic and extrinsic. Intrinsic values focus on altruism, creativity, autonomy, intellectual stimulation, esthetics, achievement, or management. Extrinsic values center not on the work itself but on those ends for which it is instrumental—life-style, pleasant surroundings, congenial associates, security, status, and purchasing power. Most people have both intrinsic and extrinsic work-value orientations, but one or the other predominates. We become painfully aware of this when we have to decide on how much of one to trade off for the other. Many workers would like more freedom or the chance to do something more interesting than their current job affords. But how many would accept a 25 percent reduction in annual income in order to do so?

The Protestant Ethic   The German sociologist Max Weber (1904) argued that the doctrines of Calvinism promoted industrial capitalism in Western Europe by inculcating a certain set of values. These values included an emphasis on the inherent goodness of work itself. A person's work was regarded as a calling. Moreover, financial success in one's work was regarded as evidence that one was blessed by God, a member of the elect few predestined to share His grace. However, money tempted the flesh, and such yearnings were to be suppressed. Protestant values called for self-restraint and deferral of gratification. By investing one's earnings, one could practice such self-denial. Over many years, repeated investment of earnings created the capital base for the Industrial Revolution.

Thus, the Protestant ethic is a cluster of values that define a "work conscience" of sorts. The values hold that people are obligated to work and that honest work—no matter how humble—is its own reward. Moreover, these values condemn laxity, idleness, and self-indulgence. Even a person's leisure pursuits should be useful, not idle play. Inner restraint dictates that enjoyment of nonwork activities must be postponed until one has earned that right.

Recent studies suggest that a secularized version of these values is a useful construct in understanding stable differences among individuals. One study (Mirels & Garrett, 1971) found that people who generally endorse the Protestant ethic (PE)—as determined by their reactions to statements about work and the pleasures of the flesh—tend to be more accepting of authoritarian leadership than those who do not endorse such values. Those who endorse the PE also tend to express interest in occupations demanding a concrete, pragmatic orientation to work, such as carpentry or veterinary medicine. They are not usually found in occupations that emphasize theoretical or abstract values or that require creativity and playful fantasy, such as music or writing.

In another study (Merrens & Garrett, 1975), subjects were given 100 sheets of paper, each of which pictured 250 circles in rows of 10. Each subject was told to draw an X in each circle with his or her nonpreferred hand and to keep working until too tired to continue. Note that subjects had no financial incentive to spur them to work, nor was the task particularly appealing. The experimenters simply waited to see how long subjects would work until quitting (the experimenters terminated the work after 30 minutes). Those who previously had scored high on a PE measure spent an average of 23 minutes on the repetitive task, compared to less than 17 minutes for low scorers, and high scorers completed 60 percent more work. A number of possible explanations, none mutually exclusive, could account for such findings. The high scorers on the PE measure may have been more driven to suppress feelings of fatigue or boredom, an explanation consistent with the value placed on self-control and discipline. High scorers might also have felt more of a moral obligation due to having committed themselves as subjects—an explanation consistent with other findings that high PE scorers accept more personal responsibility for their own actions. Finally, those who endorsed the PE might have accepted to a greater extent the legitimate authority of the experimenter, since those who value PE show a general tendency to accept systems of external authority.

A more recent study (Greenberg, 1977) found that not only did high PE endorsers work harder on a boring task, regardless of the motivational conditions, but also they increased their output following negative feedback (defined by the experimenter's report that they were doing poorly in comparison to most other subjects). On the other hand, performance by low PE scorers declined following such feedback. Both groups increased their performance following positive feedback, but for high PE scorers, the increase did not match that which occurred after negative feedback. These findings support the position of those (Wollack, Goodale, Wijting, & Smith, 1971) who suggest that work and self-esteem are closely linked in the value network of the PE. In other words, high PE scorers tend to experience guilt or loss of self-esteem when led to believe they are not working as hard as they should. Regaining a sense of self-esteem becomes contingent on working harder.

Recent surveys by Cherrington (1977) suggest that older workers are more apt to endorse the PE values than are their younger counterparts. Such values may be affected by stages of adult development. Alternatively, the affluence and liberating tendencies of our culture in recent decades may have made it more difficult to endorse the values of self-restraint and deferred gratification. Only time will tell whether the PE syndrome is a vanishing legacy of the peculiar set of forces that have shaped our history, or a dimension of individual differences that transcends history. Undoubtedly, these, like any other values, are influenced by the contemporary character of certain institutions, such as the church, family, schools, and community. That does not, however, rule out the possibility that some individuals — for whatever reasons, including innate endowment — may at any time be more susceptible than others to these influences.

IS THERE A MANAGERIAL PERSONALITY?

J. B. Miner (1978) contends that a person needs a certain set of traits and values to succeed in managerial positions in large, hierarchical, bureaucratic organizations. Over 30 years ago he began to develop, refine, and empirically validate a measure of the requisite managerial personality. He refers to the instrument as a measure of managerial role motivation, and he includes within it six scales measuring the following components:

1. *Positive response toward authority figures.* Authority is a fact of life in bureaucratic organizations. To be effective, a manager must have an approach rather than an avoidance reaction to those in authority. A tendency to flee from, or rebel against, authority structures would nip most managerial careers in the bud.

2. *A desire to compete.* Another fact of life in organizations is finite resources. The effective manager must compete with others for a share of resources — staff, budget, and capital equipment. Competing takes many forms — in sales or production, negotiation, lobbying for influence, debate. One thinks immediately of the fondness of managers for expressions and analogies from competitive sports, and the testimonials of so many executives that attribute much of their success to the lessons learned from the playing fields.

3. *Assertiveness.* The managerial role requires that a person speak out often and, sometimes, loudly. They must have a confidence in their ideas and opinions that permits forceful expression. Quiet competence is a necessary commodity, but it does not attract the attention of the powers that be.

4. *A readiness to impose wishes.* Administrators in hierarchic organizations not only respect and identify with authority figures, but they also feel very comfortable exercising power. They might solicit input from subordinates, but they have no hang-ups about making decisions that override others' preferences or that might redound to the disadvantage of others' interests.

5. *Desire to stand out from the group.* Consistent with the traits of assertiveness and competitiveness, the manager seeks a comparative edge in being noticed. The responsibilities of management require that the manager is frequently on stage. This means that failure as well as success, the *faux pas*

as well as the graceful gesture, are highly visible to others. With all the attendant risks of such visibility, the administrator in bureaucratic organizations nonetheless is stimulated rather than unnerved by the spotlight.

6. *Tolerance for routine administrative chores.* Managerial positions of whatever rank require some attention to record-keeping, paper work, ceremonial functions, reading and responding to correspondence and telephone calls. The manager need not relish these activities, but should not find them so distasteful as to cause procrastination or sloppiness.

Miner has found that scores on the composite measure of "managerial role motivation" discriminate between "fast track" and "plateaued" managers in large corporations. Managers in line functions (such as marketing, finance, and production) score higher than those who direct staff functions (such as industrial relations and R&D). Managers in traditional hierarchical organizations score higher than the more entrepreneurial-type manager in newer, loosely structured small firms or the directors of small firms that market professional services. Thus, it appears that Miner's measure is valid in measuring what it claims to measure.

Of some concern to Miner is the long-term trend in the general level of managerial role motivation among college students (see Focus on the Future).

CONCLUSIONS

We have discussed several dimensions of personality and related them to job behavior. We have stopped short of asserting that a particular personality measure would predict job performance. In general, we would caution managers against using such measures to select job applicants. Very little evidence exists to show that personality tests reliably predict quality of job performance. Rulings by courts and federal officials have discouraged the use of these tools in making hiring decisions.

Why are most personality measures poor predictors of performance? Most of them can be faked if respondents have sufficient incentive. If in seeking a sales position you are given a questionnaire attempting to measure your extroversion, you could probably tell right away that certain answers would be more consistent with widely held notions of what makes someone good at sales. If you wanted the job badly enough, you might answer, not candidly, but in a manner that would make you seem right for the job. This destroys the measure's validity.

However, there is a more basic reason why personality measures, no matter how reliable and valid in themselves, do not reliably predict job performance. Most jobs permit varying styles or approaches toward achieving final results. For example, one person may achieve success in sales because of an easy going, affable nature that appeals to potential clients.

FOCUS ON THE FUTURE

Is the Managerial Personality Type an Endangered Species?

Industrial psychologist John B. Miner has tracked scores on his measure of managerial role motivation at several college campuses over a 30-year period. His data suggest that the general level of scores started to decline around the mid-1960s and bottomed out in the early or mid-1970s, with no indication of any turnabout since then. Virtually all of the decline is accounted for by men — who generally scored higher on this measure in the 1960s, but now score no higher than women.

The decline is perhaps all the more remarkable in that it has occurred during a period of burgeoning enrollments in collegiate schools of business administration. The data suggest that students study business not because of an identification with the managerial role, but in order to achieve material success in nonmanagerial positions in accounting, investment banking, marketing research, and industrial relations.

Miner fears that the diminishing supply of those with the profile of traits and values requisite to the managerial role portends a nationwide shortfall in managerial talent. Those students in the late 1960s and early 1970s who first reflected the downturn in managerial role motivation would now approach the age and experience levels at which they become candidates for managing at levels of major responsibilities.

On the other hand, Miner has noted that his measure pertains to management in hierarchical, bureaucratic organizations. If the trend of the future lies in the development of alternative structural forms — smaller, leaner, more flexible organization forms — a different profile of traits and values might be more appropriate to success in leadership roles.

SOURCE: J. B. Miner and N. R. Smith, "Decline and Stabilization of Managerial Motivation over a 20-Year Period," *Journal of Applied Psychology* 67 (1982), 297–305.

Another person, although reserved and formal in demeanor, may succeed because of a very professional, analytic approach to markets, customer needs, and product specifications. Still another individual, while essentially shy, forces an outgoing nature because financial incentives make it worthwhile. In short, personality differences have to do with predispositions toward various job behaviors. These predispositions may be overridden by compelling incentives, or they may be adapted toward varying approaches to achieving good results on the job.

Individual counseling should help people discover their basic predispositions and how these predispositions relate to the demands of various occupations. Given this information, people have a more informed basis for self-selection into different jobs. The Strong Vocational Interest Blank, for example, is a counseling tool that compares respondents' descriptions of themselves (their likes and dislikes) with those of people who have apparently experienced reasonable levels of satisfaction in different professions and occupations. It cannot predict success in any given occupation, but it can suggest whether a person is likely to be comfortable working for very long in that occupation.

SUMMARY

Individuals do not respond identically to the same organizational environments, and the study of behavior in organizations must take account of the dimensions underlying these differences. The trait-based approach to this issue seeks to derive empirically a small number of factors, such as neuroticism and extroversion. Another approach examines differences in stable, enduring motives such as needs for achievement, power, and affiliation. A belief-based approach focuses on a person's generalized expectancy that one's own behavior does or does not control important outcomes. Finally, the Protestant ethic is an example of a value-based approach to individual differences. Various approaches have their distinctive measurement methodologies, which are useful in research and counseling but arc seldom justified as a basis for making hiring decisions.

CONCEPTS TO REMEMBER

Projective test	*n Aff*	Thematic apperception test
Neuroticism	*n Pow*	*n Ach*
Extroversion-introversion	Protestant ethic	Managerial role motivation
Internal-external locus of control	Incidental learning	Myers-Briggs Type Indicator
	Strong/weak situations	

QUESTIONS FOR DISCUSSION

1. Describe some person you know who is probably high in neuroticism. What behavior characteristics lead you to believe that this is so?
2. Describe some person you know who would probably score high in extroversion. What characteristics of that person lead you to suspect this?
3. Would a very strong need for achievement ever be dysfunctional for a manager's performance?
4. What situational factors might affect the level of a person's need for affiliation?

5. Some observers of the contemporary work scene believe that the Protestant ethic, as defined in this chapter, is on the wane. If so, what forces might account for this? Can you argue the case that it is still alive and well in the 1990s?

REFERENCES

Allport, G. W., & Odbert, H. W. (1936). Trait-names: A psychological study. *Psychological Monographs* 47(i).

Allport, G. W., Vernon, P. E., & Lindzey, G. (1951). *Study of Values*. Boston: Houghton Mifflin.

Anderson, C., Hellriegel, D., & Slocum, J. (1977). Managerial response to environmentally induced stress. *Academy of Management Journal* 20, 260–72.

Atkinson, J. W. (1958). *Motives in fantasy, action, and society*. New York: Van Nostrand Reinhold.

Behrman, D., Bigoness, W., & Perrault, W. (1981). Sources of role ambiguity and their consequences upon salespersons' satisfaction and performance. *Management Science* 27, 1246–60.

Bouchard, T. J., Jr. (1984). Twins reared together and apart: What they tell us about human diversity. In S. W. Fox (ed.), *Individuality and determinism*. New York: Plenum Press.

Bouchard, T. J., Jr., Lykken, D. T., Segal, N. L., & Wilcox, K. J. (1986). Development in twins reared apart: A test of the chronogenetic hypothesis. In A. Demirjian (ed.), *Human growth: A multidisciplinary review*. London: Taylor & Francis.

Brown, R., & Herrnstein, R. (1975). *Psychology*. Boston: Little, Brown.

Cattell, R. B. (1972). The 16PF and basic personality structure: A reply to Eysenck. *Journal of Behavioral Science* 1, 169–87.

Cherrington, D. (1977). The values of younger workers. *Business Horizons* 20, 18–20.

Cooper, R., & Payne, R. (1967). Extraversion and some aspects of work behavior. *Personnel Psychology* 20, 45–57.

Eaves, L., & Eysenck, H. (1975). The nature of extraversion: A genetical analysis. *Journal of Personality and Social Psychology* 32, 102–12.

Eitzen, S. (1974). Impact of behavior modification techniques on locus of control of delinquent boys. *Psychological Reports* 35, 1317–18.

Epstein, S. (1980). The stability of behavior: II. Implications for psychological research. *American Psychologist* 35, 790–806.

Eysenck, H. J. (1967). *The biological basis of personality*. Springfield, IL: Charles C. Thomas.

Eysenck, H. J. (ed.). (1970). *Readings in extraversion-introversion*, vol. 3. London: Staple Press.

Eysenck, H. J., (ed.). (1973). *Eysenck on extraversion*. New York: John Wiley & Sons.

French, J. D. (May 1957). The reticular formation. *Scientific American*, reprinted in T. J. Teyler (ed.), *Altered states of awareness*. San Francisco: W. H. Freeman, 1972, pp. 23–40.

Greenberg, J. (1977). The Protestant work ethic and reactions to negative performance evaluation on a laboratory task. *Journal of Applied Psychology* 62, 682–90.

Guilford, J. P. (1975). Factors and factors of personality. *Psychological Bulletin* 82, 802–14.

Hartshorne, H., & May, M. A. (1928). Studies in the nature of character. *Studies in deceit*, vol. 1. New York: Macmillan.

Kahn, R. J., Wolfe, D. M., Quinn, R. P., Snoek, J. D., & Rosenthal, R. (1964). *Organizational stress*. New York: John Wiley & Sons.

Kets De Vries, M.F.R., & Miller, D. *The neurotic organization*. San Francisco: Jossey-Bass, 1984.

Kohn, M. L., & Schooler, C. (1982). Job conditions and personality: A longitudinal assessment of their reciprocal effects. *American Journal of Sociology* 87, 1257–86.

McClelland, D. C. (1961). *The achieving society.* New York: Van Nostrand Reinhold.

Merrens, M., & Garrett, J. (1975). The Protestant ethic scale as a predictor of repetitive work performance. *Journal of Applied Psychology* 60, 125–27.

Miner, J. B. (1978). Twenty years of research on role-motivation theory of managerial effectiveness. *Personnel Psychology* 31, 739–60.

Miner, J. B., & Smith, N. R. (1982). Decline and stabilization of managerial motivation over a 20-year period. *Journal of Applied Psychology* 67, 297–305.

Mirels, J., & Garret, J. (1971). The Protestant ethic as a personality variable. *Journal of Consulting and Clinical Psychology* 36, 40–44.

Mischel, W. (1968). *Personality and assessment.* New York: John Wiley & Sons.

Mischel, W. (1977). The interaction of person and situation. In D. Magnusson & N. S. Endler (eds.), *Personality at the crossroads: Current issues in interactional psychology.* Hillsdale, NJ: Erlbaum, 1977.

Mitchell, T., Smyser, C., & Weed, S. (1975). Locus of control: Supervision and work satisfaction. *Academy of Management Journal* 18, 623–31.

Monson, T. C., Hesley, J. W., & Chernick, L. (1982). Specifying when personality traits can and cannot predict behavior: An alternative to abandoning the attempt to predict single-act criteria. *Journal of Personality and Social Psychology* 43, 385–99.

Moore, T. "Personality Tests Are Back," *Fortune,* March 30, 1987.

Rotter, J. B. (1966). Generalized expectancies for internal versus external control of reinforcement. *Psychological Monographs* 80 (1, Whole No. 609).

Seeman, M., & Evans, J. (1962). Alienation and learning in a hospital setting. *American Sociological Review* 27, 772–83.

Smith, M. B. (1963). Personal values in the study of lives. In R. W. White (ed.), *The study of lives* (chap. 14). Englewood Cliffs, NJ: Prentice Hall.

Super, D. E. (1962). The structure of work values in relation to status, achievement, interests, and adjustment. *Journal of Applied Psychology* 46, 231–39.

Tyler, L. E. (1965). *The psychology of human differences.* New York: Appleton-Century-Crofts.

Weber, M. (1904). *The Protestant ethic and the spirit of capitalism.* Translated by T. Parsons (1930). New York: Scribner.

Weiss, H. M., & Adler, S. (1984). Personality and organizational behavior. In B. M. Staw & L. L. Cummings (eds.), *Research in organizational behavior*, vol. 6. Greenwich, CT: JAI Press, 1–50.

Weinstein, N. D. (1978). Individual differences in reaction to noise: A longitudinal study in a college dormitory. *Journal of Applied Psychology* 63, 458–66.

Winter, P. G. (1967). *Power motivation in thought and action.* Unpublished doctoral dissertation, Harvard University, Cambridge, MA.

Wolk, S., & DuCette, J. (1974). Intentional performance and incidental learning as a function of personality and task dimensions. *Journal of Personality and Social Psychology* 29, 90–101.

Wollack, S., Goodale, J., Wijting, J., & Smith, P. (1971). Development of the survey of work values. *Journal of Applied Psychology* 55, 331–38.

9 Decision Making

What is a "good" decision?
What does it mean to be "rational"?
How do people make decisions?
How can decisions be made better?

Consider the following scenarios:

1. You are about to graduate from school and have been offered three jobs. All seem appealing, but it is like comparing apples and oranges since they all vary with respect to pay, location, training, initial responsibilities, and promotion potential.

2. You are a supervisor in a chemical refinery and have caught your favorite subordinate smoking in a hazardous area. You've just completed a very favorable performance evaluation of the man, but you know that his safety violation is serious enough to warrant dismissal.

3. You are vice president for strategic planning and about to make an important research and development investment decision. Five years ago, you reviewed two struggling divisions that seemed in desperate need of additional R&D funding. After extensive analysis, you chose the consumer products division over the industrial products division as the recipient of $10 million in an effort to revitalize the division. Now, consumer products is barely holding its own, while industrial products has improved its profitability slightly. You now have an additional $15 million to allocate between the two divisions.

4. Your company has been thinking about expanding and diversifying its operations. At about the same time it has come to the attention of others outside your organization, a rather attractive candidate for acquisition has come to your attention. Acquisition and merger activities have been prominent in the business news and excitement is high; but the optimism surrounding these types of strategic activities is not always well-founded. Time is running short.

5. After reviewing the quarterly sales figures, you see they are down again. One more quarter like this, and your neck will really be on the line. Your tenure as sales manager may soon be over.

People at different organizational levels and career stages constantly face these predicaments and their variations. The decisions differ—for example, the acquisition is a go/no go decision; others involve a trichotomous choice (the job offers), an allocation of funds (the R&D investment), selection of a personnel action (subordinate discipline), and an ambiguous problem with no clear solution (the sales drop-off).

More important, however, is the similarity among the scenarios. All require that a good decision be made or the repercussions could be severe.

THE QUALITY OF DECISIONS

As a manager, decision making may be your most frequent and important task. Skill in making decisions will be a major factor in your performance evaluations and rewards. It will contribute to the success or failure of the whole organization.

FIGURE 9–1

Difference between Actual and Potential Quality of Decisions

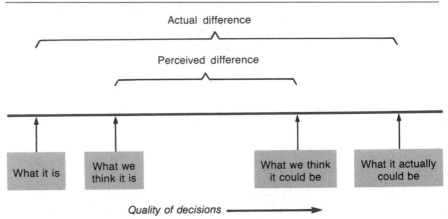

SOURCE: G. P. Huber, *Managerial Decision Making* (Glenview, Ill.: Scott, Foresman, 1980).

Most people assume they are competent decision makers. Where this assumption falls short is in the difference between what is perceived and what is real with regard to decision quality (Huber, 1980). As Figure 9–1 illustrates, it is easy to overestimate both the quality of a decision and its congruence with the ideal. The actual difference between what is and what could be is often much more substantial than we realize.

What constitutes a good decision? There are two important criteria— *quality* and *acceptance*. Quality implies that the decision will achieve some standard, goal, or objective. Acceptance means that the key actors involved in the decision, including those who will implement it, agree that the decision is appropriate.

In the short run, these two criteria may seem inconsistent. One person's preferred decision may not be another's, and some watered-down version or compromise may be needed for others to accept it. An ideal alternative may be rejected because someone calls it impractical. An early proposal, unanimously agreed on, may be far short of the quality product that could have been reached with more time and effort.

However, if a decision's quality is defined by how well it achieves its objectives, it is impossible to assess it until all the results are in. For adequate acceptance, a decision must be perceived as a good one at the time it is formulated and communicated to those who must carry it out. Thus, we need to be able to judge the quality of a decision before it is implemented—before its impact can be appraised.

Therefore, decisions should be judged by the procedures used in making them (Janis & Mann, 1977). The decision can be judged a good one if all relevant aspects of a problem are analyzed, available and pertinent information is acquired and considered in an unbiased way, and alternative courses of action are creatively derived and realistically evaluated. In the end, it may not work out well, but it will have been the best possible effort at the time it was made.

THE NATURE OF DECISIONS

Decisions may be characterized in a number of ways. First, there are fundamental distinctions between decision making, choice making, and problem solving. Second, problems can be classified as structured or unstructured. Third, decisions vary with regard to the amount of uncertainty and risk they entail. Finally, they are complex. They generate conflict within, as well as between, individuals since alternatives have multiple attributes that must be evaluated. Virtually all decisions must be made within certain constraints.

Decision Making, Choice Making, and Problem Solving

Figure 9–2 shows the differences among decision making, choice making, and problem solving (Huber, 1980). Decision making refers to the set of activities involved in diagnosing a problem and generating and selecting one alternative from among a set of alternatives. Choice making is the narrowest concept; as shown in the figure, it refers only to the stage at the end of the decision-making process, when a solution is selected. Problem solving includes decision-making activities, plus activities undertaken after the decision is made — implementation and evaluation of the chosen course of action.

Figure 9–2 also summarizes the basic stages of the entire problem-solving process. Numerous authors have provided their models of the process, but most include versions of the five stages presented in the figure: problem identification and diagnosis, generation of alternatives, evaluation and selection of alternatives, implementation of the chosen solution, and monitoring and evaluation of the results.

So, for example, the sales manager faced with low sales may go through every stage of the model. Problem identification is initiated with the realization that sales are low, as indicated by the quarterly sales figures; problem diagnosis would continue with an attempt to identify why sales are down. The sales manager would then generate, either alone or with others, alternative ideas for increasing sales. These ideas must be evaluated for cost, appropriateness, probability of success, and extent of impact. Based on these evaluations, one or perhaps more solutions will be chosen and put into effect. Ideally, then, feedback will be systematically gathered to assess the success or failure of the program.

Feedback loops are a necessary addition to this sequential problem-solving model (Bass, 1984). Models like the one in Figure 9–2 can at any

FIGURE 9–2

Decision Making, Choice Making, and Problem Solving

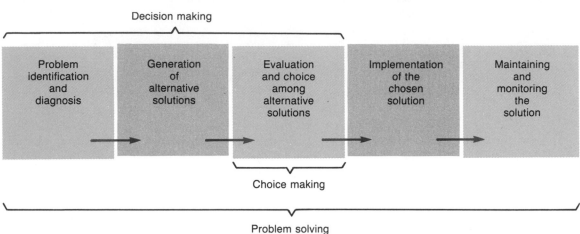

SOURCE: Adapted from G. P. Huber, *Managerial Decision Making* (Glenview, Ill.: Scott, Foresman, 1980).

point cycle back to an earlier stage. The information uncovered in carrying out one activity can signal the need to return to an earlier, seemingly completed activity.

Such repetition can make the difference between a good decision and a poor one. Too often, decision makers are reluctant to rehash old ground; they are glad to be over the hurdles of the last stage and eager to push ahead to new resolutions. However, effective decision making requires open, objective assessment of incoming information at every stage. This information may demand returning to an earlier stage and beginning the whole process again. Going back and reexamining a problem even after a decision has already been reached can improve the quality of solutions (Maier & Hoffman, 1960).

It is clear that decision making is not a smooth sequence or a strictly linear process—one jumps around, stalls, backtracks, reconsiders, quits, and starts all over again.

The Structure of Decisions

A *well-structured problem* can be defined explicitly and quantitatively, and can therefore be solved computationally. The decision, then, is easily programmed. A basic accounting problem, a financial ratio, a credit rating, or the amount that should appear on a paycheck can be routinely determined by simple decision rules or computational techniques that have already been programmed or can be logically derived. In short, there is a demonstrably correct answer to a well-structured problem.

FIGURE 9–3

Decision Tree Representations of Risky Situations

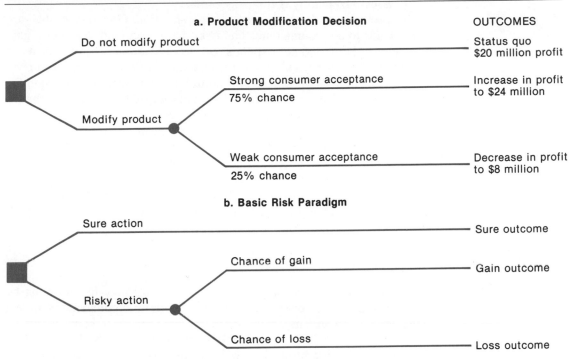

a. Product Modification Decision   OUTCOMES

Do not modify product — Status quo $20 million profit

Modify product

Strong consumer acceptance
75% chance — Increase in profit to $24 million

Weak consumer acceptance
25% chance — Decrease in profit to $8 million

b. Basic Risk Paradigm

Sure action — Sure outcome

Risky action

Chance of gain — Gain outcome

Chance of loss — Loss outcome

SOURCE: K. R. MacCrimmon and D. Wehrung (1986). *Taking Risks.* New York. Free Press, p. 12.

But most managerial problems are ill-structured (Ungson, Braunstein, & Hall, 1981). An *ill-structured problem* is not so easily programmed; the right decision cannot be clearly demonstrated. In this chapter, we will be dealing primarily with ill-structured problems for two reasons. First, in a sense, well-structured problems are not real problems at all; once such a problem is defined, the remaining steps—with the exception of implementation—are unnecessary because the computational algorithm will make the decision. Second, most problems faced by managers are ill-structured. Programs are not readily available to bail managers out of most tough decisions.

Risk and Uncertainty

Problems or decisions are further characterized by their degree of risk and uncertainty. *Risk* exists when the decision maker faces choices that carry some chance of failure. Figure 9–3 illustrates a risky situation using a decision tree in which a decision maker faces a choice to modify or not to modify the product (MacCrimmon & Wehrung, 1986). The choice to not modify—to stick with the status quo—leads predictably to a profit of $20 million. The choice *to* modify *could* lead to an even higher profit—or it could lead to a loss. To modify is the risky choice.

Figure 9–3 also shows the generic risk situation. One choice, the sure action, leads to a sure outcome. The risky action can lead to either a gain or a loss. The outcome depends on an uncertain event: consumer acceptance. *Uncertainty* exists when probabilities of events are not known, when the likelihoods of success and failure are not clear. In the example, probabilities are given at 75 percent chance of success and 25 percent chance of failure. But these probabilities are merely estimates, and their accuracy is suspect. Since the future is difficult to predict, the probabilities of different outcomes can rarely be assessed with much accuracy; most consequential decisions are made under conditions of uncertainty.

Certainty means not that the decision maker knows she will succeed—that would be lack of risk—but that she has a confident read on the probabilities (for example, 75/25) of success and failure. Risk-taking under uncertainty means that the decision maker doesn't really know the odds.

Complexity, Conflict, and Constraints

Managerial decisions typically are quite complex. Many factors must be considered, and there exist numerous and subtle interconnections among them. Multiple goals must often be met—some financial, some organizational, some personal. Furthermore, solutions typically have various advantages and disadvantages, making multiple criteria for judgment necessary.

Partly because of their complexity, important decisions generate conflict. Often, individuals from different organizational levels or units, or with different personal values and goals, will disagree. Disagreement can foster energetic, thorough, and creative problem solving. Conflict can occur at any of the problem-solving stages, from problem analysis through choice, implementation, and evaluation.

Conflict is also generated within the individual making the decision. Choices have important consequences, some positive and some negative, and the individual may feel caught in the middle when forced to select one course of action over the others. Such conflict in decision making arises in social traps (see Close-Up).

Lewin's (1935) classic analysis distinguished between three major types of intrapersonal conflict. *Approach-approach conflict* occurs when one is forced to choose between two or more attractive options, like several good job offers. Some positive alternatives must be rejected. *Avoidance-avoidance conflict* arises when one must decide between two or more unattractive options. For example, a supervisor knows he must either fire the favored subordinate who committed a serious safety violation, or cover it up and live with the knowledge that he condoned the crime and violated company policy. The third type, *approach-avoidance conflict,* exists when a single alternative

CLOSE-UP

Social Traps

Social traps are situations in which people make decisions and adopt behaviors that seem personally beneficial but have negative consequences over time or for a larger collective (the group, organization, or society). An early and prominent example is the "Tragedy of the Commons" (Hardin, 1968), in which herdsmen graze their cattle in a common pasture. Individual herdsmen seek to maximize their personal gain by grazing more and more of their cattle on the commons, but eventually the pasture is overgrazed. Short-term individual gain-seeking leads to long-term collective disaster.

> Consider some other examples (Dawes, 1988): People who do not contribute to public television are maximizing their outcomes: they can watch their favorite programs for free. But if every viewer chose that strategy, public television would fold.
>
> In Eugene, Oregon, during pollution alerts, people are asked to ride bicycles rather than drive cars. Driving a car is preferred by most commuters, and they can rationalize that one car doesn't make much difference. But if everyone chooses that strategy, pollution remains a problem.

The Indian government asks married couples to limit family size. But wives generally outlive their husbands by many years, and sons are expected to support their widowed mothers. Ignoring the government's request is the best strategy for an individual—but poverty caused by overpopulation continues to preclude the establishment of a social security system that would reduce the motivation for having large families.

In organizational decision making, social traps exist when short-run and long-run interests conflict, or when actions in the interest of one person or unit are to the detriment of another (Barry & Bateman, 1989). As examples, the executive who takes illegal or unethical courses of action for immediate personal gain could cause legal or reputational problems for the organization, and the subordinate who fails to deliver some bad news to his boss in order to avoid the fallout may cause later, larger problems. At the interorganizational level, competitors who join together in consortia may distrust one another and consequently decide to withhold money, information, and key personnel from the consortia—thereby contributing to their failure.

has both positive and negative features. To reap the advantages a particular choice may provide, one is also forced to live with the negative consequences. Drinking alcohol, eating too many fattening foods, taking a high-paying but exhausting night job during the summer, and many other personal and business decisions render these types of mixed blessings.

Finally, virtually all decisions must be made within certain constraints. We are constrained by limited time, information, or other resources (Janis, 1989). On the job, our decisions must be approved by the boss, or at least must not offend him greatly. Other managers and subordinates will have to live with our decisions; their reactions force us to compromise. We may not have the funds to implement the program we are anxious to see put into place. Trade regulations, consumer groups, and religious organizations may exert demands and hinder our actions. Even off the job, we are constrained not only by personal budgets, but by the reactions of our families, friends, and others. Only rarely can we decide to do exactly as we please.

Constraints can also be self-imposed. To the extent that decision makers fail to perform adequately the different stages of the problem-solving process, they are limiting their own ability to make optimal decisions. In the United States, the first step of the problem-solving process often is (Figure 9–2 notwithstanding) to come up with a quantifiable answer or solve the symptoms of some underlying problem. In Japan, much time is spent truly defining the problem. The focus is on what the decision is really about, not what it should be. Instead of making a choice about a particular joint venture, the Japanese might consider in which direction the business should go. The joint venture becomes only a small aspect of the larger issue. By considering broader problems and bigger issues, the Japanese seem to avoid becoming prisoners of preconceived answers (Harris & Moran, 1987).

CHARACTERISTICS OF DECISION MAKERS

Decisions differ according to their degree of uncertainty, risk, and complexity. They also differ in regard to who makes them.

Many personal differences among people have been studied for their effects on managerial decision making. We will highlight three types: perceptions, ethical values, and attitudes toward risk.

Perceptions

The way in which the decision maker perceives the problem will largely determine the decision-making strategies she employs (MacCrimmon & Taylor, 1976). For example, previous experience and current location in the organization exert important influences on perception. Prior experiences can help in selecting an appropriate solution if the prior learning experience applies to the current problem. On the other hand, the decision is hindered if the prior experience cannot successfully generalize, especially if the decision maker believes the experience to be relevant. The overconfident executive who, years ago, made an ultimately successful hiring decision based on an intuitive sizing up of the job candidate, may be ill-served by relying on such subjective assessments the next time around.

Organizational level can also affect how a problem is perceived and solved. In France, important decisions are made only by the top executives; in many U.S. firms, more decisions are made at lower levels (Harris & Moran, 1987). Managers at higher and lower levels have different goals and different information at their disposal. Upper-level managers are more concerned with the performance of the organization as a whole; lower-level managers must concern themselves with their individual work units. Similarly, those who are most removed from the level at which a decision will be implemented might overemphasize the inherent quality of the decision to the relative exclusion of practicalities. Those responsible for carrying out the decision may have the opposite bias.

A telling study of departmental perceptions of organizational problems was done years ago by Dearborn and Simon (1958). They showed that managers' diagnoses of a detailed, factual case depended on the department from which they came. Managers from the marketing department focused on sales issues, managers from industrial relations or public relations focused on human relations, and those from production focused on manufacturing problems.

Perceptual differences also arise from differences in cultural values. For example, California is a future-oriented culture, and England is more conservative and past-oriented. When trying to solve the problem of urban congestion, the British consider and prefer methods of traffic control. Californians are more likely to consider monorails and "flying cars" (Adler, 1986). Whereas Americans are quick decision makers, and being called decisive is a compliment, most other cultures downplay time urgency and some even consider length of time spent making a decision a measure of its value. For example, Americans believe that Egyptians' slow, deliberate pace is an indication of disinterest in doing business; Egyptians consider Americans an overly hasty race whose unwillingness to take more time indicates a lack of importance placed on the business relationship (Adler, 1986).

Ethics and Values

Managers also differ in their personal values. Some value bottom line considerations above all else. Others value their personal lives, or religious, moral, or ethical considerations. For example, high-level Nigerian managers give top priority in hiring and promotion decisions to family members; this process can be frustrating to American business representatives who value merit most highly (Harris & Moran, 1987). Most U.S. organizations are profit-oriented, but in Japan the organization is interested primarily in long-term growth and market share. Such differences in value systems will influence decision makers' perceptions at every stage of the problem-solving process.

Ethical considerations abound in managerial decisions characterized by uncertainty. Multiple interests and values are in conflict, and laws may be vague. Managers' decisions and actions have major consequences for the welfare of employees, consumers, and the community (Trevino, 1986). On top of these difficulties, executives sometimes face crisis conditions that demand immediate decisions and fast action. As the Focus on Management suggests, how decision makers respond reveals a lot about their personal values; and the stronger their values, the more coherent and effective their decisions can be.

FOCUS ON MANAGEMENT

Values and Crisis Decision Making

On October 17, 1989, Frank Crivello, manager of the Safeway supermarket in Aptos, California, watched a 15-second earthquake turn order into chaos (Hector, 1989). From radio reports, he quickly learned the details of one of the worst earthquakes in American history. It might be days or even weeks before electricity was fully restored, and by nightfall worried customers would be coming to his store to stock up on water, batteries, flashlights, and staples that would help them survive the next few days.

The company kept its priorities straight. Its overriding goal was to get its stores open, get people what they needed, and worry about costs later. Crivello and the other managers were determined to keep vital services like water and food supplied to panicky customers. A strong sense of community served as a guide.

Gary Spence, Safeway's highest ranking officer at division headquarters at the time, set up a phone bank and command post. Spence's team determined what supplies were needed quickly:

flashlights and batteries, candles, firewood, and canned food. Trucks at Safeway warehouses were loaded with one-gallon bottles of water and dispatched immediately. The team then went to work to get contractors out to the stores to fix structural damage and electrical systems. Meanwhile, orders went out to supply food to the Red Cross, Salvation Army, and other relief agencies.

At another store, manager Bob Powers loaded water and other essentials into shopping carts and sold them through the night in the parking lot. Drivers worked overtime, while clerks and stock workers worked 16- to 24-hour shifts. Ultimately, Crivello's store was one of the last to reopen because he had given away all of his batteries and couldn't work in the dark. But Crivello had never stopped serving the public. "We think of ourselves as part of the community," he said later. "It was an emergency . . . we dug out whatever we could find, and we stood there and gave the essentials away until they were all gone" (p. 100).

Surveys indicate cynicism and pessimism regarding American business ethics (Trevino, 1986). Executives overwhelmingly admit to compromising their personal values in order to succeed in their organizations (Lincoln, Pressley, & Little, 1982). Most report that unethical practices are accepted in their industries (Brenner & Molander, 1977), and four out of ten executives reported in a *Wall Street Journal* survey that they had been asked to behave unethically (Ricklees, 1983).

Like all other behavior, ethical (and unethical) behavior is a function of individual and situational variables (Trevino, 1986). Perhaps the most important individual factor is the person's stage of cognitive moral development (Kohlberg, 1969). Moral judgments are assessments of what is right and wrong. People differ in their assessments according to whether they are in the preconventional, conventional, or principled level of development.

In the *preconventional* level, people are concerned with their own immediate interests and the external rewards and punishments that they might receive for their actions. People do what they believe they can get away with, or what they feel will pay off most handsomely.

People who advance to the *conventional* level of moral development try to live up to what is expected of them by people who are close to them. At this level, people exhibit good behavior because family, peers, or society expect them to, and to do otherwise would let them down. Part of appropriate behavior at this level is to fulfill agreed-on duties and obligations.

Kohlberg (1969) maintains that most adults in our society are at the conventional level of development. For those estimated 20 percent who continue into the *principled* level, right and wrong are determined by self-chosen values and ethical principles. Individuals at this level see beyond norms, laws, and authority; when laws violate personal principles, people here behave according to their principles.

(Un)ethical behavior is a function of the work environment as well as the individual's personal values (Trevino, 1986). Competition, time pressures, scarce resources, reinforcements or punishments, and expectations of superiors or peers can influence the ethics of business decisions. Of course, the decison maker's level of cognitive moral development determines how *important* these situational factors are—and consequently, how much influence they will actually have.

Attitudes toward Risk

One of the most important managerial attitudes and values in decision making is risk-taking propensity. Many studies have investigated individual differences in risk taking (Bass, 1984; MacCrimmon & Wehrung, 1986). Rigid and dogmatic personalities are overly confident and more willing to take risks, women are more averse to risk taking than men in ambiguous situations, and older, more experienced managers are less willing to accept risk than younger managers. One study found that successful managers took more risks than unsuccessful managers. The researchers concluded that people who do not take risks are unlikely to get to the top—but those who do take risks should evaluate them carefully (MacCrimmon & Wehrung, 1986). They should recognize the possible losses and sources of uncertainty, and evaluate whether the possible losses are worth assuming. Then, they can take steps to *adjust* the risk by gaining more control, information, and time.

Table 9–1 shows some differences between risk averters and risk takers. Relative to risk takers, risk averters minimize their exposure to loss and prefer comfortable circumstances characterized by more information, certainty, and familiarity. The result is a decision style that minimizes risk by sharing responsibility, establishing contingency plans, and exiting from risky situations. Risk takers accept greater exposure to loss, greater uncertainty, and are more likely to participate in risky situations—which may include the acceptance of sole responsibility for outcomes.

TABLE 9–1

Characteristics of Risk Takers and Risk Averters

Key Considerations	Risk Averter Requires	Risk Taker Accepts
Loss	Low maximum loss	Higher maximum loss
	Low chance of loss	Higher chance of loss
Circumstances	Familiar environment	Unfamiliar environment
	More information	Less information
	More control	Less control
	Low uncertainty	Higher uncertainty
Decision style	Shared responsibility	Sole responsibility
	Consensus	Conflict
	Contingency plans	No contingency plans
	Exit from risky situations	Participation in risky situations

SOURCE: Adapted with permission of The Free Press, a Division of Macmillan, Inc. from TAKING RISKS: The Management of Uncertainty by Kenneth R. MacCrimmon and Donald A. Wehrung. Copyright © 1986 by Kenneth R. MacCrimmon and Donald A. Wehrung.

Regardless of whether a decision maker is naturally inclined toward risk, a person faced with a risky decision can take steps to minimize the risk (MacCrimmon & Wehrung, 1986). Risky situations can be adjusted toward less risk by seeking additional information, delaying, delegating, or otherwise sharing the risk with others. Uncertainties can be reduced through long-term contracts, lobbying with government agencies, dealing with competitors, or other actions designed to make the environment more predictable. Time can be gained by stonewalling or asking for extensions. Sharing of risk occurs through insurance, contingent contracts, collateral, performance guarantees, and joint ventures. Thus, even after making a risky choice, managers can continue to take actions to minimize the risk and obtain the best possible outcomes.

RATIONALITY

So far, we have noted that important managerial decisions are complex, uncertain, and constrained, and that decision makers are perceptually biased and influenced by subjective personal preferences regarding risk, ethics, and other values. Given all these problems, how should a manager make decisions?

The answer, of course, is rationally. Traditionally, managers are admonished to do everything they can to make sure their decisions are as rational as possible. To be a rational manager is to be objective, fair, and above reproach.

What does it mean to be rational? Historically, management scholars have relied on economic theory and the assumptions of "economic man" to provide a description of rationality in decision making. The decision maker, with complete information and without constraints, objectively evaluates alternatives and their outcomes and makes a decision maximizing expected utility.

Obviously, this description of managerial decision making defies reality. It is more *normative* (indicative of how people *should* make decisions) than *descriptive* (indicative of how people *do* make decisions). While it offers a useful standard for which the decision maker might strive, its virtual impossibility has led to the development of other useful concepts of rationality in organizational life.

Decision makers cannot maximize outcomes because of limited information and other constraints such as time and cost (March & Simon, 1958). People are limited also by their ability to process information, even if it is readily available. Rationality is therefore limited. This concept of *bounded rationality* causes the decision maker to search for and select a solution that is satisfactory rather than optimal. A related tendency, to decide on the first alternative that satisfies all minimal standards of acceptability, is called *satisficing*. Here, we accept the first alternative that comes to mind that is good enough, without bothering to compare it to other viable alternatives (Janis, 1989).

Another form of rationality is *retrospective rationality* (Staw, 1980). Here, decision makers justify the rationality of decisions that have already been made. Thus, managers often defend what they did by sounding rational rather than rationalizing; decision-making meetings are often merely forums for announcing, explaining, defending, and otherwise promoting decisions that have already been made; and decision makers often sink additional resources into a losing course of action hoping they can turn it around, thereby proving the rationality of their initial decision. As Bass (1984) puts it, "much of the action takes place after the fact. I decide, then I justify. My choice was value-driven, but I was not aware of this. Now that I have made my choice, I need to find good reasons for it" (p. 142).

Finally, *procedural rationality* refers to the effectiveness of the techniques used to make decisions (Simon, 1978). Procedural rationality exists when decision makers engage in the social and psychological processes that indicate effective problem solving. Procedural rationality occurs when the person exhibits *vigilance* (Janis & Mann, 1977). Vigilance increases the decision maker's ability to acquire and process pertinent information.

Vigilance occurs when the decision maker:

Thoroughly canvasses a wide range of alternative courses of action.

Surveys the full range of objectives to be fulfilled and the values implicated by the choice.

Carefully weighs whatever is known about the costs and risks of negative consequences, as well as the positive consequences, that could result from each alternative.

Intensively searches for new information relevant to further evaluation of the alternatives.

Correctly assimilates and takes into account any new information or advice offered, even when the information or advice does not support the initially preferred course of action.

Reexamines all the possible consequences of all known alternatives before making a final choice, including those originally regarded as unacceptable.

Makes detailed provisions for implementing or executing the chosen course of action, with special attention to contingency plans that might be required if various worst-case scenarios come to pass.

Failure to meet any of these criteria results in defective decision making. As an illustration of how uncommon true vigilance is, a study at the University of Oklahoma found that students attempting to solve ill-structured but commonplace decision problems—for example, finding a place to live—were unable to suggest high-utility action plans (Gettys, Pliske, Manning, & Casey, 1987). This study focused on only one stage of the problem-solving process (generating alternatives), using a familiar problem. The more defects that exist throughout all stages of the process, and the more difficult the problem, the more likely the decision will not be a rational one.

INFORMATION: THE RAW MATERIAL
OF DECISION MAKING

Effective decision making depends on effective information processing. Information is needed for each decision-making stage. The impetus for problem identification and diagnosis often is information indicating a drop in sales or market share, increased operating costs or employee turnover, or a gut feeling that problems loom on the horizon. Alternative solutions must be generated and assessed, using information helpful in predicting their consequences and probabilities of success. Information about constraints, costs, and political feasibility are useful in both the implementation and evaluation stages. And the important criteria on which alternatives should be judged indicate what information—sales data, costs, turnover ratios—should be collected in the monitoring stage in order to determine the success of the solution.

Information Relevance and Reliability

The information pertinent to all of the stages may be vague, inconsistent, subjective, or unavailable. For information to be useful to decision makers, it must be both relevant and reliable.

Relevance   Even if information is available, it may not be useful to the decision maker. The information has relevance when it serves a particular task and supplements the decision maker's prior knowledge (Bass, 1984). Unfortunately, people often use irrelevant information. Many investors lost substantial sums of money when they committed funds to John Z.

DeLorean's dream car, the DeLorean, and his now defunct DeLorean Motor Company (DMC). One older investor got on board because he had invested successfully in Barney Olds when he was starting Oldsmobile, and thought the DeLorean venture would be another good chance to get into a company on the ground floor. Another remembered seeing DeLorean walking his young daughter to school and figured he couldn't be all bad. These conveniently available bits of information were not as relevant as the track record of DeLorean as an entrepreneur, the success rate of new car companies, and other indicators of DMC's true viability (Levin, 1983).

Decision makers often are overloaded with irrelevant information. Information is overproduced because managers want to know as much as they can about what's going on, because staff and other personnel compete for reputations based on how much information they can produce, and because information breeds confidence in decision making. Much information is either irrelevant or redundant, breeding potentially dangerous overconfidence. Management information systems may increase managers' confidence but not improve the actual quality of their decisions (Zeleny, 1981).

Reliability   To be useful, information must be reliable or accurate as well as relevant. In organizations, numerous sources of unreliability can cause bias in the information that is presented or otherwise available to the decision maker.

Organization members perceive things, including information, as they expect to or want to. People are uncomfortable with ambiguity or uncertainty, so they provide structure or fill in the gaps that may exist in available information. Thus, information tends to lose some of its uncertainty as it moves through several decision units (MacCrimmon, 1974) and people supplement it with their own impressions and assumptions. The result is an apparent precision that is not as sound as it may seem (Bass, 1984). Similarly, it is well documented that information is lost or distorted as it is passed downward through the organizational hierarchy.

The reliability of information must be assessed; the credibility of its sources must be ascertained. This does not imply merely that the potential biases of the people who provide information must be taken into account in appraising the utility of the information. It means also that hard data such as economic and other statistics be judged for validity and for the accuracy of their assumptions and the inferences they promote.

Information Acquisition

How is information acquired for decision making? What information is actually used? Managers acquire information from people more than from written documents or other impersonal sources. They acquire information from people with whom they have direct and easy contact, both inside and outside the organization, and especially those over whom they have some control, such as subordinates and salespeople.

Thus, decision makers tend to use sources that provide lower quality information but are readily accessible. There is also a general bias toward positive, and against negative, information. Information is more likely to be used by decision makers if it supports outcomes already favored, if it avoids conflict, and if it cannot be challenged (O'Reilly, 1983). Bad news, including news that involves the possibility of interpersonal confrontations, is avoided. Good news, and information that promotes harmony, is embraced.

Negative information is often distorted or not communicated in organizations. Many laboratory studies (Tesser & Rosen 1975) have demonstrated the "mum effect," or the bias against transmitting bad news and toward reporting good news. This tendency certainly holds in organizational life as well. Many subordinates tell their bosses what they want to hear, withhold contradictory personal opinions, or neglect to report all the uncomfortable facts. The extent to which superiors will take positive feedback at face value, failing to consider that the information may be less than perfectly valid, is noteworthy. Recall the discussion in Chapter 2 of the validity of interview and survey methodologies, both of which are often conducted within a context of subordinate-to-superior communications.

Decision makers are also biased toward acquiring and using information that is vividly presented and concrete, rather than pallid and abstract. These characteristics make information more available or accessible in memory and imagination. People remember incidents in which they were personally involved and that are dramatic and have emotional impact (Nisbett & Ross, 1980). Thus, first-hand experience has a more lasting impact than reading about the same situation in a newspaper; seeing friends get fired after a merger affects one's thinking more than hearing about a merger that led to hundreds of layoffs; and learning that a tornado damaged an adjacent community affects decisions about safety precautions more than learning about a tornado that wiped out a mobile home neighborhood several states away. One study showed that students were influenced in their choices of which courses to take much more by the personalized, concrete comments of a single student than by the duller, abstract, but more valid statistical data provided by course evaluation forms (Borgida & Nisbett, 1977).

Information Processing

Having acquired at least some pertinent information, the decision maker must now process the information toward making the actual decision. People are susceptible to a variety of errors in processing information. Some biases are caused by emotional and motivational influences. Others are cognitive limitations on our ability to effectively handle large quantities of information.

Common sources of error lie in *heuristics*—judgmental rules of thumb that provide shortcuts in processing information. The following are some of the heuristics and biases to which people are commonly susceptible.

Misguided Parsimony   One important bias people have is misguided parsimony (Kanouse, 1972)—a tendency to seek a single explanation for an event. Once an adequate explanation is found, little effort is expended toward discovering other, perhaps equally or more relevant, causes. For example, a decision maker contemplating the acquisition of a foundering company would be well-served to analyze the reasons behind its weak performance. Upon realizing a serious flaw in its marketing strategy, the decision maker might be confident that she has found the key to turning things around. But misguided parsimony could prevent an adequate search for other, more important problems. The result is a poor decision—either a bad acquisition or inappropriate strategic plans for turning the company around.

Framing   The way in which options are presented is an important influence on decision makers. How decisions are framed, or phrased, affects risk preferences and decision behavior (Kahneman & Tversky, 1984).

While framing effects can be quite complex, some simple examples illustrate the point. The option of surgery (compared to radiation therapy) was deemed less attractive by physicians and patients when equivalent statistics of treatment outcomes were described in terms of probabilities of death rather than in terms of survival odds (McNeil, Pauker, Sox, & Tversky, 1982). Managers made higher (simulated) investments when an option was described with a 70 percent chance of profit than when the same option was described with a 30 percent chance of failure (Bateman & Zeithaml, 1989). Lobbyists for the credit card industry label any price differences between cash and credit purchases a cash discount rather than a credit card surcharge; consumers are less likely to accept a surcharge than to forego a discount (Thaler, 1980).

In these and other instances, options are objectively equivalent yet decision makers' choices are affected by how they are phrased. Awareness of this bias helps persuaders influence their audiences, and helps decision makers (or persuadees) avoid succumbing to the consequent irrational tendencies.

Analogies and Metaphors   Also useful to both persuaders and persuadees is understanding how analogies and metaphors sway decisions. A single analogy or metaphor often crystallizes complex problems into simple scenarios or solutions. Fear of the "domino effect" in Southeast Asia dominated foreign policy in that region in the 1950s and 1960s; a picture of an umbrella with missiles bouncing off it helped President Reagan convince the public of the merits of the Strategic Defense Initiative ("Star Wars"); and invoking the imagery of a three-legged stool convinced General Cinema executives to acquire a third line of business (a furniture retailer) that was completely unrelated to their two existing lines (Schwenk, 1984). These images were much simpler and easier to grasp than the true complexities of U.S. involvement in Southeast Asia, nuclear defense technology and strategy, and major corporate acquisitions.

Effective decision making can use analogy and metaphor in grappling with uncertainties, but also must consider carefully how the imagery is similar to and different from the current problem (Neustadt & May, 1986). Opponents to U.S. aid to the Contras sold their position by invoking an analogy to Vietnam; proponents of U.S. involvement argued that the analogy was inappropriate because of major differences between the two situations.

Anchoring and Adjustment   Anchoring occurs when people make an initial attempt to solve a problem or make a decision, and then deviate very little from their preliminary choice (Tversky & Kahneman, 1975). If some initial reference point exists, it will strongly influence the final solution. For example, professional real estate agents were given personal tours of homes and 10 pages of pertinent information and then asked to estimate prices of the homes. Of all the information at their disposal, only one item — bogus listing prices for the houses — affected their estimates. The fictitious listing prices provided an easy anchor, which was then adjusted in minor ways. The resulting, biased estimates were inaccurate, in ways that could have been costly to buyers (Northcraft & Neale, 1987).

In organizations, anchors are provided by precedents, stated or otherwise known positions of those in power, and written or unwritten norms. Ground is yielded begrudgingly from such anchor points. For these reasons, most decisions in organizations are conservative.

Making small adjustments from anchors will be successful in many situations (Hogarth, 1980). Short-term predictions of production levels, sales returns, and your boss's behavior can usually be made accurately on the basis of the recent past. Even the price of a stock can be expected to be high tomorrow if it was high today. In fact, all of the sources of error discussed above are only potentially problematic. They save us much time and effort as shortcuts in information processing. They probably result in many more correct or at least adequate decisions than faulty ones, particularly when choices are relatively easy, habitual, or embedded in stable environments. The problems arise, however, when decisions are complex, novel, risky, and embedded in turbulent environments — the domain of consequential managerial decisions.

Egocentrism and Emotion   Most of the heuristics described above are a function of constraints on cognitive capacities. That is, limited time and ability to handle complex information processing requirements leads people to invoke simple cognitive decision rules like satisficing, misguided parsimony, and anchoring adjustment. But decisions are based on considerations other than cognitive operations; they often are egocentric. People often make decisions using heuristics that give priority to satisfying their own personal motives or emotional needs (Janis, 1989).

A simple self-serving rule of thumb is used when decision makers view problems primarily from the standpoint of "What's in it for me?" The good of the organization acquires secondary importance, as decision makers push options that help them attain strictly personal goals. You undoubtedly can think of recent events in which policy makers made decisions that seem based strictly on this personal aggrandizement rule (Janis, 1989).

Emotive rules are used when people allow emotional reactions to guide their decisions. Examples are offered in Table 9–2. Note that emotional states are not necessarily negative; elation, for example, is a positive emotional reaction. If such emotive rules are guiding decisions, vigilance falls by the wayside, and losses that might otherwise have been avoidable become, instead, more probable.

THE CHOICE

Despite shortcomings in available information and potential errors in information acquisition and processing, a choice eventually must be made. To arrive at a decision, people implicitly give a value to each alternative being considered. This value reflects the sum of the values of the dimensions, as weighted by their importance, on which alternatives are judged. According to Hogarth (1980):

$$\text{Value of alternative} = \text{Sum of (Relative weight} \times \text{Value)} \\ \text{of all dimensions}$$

You can see the parallels between this model and the expectancy theory of motivation discussed in Chapter 4. The model assumes that people will choose the alternative with the highest value. This linear model has been

TABLE 9–2
Emotive Decision Rules

---

1. Impatience: "The hell with the consequences!"
2. Defensive avoidance: "I can't deal with this. Time to procrastinate or pass the buck."
3. Hypervigilant escape: "Get the hell out fast!"
4. Audacity: "Can do!"
5. Anger: "Retaliate!"
6. Elated choice: "Wow! Grab it!"

SOURCE: Adapted with permission of The Free Press, a Division of Macmillan, Inc., from *Crucial Decisions: Leadership in Policymaking and Crisis Management* by Irving L. Janis. Copyright © 1989 by The Free Press.

quite accurate in predicting individual judgments in both laboratory and such real-world settings as production-scheduling decisions, college admission office decisions, and judgments by auditors (Dawes & Corrigan, 1974; Meehl, 1955).

Decision makers sometimes employ models other than the linear model. For instance, alternatives' scores on different dimensions may or may not be able to offset one another. In deciding whether to admit a candidate to graduate school, should a person be able to overcome a low score on one dimension (such as entrance exam scores) with a high score on another dimension (such as grade point average)? Or should there be a minimum standard on both dimensions? The decision model is *compensatory* if the former approach is used, in which case a student with a poor exam score can still gain admittance if grades were high enough. On the other hand, if a person is automatically eliminated from consideration if the exam score fails to reach the minimum standard, a *conjunctive* model is operating.

When faced with the need to choose one from among a number of alternatives, the *elimination-by-aspects* model (Tversky, 1972) may be employed. Here, the dimensions are ranked in terms of importance. Next, the most important dimension is considered and any alternative that is not acceptable on the dimension is eliminated from consideration. Then, alternatives unacceptable on the second dimension are discarded, and the process continues until only one alternative remains. Tversky uses the example of buying a car, as one car after another is eliminated by virtue of not having an affordable price, then by not being American-built, then by not having an automatic transmission, and down through the list of important attributes until only one choice remains.

An *incremental* model is used when decisions involve minor changes in present policies. This occurs in part due to the cognitive bias created by anchoring, and in part because of real organization constraints. Budgets, for example, often are marked by only minor tinkering from year to year. Last year's budget provides the anchor for the decision regarding next year's budget.

Etzioni (1967) has offered a strategy of *mixed scanning* that is a synthesis of optimizing and the satisficing that occurs through routine incrementalism. Scanning refers to the acquisition and processing of information pertinent to the decision, and is essentially the same as Janis and Mann's (1977) vigilant information processing. The strategy of mixed scanning is one in which optimizing is attempted only for the most important decisions facing the organization. Satisficing and incremental processes are used for the routine decisions that arise after the major decisions have been made. In essence, the decision maker is allocating energies optimally—the hard work of vigilance and optimization is saved for those decisions for which it will really pay off.

AFTER THE CHOICE

The problem-solving process is not completed on arrival at a decision. Psychological processes continue to exert influence on the decision maker, implementation efforts begin, commitment develops, and feedback regarding the results of the decision arrives.

Psychological Responses

Once the choice is made, the decision maker typically experiences some kind of psychological or cognitive reaction. Regret is sometimes experienced, particularly when new information, including negative feedback, becomes available. Very commonly, though, the decision maker psychologically defends the chosen course of action. *Bolstering* is the umbrella term for the various psychological tactics that create and maintain the decision maker's positive outlook on the decision (Janis & Mann, 1977). Common bolstering tactics include exaggerating the favorable aspects of the choice, downplaying the risks and other negative features, and turning adverse aspects of the decision into attractive ones. For example, a demanding job that has just been chosen over a more comfortable option becomes a "fascinating challenge."

Implementation

A useful decision is not merely made—it is put into action. Decision effectiveness is determined by two broad clusters of variables: the quality of the decision itself, and skillful management of implementation (Trull, 1966). The key factors in implementation include avoiding conflict of interest, attending to potential rewards versus risk, and making sure the decision is well understood by those involved in implementing it (Trull, 1966). These and other aspects of involving others in the implementation of decisions pertain to the topics of motivation (Chapters 3, 4, and 5), job performance (Chapters 10 and 11), group processes (Chapters 16 and 17), power, politics, and leadership (Chapters 18 and 19), and organizational change (Chapter 22).

Commitment and Entrapment

Once the choice is made — particularly once it is made public, and even more so once implementation begins — the decision maker becomes committed to seeing it through. Sometimes, overcommitment develops and traps the individual, as it becomes very difficult to change the original decision.

Recall the scenario opening this chapter in which you have chosen a division to be allocated additional R&D funding, and now you are receiving negative feedback indicating that sales and profits are not increasing as hoped. Several forces are operating that would lead you to commit additional funding to the failing division. First, retrospective rationality may compel you to justify your earlier decision (Staw, 1981). No one wants to be perceived as initially wrong, or worse, as indecisive, waffling, or erratic. Add to these fears the fact that costs have increased, and lingering hope that (1) the initial investment brought the division one step closer to profitability, (2) one more push may be all it needs, and (3) approval and other rewards await if the turnaround is effected. It's easy to see how commitment increases, psychological entrapment occurs, and good money is thrown after bad.

Staw provides a number of examples of this tendency, including the R&D investment decision, the escalation of U.S. involvement in Vietnam, personal decisions to hold a stock whose price has plummeted ("It's going to turn around any day now; I just know this investment will pan out"), and finishing an advanced degree in a field that holds few job opportunities ("I can't quit now; I've already invested two years of my life"). Reversing these escalation tendencies requires gathering and using information regarding future prospects, and ignoring sunk costs. Seeking advice from an uninvolved, more objective person can be useful here.

Abandoning sunk costs could hurt your reputation; reputational damage can lead to future problems. If the future cost to reputation outweighs the cost of paying a sunk cost, then it is rational to pay it (Dawes, 1988). But such pressures on individual decision makers should be relaxed by the organization. In short, the motivation for decisions should be the attainment of future gain, not the defense of past actions.

Feedback and Evaluation

Following implementation, decisions must be monitored and evaluated. Subjective, impressionistic criteria may be used. What were the effects of the decision on the people involved? How timely was the decision, and how did it fit with the objectives and within the constraints of the firm (or individual)? Ideally, objective assessments, commonly involving cost accounting techniques, are applied in addition to personal opinion.

Despite the importance of assessing consequential decisions, rigorous evaluations often are made poorly or not at all. Valid assessments can be quite costly. Overconfident decision makers may not feel the need to test their judgments, or they may be reluctant to face the possibility of a negative evaluation.

Partly because of these psychological considerations, feedback on our decisions may fail to lead to constructive learning. Peoples' beliefs often are immune to incoming information, for several reasons: (1) we use tougher standards in criticizing evidence opposing our decisions than in criticizing supportive evidence; (2) mixed evidence reinforces our existing theories or viewpoints; and (3) when we formulate a theory, and then learn that the evidence on which it is based is false, our theory still survives (Nisbett & Ross, 1980). In short, our beliefs tend to persevere, regardless of subsequent feedback.

In addition to these tendencies, the *hindsight bias* (Fischoff & Beyth, 1976) often kicks into operation. When a person learns of an event, 20/20 hindsight makes it seem to have been inevitable. If the person "knew" things would happen as they did, there is no lesson to be learned from a bad decision. "Sure, I made the decision, but I'm not really surprised things turned out this way." A major danger to the bias of 20/20 hindsight, then, is that people fail to adequately assess past errors, and therefore don't learn important lessons from experience.

Decision makers should record not only their decisions (so that evaluations of performance can be made) but also the bases for their decisions — the information used, the assumptions made, and the procedures employed (Hogarth, 1980). Recording this information provides one form of helpful feedback on the decision-making process and ensures that learning can occur through the identification of procedural errors.

DECISION AIDS

It should be very clear that numerous pitfalls await the unwary decision maker. Fortunately, many aids, including those described in the Focus on the Future, are available to increase the probability that a well-informed, reasonably objective, appropriate decision is made.

Structuring Decisions   Standard operating procedures (SOPs) can be developed to provide solutions for well-structured problems. For ill-structured problems, computers can provide assistance, including data aggregation, time series forecasting, simulation, and input-output models. *Bootstrapping* is a useful technique that builds statistical (usually linear regression) models based on the decision maker's judgments, and then applies the models to subsequent decisions.

Another useful technique is *sensitivity analysis.* This process determines how sensitive choices are to the probability estimates and weights used in making them. The decision maker should assume that the figures used to model a problem are wrong (Hogarth, 1980). One therefore should vary the quantitative inputs to a decision model. In practice, decision makers' over-confidence (or ignorance) may cause them to select too narrow a range of input; thus, one should seek advice from critical outsiders and consider an adequate range of values (Fischhoff & Goitein, 1984). By doing so, one can determine what it would take to change the decision dictated by the original assumptions. It may be that a wide range of numerical inputs accommodate the same decision, or the decision may be shaky due to its high sensitivity to varying assumptions.

Rules of Thumb   Effective decision making need not and sometimes even should not use these technical approaches. Simple rules of thumb can often be useful. This chapter has suggested many rules of thumb

FOCUS ON THE FUTURE

Decision Simulators

Business school computer classes and corporate computer rooms have been around for many years. Recently, simulation technology has been brought to many managers, thanks to powerful personal computers and simpler software. The technology, analogous to flight simulations for airline pilots, lets managers test their decisions and make mistakes without suffering the consequences (Solomon, 1989).

With typical business decisions, most managers must quickly weigh a few options and look ahead just a couple of months. Simulations are used to train managers to think more about the long term and consider more variables and more options. And simulations allow managers to learn painlessly from mistakes. In one simulation, a team of GE employees wanted to assign more people to a project to meet an impending dead-line. The feedback showed that the extra workers took longer to learn the job, and that more people meant more communication foul-ups. Participants say they will think twice before making the same mistake in real life.

One simulation has graphics of an animated plumbing system, in which users fill little buckets with cash, inventory, and even frustration. Spending, hiring, sales, and even buildups of confidence flow through small pipes. Another simulation hits users with sudden news bulletins like accidents or vendors' price increases.

Most simulations are used in training; a few are designed for everyday use by managers at their desks. Some computer experts think that simulations will never be a standard management tool. What's your prediction?

that a decision maker should keep in mind: judge the reliability of information, maintain vigilance in information processing, beware of misguided parsimony, ignore sunk costs, be open to new evidence, record and evaluate decision processes, and learn from—rather than be blinded by—hindsight.

Other People   Other people can be invaluable as decision aids. In Asian and African cultures, different viewpoints are considered valuable because they enrich us with indispensable information. North Americans and Europeans prefer not to clutter their thinking with too many viewpoints (Maruyama, 1984), but using another person as a sounding board can help you explore and clarify ideas. Information and advice from experts can be solicited. A group may be called together to make what could have been one individual's decision. When and how to use input from others in decision making is further explored in Chapter 17, when group decision making is discussed.

Thinking   Finally, and most important, think. Whereas routine decisions can be made effectively by habit or by perfunctory analysis, complex decisions require significant mental effort.

Thinking has a number of costs and benefits (Hogarth, 1980). Thinking is hard work—it causes discomfort by highlighting uncertainties and illuminating the difficult trade-offs that must be faced. Yet thinking can also help clarify goals, preferences, and alternatives. It can help avoid procedural pitfalls that lead to consequential errors. Thinking also creates the habit of more and better thinking—that is, the more one thinks, the greater is the potential for developing better problem-solving strategies. And, thinking can help minimize the decision maker's regret if the decision does not turn out favorably. A negative outcome can be much better defended, to oneself and others, if the decision was carefully pondered.

PERSONAL INVOLVEMENT IN ORGANIZATIONAL DECISIONS

This chapter has described various aspects of individual decision making, with occasional reference to the constraints created by the organizational context. Now, we will describe aspects of personal survival regarding organizational decision making: deciding when to become involved in a decision, predicting and influencing organizational decisions, and explaining and defending individual decisions.

Becoming Involved

The manager who becomes aware of a problem or potential problem faces a decision as to whether and how to become involved (organizations face the same decision; see Close-Up). Prior to becoming actively involved, the manager might ask pertinent questions concerning his or her ability to actually do something about the problem or otherwise contribute to its solution. Important here are the resources at the manager's disposal, including political clout, and constraints, such as money and time. Bass (1984) quotes Chester Barnard's (1938) lines: "The fine art of executive decision making consists in not deciding questions that are not now pertinent, in not deciding prematurely, in not making decisions that cannot be made effective, and in not making decisions that others should make" (p. 188).

Thus, effective organizational decision makers pick and choose their issues carefully, delay if it is not timely to decide, and spread their personal risks by allowing others to contribute to decisions that could go wrong. Self-interest may be the critical factor—managers become actively involved when the decision is consequential to them, and are wise to lessen their involvement when it will gain them little.

CLOSE-UP

Getting Involved: The Role of Problem Definition

The first stage of the problem-solving process is identifying the problem. This is a perceptual and interpretative process—one that may determine whether individuals, or organizations, take any action at all. The Port Authority of New York and New Jersey provides a case in point regarding an important social issue: the plight of the homeless (Dutton & Dikerich, 1989).

The Port Authority (PA) is a government development corporation established to administer the economic and social development of the Port District, an area encompassing a 25-mile radius of the Statue of Liberty. It is a multipurpose public authority that owns and operates 35 facilities including the World Trade Center, the bus terminal, tunnels, bridges, and marine facilities, and Kennedy, LaGuardia, and Newark airports. The PA employs 10,000 people and its assets total about $5 billion.

The PA's major service is safe transportation. This service was hindered more and more by the rising numbers of homeless persons at its facilities. Over time, interpretations of the homeless problem changed, and organizational involvement in the problem changed accordingly. In 1982, homelessness was defined as a police or security issue; at that time, the local police force at the PA bus terminal (employed by the PA) dealt with the problem, in conjunction with bus terminal management; there was no coordinated, corporate-level involvement in the homelessness issue.

In 1985–86, more homeless were present in other PA facilities. In particular, problems were arising in the World Trade Center and the airports—the central components of the PA's identity. It was then recognized that the homeless problem was corporate-wide, and corporate-level staff began studying it. Even though homelessness was now understood to be a corporate problem, the PA still considered itself not to be in the social services business. But by 1987, as problems escalated and police-based solutions proved ineffective, the organization came to recognize that the issue was one for which the PA needed to accept some responsibility. It became clear that no one else was dealing with the problem, and that solving it was part of the PA's mission. The PA also became concerned with finding moral, humane solutions.

In 1987, a centralized homelessness project team was formed. As the homelessness problem hurt transportation, image, and business, it became viewed as a competitiveness issue and a regional crisis. In 1988, a major speech made the PA's commitment to the problem a matter of public record. The PA established two 24-hour drop-in centers, at a cost of $2.5 million, to serve the homeless. Other programs were also fostered; the PA was getting more and more into the business of homelessness.

Predicting and Influencing

Effectively influencing organizational decisions requires the ability to predict them. Huber (1980) highlights some of the many determinants of organizational decisions. First, the most conspicuous alternative is usually the one chosen. For solutions to be sold, they must be salient in the minds of the decision makers. If your idea is the best, don't assume it will fly; make sure it becomes obvious in others' minds. Second, the more likely decision is the one that takes the least time. If your idea is in the lead, take reasonable action to bring the decision process to a close.

Third, certain information has the greatest impact on the final decision. Hard data and vivid anecdotes are more influential than subjective impressions and dry statements; you can present and react to information accordingly. Fourth, resource availability greatly dictates which alternatives can and cannot be selected. Constraints might be designed or redesigned to fit a preferred alternative. Or perhaps a personally favored solution that exceeds budget constraints can be sold by virtue of its ability to solve other problems in addition to the one under immediate consideration.

Resource shortages also increase the role of power and politics in organizational decision making. The preferred solutions of powerful persons may override alternatives that rate highly on economic and other objective criteria. It is useful to marshall the support of powerful individuals or coalitions, and also to know which issues those persons will attempt to influence and which they will ignore. What is of great importance to a given manager may be of trivial consequence to executives who must allocate their political energies across a myriad of other issues. Power and politics in organizational life will be discussed in greater detail in Chapter 18.

Explaining and Defending

Sooner or later, most decisions must be explained and often defended. Here is a list of ingredients for the preparation of a decision report that explains and justifies the final results (Easton, 1976):

1. A background statement about the organization and its environment up to the time of decision.
2. A description of the problem, including how it came to be detected.
3. A recapitulation of the diagnostic procedures.
4. A review of the interest groups involved in and affected by the decision.
5. A statement of objectives and criteria.
6. Information on the identification, evaluation, and final choice of alternatives.
7. A statement of unfinished aspects of the decision process.

The ability to provide this information helps the decision maker assess the adequacy of his or her own decision processes. At the same time, it serves the needs of those who will be inquiring into the rationality of the decision itself.

SUMMARY

Effective decision making may be the most important skill a manager can possess. Most managers probably assume they are reasonably competent decision makers, but often there is a substantial difference between actual and potential decision quality.

Decisions differ in their degree of structure, risk, uncertainty, complexity, and conflict, and the constraints within which they must be made. The people making decisions differ also, in their perceptions, ethics, and risk-taking propensity.

Classic definitions of economic rationality and standard models of the sequential stages of decision making provide useful starting points for understanding how decisions are made. But other models better capture decision processes in organizations and what can be more realistically attained regarding rationality. Numerous disruptions, biases in information processing and acquisition, and difficulties after the decision is made, can weigh against the ultimate success of any decision.

Fortunately, most decisions work out to be adequate, if not great. Even the many psychological biases that influence decisions have advantages—they can greatly increase the efficiency of decision making while still resulting in satisfactory outcomes. When the tendencies of humans and organizations have the potential to interfere too greatly with the decision process, decision aids like bootstrapping and sensitivity analysis can increase the probability that well-informed, reasonably valid judgments are made.

CONCEPTS TO REMEMBER

Decision quality	Satisficing	Conjunctive model
Ill-structured problem	Vigilance	Elimination-by-aspects model
Risk	Reliability of information	Incremental model
Uncertainty	Heuristics	Mixed scanning
Social trap	Misguided parsimony	Bolstering
Intrapersonal conflict types	Framing effects	Entrapment
Stages of cognitive moral development	Anchoring and adjustment	Hindsight bias
	Linear model	Bootstrapping
Types of rationality	Compensatory model	Sensitivity analysis

QUESTIONS FOR DISCUSSION

1. Review a major decision you have made and at least somewhat regretted. Reflect on the process that led to your choice. What might you have done differently to have reached a more satisfactory decision?

2. Why is bolstering such a common occurrence after a decision is made?

3. Using real examples, about which you have first- or second-hand knowledge, generate some illustrations of *(a)* social traps and *(b)* escalating commitment to a previously chosen course of action. Describe how each of your examples could best be managed.

4. What does it mean to be "decisive"? What are some of the pros and cons of decisiveness?

5. Choose an important choice you must make from among several alternatives. Describe how the various models of choice apply (or don't apply) in helping you make your choice.

REFERENCES

Adler, N. (1986). *International dimensions of organizational behavior.* Boston: Kent Publishing Co.

Barnard, C. I. (1938). *The functions of the executive.* Cambridge, MA: Harvard Univ. Press.

Barry, B., & Bateman, T. (1989). The information dilemma: A social trap approach to managerial information exchange. Paper presented at the 1989 Academy of Management meeting, Washington, D.C.

Bass, B. M. (1983). *Organizational decision making.* Homewood, IL: Richard D. Irwin.

Bateman, T., & Zeithaml, C. (1989). The psychological context of strategic decisions: A model and convergent experimental findings. *Strategic Management Journal* 10, 59–74.

Borgida, E., & Nisbett, R. (1977). The differential impact of abstract versus concrete information on decisions. *Journal of Applied Social Psychology* 7, 258–71.

Brenner, S., & Molander, E. (1977). Is the ethics of business changing? *Harvard Business Review* 55, 57–71.

Dawes, R. M. (1988). *Rational choice in an uncertain world.* San Diego: Harcourt Brace Jovanovich.

Dawes, R., & Corrigan, B. (1974). Linear models in decision making. *Psychological Bulletin* 81, 95–106.

Dearborn, D., & Simon, H. (1958). Selective perception: A note on the departmental identifications of executives. *Sociometry* 21, 140–44.

Dutton, J., & Dukerich, J. (1989). Keeping an eye on the mirror: The role of image and identity in organizational adaptation. Working paper.

Easton, A. (1976). *Decision making: A short course in problem solving for professionals.* New York: John Wiley & Sons.

Etzioni, A. (1967). Mixed scanning: A third approach to decision making. *Public Administration Review* 27, 285–392.

Fischoff, B., & Beyth, R. (1975). "I knew it would happen" — remembered probabilities of once-future things. *Organizational Behavior and Human Performance* 13, 1–16.

Fischhoff, B., & Goitein, B. (1984). The informal use of formal models. *Academy of Management Review* 9, 505–12.

Gettys, C., Pliske, R., Manning, C., Casey, J. (1987). An evaluation of human act generation performance. *Organizational Behavior and Human Decision Processes* 39, 23–51.

Hardin, G. R. (1968). The tragedy of the commons. *Science* 162, 1243–48.

Harris, P., & Moran, R. (1987). *Managing cultural differences.* Houston: Gulf Publishing Co.

Hector, G. (1989). How Safeway coped with the quake. *Fortune,* November 20, pp. 100–104.

Hogarth, R. M. (1980). *Judgment and choice: The psychology of decision.* New York: John Wiley & Son.

Huber, G. P. (1980). *Managerial decision making.* Glenview, IL: Scott, Foresman.

Janis, I. (1989). *Crucial decisions.* New York: The Free Press.

Janis, I., & Mann, L. (1977). *Decision making.* New York: Free Press.

Kahneman, D., & Tversky, A. (1984). *American Psychologist* 39, 341–50.

Kanouse, D. E. (1972). Language, labeling and attribution. In Jones, E. E., Kanouse, D. E., Kelley, H. H., Nisbett, R. E., Valins, S., & Weiner, B. (eds.), *Attribution: Perceiving the causes of behavior.* New York: General Learning Press.

Kohlberg, L. (1969). Stage and sequence: The cognitive-developmental approach to socialization. In D. A. Goslin (ed.), *Handbook of socialization theory and research,* pp. 347–80. Chicago: Rand McNally.

Levin, H. (1983). *Grand delusions: The cosmic career of John DeLorean.* New York: Viking Press.

Lewin, K. (1935). *A dynamic theory of personality.* New York: McGraw-Hill.

Lincoln, D., Pressley, M., & Little, T. (1982). Ethical beliefs and personal values of top level executives. *Journal of Business Research* 10, 475–87.

MacCrimmon, K. R. (1974). Managerial decision making. In J. W. McGuire (ed.), *Contemporary management.* Englewood Cliffs, NJ: Prentice Hall.

MacCrimmon, K. R. & Wehrung, D. (1986). *Taking risks.* New York: The Free Press.

MacCrimmon, K. R., & Taylor, R. N. (1976). Decision making and problem solving. In M. D. Dunnette (ed.), *Handbook of industrial and organizational psychology.* Skokie, IL: Rand McNally.

Maier, N. & Hoffman, L. (1960). Quality of first and second solutions to group problem solving. *Journal of Applied Psychology* 44, 278–83.

Maruyama, M. (1984). *Asia Pacific Journal of Management,* January. Cited in Harris, P. & Moran, R. (1987), *Managing cultural differences.* Houston: Gulf.

March, J. G. (1978). Bounded rationality, ambiguity, and the engineering of choice. *Bell Journal of Economics* 9, 587–608.

March, J. G., & Simon, H. (1958). *Organizations.* New York: John Wiley & Sons.

McNeil, B., Pauker, S., Sox, H., Jr., & Tversky, A. (1982). On the elicitation of preferences for alternative therapies. *New England Journal of Medicine* 306, 1259–62.

Meehl, P. (1955). *Clinical versus statistical prediction.* Minneapolis: University of Minnesota Press.

Neustadt, R., & May, E. (1986). *Thinking in time.* New York: The Free Press.

Nisbett, R., & Ross, L. (1980). *Human inference: Strategies and shortcomings.* Englewood Cliffs, NJ: Prentice Hall.

Northcraft, G., & Neale, M. (1987). Experts, amateurs, and real estate: An anchoring-and-adjustment perspective on property pricing decisions. *Organizational Behavior and Human Performance* 39, 84–97.

O'Reilly, Charles A., III. (1983). The use of information in organizational decision making: A model and some propositions. In B. Staw & L. Cummings (eds.), *Research in organizational behavior,* vol. 5, pp. 103–39. Greenwich, CT: JAI Press.

Ricklees, R. (1983). Ethics in America. *The Wall Street Journal,* Oct. 31–Nov. 3, p. 33.

Schwenk, C. (1984). Cognitive simplification processes in strategic decision making. *Strategic Management Journal* 5, 111-28..

Simon, H. (1978). Rationality as a process and as product of thought. *American Economic Review* 68, 1–16.

Solomon, J. (1989). Now, simulators for piloting companies. *The Wall Street Journal,* July 31, p. B1.

Staw, B. M. (1980). Rationality and justification in organizational life. In B. Staw & L. Cummings (eds.), *Research in organizational behavior,* vol. 2, pp. 45–80. Greenwich, CT: JAI Press.

Staw, B. M. (1981). The escalation of commitment to a course of action. *Academy of Management Review* 6, 577–87.

Tesser, A., & Rosen, S. (1975). The reluctance to transmit bad news. In L. Berkowitz (ed.), *Advances in experimental social psychology* 8, New York: Academic Press.

Thaler, R. (1980). Toward a positive theory of consumer choice. *Journal of Economic Behavior and Organization 1, 39–60.*

Trevino, L. K. (1986). Ethical decision making in organizations: A person-situation interactionist model. *Academy of Management Review* 11, 601–17.

Trull, S. G. (1966). Some factors involved in determining total decision success. *Management Science* 12, 270–80.

Tversky, A. (1972). Elimination by aspects: A theory of choice. *Psychological Review* 79, 281–99.

Tversky, A., & Kahneman, D. (1975). Judgment under uncertainty: Heuristics and biases. *Science* 185, 1124–31.

Ungson, G., Braunstein, D., & Hill, P. (1981). Managerial information processing: A research review. *Administrative Science Quarterly* 26, 116–34.

Zeleny, M. (1981). Descriptive decision making and its applications. *Applications of Management Science* 1, 327–88

SECTION TWO

Cases

ATLANTIC COUNTY DIVISION OF BEACH SAFETY

The Atlantic County Division of Beach Safety employs 100 trained lifeguards during the summer months on the county's ocean beaches. The lifeguard corps is mainly comprised of young college-age males and females who are strong swimmers and have completed specific courses in swimming, water safety, and lifesaving. Officials in the Division of Beach Safety are proud of the beach patrol, as it was ranked second in the nation on the quality of its performance.

Last summer, however, the lifeguards exhibited a lack of motivation and complained about the terms of their employment and working conditions but continued to work effectively. Their discontent centered on the issue of inadequate wages. Compared with other ocean lifeguards, they were receiving one to three dollars less per hour. Compared with other Atlantic County employees, the lifeguards were the lowest workers on the pay scale. Entry-level secretaries, for example, received higher pay than the lifeguards.

To reasonably resolve their pay problem, the lifeguards met with their immediate supervisors and were told, "We can do nothing about your low pay. The Division of Beach Safety sets your wage rates, not us. We have many

SOURCE: J. M. Champion and J. H. James, eds. *Critical Incidents in Management* (Homewood, Ill.: Richard D. Irwin, 1985), pp. 155–57.

FIGURE C–1
County Government Organization

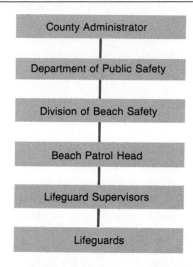

applicants for lifeguard jobs, and jobs are scarce in the summer. You are lucky to have your jobs; don't rock the boat. If you still want to try and do something about your pay, see the head of the Division of Beach Safety or the head of the Department of Public Safety."

After appropriate appointments had been arranged, the head officials of beach safety and public safety, accompanied by staff members, came to a lifeguard meeting at the main lifeguard station. In reply to demands for increased pay, Sally Wingate, head of the Department of Public Safety, stated, "There's nothing I can do to alter the adopted budget. Remember that volunteer lifeguards originally did your jobs. Being a lifeguard puts you where the action is and it doesn't hurt your tan, either! After all, we do pay minimum wages. You'll have to see the county administrator about any budget changes."

At a meeting the following week, the county administrator, Roy Hamilton, heard about the lifeguards' request for increased pay and responded, "This year's county budget has been completed and approved. Unfortunately, we were constrained by the tax dollars available. Funds were sufficient to support raises for most other employees. Have a good summer."

Events moved swiftly. Feeling frustrated, rebuffed, and unappreciated even though their daily work involved life-and-death situations, the lifeguards sought legal advice, learned that they could strike without breaking the state law (because they were not unionized), and decided to "go public" with their grievance. The strike was set for Saturday on the Fourth-of-July weekend, the busiest day of the year. Area newspapers and television and radio stations were informed about the strike.

On the designated strike day, all lifeguards showed up at the main lifeguard station. More than 75 percent of them supported the strike and remained in front of the main station, refusing to go to appropriate guard stations along the beach. People began to fill the beaches and the water. The probability of accidental injury and drowning increased steadily along the crowded, unguarded ocean shore.

As the danger increased, two lifeguard supervisors contacted Bill King, chairman of Atlantic County's board of commissioners, who sensed both the immediate dangers and the long-run organization implications.

King instructed Hamilton to decide on prompt action for restoring safety to the county's public beaches, and to develop some specific policy and procedure recommendations dealing with relevant underlying issues such as personnel policy and operational policy. Hamilton knew that he must decide and act quickly on the critical beach safety problem. He also knew that afterwards he must develop recommendations for compensation policy and grievance handling procedures, among others, for the next meeting of the county commissioners.

Questions   Could the strike have been prevented? Why or why not? What steps should King take now?

CONTRADICTORY STAFF ADVICE

The administrator of the state mental hospital learned that keys to security wards for dangerous criminals had been lost or stolen when he received an early morning telephone call on May 1 from the hospital's night administrator. Since duplicate keys were available in the hospital safe, the administrator, Mr. Jackson, knew that loss of the keys would not interfere with the hospital's routine functioning, but he decided to call a general staff meeting the next morning to consider the problem.

At the meeting, Jackson explained about the missing keys and asked for suggestions. The assistant administrator suggested that the matter be kept confidential among the staff since public knowledge could lead to damaging publicity and a possible investigation by Department of Health and Rehabilitative Services officials.

SOURCE: J. M. Champion and J. H. James eds., *Critical Incidents in Management* (Homewood, Ill.: Richard D. Irwin, 1985), pp. 56–57.

The head of security for the hospital reported that only two keys were missing. Although he could not tell if the keys had been stolen or lost, he thought they were probably stolen. He emphasized that the missing keys were "master keys" that could open the doors to all security wards where the most dangerous criminals were housed. In his opinion, immediate replacement of the locks on those doors was required.

The director of accounting estimated the cost of replacing the locks at more than $5,000. She reminded the group that operating costs already exceeded the hospital's operating budget by about 10 percent due to inflation and other unexpected expenses, and that an emergency request for a supplemental budget appropriation to cover the deficit had been sent to the Department of Health and Rehabilitative Services the previous week. She concluded that no funds were available in the budget for replacing the locks, and an additional $5,000 request might jeopardize the request for supplementary operating funds already submitted. Besides, since it was early May, the hospital would begin operating under the budget for the next fiscal year in approximately 60 days. The locks could be replaced then and the costs charged against the new budget.

Another staff member reasoned aloud that if the keys had been lost, any person finding them would probably not know their purpose and that if the keys had been stolen, they probably would never be used in any unauthorized way.

Jackson thanked the staff members for their contributions, ended the meeting, and faced the decision. He reflected that behind the doors to the security wards were convicted first-degree murderers and sexual psychopaths, among others. He also remembered his impeccable 13-year record as an effective hospital administrator. The thought occurred to him that perhaps the most important action would be to find and place the blame upon the person who was responsible for the disappearance of the two keys.

As he continued his deliberation, Jackson realized that each staff member's suggestion reflected his or her individual profession or specialty. These divergent and contradictory recommendations, taken together, produced no solution. Jackson saw two critical requirements. He recognized an immediate need to decide upon and implement temporary procedures to guarantee containment of the mental patients. Moreover, he needed to develop an organizational response policy for future incidents that threatened to compromise the mental patient security system. Jackson didn't know how best to proceed.

Questions How should Jackson structure his decision-making process? What pitfalls should he beware of?

CENTER CITY ENGINEERING DEPARTMENT

The Engineering Department of Center City employed approximately 1,000 people, all of whom worked under the provisions of the Civil Service System. Of these employees, about 100 worked in the design division. Parker Nolton, an associate engineer, had been employed in the design division for 19 years and was known personally by virtually everyone in the division, if not in Center City itself. Nolton had held the position of associate engineer for seven years on a provisional basis only, for he had never been able to pass the required civil service examinations to gain permanent appointment to this grade, although he had taken them often. Many of his co-workers felt that his lack of formal engineering education prevented him from passing the examinations, but Nolton felt that his failures were the result of his tendency to "tighten up" when taking an examination. Off the job, Nolton was extremely active in civic affairs and city-sponsored recreational programs. During the past year, for example, he had been president of the high school Parent Teacher's Association, captain of the bowling team sponsored by the Engineering Department in the Municipal Bowling League, and a member of the managing committee of the Center City Little League.

As Center City grew and the activities of the engineering department expanded to keep pace with this growth, younger men were hired into the department in relatively large numbers. Among those hired were Ralph Boyer and Doug Worth. Both of these young men were graduate engineers, and had accepted the positions with the engineering department after fulfilling their military obligations. Ralph Boyer had been an officer in the Army Corps of Engineers. In order to give the new men opportunities to achieve permanent status in the Civil Service System, examinations were scheduled with greater frequency than they had been in the past. Nolton's performance on the examinations continued to be unsatisfactory. The new men, however, passed the exams for successively higher positions with flying colors. Ralph Boyer in particular experienced marked success in these examinations and advanced rapidly. Three years after his initial employment, he was in charge of a design group within the design division. Parker Nolton, in the meantime, had been shifted from the position of a project engineer to that of the purchase order coordinator. The position of purchase order coordinator was more limited in scope than that of a project engineer, although the responsibilities of the position were great. He continued to be classified as an associate engineer, however.

Ralph Boyer continued his successful career and soon qualified for the position of senior engineer. A new administrative group that had been created to meet the problems that arose in the design division because of the expanding activities of the engineering department was placed under his direction. Doug Worth, too, was successful in his examinations and was shortly promoted to the grade of associate engineer and transferred into the administrative group headed by Ralph Boyer.

One of the functions under the new administrative group was that of purchase order coordination. This relationship required that Parker Nolton report to Ralph Boyer. Nolton, however, chose to ignore the new organizational structure and dealt directly with the chief engineer, an arrangement which received the latter's tacit approval. Nolton was given a semiprivate office and the services of a junior engineer to assist him in his activities. His assistant, John Palmer, soon requested a transfer on the grounds that he had nothing to do, and there was no need for anyone in this position. Nolton, on the other hand, always appeared to be extremely busy and was continually requesting additional manpower and assistance to help him with the coordination of purchase orders.

Some four months after the organizational changes noted above had taken place, the chief engineer left the company and his replacement, Stan Matson, was appointed from within the division. Matson was the logical successor to the position; his appointment came as no surprise and was well received by all the employees. His appointment was shortly followed by the assignment of Ralph Boyer to a special position which took him completely out of the design division. Doug Worth was assigned to the position thus vacated, supervisor of the administrative group, and consequently inherited the supervision of Parker Nolton's activities. This assignment, initially made on a provisional basis, was soon made permanent when Worth passed the required examinations and was awarded the grade of Senior Engineer. Doug Worth had never worked closely with Parker Nolton but had been on cordial terms with him since his arrival in the engineering department. He had had contact with Nolton in several recreational activities in which they both had participated.

During the months which followed, Parker Nolton continued his direct reporting relationship with the chief engineer, now in the person of Stan Matson, and never consulted or advised Doug Worth regarding the progress of his activities as purchase order coordinator. His former assistant, John Palmer, had been transferred and had been replaced by an engineering aide. Both the aide and Nolton appeared to be busy most of the time, and Nolton was still requesting more manpower for his activity through formal channels. When occasions arose which required that Doug Worth check on Nolton's activities, he was always forced to go to Nolton's office for information. Nolton always claimed to be too busy to leave his own office. During the conversations which occurred when Worth visited Nolton, Nolton frequently gave the impression that he regarded Worth's activities and interest as superfluous. Several times he suggested that in future situations Worth just send the inquiring party directly to him if questions arose about his activities. He often made the comment that he knew everyone in the department, and often it was better to handle many situations informally rather than through channels.

Doug Worth was concerned with Nolton's attitude, for he did not feel that he could effectively carry out his responsibilities as supervisor of the administrative group if he did not know the current status of activities in all of the functions under his control. Consequently, he attempted to gain more cooperation from Nolton by approaching the subject at times when the two men were engaged in common off-hours recreational activities. These attempts were uniformly unsuccessful. Nolton always quickly brought the conversation around to the standing of the bowling team, the progress of the P.T.A., or any other unrelated subject close at hand.

After several attempts to talk with Nolton in a friendly way off the job, Worth concluded that the situation as it currently stood was intolerable. While he realized he must do something, Worth felt he understood Nolton's attitude and reactions and was sympathetic. After all, Nolton had been in the department for years and had been relatively successful. He knew all the "ropes" and had many friends. Worth reflected that it must be a blow to a man like Nolton to have to report to young, relatively inexperienced men. Worth had faced similar problems during his military career, when he had more experienced men many years his senior under his command. After much thought, he decided his best approach would be to appeal to Nolton in a very direct manner for a greater degree of cooperation. Thus, Worth approached Nolton on the job and suggested that they have a talk in his private office where they would not be disturbed by all the activity in Nolton's office. Nolton protested that he could not take time away from his duties. Worth was firm, however, and Nolton reluctantly agreed to come to Worth's office, protesting all the way that he really could not spare the time.

During his opening remarks to what Worth had planned as a sympathetic discussion of the situation, Worth referred to "the normal relationship between a man and his superior." Nolton's reaction was violent. He stated that he didn't regard any young upstart as a "superior," especially his. He told Worth to run his own office and to let him, Nolton, run his. He concluded by stating "if you haven't anything more to say, I would like to get back to my office where important work is being neglected." Worth, realizing that nothing more could be accomplished in the atmosphere which prevailed, watched in silence as Nolton left.

Doug Worth subsequently reported his latest conversation with Nolton to Stan Matson, the chief engineer. He also related the events which had led to this conversation. In concluding his remarks, he stated that he could no longer take responsibility for Nolton's actions, because Nolton would neither accept his guidance, nor advise him of the state of his work. Matson's reply to this last statement was "yes, I know." This was the only comment Matson made during the interview, although he listened intently to Worth's analysis of the situation.

At the next meeting of the supervisory staff of which Worth was a member but Nolton was not, Worth proposed that Nolton be transferred to the position of design drafting engineer, in effect a demotion. As Worth was explaining the reasons for his proposed action regarding Nolton, one of the other members of the supervisory staff interrupted to proclaim very heatedly that Nolton was "one of the pillars of the entire engineering department," and that he would be violently opposed to the demotion of "so fine a man." Following the interruption, a very heated, emotional discussion ensued concerning the desirability of demoting Nolton.

During this discussion Stan Matson remained silent; yet he reflected that he probably should take some action during the meeting regarding the Nolton situation.

Questions   How can you account for the behavior of Nolton? of Worth? of Boyer? What advice would you give Matson?

DEL RICE

Del Rice is the assistant manager of Sac County Federal's largest branch. He is 31 years old and has been employed by the institution for six years. After a brief orientation period as a teller he was given further training and assigned to his present position, in which he has worked for nearly five years. Two years ago he was elected by the board to become an assistant vice president. He does a good job in planning work and in supervising his employees. As an administrator he is competent. He gets along unusually well with his employees, the customers, the general public, and his branch manager. He is president of the local Savings and Loan Institute chapter, where he has taken many courses. Civic duties make time-consuming demands on him.

The branch manager, Amos Turner, is 68 years old. He is a senior vice president and director of the association, one of the few remaining members of the initial investors who founded the association almost 40 years ago. Turner is one of the most widely respected and popular members of the

Reprinted with permission from Edgar G. Williams, *People Problems* (Bureau of Business Research, Indiana University Graduate School of Business, Bloomington, Ind., 1962).

community in that section of the city where the branch office is located. He has literally hundreds of personal friends and acquaintances and is strongly motivated by a desire to have the association render the best possible customer service tailored to suit their individual needs.

Following Rice's assignment to the branch, Turner assigned more and more of the internal functions to the young man. Now he does little but talk to people who come to him for personal services, and he takes some loan applications. Turner has been pleased with Rice's work and has recommended salary increases for him at the end of each salary review period.

More than one of the vice presidents at the main office object strongly to Rice's attitude concerning matters affecting their respective departments. The chief loan officer maintains that Rice does not obtain sufficient information about the property or the credit of loan applicants on which to make a reasonable decision, despite continuing requests on his part for the assistant manager to obtain more information. He also says that Rice wants to process every loan application that originates at his branch as a prime loan with respect to the terms offered the borrower even though the risks involved may be marginal.

The personnel manager says that Rice constantly harasses him to provide additional personnel for his branch, maintaining that his employees have to work harder and longer than others in the association, although there is a work load as nearly equitable as the personnel manager has been able to devise.

The controller says that Rice too readily breaks minor rules that have been established for internal control in order to accommodate unusual requests from his customers. These men summarize their views by saying that Rice has a bad case of "branchitis."

The supervisor of branch operations, Rex Daily, receives these complaints from the department heads. He says that he has checked out all of the complaints, found most of them to be true, and has spent many hours with Rice trying to explain to him how he can improve his management of branch affairs and at the same time be more consistent with the established policies of the association. Like the department heads, he has found Rice's responses to be argumentative or consisting of wisecracks about the "experts" at the main office who "pick on" the branch personnel.

A new branch is to be opened within two months in an area that is a logical extension of the general area now being served by the branch headed by Turner and Rice. Rice has informed Daily that he wants very much to be named as the manager for the new branch. (Other branches have been opened since he has been with Turner, but he has never before requested consideration.)

Rice told Daily that all of the people in his community and especially his personal friends expect him to get the appointment. He also said that he considers this to be a turning point in his career with the association.

Turner has told Daily that he considers Rice to be one of the two best-qualified men for the job and will consent to but not urge his selection for the post because of the difficulties that losing the young man would cause him in his own branch.

Rice apparently knows his superior's attitude because he referred to it when making his request that Daily recommend him for the job at the new branch manager's office. Daily realizes that with Turner taking a neutral position, his recommendations will undoubtedly be accepted by the managing officer.

Questions   Which motivational and/or personality concepts do you find most useful for understanding Del's job behavior? Illustrate with examples. If you were Rex Daily, would you recommend Rice? Explain why or why not.

The Individual and the Organization

Patterns of Conflict and Accommodation

10 Individual Performance in Organizations

What factors combine to determine individual performance?

How do these factors interact with each other in determining performance?

How important are nonmotivational factors in determining individual performance?

Why is it useful to distinguish between in-role and extra-role performance?

To this point, we have concerned ourselves with some fundamental psychological processes that underlie behavior in organizations. Many people think of this as "motivation." Whether one speaks of psychological need states, outcomes of behavior, attitudes about work, or differences among individuals in values and motives, the reference is to matters we consider motivational in nature.

It is now time to place these motivational matters into a larger framework of variables that determine individual performance.

It is helpful to distinguish between two different types of performance. *In-role* performance consists of those functions or contributions that are required by the job description or qualify contractually for compensation from the organization's formal reward system. In-role performance is usually what we have in mind when we refer to a person's productivity. For a professor, in-role performance consists of preparing for and teaching classes, advising students during office hours, conducting research and writing papers, and various forms of administrative chores specified by the system. For an industrial sales representative, in-role performance includes calling on present and potential clients, providing those clients with technical information and services, and sending routine written reports to the home office. Typically some minimally acceptable levels can be specified for in-role performance, and performance beyond the minimum often qualifies for increased rewards.

Extra-role performance consists of those functions or contributions that are not required by the system and for which there is no contractual guarantee of increased reward. In other words, extra-role performance is, to large degree, discretionary insofar as the individual is concerned. It consists of types of performance that a person would not be disciplined for not doing and would not be automatically rewarded for doing. The professor who reads a colleague's manuscript and makes suggestions for improving it performs in this extra-role capacity. The product manager who helps someone in industrial relations learn a new software package contributes in extra-role fashion.

A MODEL OF IN-ROLE PERFORMANCE

An instructive model of in-role performance borrows somewhat from the work of Porter and Lawler (1968), with some modification for our purposes.

The model is shown in Figure 10–1. The important variables are:

1. *Motivation*—the strength of the desire, intention, and commitment of the individual to perform a task at a specific level of quality or rate of output.
2. *Effort,* the most immediate effect of motivation, which may be interpreted in either physical, mental, or psychological terms.

FIGURE 10–1

Model of Factors Underlying Individual Performance

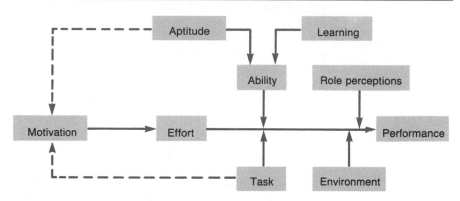

3. *The task,* including the methods, tools, and techniques used.

4. *Ability,* determined by the experience or practice gained in prior task performance, along with the person's innate aptitude for the task.

5. *The environment,* or the physical dimensions such as lighting, heat, humidity, noise, and crowding which have been shown empirically to affect performance.

6. *Role perceptions,* defined as the individual's idea of what the job requirements are.

7. *Performance itself.*

Before continuing to analyze this model, it's important to understand that the variables are not independent of one another. Motivation affects how much and how well a person will practice a task. Greater aptitude for a task may spark a higher level of motivation to perform well. Differences in tasks correlate to some degree with motivation, and differences in environment may engender different levels of motivation. Also, some of these variables moderate the effects of other variables on performance. Specifically, the nature of the environment or the person's ability will determine just how much effect motivation has on performance.

There are no studies that examine all combinations of various levels of each of the above-mentioned variables. Although some experiments have simultaneously varied the levels of ability, motivation, and a particular characteristic of the environment for a particular type of task, it would be risky to generalize the results of other aspects of the environment or to other types of tasks. Therefore we will piece together results from many different studies and derive tentative, cautious inferences about general relationships between these performance variables.

MOTIVATION

Without question, motivation is an important variable in the model shown in Figure 10–1. If motivation is the immediate determinant of effort level, then motivation must be accorded some primacy in our framework, for without effort, no amount of ability, no ingenuity of task design, no environment could yield performance. At any given level of motivation below the maximum possible level, an increase in motivation, other factors being the same, probably translates into some increase in performance. With that in mind we'll address two issues. First, what is the characteristic *baseline* level of motivation for someone employed to perform a specific job? Most individuals must work for a living; they expect work to be an important part of their lives, and they usually exercise some choice over what job they have. What level of motivation can be expected from the start? When should costly or unusual interventions be undertaken in the workplace to increase such motivation? How much of an increase is possible, given the baseline? Can such an increase be sustained? What are the comparative improvements in performance that might be expected if a given amount of resources such as money, time, or management effort were devoted to improve other—nonmotivational—factors such as training, task modification, and improved work environment?

Most adults begin work with a baseline motivation level that is at least moderately high. This level is usually sustained for most of his or her working career. In other words, if there existed a "zero" level of motivation at one extreme, and 10 represented the most intense motivation imaginable, we could peg the baseline motivation level for most people at between five and eight.

Surveys of job attitudes repeatedly show that most people like their jobs (we will examine these findings in greater detail in Chapter 13). A majority of respondents report that they would continue to work at the same job, even if they were so well off financially that they didn't need money. This is not to say that job attitudes or intentions accurately mirror the level of effort people put forth on the job. Rather, it shows that most people accept the requirements of work and a readiness to do what is reasonably expected of them without inordinate pressure to perform. Of course, if people's conceptions of fairness are outrageously violated or if they feel abused, their response may well be a reduction in their characteristic baseline motivation level. But this would represent an abnormal work situation. In such situations the issue is one of restoring the natural baseline level of motivation, not of pushing it beyond its normal state.

Experiments by Orne (1962) are relevant to the issue of baseline motivation. Orne was concerned that many laboratory experiments using college students in psychological research were yielding misleading results. In particular, he wondered if many human subjects were predisposed to "help" the experimenter by behaving the way they thought the experimenter wanted them to behave, rather than responding as they would in natural situations. To examine this question, Orne contrived a set of exceedingly dull tasks (duller than most jobs people would ever do). He wanted to see how long subjects would continue working on these tasks without any pay or any task interest. One experiment asked subjects to perform thousands of simple computations on two-digit numbers until the experimenter gave the signal to stop. Five and a half hours later the experimenter — not the subjects — gave up. Even though the experimenter came in periodically and tore up their work, the subjects continued to perform the task unless the experimenter said to stop.

Orne's point was that the subject in a psychological experiment is willing to go to great lengths to please the experimenter. Perhaps this poses problems for some psychological research, but it would appear to represent a boon for most employers. The findings suggest that when people commit themselves to a situation, they generally accept "the rules of the game" and the authority structure of the situation, and then apparently try to conform to what they conceive as reasonable expectations.

Assuming that the baseline level of motivation is substantial, could it still be increased by special measures? The answer is an unequivocal Yes. For example, in a study by Levi (1967), a steeply progressive wage incentive was introduced to a small group of female clerical workers, who were already exhibiting satisfactory levels of effort and performance. Given the workers' level of experience, we can assume that ability was not changed, nor were any obvious changes made in the task or physical environment. Over a period of several days, work output increased by over 100 percent, with no decline in quality. We can assume that most, if not all, of this increase resulted from greater effort through greater motivation. Thus, the baseline level of motivation clearly left significant room for further increase. But, this increase in effort had its costs. The workers soon showed signs of burnout — they complained of exhaustion, headaches, and muscular aches at the end of the workday. Furthermore, the study showed that the level of effort they were exerting was causing serious physiological as well as psychological stress. In other words, it is questionable whether this super level of motivation could have been sustained very long.

In the next chapter we will examine some programs designed to increase performance, most of them through increasing motivation and effort. When such programs are successful — and they are not invariably successful — the most significant and dramatic increases in effort and performance are short-lived. The first few weeks or months may produce spectacular gains, but thereafter the trend shows a decline. An improvement over the initial baseline may still exist after many months, and it may be cost-justified. But in general, massive increases over the baseline cannot be long sustained. We may speak of "giving 100 percent," but we cannot realistically hold that as our model for day-in, day-out job effort. Super high levels of motivation are interesting precisely because of their rarity and seem automatically to generate psychological and physiological processes that render them short-lived.

Certainly, attempts to increase job motivation are necessary. In some situations the normal motivation baseline has been impaired, and sound interventions are needed to restore it. Even when the baseline motivation level is relatively high, certain incentives, contingencies, and management practices can increase it further, yielding higher levels of effort that can be significant and sustainable. However, managers should be careful not to overestimate the gains to be derived from such programs. In quite a few instances, unfulfilled, unrealistic expectations have led organizational officials to discount the very real, though incremental, improvements that motivational programs might have yielded. Instead of building impractical hopes, it's a good idea when contemplating the investment of resources in motivational programs to at least consider whether an equivalent expenditure of resources on other factors might bring greater returns with respect to performance gains. It is also important to recognize that the ultimate effect of any given change in motivation will also depend on the condition of the task, workers' abilities, and environment.

THE TASK

Around the turn of the century, an engineer by the name of Frederick Taylor undertook some simple experiments at the Bethlehem Steel Company. Taylor had noted how unsystematic most workers were in performing their various tasks, such as loading pig iron onto a railroad car. Apparently the men were told what to do, but never given any standard instructions as to the best way of doing it. Taylor believed that for any task, there existed a "one best way" of doing it, a way that would provide for maximum productivity or efficiency and minimum fatigue.

For one of his experiments, Taylor selected a worker to whom he gave the pseudonym "Schmidt." By all accounts, Schmidt was a hard worker, not known for "goldbricking." Schmidt seems to have been a man of enormous physical stamina, for he ran several miles to and from work, and after work hours labored at building a house for himself and his family. Taylor, who by careful study and observation had devised an efficient method for loading pig iron, enlisted Schmidt's cooperation in performing an experiment. Schmidt was to do precisely as Taylor instructed, with respect to every movement, the choice of shovel, and when to pause for rest. Schmidt did precisely as he was told. (We should add that Taylor also agreed to pay Schmidt according to how much pig iron he loaded, so this motivational factor must be noted.) The result of the experiment was that Schmidt, who previously had been able to load an average of 12.5 tons a day, was now able to load 47 tons a day — nearly a fourfold increase. And Schmidt still had the energy to run home after work and build his house.

No doubt Taylor's financial incentive raised Schmidt's motivation level somewhat. However, Taylor's account of this experiment (Taylor, 1911) strongly implies that Schmidt's baseline motivation level was already quite respectable. The increase in output could be attributed not to change in motivation, but to change in the task—the design, method, sequence of operations, and use of specific tools.

At about this same time, Frank and Lillian Gilbreth began using film to do time and motion studies in order to identify the most efficient methods of doing jobs such as bricklaying. The Gilbreths' findings led to productivity increases of over 200 percent in bricklaying and even greater increases in some other tasks.

The productivity increases registered by Taylor, the Gilbreths, and countless other industrial engineers and efficiency experts are especially impressive when compared to the measurable gains produced by various kinds of motivational techniques. Among the latter, it is quite uncommon to encounter output increases of 25 percent or more. Wyatt, Frost, and Stock (1934) reported productivity gains of 25 to 45 percent when they introduced bonus and piece-rate pay systems to a group of candy factory workers who had previously worked on a straight-line pay system. According to Opsahl and Dunnette (1966), however, the effect of installing incentive pay plans has varied widely from plant to plant and often does not lead to any increase at all in production. Goal-setting programs have been known to increase production by 50 percent above the baseline, but effective goal-setting may succeed due to task modification as well as motivational processes.

At least one program (Locke, Sirota, & Wolfson, 1976) intended to increase output through higher motivation was found to raise productivity *in spite* of the fact that the evidence suggested lower morale (and possibly lower motivation) brought about during the operation of the program. The data strongly suggested that the real reason for productivity improvement was alteration of the various tasks, primarily the elimination of redundant operations and reduction of overlap in job duties among different workers.

In many instances task modification yields much greater performance gains than increased motivation, and it seems probable that any increase in motivation will have much greater impact on performance when the task is optimally designed. Increased motivation on the part of a typist will result in a much greater increase in number of words and pages than would the same motivation change in the case of someone writing those words with a pencil. Thus, the effects of formal or informal performance incentives will be magnified when the design of the task has been perfected within the current state of the art or technology.

Interdependence of Task Design and Motivation   When the redesign of a task promises greater efficiency—because of elimination of redundant operations and simplification of the steps involved—the effect of the design on productivity must also take into account the possible effect on motivation. A more simplified task is sometimes a less interesting—and therefore less motivating—task. If the simplified task requires a repetitive response, the phenomenon of *habituation*—the buildup of resistance to that response— occurs. Eventually, task avoidance results, in the forms of unauthorized breaks, tardiness, unexcused absenteeism, or at least a slow-down in performance.

Trist and Bamforth (1951) have documented the unforeseen effects of theoretically superior task design on motivation. Their studies report the experiences of British coal mines when the longwall method of coal-getting was introduced. The new method, brought about by the technological development of the face conveyor, appeared in design to be vastly superior to the traditional method. However, the arrangements used to implement the longwall method broke up the cohesion of the mining teams. It gave each miner a very specialized task to perform, whereas in the traditional method the miners had all performed a variety of operations. In effect, the longwall method replaced flexible, autonomous work groups with the assembly-line method. "There was no question that one of the most disliked features of the conventional longwall system was its tying the worker to a single, narrowly defined task" (Katz & Kahn, 1966). Absenteeism soared, worker cooperation diminished, numerous breakdowns occurred, and productivity came nowhere near what was expected. Later, modifications of the longwall system restored some of the characteristics of the old methods and finally the predicted increases in efficiency came about.

We now recognize that task simplification, past some point, adversely affects the baseline level of motivation, and this effect may more than offset the inherent superiority of design in an ultrasimplified method. Many programs have aimed at improving motivation by deliberately redesigning jobs to make them less simplified. We shall postpone until the next chapter any overall assessment of such programs, but we should point out here that: (1) A simplified task may indeed lower motivation, yet still increase productivity, simply because a lesser level of effort is nonetheless used much more efficiently; and (2) task simplification does not always adversely affect motivation. Even when such is the case, it is conceivable that compensating arrangements such as incentive pay and goal-setting can offset any otherwise negative effect on motivation.

ABILITY

The person of modest ability who, by sheer effort, outperforms others of grander talents, becomes something of a folk hero. The tortoise that finished ahead of the hare, the Little Engine That Could, the Cinderella team in the NCAA final basketball four, represent only the more legendary instances. Peters and Waterman's (1982) *In Search of Excellence* makes the valid point that corporate success probably depends more on the contribution a company gets from the rank and file than the exploits of the few most gifted performers.

Nonetheless, we can scarcely afford to overlook the importance of ability in our model of performance. Motivation determines the quantity or intensity of effort, but ability determines what the quality of such effort will be.

Ability is the result of *aptitude* and *learning.* Aptitude refers to individual differences in the facility for learning and mastering a task. It represents a person's potential for performance, his or her latent ability that may lie fallow until the proper amount of training, experience, and motivation transform it into actual performance. A person with greater aptitude for a task will learn the task more easily, make faster progress, and exhibit a higher level of stable performance (see the Close-Up that follows for a qualifying note to this statement).

There exists no consensus on the number of different kinds of aptitudes, although Fleishman (1954) and Dunnette (1976) have offered useful observations on empirically derived aptitude factors. Some aptitudes — such as those for abstract reasoning, facility with numbers, deductive logic, and

---

CLOSE-UP

Typical versus Maximum Performance

Is a person's maximum performance a good predictor of typical performance? Obviously, for any one person, the maximum would exceed the typical level of performance. But across persons, are those who are capable of higher maximum output also those with generally higher day-to-day performance?

To answer this question, a research team obtained data from 635 newly hired cash register operators and 735 experienced operators employed by 12 different supermarket chains. Cash register systems made possible measures of speed (items checked per minute) and accuracy in typical performance over four consecutive one-week periods. During this period, operators were also given a test of maximum performance in processing a shopping cart of 25 items.

The correlations between typical performance and maximum performance were generally very low, in terms of both speed and accuracy. The correlation was slightly higher for experienced than for newly hired operators. Interestingly, and contrary to prediction, supervisor ratings of the operators were more related to maximum than typical performance.

The researchers conclude that "typical and maximum performance measures clearly do not yield comparable information about the relative performance of cashiers," and suggest that maximum performance is primarily determined by ability, with motivational or personality factors having more effect on typical performance.

SOURCE: P. R. Sackett, S. Zedeck, and L. Fogli, "Relations between Measures of Typical and Maximum Job Performance," *Journal of Applied Psychology* 73 (1988), 482–86.

verbal comprehension and fluency—are related to general intelligence. Others, such as eye-hand coordination, reaction time, manual dexterity, and peripheral vision are grouped as physical and motor skills. The job of a computer programmer draws mainly on aptitudes of an intellectual nature, the operation of earth-moving equipment uses primarily motor skills, and a typist or automotive mechanic exercises some of both.

Industrial psychologists have contributed enormously to the development of instruments that measure job-related aptitudes. These instruments, called selection tests, enable employers to identify individuals who possess an abundance of the aptitudes relevant to job performance. The most refined instruments generate a pattern of scores by individuals on various aptitude measures, and these patterns can be correlated with the jobs that require particular blends of abilities. Thus, such measures help not only in the decision to hire, but also in the placement of individuals in specific jobs within an organization. These instruments can also predict which persons will benefit most from training programs.

One of the hotly debated issues of recent times concerns the role of general intellectual ability in determining performance in virtually any job (see Close-Up, "The g Factor"). Dunnette (1972), in summarizing the empirical research literature on the expectancy theory of job motivation, noted that:

> In those experimental studies that used performance on a simple repetitive task as a dependent variable and that also obtained measures of ability, a brief aptitude or general intelligence test almost always accounted for much more variance in performance than did the motivational variables. [p. 91]

Hunter and Schmidt (1983) have shown that improved selection based on valid aptitude measures would save the federal government as much as $15 billion per year, and have estimated conservatively that proper use of such instruments would contribute $80 billion per annum to the nation's economy. Before investing substantial amounts of money in programs aimed at increasing motivation, organization officials should consider whether they have exhausted the gains from the use of valid selection and placement tools.

Learning   Consider the following study, conducted by Cherrington, Reitz, and Scott (1971). Ninety undergraduate students, in groups of seven to nine, were brought into a laboratory and given stacks of tests to score. All students were guaranteed at least $1 per hour and told that each of them had a 50 percent chance of receiving a $1-per-hour bonus. At the end of one hour of work, half of the students in each group were chosen randomly to receive the bonus. The random selection ensured that half of the students were appropriately rewarded, in the sense that whether they received the bonus buck was directly related to whether they

CLOSE-UP

The g Factor

A popular point of view holds that the intelligence required for various jobs comes in varied, independent forms. For example, the type of intelligence needed in an effective loan officer is different from the "smarts" that contributes to good performance by a quality control inspector.

A related view, set forth in Roger Peters's *Practical Intelligence: Working Smarter in Business and the Professions* (Harper & Row, 1987), which also argues for "multiple intelligences," contends that the practical intelligence so important in many jobs is quite distinct from the "school smarts" measured by standard IQ tests.

Psychologist R. J. Herrnstein emphatically disagrees. Pointing to the analyses by J. E. Hunter and F. L. Schmidt of a massive accumulation of data, Herrnstein contends that intelligence as measured by IQ is the single most valid predictor of job performance. Its validity is greatest for more complex jobs, but has some validity even for the simplest jobs.

According to L. S. Gottfredson, tests of specialized mental abilities predict performance only to the extent that they contain the "g factor" — a measure of general mental ability. This factor is a very general capacity for abstract thinking, problem solving, and the capacity for learning and assimilating complex ideas. The g factor is broader than mere academic ability and, in fact, includes what is more popularly regarded as practical intelligence.

Measures of motor skills and background factors may add to the validity of IQ tests as predictors of performance for certain positions. But in the absence of information about such factors, any reliable intelligence measure containing the g factor contributes information predicting performance in virtually any job, even so-called low-level jobs.

SOURCE: R. J. Herrnstein, "Brains in the Workplace," *Fortune,* June 22, 1987; L. S. Gottfredson, "Reconsidering Fairness: A Matter of Social and Ethical Priorities," *Journal of Vocational Behavior* 33 (1988), 293–319.

performed above average. At the same time, half of the subjects were inappropriately rewarded — i.e., below-average performers got the bonus, above-average performers didn't.

Of particular interest to the researchers was the performance of the students during the next hour of work. Following the logic of reinforcement concepts, the researchers expected that the appropriately rewarded workers would show higher productivity than the inappropriately rewarded group. Their predictions were indeed borne out, as seen below:

	Number of Tests Scored	
Performance	Appropriately Rewarded Subjects	Inappropriately Rewarded Subjects
First hour	291.6	280.9
Second hour	428.4	385.9

The appropriately rewarded subjects showed 11 percent higher productivity in the second hour than the inappropriately rewarded persons. But note that the inappropriately rewarded group actually registered a whopping 37 percent increase in productivity over the first hour. Consider the implications of this. The inappropriate reward manipulation represents a simulation, on a small scale, of the most perverse organizational reward system imaginable—lower performers get a bonus while higher performers do not. Presumably, such a condition would put a damper on one's motivation. Yet precisely such a condition was accompanied by an increase in output over three times as much as the increase due to differences in the appropriate-inappropriate reward systems. One must assume that the increase within the inappropriate reward group was due to learning or experience.

Every task has a characteristic learning curve—a graph of performance against repeated intervals of task practice. For very simple tasks, the learning curve would show a very steep progression, then reach a stable and more or less flat line of performance with continued practice. More complex tasks tend to show an S-shaped curve, with slow initial gains followed by more rapid improvement. Learning curves on complex tasks may also reflect a plateau, a period of no apparent improvement after initial gains, with an eventual "breakthrough" to a higher level. For any given task, individuals with very high aptitude for the task will show more rapid gains and reach a higher level of stable performance than others. Figure 10–2 illustrates the difference between the learning curves for the two types of tasks.

Properly implemented motivational techniques may produce performance gains that complement those due to learning and experience, as apparently was the case in the Cherrington, Rcitz, and Scott study. Also, applications of operant concepts may dramatically speed up the acquisition of skills, as was discussed in Chapter 4. Managers should not overlook the potential improvement in individual task performance that can be effected by systematic, intensive training programs. Peters and Waterman (1982) noted that a heavy investment in employee training was a characteristic common to excellent corporate performers. This type of education was important in companies as varied as McDonald's, which sponsors a "Hamburger University," and IBM, which provides a 15-month regimen of basic sales training.

The contribution of learning or practice on job performance varies somewhat depending on the complexity of the job, but overall the effect is significant for levels of experience up to 12 years.

PHYSICAL ENVIRONMENT

Noise   The effects of noise on individual task performance are neither easy to summarize nor easy to predict (Plutchik, 1959; Cohen, 1980). The relationship between background noise and performance appears to be

FIGURE 10–2

Learning Curves for Simple and Complex Tasks

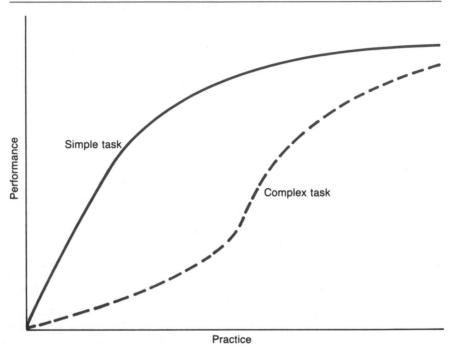

moderated by the character of the noise—its frequency, volume, and predictability. Additional moderator variables include the task (whether cognitively simple or complex) and the workers' individual personalities.

Noise acts as a stressor, and thus contributes to the general level of physiological arousal of the individual. Up to some point, increases in arousal improve performance because of the overall energizing effect on behavior. Past some point, further increases in arousal interfere with performance as behavior becomes less precise and less sensitive to subtle discriminative cues. The point at which noise becomes a detriment to performance depends, in part, on the task. With cognitively simple or repetitive tasks, intermittent noise—if not too intense or shrill—facilitates performance. This is especially true for persons who score high in extroversion; such persons have a relatively strong need for stimulation. Performance on tasks demanding concentration and a high rate of information processing is more vulnerable to the effects of noise. Loud noise usually impairs performance on tasks involving high levels of skill, resulting in greater frequency of errors and lapses in responding (Broadbent, 1978). Furthermore, abnormal noise levels cause increased variability in performance over time (Park & Payne, 1963).

FIGURE 10–3

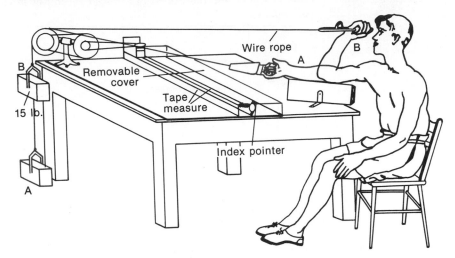

SOURCE: N. H. Mackworth, "High Incentives versus Hot and Humid Atmospheres in a Physical Effort Task," *British Journal of Psychology* 38 (1947), 90–102.

Even when high-intensity noise does not affect performance, it produces symptoms of discomfort, irritability, and distraction (Plutchik, 1959). Even when the effects of noise are not immediately reflected in task performance, there are after-effects that include lessened tolerance for frustration, lower incidence of altruistic or charitable behaviors, and fatigue (Cohen, 1980).

Fortunately, there is evidence (Cohen, 1980) that the adverse effects of noise, whether on task performance or the delayed after-effects, are substantially reduced by interventions that increase the sense of personal control or predictability of the noise. Curiously, people are less bothered by noise when they believe they can terminate it, regardless of whether they actually exercise that option.

Heat and Humidity   A classic study by Mackworth (1947) demonstrated the effect of hot and humid conditions on a physical task. The task consisted of raising and lowering a 15-pound weight by means of a pulley that the subject operated with one arm while seated at a table. The subject was instructed to raise and lower the weight in time to a metronome and continue to do so until unable to work any longer (see Figure 10–3).

Some of the subjects in Mackworth's experiment were given incentives to perform by goal setting, continuous feedback, and verbal encouragement from the experimenter, while other subjects were not provided with such incentives. Also, from data accumulated during practice sessions spread over two weeks, Mackworth could classify some of the subjects as high ability and others as average ability.

FIGURE 10–4

Level of Ability and the Effects of Stronger Incentives in Hot and Humid Atmospheres

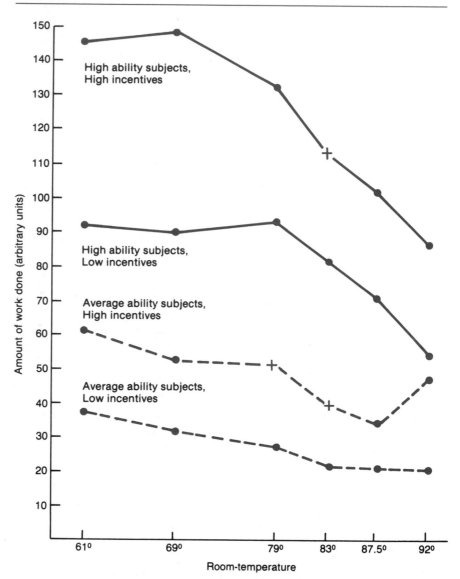

SOURCE: N. H. Mackworth, "High Incentives versus Hot and Humid Atmospheres in a Physical Effort Task," *British Journal of Psychology* 38 (1947), 90–102.

The results showed an overall drop-off in performance of about 40 percent as room temperature increased from 69 degrees to 92 degrees (Figure 10–4). The decline in performance was larger for those subjects given motivational incentives and for the high-ability subjects. While there was an overall positive performance effect attributable to the incentives, that effect was greatest at standard heat and humidity conditions and smallest under conditions of extreme heat and humidity. Similarly, the overall effect of ability was maximized at normal conditions and diminished as the environment became increasingly hot and humid. The moral seems rather clear: whatever good effects managers are able to obtain from selecting high-ability performers and motivating them with incentives, these effects can very nearly be washed out by unfavorable physical environments. Motivation and ability produce their maximum returns when the environment is properly maintained.

DeNisi (1983) reports a study by Fine and Kobrick (1978) that shows that heat can also impair performance on mental tasks. Some male soldiers worked on tasks such as decoding messages and recording weather data in a 70-degree environment and others worked in a 95-degree condition. For the first three hours, the differences in performance were not enormous. But at the five-hour mark, the soldiers working under intense heat made twice as many errors as the group in the standard condition. This differential persisted at seven hours.

Other factors of importance in the physical environment include the level and quality of illumination, amount of physical space (or, conversely, the extent of crowding), and the availability of specially designed chairs, shoes, gloves, optics, and other such devices that help minimize fatigue on specific tasks. The related fields of ergonomics and human factors engineering have made massive contributions to industry by analyzing and researching the design of physical conditions at work.

Research strongly suggests that substandard physical conditions can impair individual task performance, and the longer the time period under consideration, the more likely such impairment will be manifest and the more cumulative it becomes. Furthermore, research indicates that the more substandard the environment, the smaller the gains to be derived from motivational incentives and individual skill level.

ROLE PERCEPTIONS

An old adage tells us that the best way to get someone to do something is to tell him exactly what we want him to do. People may be predisposed (motivated) and eminently qualified to carry out our wishes, but their talents and good will are lost unless they know exactly what we expect from them.

The issue of role perceptions in relation to individual job performance has to do not so much with performance on a single task, but rather the relative emphasis and urgency to be accorded to a collection of tasks that comprise a role. The retail clerk, the personnel assistant, the plant manager, the maintenance engineer, and the janitor, have not just one task to do, they have a variety of chores. Their overall performance depends not only on their motivation to perform, their aptitude, and the physical environment, but also on how they allocate their time and other resources among the competing tasks. An industrial sales representative who devotes either too much or too little time to reading technical reports is not apt to be judged an outstanding performer. Ultimately, the worker must understand the legitimate role expectations of his or her behavior as held by supervisors and co-workers.

There are three potential breakdowns in role perceptions. One is *role ambiguity,* which exists when a person is in doubt as to what others' expectations are. The effects of this condition include tension, lowered self-esteem, lower job satisfaction (Kahn, Wolfe, Quinn, Snoek, & Rosenthal, 1964), and—more significantly for our purposes here— generalized hesitation and tentativeness. Essentially, role ambiguity has an adverse motivational affect and can even hurt a person's baseline motivation level. If a person is not sure what he or she is supposed to be doing, the person will be rather cautious and tentative about doing anything. The result could be wasted effort or even punishment for doing the wrong thing.

A second role pathology is *role conflict,* defined as incompatible or inconsistent expectations of one's behavior by various other parties. Again, Kahn et al. (1964) have amply reported the tensions and sense of futility engendered by being caught in the middle between agents who have diametrically opposing demands on an individual's job behavior. A nurse, for example, may be instructed by the head nurse to distribute attention over an entire ward of patients, while a politically powerful physician insists that special concern be given to one or two particular patients. As with role ambiguity, role conflict leads to hesitation and vacillation rather than unrestrained effort.

Finally, role perceptions may simply be downright wrong. Even when an employee feels no ambiguity or conflict concerning his or her role, the person may nonetheless have a distorted concept of which tasks are really important or how best to achieve them. Talented, motivated individuals may squander their energy on trivial chores, resulting in something less than good or even satisfactory performance.

Role pathologies may represent occupational hazards in some situations. Role conflict, for example, is virtually inevitable for industrial foremen caught between demands for maximum output and maximum quality, as well as other demands for employee comfort and safety. Role ambiguity must be expected in jobs that involve unstructured tasks, such as those for managers, consultants, and newly created jobs.

However, many problems pertaining to role perceptions can be minimized by leadership that provides structure (leadership structuring will be addressed in depth in Chapter 19), by provisions for regular and timely feedback, by many forms of indoctrination and training, and by a variety of intervention programs (as discussed in the next chapter and in the concluding chapter on organizational change and development).

EXTRA-ROLE PERFORMANCE: ORGANIZATIONAL CITIZENSHIP BEHAVIOR

Katz and Kahn (1978) have argued that, in addition to attracting and retaining members who render satisfactory or better in-role performance, effective organizations must also evoke "innovative and spontaneous behavior: performance beyond role requirements for accomplishments of organizational functions" (p. 337). Their notion of "spontaneous" behavior refers to countless informal acts of cooperation, helpfulness, and goodwill: "Within every work group in a factory, within any division in a government bureau, or within any department of a university are countless acts of cooperation without which the system would break down. We take these everyday acts for granted, and few of them are included in the formal role prescriptions for any job" (p. 339).

Organ (1988) has provided a category system for the *extra-role* forms of performance, which he refers to as *organizational citizenship behavior* (OCB). OCB consists of those contributions rendered by members that are not enforceable requirements of the job and which are not compensated by contractually guaranteed incentives. Types of OCB include:

1. *Altruism.* This category includes those contributions rendered by helping a specific individual (e.g., a colleague) with an immediate work-related problem, such as showing a new hire how to use a tool or helping someone catch up with a backlog of work.

2. *Courtesy.* This form of OCB includes all of those gestures that involve consideration of others and that *prevent* problems from occurring. A fact of life in organizations is interdependence: What you do and decisions you make affect others down the line. Courtesy consists of judicious timing in consulting with those who will be affected by your actions, providing advance notice, respecting others' claims for (and need of) commonly shared resources.

3. *Sportsmanship.* An important part of OCB is *forebearance,* or some things that one *refrains* from doing. If interdependence is one fact of organizational life, another is that everyone occasionally must endure a certain degree of frustration, inconvenience, or even stress. In some sense, we all have a right to register our grievance when events work some hardship on us. But an excess of such complaints could overload administrative capacity and exhaust administrators' stamina. Energies get diverted from productive operations to protracted legalisms and arguments. Thus, "they also serve who only stand and wait"; people who endure with grace and good spirit the occasional impositions and inconveniences, when they might have initiated lengthy appeals, contribute a form of OCB.

4. *Civic virtue* (Graham, 1986). Another form of OCB is represented by responsible, constructive involvement in the political process of the organization. Thus, good contributors attend meetings, read their in-house mail, keep abreast of developments in the organization and issues affecting

it, and offer opinions and suggestions at the appropriate time and in the proper form.

5. *Conscientiousness.* Organizations have rules and policies that require acceptable levels of compliance with respect to attendance, punctuality, neatness, care for organizational property, and use of company time. But, by their very nature, rules and the machinery of discipline can enforce only the minimum; they cannot enforce beyond that. Thus, another form of OCB is measured by the extent to which a person goes beyond the minimum and complies with the spirit as well as the letter of the rules.

Over a long period of time and across quite a few people, these OCB categories contribute to an organization's effectiveness. Yet they seldom show in any conventional measure of an individual's productivity. At the margin, OCB might even occur at some expense to an individual's credited productivity; for example, the time I take to help you with your immediate problem is taken away from my own work.

A moment's reflection on typical examples of the OCB categories leads one to speculate that much of OCB is not heroic, but mundane. As Katz and Kahn (1978) put it, we "take them for granted," because individual instances of OCB seem almost trivial or commonplace in nature. Yet that very characteristic means that they are largely a matter of *willingness* or intent or inclination to do them — they do not generally require much skill, expertise, or physical resources. Thus, our model of OCB determinants, or extra-role performance, would look something like Figure 10–5. Whatever the motivational dynamics that underlie effort directed toward OCB, that effort should lead in a more straightforward manner to actual OCB.

As we shall see in Chapter 13, those attitudes that make up job satisfaction have a closer relationship to OCB than they do to in-role productivity. And recent research (e.g., Organ & Konovsky, 1989; Farh, Podsakoff, & Organ, 1990) strongly suggests that the fairness factor within job satisfaction is particularly important. The inclination to contribute in the many day-to-day, humble, uncredited forms is a function of how much a person believes that leaders and colleagues strive for long-run fairness in treatment of others. Aside from job satisfaction, certain aspects of personality would probably also enter into the determination of at least some forms of OCB. Research is just now underway in an effort to identify what these personality traits would be. Work by McCrae and Costa (1987) indicates that something akin to "agreeableness" is a stable dimension of individuals that cuts across all walks of life. People who score high on this dimension are easy to get along with, unselfish, kind, sympathetic toward others; the implications for altruism and courtesy are obvious. McCrae and Costa's data also point to a factor suggestive of "conscientiousness." Those so characterized are careful, persistent, thorough, reliable, self-disciplined, quite evocative of the type of OCB that has the same name.

FIGURE 10–5
Model of Determinants of Organizational Citizenship Behavior

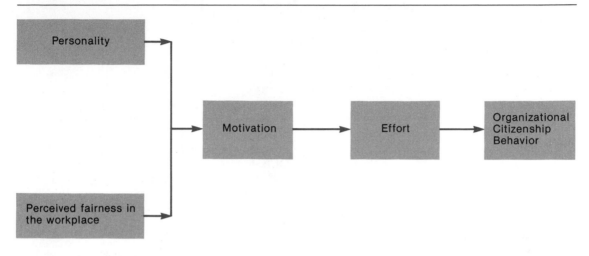

MANAGING THE POOR PERFORMER

Managers often must contend with the problem of an individual who either neglects or handles poorly some part of the job. Such problems include the sales representative who turns in late or incomplete written reports, the production scheduler who never seems to coordinate plans with foremen, the secretary who continually misfiles important information, the marketing manager who does not use marketing research data in promotion campaigns, or technical specialists who fail to communicate clearly with operating people. In other words, the problem is often not unsatisfactory overall performance, but a discrepancy with respect to some particular aspect of the job.

Mager and Pipe (1970) have offered a slim, readable, and amusing volume to aid the manager frustrated by such performance problems. Their framework takes the form of a flowchart, as shown in Figure 10–6.

The first step in Mager and Pipe's analysis is to describe the performance discrepancy. This step may not be as easy as it sounds. Managers are sometimes frustrated with a subordinate, but have never gotten past their frustration to define the problem in precise, operational terms.

The next step requires that the administrator make an explicit judgment as to whether the discrepancy is important. The answer need not always be affirmative. A manager will often be vexed by some subordinate pecadillo on aesthetic, cosmetic, or personal value grounds, but objectively the worker's performance offers no real threat to organization function. For example, an engineer's reports may be studded with

FOCUS ON INTERNATIONAL OB

Organizational Citizenship Behavior in the Pacific Rim

Bureaucratic structures in the United States have a "constitutional" character that limits managerial control over individuals to well-defined roles. The concept "organizational citizenship behavior" (OCB) is thus quite meaningful in the context of such structures as a reference to discretionary individual contributions that extend beyond formal role obligations.

Does the OCB concept have similar — or any — meaning in other cultures? Farh, Podsakoff, and Organ (1988) addressed this question in a study of supervisory ratings of 195 Ministry of Communications employees in Taiwan. They found that the ratings broke down into the same two factors — the

more personal OCB form of "Altruism" and the impersonal variety "Generalized Compliance" — that had emerged from previous studies in the United States. Also, the correlations of these two OCB factors with subordinate job satisfaction replicated the results of studies in American firms. The authors conclude that the OCB construct is not culture-bound and is not an artifact of a particular language.

SOURCE: J. Farh, P. M. Podsakoff, and D. W. Organ, "Organizational Citizenship Behavior in the Pacific Rim: A Constructive Replication and Extension of U.S. Studies." Paper presented at Academy of Management meetings, 1988, Anaheim, CA.

misspellings and grammatical errors, thus inviting the rage of the boss, yet the reports are easily understood by their target readers.

If the performance discrepancy is important, the flowchart proceeds to examine whether the problem is one of lack of ability and, if so, whether or not training or practice or ultimately redesign of the job or transfer may be indicated; or a problem of motivation. If lack of desire rather than lack of ability is the cause of the problem, the flowchart sorts out the various reasons for insufficient motivation: Is performance of the task in question actually punishing? Is nonperformance rewarding? Is there any recognition or reinforcement for performance? Finally, the analyst must not overlook the question of whether or not there are obstacles in the way of performance. The person may have the ability as well as the desire to do what is expected, but may be hampered by inadequate tools, lack of information, little cooperation from others, or uncontrollable interruptions or distractions.

CONCLUSION

The major theme of this chapter is that motivation is only one of several factors that determine the level of individual performance. Motivation cannot be discussed in a vacuum without reference to these other variables. Some of these factors influence motivation, either positively or negatively.

FIGURE 10–6
Performance Problems

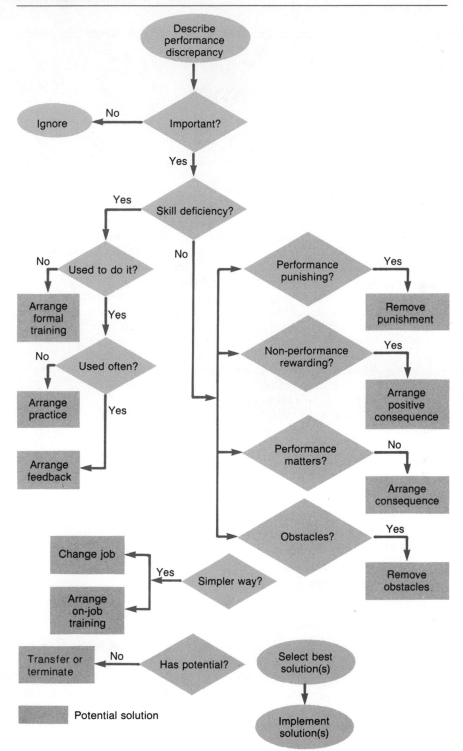

SOURCE: R. F. Mager and P. Pipe. *Analyzing Performance Problems* (Belmont, Calif: Lear Siegler, Inc./ Fearon Publishers, 1970), p. 3.

FOCUS ON THE FUTURE

Telecommuters and the Electronic Cottage

An increasing portion of individual work performance will occur in the home. Along with the trend toward more of the labor force performing information-handling jobs, the technology—micro computers, modems, fax machines—spawned by and contributing to this trend will allow more employees to telecommute.

In 1984, there were an estimated 100,000 telecommuters working for 400 companies. As of 1990, that number has grown to 7–10 million. Up to 20 percent of Fortune 500 companies will have formal telecommuting programs by the mid-1990s, and experts predict that 15 million people will telecommute by the end of the decade. The state of California has begun a program aimed at having 10 percent of the state's workforce spend two to four days a week working out of their homes; the rationale: to reduce the smog and congestion of state highways.

Among the touted benefits of telecommuting: reduction of office-related costs; increased work-autonomy for the individual; improved quality of life by eliminating the hassles of commuting to and from work; more flexibility for the family; reduced need to relocate. Possible disadvantages: isolation of the employee from co-workers and, according to union leaders, less collective security for individual workers.

The trend toward telecommuting poses obvious implications for supervision and management. Supervisors, having less opportunity to monitor the process of work, must think more in terms of projects, goals, and deadlines. Clarity and precision of communicated expectations will become particularly critical.

SOURCES: M. Antonoff, "The Push for Telecommuting," *Personal Computing,* July 1985; J. A. Savage, "California Smog Fuels Telecommuting Plans," *Computerworld,* May 2, 1988.

Moreover, the contribution of motivation to performance may be amplified or effectively nullified, depending on the condition of such non-motivational factors as the task, worker ability, environment, and role perceptions.

SUMMARY

Individual in-role performance is a function of motivation, the task, ability (which is a composite of aptitude and learning), the physical environment, and role perceptions. Motivation underlies the effort that a person expends on job performance. The other factors determine how efficiently effort is translated into performance as well as having various effects on motivation. In most cases the baseline motivation level is reasonably healthy, though that level can be improved. Investment of managerial and organizational resources to improve performance should follow a systematic consideration of the comparative costs and benefits of interventions to increase motivation—reengineering or reconfiguring the job itself, improving the selection of persons with job-relevant aptitudes, training people in the skills essential to satisfactory or superior performance, improving the physical environment in which the job is done, and communicating more clearly the expectations or requirements associated with the job. The manager must examine the determinants of performance as a set of interrelated variables. As an example, the effect of increased motivation on performance will be magnified by additional improvements in ability or environment.

Extra-role performance in the form of organizational citizenship behavior generally depends less than in-role performance on nonmotivational factors. Evidence to date suggests it is largely a function of the fairness a person attributes to the system and certain stable dimensions of personality.

CONCEPTS TO REMEMBER

Baseline motivation level	Organizational citizenship	Role perceptions
Aptitude	behavior	Role conflict
Learning curve	Role ambiguity	

QUESTIONS FOR DISCUSSION

1. What types of people would we expect to have a rather high baseline level of motivation? Why? What kinds of experiences or conditions might damage the baseline level of motivation?

2. How does the role of the leader or supervisor fit into the models of in-role and extra-role performance?

3. How do the various factors in the model of in-role performance apply to the job of a *(a)* bank loan officer, *(b)* sales manager, *(c)* grocery store cashier, *(d)* air traffic controller?

4. How important is technology in relation to the in-role performance model? Be specific in identifying the parts of the model influenced by technology.

5. Explain why motivational forces have a more direct tie to a person's organizational citizenship behavior than to in-role productivity or technical excellence.

REFERENCES

Broadbent, D. E. (1978). The current state of noise research: Reply to Poulton. *Psychological Bulletin* 85, 1052–67.

Campbell, J. P. (1976). Motivation theory in industrial and organizational psychology. In M. D. Dunnette (ed.), *Handbook of industrial and organizational psychology,* pp. 63–130. Skokie, IL: Rand McNally.

Cherrington, D. L., Reitz, H. J., & Scott, W. E., Jr. (1971). Effects of reward and contingent reinforcement on satisfaction and task performance. *Journal of Applied Psychology* 55, 531–36.

Cohen, S. (1980). Aftereffects of stress on human performance and social behavior: A review of research and theory. *Psychological Bulletin* 88, 82–108.

DeNisi, A. S. (1983). Performance in organizations: Determinants, appraisals, and applications. In R. Baron (ed.), *Behavior in Organizations,* pp. 237–73. Boston: Allyn & Bacon.

Dunnette, M. D. (1972). Performance equals ability and what? Mimeographed paper, University of Minnesota, Minneapolis. Cited in J. P. Campbell (1976), Motivation theory in industrial and organizational psychology. In M. D. Dunnette (ed.), *Handbook of industrial and organizational psychology,* pp. 63–103. Skokie, IL: Rand McNally.

Dunnette, M. D. (1976). Aptitudes, abilities, and skills. In M. D. Dunnette (ed.), *Handbook of industrial and organizational psychology.* Skokie, IL: Rand McNally.

Farh, J. L., Podsakoff, P. M., & Organ, D. W. (1988). Organizational citizenship behavior in the Pacific Rim: A constructive replication and extension of U.S. studies. Paper presented at Academy of Management meetings, 1988, Anaheim, CA.

Fine, B. J., & Kobrick, J. L. (1978). Effects of altitude and heat on complex cognitive tasks. *Human Factors* 20, 115–22.

Fleishman, E. A. (1954). Dimensional analysis of psychomotor abilities. *Journal of Experimental Psychology* 48, 437–54.

Gottfredson, L. S. (1988). Reconsidering fairness: A matter of social and ethical priorities. *Journal of Vocational Behavior* 33, 293–319.

Graham, J. W. (1986). Organizational citizenship informed by political theory. Paper presented at Academy of Management meetings, Chicago, IL.

Herrnstein, R. J. (1987). Brains in the workplace. *Fortune,* June 22, 183–84.

Hunter, J. E., & Schmidt, F. L. (1983). Quantifying the effects of psychological interventions on employee job performance and work-force productivity. *American Psychologist,* 38, 479–86.

Kahn R. L., Wolfe, D. M., Quinn, R. P., Snoek, J. D., & Rosenthal, R. A. (1964). *Organizational stress.* New York: John Wiley & Sons.

Katz, D., & Kahn, R. L. (1978). *The social psychology of organizations.* New York: John Wiley & Sons.

Levi, L. (1967). *Stress: Sources, management, and prevention.* New York: Liveright.

Locke, E. A., Sirota, D., & Wolfson, A. D. (1976). An experimental case study of the successes and failures of job enrichment in a government agency. *Journal of Applied Psychology* 61, 701–11.

McDaniel, M. A., Schmidt, F. L., & Hunter, J. E. (1988). Job experience correlates of job performance. *Journal of Applied Psychology* 73, 327–30.

Mackworth, N. H. (1947). High incentives versus hot and humid atmosphere in a physical effort task. *British Journal of Psychology* 38, 90–102.

Mager, R. F., & Pipe, P. (1970). *Analyzing performance problems.* Belmont, CA: Lear Siegler, Inc./Fearon Publishers.

Opsahl, R. L., & Dunnette, M. D. (1966). The role of financial compensation in industrial motivation. *Psychological Bulletin* 66, 94–118.

Organ, D. W. (1988). *Organizational citizenship behavior: The good soldier syndrome.* Lexington, MA: Lexington Books.

Organ, D. W., & Konovsky, M. (1989). Cognitive versus affective determinants of organizational citizenship behavior. *Journal of Applied Psychology* 74, 157–64.

Orne, M. T. (1962). On the social psychology of the psychology experiment: With particular reference to demand characteristics and their implications. *American Psychologist* 17, 776–83.

Park, J. F., & Payne, M. C. (1963). Effects of noise level and difficulty of task performance in performing division. *Journal of Applied Psychology* 47, 367–68.

Peters, T. J., & Waterman, R. H., Jr. (1982). *In search of excellence.* New York: Harper & Row.

Plutchik, R. (1959). The effects of high intensity intermittent sound on performance, feeling, and physiology. *Psychological Bulletin* 56, 133–51.

Porter, L. W., & Lawler, E. E. III. (1968). *Managerial attitudes and performance.* Homewood, IL: Richard D. Irwin.

Sackett, P. R., Zedeck, S., & Fogli, L. (1988). Relations between measures of typical and maximum job performance. *Journal of Applied Psychology* 73, 482–86.

Taylor, F. (1911). *The principles of scientific management.* New York: Harper & Row.

Trist, E. L., & Bamforth, K. W. (1951). Some social and psychological consequences of the longwall method of coal-getting. *Human Relations* 4, 3–38.

Vroom, V. H. (1964). *Work and motivation.* New York: John Wiley & Sons.

Wyatt, S., Frost, L., Stock, F.G.L. (1934). Incentives in repetitive work: A practical experiment in a factory. Medical Research Council, Industrial Health Research Board, Report N. 69. London: Her Majesty's Stationery Office, pp. 1–24.

11 Job Motivation Programs
Methods of Application

What are the motivational objectives of a compensation system?

What methods are used to achieve these objectives?

What have been the recent developments in compensation programs?

What are the most popular noncompensation programs for applying motivation concepts?

What are the theoretical bases for these programs?

What are the limitations of these programs?

Our task now is to examine the methods by which organization objectives are linked to the interests of individual participants. As we have noted in the previous chapter, the baseline motivation level of organizational participants is often substantial. Still, a number of programs exist that, when appropriately administered, increase job motivation well beyond that baseline.

COMPENSATION PROGRAMS

From a motivational standpoint, the ideal compensation program accomplishes three objectives. First, it establishes a standard level of pay high enough to meet the going market rate in the industry or community. Thus, the organization is able to attract sufficient numbers of qualified personnel for its various jobs. Second, the pay program provides for internal equity such that participants believe they are fairly paid in outcomes for their comparative inputs. Third, the pay system provides incremental rewards for above-average performance or productivity.

Unfortunately, these objectives often conflict with each other. The methods used to achieve any one of them complicates the management of the others.

The Market   Prospective employees must first be motivated to enter the organization. Thus, the pay system must meet the rate established by the supply and demand for categories of personnel in the locality. Some companies actually offer starting salaries well above the market rate to attract a large number of interested applicants and then select very carefully from them. The assumption behind this strategy is that by attracting and choosing the most competent employee, in the long run unit labor costs will actually be lower.

Katz (1964) has used the term *instrumental system reward* to describe those rewards that accrue to individuals by virtue of their membership in the system. A standard or starting salary that comfortably exceeds the market rate is such a reward. Katz contends that such rewards, while inducing people to enter and subsequently remain, do not motivate performance beyond that minimally necessary to retain membership. From a strictly motivational standpoint, that is a logical argument. However, if generous base pay enables the firm to choose only those with the very highest skills, then those skills exercised at a baseline motivation level might well result in greater productivity than a group of average-skilled persons highly motivated by incremental pay gains based on performance.

Equity   An important human motive is that of realizing fairness or equity in exchanges with others. This seems to be an especially strong motive with respect to compensation.

Equity theory (e.g., Adams, 1965) proposes that individuals define and assess equity by the criterion that their ratio of outcomes (pay) to inputs (effort, training, experience, hazards, responsibilities) approximates the ratio of outcomes to inputs for relevant comparison persons (such as others in the organization). That is, we do not object to others being paid more than we are paid, provided those others are contributing manifestly more and their jobs require more experience, expertise, or stress. But we resent it when others receive significantly higher pay for contributing essentially the same value of inputs that we contribute.

Equity theory identifies several behavioral and perceptual means by which a person might resolve the tension caused by felt inequity. A characteristic response to pay inequity, and to the bitterness aroused by it, is to redefine one's relationship to the organization. A person might still perform at an acceptable (perhaps even higher) level of personal productivity if the person is intrinsically reinforced by the job. But the person will probably not feel obliged to render services that are not mandatory. Specifically, someone smoldering with chronic feelings of pay inequity is unlikely to perform discretionary, spontaneous acts of cooperation, helping others, or other forms of organizational citizenship behavior described in the previous chapter.

Job evaluation is the usual method by which companies formulate an internal pay structure that is accepted as equitable. Job evaluation evaluates the job (not the individual) in terms of the requirements it poses for any person performing the job at a minimally satisfactory level. This is not the appropriate place to present a thorough discussion of the intricacies of job evaluation (the interested reader may consult Belcher & Atchison, 1987, or Schuler & Youngblood, 1986). Briefly, however, the process works as follows: First, a classification system is formulated that includes all of the important factors or inputs that are required to perform the jobs in the organization. Most job evaluation plans include half a dozen or more such factors, such as degree of physical exertion required, degree of exposure to safety hazards, amount of formal education, budgetary responsibility, responsibility for the performance of others, special aptitudes, and related work experience. Second, each factor is defined in terms of some continuum or scale, typically on a five-point scale (e.g., for the education factor, a 1 would translate into a high school diploma or less, a 5 would represent graduate degree or doctorate in a specialized field). Third, to each place on the scale for each factor some point value is assigned, such as 50 points for high school diploma or less and 400 points for graduate degree. Finally, from observations or descriptions of what each job requires in terms of the amounts of the various factors, a total point value is determined for each job. The expectation is that average or standard compensation for any given set of jobs will be directly proportional to the point value arrived at from the analysis of how much the job requires of each of the relevant factors. Keep in mind that we are *not* talking about allocating points or dollars based on level of performance or productivity within a job. The purpose in job evaluation is to evaluate the monetary worth of the requirements dictated by the job for satisfactory performance by anyone.

FIGURE 11–1

Scatterplot of Jobs' "Worth" against Standard Hourly Pay

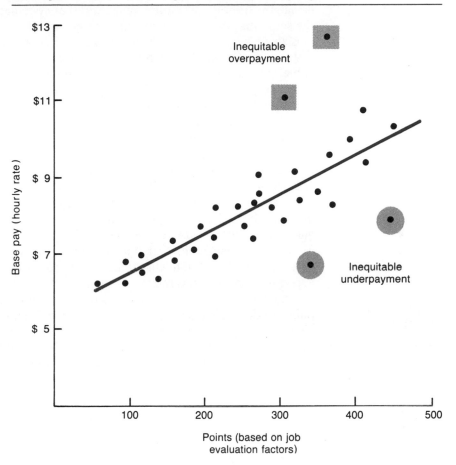

The results of job evaluation could be summarized by a graph such as that seen in Figure 11–1. As expected, there is a general trend such that the greater the requirements of the job (as reflected in points along the horizontal axis), the greater the accompanying standard or average pay scale (the vertical axis). To the extent that the dots representing different jobs all lie on or near that trend line, pay equity has been achieved. But note that certain jobs fall well above the trend line; that is, they are assigned pay rates higher than expected from the job evaluation. Some other jobs fall well below the trend line, which means that people doing these jobs are inequitably underpaid in comparison to those above the line.

Why can total equity not be achieved, at least within the measurable limits of job evaluation? If the job evaluation program is of recent vintage, the pay system may reflect the accumulated past practices of unsystematic compensation practices. Equity might eventually be achieved by bringing jobs below the line up to it and allowing inflation and attrition to permit the line itself to catch up with those presently overpaid. Otherwise, the deviations from the trend line may represent systematic discrimination, in the sense that those jobs below the line are mainly held by minorities, and jobs above the line are usually filled by a favored group, for example, white male Anglo-Saxon Protestants. A third reason is the market. Those in "objectively overpaid" jobs are performing services in demand relative to the supply of persons willing and able to provide such services in the area or industry. The deviations below the trend line represent employee services that are in abundant supply relative to the demand.

Labor market conditions often present organizations with the dilemma that equitable pay, as defined by the job evaluation program, is not consistent with the pay structure needed to attract and retain certain types of labor at competitive and cost efficient rates. Equity might imply that librarians and heavy equipment operators be paid the same, if their respective contributions are the same, yet the going rate for hiring heavy equipment operators might be considerably more than that for librarians. To offer the same salary to both would mean either that jobs involving the use of heavy equipment would go unfilled or that the organization would be spending more than necessary to attract and retain librarians.

Advocates of a strict equity approach to compensation have recently rallied under the banner of "comparable worth." This doctrine argues that dissimilar jobs can be compared in terms of their intrinsic worth or contribution and should be paid accordingly. Would such an approach ignore market realities? The proponents of comparable worth reply that market forces often represent systematic collusions among large institutions. This enables them to impose their patterns of intentional or unintentional discrimination against women and minorities on the market. Thus, the argument goes, institutions enforce inequitable underpayment on jobs typically performed by women, and the corrective is legislation that would require employers to base compensation strictly on a sound program of job evaluation. Therefore, it is not sufficient merely to pay men and women the same for doing the same job, nor to allow women to compete for the higher-paying jobs filled mainly by males; rather, all jobs should be paid according to their inherent value. These arguments were advanced when the American Federation of State, County, and Municipal Employees brought suit against the state of Washington in 1982. The U.S. District Court judge found such arguments persuasive and ordered the state to immediately bring all members of predominantly female job categories up to their "evaluated worth." The state figured the cost of compliance at $400 million in 1984 alone and $60 million per year afterward.

Minnesota passed a law in 1984 that incorporates the concept of comparable worth as applied to state employees. Men and women performing different work but of comparable value—as measured by job evaluation techniques—must be compensated the same. In Canada, the province of Ontario passed similar legislation in 1987 to apply not only to public sector employees, but also to private companies with 10 or more employees. Organizations must have achieved comparable worth in compensation plans by January 1990. No firms are permitted to cut anyone's wages to achieve pay parity in male-dominated and female-dominated jobs, but are allowed to phase in the parity by adding on 1 percent of the previous year's payroll annually until the difference is made up.

Incremental Rewards Whatever the standard pay rate, a pay system motivates effort for incremental performance (i.e., performance beyond that deemed satisfactory or essential to continued membership in the system) to the extent that incremental compensation is contingent on such performance.

The expectancy model of motivation (Chapter 4) has, perhaps more than other approaches to job motivation, lent itself to the discussion of how pay affects work motivation. For compensation to motivate effort for incremental performance, the individual must view such performance as clearly instrumental to greater pay. This implies that better performance will be recognized, accurately assessed, and contingently rewarded. Also, the increment in pay must be sufficient to represent a large positive valence; for example, a 1 percent pay gain for 20 percent increase in productivity would presumably not constitute sufficient incentive value. Furthermore, the individual must expect that a sizable increment in effort would result in a proportionate increase in measurable performance.

Several types of incremental pay plans have been formulated and used by organizations to elicit incremental performance. *Piecework* plans pay employees on the basis of a fixed amount of money for each unit of output. Per unit pay is derived from industrial engineering analysis of the amount of time and effort normally required to produce a single unit of output. Such plans are rarely found today in large organizations for full-time workers, because every change in the overall pay scheme (e.g., cost-of-living increases) requires a recalculation of the per unit pay. Also, such a plan makes it possible for a worker's earnings to fluctuate dramatically from one pay period to another. *Bonus* plans, on the other hand, provide a standard hourly or weekly pay rate for performance up to some standard level (again derived from cost accounting information and analysis of industrial engineering data). Productivity beyond the norm results in proportionate pay increments.

Piecework and bonus plans are limited in their applicability by several factors. First, each person's output must be measurable in a fairly objective fashion. Second, variations in output must be attributable to, and controlled by, the skill and effort of the individual worker. Thus, such plans would lose motivational impact if most of the variance in an individual's output were caused by forces outside his or her control, such as the speed of the production line, shortages of materials, or dependence on others' work to complete a unit of output. Psychologically, the expectancy that increased effort would result in increased performance is curtailed. Furthermore, industrial workers have become suspicious of such plans over the years—they fear that productivity beyond the standard brings negatively valent outcomes in its train. The fear is that management will react to high bonus earnings by recalculating a higher level of standard productivity. This concern, in turn, leads work groups to pressure their members to restrict output below what is feasible, and so individuals feel that increased production—while leading to higher pay—will also cause estrangement from co-workers.

For service, administrative, professional, or managerial jobs in which performance cannot be measured by quantifiable output, *merit pay* plans are devised to motivate greater effort with incremental monetary reward. Such plans provide periodic increases in pay—beyond those increases naturally accruing due to seniority, cost-of-living adjustments, or across-the-board raises—contingent on an individual's overall performance. Since performance is not directly measurable, a subjective assessment of the amount and quality of the individual's contributions may be rendered by the immediate superior or through a systematic performance appraisal program. In any case, since the appraisal is subjective, the rater and ratee have ample opportunity to disagree over the value of the individual's performance. Furthermore, since the appraisal can be influenced by many perceptual distortions (Chapter 6), it is easy to imagine how any given individual, in spite of the existence of a merit pay program, may conclude that only the most tenuous linkage connects performance with pay.

Lawler (1971) has concluded that organizations should use merit pay as a motivational device only when individual performance is easily measurable, or, failing that, when the trust level prevailing in the organization is reasonably high. Also, he argues that such systems are pointless unless the amount of incremental pay contingent on performance is quite substantial. The evidence reviewed by Lawler (1971) suggests that many organizations do not succeed in linking pay to individual performance, even when they publicly claim to use a merit pay system.

Leventhal's (1980) model of social justice offers some insight into why incremental pay systems are likely to be constrained within a limited range. Leventhal notes that fairness in distribution of outcomes can be defined by differing, even competing rules, and that individuals vary considerably in what they believe to be the proper weights assigned to various inputs. Some would put the predominant weighting on measurable productivity; others would emphasize effort; many would argue for the importance of tenure or seniority as an input (this factor is often the major determinant of pay in Japanese companies); still others would "let the market decide"—firms should pay what they must to hold on to those who could be recruited by competitors.

Leventhal argues that, in some instances, even equality of pay—at least within same-tenure cohorts of a group—might be defended as at least a baseline level of fairness. When individual contributions are difficult to measure and cohesion in the group is considered of major importance, managers (especially women managers, it appears) will start with equality as the operating rule of equity and deviate from that only when compelling circumstances dictate.

Recent Developments in Compensation Programs

In the late 1960s and 1970s many firms experimented with nonmonetary motivation programs, some of which will be noted later in this chapter. During this era, the assumption seemed to be that, at least in the Western industrialized world, a stage of general affluence had been attained and salary had been eclipsed by other aspects of work — notably, the importance of intrinsic satisfaction and the motive of psychological growth. The implicit reasoning beneath this assumption apparently held that pay dealt mainly with "lower order" needs such as creature comforts and security, which most people now took for granted; otherwise, pay was regarded as a "hygiene factor" to be managed competently, but not reckoned as a major motivational tool.

We can now see the naiveté of such a view. Needs—even at the most basic level—are subjective and comparative, not absolute. A personal income that would have meant affluence by historic standards or in other parts of the world is not affluence to those with a different comparison. Furthermore, income is inextricably intertwined with many psychological motives other than security and creature comforts; it touches on self-esteem, personal relationships, and measures of achievement. A 1981 poll by *Psychology Today* of its readers (who probably exceeded the national average in personal income) evoked responses from 20,000 people testifying to the complex symbolic importance of money. While 40 percent of responders felt they were "doing okay," 23 percent reported they were "struggling" and only 12 percent described themselves as "comfortably affluent" or "rich." Regardless of personal income—whether less than $10,000 or more than $100,000—readers felt they needed at least that much to live comfortably and more to feel rich. Over two thirds of respondents reported having experienced anxiety, depression, or anger in the recent past in association with money; at the same time, nearly half said they had also experienced happiness or excitement in connection with money. The majority of respondents agreed that income is a major index of success.

In the 1980s, the pendulum swung back to more focused attention to pay as a medium of job motivation. Among the trends and innovations seen in corporate compensation programs in the last decade:

Merit Pay Plans with Teeth   The vast majority of U.S. and Canadian firms report having merit pay plans for their personnel. But according to research by Painter, Sutton, and Burton (1982) and Foulkes (1980), only a small component of pay increases under these plans are actually based on performance. In fact, for both union and nonunion workers, tenure is the overwhelming determinant of actual pay. Annual increases consist primarily of cost-of-living adjustments. The "merit" component is essentially contingent on receiving a performance rating of "satisfactory," which the majority of employees receive.

In 1985, *The Wall Street Journal* reported that "pay-for-performance is one of the hottest management and labor trends around, according to compensation consulting firms." Corporations that had merely paid lip-service to the merit pay idea began earnest efforts to differentiate high from average from low performers and to increase the variance in pay increases accordingly. One such plan implemented at BankAmerica's credit-card division ranks all 3,500 employees on about 200 specific criteria and lumps personnel into five groups or quintiles. Those in the top 20 percent on the quantitative measures get raises at least 40 percent higher than those in the bottom group, and the latter have a limited time in which to improve their ratings and move up in the rankings.

Such programs have their pitfalls. The devices by which employee performance is calibrated can be quite arbitrary; even when such is not actually the case, those who receive lesser benefits often have that perception. Some managers believe that the extra satisfaction experienced by the few top performers is more than offset by lower morale among the rest of the group. Collegiality suffers from the competitive climate, and subtle processes that depend on cooperation begin to deteriorate. Wide variances in pay increases, when compounded from one year to another, are felt to reflect distinctions not merely in productivity but in class of citizenship, and those who feel relegated to second-class citizenship have a lessened sense of commitment. Nonetheless, many companies are committed to the philosophy of "pay for performance," while searching for methods to limit the abuses and grievances attendant to it.

Cash Bonus Plans   Even a substantial pay increase, when spread out over 12 or 52 paychecks, loses some of its wallop. Thus, some compensation experts (Lawler, 1976) have argued that providing the entire increase in a one-shot cash payment increases the *valence* of the increase. Theoretically, the increase should have more motivational value when the money comes in one big lump. And, in fact, increasing numbers of firms in the 1980s experimented with this arrangement.

The catch in such programs, in practice, is that the cash part of the pay increase does not factor into base pay. So, if you start with a base of $36,000 and get a 10 percent cash bonus of $3,600, then your percentage next year is again figured from the $36,000 base—not $39,600. Also, certain benefits that are figured on base pay, such as company contributions to employee retirement plans, would be lower with such programs. Thus, when one large U.S. corporation adopted the cash-bonus plan in the mid-1980s, the result was—according to published accounts—a negative effect on the morale of the middle managers and professional staff included in the plan.

One argument in favor of the cash-bonus idea is that, since the increase is *not* factored into base pay, such programs do not create such glaring distinctions in citizenship. Arguably, people are more sensitive to distinctions in base pay than to variance in one-shot payments. Furthermore, the cash-bonus method avoids the unintentional compounding of inequity when the maximum increase available for merit varies from one year to another. If I, as top performer in a "good year" for the company overall, receive a 20 percent increase and this is added to my base, I will maintain my pay advantage over you if your superior performance occurs in lean years for the company when the maximum increase is less than 10 percent. Perhaps a "middle-way" approach with such plans is to factor into base pay any increases granted as cost-of-living adjustments or attributable to satisfactory performance with increased tenure, while using the lump-sum portion to reward the exceptional performance of a few.

Skill-Based Pay   The doctrine of comparable worth that underlies job evaluation dictates pay according to the skills the job requires of the person performing it. Skill-based pay introduces a somewhat different principle — that the *individual* should also be compensated according to the number and type of skills relevant to *other jobs* in the department or company. Theoretically, this provides the incentive for employees to increase their versatility. A workforce with skills applicable to many jobs provides a flexibility that could give a significant competitive edge to firms in turbulent market or technology environments. Furthermore, continually learning new competencies no doubt provides an important way to satisfy many psychological growth needs.

The downside of such programs is that the firm might invest substantial resources — first in providing training, second in compensation for attained skills — without ever recouping its investment from the individual's actual use of the acquired skills on the firm's behalf. At worst, a company might train an employee in skills not used until the individual takes a position with a competing firm.

Again, a "middle way" approach comes to mind, one that in practice is the preferred route: cash bonuses paid to employees who master any of a designated list of skills beyond those used in the current job.

Expansion of Stock Ownership Plans   Until recently, stock options and restricted stock shares were available only to a few top corporate officers. *The Wall Street Journal* (October 3, 1988) reports that four or five times as many employees as in the past are now eligible for stock options.

One reason for this development, in an era of hostile takeovers, may be the desire to place more stock in friendly hands. But such a program also gives more employees a sense of being a "stakeholder" in the success of the firm. The sense of proprietorship strengthens commitment, increases psychological identification with the company, and provides the incentive to contribute in many ways, not just for brownie points and short-run benefits.

During the 1980s one favored device for transferring stock ownership to the rank-and-file workforce has been Employee Stock Ownership Plans (ESOPs), made possible by special legislation in the previous decade. ESOPs permit the firm or its owner to borrow money to create stock for employees. The money can be used to purchase new assets to expand or modernize operations; as the money is paid back, shares of stock go to employees. Originally both the interest *and the principle* of the loan were tax deductible when repaid. For growing firms, or owners who wanted to retire and transfer ownership to employees, ESOPs were especially attractive, and Rosen, Klein, and Young (1986) have reported on the success of ESOPs at firms such as W. L. Gore (maker of Gore-Tex) and Lowe's Companies (a chain of home improvement and building supply stores in the Southeast).

More recently, accounts of abuse of ESOPs have appeared in the media. Some firms have used them for reasons not intended by framers of the original legislation—to finance leveraged buyouts or purely as tax dodges without providing the normal safeguards for employee retirement plans.

Expansion of Profit-Sharing Plans   In 1887, Procter & Gamble adopted a plan to divide profits between shareholders and employees in the same proportion that labor costs stood to total costs. A century later, according to Tom Peters ("Tom Peters on Excellence," Feb. 18, 1987), only 15 percent of the U.S. labor force participates in a profit-sharing plan. However, there are indications that the proportion is increasing, and firms that have practiced profit-sharing for management and professional staff now increasingly extend this to clerical, blue-collar, and entry-level employees. Moreover, unions have recently agreed to such plans (along with greater employment security) as a trade-off for higher base pay. From management's viewpoint, this converts a portion of wages and salary expense to variable costs rather than fixed costs.

Drawing from an expectancy model of motivation, theorists have long argued that a drawback of profit-sharing plans is that the individual sees little or no link between his or her own effort and firm profits—which depend on many factors beyond the individual's control. Theoretically, profit-sharing plans should minimally effect the work behavior of most employees. In a strictly rational sense, that argument is compelling. But perhaps something more than cold, means-end rationality is at work here. The basic idea is that "we're all in this together"—the goals and interests of top officials, line managers, staff, and hourly workers are all congruent. What benefits one benefits all. A broader and deeper sense of involvement is the key, not a logical or realistic calculation of how individual effort now influences quarterly profits.

The All-Salaried Workforce   Compensation practices have long made a distinction between hourly and salaried employees. Hourly employees lose pay for any loss of scheduled work time, whether it be an hour or a day. They generally qualify for fewer benefits and incentives than salaried workers. The only advantage is overtime pay when working more than the standard 40 hours per week. The result of this distinction in compensation is often a correlated distinction in implied class of citizenship, as reflected in work attitudes and sense of identification with the firm.

A few years ago, American Steel & Wire Corp. in Ohio put all employees on straight salary—employees are paid even for missed time. The vice president for human resources was warned that absenteeism would soar, but the opposite occurred; absenteeism and turnover are presently lower than the industry average. The argument for the all-salaried workforce is that it builds trust, makes everyone feel like a first-class citizen, and thereby builds commitment.

Flexible Benefit Plans   In 1985, Steelcase, Inc., a Michigan-based office furniture company, joined the growing ranks of employers who offer a "cafeteria-style" benefits plan. At Steelcase, participants receive a designated number of benefit dollars and can distribute them across a menu of choices. Single parents can opt to assign some of their benefit dollars to child-care; benefit dollars not spent on medical or insurance plans can be put into retirement accounts or even taken home in cash. Steelcase reports that the plan has actually saved money, while improving morale because of increased control exerted by participants over the total pay package. This supports the contention of Lawler (1976)—a longtime advocate of cafeteria-style plans—that, because of individual differences, such choice increases the resultant valence of pay outcomes.

The major obstacle to such plans is "adverse selection"—the tendency for the healthiest and youngest to opt out of medical care benefits and take the equivalent dollars in other forms, leaving only the higher risk groups covered by medical insurance. Flex-type benefit plans therefore must set certain constraints on the allocation of benefit dollars to certain categories.

NONMONETARY MOTIVATION PROGRAMS

Over the last two decades, organizations have gone beyond compensation in their attempts to apply motivation theories to the work scene. The most widely used programs have been (in no particular order) *organizational behavior modification*, or programs emphasizing positive reinforcement; *job redesign*, sometimes called job enlargement or job enrichment; and *management by objectives*. The majority of firms among the Fortune 500 have had experience with one or more of these programs, on varying scales of involvement. Public, nonprofit organizations—such as state and local governments, hospitals, and school systems — have also experimented with versions of these programs. All three have gone through periods of faddism, and none today attracts the publicity accorded to them when they first burst on the scene and were the "in" thing to do. However, they all continue to be widely used in various forms, perhaps in more eclectic and decentralized fashion than before.

ORGANIZATIONAL BEHAVIOR MODIFICATION: USING POSITIVE REINFORCEMENT

Organizational behavior modification (OB Mod) applies operant concepts and principles to work settings. These concepts come primarily from the work of B. F. Skinner (1953). These concepts had been systematically and effectively applied in mental health and educational institutions before they became popular in industry. Nord (1969) drew attention to the broad relevance of operant principles for the work environment, and Luthans and Kreitner (1975) demonstrated the compatibility of reinforcement concepts with the more popular schools of management thought.

OB Mod does not concern itself directly with motivation as an explanatory construct. Nor does it have recourse to other internal states such as attitudes or personality traits as representing ultimate causes of behavior. First and foremost, it concerns the observation of behavior itself. Second, it assumes that such behavior is lawfully related to the observable antecedent stimuli of that behavior and the immediate consequences of behavior. To modify behavior, you modify the contingencies and schedules of reinforcement rather than trying to change attitudes.

Stages in Program Development

The methods used to implement a program of organizational behavior modification (OB Mod) have been amply described and illustrated by Lawrence Miller (1978), who has served as a consultant to many companies in the design of such programs. As Miller notes, the first step is *pinpointing,* or defining very precisely in operational terms the work behavior that is to be modified. OB Mod cannot be applied to such vague, catch-all goals as "working harder" or "more effective service." Miller observes that many managers are unsatisfied with employees' performance, but have not analyzed their dissatisfaction to the point of identifying specific behaviors they would like to see changed. This process may be the most difficult step in OB Mod. Only when officials can define the target behavior in measurable terms, such as "attend to the customer within five minutes of his/her entering your area of the store" or "wear your safety visor," will OB Mod be feasible.

The second step consists of a *baseline audit.* Officials must determine how frequently the target behavior occurs before there is any intervention. This knowledge is needed to serve as a comparison for subsequent performance levels. Such information enters into any cost/benefit analyses of potential gains. It also documents in convincing, quantitative terms the state of present performance and may supply the "shock treatment" needed for managers who have complacently overestimated their units' performance.

Next, a *criterion* or standard must be set. This is the ultimate goal toward which subsequent efforts are aimed. A standard may already exist; if not, one has to be set on the basis of observation and judgment. The standard should be realistic and attainable, but sufficiently higher than present practice to make the OB Mod program cost effective.

The next step is to *"consequate"*—choose a reinforcer. Officials have to specify a consequence for reinforcing an instance of the desired behavior. Several considerations enter into this choice: the reinforcer must be flexible and timely so that it can be delivered as soon after the behavior as possible; it must be something that does not quickly lead to satiation on the part of the employees; it must have broad appeal to the group in question. In many OB Mod programs, group leaders and supervisors are trained to use social reinforcement in the form of praise coupled with quantitative feedback—for example, "Roy, I see you're now holding scrap rates to less than 5 percent, and that's just super." In other programs, improvements are posted conspicuously on wall charts or bulletin boards. Some elaborate programs translate the feedback into points or stamps that can be accumulated and later exchanged for merchandise or privileges of the employee's choice. Miller (1978) suggests that reinforcer surveys be periodically administered (possibly by inclusion in a more general survey) with questions such as:

I would work harder if _____.
If my boss would _____ I would enjoy working here.
My job would be more rewarding if _____.

Responses to such items offer clues as to the types of reinforcers that may prove effective.

Whatever the reinforcers chosen, they should be mediated by the supervisor. This practice makes the supervisor's attention a conditioned reinforcer; it strengthens the social reinforcement by the manager for those later occasions when it has to serve as the major source of ongoing reinforcement.

At the onset, the reinforcers chosen may have a very contrived tone; that is, they are artificial—not naturally occurring consequences of the behavior. Some critics of OB Mod call this the gumdrop syndrome. Often, however, contrived reinforcers are necessary if the desired behavior does not have the initial strength required to generate more natural reinforcers.

From this point, the program moves to the *shaping* stage. If the target behavior occurs only 50 percent of the time and the standard is 95 percent, it would be unrealistic to wait until the standard is reached before providing reinforcement. It is unlikely that such an immediate improvement will occur;

therefore, any intermediate gains will go unreinforced and the efforts made to achieve such gains would undergo extinction. Rather, officials have to use the method of successive approximations. As Miller (1978) notes, two conditions are required for doing this: (1) some variability in present rate of responding, and (2) selective reinforcement. Initially, any improvement, no matter how small, over the average baseline value is reinforced liberally and frequently. As responding begins to stabilize at a slightly higher rate, only further improvement beyond that level is reinforced. By stages, the criterion of reinforcement is gradually moved toward the ultimate standard.

Once the target behavior approaches the standard or criterion level with some consistency, an important decision arises. Should the contrived reinforcers used up to this point be continued, or does the target behavior now have the strength to generate more noncontrived reinforcers — pride in one's work, covert self-reinforcement, respect from peers and superiors, the gleaming smile of a customer, a high-quality finished product? At the very least, OB Mod practitioners recommend stretching the ratio of contrived reinforcers. This means using them less frequently on a variable ratio schedule. A given amount of reinforcement is contingent on increasingly larger numbers of responses. This step offers several advantages: more economical use of the reinforcer; less likelihood of satiation; and, as we noted in Chapter 4, promotion of greater resistance to extinction.

At Emery Air Freight (see Close-Up), officials tried to phase out the contrived reinforcers, but found that the target behaviors declined in frequency when not followed by quantitative feedback. Emery's managers concluded that noncontrived positive consequences of the selected areas of performance would not be able to sustain the improvements and elected to continue to provide precise feedback.

In contrast, Luthans, Paul, and Baker (1981) report a case in which contrived reinforcers were not needed indefinitely. In this experience with OB Mod in a large department store, officials targeted three behaviors of sales personnel: assisting a customer within five seconds after the customer arrived in the sales area (or at least within five seconds after concluding business with a prior customer); stocking shelves to 70 percent capacity with appropriate merchandise; and staying within nine feet of the store area of responsibility. For 20 days, researchers performed the baseline audit measuring these behaviors for sales personnel in 16 departments. For the next 20 days, contingencies were introduced in eight of those departments, using contrived reinforcers exchangeable for time off with pay. During this period the targeted behaviors increased dramatically for the eight departments given the extra incentives, while remaining at virtually the same level for the control departments not exposed to the contingency. When the contingency was withdrawn, the improvements in the targeted behaviors remained essentially intact for three weeks. The authors conclude that the increase in targeted behaviors led sales personnel to experience the reinforcing effects of positive customer reactions and greater success in

CLOSE-UP

OB Mod at Emery Air Freight

This company realizes significant savings when small shipments intended for the same destination are shipped together in containers rather than separately. Company policy strongly encouraged this procedure, and many operating officials believed it was being followed almost all the time.

A performance audit showed, however, that containers were, in fact, used only about 45 percent of the time. Emery set a target goal of using containers 95 percent of the time, representing a savings of $650,000 annually over baseline performance.

Emery provided its operating managers with programmed instruction workbooks on the use of positive reinforcement. Managers began a systematic program of awarding praise and other social reinforcers to workers for any improvements over baseline performance level. In addition, workers were given printed forms for recording their own behavior, thus providing a continuous record of feedback. In the early stages, supervisory praise was given frequently; as performance increased and approached the target level, praise was given with gradually decreasing frequency, and the self-recorded feedback provided most of the reinforcement.

Emery tried positive reinforcement in other operations, too, such as sales and customer service. In each case, the result was dramatic improvement over initial performance levels. In the three years of applying positive reinforcement principles, Emery estimates it saved over $3 million.

Emery found that eventually praise from supervisors began to lose its effect. In fact, sheer repetition led in some cases to the risk that praise would become an irritant rather than a reinforcer. To overcome this problem, supervisors made use of other reinforcing options, such as letting a worker switch temporarily to a more enjoyable task after completing a less enjoyable one, providing release time contingent on good performance, and sending personal letters of commendation from executives to the employee's home. Still, however, the bread-and-butter reinforcer that sustained the performance was the immediate, precise feedback that workers received.

SOURCE: Emery Air Freight, "At Emery Air Freight: Positive Reinforcement Boosts Performance," *Organizational Dynamics* 1 (1973), 41–50.

sales. Thus, the contrived reinforcers acted as a "way station" to improve certain behaviors that, once stabilized, created their own noncontrived reinforcement.

Criticisms of OB Mod

Formal programs of positive reinforcement have generated some controversy, whether in spite of or because of their apparent success. Some critics see such practices as demeaning, suggesting that application of operant concepts to work is manipulation that violates human dignity.

Positive reinforcement is, of course, a form of manipulation—if it is successful. Any tactic that influences behavior must, by definition, be considered manipulation. But organizations, in order to function, must influence the behavior of their members. Thus, the charge of manipulation would apply to any organization that succeeds in coordinating collective effort to some common goal.

Skinner (1972) has reminded us that we inevitably control each other's behavior. We respond to each other in ways that either strengthen, punish, or extinguish prior behavior. We cannot avoid exerting such influence. The important criterion is whether such influence is constructive to the parties affected. Skinner suggests that we should not leave such influence to chance. It is more rational for a social system to plan its contingencies of reinforcement. This makes it possible for all parties—managers and workers alike—to be positively reinforced, and the organization contributes to the larger culture.

OB Mod uses artificial reinforcers, not as ends in themselves, but to strengthen constructive behaviors that eventually will generate their own noncontrived reinforcers. Thus, contrary to what some critics argue, OB Mod does not overlook the importance of intrinsic rewards from work. The "gumdrop stage" is not a permanent condition, but a means of reaching a more desirable state in which people experience satisfaction from the constructive consequences of their own competence.

Some managers believe that if workers are fairly paid, "then they ought to do what is expected of them without any extra reward." Unfortunately, good wages, distributed in an across-the-board fashion, function primarily to attract and hold workers. In the absence of some more precise contingency, the paycheck at the end of the week has little effect on job behavior earlier in the week. History teaches us that when organization officials do not use immediate positive reinforcement, they inevitably resort to aversive forms of control, which often have longer-run ill effects for both the manager and those managed.

The most conspicuous limitation of OB Mod concerns the type of work behavior for which it is suited. It is best applied to work behavior that can be precisely defined, quantitatively measured, and frequently repeated. Thus it pertains most readily to simple, routine, recurring task responses. Formal programs of positive reinforcement could not be easily applied to more unstructured tasks, to jobs that require creative responses, or to significant but rarely occurring job behaviors. Operant concepts, in a theoretical sense, do have relevance to such dimensions of work, but it would be difficult to design and administer a program applying the concepts to such types of work.

JOB REDESIGN

The major premise underlying job redesign as a motivational program is that job motivation is sustained primarily by the job itself. Put another way, the important rewards are the intrinsic rewards generated by task effort.

A number of partially overlapping conceptual and philosophical frameworks converge in the notion of job redesign. The most direct and immediate implications for this approach came from Herzberg's (1966) two-factor theory. Herzberg maintained that job-extrinsic factors—such as salary, conditions surrounding the job, supervision, and relations with co-workers—serve mainly hygienic functions: when well-managed, they prevent the disease of dissatisfaction that arises from feelings of inequity or physical discomfort. In doing so, the hygiene or extrinsic factors meet the basic, lower-order needs to feel secure and to avoid pain. Having met such needs, they can do no more. Only the job itself, the task, can provide the means of satisfying the higher-order needs for stimulation and psychological growth. And the job can do this only if it is enriched.

Herzberg questioned the trend in modern industry toward work simplification. The techniques introduced by Frederick Taylor and other apostles of scientific management, then carried forward by industrial engineers, had called for a fractionization of work into jobs that consisted of highly repetitive cycles of simple operations. When used on a vast scale—as in the assembly lines of automobile plants—these techniques boasted not only of the advantages of mechanical efficiency, but also of very short training times for new workers. The increased production made possible by this system, in turn, made it possible to pay higher wages to workers.

By the mid-1950s, some observers began to wonder if work simplification was causing certain dysfunctions that more than offset the virtues of mechanical efficiency. At this time, concern centered around the problem of repetition. British psychologists had explored the industrial applications of the phenomenon of *response-produced inhibition*. When an organism repeats a stereotyped response, an inhibition builds up against further repetition of that response. This inhibition has nothing to do with muscular fatigue; rather, it is a feedback mechanism from the central nervous system. British studies had shown that, on certain repetitive tasks, many workers exhibited intermittent deficits in response that could be accounted for only by this principle.

The obvious antidote to response-produced inhibition was some opportunity for *alternating response*. Response-produced inhibition dissipates rapidly when an alternative response is performed. Thus, the first attempts at job redesign (actually preceding Herzberg's theory) introduced variety into the task by *job enlargement*. Programs of job enlargement required the worker to alternate periodically between different responses, giving the worker more different things to do. Early studies suggested that job enlargement (or horizontal job loading) produced generally positive results, at least initially, in the form of better morale, less absenteeism, and greater production. The casual, uncontrolled nature of the studies, however, precluded any confident conclusions. Moreover, a few of the published studies described disappointing results, and a selective bias may have led companies to report only successful programs.

Herzberg contended that job enlargement offered little in the way of motivational potential. The job must be "enriched"—it must provide the worker an opportunity to experience a sense of achievement on the job. This meant building into the job complexity, autonomy, and challenge. Whereas job enlargement called for horizontal loading, job enrichment implied vertical job loading. The latter involves not only alternating operations, but also responsibility for planning the operations and evaluating the product of the operations.

While Herzberg's two-factor theory of job motivation provided the initial stimulus for job redesign programs, his model did not offer systematic criteria for defining what constitutes an enriched or intrinsically motivating job. Furthermore, the dogmatic tone of some of his statements—the idea that only mentally ill persons would not respond favorably to job enrichment, preferring satisfaction based on hygiene factors—did not seem to square with the results of some attempts at job enrichment. Thus, while giving due credit to Herzberg for redirecting attention to the job itself as motivator, researchers and practitioners in the 1970s looked to a different source for guidance and inspiration when redesigning jobs.

The Hackman-Oldham Job Characteristics Model

Hackman and Oldham (1976) have presented a model specifying five "core characteristics" of a job, the effects of these characteristics on psychological states, and the outcomes realized when the psychological states are activated (see Figure 11–2). Three of the core characteristics combine to account for the psychological state of "meaningfulness": *skill variety*—the mix of skills required of (and valued by) the individual; *task identity*—the extent to which a job provides a "sense of closure," such that a person's efforts have resulted in an identifiable and visible contribution; and *task significance*—the degree to which the result "matters," demonstrably affecting others inside or outside the organization. The job of camera repair technician would probably rate high in all three of these characteristics. The repairman must use a mix of valued skills (diagnostic, conceptual, technological) to perform a task with strong identity (start with a broken camera, end with a fully functioning camera) that has considerable significance (to a customer who can now come back from vacation or family reunion with a treasure trove of snapshots). The repairman's work, then, would be experienced psychologically as quite meaningful.

According to the Job Characteristics Model, meaningfulness alone does not provide intrinsic motivation potential. Meaningful work must also provide *autonomy,* otherwise the sense of personal responsibility—of the person as agent of causality—is lacking. Finally, *feedback,* providing knowledge of results, must be present so that the outcomes of work effort can act as rewards.

Theoretically, the greater the feeling of meaningfulness in the work, the sense of personal responsibility, and knowledge of results, the greater the resultant level of intrinsic motivation—which in turn is predicted to manifest

FIGURE 11–2
Hackman & Oldham's Job Characteristics Model

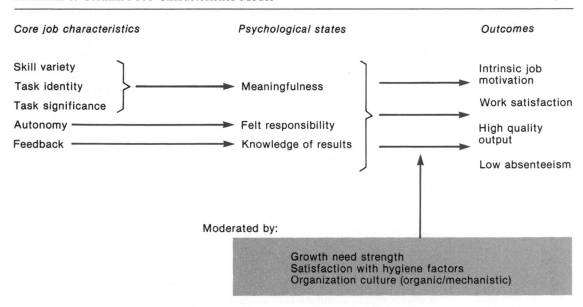

itself in higher quality of work, low rate of absenteeism, and high job satisfaction.

However, the Job Characteristics Model spells out the limits within which the core characteristics determine attitudinal and behavioral outcomes. The relationships hold only to the extent of the individual's *growth need strength,* that is, the strength of the motive for experiencing psychological growth. The model recognizes that not all people have this need in abundance, and even among those who do, many prefer to realize their growth in nonwork domains of their life. And the model does not characterize such people as mentally ill or otherwise requiring treatment; they are just different from those who seek to grow through work experience.

Furthermore, the Job Characteristics Model assumes that, even among those with considerable growth need strength, a precondition for intrinsically motivating tasks to lead to positive outcomes is the absence of any festering problems pertaining to hygiene factors. For example, widespread perceptions of pay inequity or inconsiderate supervision would, according to the model, prevent the realization of the potential positive effects of enriched jobs.

Finally, the model asserts that only certain organizational cultures or climates provide the necessary supportive environment in which intrinsic job motivation can be sustained. A mechanistic structure, with heavy emphasis on formal rules and procedures, works at cross purposes with the ethos of intrinsically motivating tasks. An organic structure, which relies on more informal and ad hoc modes of coordination, coheres more naturally with intrinsically motivating tasks.

Hackman and Oldham's *Job Diagnostic Survey* (JDS) represents a major development linking their ideas to both research and application. The JDS provides instruments (in the form of questionnaires) for assessing in a prospective firm the current levels of the core job characteristics, the intervening psychological states, the attitudinal outcomes, and the three moderating factors (growth need strength, satisfaction with hygienes, and organic/mechanistic climate). Thus, the JDS provides the data with which to determine whether jobs are already intrinsically motivating, and if not, whether conditions are favorable for job enrichment/job redesign to "take."

Methods for Implementing Job Redesign/Enrichment   The "work module" concept provides an overarching principle to the implementation of job redesign programs. This concept calls for grouping together logically related tasks to define a natural, meaningful area of responsibility for an individual. Often the logical basis for grouping tasks consists of customer or client relationships. For example, a keypunch operator, instead of specializing within a narrow category of in-basket work (such as cost data), will handle all data transcription for a particular department or branch. The keypunch operator would communicate directly with the people affected in order to understand their particular needs and to plan accordingly. The operator is also responsible for ensuring the quality of the finished work. Thus, the operator uses interpersonal, conceptual, organizational, and technical skills; can see the impact of the work on others; and performs a function with interpretable identity.

A close cousin to the work module concept is that of "nesting": putting together individual jobs that complement each other. This gives the work group and the individual a second-order sense of job meaningfulness. The keypunch operator noted above, instead of being thrown together with others who keypunch, is grouped with those who provide complementary services — such as programming, report writing, library research — in handling management information systems needs for a designated department or branch. In some instances, the nesting of related jobs lays the foundation for *autonomous work groups* or *self-managed work groups* in which individuals learn each other's jobs, rotate from one job to another, provide for their own internal organization, and even make their own personnel decisions, without direct supervision.

Another motif pervading job redesign programs is the systematic *unblocking of feedback channels.* Periodic reports flow back and forth directly between the individual and the parties affected by his or her work — not up one side of the hierarchy and back down another. The quicker the positive feedback, the more it reinforces the effort that went into the work; the more timely the negative feedback, the better the chance for constructive adjustments.

Research

Studies show that employees' reported perceptions of the core task characteristics correlate positively with job satisfaction and reported levels of work effort. To a somewhat lesser extent, descriptions of job characteristics correlate with attendance and independent measures of performance (e.g., supervisory evaluations). Other research has shown that subjects' reported descriptions of these task attributes are capable of discriminating between jobs officially classified at different salary grades. Moreover, while the bulk of the relevant research is from nonexperimental field surveys yielding only correlational data, the limited evidence from field experiments suggests that actual changes in the direction of job enrichment yields increases in employee perceptions of task characteristics. Thus, at least in some gross, overall sense, subjects' responses to the JDS reflect reasonable measurement validity.

Research on the moderators presumed to condition the effects of task characteristics have been almost entirely limited to the growth need strength factor. Even there, the results are only weakly supportive, mainly with respect to reports of intrinsic motivation and work satisfaction. At least one study (Steers & Spencer, 1977) did find that level of achievement motivation moderated the effects of task characteristics on performance. Task autonomy and identity were positively related to the rated performance of those with high need for achievement, but essentially unrelated to performance of those low in achievement needs.

Results of Job Redesign Programs

Scores of firms have undertaken some form of job redesign. Notable examples include Texas Instruments, Corning Glass, IBM, AT&T, Procter & Gamble, Maytag, Buick, Motorola, Monsanto Chemical, and Scott Paper Company. In Europe, programs by Volvo and Saab-Scania (Sweden) and Philips (Netherlands) have attracted much attention and discussion. Some experiments have been carried out on a small scale, with selected groups thought to be most in need of radical improvement; in other instances, as with the Gaines Foods Company and Scott Paper Company (and the General Motors' Saturn plant to be located in Tennessee), entirely new plants have been designed and constructed in order to carry out comprehensive reforms in job structure.

The majority of firms that have experimented with job redesign describe the projects as successful. This is to be expected; a management team that has invested large sums of stockholders' money in any project, attracted media attention, and put the prestige of the firm on the line will certainly want to interpret the results as justifying the costs. Since most assessments of these programs come from uncontrolled case studies, the evidence for success or failure is generally ambiguous. Therefore, it would not be surprising if officials overestimated the benefits of the programs.

CLOSE-UP

Where's the Enrichment?

Researchers introduced a job enrichment program in three clerical work units of a federal agency. Productivity increased, but it soon became clear that this was not due to motivational or attitudinal forces. Instead, the productivity increase was due to more efficient use of manpower, elimination of redundant operations, feedback, and competition. Attendance improved initially because workers expected higher pay would also be forthcoming. When workers realized that pay would not increase, many of them were irate. The authors concluded: "It was clear . . . that these employees viewed their jobs instrumentally, that is, as a means to an end. . . .

It was not that they were indifferent to the work itself, they clearly preferred interesting to dull work. But in their hierarchy of values, the extrinsic rewards came first."

SOURCE: E.A. Locke, D. Sirota, and A. D. Wolfson. "An Experimental Case Study of the Successes and Failures of Job Enrichment in a Government Agency," *Journal of Applied Psychology* 61 (1976), 701–11.

Culling the evidence available from studies that used fairly objective measures of relevant criteria before and after job redesign, the following seems to be a fair statement:

1. There is not a consistently strong improvement in productivity. When productivity did improve, the increase could have been accounted for by nonmotivational factors, such as newer and better plant and equipment, greater flexibility of operations, and improved scheduling of materials flow in the work process.

2. Studies report a more consistent improvement in quality of finished products.

3. The majority of instances show some improvement in work attendance. The inference is that increased worker satisfaction mediates this effect.

4. Some programs have yielded a mix of positive and negative effects, with the latter more or less cancelling out the former.

It is difficult to sort out the results because management can hardly redesign jobs without changing other variables in the work environment at the same time. To restructure jobs usually means that you also change technology, patterns of social interaction, and the character of supervision. Neither positive nor negative effects of the program as a whole can easily be attributed to any one variable.

Some would argue that job redesign seldom gets a fair chance to prove itself. Unions have offered only lukewarm support for the concept. Leaders of organized labor have criticized "demeaning work" and called for work that preserves the worker's dignity. But in serious collective bargaining the

FOCUS ON INTERNATIONAL OB

Culture and Job Redesign

Hofstede (1980) has noted that job redesign programs in the United States have emphasized the enrichment of individual jobs, while counterparts to these programs in Sweden and Norway have concentrated on restructuring work on the basis of groups. Why the difference? Hofstede suggests it is no accident, but a logical outgrowth from the cultural differences between these countries. Hofstede's study of the beliefs and values of 40 countries indicates that the United States scores high in a dimension of "masculine" values—defined by an orientation toward independence, productivity, hard measures of performance, andpersonal ambition. Scandinavian countries, bycontrast, lean toward the "feminine" end ofthe continuum, with stress on interdependence, quality of life, service, and sympathy for the less talented.

Furthermore, the prospects for job enrichment would seem to be quite limited in cultures with strong values favoring uncertainty avoidance, such as Greece and Japan, because such values predispose employees to favor security and lifetime employment over interesting and challenging work.

SOURCE: Geert Hofstede, "Motivation, Leadership, and Organization: Do American Theories Apply Abroad?", *Organization Dynamics*, Summer 1980. Reprinted in H. W. Lane and J. J. DiStefano, *International Management Behavior* (Scarborough, Ontario: Nelson Canada, 1988), 105–31.

definition of *quality of work life* zeroes in on pay, benefits, safety, hours of work, and job grades. Some unionists, such as William Winpisinger (1973), are frankly and outspokenly suspicious of management's ulterior motives in the push for job enrichment. Is it merely a disguised effort to get more work for less pay, or even to undercut the influence of the union? Certainly job redesign plays havoc with the well-defined job descriptions that presently limit management's ability to manipulate work assignments and responsibilities. Furthermore, if management and labor find it hard to agree on concrete issues such as pay and benefits, it would be much more difficult to agree on something as elusive as "intrinsic job rewards." Therefore, unionists have not generally embraced programs for job enrichment, although the posture of labor leaders has softened somewhat due to economic distress in such industries as autos and steel.

In some instances, the initial success of job redesign programs has threatened lower-level supervisors and managers. Job redesign builds into the job certain dimensions of work that previously were in the domain of supervisory responsibilities. If this downward shift in responsibility works, lower-level managers wonder if they may soon be expendable. At the very least, redesigned jobs that give workers more autonomy and discretion affect a manager's sense of control. Foremen and supervisors might interpret job enrichment as simply one more step in the erosion of their authority, while their responsibilities remain as great as ever. Not surprisingly, lower-level managers, after initial endorsement of job-redesign programs, often become less cooperative in the extension and consolidation of the changes made.

Beyond the question of enlisting the active support of organized labor and lower levels of management looms a more fundamental issue brought to light by results of some programs: A sizable minority of the labor force still places greater priority on the extrinsic rewards of pay, benefits, and working conditions than on the intrinsic rewards of work.

Our conclusion is that increasing the intrinsic rewards of task effort holds vast potential for enhancing job motivation, but realizing this potential involves grappling with prickly political, institutional, and cultural dilemmas. The theoretical framework supporting job redesign is not in question; rather, we have underestimated the difficulties of applying that framework in complex settings. Results of the more successful programs have been sufficiently encouraging for us to believe that efforts along these lines will continue and that some of the major problems will be resolved.

MANAGEMENT BY OBJECTIVES

Programs of OB Mod and job redesign evolved in response to conceptual frameworks that preceded them. By contrast, management by objectives (MBO) represents a case in which practice ran far ahead of formal theory and research. Indeed, much of the research supportive of MBO not only came after years of implementation by hundreds of organizations, but was actually independent of any concern with MBO.

Credit is usually given to Peter Drucker for the embryonic formulation of MBO. In *Practice of Management* (1954), Drucker stressed the importance of having managers at every level work for clearly defined objectives that were integrated across levels. Integration and consistency of these objectives would result from collaboration between superior and subordinate officials in setting quantitative performance goals.

Carroll and Tosi (1973) give credit also to Douglas McGregor for popularizing a goal-oriented approach to managing. McGregor (1960) criticized many existing methods of appraising the performance of managers. He argued that all too often, managers were evaluated on the basis of style, personality characteristics, or irrelevant "halo" factors rather than results. Furthermore, performance review discussions often made both superior and subordinate officials uncomfortable, since they focused on weaknesses rather than strengths. McGregor suggested that a more positive motivational climate would result from evaluating performance against well-defined quantitative goals, worked out in advance by boss and subordinate in discussion. This would leave subordinates latitude for using their own style or methods for achieving the goals. The criterion of performance would be measurable results. Appraisal would provide feedback of actual performance in comparison to the goal.

Numerous versions of MBO (also called *management by results* and *goals management*) were already being practiced when theoretical and empirical work on goal setting came to light in the late 1960s. Locke (1968) argued that the immediate determinant of task behavior is conscious intentions, which in turn derive from values and from cognitive maps that link behavior and its outcomes to the realization of those values. Goals serve to make intentions clear and explicit. Feedback and incentives are important because they stimulate goal setting or lead a person to accept an external goal. Participating in setting a goal is important to the extent that it leads to acceptance of the goal.

Results of laboratory experiments by Locke and his associates support the hypothesis that specific, precise goals ("Increase your output by 10 percent") lead to greater productivity than general ("Do your best") goals. Demanding goals ("Increase your performance by 20 percent") result in higher productivity than easy goals ("Increase your output by 5 percent"), provided the subject accepts the goal. If the subject does not reject or abandon the goal as impossible or unrealistic, difficult goals lead to higher performance, whether or not the goal itself is actually reached. A study by Latham and Saari (1979) supports the prediction that whether a subject is assigned the goal or personally sets it makes little difference as long as goal difficulty is the same. Some evidence from both lab and field studies suggests that participation results in more demanding goals.

McClelland's (1961) work on the theory of achievement motivation also supports the basic concepts of MBO. Managers as a group usually score rather high on this motive. Two characteristics of people who are strongly motivated by the need to achieve are (1) a tendency to set moderately difficult, but attainable, personal goals, and (2) a compulsive need for quick, precise feedback on the performance. MBO, then, creates a task environment that capitalizes on the motivational characteristics of managers.

The MBO Process

MBO has no pure or definitive prototype. The format and structure of the program invariably include features to fit the prevailing conditions in an organization. Nonetheless, MBO consultants typically design a program involving the following sequence of events:

1. The subordinate manager works up a written statement as a provisional draft of his or her objectives for the coming period (year, six months, or quarter). This statement anchors the objectives in measurable terms. Any objective judged to be important is linked to a quantifiable index. The subordinate, in effect, says, "These are the criteria by which I choose to be judged."

2.   The subordinate submits this statement to the superior for review. Their joint discussion, which may lead to modifications of the subordinate's original statement, results in the final and formal statement of the objectives.

3.   Periodic but frequent joint reviews by superior and subordinate discuss progress to date and assess the distribution of time and effort toward various component goals. This provides feedback to the subordinate as to which objectives need more or less emphasis. A regional sales manager, for example, may confirm that he or she is making rapid strides toward meeting the overall sales objectives but is running behind in the effort to meet the goal of obtaining orders from 25 new industrial customers. These interim review sessions help to fine-tune the direction of subsequent efforts.

4.   At the end of the period for which goals were set, superior and subordinate discuss the latter's performance in a more comprehensive fashion. Analysis concerns the reasons why some or all goals were not met — ideally in a constructive fashion for purposes of future planning. Some goals may, in retrospect, be judged as unrealistic; unforeseen developments (e.g., a strike, an economic downturn, or a change in corporate policy by top management) may have led to constraints that handicapped the subordinate's performance; or the subordinate might have pursued the wrong strategies. The review provides the basis for defining objectives for the upcoming period.

An important issue concerns the question of whether MBO is tied to decisions about compensation. On one hand, it seems logical that managers will be more personally involved in the setting and pursuit of goals if their performance in comparison to the goals determines their salary. On the other hand, one can argue that to tie compensation to MBO may subvert and distort the goal-setting process. Subordinates might concentrate the goal-setting on areas of operation where they knew they could look good rather than honestly aiming at target goals that would benefit the organization as a whole.

Assessment of MBO   Research in the form of correlational field studies has sought to determine which elements of the MBO process have the most favorable effects on participants. Findings reported by Carroll and Tosi (1973) suggest that the degree of subordinate influence is not an important factor in the perceived success of the program. Difficulty of goals set has an uneven relationship with participant motivation: Difficult goals seem to stimulate the more mature and self-confident manager, but have a discouraging effect on less experienced subjects. More consistently positive relationships with program criteria are noted for the *clarity* of goals set, the *perceived relevance* of the goals, and the *frequency of feedback.*

Other research has attempted to evaluate the overall effect of MBO. Many studies report increased productivity, better planning, improved attitudes toward performance appraisal, and increased morale of managers. Unfortunately, these findings come from uncontrolled case studies comparing pre-MBO data with trends immediately after MBO. Also, many of the criterion measures come from responses to interviews. We should not ignore such findings, but clearly we have to qualify them.

Perhaps the most ambitious and rigorous test of an MBO intervention is that conducted by Muczyk (1978). His study compared the performance of 13 branch banks that underwent MBO to an identical number of control branch banks not exposed to MBO. The criteria were hard measures of overall financial performance, as well as attitudinal measures. Measures were taken at the beginning of the study, six months later, and 12 months after the start. The experimental and control banks were matched for market area and size to minimize any differential advantage of one group over the other. Muczyk found no significant effects attributable to MBO at either the 6-month or 12-month checkpoints in either financial performance or attitudinal criteria. Banks that underwent MBO did improve their performance over baseline levels, but so did the other banks. Muczyk qualified his findings by noting that MBO was introduced only from the middle-management ranks down; the preferred strategy is to include top-level management. Moreover, officials participated on a voluntary basis, so that "the normal pressures exerted by top management on behalf of the success of a program introduced on a more permanent basis were absent" (p. 327).

Limitations of MBO

We might note first of all that MBO, in both its conception and application, is almost entirely for managers. OB Mod and job redesign have found readiest application to operative, nonmanagerial employees. MBO, by contrast, has found little or no application with nonmanagerial, nonprofessional workers except for sales personnel. There is nothing inherent in any of these programs that would logically and necessarily exclude any groups from treatment, but MBO lends itself more easily to subjects with substantial levels of responsibility and authority.

Even among MBO interventions otherwise judged successful, a consistently voiced objection is to the amount of paperwork involved (Carroll & Tosi, 1973; Webber, 1979). The mechanics of the goal-setting, feedback, and review processes generate an enormous number of forms for documentation. Most managers consider such paperwork an irritant and a distraction.

Participants often feel that MBO distorts the nature of their performance by placing excessive emphasis on performance dimensions that easily lend themselves to quantitative expression. They feel that they hurt their personal interests if they spend much time on tasks that are important

CLOSE-UP

Improving Productivity

Industrial psychologists Raymond A. Katzell and Richard A. Guzzo reviewed 207 recent American experiments using some type of motivational program. A sampling of their findings is given below, showing the proportion of programs in each category that achieved positive results on various criteria. The authors caution that some of the experiments undoubtedly suffered from flaws in research design and that studies with unsatisfactory results are less likely to have been reported. Still, the findings attest to the considerable potential that such programs have to offer.

Proportion of Programs Achieving Positive Results

Program	Output	Criterion Absences/Turnover	Attitudes
Goal setting	21/22	6/9	7/10
Job redesign	22/25	8/10	7/10
Pay incentives	18/20	7/9	3/4
Feedback	26/28	6/10	4/6
Work schedules	11/18	8/11	7/9

SOURCE: R. A. Katzell and R. A. Guzzo, "Psychological Approaches to Productivity Improvement," *American Psychologist* 38 (1983), 468–72.

but difficult to measure. A regional sales manager can set precise goals for total sales, number of new accounts, administrative costs per dollar of sales, and sales revenue from new products. On the other hand, it is not so easy to set specific goals for customer service and subordinate development. A half day spent in consultation with a potentially big customer may be more important than a dozen routine phone calls to existing clients, but there is no obvious means to measure and document this. Ridgeway (1956) found that what is formally measured attracts attention and effort at the expense of what is not measured. People assume that what is measured is what really counts. While MBO programs include intensive training on how to set clear goals for all areas of performance, it does not provide magic formulas for measuring intrinsically subjective or qualitative dimensions.

In some organizational climates, if MBO is imposed on subordinates resentful and distrusting of the hierarchy, it may be viewed as a "club" to force people toward unrealistic goals. The numbers associated with the objective-setting and review process exert a special tyranny of their own without considering mitigating circumstances. The result is that managers direct their ingenuity toward finding ways to beat the statistics game rather than make substantive contributions.

As with OB Mod and job redesign programs, the results produced by MBO depend on how it is introduced and implemented, on the support demonstrated by top-level managers, and on the existing climate of the organization. Evaluating the program itself apart from these other variables in field settings is well nigh impossible. The best that can be said is that MBO can produce increased job motivation among managers, but there is no guarantee that it will do so if barriers work against it.

Nonmotivational Objectives of MBO

Our focus has been on MBO as a program for increasing managerial job motivation, but MBO addresses other purposes. Many practitioners see it primarily as an effective means to ensure managerial control over system performance. Others view it foremost as an aid to planning. Many consultants stress its benefits as a developmental tool for junior managers. Some emphasize the performance-appraisal feature of MBO. Of course, motivation enters into all these issues to some extent. Nonetheless, numerous instances of MBO, while not ignoring its motivational implications, emphasize its impact on planning, control, and development of subordinate managerial skills.

CONCLUDING OBSERVATIONS

While we have discussed these programs as if they were totally distinct from one another in practice and philosophy, they do overlap to some extent. OB Mod, for example, clearly contains elements of goal-setting and feedback emphasis most often associated with MBO. Job redesign attempts to increase the total amount of reinforcement for work effort by drawing on the noncontrived reinforcers made possible by job enrichment. In some respects, MBO redesigns or enriches the jobs of lower-level managers and captures the reinforcing quality of precise feedback.

We draw attention to these underlying similarities to forewarn the reader against partisan claims that any one model or program of job motivation has a monopoly on validity or practical benefits. OB Mod, job redesign, and MBO do not reflect antagonistic concepts but rather different points of emphasis. There is no reason—philosophical or practical—why they cannot complement each other.

Furthermore, like the character who was shocked to realize he had been "speaking prose all his life without knowing it," many organizations practice the core components of one or more of these programs without calling them by their popular names or even knowing that such programs exist. It would represent a wild oversimplification to say that one firm practices MBO and another absolutely does not, or that one company has adopted OB Mod and another avoided it. One could scarcely imagine an organized setting in which, at least informally, officials were not setting goals, reinforcing superior efforts, or enriching the jobs of promising employees who are capable and desirous of greater challenges.

SUMMARY

Organizations have used a variety of programs in the attempt to apply motivational principles to job behavior. The most widely used approach is the compensation system. Ideally, a pay program attracts and holds the people needed for various jobs, establishes equity across different job categories, and provides incentives for above-average performance. However, these objectives often come into conflict with each other.

The most popular noncompensation programs include organizational behavior modification (OB Mod), job redesign, and management by objectives (MBO). OB Mod procedures draw from the concepts of operant psychology; job redesign is based on the premise that employees seek to satisfy psychological growth needs at work; and MBO is supported by the demonstrated effects of goal setting. Each program, however, can also be supported by other theoretical frameworks. Empirical assessment of these interventions has produced inconclusive results; none of these approaches has a guarantee of success, in part because so much depends on the institutional context in which they are introduced. They represent not cookbook formulas, but guidelines that must take account of the technological and political constraints specific to the organization.

CONCEPTS TO REMEMBER

ESOPs	Noncontrived reinforcer	Instrumental system reward
OB Mod	Stretching the ratio	Comparable worth
Pinpointing	Job redesign	Job evaluation
Baseline audit	Intrinsic rewards	Job enlargement
Reinforcer survey	Two-factor theory	Job enrichment
Contrived reinforcer	Response-produced	MBO
Shaping	inhibition	Job Characteristics Model

QUESTIONS FOR DISCUSSION

1. Explain why, in practice, the three objectives of a firm's compensation plan can seldom be achieved simultaneously. What considerations should guide officials when faced with conflicts between the objectives?

2. Are OB Mod and job redesign incompatible with each other? Frame your answer in both theoretical and practical terms.

3. If a job-redesign program leads to increased productivity and profits, should the increased earnings be shared with those performing the redesigned jobs? Why or why not?

4. Compare and contrast MBO with job redesign.

5. Discuss the difficulties of evaluating the effectiveness of any intervention aimed at increasing job motivation.

REFERENCES

Adams, J. S. (1965). Inequity in social exchange. In L. Berkowitz (ed.), *Advances in experimental social psychology*, vol. 2. New York: Academic Press.

Bettner, J. (1988). Firms give stock options to wider range of workers in effort to instill loyalty. *The Wall Street Journal,* Oct. 3.

Carroll, S. J., Jr., & Tosi, H. L., Jr. (1973). *Management by objectives.* New York: Macmillan.

Dolan, C. (1985). Many companies now base workers' raises on their productivity. *The Wall Street Journal,* Nov. 15.

Drucker, P. (1954). *The practice of management.* New York: Harper & Row.

Emery Air Freight. (1973). At Emery Air Freight: Positive reinforcement boosts performance. *Organizational Dynamics* 1, 41–50.

Foulkes, F. K. (1980). *Personnel policies in large nonunion companies.* Englewood Cliffs, NJ: Prentice Hall.

Hackman, J. R., & Oldham, G. R. (1975). Development of the Job Diagnostic Survey. *Journal of Applied Psychology* 60, 159–70.

Hackman, J. R., & Oldham, G. R. (1976). Motivation through the design of work: Test of a theory. *Organizational Behavior and Human Performance* 16, 250–79.

Herzberg, F. (1966). *Work and the nature of man.* Cleveland: World.

Katz, D. (1964). The motivational basis of organizational behavior. *Behavioral Science* 9, 131–46.

Katzell, R. A., & Guzzo, R. A. (1983). Psychological approaches to productivity improvement. *American Psychologist* 38, 468–72.

Latham, G. P., & Saari, L. M. (1979). The effects of holding goal difficulty constant on assigned and participatively set goals. *Academy of Management Journal* 22, 163–68.

Lawler, E. E. (1971). *Pay and organizational effectiveness.* New York: McGraw-Hill.

Lawler, E. E. (1976). New approaches to pay: Innovations that work. *Personnel* 53, 11–23.

Leventhal, G. (1980). What should be done with equity theory? New approaches to the study of fairness in social relationships. In K. G. Gergen, M. S. Greenberg, & R. H. Willis (eds.), *Social exchange: Advances in theory and research.* New York: Plenum Press, 27–55.

Locke, E. A. (1968). Toward a theory of task motivation and incentives. *Organizational Behavior and Human Performance* 3, 157–89.

Locke, E. A., Sirota D., & Wolfson, A. D. (1976). An experimental case study of the successes and failures of job enrichment in a government agency. *Journal of Applied Psychology* 61, 701–11.

Luthans, F., & Kreitner, R. (1975). *Organizational behavior modification.* Glenview, IL: Scott, Foresman.

Luthans, F., Paul, R., & Baker, D. (1981). An experimental analysis of the impact of contingent reinforcement on salespersons' performance behavior. *Journal of Applied Psychology* 66, 314–23.

McClelland, D. C. (1961). *The achieving society.* New York: Van Nostrand Reinhold.

McGregor, D. (1960). *The human side of enterprise.* New York: McGraw-Hill.

Miller, L. (1978). *Behavior management.* New York: John Wiley & Sons.

Muczyk, J. P. (1978). A controlled field experiment of measuring the impact of MBO on performance data. *Journal of Management Studies* 15, 318–19.

Nord, W. R. (1969). Beyond the teaching machine. The neglected area of operant conditioning in the theory and practice of management. *Organizational Behavior and Human Performance* 1, 375–401.

Painter, B., Sutton, S., & Burton, S. (1982). *Provincial worklife survey: A pilot project.* Vancouver: Sociotechnical Systems Group, B. C. Research.

Peters, T. (1987). Profit-sharing a key to employee involvement. "Tom Peters on Excellence," *Bloomington Herald-Telephone,* Feb. 18.

Ridgeway, V. F. (1956). Dysfunctional consequences of performance measurements. *Administrative Science Quarterly* 1, 240–47.

Rosen, C., Klein, K. J., & Young, K. M. (1986). *Employee ownership in America: The equity solution.* Lexington, MA: Lexington Books.

Rubenstein, C. (1981). Money & self-esteem, relationships, secrecy, envy, satisfaction. *Psychology Today,* May.

Schuler, R. S. (1983). *Effective personnel management.* St. Paul, MN: West Publishing.

Skinner, B. F. (1953). *Science and human behavior.* New York: Macmillan.

Skinner, B. F. (1972). *Beyond freedom and dignity.* New York: Alfred A. Knopf.

Steers, R. M., & Spencer, D. G. (1977). The role of achievement motivation in job design. *Journal of Applied Psychology* 62, 472–79.

Webber, R. (1979). *Management: Basic elements of managing organizations.* Homewood, IL: Richard D. Irwin.

Winpisinger, W. W. (1973). Job satisfaction: A union response. *AFL-CIO American Federationists* 80, 8–10.

12 Punishment and Discipline in Organizations

What are the arguments for and against the use of punishment in organizations?

What is the process by which punishment affects behavior?

Under what conditions is punishment most likely to have desirable effects on behavior?

How do managers discipline?

It is remarkable how little is written or said about the topic of punishment in organizational settings. Extended discussions about job motivation illustrate the methods of eliciting desired behavior, but overlook the fact that organizations also must eliminate undesired behavior.

Punishment and disciplinary measures are, indeed, frequently used in organizations. For many first-line supervisors and managers who have little control over organizational rewards (such as salary raises, promotions, and benefits), punishment and discipline (or their threat) are the most immediate tools available for shaping the behavior of subordinates. One could argue that, day in and day out—whether intentionally or unintentionally—punishment is used far more often than reward in attempts to influence behavior.

Even when officials have ample means of rewarding exemplary performance, they often encounter dysfunctional behaviors in the form of excessive absenteeism, rowdiness, damage to company property, falsifying records, theft, violation of safety rules, sexual harassment, and substance abuse. Sooner or later, managers must take note of such problems and try to correct them—most likely by disciplinary actions.

Why, then, the relative silence on this seemingly important topic? First of all, punishment is controversial. There is little debate over whether to reward good behavior or performance, but heated arguments are raised over whether to punish ineffective or undesirable behavior. This controversy is reflected in popular discussions about child rearing, the penal system, and our permissive society. Second, punishment is not a pleasant topic; it suggests problems, tensions, and a host of other disagreeable matters. Finally, punishment is considerably more complex and unpredictable than rewards in its effects on behavior. This complexity makes it difficult to predict whether the effect of punishment on behavior will be constructive, undesirable, or nonexistent.

Punishment occurs when an aversive consequence (C^-) follows a response. An aversive consequence is one whose removal is reinforcing; the *removal* of an aversive stimulus *reinforces* the behavior that precedes the removal. The next time you are in a crowded elevator, notice the behavior of the people around you. What do they do? Usually they gaze at the lighted numbers above the elevator door, even when their destination is several floors away. What conceivable interest could people have in doing this? Quite simply, it represents behavior sustained by the removal and avoidance of an aversive stimulus: close eye contact with strangers. In our culture, we ordinarily experience some discomfort in face-to-face encounters with strangers in close quarters. Because looking up at the numbers removes this discomfort, this behavior is strengthened in such settings.

Schematically, we may represent a punishment episode as follows:

$$A \rightarrow B \rightarrow C^-$$

Given some antecedent situation (crowded elevator), some behavior (close eye contact) is followed by an aversive consequence (embarrassment, awkwardness). The A is important here: it signifies that the behavior is followed by an aversive consequence on certain well-defined occasions. When walking around a city square or in a long corridor, eye contact with strangers several yards away is not uncomfortable. Even in crowded quarters, eye contact poses no problems if those around you are friends.

Discipline is a *deliberate attempt to punish.* The boss who chews out a tardy employee is clearly making a deliberate attempt to make that person experience aversive consequences for such behavior. The official who calls a technical foul on an unruly coach consciously imposes a penalty for unsportsmanlike conduct.

Not all instances of punishment (even in organizations) constitute discipline, as we have defined it. For example, punishment occurs when a student asks the instructor a question and the instructor's response puts the student "on the spot." The instructor may not have intended to do this (we try not to punish intellectual curiosity, since that is the presumed goal of educational systems), but the answer had that effect. Many constructive behaviors occur less frequently than desired simply because of unintended aversive consequences that follow such behaviors.

By the same token, not all disciplinary measures constitute punishment. In some organizations, excessive unexcused absenteeism is disciplined by suspending the person from work for a few days—the person is disciplined by doing more of what he or she was disciplined for to begin with! When disciplinary measures involve consequences that actually are not aversive to the person disciplined, then no punishment has actually occurred.

THE PSYCHOLOGICAL DYNAMICS OF PUNISHMENT

Psychologists agree about the process by which punishment affects behavior. To illustrate the process by which punishment works, consider the example of an office clerk who likes to prop his feet up on the desk. The clerk's supervisor views this as undesirable behavior. Perhaps the supervisor doesn't think it looks appropriate to visitors and management officials who occasionally pass through. So the supervisor walks over to the clerk's desk and gives him a verbal reprimand. Thus far, we have the situation shown below:

$$A \text{ (work environment)} \rightarrow B \text{ (undesired behavior of propping feet on desk)} \rightarrow C^- \text{ (reprimand)}$$

An aversive consequence, such as the reprimand, usually triggers an emotional response of some kind. The emotional response may be felt or experienced as fear, guilt, or anxiety. The emotional response is itself aversive. That is, anything we do that terminates or avoids such feelings will be reinforced by the removal of the aversive feeling.

FOCUS ON INTERNATIONAL OB

Humiliation: Punishment in China

The Chinese use a variety of methods to reward good workers, including citations as a "model worker" and the provision of extra rewards, such as a television set or a bonus. But, in an economic system that prohibits firing, how do they discipline employees for unsatisfactory work behavior?

Managers at the Xian Department Store, which employs about 800 people, decided to give special recognition to their "40 Worst Shop Assistants."

The store's general manager, Xiao Xingcai, concedes that "service in China has been bad for a long time." Retail salesclerks there have a reputation for rudeness to customers. Xingcai set up a ballot box at the customer service desk and urged shoppers to vote for the worst salespeople. Customers responded all too willingly. Managers sorted through the ballots, adding some of their own observations, and picked the 40 Worst, who then had to write self-criticisms analyzing their deficiencies and forfeit their monthly bonus. Each of the 40 received a plaque, with picture, posted in their workplaces proclaiming him a member of the "40 Worst."

One of the recipients responded, "I accept my punishment, since my error hurt the store's reputation. Today, I view my little three-foot shop counter as a window of socialist civilization." By losing her bonus, she lost nearly one fourth of her monthly income. Just a few months earlier, she had been regarded as one of the store's top salespeople.

Several other organizations have made inquiries about the store's new method of discipline. A related plan, to select the "Worst Manager," has stalled, however.

SOURCE: *The Wall Street Journal,* January 24, 1989 (Staff reporter Adi Ignatius).

Recall that an emotional response to an unconditioned stimulus (in this case, the reprimand) can come under the control of other stimuli that immediately precede the unconditioned stimulus. Thus, if the clerk feels guilt or anxiety as a result of the reprimand, the emotional response should also be triggered in the future by those events that preceded the reprimand. So, the next time the clerk props his feet on the desk, either the raising of the feet or the feel of the heels on the desk should trigger the emotional response previously evoked by the reprimand. In other words, the initial components in the behavior produce consequences (in the form of sensations) that trigger the conditioned emotional response. Since this emotional response itself is felt as aversive, any act that terminates it will be reinforced. If the clerk lowers his feet and moves the chair closer to the desk or stands up, he no longer feels anxiety. He is *negatively reinforced for doing something else that eliminates or avoids the aversive consequence* created by a negative emotion.

Now let us see what can go awry in this complex process. First, consider the reprimand itself. Can we be certain that it is aversive? To some people it may not be. Since it gives the offender some attention, it could conceivably act as a reinforcer, especially if the clerk had a very dull job and any break in the routine offered a bit of variety. If the reprimand is not aversive, it will not generate the emotional response that suppresses the undesired behavior.

Second, even if the reprimand is aversive, it may occur too late after the response to come under the control of immediate antecedents of the undesired behavior. If the clerk had his feet propped up on the desk for 45 minutes before the supervisor intervened, the events leading up to propping the feet may be totally unaffected by any resulting emotional response.

Third, let us assume the clerk is a very nervous, anxiety-prone sort of person. The reprimand may trigger a strong emotional response — much stronger than the supervisor intended. The anxiety response may be so strong and intense that it "spreads" to much of the surrounding work environment — that is, the entire immediate work setting acquires the power to evoke an anxiety response. The anxiety may prevent the foot-propping, but it also may prevent the clerk from effectively concentrating on his job.

The clerk may discover, on the other hand, that propping the feet is followed by a reprimand only under certain conditions — when the supervisor is nearby, when the supervisor is not preoccupied with other matters, when the supervisor seems to be in a foul mood. So the clerk simply learns to discriminate between the antecedents that define occasions when a particular response is or is not punished. The foot-propping is suppressed only in the presence of certain well-defined cues. In the conditions described above, punishment either would not have its intended effect of suppressing the response or would have unintended effects that may offset the value of any deterrent effect. It is difficult to predict the actual effect, precisely because the process is so complex.

THE CASE AGAINST PUNISHMENT

Many people argue that punishment should be avoided as a means of trying to influence behavior. Their objections to punishment are prompted, at least in part, by humanistic considerations or ideology, but also include the following arguments:

1. For punishment to be at all effective, there must be continued monitoring or surveillance of behavior, which is a very wasteful use of high-priced managerial time.
2. Punishment never really extinguishes or eliminates undesirable response tendencies, but only temporarily suppresses them. These tendencies reappear with full force when the threat of punishment is removed.
3. Punishment has undesirable side effects. It may cause resentment and hostility toward the punisher, creating a "get-even" mentality through sabotage, restricting work output, or doing things that make the punisher

look bad. The fear associated with the punishing agent may lead the punished person to avoid the manager's very presence; this, in turn, makes it more difficult for the manager to play the desired role of coach, teacher, or counselor. The reaction to punishment might be more extreme, causing rigidity and inhibition in the offender because of the anxiety aroused. This can make it more difficult for the person to learn new behavior, including very desirable behavior, or to adapt to change.

If punishment is so ineffective in changing behavior and has such undesirable side effects, why do people use it so much? Why haven't they learned over the centuries to use other methods in place of punishment? Skinner (1953) believes that punishment is still used mainly for one reason: its use is reinforcing to the punisher. Since applying an aversive consequence immediately, although temporarily, suppresses the undesired behavior that offends the punisher, the punishing behavior is reinforced by the cessation of the undesired behavior. Since the immediate consequences of one's behavior are the most influential in shaping it, the punisher continues to punish when confronted by undesired subordinate behavior.

One could also argue that if the controlling agent feels angry and frustrated by subordinate performance, the act of punishment may be reinforcing by providing the agent with an opportunity to "blow off steam" and ventilate feelings. Punishment may also give some people a feeling of power, which is reinforcing. Finally, punishment is often the "easiest" thing to do, since it does not require a great deal of thought.

If punishment is to be avoided, what do the critics suggest that we use in its place? They offer several possibilities:

1.   Try extinction. Find out what reinforcers (sometimes subtle ones) are sustaining the undesired behavior. What does the subordinate gain from such behavior? Praise and recognition from peers? Then convince those peers to cooperate with you (sometimes easier said than done) by ignoring the unruly behavior. When such behavior is not reinforced, it will eventually lose strength and extinguish itself.

2.   Use environmental engineering—rearrange the features of the environment so that the antecedents do not evoke the undesired response. Skinner (1953) tells of a manager who had a traffic problem caused by employees hurrying down the corridor as soon as the end of the workday was signaled. The manager solved the problem by placing wall mirrors along the corridor. The stimulus situation that had evoked stampeding down the hallway was transformed into one that encouraged a more leisurely and orderly walk-and-stop sequence.

One of the authors used a cafeteria's rest room while waiting for lunch. On the inside of the stall door was a small blackboard, with a piece of chalk attached to a string. Apparently, the owner was trying to use environmental engineering to encourage behavior less costly and troublesome than the usual obscene graffiti semipermanently etched on the walls and doors.

3.   Along lines similar to the strategy offered above, reward either desirable or neutral behavior that is physically incompatible with the undesired behavior. If people are reinforced by what occurs at their work stations, they will have less cause to loiter in the employee lounge.

4.   Simply allow adjustment, development, or maturation to take its course. With biological maturation, young children eventually learn not to throw fragile objects, cry, or wet the bed. Punishing such behavior may not speed up this process, and may cause emotional problems if applied to behavior over which the child has insufficient biological control or experience. Similarly, new or inexperienced employees make many mistakes that, given a reasonable period of adjustment, they will learn to avoid. Punishment may not hasten this process, and if it causes undue anxiety, it can actually retard the process.

REBUTTAL TO THE CASE AGAINST PUNISHMENT

It has probably occurred to the reader that, however desirable the use of nonaversive control may be, there are nevertheless some weaknesses in the case against punishment.

1.   As Bandura (1969) points out, much of our healthy behavior is acquired due to naturally punishing contingencies. We learn how to ride a bike, not to run on slick floors, not to drive fast on icy roads, not to wear heavy clothing in the summer, not to run immediately after a heavy meal, all because nature punishes us. Furthermore, we usually learn these things rather quickly and without any emotional scars. Apparently, then, nature uses punishment very effectively. Natural punishments may hold some clues for the effective use of punishment and discipline in organizations.

2.   Some of the recommended alternatives to punishment are not always feasible, economical, or equitable. For example, if the undesired behavior is intrinsically reinforcing, it will be difficult, if not impossible, to use the extinction procedure. There is no way you can allow the response to occur without its being reinforced. If a security guard goes to sleep on the night shift or a bus driver uses hard drugs, it is hard to imagine how these behaviors can be allowed to occur in the absence of reinforcement, for in a sense such activities are their own reinforcement. Rearrangement of the physical environment may be out of the question due to technological constraints or economic considerations. Singling out frequent offenders and rewarding them for doing other things may appear inequitable to the majority of subordinates who have been conscientious all along. And the maturation or adjustment period may simply take too long for the manager who is pressed for immediate results.

CLOSE-UP

Bagging It

Aversive control is not only frequently relied on, but it also typically is administered ineffectively. A common practice employed by many managers when they punish group members is called "bagging it." Supervisors who "bag it" avoid dealing with dysfunctional group member behavior directly when they observe it by depositing the incident into an imaginary bag that they carry on their back. As the incidents of undesirable behavior accumulate, the manager's "bag" becomes more and more difficult for him or her to carry. Then one day, usually without much warning or provocation, the manager "unloads the bag" on a group member. As one might expect, the result of this emotional display by the supervisor is seldom very functional.

SOURCE: W. E. Scott, Jr., and P. M. Podsakoff, *Behavioral Principles in the Practice of Management* (New York: John Wiley & Sons, 1985), pp. 171-72.

FACTORS DETERMINING WHETHER PUNISHMENT IS EFFECTIVE

Solomon (1964) contends that the critics of punishment have sometimes been too dogmatic in their denunciation of its use. While punishment may be ineffective in changing behavior and it could produce unwanted by-products, there is nevertheless considerable evidence that punishment can be an effective tool under certain conditions. What are the conditions that make for efficacious punishment?

1.   Punishment is more effective *if it is applied before an undesired response has been allowed to gain strength.* The longer an undesired response is allowed to occur unpunished, the stronger it becomes, and thus the more resistant it becomes to any method of behavioral control. The irony is that many well-intentioned managers will look the other way, or forestall any kind of confrontation, when they witness a rule violation. Their hope is that things will take care of themselves and that the subordinate will stop doing it. When the subordinate persists in repeating the offense, the manager finally runs out of patience and moves in to correct the situation with discipline. Unfortunately, the offense may now be a strongly ingrained response and highly resistant to external control. The manager should have acted earlier.

2.   Other things being equal, punishment is generally *more effective when it is relatively intense and quick*—that is, administered as soon after the undesired response as possible. When punishment is applied in a program of gradually increasing intensity, people can adapt to the punishment. Ironically, many official disciplinary programs—well intentioned and apparently based on humanitarian considerations—begin with very

mild and sometimes delayed punishment, with gradually more severe punishment (culminating in dismissal) after repeated occurrences. This may be much less effective (and ultimately less humanitarian) than moderately severe punishment of early offenses.

To maximize the association between the behavior and its consequences, punishment should quickly follow the undesired response. The speedier the punishment, the greater information value it has to the recipient and the more it seems like a natural and automatic result of the behavior.

3.   Punishment should *focus on a specific act, not on the person* or on the general patterns of behavior. Punishment should be dispensed in an impersonal manner, not as a means of revenge or as a way to vent frustrations. The more impersonal the administration of discipline, the less likely the person being punished will experience the kind of humiliation or rage that strains the relationship between manager and subordinate.

Unfortunately, the tactic frequently used by supervisors — ignoring early offenses, trying to be patient in the hope of preventing an argument — almost guarantees that when the offense occurs repeatedly, the manager will finally run out of patience and apply discipline in an emotional, personal manner. The manager is likely to resent having his or her patience tried, and discipline has all the overtones of arbitrariness and pettiness. No wonder that the person punished feels a need to "even the score" or to reassert strength and status. On the other hand, the manager who takes some disciplinary action — however mild — when a violation first occurs is more in control of his or her own emotions and is able to punish in an impersonal manner.

4.   Punishment should be *consistent across persons and across time*. The more consistently discipline is administered, the less it will appear to be arbitrary or personal. Unfortunately, as Rosen and Jerdee (1974) have found, organization officials tend to be inconsistent. They let minor infractions pass unnoticed when other things are running smoothly, when there is a big push to speed up production, or when the supervisor is not experiencing much pressure from above. Also, managers understandably (though often regrettably) apply different patterns of enforcement to those with longer (as opposed to shorter) job tenure, or to employees with hard-to-replace (as opposed to easy-to-replace) skills. The net effect of such selective discipline is that when people are punished, they believe "it's not what I did, it's who I am." Consequently, it is not surprising that punishment creates unwanted emotional side effects.

5.   Punishment should *have information value*. This is accomplished when discipline: is administered following early instances of undesired behavior; follows quickly after such behavior; is intense; and is consistent. In addition, disciplinary measures should be accompanied by an explanation of why the

---

CLOSE-UP

Just Cause

Beach (1985) has noted the paradox that, although collective bargaining has exerted a powerful and pervasive influence on the administration of industrial discipline, labor-management agreements seldom discuss the topic in any detail. Most labor contracts "merely state that management has the right to discipline, suspend, or discharge for just cause and that employees have the right to submit grievances if they consider an action unfair." Among the questions that determine just cause are the following:

Did the employee have prior knowledge that a particular conduct could be subject to disciplinary action?

Was the rule that the individual violated reasonably related to the efficient and safe conduct of the business?

Was management's action consistent, one employee compared with another?

Did management determine accurately whether, in fact, the employee had violated the rule?

Was the penalty assessed reasonably related to the seriousness of the offense?

SOURCE: D. S. Beach, *Personnel: The Management of People at Work,* 5th ed. (New York: Macmillan, 1985), p. 375.

---

behavior is not desired, how it can be corrected, and the expected consequences of continued violations (this does not imply that discipline should be carried out either apologetically or threateningly). Again, it is important that supervisors or managers act before losing patience; they are better able to make discipline an educational experience if they have control over their own emotions.

Another ingredient of the information value desired in discipline is guiding the offender into acceptable modes of behavior that will be rewarded. One of the criticisms cited earlier is that punishment only suppresses rather than extinguishes unwanted behavior. In answer to this criticism, *punishment can be used to temporarily suppress an unacceptable response. This creates an opportunity to guide the person into different behavior that will be strengthened by rewards* (Solomon, 1964).

6. Punishment is most effective when it occurs in the *context of a warm or nurtured relationship.* Among other things, this means that the manager should be a source of rewards (for example, good feedback, friendly interaction) as well as punishment. This offsets the tendency for punishment to cause avoidance of the punishing agent.

To support the statement above, Arvey and Jones (1985) report on two organizational programs that used "mixed-consequence" systems—positive reinforcement for work attendance and punishment for excessive absenteeism. Both programs showed substantial reductions in absenteeism.

THE HOT STOVE RULE

Much of what we have said about the factors maximizing the effectiveness of punishment is summarized in Douglas McGregor's "Hot Stove Rule" of discipline (see Strauss & Sayles, 1967). McGregor observed that nature punishes our behavior very effectively. We learn quickly from nature, and we learn without serious emotional problems. If we get too close to the hot stove and accidentally touch it, the reaction is immediate. What is it about the hot stove that makes it such a good teacher? It is swift; the association between our behavior and its consequences is undeniable. It is relatively intense on the very first instance of our improper response. It is impersonal; the hot stove has nothing against us personally and doesn't lose its temper. Our behavior, our specific response, is singled out. The hot stove is unerringly consistent; regardless of who touches it or when, the result is the same. Finally, an alternative response is available: move away from the stove.

The point, then, is to strive to emulate nature in carrying out disciplinary measures.

THE IMPORTANCE OF EXPLAINING THE RULES

A study by Walters and Cheyne (1966) demonstrates that cognitive structuring—providing a clear, cogent rationale for the punishment contingencies—determines to a great extent the effectiveness of punishment procedures. In their study, 84 first-grade boys were given some toys to play with. Some of the boys were told beforehand that there were some toys they should not handle; others were given reasons why they should not play with them. In addition, the boys were punished either "early" (as soon as they began to reach for the prohibited toys) or "late" (three seconds after they had picked a prohibited toy off the table). The intensity of the punishment was also varied: the punishment was either a 54-decibel noise or a 96-decibel noise. When no cognitive structuring had been provided—when no reasons were given why the boys should refrain from playing with certain toys—late punishment or low-intensity punishment had little effect on the subjects' behavior, compared to early/high-intensity punishment. However, when cognitive structuring had been provided, even late/low-intensity punishment was highly effective.

The implications of the Walters-Cheyne study for punishment in organizational settings should be obvious. High-intensity punishment is often ruled out for practical reasons arising from labor contracts, legal constraints, and other factors (see Close-Up). In addition, there are numerous reasons why punishment cannot be administered as quickly as theory would suggest. It becomes all the more important, then, for administrators to provide, in advance, clear and persuasive reasons why certain rules exist or why certain behaviors cannot be tolerated. The study by Walters and Cheyne suggests that if this step is taken, mild, delayed aversive stimuli can effectively reduce the frequency of undesired responses.

VICARIOUS PUNISHMENT

Albert Bandura has concluded from many years of research into behavior modification that "virtually all learning phenomena resulting from direct experience can occur on a vicarious basis through the observation of another's behavior and its consequences for them" (Bandura, 1969, p. 118). We learn from observing competent models what kinds of behavior meet with success or other forms of reward. Similarly, we learn about the contingencies of aversive control by observing others. We are less likely to imitate those behaviors for which we see others punished.

A study by Di Giuseppe (1975) of boys five to eight years old showed that vicarious punishment is governed by much the same principles as directly experienced punishment. Boys who were reprimanded for touching a toy (supposedly belonging to another child) were less likely to handle that toy when the experimenter left the room (as recorded by an observer behind a one-way glass); those reprimanded "early" (as soon as they reached for the toy) were less likely to return to it (when the experimenter left) than those who were reprimanded "late" (after actually handling the toy). Other subjects saw a film in which a boy like themselves was either not reprimanded, reprimanded late, or reprimanded early. When each of these subjects was left in the room with the toy, the effects of vicarious punishment were almost identical to the effects of direct punishment. Those who had seen the boy punished in the film were less likely to handle the toys later; and those who had witnessed immediate punishment were less likely to transgress than those who had seen delayed punishment administered.

Schnake (1986) conducted a study in which students were recruited through a university placement office for short-term jobs doing clerical work and assigned to one of five groups. In four of the groups, a confederate of the experimenter deliberately worked at a slower pace than the others (the subjects). In two of the groups that included the confederate, the "supervisor" (actually, the researcher) threatened to cut the confederate's pay; in two other groups, the researcher actually carried out this threat. The student workers could clearly see and hear the supervisory treatment of the confederate. The results showed that groups witnessing the actual punishment produced at a significantly higher rate than either the control group (which contained no confederate and no episodes relating to punishment) or the groups that heard the threat of punishment. The effect of the vicarious punishment on productivity held up through the following week, after which the experiment concluded. Moreover, neither the punishment nor its threat showed any adverse affect on reported satisfaction with this short-term job.

WHEN, WHY, AND HOW MANAGERS DISCIPLINE

Not too surprisingly, managers most often resort to disciplinary actions in the context of a general syndrome of low subordinate performance, especially when that includes excessive absenteeism (Szilagyi, 1980; Podsakoff, 1982). However, managers do appear to take into account other factors besides poor performance. The decision to punish depends on the perceived actual or potential consequences of the low performance and previous performance record (Arvey, Davis, & McGowen, 1982). This pattern is consistent with what we would predict from an attributional analysis (Chapter 6). It seems that supervisors intuitively work through the process of assigning internal versus external causes of poor performance. Recall that we tend to assign greater internal cause or blame (i.e., lack of effort or gross negligence) to behavior that has serious consequences, while we presume external causes — such as the situation or context — if the behavior is inconsistent with previous observations (i.e., prior performance record is satisfactory).

The larger the subordinate group, the more likely a manager will use formal as opposed to informal modes of discipline (Podsakoff, 1982; Beyer & Trice, 1984). A large subordinate group can render the supervisor more interpersonally distant from most of the individual subordinates, making it less unpleasant for the supervisor to use formal sanctions. At the same time, a large group makes it more difficult for the boss to use informal methods of influence based on a personal relationship. In support of this inference are the results reported by Beyer and Trice (1984), who found that supervisors who worked closely with small groups of subordinates outside company premises were less likely to discipline. Apparently in such situations the supervisor finds disciplinary measures more unpleasant, and the closer relationship with each individual provides more informal means of influence.

Research strongly suggests that managerial use of disciplinary measures depends on the support and guidance of specific company policy. A study by Beyer and Trice (1984) took place in an organization that had an extensive and detailed policy specifying how and when to administer discipline to employees suspected of having drinking problems. A somewhat less detailed policy dealt with absenteeism, and there was only a vague policy statement concerning the treatment of sexual harassment. Managers carried out more disciplinary actions for problem drinking than for the other offenses, probably because they knew precisely how to proceed, were more confident of support by their superiors, and could more easily legitimize their actions to other subordinates and themselves.

Somewhat disturbing is the finding that "even among experienced human resource management professionals, differences exist in terms of the criteria used in making disciplinary decisions" (Klaas & Wheeler, 1990). Personnel managers seem to adhere more to something like a "rule of law" and withold sanctions unless they can support them by previous consistency in the application of company policy. By contrast, line managers react most sensitively to employee offenses that are accompanied by a manner of insubordination, such as explicit defiance of the manager's authority.

Kipnis, Schmidt, and Wilkinson (1980) report that managers most frequently resort to sanctions when other means of influence prove unsuccessful. Apparently administrators themselves recognize the complexity and unpredictability of the disciplinary process and therefore exhaust other methods before attempting the use of punishment.

CASE STUDY

In an article published in the *Harvard Business Review* (1964), John Huberman recounts the experiences a large plywood mill had with disciplinary measures. Originally small, the company experienced a gradual increase in the size of its operations and its work force. As increased size led to greater distance between top management and first-line foremen, many policy issues became uncertain. One of these was the issue of how to deal with work performance and disciplinary matters.

1. As a result of the uncertainty, foremen had a tendency to delay action. They would let minor infringements of the rules go by. Presumably, their underlying motive was to avoid unnecessary confrontations in the hope that their benign inaction would be appreciated and reciprocated with good behavior. Of course, the opposite effect occurred. "A few individuals . . . would then start to test just how far they could go."
2. "After several annoying incidents, a foreman would get sufficiently angry to decide on immediate discharge." When failure to discipline early offenses led to repeated offenses, the foreman lost patience and felt personally wronged; when he finally took disciplinary action, he did so without having control over his own emotions. Predictably, the reaction of the individual being disciplined was anger and resentment.
3. "Vigilant supervision was required to make sure that the . . . individual [who had been disciplined] would not act out his annoyance over the punishment by lowering production or quality. . . . On return from suspension, the man obviously had to save face . . . to inform everyone how pleasantly and usefully he spent the 'time off.'" The disciplined person sought vengeance at being treated in a way he perceived as arbitrary, personal, and capricious. Discipline was noncontingently followed by reinforcement: first, from the union, in the form of full benefits and, in effect, a paid vacation; and later from being able to tell peers how he had given the company its comeuppance.

Eventually the company turned to a program that Huberman calls "discipline without punishment." Actually, the program was more like "punishment without discipline." Essentially it was a series of steps involving, on a first offense, a casual reminder and a note of correction (except for such severe violations as theft and fighting); on a second offense, a discussion with the individual in the foreman's office; on a third offense, a repetition of step two, but with the shift foreman also present and posing questions about alternative placement through vocational counseling provided by the personnel office. If unsatisfactory work behavior persisted, the offender was sent home for the day, with full pay—the latter being an expression of the company's sincere wish to see him become a productive member of the organization. If this measure proved unavailing, any future incident within a reasonably short time period would result in dismissal, not as a punitive act but as a realistic recognition that the individual and the organization did not have a viable relationship with each other.

The results in the first few years following the introduction of this program were considered highly satisfactory by plant management. Only three workers had experienced the fourth stage of being sent home with pay, and no workers had to be terminated (though two of the three left voluntarily a few weeks after returning to work from the suspension).

Several features of the new program should be noted. The program made very clear what steps foremen had to take at each stage of worker violations. Because they had a definite, companywide policy to follow, there was no reason for foremen to let early incidents go by without taking some action. The steps could be taken without emotional involvement by the disciplining parties. The desire for revenge and one-upmanship was deflated by giving suspended workers their day's pay in advance. The possibilities for subsequent noncontingent rewards from the union and peers were largely eliminated.

And yet the steps prescribed for countering employee infractions were, in fact, aversive. Being reminded of an offense, conducted to the boss's office (some unions will not allow this unless the union steward is also present), counseled to consider other employment possibilities, sent home (even at cost to the company) are hardly cause for rejoicing. When your rationale for hostility and recrimination is cut out from under you, you can focus your negative feelings only on yourself.

STYLES OF DISCIPLINE

Shull and Cummings (1966) found evidence of considerable variation among managers' philosophy and style of discipline. The authors presented a number of executives with a written case in which four workers all committed the same infraction—arriving late for work for the third time—but had different lengths of service, previous work performance records, and reasons for being late. The executives responded to the question of whom they would dock (the plant rule was a $5 fine for three late shows within a six-month period) and why. Some of the respondents—dubbed "pure humanitarian" by the authors—would fine none of the men. Others—the "pure legalistic"—would follow the rule to the letter, fining all four workers, regardless of the

FOCUS ON MANAGEMENT

How to Fire Someone

According to *Fortune* columnist Walter Kiechel, "Firing people has become such a common, if still unpleasant, exercise in the executive manual of arms that a substantial body of wisdom has accumulated on the subject." Recommendations from consultants and those who have learned from experience include:

1. Prepare for the possibility of discharge early, from the day of hiring. "The key to relatively guilt-free firing is having behind you a performance appraisal system that let the individual know where he stood every step of the way." Keep records of every observed instance of unsatisfactory performance or violations and of every step taken to deal with the problem.

2. Check with your legal department to see if discharge would, in that particular context, be considered discriminatory or a breach of contract.

3. Have someone else from management or the human resources department present as a witness.

4. Choose a neutral location, for example, a conference room. Giving the bad news in the subordinate's office or workstation would seem like a gross invasion of privacy; if you choose your own office, you won't be able to exit gracefully should the proceedings become unpleasant. Since the termination is official business, neither a bar nor a restaurant is appropriate. Also, making the announcement on a superficially social occasion might imply that your decision is tentative or inconclusive.

5. The session should take no longer than 15 minutes. Give the person a chance to respond, and avoid becoming hostile or defensive if the person reacts in anger. Indicate your availability to discuss the matter after the person has had a chance to absorb the impact, but leave no doubt that your decision is final and irrevocable.

6. Provide him or her with a written statement of any severance benefits and any help you or your organization is prepared to give in the form of outplacement.

SOURCE: W. Kiechel III (1986). "Office Hours," *Fortune*, March 31, 1986, 166-67.

extenuating circumstances. These two groups accounted for most of the responses. A few executives, however, believed in a more clinical or judicial approach to discipline. They seemed to recognize the need for maintaining standards but could not accept a mechanical enforcement of rules, which they regarded primarily as general principles that were not necessarily applicable to every individual case. The violations were interpreted in the context of the worker's probable intentions and past service and the probability of repeated offenses considering what was known about the worker's character.

A survey of 526 hourly employees of a chemical refinery (Arvey et al., 1982) found that 96 percent of the respondents believed the system of discipline should "be run by the book," with no exceptions and everyone treated alike. Yet, in apparent contradiction, 44 percent believed the system should consider the circumstances surrounding any particular incident before determining the precise form of sanction. We don't want favoritism (especially as granted to others), but we do want extenuating circumstances noted (as applied to ourselves).

Because there are such diverse managerial codes of justice, disciplinary judgments are frequently matters of controversy. Depending on one's orientation, one can cite disciplinary precedents based on parity (all violations treated alike, whether all enforced or all glossed over) or equity (a person's outcomes should correspond to his or her inputs in the form of service, effort, and value). Either standard can be eloquently defended or vigorously challenged, because our legal system and cultural norms seem to endorse both. Since neither standard will be universally accepted as fair by all parties, the administration of discipline is never likely to be a favorite managerial responsibility. Focus on the Future highlights an employee appeals process to challenge disciplinary actions that are perceived as unfair.

CONCLUDING COMMENT

We do not advocate the indiscriminate use of punishment to whip subordinates into shape. Feasible alternatives to its use — for example, the positive approach of rewarding acceptable behavior or of changing the conditions that evoke the undesired response — are certainly preferred. Punishment, despite the best efforts of well-intentioned managers to follow the principles outlined in this chapter, remains a risky and unpredictable enterprise because of the complex manner in which aversive stimuli affect behavior.

A basketball coach was asked why he chose to emphasize defense rather than offense. His answer was, "Offense is very complicated, whereas defense is basically simple; and I'm not too smart, so I emphasize the simple things." If a manager keenly feels the limitations of human intelligence in administrative matters, he or she is well advised to emphasize the "simpler" positive reinforcement strategies (although it often requires considerable thought and planning to discover ways to use the simple methods).

For obvious reasons, empirical research on the effects of punishment on human behavior has been somewhat limited. The professional ethics that govern the conduct of research on human subjects rule out the use of anything but mild, innocuous punishment in experiments. Thus, what we know about the effects of punishment — aside from our naturalistic observations — derives mainly from studies with lower organisms and studies that use mild electric shock, loss of bonus money accumulated during the experimental period, verbal rebuke, or similar aversive stimuli in experiments with children and college students.

Nevertheless, the fact remains that administrators do use punishment and sometimes have to, even if only as a last resort. For some time to come, discipline in organizations is likely to be one of the responsibilities of managers. If the administrator can closely imitate the hot stove, the exercise of discipline can have a constructive effect on the behavior of organization participants and need not result in hostility, rigidity, or the alienation of subordinates from organization goals.

SUMMARY

Punishment of a response occurs when the response is followed by aversive consequences. The processes by which punishment affect behavior are quite complex, and thus the overall effects of punishment on behavior are harder to predict than are the effects of reward. Critics of aversive conditioning techniques argue that punishment requires surveillance to be effective, that punishment suppresses rather than extinguishes undesired response tendencies, and that it often causes destructive side effects. These critics suggest that the prevalence of punishment is sustained primarily by its immediate but temporary reinforcement of the punisher. Alternatives to punishment include extinction, environmental engineering, reinforcing competing but acceptable responses, and allowing maturation to occur at its natural pace.

Punishment is more effective when applied to weak responses, when the aversive consequence is relatively intense and quickly follows the response, if focused on the act rather than the person, is consistent across time and persons, contains or is accompanied by information, and occurs in the presence of a warm relationship. These conditions are summarized in McGregor's Hot Stove Rule of discipline in organizations. These conditions also explain why naturally occurring punishment is effective without producing dysfunctional side effects.

CONCEPTS TO REMEMBER

Hot Stove Rule	Pure legalistic	Parity
Cognitive structuring	Clinical/judicial	Equity
Vicarious punishment	Disciplinary style	Just cause
Pure humanitarian	Corporate due process	

QUESTIONS FOR DISCUSSION

1. Some behaviors in organizations are rewarded by one set of reinforcing agents (such as peer groups) and punished by another set of agents (superiors). What determines whether the behaviors in question will be maintained, strengthened, or weakened?

2. Some individuals seem to respond positively (in the desired direction) to disciplinary measures, some negatively, others to "shrug it off." How can we account for these differences?

3. Review the section of this chapter reporting on studies of how managers actually discipline. In what respects do managers seem generally to follow the theoretically most effective methods of punishment? In what respects do managers generally seem to depart from such methods?

4. "In the long run, punishment, unlike reinforcement, works to the disadvantage of both the punished organism and the punishing agency" (Skinner, 1953, p. 183). Discuss.

5. Unions, legislation, and the bureaucratization of organizations have limited or proscribed the use of a number of punitive measures by managers. What techniques of punishment — what kinds of aversive stimuli — are generally available to managers? Which of these can be tailored to fit the Hot Stove Rule?

REFERENCES

Arvey, R. D., & Jones, A. P. (1985). The use of discipline in organizational settings: A framework for future research. In Cummings, L. L., & Staw, B. M. (eds.), *Research in organizational behavior,* vol. 7. Greenwich, CT: JAI Press, Inc., 367-408.

Arvey, R. D., Davis, G. A., & McGowen, S. (1982). Discipline in organizations: A field study. University of Houston Technical Report, NR 170-914, TR#2, September, 1982.

Bandura, A. (1969). *Principles of behavior modification.* New York: Holt, Rinehart & Winston.

Beach, D. S. (1985). *Personnel: The management of people at work,* 5th ed. New York: Macmillan.

Beyer, J. M., & Trice, H. M. (1984). A field study of the use and perceived effects of discipline in controlling work performance. *Academy of Management Journal* 27, 743-64.

DiGiuseppe, R. (1975). Vicarious punishment: An investigation of timing. *Psychological Reports* 36, 819-24.

Ewing, D. W. (1989). Corporate due process lowers legal costs. "Manager's Journal," *The Wall Street Journal,* October 23, 1989.

Huberman, J. (1964). Discipline without punishment. *Harvard Business Review* 42, 62-68.

Ignatius, A. (1989). Now if Ms. Wong insults a customer, she gets an award. *The Wall Street Journal,* January 24, 1989.

Kiechel, W. III. (1986). How to fire someone. "Office Hours," *Fortune,* March 31, 166-67.

Klaas, B. S., & Wheeler, H. N. (1990). Managerial decision making about employee discipline: A policy-capturing approach. *Personnel Psychology* 43, 117-34.

Kipnis, D., Schmidt, S. M., & Wilkinson, I. (1980). Intraorganizational influence tactics: Explorations in getting one's way. *Journal of Applied Psychology* 65, 440-52.

Podsakoff, P. M. (1982). Determinants of a supervisor's use of rewards and punishments: A literature review and suggestions for further research. *Organizational Behavior and Human Performance* 29, 58-83.

Rosen, B., & Jerdee, T. H. (1974). Factors influencing disciplinary judgments. *Journal of Applied Psychology* 59, 327-31.

Schnake, M. E. (1986). Vicarious punishment in a work setting. *Journal of Applied Psychology* 71, 343-45.

Scott, W. E., Jr., & Podsakoff, P. M. (1985). *Behavioral principles in the practice of management.* New York: John Wiley & Sons.

Shull, F. A., & Cummings, L. L. (1966). Enforcing the rules — how do managers differ? *Personnel* 43, 33-39.

Skinner, B. F. (1953). *Science and human behavior.* New York: Macmillan.

Solomon, R. L. (1964). Punishment. *American Psychologist* 19, 239-53.

Strauss, G., & Sayles, L. (1967). *Personnel: The human problems of management.* Englewood Cliffs, NJ: Prentice Hall.

Szilagyi, A. D. (1980). Causal inferences between leader reward behavior and subordinate performance, absenteeism, and work satisfaction. *Journal of Occupational Psychology* 58, 195-204.

Walters, R. H., & Cheyne, J. A. (1966). Some parameters influencing the effects of punishment on social behavior. Paper presented at the Annual Meeting of the American Psychological Association, New York.

13 Job Satisfaction

Why is job satisfaction important?
How is job satisfaction measured?
What is the extent of job satisfaction in the labor force?
What groups in the labor force express the most job satisfaction?
What are the causes and effects of job satisfaction?
What are the causes and effects of job dissatisfaction?

As we noted in Chapter 1, one criterion by which we evaluate an organization is performance. For a manufacturing firm, this might be share of the market or return on investment; for a hospital, the quality of health care provided; for local government, the efficiency with which services are provided to the community. Whatever the actual measure might be, we evaluate the management of an organization according to some criterion of effectiveness.

To an increasing extent, organizations also consider job satisfaction a criterion of organizational functioning. Why is job satisfaction important? One reason stems quite simply from certain value judgments. People spend a sizable proportion of their waking lives at work. From any minimally humanitarian point of view, we would want that time to be more or less pleasant, agreeable, and fulfilling. Few people actually have the choice of working or not working. Of those who have to work, most have only limited options as to where to work. Given such constraints, much of the population would find little cheer in their lives if the workplace offered no satisfaction.

A second reason for attaching considerable importance to job satisfaction is its relationship to mental health. Discontent often has a "spillover" effect on otherwise unrelated portions of our lives. Dissatisfaction with one's job seems to have an especially volatile spillover effect. People who feel bad about their work are apt to feel bad about many other things, including family life, leisure activities—even life itself. Psychiatrists tell us that most of their patients express negative feelings about their jobs. Admittedly, the direction of causation may sometimes run the opposite way. Unresolved personality problems or maladjustment may indeed be the cause of a person's inability to find satisfaction in work. Nevertheless, anyone who has had to live with a parent, spouse, or roommate who didn't like his or her job knows how tense relationships with that person can be. Both casual observation and scientific study provide compelling evidence that job satisfaction is an important component of overall psychological adjustment.

Evidence also points to a relationship between job satisfaction and physical health. According to one study (Palmore, 1969), people who like their work are likely to live longer. Again, complicating factors preclude a hasty conclusion that job satisfaction, per se, is the causal factor, since people with greater job satisfaction also tend to have greater incomes and more education, and thus may coincidentally enjoy greater advantages and knowledge that promote longevity. Nonetheless, chronic dissatisfaction with work is a stressor, and stress eventually takes its toll.

Level of job satisfaction does not invariably determine the general quality of life. The spillover phenomenon appears to characterize many of those with advanced educational attainments, as well as those who strongly identify with a profession. For some others, the "segmentalist hypothesis" (Kabanoff, 1980) more accurately describes their orientation: Some people sharply delineate their work roles from family, community, or personal affairs, and their enjoyment of leisure is little affected by their attitudes about work. Job satisfaction does not always generalize to satisfaction with life itself.

Later in the chapter we will examine the reasons why employing organizations find it in their own self-interest to concern themselves with the job satisfaction of participants.

WHAT IS JOB SATISFACTION?

The term *job satisfaction* did not come into currency until recently. In the management literature published before 1950, the more common word was *morale*. This usage probably derived, as did so much of the nomenclature of early management concepts, from the military tradition. In any case, the concept of morale was imprecise. Child (1941) noted different conceptions of morale. One had to do with "a condition of physical and emotional well-being in the individual that makes it possible for him to work and live hopefully and effectively" (p. 393). Other interpretations concerned commitment to the goals of the group or organization or the esprit de corps of the group as a whole.

During the 1950s, the term *morale* gradually fell into disuse in scholarly literature. *Job attitudes* replaced it, probably because the instruments used to measure morale came from the techniques of attitude scale construction as developed in psychology. Moreover, the prevailing view in the 1950s was that job attitudes are a function of the extent to which a person's needs are satisfied by work experience. Thus, the phrases "job satisfaction" and "job attitudes" have become roughly synonymous.

In essence then, job satisfaction represents the constellation of a person's attitudes toward or about the job. In general, job satisfaction is the attitude toward the job as a whole. It is a function of satisfaction with different aspects of the job (supervision, pay, the work itself) and of the particular weight or importance one attaches to those respective components.

Like any other attitude, job satisfaction is a mixture of beliefs, feelings, and behavior tendencies. Presumably, attitude scales purporting to measure job satisfaction measure these. Recently, as a result of sophisticated analyses of life satisfaction data (Campbell, 1976), there is evidence that job satisfaction scales reflect more of the belief or cognitive component of job attitudes than of the affective or emotional component (Organ & Near, 1985). When people respond to job attitude measures, they assess the job and its characteristics, but only to a lesser extent do they report their happiness or unhappiness actually felt on the job. One could assess a job positively and still not be happy on a typical workday. Assessments and feelings would be expected to have some correlation with each other, as we saw in the "consistency principle" of attitudes in Chapter 7. But the correlation is neither invariable nor absolute. Thus, the reader and the manager should exercise caution in interpreting the findings from typical job satisfaction measures. A high level of job satisfaction, as conventionally measured, does not necessarily correspond to the original notion of morale, if by the latter term we refer to the energizing effects of strong positive emotions. A growing body of opinion (e.g., Scarpello, 1988; Organ, 1988) regards job satisfaction measures as reflecting a general notion of "fairness" more than anything else. That is, much of the distribution of job satisfaction scores corresponds to an evaluation of the job and its various aspects against some intuitive idea of what they "ought" to be.

Nonetheless, researchers and practitioners alike have used job satisfaction measures to advantage. Researchers can investigate the effects of leadership style, organization structure, and task characteristics on job attitudes. Managers can spot trends in job attitudes that do not show in behavior until much later, and thus take necessary action to prevent widespread turnover or grievances. Managers can also assess the effects of reward systems, changes in policies, and new programs.

Both the researcher and the manager have at their disposal a number of well-developed, standardized instruments for studying job satisfaction (see Close-Up). Perhaps the most widely used is the *Job Descriptive Index* (Smith, Kendall, & Hulin, 1969), or JDI. This scale provides separate measures for satisfaction with the work itself, supervision, pay, promotions, and co-workers. It is quite simple in its format and administration and, over the years, its reliability has been well documented. Its widespread use has led to the development of a statistical base of "norms" against which the satisfaction of any particular group can be compared. Scott's (1967) *Semantic Differential* scale, though not nearly as widely used as the JDI, has the possible advantage of measuring more of the respondent's emotional state, as distinguished from the cognitive assessment of the job. Thus, Scott's measure probably is more faithful to the concept of morale as originally defined and as used intuitively by the layman.

THE EXTENT OF JOB SATISFACTION IN THE LABOR FORCE

What percentage of the nation's workers are satisfied with their jobs? Which groups are more or less satisfied than other groups? Are people's attitudes toward their jobs becoming more or less favorable? A number of nationwide surveys of the labor force have addressed these questions.

The longest-running series of job satisfaction surveys is conducted by George Gallup, probably the foremost name among professional pollsters. The Gallup organization uses the simple, direct method of asking people whether they are, on the whole, satisfied or dissatisfied with their present jobs. From 1949 to the 1970s, only a small proportion of workers—20 percent at most, and usually less—have responded with "dissatisfied." These figures come as quite a surprise to most people. Contrary to many opinions, the vast majority of the nation's workers seem to feel at least moderately pleased with their jobs. They may have specific gripes about work (a favorite and

CLOSE-UP

A Sampler of Job Satisfaction Measures

Researchers have developed a variety of formats for constructing job satisfaction scales. Shown here are illustrative items from several widely used instruments.

Job Descriptive Index (JDI)
(Smith, Kendall, & Hulin, 1969)

Think of the pay you get now. How well does each of the following words describe your pay? "Y" if it describes your pay, "N" if it does not describe your pay, "?" if you cannot decide.

_____   Adequate
_____   Less than I deserve
_____   Highly paid

Minnesota Satisfaction Questionnaire
(Weiss, Dawis, England, & Lofquist, 1967)

Are you very dissatisfied (VD), dissatisfied (D), neither dissatisfied nor satisfied (N), satisfied (S), or very satisfied (VS), with this aspect of your job?

	VD	D	N	S	VS
The working conditions	___	___	___	___	___
The chances for advancement	___	___	___	___	___
The chance to use my abilities	___	___	___	___	___
My pay and the amount of work I do	___	___	___	___	___
The feeling of accomplishment I get	___	___	___	___	___

traditional indoor sport of Americans), and they usually see plenty of room for improvement, but overall, they like their jobs. Gallup's findings are supplemented by other surveys of varying scope and representativeness (for a review of these, see Herzberg, Mausner, Peterson, & Capwell, 1955). With almost uncanny consistency these studies show 70 to 85 percent of workers as saying that they were satisfied with their jobs.

No doubt these figures overstate somewhat the "true" level of job satisfaction prevalent in the country. Some of the "satisfied" responses probably reflect a state of simply having come to accept the job one has, whatever its imperfections, if one had little prospects of improving on it. Also, as we noted in Chapter 7, some attitudes are passive, seldom even registering in consciousness until someone asks us about them. Some of the people who tell pollsters they are satisfied with their work might have few other occasions to reflect on their job attitudes. Finally, one could argue that, in the absence of any definite attitudes about work, possibly even for people with moderately unfavorable sentiments about their jobs, some individuals just do not want to come right out and say (even to themselves) that they are

---

CLOSE-UP *(concluded)*

Scott's Semantic Differential Scale
(Scott, 1967)

Check the position between each pair of adjectives that best describes how you feel at work.

Me at Work

Appreciated	___	___	___	___	___	___	___	Unappreciated
Satisfied	___	___	___	___	___	___	___	Unsatisfied
Interested	___	___	___	___	___	___	___	Bored
Informed	___	___	___	___	___	___	___	Uninformed
Valuable	___	___	___	___	___	___	___	Worthless
Penalized	___	___	___	___	___	___	___	Rewarded

Bullock's Scale
(Bullock, 1952)

Indicate whether the statements below describe something that is very good, good, fair, poor, or very poor about your job.

	VG	G	F	P	VP
This company as a place to work	___	___	___	___	___
Chances of steady work	___	___	___	___	___
Credit given by my supervisor for doing a good job	___	___	___	___	___

---

actually dissatisfied; in other words, it may be more socially desirable to respond "satisfied" than "dissatisfied."

Still, even noting such qualifications, the evidence from polls and surveys suggests that the majority of job holders evaluate their work experience in reasonably favorable terms.

Recent Trends: Better or Worse?

In the early 1970s, the extent of job satisfaction became a matter of some controversy. The most publicized position—portrayed in books, magazines and newspapers, and on television—purported to show a crisis in job morale, a crisis reflected not only in surveys of job attitudes, but also in such behavioral indicators as increased absenteeism, higher turnover, and declining economic growth and labor productivity. *Work in America* (1973), a special report to the secretary of the Department of Health, Education, and Welfare, commented at length on "job alienation," with particular reference to "blue-collar blues," "white-collar woes," the dissatisfaction of younger workers, and the prevalence of negative attitudes among women and minority workers. Sheppard and Herrick's *Where Have All the Robots Gone?* (1972), based largely on a study of approximately 1,500 workers, painted a similarly dismal picture of the typical worker's job attitudes. Judson Gooding's *The Job Revolution* (1972) conveyed the same message. These three books agreed that job satisfaction was spiraling downward and that the major cause was "sterile" work that offered too few people opportunity for psychological growth and fulfillment. The correct approach, they urged, lay in a concerted program of job redesign in industry and business to render work more meaningful, interesting, and enriching.

Not all observers agreed that job attitudes had come to such a sorry state. Gallup's survey results, while showing a dip in the period 1963–71, suggested that the extent of job satisfaction had remained stable over the years since 1949, and if anything had risen between 1949 and 1971, especially for blacks. In fact, even in the Michigan study cited by Sheppard and Herrick, no more than 25 percent of any single subgroup of workers expressed negative attitudes toward work. The overall figure for the entire sample was about 14 percent — remarkably close to the 13 percent Herzberg et al. (1955) found as a median figure in their review of earlier studies.

What about behavioral indicators of job attitudes, such as turnover and absenteeism? The quit rate among employees surveyed by government agencies did increase steadily through the 1960s. One must, however, take into account the unemployment level throughout this period to place the trend in proper perspective. People are more apt to quit their jobs — even jobs they would otherwise be satisfied with — when they have good prospects of finding better jobs. The job market became increasingly favorable for workers as the nation's economy enjoyed the longest period of sustained growth since World War II. The expansionist fiscal policies of the Kennedy-Johnson administrations, compounded by the increasing U.S. involvement in Vietnam, led to a shortage of workers. As the economy entered a severe recession in 1974–75, quits became less frequent.

It should be pointed out that, after correcting for unemployment level, there remains a slight trend toward a higher quit rate. For a given level of unemployment, turnover seems to have been slightly greater since 1963 than it was before that time. This observation reflects another trend during the 1960s and 1970s, namely the growing proportion of younger workers in the labor force. People switch jobs more frequently during the early years of their careers.

Nonetheless, while the evidence does not argue for a crisis of widespread job alienation, it does appear that job satisfaction in the labor force crested sometime in the early to mid-1960s, declined somewhat in the late 1960s and early 1970s, probably increased marginally in the late 1970s, and declined slightly again during the 1980s. Some survey data (see Focus on Management) suggest that disaffection among managers has consistently declined since the early 1970s. As of this writing, job satisfaction in the nation's labor force almost certainly does not match that of the early 1960s (see Figure 13–1).

FOCUS ON MANAGEMENT

The Trend in Managerial Job Satisfaction

The Opinion Research Corporation, averaging data from its annual surveys, reports spreading disaffection among the managerial ranks during the period 1970–1984, as shown below. While job attitudes remain more favorable among managers than within hourly or clerical groups, the downward trend in managerial commitment and loyalty to the company is unmistakable.

Percent who rate their companies favorably

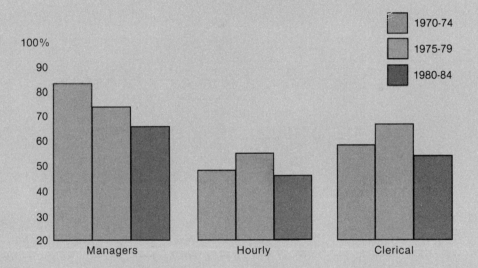

While no studies yet can pinpoint the precise reasons for growing managerial disaffection, the opinion among some consultants is that the wave of mergers and cutbacks—which resulted in a net loss of nearly 500,000 managerial and professional jobs between 1979 and 1985—during the period of these surveys has adversely affected management morale. Before 1970, layoffs affected primarily hourly employees. Recently, managers at almost all levels sense that they and their jobs are expendable.

Even the survivors of the takeovers and downsizing programs get the message; they have little input into the decisions that affect their jobs, and any loyalty they exhibit might not be reciprocated. One sign of this diminished loyalty and commitment is that increasing numbers of executives now refuse to relocate when asked to accept a transfer.

SOURCE: T. F. O'Boyle, "Loyalty Ebbs at Many Companies as Employees Grow Disillusioned," *The Wall Street Journal,* July 11, 1985.

FIGURE 13–1

Job Satisfaction in the Nation's Labor Force: Trends over Time

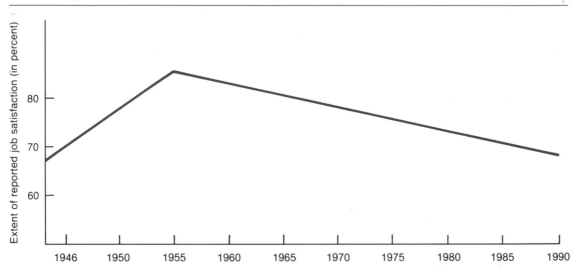

How can we explain the slight downward trend since 1960? Probably the strongest contributing factor derives from changes in the age structure of the labor force. Until 1960, the post-World War II labor force steadily became older. In 1960, the proportion of workers aged 20–34 numbered just over 30 percent; by the mid 1970s, that figure reached 40 percent as members of the postwar baby boom had begun to mature and enter the labor force. And, survey after survey shows that younger workers, particularly those under 30, tend to report less job satisfaction than older employees. It is a demographic fact of life. By the mid-1980s, however, the work force had begun to show a reversal of this trend. That factor alone would predict greater job satisfaction in the years ahead, other things equal.

Which Groups Are Most Satisfied?

While both historical and current analyses testify to a reasonably high level of job satisfaction in the labor force as a whole, clear-cut patterns of variation do exist. Among the differences between groups are those pertaining to age, length of tenure, occupational level, race, and sex.

Herzberg's review in 1955 showed a consistent trend in job attitudes according to age and length of service (see Figure 13–2). When people begin work (typically in their late teens or their early 20s), they appear to do so with considerable enthusiasm. This enthusiasm soon wanes, giving way to steady decline in job morale, which reaches its lowest depths in the late 20s or early 30s. Attitudes then become increasingly positive, at least well into the 50s. The trend after that is less certain. Some studies suggest that the level of job satisfaction continues to climb or at least hold steady; others point to another

FIGURE 13–2
Age and Job Satisfaction

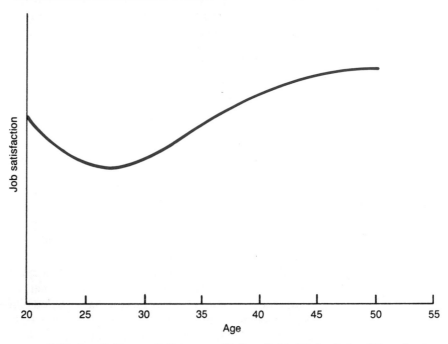

SOURCE: F. Herzberg, B. Mausner, R. Peterson, and D. Capwell, *Job Attitudes: Review of Research and Opinion* (Pittsburgh: Psychological Service of Pittsburgh, 1955).

decline — possibly due to concern about health, approaching retirement, or the end of the road as far as career advancement is concerned. In any case, the point seems well established that workers under age 30 are less satisfied than those over 30. Sheppard and Herrick's (1972) data showed that among workers aged 20–29, 24 percent expressed negative attitudes toward work as opposed to 13 percent in the 30–44 age bracket and 11 percent in the 45–54 range.

Why is this the case? Herzberg and his associates suggested a number of plausible reasons. When you evaluate anything — be it a job, a meal, a car, or a movie — you do so by comparing the object to others you have experienced. When you take your first full-time job, you have no prior job with which to compare it. How do you evaluate it? Probably by comparing it with the next closest thing — school. School life is characterized by variety, a wide circle of acquaintances, frequent opportunities for achievement, changes in activities, and a number of significant events (getting a driver's license, a first date, making a varsity athletic team, graduation, and so on). Most jobs suffer by comparison with the colorful world of academic life (more colorful in retrospect, of course). Few jobs offer that kind of variety and change of pace.

Second, and perhaps related to the foregoing consideration, is the nature of the *expectations* people bring to their first job. Not infrequently, those entering the world of work anticipate that life will become better in every respect—more freedom, continually improving financial position, involvement in interesting actitivities, opportunity to travel, and respect for the status of an adult, full-time worker. In cases when these expectations defy reality, those individuals will spend much of the next decade experiencing some disillusionment. After some point, expectations are modified and adjusted downward, and the job is seen in a more positive perspective.

We hasten to remind the reader that even among this least satisfied age group, a majority are satisfied. The failure of realizing early expectations often means simply a diminished enthusiasm rather than outright dissatisfaction.

Professional and managerial workers report the highest level of job satisfaction. Unskilled manual workers in the heavy industries, such as the automotive and steel industries, report the greatest dissatisfaction. In between those two extremes are clerical and sales workers and skilled blue-collar workers.

Blacks and other minorities are less likely to be satisfied with their work than are whites, probably because the former are overrepresented in marginal occupational categories and in unskilled blue-collar jobs. However, whereas Gallup found that in 1949 nearly half of black workers surveyed expressed job dissatisfaction, in 1971 only about a fourth of the black workers surveyed voiced negative work attitudes. The long-term trend has without question been one of increased job satisfaction in this group.

Sex differences in job satisfaction show less consistency. Published studies up until the mid-1950s showed no clear-cut differences between males and females. Sheppard and Herrick's findings in 1972 showed females to be less satisfied than males, the difference reaching its maximum extent among workers under 30. It would appear that women, especially young women, are less likely to be satisfied with just any form of employment. They are more sensitive than women workers of preceding generations about working under conditions inferior to those of males with the same qualifications as their own. Despite some years of affirmative action programs, equality of treatment between the sexes with respect to job opportunities has not been fully achieved.

CAUSES OF JOB SATISFACTION

One analytic approach to the sources of job satisfaction is to look at the groups that seem most satisfied—professionals and managers—and to see what they have that other workers don't have, or don't have in as great measure.

First, the most satisfied groups typically earn higher salaries than do other occupational groups. This is not to say that money is the only source, or even the most important source, of job satisfaction. Many people would probably agree that insufficient pay or the perception of inequitable pay is a more decisive determinant of dissatisfaction than sufficient or fair pay is of satisfaction. Nevertheless, as we noted in Chapter 11, money has rich, complex symbolic meaning to most of us. It represents far more to individuals than the material goods and services it can command. Income level is inextricably associated with social status, independence, lifestyle, and the worthwhileness of what one is doing. Certainly relative pay—one's pay as compared to significant comparison groups—seems to count for something in calculating job satisfaction.

Second, professionals and managers enjoy more autonomy in their work than do other groups. They set their own hours, their own pace, and most of the time they are free from close supervision. They unilaterally make a large number of decisions about how they do their work.

Third, and perhaps most important, professionals derive a greater measure of intrinsic rewards from work. Their work is varied and stimulating. It offers challenge, the chance to use valued skills and knowledge, and opportunity for continual self-development and growth. In brief, professional and managerial jobs generally score higher on the dimensions (noted in Chapter 11) defining intrinsically motivating tasks. Study after study shows that professionals and managers report greater satisfaction of their needs for achievement and self-actualization than do other occupational groups.

Another method of ascertaining the major causes of job satisfaction is to ask people to rank order various aspects of work in terms of their importance. Herzberg et al. (1955) averaged the findings of 16 such studies, involving a total of over 11,000 employees. The first-ranked factor was security; the second was "interest from intrinsic aspects of the job"; the third was opportunity for advancement; and the fourth was considerate and appreciative supervision. Wages ranked seventh.

Almost two decades later, Sheppard and Herrick found some changes in the ranking of job dimensions. "Interesting work" was ranked first; second, third, and fourth, respectively, were enough equipment, information, and authority "to get the job done." "Good pay" ranked fifth. Job security, so important in the 1940s and early 1950s, had dropped to seventh. Workers continued to place a high value on the inherent interest afforded by the job. They remained sensitive to styles of supervision, especially with regard to consideration displayed, but also with regard to structuring the work environment. (An extended discussion of the effects of leadership styles on job attitudes is deferred until Chapter 19.) Economic benefits were still accorded substantial importance. Job security apparently matters a lot when you don't have it (the experience of many workers in the 1930s), but not when you've got it (as did more of the labor force in the 1970s). More recently, job security has undoubtedly taken on increased importance among workers in industries—such as steel and auto—adversely affected by international competition.

FOCUS ON INTERNATIONAL OB

Rewards People Want from Work: Cultural Differences

A study of work goals of 19,000 employees of a large multinational electrical equipment manufacturer with operations in 46 countries found that, in all countries, the five most important goals concerned individual achievement, the immediate work environment, pay, and conditions of work. Some of the major differences among cultural groups:

English-speaking countries placed relatively greater emphasis on individual success and relatively less importance on security.

French-dominated cultures, compared to the English, attached greater significance to security and ranked challenging work lower in priority.

Scandinavian countries reported less concern about personal status and recognition and more concern that work not interfere with family and personal life.

Latin and southern European groups placed highest emphasis on job security and fringe benefits and, in comparison with other countries, considered individual career success less important.

The Japanese wanted challenging work, but rated upward mobility lower than English groups, and they considered good working conditions and a friendly work environment very important.

SOURCES: D. Sirota and M. J. Greenwood (1971). *Understanding Your Overseas Workforce. Harvard Business Review* 14 (January–February), pp. 53–60. Reported in N. Adler (1986), *International Dimensions of Organizational Behavior* (Boston: Kent Publishing, Inc.).

It is important not to overlook the role of the work group in determining job satisfaction. The Hawthorne researchers in the 1920s and 1930s (Roethlisberger & Dickson, 1964) found that people working on isolated jobs were more apt to express irritation, dissatisfaction, or feelings of depression on the job. A later study of automobile industry workers (Walker & Guest, 1952) found that isolated workers disliked their jobs. Seashore (1954) noted that cohesive industrial work groups were less likely to be adversely affected by pressure for production and expressed less anxiety about their jobs than noncohesive work groups. The opportunity for pleasurable interaction with co-workers appears to atone for considerable shortcomings in other features of jobs, such as uncomfortable working conditions or tedious work. Interviews with those rare specimens who win enough money in lotteries to retire, yet soon return even to unskilled jobs, find that a frequently cited reason for going back to work is simply to be back with friends at the job.

The weights of the above-mentioned job attributes in contributing to job satisfaction or dissatisfaction vary considerably from one individual to another. For example, autonomy and the intrinsic interest of the work itself matter more to younger workers and highly educated employees than to their opposites. Job security and pay take on increased importance for workers over age 40 (Herzberg et al., 1955). Variety in the job means more to extroverts than to introverts.

The Person   As Gurin, Veroff, and Feld (1960) have noted, the dominant tradition in research and theory has been to construe individual job satisfaction as largely the result of environmental variables. Thus, research has tried to ascertain the effects of pay, supervision, co-workers, formal policies, and task characteristics on satisfaction. By contrast, the effect of personality or "dispositional" variables on satisfaction has not received much emphasis until recently.

Yet there is reason to believe that a person's characteristics substantially determine work satisfaction. We have noted that younger workers more often report dissatisfaction than older workers. Presumably this arises from differences in expectations, patience, and adjustment. If so, and if employees within any given age group also vary in characteristic expectational level, then this dimension of individual differences obviously contributes to level of satisfaction. Of course, differences in expectations might themselves represent the effects of differential environments, past or present. But it is also conceivable — and, in terms of our everyday experience, quite intuitively plausible — that certain persons are simply prone to expect more than others from their work.

Expectations aside, some people tend to "make the best of the situation." Like the Apostle Paul, they "have learned in whatsoever state I am, therewith to be content" (Philippians 4:11). Their characteristic mood tilts toward cheerfulness, even when beset by problems and hassles. Similarly, there are those persons who have a low threshold for frustration and actually search for things to be upset about. Indeed, some of the early scholarship on job satisfaction (as summarized in Herzberg et al., 1955) interpreted job dissatisfaction as primarily a manifestation of neuroticism or maladjustment on the part of the person.

A recent study by Schneider and Dachler (1978) provides some relevant data. They administered a job satisfaction measure (the Job Descriptive Index) to 847 utility workers on two occasions, separated by a 16-month interval. Averaging across the five component measures of satisfaction, Schneider and Dachler found a correlation of .57 between a person's initially reported satisfaction and the satisfaction reported nearly a year and a half later. This represents a strikingly high coefficient of stability in reported job attitudes when one considers not only the inherent random error in such a measure, but also — and more significantly — the magnitude of changes that one would expect to occur during that time. Surely a considerable number of persons experienced negative events, such as promotions not received, low salary increases, protracted hassles with co-workers or clients, changes in supervision, and unwelcomed additions in job duties and work load. Just as surely, quite a few employees were "on a roll" during this time and prospered in many ways. Yet, knowing an individual's satisfaction level at the outset, one could have predicted quite well that person's satisfaction much later.

Staw and Ross (1985) found that, even among workers who changed places of employment, a person's initially reported satisfaction correlated significantly with their satisfaction as measured five years later.

Even more impressive is evidence from a study by Staw, Bell, and Clausen (1986). They attained access to data collected in the 1950s in a study that had included high school counselors' ratings of the typical mood states (e.g., cheerfulness, irritability, congeniality) of adolescents. Those ratings correlated in excess of .30 with job satisfaction of the same people reported *several decades later*. In fact, those ratings of generalized attitudes predicted people's job satisfaction up to 30 years later as well as, if not better than, any single factor in the person's current job.

Arvey, Bouchard, Segal, and Abraham (1989) took this analysis one step further in a study of 34 monozygotic (identical) twins separated at birth and reared apart. The researchers found that genetic factors could explain about 30 percent of the variation in job satisfaction, even when controlling for job characteristics. The influence of genetic factors registered most clearly in the measures of general satisfaction and satisfaction with intrinsic dimensions of work, with weaker effects on satisfaction with extrinsic rewards (such as pay and job security). The authors conclude that "the organization may have somewhat less 'control' over job satisfaction than is commonly believed, particularly with respect to intrinsic satisfaction" (Arvey et al., 1989, p. 191).

The point is not that job environment has little effect on satisfaction. Rather, individuals seem to differ in their predisposition to be satisfied or dissatisfied and also in their sensitivity to favorable or unfavorable characteristics of the work situation. Figure 13–3 depicts the relationship between job environment and satisfaction for three hypothetical individuals. Persons A and B both appear as moderately sensitive to the effects of job environment, given the slopes of the curves. The difference between them lies in the intercept: A is more likely to exhibit positive satisfaction for any given job situation. Person C, on the other hand, is little affected by differences in work environment; C's job satisfaction is almost constant over a wide range of variation in the favorability of work surroundings.

What are the implications of these differences for the administrator? Perhaps the most obvious is the confirmation of the old adage, "You can't please all the people all the time," or, at the very least, it may be prohibitively expensive to try to do so. More important, these differences could be made functional for the organization. Certain tasks, especially those requiring a climate of congeniality or cordial interaction with outsiders, could be well-suited to those individuals predisposed to be satisfied. On the other

FIGURE 13–3

Relationship between Work Environment and Job Satsifaction for Three Different Individuals

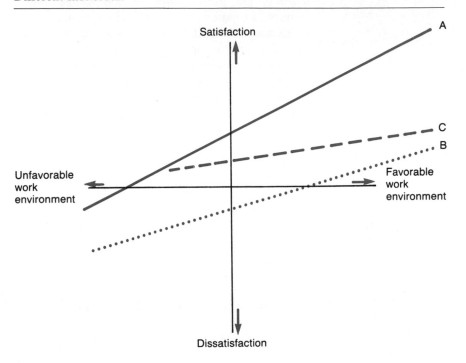

hand, chronically dissatisfied types may have their place, too: for example, to function as devil's advocates in task settings in which complacency is to be avoided.

JOB DISSATISFACTION

Should we conceptualize job dissatisfaction as simply the opposite of job satisfaction? If so, do the causes of job dissatisfaction represent merely the opposite (or absence) of those things that create satisfaction? If autonomy, stimulation, and intrinsic interest lead to job satisfaction, does their absence cause dissatisfaction?

Herzberg (1966) argued that, contrary to intuitive logic, job satisfaction and dissatisfaction are not mirror opposites, nor are they generally caused by opposite things. He based his conclusions on a study that asked people to write stories about occasions on which they felt especially good about their work and similar stories about when they felt bad about the job. Analysis of the stories showed that, when achievement or the work itself were mentioned, they were likely to write an episode of feeling good. References to conditions surrounding the job, pay, and supervision, on the other hand, were more likely to appear in stories about feeling bad. From this, Herzberg concluded that job *content* determined satisfaction. Lack of interesting work did not create dissatisfaction, but simply prevented positive attitudes from occurring. On the other hand, job *context* determined dissatisfaction. Inconsiderate supervision, wage inequities, or poor working conditions could lead to dissatisfaction. Correcting such problems only removed dissatisfaction and did not bring about satisfaction.

Critics have hounded Herzberg mercilessly for methodological shortcomings. Since his methods consisted of the critical incident or story-telling technique, his findings were vulnerable to the charge that subjects simply allowed defense mechanisms to distort their memories. In other words, people may have taken credit for the good times by writing about things they did themselves (achievement, advancement, the work itself), while attributing the causes of the bad experiences to people or things around them (boss, co-workers, compensation policies, irrational rules).

However, subsequent findings by other researchers lend some support to Herzberg's conclusions. Schriesheim (1978) found that the best predictors of prounion voting were critical attitudes about economic issues (pay, security, and company policy). Attitudes concerning noneconomic facets of the job (job autonomy, opportunity for accomplishment, variety) did not predict voting behavior so well. The correlation between satisfaction with economic issues and prounion voting was $-.74$, while the correlation with satisfaction on the noneconomic matters was only $-.38$.

Hamner and Smith (1978) found that the best predictors of union activity among work units were negative opinions about supervision.

A Gallup Poll survey (Gallup, 1978) asked people who described themselves as generally satisfied or dissatisfied with their jobs to give reasons for their answers. Of those who described themselves as satisfied, more persons (39 percent) mentioned "enjoy my work" than any other reason. Those who said they were dissatisfied most frequently cited "poor wages" (34 percent). (However, 20 percent of the dissatisfied group did cite "boring job" as a factor causing their discontent.)

These studies and others suggest a model that defines four categories of satisfaction and dissatisfaction:

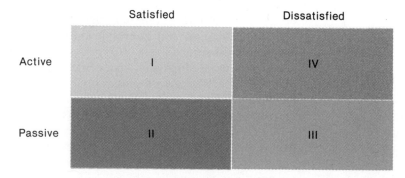

The satisfied-dissatisfied dimension is defined by whether the person's job attitudes are generally positive or negative. The active-passive distinction refers to the frequency with which the attitude is aroused and actually becomes a force on job behavior. A passive attitude more or less stays in the background of consciousness and is expressed only when external stimuli awaken it. For example, a person with a passive job attitude might be conscious of that attitude only when an interviewer asks about it, or when some unusually good or bad job incident occurs. An active attitude, on the other hand, is one that is more often intruding into consciousness; it has a stronger effect in filtering the perception of external stimuli and mediating the effects of stimuli on overt behavior.

We suspect that more people would fall into Category II than any other. Such persons, if asked "On the whole, would you say that you are satisfied or dissatisfied with your present job?" would unhesitatingly answer "satisfied." That is, they have no serious complaints about the way the company or its officials treat them. They could see room for improvement, they might wish they had a more exciting job or prospects for a more dynamic career, but they'll take what they have and regard the intermittent periods of real involvement as a bonus. We suspect, furthermore, that workers over 35 would be disproportionately numbered in this group.

Those in Category III, the Passively Dissatisfied, represent a smaller group—a group that might actually respond "satisfied" to a Gallup Poll, because they are not sufficiently involved to offer even mild protest. It is a personal, somewhat private matter to them, arising from vague doubts about whether the job is as good as it ought to be.

Those in Quadrant IV represent a small minority in the general labor force, although constituting a majority at times in specific organizations. They have no qualms about describing themselves as dissatisfied. They will voice their complaints, press grievances, lead the way into union activity, even engage in forms of sabotage. The reasons for their acute dissatisfaction stem not from unstimulating jobs (or at least not that alone), but because of what they regard as inequities in pay, benefits, supervision, or company policies.

The "actively satisfied" in Quadrant I represent those who genuinely enjoy what they do and are intensely involved in the job. Satisfaction is more than making peace with the job; it is a characteristic mood state that involves spreading the good mood to others. These people are a sizable minority in the work force, dominated by professionals and skilled workers, but well represented in all kinds of vocations. They are the ones who do the little extras, like helping others in a pinch and working for the general welfare of the group, but not necessarily producing more in a narrowly quantitative sense.

CONSEQUENCES OF JOB SATISFACTION AND DISSATISFACTION

Turnover

Empirical studies have firmly established that the satisfied employee is less likely than the dissatisfied counterpart to quit the job over a given period. The actual strength of the relationship between satisfaction and turnover varies considerably from one organization to another and from one time period to another. Even dissatisfied employees try to hold on to their jobs when labor mobility is low or downturns in the economy make alternative work hard to find. Conversely, individuals who strongly like their present jobs can be tempted by prospects of better pay, career advancement, or other opportunities existing elsewhere. The level of unemployment determines much of the variance in job turnover. On the whole, however, the satisfied tend to stay and the dissatisfied to leave. Those actively dissatisfied are the most likely to leave.

Rusbult, Farrell, Rogers, and Mainous (1988) presented some interesting findings regarding the effects of *decline* in job satisfaction. Drawing from work by Hirschman (1970), they theorized that a person would respond to decreasing job satisfaction in one of four ways: *exit* (quit, or actively search for a different job); *voice* (take active and constructive steps to improve work conditions by discussing problems with co-workers and supervisor); *loyalty* (passively but optimistically wait for conditions to improve, while still supporting the organization and contributing to it); and *neglect* (lowered involvement marked by reduced effort and a "don't care" syndrome). The greater the *prior* level of job satisfaction before it declined, the greater the likelihood that people would choose either voice or loyalty in response to adverse conditions. The lower the original satisfaction, the more likely that members chose either exit or (failing that option) neglect. The better the alternatives, the more likely that a decline in satisfaction would lead to exit.

Absenteeism

On any given day, about 4 percent of the labor force fail to show up for work, costing U.S. business an estimated $30 billion per year (Johns, 1987). The decision not to show up for work on a given day represents a temporary decision to quit. Thus, since turnover is inversely related to level of job satisfaction, so is absenteeism. And, dislike of the work itself best predicts a person's rate of absences; attitudes toward co-workers, supervisor, and benefits have less effect on work attendance.

However, just as the relationship between quit rate and job attitudes varies as a function of other complicating variables, so too the prediction of absence rate from job satisfaction must also take other factors into account. The relationship may be quite negligible when total absences for all reasons are computed. However, total absence figures are heavily weighted by long illnesses, which tend to produce large numbers of consecutive days absent. Job attitudes predict much better the *frequence* of absence—especially unexcused absence due to minor ailments—than they predict total days absent.

Job satisfaction aside, absence rates decline in periods of high unemployment and increase when employees can easily earn overtime pay. Furthermore, evidence accumulates that both national and local "work cultures" may determine the degree to which an individual feels justified in responding to discontent by going AWOL: Japan and Switzerland, for example, consistently report lower rates of worker absences than the United States, while English and Italian workers are absent more often. Studies of large manufacturing plants reveal large and stable differences among different departments that could hardly be attributed to differences in work satisfaction or demographics.

Finally, some studies strongly support the notion that a person's *past* absence record (including days absent in school) predicts *future* absenteeism. We can think of several explanations for this finding. Conceivably absence is a learned behavior, shaped at an early age. Recall, too, the persuasive body of evidence pointing to the individual as a determinant of job satisfaction; either certain traits lead to absence indirectly because of their influence on job attitudes, or perhaps the traits that underlie satisfaction are simply the same characteristics that predispose a person to stay home from work.

Union Activity

As we noted above, ample evidence exists to document the relationship between job attitudes and various forms of union activity: voting for union representation, attending meetings, supporting the union cause, and participating in work stoppages. Active dissatisfaction, frequently stemming from perceptions of serious inequities regarding pay, supervision, and work conditions, seems to initiate and sustain these activities. Furthermore, as Schriesheim (1978) noted, these attitudes probably develop over a period of months or even years, and "it seems unlikely that they can be changed in the course of a brief election campaign" (p. 551).

Productivity?

Does increased job satisfaction lead to higher productivity? Does job dissatisfaction hurt productivity? These questions have nagged at managers and industrial psychologists alike for nearly half a century.

Popular opinion views job attitudes as having a direct effect on performance—it seems logical that more positive feelings about work would lead to greater output and higher quality (see the Close-Up). Unfortunately, four decades of research give little basis for such a conclusion.

CLOSE-UP

Managers' and Union Leaders' Beliefs about Job Satisfaction

In a mail survey, 563 top-level managers and 69 union officers were asked their opinions on the nature, causes, and extent of job satisfaction. The percentages of each group expressing strong agreement (SA), agreement (A), and disagreement (D), with the survey's statements of opinion suggest a fairly high degree of correspondence between management and union thinking about worker satisfaction—even with respect to the dubious hypothesis that satisfaction directly leads to higher productivity.

	SA	A	D
Work should be a rewarding part of life, not a form of drudgery.			
Unions	41%	55%	0%
Management	45	53	1
Workers are better educated today and therefore demand more from their job.			
Unions	20	65	12
Management	12	74	12
Most workers are satisfied with their work.			
Unions	0	45	52
Management	1	54	43
If workers were more satisfied with their jobs, there would be greater productivity.			
Unions	25	62	10
Management	17	70	12

SOURCE: R. A. Katzell and D. Yankelovich, *Work, Productivity, and Job Satisfaction* (Washington, D.C.: The Psychological Corporation, 1975).

An exhaustive review of studies concerning the relationship between job satisfaction and job performance is beyond the scope of this chapter. The interested reader may consult a number of excellent reviews elsewhere (Brayfield & Crockett, 1955; Vroom, 1964; Iaffaldano & Muchinsky, 1985; Petty, McGee, & Cavender, 1984).

For illustrative purposes, however, let us cite the experiences of researchers at the Survey Research Center of the University of Michigan. In 1950, they began a large-scale investigation into the types of supervision that result in individual satisfaction and productivity. Their guiding assumption was that morale acted as an intervening variable between supervision and performance. That is, certain supervisory styles would affect job attitudes, and these, in turn, would affect performance. In their first study, which dealt with female clerical workers in an insurance company, the researchers succeeded in identifying certain supervisory styles that were reliably associated with higher than average productivity. To their surprise, the productive groups showed no greater job satisfaction than did the less productive groups. Further studies of 300 railroad laborers and 6,000 workers at a tractor factory yielded the same findings. In none of these studies did satisfaction significantly predict performance. In fact, no single subcomponent of satisfaction—with the job itself, with the company, with supervision, or with pay and promotion opportunities—accounted for any reliable share of the variance in productivity (Kahn, 1960). Thus, while job attitudes bear a measurable relationship with turnover and absenteeism, little evidence supports the case for a strong, direct link between satisfaction and on-the-job productivity.

Why are satisfaction and performance not closely related? Deficiencies in measures of performance might provide one explanation. Many jobs do not lend themselves to objective, concrete performance measures, and subjective ratings by superiors or peers have to serve as surrogate measures. Such rating scales often exhibit unreliability and low levels of agreement among different raters. In fact, Vroom (1964) found that, in those studies using objective performance criteria, a slightly higher relationship between performance and satisfaction emerged. Nevertheless, the actual correlation was still very low.

A second explanation could be that, in many instances, individual performance level simply cannot vary to any great extent. A worker paced by an assembly line or other technological constraints can hardly work faster or harder than the total flow of work. On jobs that require coordination among several people, the fastest worker is apt to be limited by the pace of the slowest. In short, many work situations are pegged to a certain minimally acceptable performance level, with the consequence that administrators place no premium on, or even discourage, a disruptingly higher level of performance by a few individuals.

More generally, however, the cumulative impact of empirical studies has forced organizational theorists and researchers to revise their thinking about the linkage between satisfaction and performance. That some linkage does exist is argued by a generally positive, albeit very low, correlation between the two variables. The consensus of evidence and opinion on just how the two are connected is represented by Lawler and Porter's (1967) theoretical scheme (see Figure 13–4). In their model, satisfaction comes from rewards. Rewards, in turn, break down into two types: extrinsic rewards, such as salary increases and other reinforcements controlled by the organization; and intrinsic rewards, the gratification of having done a job well or of having used one's abilities to solve a problem. Rewards may or may not flow from performance in any predictable fashion, but intrinsic rewards are likely to be more closely connected to performance than are extrinsic rewards. The latter may accrue to employees in an across-the-board fashion. Even if organization officials attempt to reward merit, they may find it difficult to

FIGURE 13–4

The Lawler-Porter Model of the Relationship between Performance and
Satisfaction

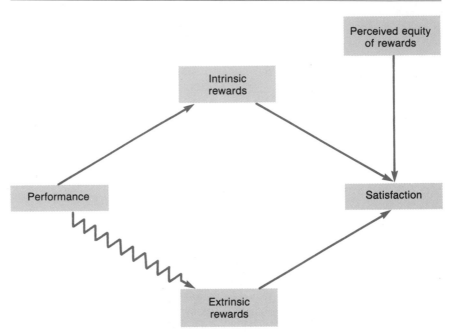

SOURCE: Adapted from E. E. Lawler III and L. W. Porter, "The Effect of Performance on Job Satisfaction," *Industrial Relations* 7 (1967), pp. 20–28.

measure performance reliably. For some jobs extrinsic benefits are
determined by a union contract or by the government, leaving little flexibility
in the reward system for recognizing the star performers. Finally, some
determinants of job satisfaction (such as peer-group relations) are simply by
their very nature not apt to be contingent on performance.

Thus, in many cases we cannot expect much correlation between job
satisfaction and performance. If a job holds little potential for intrinsic
rewards, and if extrinsic rewards bear little relationship to individual
performance level, the resultant connection between performance and
satisfaction is weak. In any case, whatever connection does exist is due, not
to the causal effect of satisfaction on performance, but to the fidelity with
which rewards follow performance.

Should an organization strive for a high positive relationship between
satisfaction and performance? On the one hand, the answer is yes, since
satisfied people tend to stay. If the performance-satisfaction connection is strong, those who stay will be the more productive employees;
turnover will more likely occur among the less productive people. How,
then, can organization officials make the connection stronger? The
Lawler-Porter model indicates two methods: (1) correct the reward system

so top performers receive proportionately higher extrinsic rewards; and/or (2) modify the task so it becomes capable of yielding intrinsic rewards for performance. The latter method amounts to a program of job enrichment.

Not all organizations have performance problems; some companies would be satisfied with routine, minimally acceptable individual performance if they could just count on a sufficient number of people showing up for work at the start of each shift. An indirect and discriminative strategy centered on the reward system would not be suitable for such companies. It would make more sense to launch a frontal assault on their job attitude problems.

Is There a Case for "Satisfaction Leads to Performance"?

Behavioral scientists seem to derive a perverse joy in disproving conventional folk wisdom. The more they can knock common sense truisms into a cocked hat, the more they seem to justify their calling. Organizational psychologists in the last two decades have relentlessly hammered away at the naive belief that a person will perform better because of greater job satisfaction. Researchers have marshaled data from scores of studies demonstrating just how tenuous the empirical linkage is between job attitudes and productivity criteria.

If research evidence offers little support for the notion that satisfaction leads to performance, why do legions of experienced managers persist in the belief? These practitioners cannot be easily dismissed as obtuse victims of their own delusions. Many have made successful careers from perceptive observations and good judgment. How do we square our findings with the fact that intelligent practitioners believe that greater satisfaction leads to better performance?

Organ (1977) has suggested that a key to resolving this paradox lies in the word *performance*. If by performance we mean something like quantity of output, creative solutions, or quality of craftsmanship, then we are talking about the type of individual performance that industrial psychologists have, with some success, tried to measure. And for such measures, we agree with the generally accepted conclusion that satisfaction does not appear to determine — in any appreciable or straightforward fashion — the level of contribution.

But does the manager define performance solely in this manner? We suspect that managers have much more in mind when they use the term. They use the word as a blanket term for a veriety of "citizenship behaviors" that include helping a fellow employee; graciously accepting temporary frustrations; cooperating in carrying out changes pushed down from higher ranks; saying good things about the department, the organization, or the supervisor; "coming through in the clutch" (e.g., making a special effort to show up for work in extremely bad weather); keeping the workplace clean; acting as a peacemaker to defuse conflict between other workers — the list could go on and on. These things could be done "for" the supervisor, "for" the work group, "for" the organization, or simply "for" the individual's personal reasons. But they are behaviors valued by organization officials, and they are done to a great extent by some, less by others, and almost not at all by more than a few. The practicing manager apparently believes they will be done more often by satisfied people.

There are at least two different conceptual frameworks from social psychology that would support this belief. One, social exchange (Adams, 1965; Blau, 1964), asserts that people generally feel bound by the prescriptions of social justice and reciprocity. If people derive satisfaction at work because of what their supervisors have done for them, they feel an obligation to reciprocate. Increased productivity may represent the most obvious form of reciprocity, but many work situations make this impracticable, and in any case the individual seeking to reciprocate may not have the requisite skills for marked improvement in productivity. The person's work may depend so much on others' efforts or external constraints that greater effort toward productivity would be futile. Often, the individual rightly suspects that superiors would show more appreciation for other things: loyalty, compliance, solid citizenship — or all those little things we enumerated above.

Katz and Kahn (1966) have written convincingly on the importance of nonprescribed, spontaneous behavior of people in organizations. No design of an organized system of roles can hope to anticipate all of the contingencies and urgencies that arise in day-to-day functioning. Consequently one cannot write into any job description the requirement that the incumbent respond in citizenship fashion to such urgencies. In fact, many such responses go unnoticed, or at the very least are difficult to measure and credit to a specific individual. Furthermore, it is not so much the isolated occasion of these responses, but their aggregative or cumulative effect that lubricates the social machinery of organization units, making them more viable and effective. Thus, managers are doubly appreciative of consistent response as a "good soldier," since they can neither specify nor require such behavior.

There are boundary conditions around the reciprocating motive. We feel the obligation to reciprocate only to the extent that others appear to have acted on their own volition in doing us a good turn. Moreover, we bristle at the thought that someone has tried to manipulate us, or strategically tried to put us under a sense of obligation for concealed, ulterior purposes. Overwhelming benefactions that we cannot hope to repay may arouse guilt or ego-defensive attitudes, leading us to suppress feelings of indebtedness.

Nonetheless, with due recognition to these boundary conditions, the layman's "gratitude" theory that satisfied people do more of certain valued behaviors has support from a respectable body of theory. Bateman and Organ (1983) found empirical support as well. Supervisors of nonacademic staff members of a university rated their subordinates on the extent to which they exhibited a variety of citizenship behaviors—keeping the workplace clean, helping out in a pinch, making sacrifices to work through temporary disruptions, complying with the rules, and so on. Bateman and Organ found a strong positive correlation between the ratings and the satisfaction reported by the employees. A study of employees of two banks by Smith, Organ, and Near (1983) produced similar findings.

A second body of literature that argues for a relationship between job attitudes and citizenship behaviors concerns the effects of generalized mood state. A series of studies (e.g., Levin & Isen, 1975; Isen, Clark & Schwartz, 1976) have found that an unexpected turn of good fortune disposes people to be more altruistic toward the plight of others. For example, individuals who receive a windfall in the form of finding a $5 bill on the sidewalk are subsequently more likely to help a passerby pick up dropped groceries or give a lift to a stranded hitchhiker. It is conceivable that this tendency represents, in part, just another form of attaining equity: in this case, "equity with the world" (Austin & Walster, 1975). But a study by Rosenhan, Underwood, and Moore (1974) suggests that something more is at work. They asked some third-grade children to think for one minute about a recent event that had made them happy; others to think about an event that made them sad; and a control group simply to count out loud to 30. Immediately afterward, each child was given 25 pennies. The researchers then gave the subjects an opportunity to put some of their pennies into a bag, ostensibly for their classmates who could not participate. Those children who had thought about a happy occasion donated more pennies than the ones who simply counted to 30, who in turn gave more than those who had ruminated over an unhappy experience. The authors concluded that negative affect (unhappiness or resentment) increases the psychological distance between the self and others, while positive affect (a good mood) decreases such distance. They describe as "striking" the tendency of affect, whether positive or negative, to generalize from whatever caused it to other stimuli, notably other persons, in the immediate situation.

A study by Organ and Konovsky (1988) sought to determine if mood state accounted for organizational citizenship behaviors. Their findings fail to support this reasoning. Whether a person characteristically experienced a positive or negative mood at work was unrelated to supervisors' ratings of their contributions in the form of altruistic gestures toward others, or their conscientiousness as reflected in attendance, punctuality, and adhering to the spirit as well as the letter of workplace rules. Rather, the data suggested more of a "fairness" interpretation. Regardless of typical mood state (which might have little to do with the work environment), those employees who felt that their pay and position met reasonable expectations in comparisons with others were more likely to be rated by supervisors as superior in terms of citizenship contributions.

Thus, if we think of job satisfaction as something akin to a generalized sense of fairness—in treatment by the boss, in the distribution of rewards, in the way the larger system works—and think of that form of performance that appears in discretionary acts of good citizenship in the workplace, then perhaps practicing managers do have a defensible case for the belief that "satisfaction leads to performance" (Organ, 1988).

SUMMARY

Job satisfaction of participants is one criterion by which we evaluate organizations. The importance attached to this criterion derives from humanistic values, the effects of job experiences on mental and physical health, and the overall quality of life (although, for many persons, job experiences may not critically determine general life satisfaction).

General job satisfaction, as well as satisfaction toward specific facets of the job, is measured by standardized attitude or opinion surveys. Surveys repeatedly show that 75 to 85 percent or more of the country's labor force report being generally satisfied with the work they do. Data suggest that the current extent of satisfaction is slightly less than in the early 1960s. This decline appears to be largely attributable to the greater proportions of young workers in the labor force and partly due to the dissaffection of some managerial groups; however, the data have never suggested the existence of a "job alienation" crisis. Job satisfaction is highest among professional and managerial workers. Income, autonomy, intrinsic psychological rewards, and social gratification are major determinants of satisfaction. Perceived inequities about pay, policies, working conditions, and supervisory treatment appear to be the major sources of active dissatisfaction.

Job attitudes predict with some reliability the extent of turnover, absenteeism, and union activity. Job satisfaction apparently does not exert much influence on conventional measures of performance. However, there is reason to believe that satisfaction in terms of beliefs of workplace fairness does influence a number of "citizenship behaviors" valued by organizational officials.

CONCEPTS TO REMEMBER

Spillover hypothesis	Morale	Citizenship behaviors
Segmentalist hypothesis	Job alienation thesis	Active-passive dimensions
Job Descriptive Index	Lawler-Porter model of	of job attitudes
Gallup surveys of job	satisfaction and	
satisfaction	performance	

QUESTIONS FOR DISCUSSION

1. What could be done by employers to prevent the "trough" in job satisfaction that seems to characterize younger workers? What could be done by schools and colleges?

2. If member job satisfaction is a criterion for evaluating organizations, should the satisfaction of subordinates also be a criterion for evaluating supervisors and managers? Defend your position.

3. What might cause a person to be actively rather than passively satisfied with a job? Actively versus passively dissatisfied?

4. Why do so many people believe "satisfaction causes performance"?

5. Is it fair to stockholders when profit-seeking organizations try to increase member satisfaction beyond the point of demonstrable savings to the firm?

6. Identify from your own experience or observations a work situation where morale was very poor and one where it was very good. What seemed to be the major causes in each case?

REFERENCES

Adams, J. S. (1965). Inequity in social exchange. In L. Berkowitz (ed.), *Advances in experimental social psychology,* vol. 2. New York: Academic Press.

Adler, N. (1986). *International dimensions of organizational behavior.* Boston: Kent Publishing, Inc.

Arvey, R. D., Bouchard, T. J., Segal, N. L., & Abraham, L. M. (1989). Job satisfaction: Environmental and genetic components. *Journal of Applied Psychology* 74, 187-92.

Austin, W., & Walster, E. (1975). Equity with the world: Transrelational effects of equity and inequity. *Sociometry* 38, 474-96.

Bateman, T. S., & Organ, D. W. (1983). Job satisfaction and the good soldier: The relationship between affect and employee "citizenship." *Academy of Management Journal* 26, 587-95.

Blau, P. (1964). *Exchange and power in social life.* New York: John Wiley & Sons.

Brayfield, A. H., & Crockett, W. H. (1955). Employee attitudes and employee performance. *Psychological Bulletin* 52, 396-424.

Bullock, R. P. (1952). *Social factors related to job satisfaction.* Columbus, Ohio: Bureau of Business Research, Ohio State University.

Campbell, A. (1976). Subjective measures of well-being. *American Ppsychologist* 31, 117-24.

Child, I. L. (1941). Morale: A bibliographical review. *Psychological Bulletin* 38, 393-420.

Gallup, G. H. (1972). *The Gallup Poll.* New York: Random House.

Gallup, G. H. (1978). *The Gallup Poll,* 1972-77, vol. 1.

Gooding, J. (1972). *The job revolution.* New York: Walker.

Gurin, G., Veroff, J., & Feld, S. (1960). *Americans view their mental health.* New York: Basic Books.

Hamner, W. C., & Smith, F. J. (1978). Work attitudes as predictors of unionization activity. *Journal of Applied Psychology* 63, 415-21.

Herzberg, F. (1966). *Work and the nature of man.* Cleveland: World.

Herzberg, F., Mausner, B., Peterson, R., & Capwell, D. (1955). *Job attitudes: Review of research and opinion*. Pittsburgh: Psychological Service of Pittsburgh.

Hirschman, A. O. (1970). *Exit, voice, and loyalty: Responses to decline in firms, organizations, and states*. Cambridge, MA: Harvard University Press.

Iaffaldano, M. T., & Muchinsky, P. M. (1985). Job satisfaction and job performance: A meta-analysis. *Psychological Bulletin* 97, 251-73.

Isen, A. M., Clark, M., & Schwartz, M. F. (1976). Duration of the effect of good mood on helping: Footprints on the sands of time. *Journal of Personality and Social Psychology* 34, 385-93.

Johns, G. (1987). The great escape. *Psychology Today* (October), 30-33.

Kabanoff, B. (1980). Work and nonwork: A review of models, methods, and findings. *Psychological Bulletin* 88, 60-77.

Kahn, R. L. (1960). Productivity and job satisfaction. *Personnel Psychology* 13, 275-87.

Katz, D., & Kahn, R. L. (1966). *The social psychology of organizations*. New York: John Wiley & Sons.

Katzell, R. A., & Yankelovich, D. (1975). *Work, productivity, and job satisfaction*. Washington, D.C.: The Psychological Corporation.

Landy, F. J. (1978). An opponent process theory of job satisfaction. *Journal of Applied Psychology* 63, 533-47.

Lawler, E. E. III, & Porter, L. W. (1967). The effect of performance on job satisfaction. *Industrial Relations* 7, 20-28.

Levin, P. F., & Isen, A. M. (1975). Further studies on the effect of feeling good on helping. *Sociometry* 38, 141-47.

O'Boyle, T. F. (1985). Loyalty ebbs at many companies as employees grow disillusioned. *The Wall Street Journal,* July 11.

Organ, D. W. (1977). A reappraisal and reinterpretation of the satisfaction-causes-performance hypothesis. *Academy of Management Review* 2, 46-53.

Organ, D. W. (1988). A restatement of the satisfaction-performance hypothesis. *Journal of Management* 14, 547-57.

Organ, D. W., & Konovsky, M. A. (1988). Cognitive versus affective determinants of organization citizenship behavior. *Journal of Applied Psychology* 73.

Organ, D., & Near, J. (1985). Cognition versus affect in measures of job sastisfaction. *International Journal of Psychology* 20, 241-53.

Palmore, E., (1969). Predicting longevity: A follow-up controlling for age. *Gerontology* (Winter), 103-8.

Petty, M. M., McGee, G. W., & Cavender, J. W. (1984). A meta-analysis of the relationships between individual job satisfaction and individual performance. *Academy of Management Review* 9, 712-21.

Roethlisberger, F. J., & Dickson, W. J. (1964). *Management and the worker*. New York: Wiley Science Editions.

Rosenhan, D. L., Underwood, B., & Moore, B. (1974). Affect moderates self-gratification and altruism. *Journal of Personality and Social Psychology* 30, 546-52.

Rusbult, C. E., Farrell, D., Rogers, G., and Mainous, A. G. III. (1988). Impact of exchange variables on exit, voice, loyalty, and neglect: An integrative model of responses to declining job satisfaction. *Academy of Management Journal* 31, 599-627.

Scarpello, V. (1988). Pay satisfaction and pay fairness: Are they the same? Paper presented at meetings of Society for Industrial and Organizational Psychology, Dallas, TX.

Schneider, B., & Dachler, P. (1978). A note on the stability of the job descriptive index. *Journal of Applied Psychology* 63, 650-53.

Schriesheim, C. (1978). Job satisfaction, attitudes toward unions, and voting in a union representation election. *Journal of Applied Psychology* 63, 548-52.

Scott, W. E., Jr. (1967). The development of semantic differential scales as measures of "morale." *Personnel Psychology* 20, 179-98.

Seashore, S. (1954). Group cohesiveness in the industrial work group. Ann Arbor: University of Michigan, Institute for Social Research, Survey Research Center.

Sheppard, H. L., & Herrick, N. Q. (1972). *Where have all the robots gone?* New York: Free Press.

Sirota, D., & Greenwood, M. J. (1971). Understanding your overseas workforce. *Harvard Business Review* 14, (January–February), 53–60.

Smith, C. A., Organ, D. W., & Near, J. P. (1983). Organizational citizenship behavior: Its nature and antecedents. *Journal of Applied Psychology* 68, 653-63.

Smith, P. C., Kendall, L. M., & Hulin, C. L. (1969). *The measurement of satisfaction in work and retirement: A strategy for the study of attitudes.* Skokie, IL: Rand McNally.

Staw, B. M., Bell, N. E., & Clausen, J. A. (1986). The dispositional approach to job attitudes: A lifetime longitudinal test. *Administrative Science Quarterly* 31, 56-77.

Staw, B., & Ross, J. (in press). Stability in the midst of change: A dispositional approach to job attitudes. *Journal of Applied Psychology.*

Vroom, V. H. (1964). *Work and movitation.* New York: John Wiley & Sons.

Walker, C. R., & Guest, R. H. (1952). *The man on the assembly line.* Cambridge, MA: Harvard Univ. Press.

Weiss, D. J., Dawis, R. V., England, C. W., & Lofquist, L. H. (1967). *Manual for the Minnesota studies in Vocational Rehabilitation,* vol. 22. Minneapolis: University of Minnesota.

Work in America. (1973). Report of a special task force to the secretary of health, education, and welfare. Cambridge, MA: MIT Press.

14 Stress in Organizations

What are the different meanings of stress?

What is the relationship between stress and health?

What is the relationship between stress and thought?

What is the relationship between stress and emotions?

What is the relationship between stress and performance?

What are the major stressors in organizations?

How does one manage stress?

Picture a 48-year-old male executive, graying at the temples, seated at a desk. His shirt-sleeves are rolled up; his collar is open, his tie is loosened. His facial muscles appear taut; he props his elbows on the desk with hands clenched together so tightly that the veins in his forearms stand out. He looks away from his desk—which is littered with papers, an ashtray overflowing with cigarette butts, and four coffee-stained Styrofoam cups—and winces at the relentless sweep of the hands on the wall clock. Picking up a pencil, he snaps it in impotent rage.

This image represents the stereotype of job stress and it illustrates some widely held assumptions about stress: stress increases with a job's level of responsibility; it is marked by tension and anxiety; it causes a breakdown in performance; and it is caused by the pressures of time and of other people's demands on us.

These assumptions are, at best, oversimplified. Just how valid they are depends on what we mean by stress—and the word means different things to different people. The vernacular and technical meanings of stress have become thoroughly confused, probably because they overlap. As a result, many people misunderstand the relationship between stress and feelings, stress and thought, stress and illness, stress and adaptation, stress and performance—even stress and life. This chapter will attempt to sort out these various meanings.

STRESS AS AN EVERYDAY TERM

In everyday usage, stress usually implies something unpleasant. We may use the term to describe a situation, such as a traffic snarl or the pressure to complete a term paper due the next morning. The word might describe the emotions aroused by such situations—fear, irritation, or frustration. Certain physical symptoms are associated with stress—tightness in the stomach, a stiffened neck, sweating under the arms, jittery hands.

Our popular "model" of stress resembles that of Figure 14–1: elements in a sequence defined by an undesired circumstance, an uncomfortable state of mind, and an unpleasant mixture of physical sensations. We would also probably acknowledge some feedback effects: as we become aware of the

FIGURE 14–1

A Model of the Popular Meaning of Stress-Distress

Unpleasant situation

Uncomfortable state of mind ⟶ Disturbing physical symptoms

physical sensations (clammy hands, racing pulse), our emotional state (anxiety) becomes more acute; as we become more anxious, we find ourselves doing things (acting impulsively, making mistakes) that aggravate the problem. In effect, we equate stress with distress.

There is nothing inherently wrong with this model. It is wrong only when we use this meaning of stress, instead of the technical meaning, as a scientific construct in statements about relationships between stress, on the one hand, and illness, performance, and adaptation on the other. When we shift to a scientific meaning of stress, we find that pleasant as well as unpleasant events can cause illness; that positive as well as negative feelings and emotions can accompany stress; that adapting to stress does not negate its toll on the body; that performance itself can add to stress, but is not necessarily affected by it.

STRESS AS A SCIENTIFIC CONSTRUCT

Stress became a scientific construct in the research and writing of Professor Hans Selye. He discovered that whether he subjected laboratory rats to extreme cold, injected chemical irritants into their tissue, or just held them as they struggled to get loose, the animals' physiological processes showed certain common reactions. Of course, specific effects were associated with each particular treatment as well, but Selye was interested in the common denominators — the invariant response of the organism's body to any demand placed on it (see Figure 14–2). The common features constituted what Selye labeled the General Adaptation Syndrome, or G.A.S. — the syndrome by which a state of stress is manifested.

The nonspecific response of the body to some environmental demand, or stressor (which could be a germ, an overload on a group of muscles, a loud noise, extreme heat or cold) involves the body's endocrine system. It begins with the pituitary, a cherry-sized organ resting at the base of the brain. The pituitary signals the alarm state of the G.A.S. by sending a chemical messenger in the form of the hormone ACTH to the adrenals. During this stage the body is, in a sense, in retreat, experiencing a temporary and minor loss of efficiency until it can rally its forces of resistance. The adrenals, in response to ACTH, initiate the second stage of the G.A.S., the resistance stage, by secreting their own hormones, adrenaline and noradrenaline, collectively called the catecholamines. The catecholamines enter the bloodstream and trigger a succession of changes in the body chemistry — in the level of fatty acids in the blood and in the blood's clotting chemistry — and also alter the digestive processes. These events during the resistance stage eventually enable the organism to neutralize, isolate, or minimize the damage to the organism as a whole. The body seems to adapt to the demand.

However, Selye believes that from birth, any organism has only a fixed, limited amount of adaptation energy. Every stress response of the body uses up some of this precious asset. Whatever is used up cannot be replaced. Thus, the resistance state of the G.A.S. cannot continue indefinitely.

FIGURE 14–2
Stress as a Scientific Construct Formulated by Hans Selye

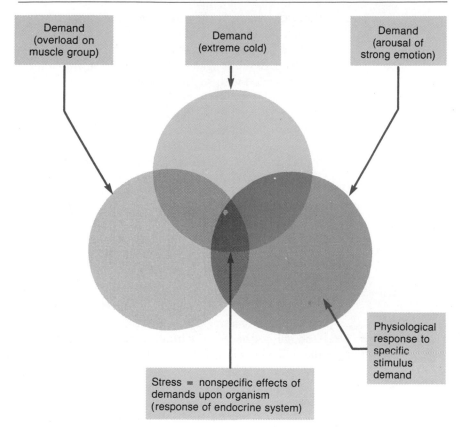

Subjected to an environmental stressor of sufficient strength for a sufficiently long time, the adaptive energies of the organism are depleted, and exhaustion or collapse – the third and final G.A.S. stage – follows.

The exhaustion may take the form of depression or some other temporary lapse and may necessitate bed rest. This appears to allow the body to transfer some of its fixed store of adaptation energy from "long-term reserves" (analagous to a savings account) to a short-term available supply (like a checking account). But this is a transfer, a borrowing, that cannot be repaid. If the process continued, eventually the entire stock of adaptation energy would drop to nothing, and life could not go on. Thus, adaptation is a costly business. To adapt, in this sense, to a stressor does not mean that the stressor does no harm. Adaptation is the essence of stress itself, at least in a physiological sense.

To summarize, stress as a scientific construct represents the invariant, nonspecific reaction of the body to any environmental demand – whatever form that demand may take.

STRESS AND ILLNESS

The adrenals play a significant role in providing resistance to agents that threaten the body. We are constantly exposed to, and ever transporting within us, microbes that could potentially wreak havoc to our tissues. This seldom happens because the endocrine system, in which the adrenals are involved, defends against these microbes. But what if the endocrine system is overloaded with so many demands that it cannot deal with all of them?

To address this issue, let us examine Table 14–1, which shows a list of changes or events that can occur in a person's life. Each event is assigned a number that serves as a rough measure of the relative degree of adjustment demanded by the event. The weighting scheme was derived through studies by Professors T. H. Holmes and R. H. Rahe (1968) and colleagues at the University of Washington. Their studies asked people of varying ages and from several different cultures to compare events with each other in terms of the degree of adjustment required. It seems to be universally agreed that the death of a spouse requires more adjustment on the part of the surviving spouse than any other single event. The table can be used to provide a rough measure of the degree of adjustment a person has to make during a given period of life. Simply add up the number of points associated with each event experienced during, say, a year.

Holmes and his co-workers found that once a person "earns" 200 or more points in a single year, there is at least a 50-50 chance of a fairly serious (though not necessarily life-threatening) breakdown in health occurring in the following year. One who totals 300 or more points in a year runs that risk factor up to about a 75 to 80 percent chance. The illness brought on by such demand for adjustment can appear as digestive ailments, respiratory problems, kidney malfunction, almost any breakdown in the body's economy.

What is the explanation for this relationship? Significant changes in one's immediate life environment trigger a rapid succession of new situations with which one has to cope. The endocrine system provides the adaptation energy for the sustained arousal and vigilance needed to cope with the novelty, uncertainty, or conflict occasioned by the new situations. But remember it is this same endocrine system that provides the basis for resistance to any agent (e.g., bacteria) that threatens the body. If the endocrine system is constantly marshaling the body's energy for adjustment, the capacity for resisting those lurking microbes will be exhausted. Thus, wherever the body is most vulnerable, a breakdown can occur. (For a very readable account of the effect of life changes on illness, see Alvin Toffler, *Future Shock,* 1970, pp. 289–304.)

You should note that a number of the events listed in Table 14–1 are positive, ordinarily regarded as occasions for pleasure or celebration. The layman's definition of stress as something to be avoided hardly seems to describe marriage, the birth of a child, promotion, outstanding personal achievement, sudden drastic improvement in financial position, moving to a

TABLE 14–1

Social Readjustment Rating Scale

Life Event	Scale Value
Death of spouse	100
Divorce	73
Marital separation	65
Jail term	63
Death of a close family member	63
Major personal injury or illness	53
Marriage	50
Fired from work	47
Marital reconciliation	45
Retirement	45
Major change in health of family member	44
Pregnancy	40
Sex difficulties	39
Gain of a new family member	39
Business readjustment	39
Change in financial state	38
Death of a close friend	37
Change to a different line of work	36
Change in number of arguments with spouse	35
Mortgage over $10,000	31
Foreclosure of mortgage or loan	30
Change in responsibilities at work	29
Son or daughter leaving home	29
Trouble with in-laws	29
Outstanding personal achievement	28
Wife begins or stops work	26
Begin or end school	26
Change in living conditions	25
Revision of personal habits	24
Trouble with boss	23
Change in work hours or conditions	20
Change in residence	20
Change in schools	20
Change in recreation	19
Change in church activities	19
Change in social activities	18
Mortgage or loan less than $10,000	17
Change in sleeping habits	16
Change in number of family get-togethers	15
Change in eating habits	15
Vacation	13
Christmas	12
Minor violations of the law	11

SOURCE: From L. O. Ruch and T. H. Holmes, "Scaling of Life Changes: Comparison of Direct and Indirect Methods," *Journal of Psychosomatic Research* 15 (1971), p. 224.

bigger home in a better neighborhood, or graduation from college. Yet, to the extent that these events demand adjustments, they are stressful in Selye's sense, and if enough of these are bunched together, they can produce health problems.

STRESS AND THOUGHT

Selye sees stress as a nonspecific response of the endocrine system to any demand placed on the organism. Thus, many episodes of stress occur without the organism being aware either of the stressor or of the stress reaction itself. A cold room or an overloaded muscle will trigger the endocrine activity that constitutes stress, regardless of whether the person interprets the situation as stressful. Therefore, the relationship between stress and thought is neither perfect nor direct. As a species, we are fortunate that such is the case. We could not possibly attend to every instance of our system's need to adapt to environmental demands. The stress response provides the necessary (though sometimes costly) adaptation energy without us having to think about it.

Nonetheless, cognitive processes (perceiving, labeling, interpreting, and evaluating) do have their place in the dynamics of stress. Stress often influences the content and style of our thinking. Also, our thoughts about a potential stressor may initiate an emotional response which itself constitutes an additional, independent stressor. Finally, for better or worse, our interpretation and assessment of potential stressors may affect our behavior.

The discharge of stress hormones usually brings about a state of generalized arousal. When this occurs in moderation, it may sharpen our thinking, helping us to concentrate. For example, some people say that a cold shower helps them "get the juices flowing" so that they can think logically and efficiently. Others arrange their work environments so that there is always some stimulus (for example, reminder of a deadline) inducing just enough psychological pressure to maintain vigilance and alertness.

However, when stress-induced arousal reaches a certain level, "thoughts and action become more primitive" (Weick, 1975). We become less sensitive to subtle aspects of our environment and more prone to think in terms of absolutes. A person working in a state of fever-pitched arousal may think that the work being completed must be perfect or the effort is a failure. Similarly, a highly aroused manager easily falls into the trap of evaluating people as all good or all bad. Alternatives are defined in mutually exclusive terms: it's either this way or that, one or the other, black or white, no in-between.

Simplistic thinking may be useful when the original stressor or the tasks themselves are simple. Seldom, however, is this the case in today's organizations. Stressors in the work situation are more apt to arise from complex situations. Primitive, simplistic thought patterns are clearly inadequate. As Weick (1975) argues, "These 'terrible simplifications' which occur after an increase in arousal are what make stress appear to be a bad thing. It's not the stress itself that causes havoc, but rather the simplifications in analysis and action that follow it. These . . . produce the states of confusion and panic typically associated with stress" (p. 37). The stress response, then, affects the quality of thought. But the sequence can also work the other way: our thoughts can precipitate the stress.

The stress response was essential to the early versions of homo sapiens, not only in adapting to the immediate demands of the environment (such as temperature extremes or bacteria), but also as an aid to coping with imminent or *anticipated* dangers. In a confrontation with a large animal predator, an anticipatory stress response would provide the adrenalin enabling quick escape or a change in blood chemistry lessening the loss of blood from a mauling. This anticipatory stress response occurs in advance of the dangerous event, following *recognition* of the predator, *interpretation* of its strength and movement, and *assessment* of the danger.

Having inherited our ancestors' basic cognitive and hormonal characteristics, we are capable of this same anticipatory stress response triggered by the perception of threat. The difference — and the problem, so often — is that our environment lacks the simplicity of the cave dwellers' environment. Their anticipatory stress responses were likely to be cued only by unequivocal, direct physical dangers. It usually was quite clear whether something was a threat. Most of the "dangers" we confront today, however, pose no real physical danger at all. Yet, we define them as threats because they may seem to endanger our self-esteem, status, economic security, or relationships with others. Furthermore, the stress response is triggered by these dangers, even if they have no objective or factual basis. Unfortunately, the stress response serves no useful purpose in coping with these different psychological (as opposed to physical) sorts of dangers.

Thus, how we think about a situation may determine its stress potential as much as, or more than, the situation itself. If you regard the outcome of an interview with a client as a life-or-death matter, your stress response will be much greater than if you think of the interview as just one game in a long season.

A study by Kobasa, Maddi, and Kahn (1982) demonstrates the significance of cognitive appraisal as a mediator of stress. Using a measure of life change events very similar to that shown in Table 14–1, the researchers monitored the frequency and severity of such life change events over five years in a group of several hundred middle- and upper-level managers in a large utility company. The researchers also measured the frequency and seriousness of illness experienced by these managers.

Over the five-year span, there was a modest overall correlation between the measures of stressful life events and illness, consistent with many previously published studies. However, many of the managers who experienced a rather high level of potentially threatening life events were virtually unscathed by any symptoms of physical disorders, while others who experienced the same number and type of events had frequent and, in some cases, serious health problems. Why did the same objective situations prove debilitating for some, but innocuous to others? Kobasa et al. (1982) and Kobasa (1979) found that the "hardy" subject characteristically had a *conception* of life change events different from that of the others. Hardy subjects generally had a sense of greater *internal control*. Even though the events might have been initiated by other agents or forces, they felt they could take charge of the situation and shape its ultimate course. They also perceived *meaningfulness* in the events, a sense that they fit into a coherent, larger structure of their lives. Finally, they defined these events as *challenges* — welcome tests of their competence, rather than as dangers or threats. By contrast, the managers who reacted to stressful life events with physical breakdown generally lacked the sense of internal control, could not discern meaning in the demanding situations, and regarded unexpected change as a threat to their interests.

We should not infer from this study that a person has an infinite capacity for adjustment, provided his or her "head is right." Demanding situations can cause breakdowns, regardless of how or whether a person perceives them. The point is that an individual's interpretation of the situation can either augment or reduce the stress potential of the situation.

EMOTIONAL STRESSORS

Some of Selye's experiments with laboratory animals — subjecting them to cold temperatures or injecting them with a foreign substance — seem to have little to do with stress as we think of it in organizations. But a series of his studies do have direct relevance to us. When he held a rat so that it could only struggle in futility and not get away, Selye found the same physiological response (the G.A.S.) that occurred with direct assaults on their bodies. Yet in forcibly immobilizing the animal, he did not injure it. The stress response of the adrenals seemed to be mediated not by injury but by strong emotions (in this case, something like anger or frustration). We, as human beings, are susceptible to very strong emotional responses as well. And our responses can come under the control of subtle cues in the form of words, symbols, and other social stimuli.

The emotions are governed by a primitive part of the lower brain called the hypothalamus (which also regulates some other functions, including hunger and body temperature). Under conditions of emotional arousal, the hypothalamus sends messages to the pituitary that trigger much the same sequence of events as described by Selye's G.A.S. Consider the example of a critical superior lashing out at a subordinate's mistakes. The words, the tone of voice, the facial expressions of the boss are the sorts of cues that (in most of us) evoke strong emotional responses — anger, fear, or anxiety. Thus, the stress response of the body is triggered. However, the stress response of the body evolved eons ago to enable the body to fight or run, and neither response is appropriate in this context. The quickened pulse, the increased sugar and fat levels in the blood, the quickened clotting time of the blood, the constriction of the blood vessels—all part of the eventual effects of the adrenal response—do no good; they are a waste of the body's fixed store of adaptation energy, and they wear down our own internal resources.

We should emphasize, however, that:

1. The stress response may occur without any strong emotional response necessarily becoming involved.
2. *Any* strong emotion can trigger the stress response.

The surprising fact to most is that the various emotions—fear, anger, ecstasy, thrill, hilarity—involve virtually the same internal physical responses. The distinctions between them are made by external cues and their interpretation by the information-processing centers of the brain—not by the hormones. For example, one study (Levi, 1972) found that whether people watched a horror movie, an anger-provoking film, or a comedy, the stress response (as measured by the level of adrenaline in the subject's urine) was about the same. In all three instances, the stress response was significantly greater than that which followed a dull documentary film. Thus, it is the strength of the emotion, not the label we put on it, that determines the stress response.

The serious emotional stressors most likely to be triggered in the work environment are frustration, anxiety, and depression.

Frustration

As an objective condition, the term *frustration* denotes any obstruction between behavior and its goal or any interference with ongoing instrumental behavior. As such, frustration is obviously endemic in organizational life. The existence of a hierarchy, of competition, and of constraints on behavior guarantee that frustration will be frequent. This need not be something to lament, however, because frustration often has positive effects on behavior. For example, our repertoire of instrumental behavior would not grow if we were never frustrated, because without frustration we would seldom try new methods for achieving our ends. Frustration can occasion perceptual as well as behavioral change, too: our built-in assumptions and biases for viewing situations usually go unexamined until actions based on those assumptions prove ineffectual. Finally, frustration sometimes provides the moderate arousal of energy that helps us focus our attention on a task.

These positive consequences are more likely when frustration is temporary or intermittent, when alternative responses are available or substitute goals can suffice, or when the person's past experience has led him or her to develop a frustration tolerance.

When frustration is prolonged and the limit of frustration tolerance has been reached and passed, we use the word frustration to signify an inner emotional state. For example, suppose you need to print out a report that your boss absolutely needs in the next hour. You find that the printer will not work. Objectively, frustration has occurred, since the nonfunctioning printer represents an obstacle to your immediate goal. The immediate effect on your state of mind is concern, maybe annoyance, but nothing serious. You check the settings on the printer, repeat the procedure, fiddle with the machine. If repeated attempts to print the report fail, eventually you run out of alternatives and you begin to experience frustration in an inner, emotional sense. Your behavior might well degenerate into primitive forms, such as slapping the printer or the computer, or mindlessly repeating responses that do not work. You might curse any work associate so unfortunate as to be near you at this moment, or you might just cry.

Frustration and Aggression   The link between frustration and aggression, or behavior directed toward the harm of another person or object, has attracted the attention of psychologists for quite some time. Early in the century, aggression was thought to be caused by some built-in instinct in animals and humans, but this explanation soon proved unsatisfactory. Ethological studies of animals in their natural habitats showed aggression to be quite rare except in order to obtain food. Later it was argued that frustration is always a cause of aggression and that aggression is always preceded by frustration. This position seemed to be extreme since (1) people appear to be able to endure a variety of frustrating events daily without showing aggressive behavior, and (2) aggression can be instrumental and can be strengthened by reinforcing consequences that only remotely relate to frustration—for example, browbeating subordinates in order to gain a psychological advantage.

The currently held view is that frustration generates a predisposition to aggress (often labeled anger), but that other factors determine whether aggression takes place and what form the aggression takes. It seems plausible to view aggression as a "last resort" after other methods of coping have failed. Thus, up to a point, the tendency to aggress will vary directly with the duration of frustration, the number of unsuccessful responses, and the strength of the responses interfered with. The tendency to aggress will vary inversely with the number of alternative instrumental responses available for dealing with the situation.

Among the factors that determine the occurrence of aggression are whether punishment for aggression is anticipated, whether one's peer group approves of the aggression (and offers possible support in resisting punishment), and the extent to which aggression has been strengthened by reinforcement in the past. The last factor is a subtle but important one, because organization officials sometime unwittingly reinforce aggressive behavior. When noisy outbursts by subordinates threaten an administrator's control, the administrator may be inclined to give in—remove the source of frustration. This means, of course, that when confronted by further frustrations, these subordinates are likely to use aggression again. On a smaller scale, the same thing happens when we get our soft drink after kicking the vending machine. Aggression sometimes gets the job done.

Aggression is also more likely to occur when frustration is unanticipated or is *perceived as arbitrary*. The emphasis here is on the point of view of the person being frustrated. For very good and compelling reasons, administrators are often forced to institute changes that are frustrating to lower-ranking participants. If the rationale behind such measures is not communicated, aggression may result. Changes are less likely to be perceived as arbitrary if participants have had some form of input, are told what considerations led to the changes, or if the decision makers themselves are sharing the burdens imposed by the changes.

As noted above, the anticipation of punishment can inhibit aggression. Even a severely frustrated technician usually doesn't punch the boss, because the consequences may be quite costly. However, both the target and the form of aggression can be *displaced:* automobile assembly line workers have ripped car upholstery or jammed the production line; some individuals may vent aggression on a co-worker; and others wait until they're home and then take it out on their family.

The administrator must avoid reinforcing illegitimate, unconstructive forms of aggression. Otherwise, he or she will only have to face more and more of it in the future, particularly as more reasonable employees learn by observation that "it pays to get tough." Yet, the administrator must be careful not to bottle up direct aggression only to have it displaced onto other persons or take the form of sabotage. What is the way out of this dilemma? Levinson (1959) suggests that the organization provide official channels for the discharge of aggression. One example is the grievance procedure of unionized organizations. Other forms could include such things as a "corporate ombudsman"—an official flak-catcher—to hear appeals from those who believe their work or treatment involves intolerable frustration. Ultimately, of course, such devices are of little value unless organization officials make a determined effort to keep participants' frustration within manageable bounds, communicate in advance the rationale for frustrating changes, and show a willingness to help bear the cost of organization frustrations. Grievances that never get fully processed and ombudsmen who carry no real clout cannot stretch to infinity the frustration tolerance of employees. If frustrated persons never or very seldom get any substantive relief by using such channels, their aggression will take other, less desirable channels.

Anxiety

Psychologists have found it difficult to agree on a succinct definition of anxiety as an emotional stressor. Attempts to define anxiety have often taken the form of distinguishing between anxiety and fear or between anxiety and frustration. Whereas fear is the reaction to immediate, present danger, anxiety is the reaction to anticipated harm, whether physical or psychological (such as loss of self-esteem or loss of status). Whereas frustration is interference with instrumental behavior, anxiety is the feeling of not having appropriate responses or plans for dealing with anticipated harm.

The distinctions seem subtle, but most people seem to understand quite well what they mean when they say that they are anxious: the sense of dread, foreboding, and apprehension that gnaws at their insides and darkens their outlook on things in general. Sometimes the cause of anxiety is uncertain; the threat is vague, and the potential danger is itself ambiguous. This, of course, renders anxiety all the more unsettling, since it makes any instrumental coping response harder to select.

What causes anxiety in organizations? Differences in power, which leave people feeling vulnerable to administrative decisions adversely affecting them; frequent changes, which make existing behavior plans obsolete; competition, which inevitably makes some persons lose face, esteem, and status; and job ambiguity (especially when this is coupled with pressure). To these may be added some related factors, such as lack of job feedback, job insecurity, and responsibility for important outcomes coupled with dependence on others to achieve those outcomes.

The 1980s saw quite a few developments that would almost certainly add to chronic anxiety in the workplace. Corporate downsizing and restructuring have stricken hundreds of thousands from the payroll, leaving middle-aged managers and professionals stranded in the marketplace. Deregulation and global competition in many industries has forced a quickened corporate response to the external environment, with millions of employees at all levels unsure how changes will affect their work and lives. More decisions must be made under time pressure before complete information is available.

Personal, nonorganizational factors come into play as well, such as physical illness, problems at home, unrealistically high personal goals, and estrangement from one's colleagues or one's peer group.

Of course, all causes of anxiety cannot be eliminated in our imperfect world of imperfect organizations managed by imperfect people, nor is all anxiety deleterious to health or performance. Moderate anxiety mobilizes and focuses our energy, sharpens our sensitivity to information in the environment, and is often a prelude to the formulation of innovative, creative solutions.

When anxiety is severe and prolonged, people often resort to dysfunctional coping mechanisms. The individual begins to direct attention to the internal sensations of anxiety at the cost of dealing rationally with the source of the anxiety. This may lead to alcoholism, drug abuse, excessive absenteeism, or other forms of escapism. Since such responses do temporarily alleviate emotional stress, they are reinforcing and can become chronic.

A complicating variable in the optimal handling of anxiety is an unwillingness to admit to it. Particularly among men, there seems to be the attitude that talking about anxiety is a sign of weakness. This is unfortunate, for many causes of apprehension could undoubtedly be laid to rest if they were voiced.

What can administrators do to help keep anxiety within manageable bounds? They can reinforce its expression, so that if it is groundless it can be dispelled. They can, where possible, avoid initiating changes that uproot people from cohesive groups. The Hawthorne studies (Roethlisberger & Dickson, 1964) showed that nagging personal worries were much less debilitating to female workers when they were allowed to form natural work groups. Increasing job performance feedback, providing information before significant organization change, and avoiding unnecessary competition are all means of mitigating stressful anxiety.

Some individuals — those characterized as high in neuroticism — seem to be particularly vulnerable to anxiety. One might even say that such persons carry a pool of free-floating anxiety around with them, such that even mild stimuli will trigger a strong anxiety response. These people seem to have a pronounced conditionability of this emotional response to a vast range of everyday physical and social cues. In these individuals, anxiety may be regarded as a trait, as well as a reaction to a specific situation.

Depression

> It can steal up as insidiously as a November fog, chilling the heart, sapping the will even to get out of bed in the morning. Victims often experience it as a terrifying aloneness, a sense of being strangely "outside" themselves, like ghostly spectators of their own lives . . . life bereft of the smallest consolation . . . day after day the same smothering "heaviness" in things . . . . [*Newsweek,* May 4, 1987]

All of us experience occasional episodes of what we refer to as depression. Such episodes tend to coincide with illness, a prolonged struggle with some problem, or the experience of some loss — whether the loss of a close friend, a relative, or a job.

With most of us, depression in this acute stage is probably useful, though hardly comfortable, for the mind-body system. Depression slows the system down. It works like a safety valve to prevent us from continued futile struggle that can only overtax our capacities. The depression that comes with a bad cold, for example, becomes a cue to disengage from the crowd, leave work a bit early, put vexing chores on hold, or postpone some mundane tasks. This recess allows the body to transfer adaptation energy from the long-term stores to an accessible pool.

For most of us, the depressive episode is self-limiting. After a few days at most, feelings of renewed energy, confidence, and optimism take hold, and life resumes its normal course. Certain people, however, do not escape the depressive episode. Depression for them becomes chronic, and they seem to sink deeper and deeper into apathy and self-defeating behavior. These people are the true depressives. For them, the event that caused the acute phase of depression was simply a trigger. Chances are that sooner or later, their physical and psychological makeup would have brought forth such a response.

An estimated 30 to 40 million Americans (twice as many women as men) will experience clinical depression, and at least a third of those will have recurrences of this most common form of mental illness. Although the condition is eminently treatable, only one in five victims seeks professional help, probably because they don't recognize the problem for what it is or they attribute it to a failure of personal will.

According to the National Institute of Mental Health, the incidence of depression is on the increase, especially among those aged 25 to 44.

Flach (1974) and Kline (1974) have provided detailed descriptions of the chronic depressive's symptoms:

Sleep disturbances, especially waking up after an hour or two of sleep and being unable to get back to sleep.

Loss of appetite.

Decreased sex drive.

Aversion to social contacts.

Indecision and procrastination (a depressed person may have extreme difficulty even deciding what to wear, what to order from a menu, or how to answer a letter).

A change in dress or appearance, especially toward untidiness.

Fatigue and poor concentration.

In general, and most pervasive, reduced enjoyment of all the things that used to give pleasure.

A general sense of being trapped; helplessness; guilt.

In Western culture, guilt especially figures in the depressive syndrome (this does not seem to be the case among non-Western depressives). Indeed, one notes a paradox: depressives feel they cannot control events around them, yet at the same time they blame themselves for the way events turn out (Abramson & Sackheim, 1977). A clue to unravelling this paradox comes from Janoff-Bulman (1979): depressives blame themselves, not merely for their behavior, but also for their character — the kind of people they perceive themselves to be — and this they feel hopeless to change.

Obviously, the depressive syndrome will affect a person's work. The depressive will have difficulty summoning the energy to confront the everyday challenges of work; will be easily distracted; will put off making even routine decisions. Alcoholism may exacerbate the situation. The reactions of work associates are predictable: expressions of anger or irritation, or perhaps well-intentioned pep talks. Neither is likely to help much.

The person who has never experienced chronic depression can't empathize with the depressive. The nondepressed see the problem as a lack of willpower or "get-up-and-go." They soon give up on the depressive as a loser. They simply cannot comprehend the nature of the affliction. Of course, as work associates and even family members turn away, the depressive's vicious cycle intensifies, with deeper feelings of inadequacy, guilt, and alienation. If the cycle is uncorrected, it may develop into such extreme forms as chronic alcoholism or even suicide. Even short of such tragedies, the result will be the loss of the contributions of an effectively functioning person.

A major breakthrough in the treatment of depressives occurred in 1957 with the discovery of tricyclic antidepressant drugs (Flach, 1974). These drugs are not "uppers," or central nervous system stimulants. They have no effect whatever on the nondepressed; even among the depressed, they still permit the experience of normal or appropriate emotional responses, such as grief for a lost loved one. Rather, the tricyclics seem to activate some biochemical processes in the brain—processes that normally occur in the nondepressed, but are inhibited in the depressive—so that depression becomes self-limiting. The tricyclics, moreover, do not act as a placebo; they help even those patients who don't think they will do any good ("The medicine won't bring my wife back, will it?" "How will it get my job back?", "My failures are a fact, no drug can erase them.") At the very least, therapists find this medication gives the client an emotional toehold, so that other forms of therapy (such as counseling) have a better chance of providing help. (Other antidepressants, such as lithium and mono-amine oxidase inhibitors, or MAOs, have also proved effective in many cases.)

Thus, the manager should try to recognize any serious bouts with depression in an associate, try to refrain from writing off the individual as a loss, and seek intervention by a professional (especially a psychiatrist, who can prescribe drugs). With appropriate treatment, the prospects for recovery are considerable.

Burnout

Something akin to depression—not as serious but probably much more common—is the condition increasingly described as "burnout." It refers to a syndrome that is usually associated with work and includes such features as physical exhaustion, sleep disturbances, the utter absence of any positive reinforcement from any aspect of work, feelings of hopelessness and futility, and a cynical attitude about everything associated with the job. Increasingly, researchers (Maslach & Jackson, 1981; Gaines & Jermier, 1983) point to *emotional exhaustion* as the core component of the burnout syndrome.

Anyone exposed to chronic job stressors provides an easy target for burnout, but it seems to occur with particular frequency among those whose work requires constant interaction with clients who have problems. Police officers, inner-city public school teachers, social workers, and emergency room health care workers in big cities face an occupational hazard in the form of burnout. These jobs often attract idealistic types who are motivated by the ideal of service, but due to repeated frustrations in trying to help their clients—sometimes because of the constraints of a mindless bureaucracy, often because of the clients themselves—they are worn down by their vicarious suffering and discouraged by finding that much effort and sacrifice on their own part often changes nothing in the client's situation.

If, as some believe, the pace of change and information overload increases into the 1990s, we might well find burnout a common malady among professionals and managers in both public and private sectors.

SOURCES OF STRESS IN ORGANIZATIONS

Given Selye's meaning of stress, any organization, condition, or event that places on a person a demand to adapt is a stressor. Nonetheless, we can identify certain job-related stressors that are particularly prevalent. These sources of stress are job overload, role conflict and ambiguity, organization politics, and Type A behavior.

Job Overload

Probably every member of an organization has some rough, subjective notion of what constitutes an optimal amount of work. Even if we cannot measure this ideal quantity of work, we know when our agenda of tasks approximates it. On the one hand, we have enough to keep busy. On the other hand, we have time to attend carefully to what we are doing. After work, we have enough energy left over to take care of personal business and enjoy leisure-time pursuits.

When the workload interferes with these ideal conditions, overload has occurred. Everyone experiences overload from time to time, but in some jobs it is chronic. As such, it eminently classifies as a stressor, since it represents a pressing demand on the organism to adapt.

We can distinguish between different types of overload. The simplest — and probably the easiest to cope with — is working long hours on a single task or a group of closely related tasks. Self-employed professionals, small-time entrepreneurs, and farmers come to mind here. They often have long workdays, they sacrifice some leisure time, but the work has focus and their efforts accumulate.

A more vexing form of overload arises when deadlines and time pressures enter the picture. Of course, deadlines per se do not create undue stress, but when one perceives them as unreasonable, they do act as stressors. Kiev and Kohn (1979) found that both middle- and upper-level managers reported this as the single most frequent stressor in their jobs.

Yet there is no question that time pressures, even when they exceed our preferences, do enhance productivity. A longitudinal study of scientists and engineers (Andrews & Farris, 1972) found such pressures to relate positively to several aspects of performance, including innovativeness and overall productivity. The study also revealed that, like many of us, scientists and engineers prefer tight deadlines to no time limits at all. We seem to recognize that we need such external prods to combine with self-discipline.

Qualitative overload exists when the job's requirements outstrip the employee's skills. This problem arises frequently when the novice—whether bank teller, nurse, or pathologist—is assigned "tough cases" worthy of the seasoned veteran. It also results from assigning individuals to jobs for which they are not equipped, although they persist in the struggle because of the prospects of high income or social status. Sometimes this problem simply represents the unfortunate judgment of personnel managers. While such mismatches are often corrected—although at great expense to the employee's self-confidence—a person frequently will struggle to achieve barely acceptable results, working twice as hard under twice as much tension as a fully qualified person.

Finally, there is a different type of overload: being overwhelmed by a plethora of separate, essentially unrelated tasks. The problem is not simply long hours or that any one task carries a fast-approaching deadline or strains the person's skill. The root of the problem lies in the externally imposed demands for attentional shift and the interruption of response sequences. The "start-up cost" of shifting one's concentration is, in itself, a considerable stressor. This type of stressor characterizes the job often defined as *general administration* and is especially likely to occur with lower-level supervisors. It can become a pathological condition when the individual:

1. Cannot or will not delegate chores to subordinates.
2. Has no clear sense of where the job's real responsibilities begin and end.
3. Cannot refuse a new imposition for fear of reprisal, of alienating someone, or of creating a bad image.

This type of overload typically does not develop overnight. It evolves in an insidious fashion as an individual accedes to—or even volunteers for—a series of what seem to be finite, limited services. As the person strives in good faith to perform these services effectively and expeditiously the message comes across that "this is a person we can count on." What seem to be one-shot episodes gradually become ongoing expectations. The role has expanded because the individual, by adopting a flexible posture toward the discretionary boundaries of the job, has pushed out its limits to include a greater variety of responsibilities. Soon the individual finds the organizational role crowding into other life roles (such as the family member role). He or she stews over the disarray of unfinished business, and becomes overburdened by the items on the "guilt shelf." In an ideal situation, organizations would provide occasional short-term "moratoria" for overloaded employees to take stock of accumulated commitments, prune away

FOCUS ON THE FUTURE

Job Sabbaticals in the 90s?

One possible antidote to occupational burnout is the sabbatical, heretofore the treasured privilege of professors (or, as one wag called it, "the leisure of the theory class"). Consultant Diana Hewitt (Hewitt Associates, Lincolnshire, Ill.) believes that employers are "reacting to stress and job burnout." McDonald's provides eight weeks of unrestricted time off at full pay for every 10 years of full-time service, and 90 percent of those eligible take it. Martin E. Segal, a New York consulting firm, provides two months off at full pay plus $1,500 for travel expenses, but requires that one month be spent in research or study.

Consultant Marilyn Moats Kennedy believes that, even when no provision exists for paid time off, an increasing number of professional and managerial employees (those most able to afford it) will request leaves of absence for three to six months every 10 years or so. And there are indications that more employers will be receptive to such requests. IBM has announced a program offering a year of personal leave for those with 10 years or more of tenure with the company. The program is intended for those who need to care for a new child or sick relative; those who exercise this option get company benefits while on leave and are guaranteed jobs when they return to work.

SOURCE: *The Wall Street Journal,* December 15, 1989; *USA Today,* October 18, 1988.

---

those that are dangling at the edges, and pare them down to a manageable set of high-priority tasks. University professors do something like this when they take sabbatical leave. They have a polite excuse for shedding a stock of obligations, and they can return with a more foresighted resolve to exercise discretion in taking on responsibilities. Unfortunately, an extended sick leave or resignation are often the only ways a manager can accomplish the same thing (see Focus on the Future).

Role Conflict and Ambiguity

Robert Kahn and his research colleagues at the Survey Research Center of the University of Michigan (Kahn, Wolfe, Quinn, Snoek, & Rosenthal, 1964) have found that role conflict and ambiguity represent significant sources of stress in large organizations. They define role conflict as the "simultaneous occurrence of two (or more) sets of pressures such that compliance with one would make more difficult," or impossible, compliance with the other. For example, a supervisor may be pressed by superiors to maximize production from subordinates, yet at the same time to avoid morale problems that may lead to absenteeism, turnover, or grievances processed by the union. Sales executives are sometimes put in the position of having to violate the law or business ethics to achieve the product market penetration demanded by superiors.

Kahn et al. found role conflict to be associated with greater levels of interpersonal tension, lower job satisfaction, lower levels of trust and respect for persons exerting the conflicting role pressures, and decreased confidence in the organization. Role conflict cannot be eliminated from organizations. Kahn suggests, however, that it could be kept within reasonable bounds if organization design took due account of the relationships between various roles.

Role ambiguity is the uncertainty surrounding one's job definition: uncertainty concerning the expectations held by others for one's job performance, the steps necessary to go about meeting those expectations, and the consequences of one's job behavior. As Kahn notes, "efficient goal-directed behavior is based on predictability of future events" (Kahn et al., 1964, p. 72). To this might be added the observation that instrumental behavior depends on clarifying what goals are relevant and on what behavior is essential to move toward those goals. A person with a high degree of role ambiguity simply has no plans to guide behavior.

Individuals seem to differ vastly on the extent to which they find role ambiguity stressful. Regardless of intelligence or competence, some people seem to demand a high degree of structure in their lives, while others tolerate — and even thrive on — ambiguity.

In addition to individual differences that determine the degree of stress caused by role ambiguity, there are factors in the job environment that make ambiguity more or less aversive. One of these seems to be the general level of pressure induced by organizational demands. When the stakes or consequences associated with instrumental role performance are very great, ambiguity is most aversive. When the job climate is more supportive, ambiguity seems to be more tolerable, and sometimes even preferable to highly structured roles. This should not be surprising, since greater amounts of freedom, autonomy, and discretion in one's job must inevitably mean some increase in role ambiguity.

Thus, where role ambiguity is unavoidable — due to the very nature of the job or task — the administrator can ameliorate the resultant stress either by trying to provide a more supportive climate or by giving special attention and guidance to those persons with a low tolerance to ambiguity.

Organizational Politics

A survey of over 2,500 middle- and upper-level managers by Kiev and Kohn (1979) found that respondents pointed to the "general political climate" of the organization as the third most frequently cited source of stress (the first two were, respectively, "heavy workload" and "disparity between what I have to do on the job and what I would like to accomplish"). This finding reflects the inescapable reality that in organizations, one depends on others. To achieve virtually anything of substance, you have to elicit the cooperation of other people. Failure to recognize and manage these dependencies will doom one to chronic frustration and resentment.

Organizational politics becomes most stressful to those who temperamentally are ill-equipped to cope with it. Often this is the type of person who needs to achieve but has little need for power, whose rigid set of values defines any form of concession as "selling out." As this person runs into one obstacle after another in the pursuit of achievement, "politics" becomes the focus of nightmares and impotent rage.

This is not to say that politics causes stress only for "unreasonable" people. The point, rather, is that you cannot manage this source of stress simply by demeaning politics as something beneath you. It is an inevitable condition of organizations when different people want different things and reach a consensus only by give-and-take and forming coalitions.

Type A Behavior

Sometimes the organizational environment provides the demands that trigger the stress response. In other cases, it serves as the arena in which individuals place demands on themselves. The latter circumstance seems best to characterize the stressful syndrome that Friedman and Rosenman (1974) call *Type A behavior.*

The Type A syndrome is one of chronic, combative struggle with the social and physical environment. The Type A strives to do things quickly, to do several things at once, to achieve the maximum efficiency and output in the time available (see Close-Up). The Type A eats fast, walks fast, will try to read mail while carrying on a telephone conversation, or will dictate to a recorder while driving—anything to squeeze more from the seconds and minutes. Friedman and Rosenman describe one Type A who used two electric razors, one on each side of the face to get a head start on the workday.

Any person or object that threatens the Type A's control over the pace of events becomes the focus of barely suppressed hostility. The Type A tends to interrupt and finish sentences for someone who speaks very slowly (Friedman finds this a useful test for diagnosing whether a client is a Type A); to break in and finish a task for a subordinate who doesn't work quickly; to grip the steering wheel so tightly that knuckles turn white when a slow driver ahead cannot be passed; to pace impatiently when a push of the button does not immediately bring the elevator.

Glass (1977), from a series of laboratory experiments using college students as subjects, has elaborated on this behavioral syndrome. Both Type As and their counterparts—the more deliberate, easygoing type Bs—will work fast when given a difficult goal or time limit, but the Type A, unlike the B, works just as fast when there are no time pressures. Also, when placed

---

CLOSE-UP

Type A Behavior: The Tell-Tale Indicators

A variety of questionnaires have been developed to measure Type A syndrome. While those measures are useful for some purposes, they are not as reliable for predicting coronary disease as are clinical assessments by trained interviewers. These interviewers typically look for such Type A clues as the following:

1. A subject's tendency to accentuate key words in ordinary speech, even when there is no need for it, or the tendency to utter the last few words of sentences more rapidly than the opening words.

2. A tendency to hurry the speech of the interviewer, by nodding the head vigorously, saying "uh huh, uh huh," repeatedly, or even attempting to finish the interviewer's sentences.

3. Characteristic gestures or nervous tics, such as clenching the fists, banging one fist into the other palm to emphasize a point, habitually clenching the jaw, or frequently jerking the corners of the mouth backward and exposing the teeth.

4. An obsession with translating and evaluating his or her activities, as well as others', in terms of numbers.

5. The habit of always moving, walking, and eating rapidly.

6. Extreme impatience with repetitious chores, such as writing checks, making out bank deposit slips, or signing travelers' checks.

7. A general insensitivity to unobtrusive aesthetic details, such as flowers, pictures, dress, wallpaper patterns, or the fine textures of materials and surroundings.

8. Frequent use of Anglo-Saxon obscenities.

9. Rapid blinking (over 30 times per minute).

10. Rapid, vigorous finger-tapping or knee-jiggling.

SOURCES: M. Friedman and R. Rosenman (1974), *Type A Behavior and your heart* (New York: Knopf); M. Friedman and D. Ulmer (1984), *Treating Type A behavior and your heart* (New York: Knopf).

---

on a treadmill to test aerobic conditioning, Type As suppress any feelings of fatigue as the angle and speed of the treadmill approach the limits of their aerobic capacity.

In his novel *The Hurricane Years,* Cameron Hawley has given us a character, Judd Wilder, who personifies the Type A. Wilder, an executive for a carpet company, is driving from New York to corporate headquarters in Pennsylvania, trying to deliver proofs of the stockholders' report by 8:30 p.m. that evening. There is no compelling reason why the report has to arrive at that time; it is simply one of the innumerable goals Wilder instinctively and unceasingly sets to stretch himself to the limit. Behind the wheel, he experiences a massive heart attack. Rushed to a county hospital, he comes under the care of Dr. Aaron Kharr, who soon recognizes the type: "inherently aggressive, competitive, energetic, and ambitious. . . ."

Not surprisingly, Type As thrive in an atmosphere of tight deadlines and goal setting. Given such jobs, they actually turn out quite a bit of work. They often excel in middle-management and sales jobs, but seldom make it to the top of the organization. The reasons: they cannot comfortably dwell at length on really critical issues before reaching a considered judgment, and their easily aroused impatience and hostility aggravate their co-workers.

In a predictive longitudinal study of several thousand 39- to 59-year-old males, Friedman and Rosenman (1974) found that those clinically categorized as Type As ran at least double the risk of Type Bs of experiencing premature coronary artery disease. Unrelenting combativeness and the hostility and rage evoked by frustration cause the body to produce high levels of adrenal hormones. These hormones, when not serving the fight-or-flight response for which evolution designed them, increase the clotting elements in the blood that may accelerate the formation of arterial plaque.

Recent research at Duke University Medical Center (Wood, 1986) suggests that hostility is the truly "toxic component" of the Type A behavior syndrome. Anger and irritation seem to represent the pathogenic elements of coronary-proneness. In fact, researchers found that a simple questionnaire measure of the frequency and intensity with which a person experienced hostile rage (whether openly expressed or not) predicted coronary disease better than the usual measures of Type A tendencies. Thus, the individual who likes to operate at a fast pace need not fear the worst, provided he or she does not respond to a forced slowdown with anger.

Certain characteristics of organizational environments clearly cater to such a stress-prone profile. However, we would indict organizations unfairly if we blamed them for this behavior. Type As show this cluster of traits in many settings — at parties, on a sailboat, at a backyard family outing, even in bed. On the other hand, while Type Bs respond with haste and struggle to difficult, pressing circumstances, they have no problem dropping back to a more measured tempo under less harried conditions.

Fortunately, we now have reason to believe that people can alter their Type A tendencies. Friedman and Ulmer (1984) carried out a four-year experimental program with more than 1,000 heart attack victims and successfully treated the Type A condition. In so doing, they cut the risk of a repeat heart attack by over 50 percent in comparison with a control group that underwent the more conventional treatment of diet, exercise, and reduction of risk factors.

Occupational Differences

Studies by the National Institute on Workers' Compensation and the American Institute of Stress reveal a consistent clustering of certain types of jobs that account for a disproportionate share of worker compensation claims and stress-related illness. Some of these occupations are noteworthy for their constant physical hazards, as in the case of miners and police officers. But the more characteristic feature of jobs correlated with such symptoms as high blood pressure is the combination of *high psychological demand* and *low decisional control*. In other words, the "killer jobs" expose people to high levels of pressure and responsibility while giving them little authority or few resources to deal with the problems. Contrary to popular stereotype, CEOs, high-ranking corporate officials, surgeons, bankers, and CPAs are not the coronary-prone occupations; true, these vocations impose considerable job pressures, but they provide the training, power, and staff with which to manage the problems. On the other hand, waitresses, cashiers, telephone operators, customer service representatives, and inner-city school teachers face a stream of problems—usually from outside parties—but have few options other than to absorb them and stoically accept the abuse.

STRESS AND PERFORMANCE

For many years, people have pondered how stress affects performance. Some would argue that stress has a negative effect, citing the case of a young executive whose work deteriorates under the critical glare of a cruel boss, or the student whose As drop to Cs during her parents' bitter separation. Others take the opposite view, that stress brings out a person's mettle; they name a destitute composer who produces a masterpiece while nursing a deathly ill child, or the writer whose best work is created in noisy surroundings under a pressing deadline. Still others present a more complex view: moderate stress improves performance while extreme stress undermines performance. Finally, some thinkers see this issue as defined by moderator variables: the effects of stress depend on the situation, the task, or the person.

What seems to be missing from these views is the consideration of performance itself as a stressor, as part of the total demands made on the organism. Consider, for example, a study of clerical workers conducted by Levi (1967). Preliminary observation showed that 12 women normally processed about 160 invoices per hour. Suddenly the researchers intervened and offered a steeply progressive system of incentives above the monthly wages. Production increased by over 100 percent, with no increase in errors. But urine samples taken from the workers showed a significant elevation of the stress hormones, noradrenaline and adrenaline. Also, the subjects complained of exhaustion and muscular aches after completing the workday. When the researchers withdrew the incentive, stress hormones returned to baseline levels, and somatic symptoms declined.

How do we interpret these findings? It would appear that an individual, given reasonable workloads and standard work conditions, establishes an equilibrium of effort. If a person significantly departs from this balanced condition, the resulting demand triggers the stress response.

What if performance is not increased, but simply maintained while surrounding conditions deviate from the equilibrium? A study by Glass and Singer (1972) suggests what may happen. They gave subjects some clerical tasks to perform under conditions of random, intermittent, irritating noise, while others worked under standard conditions. The noise had no effect one way or the other on either quantity or quality of performance. But after the noise had ceased, and after the people had finished the assigned task, some interesting findings came to light. When given a puzzle to solve—and unbeknownst to the subjects, the puzzle had no solution—those who had worked with the noise showed less tolerance for the frustration of working on the solutionless puzzle. They gave up sooner than the people who earlier had worked under less vexing circumstances.

When you have to work in the presence of significant stressors—noise, interruptions, or strained relationships with work associates—you have a choice. You may elect to exert the same overall level of demand on yourself, in which case performance probably will show some deterioration (the more difficult the task, the sooner this will become manifest). Or, you may expend a higher level of mental and physical effort to maintain (or even increase) performance level—and this increases the total demand placed on you. Eventually, there must be a letdown, but it may not show on the job. It might be reflected in less tolerance for delays on the ride home, or by the inability to remember your gym locker number or what you were supposed to get at the grocery store. Still another possibility is that you simply endure a chronic level of demand to maintain normal functioning. But eventually the accumulated demands temporarily exhaust the endocrine system, which is then overcome by a virus to which it can no longer present a solid shield of immunity. Any of an array of illnesses results.

Cohen (1980) has reviewed many studies documenting the effects of stress on behavior. The stressors studied include noise, exposure to electric shock, crowding, bureaucratic harassment, discrimination, and information overload. These studies generally find no immediate negative effects of stressors on performance. Rather, the evidence suggests that subjects in some way adapt so they can maintain performance, at least temporarily.

This adaptive process exacts a considerable and cumulative toll, which generally is not evident until after termination of the stressors. A subject's depletion of psychic reserves manifests itself in lowered frustration tolerance and in less efficient performance on tasks performed after the original stressor has ceased. Also, subjects maintaining their performance while beset by environmental stressors display less sensitivity afterwards to the needs of others (for example, subjects are less likely to help a stranger). Fortunately, the effects of stress are mitigated by any device that makes the stress more *predictable* or provides some potential for *personal control* over the timing or magnitude of the stressor.

In sum, it is the combination of stressors, the aggregate demand on the mind-body system, that we have to consider. Dramatic, sustained levels of performance beyond "normal" represent one such demand. So does maintaining performance under "abnormal" conditions. The more pertinent question is not, What is the effect of stress on performance? (since that can hardly be predicted) but, What is the eventual effect of *sustaining performance* under the load of increased environmental stressors?

MANAGING STRESS

Organizational Responses

Corporate officers have good reason for concern about stress in the workplace, aside from its effect on morale or the burnout of valuable staff. They know that an increasing number of employees now take to the courts, sometimes successfully, with claims of job-induced stress. From 1982 to 1986, damage suits against employers for stress-related illness increased five-fold (Roberts & Harris, 1989). In 1988, U.S. workers filed a record number of stress-related workers' compensation claims, some of which targeted inconsiderate, unreasonable pressure from supervisors. Such actions accounted for 14 percent of all occupational-disease claims, as opposed to 5 percent in 1980.

Ivancevich, Matteson, Freedman, and Phillips (1990) provide a progress report of the commitment of American corporations to programs for managing stress. Most of the early examples of such programs could be described as *reactive* rather than preventive. While they were well-intended, their focus was on identifying individuals with symptoms suggesting stress or burnout, referring the person to a health-care professional for counseling or other treatment, and trying to teach the individual practical methods for coping with stress. Union leaders charge that such programs favor white-collar and managerial employees; they also suggest that stress-management should try to change work operations that create the stress, rather than treat physical and emotional symptoms as the result of some deficiency in the individual.

Perhaps in response to such observations, the later generation of organizational stress-management programs have a more preventive, group-based orientation. Such programs include stress-management seminars, exercise programs, on-site monitoring of cholesterol and hypertension levels, nutritional counseling, and representative employee committees to make recommendations for constructive changes that mitigate pressure, hazards, and tension in the workplace (Murphey & Hurrell, 1987).

We have scant knowledge about the actual benefits of stress management programs. Ivancevich et al. (1990) describe present knowledge as "largely based on anecdotes, testimonials, and methodologically weak research." On the positive side, there is evidence of a slowly increasing commitment to rigorous evaluation of worksite interventions to manage stress.

FOCUS ON MANAGEMENT

Executive Stress: A Survey

The chairman of a large textile company says that he exercises and runs around with wild women. Another chief executive officer who owns a ranch reports that he likes to look at the cows and drink Dr. Pepper. Other top-level managers have their own favorite methods for relieving job stress.

These findings come from a Gallup poll of 327 chief executives of large corporations, 312 CEOs of medium-sized companies, and 206 small business proprietors. The poll, conducted for *The Wall Street Journal,* revealed that owners of small businesses were more than twice as likely as leaders of large firms to cite job stress as a problem. The relationship between degree of managerial stress and size of company was almost perfectly inverse. Furthermore, the major causes of stress, as well as the amount, varied with firm size: Executives of larger companies cited employee problems as the most frequent stressor, while small business owners attributed their distress to cash-flow and other financial strains.

A majority of the respondents from all types of organizations mentioned exercise (golf, tennis, hunting, jogging) as a means of coping with job tensions. Most of the executives also thought it important "not to bottle it up," but to occasionally scream or kick the desk. They also emphasized the value of a long-run perspective ("Judge your career on a year-to-year basis and not on things that happen in daily operations").

Whereas 48 percent of the managers under age 45 complained of stress, only 29 percent of those over 45 reported stress as a significant problem.

While a substantial percentage of the executives experienced stress to the extent that they suffered physical problems (e.g., insomnia) or often found it difficult to relax at home, only a tiny minority said they would be happier in a less demanding job.

SOURCE: Roger Ricklefs, "Many Executives Complain of Stress, but Few Want Less-Pressured Jobs," *The Wall Street Journal,* September 29, 1982. Reprinted by permission of *The Wall Street Journal,* Dow Jones & Company, Inc., September 29, 1982. All rights reserved.

Individual Response

We can scarcely speak of eliminating stress at work. Since stress is a state of the organism under environmental demands, and since work—even the best, most absorbing work—presents demands of some nature, we have to take the more feasible tack of managing these demands (see Focus on Management).

1. *Assess the trade-off.* The essential task of managing is to allocate your resources for the best return. If something costs 50 percent more but gives you only 2 percent more satisfaction, you look for a better bargain.

Most managers and professionals agree that 80 percent of your success or accomplishments in a job come from 20 percent of the things you do. If that is the case, and if you can identify that 20 percent, then obviously it makes sense to spare no demands on yourself to do those parts of the job well. Long hours, skipped lunches, extra coffee, worry, strain—they take some toll, but the payoff justifies them. But what about the 80 percent of the job that determines only 20 percent of your success (however you choose to define it)? Those parts of the job have to be done, but it makes no sense to wear yourself down doing them any faster or better than necessary.

The very flexible person indiscriminately takes on added duties without assessing the trade-off and becomes the victim of overload. The very rigid person brooks no compromises and does not consider whether minor concessions could promote essential aims. He or she becomes the victim of impotent rage when thwarted by dependence on others. The Type A presses to the limit of endurance without regard to external urgency and becomes the victim of an addiction to his or her own adrenaline.

The reader may object that not all stressors are matters of choice. True enough. But a considerable proportion are either of our own making or are magnified by our unwitting collaboration. You probably cannot prevent the tire that punctures on the way to work. But you can decide if the consequences of being late call for a frenzied struggle; and when you get to work you can decide whether the day's agenda justifies a breakneck pace to make up for lost time.

2. *Balance the load.* As we have emphasized above, the important consideration is the aggregate demand placed on the organism. Heavy job demands may be compensated by lesser demands elsewhere. The executive who works long hours and competes ferociously but enjoys a tranquil family life and relaxing hobby may suffer less stress than someone who glides through a nine-to-five routine and spends the rest of the waking hours in bitter disputes with spouse and kids. Vacations and occasional long weekends provide some compensation, but not if they demand a frenetic pace and offer no opportunity to reflect and drop one's guard.

3. *Fine-tune the mind-body system.* The organism's stress response proved functional in the slow evolution of the species so long as the major threats encountered were physical—such as a germ, a falling tree, or a predator. Such threats called either for resistance via the immune system or the quick burst of adrenaline that enabled a person to fight or run. From time to time, we still need to fight or run, and we certainly still need our immune system. But on many occasions the stress response is triggered by conditioned emotional responses and other reactions to verbal, social, and symbolic stimuli. On those occasions the stress response represents a waste of the organism's resources. What the mind-body system requires is some sort of fine-tuning to inhibit wasteful stress responses.

One such conditioning factor seems to be contacts with others. James J. Lynch (1977) assembled data that argue strongly for the protective role of human companionship. He found that the age-adjusted death rates for persons who are divorced, single, or widowed significantly exceed those for married persons, and that the difference is consistent over a large number of diseases and specific causes of death. He also cited laboratory findings that show that the pulse rates of animals exposed to noxious stimuli (such as loud noises previously paired with electric shock) is substantially moderated by the physical presence of a human being. Back and Bogdonoff (1964) found that a threatening interview evokes a sharper physiological stress response among subjects interviewed alone than among those accompanied by an acquaintance.

It is not yet clear exactly how companionship serves this protective role. But findings suggest that the individual firmly anchored in close, supportive relationships has a powerful ally in managing stress. The effects are not simply psychological; they are also physiological and can be objectively quantified.

Moderate exercise constitutes a second conditioning factor. Exercise itself is a stressor. But taken in small, regular doses, evidence suggests that the effect is to tone the mind-body system and dampen the stress response to the day's succession of minor problems and irritations. An aerobically conditioned individual not only has a lower resting pulse rate, but also responds to sudden crisis with a less pronounced rise in heart rate.

Herbert Benson (1974), drawing on the evidence that various forms of meditation have beneficial physiological effects, has suggested that managers practice the "relaxation response." A session takes only 20 minutes, about the length of a coffee break. All you need to do is take a comfortable position in a quiet place, close your eyes, try to relax all your muscles, and focus your attention on the rhythmic sound of your breathing. Benson emphasizes the importance of not forcing the response or worrying about "how well you're doing," but simply practicing it with a passive attitude. He has used this technique with considerable success in treating hypertension. This relaxation response evokes many of the physiologic changes (such as decreased oxygen consumption, lower pulse rate, and reduced muscle tension) found with other forms of meditation. These effects become stable, lasting well beyond the duration of the relaxation period. They fine-tune the body by "alleviating the effects of the environmentally induced, but often inappropriate, fight-or-flight response" of the endocrine system.

Many people have their own forms of "relaxation response" or "meditation." Prayer, appreciation of simple rituals, solitary reflection in a personal retreat—all appear to capture the essence of the relaxation response.

CONCLUSION

Managers have a dual responsibility: they must manage their own stress and manage the demands placed on others. Ethical as well as pragmatic considerations enter into any approach to balancing these responsibilities.

The martyr who spares everyone else by burning up his or her own resources will probably not realize the optimal contribution of the work group. The supreme egoist who deflects every imposition onto others will sooner or later become estranged from the salubrious bonds of fellowship. With stress, as with so many issues, equity and moderation seem to represent the best guidelines.

However, we would venture to say that more administrators — especially at lower or middle ranks — err in the direction of neglecting to manage their own demands, accepting and imposing excessive demands on their own reserves. Whether this follows from pride, a sense of noblesse oblige, or genuine concern for those around them, in the end it probably becomes a self-defeating process, because managers under inordinate stress tend to create unintended stress for those around them. Supporting this hypothesis is the observation, from study after study, that higher-level managers report less stress and enjoy better health than those of the same age at lower echelons. We suspect that those who manage their own demands put to better use their total resources — including the energy and vitality of others.

SUMMARY

The popular and scientific meanings of the term *stress* overlap, but do not coincide. In everyday discourse, we use it to refer to situations and emotions that combine to produce distress. Selye developed the construct to refer to the nonspecific response of the organism's endocrine system to any demand placed on it — regardless of how those demands are evaluated or whether they produce uncomfortable feelings. Illness follows when the total set of demands over time impairs the immune function of the endocrine system. Emotional stressors include frustration, anxiety, depression, and any other strong emotion. Job-related stressors that create particular problems are job overload, organizational politics, role conflict, role ambiguity, and Type A behavior. In general, the high-stress occupations are those that expose individuals to high levels of psychological demand while providing little decisional control over events. Stressors may or may not affect performance, but the struggle to maintain performance under adverse circumstances adds to the total set of demands on the organism. Approaches to managing stress include an increasing number of corporate programs to identify casualties of stress and interventions to reduce or prevent excessive pressures in the workplace. The individual's responsibilities for managing his or her own stress include assessing the trade-offs between additional self-imposed demands, compensation, and moderating the body's inappropriate stress responses. The latter appears to be accomplished by close relationships, reasonable exercise, and various forms of meditation or related behavior.

CONCEPTS TO REMEMBER

Stress	Anticipatory stress response	Anxiety
General Adaptation	Frustration	Role conflict
Syndrome	Frustration tolerance	Role ambiguity
Alarm reaction	Depression	Role set
Resistance	Aggression	Job overload
Exhaustion	Displaced aggression	Type A behavior
Endocrine system	Burnout	Stress management

QUESTIONS FOR DISCUSSION

1. Provide several definitions of the often-used term *stress tolerance*.

2. What might cause people to view frustration on the job as arbitrary, even though there really is a good reason for the events causing the frustration?

3. One author has referred to guilt and anxiety as "useless emotions." Do you agree?

4. What are the various ways in which a cohesive work group aids its members in the management of stress?

5. Over the course of the last decade, what developments have tended to increase stress? To decrease it? What developments in the next decade do you foresee that will add to or diminish work stress?

REFERENCES

Abramson, L. Y., & Sackheim, H. A. (1977). A paradox in depression: Uncontrollability and self-blame. *Psychological Bulletin* 84, 838–51.

Andrews, F. M., & Farris, G. F. (1972). Time pressure and performance of scientists and engineers: A five-year panel study. *Organizational Behavior and Human Performance* 8, 185–200.

Back, K. W., & Bogdonoff, M. (1964). Plasma lipid responses to leadership, conformity, and deviation. In P. H. Leiderman & D. Shapiro (eds.), *Psycho-biological approaches to social behavior*. Stanford, CA: Stanford University Press.

Benson, H. (1974). Your innate asset for combatting stress. *Harvard Business Review,* July–August, pp. 49–60.

Cantril, H. (1957). Perception and interpersonal relations. *American Journal of Psychiatry* 114(2), 27–29.

Cohen, S. (1980). After effects of stress on human performance and social behavior: A review of research and theory. *Psychological Bulletin* 88, 82–108.

Depression (1987). *Newsweek,* May 4.

Flach, F. F. (1974). *The secret strength of depression*. Philadelphia: J. B. Lippincott.

Friedman, M., & Rosenman, R. H. (1974). *Type A behavior and your heart*. New York: Alfred A. Knopf.

Friedman, M., & Ulmer, D. (1984). *Treating Type A behavior and your heart*. New York: Knopf.

Gaines, J., & Jermier, J. M. (1983). Emotional exhaustion in a high stress organization. *Academy of Management Journal* 26, 567–86.

Glass, D. C. (1977). *Behavior patterns, stress, and coronary disease*. Hillsdale, NJ: Laurence Erlbaum Associates.

Glass, D. C., & Singer, J. E. (1972). *Urban stress*. New York: Academic Press.

Hawley, C. (1968). *The hurricane years*. Greenwich, CT: Fawcett Publications.

Holmes, T. H., & Rahe, R. H. (1968). The social readjustment rating scale. *Journal of Psychosomatic Research* 2, 213–18.

IBM guarantee: Leave job and keep it. *USA Today,* October 18, 1988.

Ivancevich, J. M., Matteson, M. T., Freedman, S. M., & Phillips, J. S. (1990). Worksite stress management interventions. *American Psychologist* 45, 252–61.

Janoff-Bulman, R. (1979). Characterological versus behavioral self-blame: Inquiries into depression and rape. *Journal of Personality and Social Psychology* 37, 1798–1809.

Job sabbaticals loom as popular perk of '90s. *The Wall Street Journal,* December 15, 1989.

Kahn, R. W., Wolfe, D. M., Quinn, R. P., Snoek, J. D., & Rosenthal, R. A. (1964). *Organizational stress*. New York: John Wiley & Sons.

Kiev, A., & Kohn, V. (1979). *Executive stress: An AMA survey report*. New York: AMA-COM.

Kline, N. (1974). *From sad to glad*. New York: G. P. Putnam & Sons.

Kobasa, S. (1979). Stressful life events, personality, and health: An inquiry into hardiness. *Journal of Personality and Social Psychology* 37, 1–11.

Kobasa, S., Maddi, S., & Kahn, S. (1982). Hardiness and health: A prospective study. *Journal of Personality and Social Psychology* 42, 168–77.

Levi, L. (1967). *Stress: Sources, management, and prevention*. New York: Liveright.

Levi, L. (1972). Stress and distress in response to psychosocial stimuli. *Acta Medica Scandinavica,* Supplement 528, 119–42.

Levinson, H. (1959). The psychologist in industry. *Harvard Business Review* 37, 93–99.

Lynch, J. J. (1977). *The broken heart: The medical consequences of loneliness*. New York: Basic Books.

Maslach, C., & Jackson, S. E. (1981). The measurement of experienced burnout. *Journal of Occupational Behavior* 2, 99–113.

Murphy, L. R., & Hurrell, J. J., Jr. (1987). Stress management in the process of occupational stress reduction. *Journal of Managerial Psychology* 2, 18–23.

Ricklefs, R. (1982). Many executives complain of stress, but few want less demanding jobs. *The Wall Street Journal,* September 29.

Roberts, M., & Harris, G. T. (1989). Wellness at work. *Psychology Today,* May 1989, 54–58.

Roethlisberger, F. J., & Dickson, W. J. (1964). *Management and the worker*. New York: Wiley Science Editions.

Ruch, L. O., & Holmes, T. H. (1971). Scaling of life change: Comparison of direct and indirect methods. *Journal of Psychosomatic Research* 15, 221–27.

Selye, H. (1956). *The stress of life*. New York: McGraw-Hill.

Toffler, A. (1970). *Future shock*. New York: Random House.

Weick, K. E. (1975). The management of stress. *MBA* 9, October, 37–41.

Wood, C. (1986). The hostile heart. *Psychology Today,* September, 10–12.

15 Careers

What does it mean to have a successful career?
What are the problems faced by employees in managing their careers?
What are the problems of career management faced by organizations?

Do you ever wonder what your career holds in store for you? Do you wonder whether you will be a "success" or a "failure"? Do you reflect on your strengths and weaknesses, and on what career might be right for you? Is your career more or less important than family, friends, and nonwork pursuits?

These are weighty questions. Most of us consider such questions on occasion, but few make a concerted effort to expand their career options and examine ways to attain personal goals. People tend to be passive, letting others initiate important career decisions rather than make decisions themselves on the basis of their own interests and goals (Roe & Baruch, 1967). Professionals and administrators probably make higher-quality decisions about their subordinates and their capital assets than they do in managing their own careers (Hall, 1976).

In this chapter, we will discuss careers from the standpoint of both the individual and the employing organization. After completing the chapter, you may not have answers to the difficult questions posed in the first paragraph, but you will have been exposed to important research and current thinking about careers. This exposure should prod you to think about the issues and help you make optimal career decisions and anticipate and cope with career-related problems.

The chapter is organized into six major sections: general perspectives on careers, the nature of career progressions, the primary stages of careers, socialization, career management by the organization, and career management by the individual.

PERSPECTIVES ON CAREERS

Before describing how careers unfold and how they can best be managed, it is important to articulate the basic premises that pervade our discussion. Some of the more important premises will emerge when we examine why careers are important, the meanings of career success and failure, and where responsibility for career management resides.

The Importance of Careers

Careers are important because they represent peoples' entire lives in the work environment (Hall, 1976), and work largely determines overall quality of life. Careers are a prime concern of employees, and managers should remember that subordinates see administrative policies in relation to their personal careers. They often are more concerned with pay scales, job opportunities, chances for promotion, and other tangible aspects of careers than with what is best for the company. Since organizational effectiveness is influenced by the organization's ability to help meet the needs of its membership (Cummings, 1978), decision makers should consider career-related issues in establishing management practices.

Work is viewed as central to the achievement of social equality (Hall, 1976). Job hiring and promotion practices for women, minorities, working mothers, and older employees have had high visibility in recent years. Job quality (not simply employment per se) is a means to upgrade peoples' lives and may become more a subject of legislation in coming years. Thus, careers are vehicles for social reform and are coming under more public scrutiny than ever before.

Career Success and Failure

Success in a career does not necessarily imply a company presidency, being on the fast track for promotions, or making a six-figure salary. At the same time, failure does not necessarily connote the absence of those achievements. If an individual defines success and failure in those terms, she can use those criteria to draw conclusions about her own success or failure, but the same criteria cannot be applied to everyone.

In other words, different people define success differently, using different criteria. People can be classified according to their *career anchors,* or self-perceptions of their motives, talents, and values (Schein, 1978). These self-concepts guide, stabilize, and integrate peoples' careers and provide meaningful inner standards of career success. Table 15–1 summarizes the characteristics of five career anchors, as well as career paths typical of people holding the different anchors.

Some individuals hold as their primary concern technical competence in some functional area like accounting, engineering, or information systems. People with this *technical* career anchor disdain general—but can live with functional—management. They define success by ever-increasing challenges and from feedback that they are expert in their field.

On the other hand, individuals with the *managerial anchor* thrive on the analytical, interpersonal, and emotional skills of management. These people measure their success by income, rank, and promotions—indications of responsibility.

Other career anchors are security, autonomy, and creativity. A *security* anchor typifies the organization man (Whyte, 1956), the conformist who defines success by stable, secure work and home situations. People with *autonomy* anchors consider themselves successful to the extent they can determine their own schedules, work habits, and lifestyles. Finally, the *creativity* anchor, central to most entrepreneurs, represents a need to build something of one's own. Financial success is important, but the real success criterion for these individuals is creative accomplishment.

Thus, career success is best assessed by the individual (see Focus on International OB for a pertinent international study). This ethic of self-evaluation is consistent with recent social movements that emphasize the right to self-determination (Hall, 1976). Raising the mandatory retirement age, career opportunities in traditionally male or female-dominated jobs, and an increased willingness of employees to refuse promotions (and of employers to accept such refusals) all recognize the individual's responsibility to make his or her own life choices.

TABLE 15–1
Career Anchors

Career Anchor	Characteristics	Typical Career Paths
1. Technical/functional competence	1. Excited by work itself 2. Willing to forego promotions 3. Dislikes general management and corporate politics	1. Research-oriented positions 2. Functional department management jobs 3. Specialized consulting and project management
2. Managerial competence	1. Likes to analyze and solve knotty business problems 2. Likes to influence and harness people to work together 3. Enjoys the exercise of power	1. Vice presidencies 2. Plant management and sales management 3. Large, prestigious firms
3. Security and stability	1. Motivated by job security and long-term careers with one firm 2. Dislikes travel and relocation 3. Tends to be conformist and compliant to the organization	1. Government jobs 2. Small, family-owned businesses 3. Large government-regulated industries
4. Creativity/entrepreneurship	1. Enjoys launching own business 2. Restless; moves from project to project 3. Prefers small, up and coming firms to well-established ones	1. Entrepreneurial ventures 2. Stock options, arbitrage, mergers and acquisitions 3. General management consulting
5. Autonomy and independence	1. Desires freedom from organizational constraints 2. Wants to be on own and set own pace 3. Avoids large businesses and governmental agencies	1. Academia 2. Writing and publishing 3. Small business proprietorships

SOURCE: Edgar Schein, *Career Dynamics,* © 1978, by Addison-Wesley Publishing Co., Inc., Reading, Massachusetts. Adapted material from pages 124-160. Reprinted with permission of the publisher.

Responsibility for Career Management

Responsibility for career management lies with both the individual and the organization, but it is not safe to assume that both sides accept this responsibility. Commonly, both parties abdicate the responsibility and assume that the other is doing its share. For the individual, the *safest* assumption is that the organization is not going to automatically take care of his or her career needs. Similarly, the organization might best assume that employees are not properly attending to their own personal career management strategies. Both the individual and the organization are responsible for facilitating career success.

The *organization's* staffing needs and career movement policies can affect career opportunities of employees. The *individual* must perform three tasks: (1) assess his or her skills, interests, and potential; (2) identify career objectives and develop a realistic career plan; and (3) prepare for career and for specific target positions by obtaining the necessary training and experience. Even a conscientious effort to tackle these tasks may not result

FOCUS ON INTERNATIONAL OB

Career Success among European Executives

A study at INSEAD (European Institute of Business Administration) of Fontainebleau, France surveyed 150 European executives (Derr & Laurent, 1989). The executives reported their personal definitions of career success. The top five definitions were:

1. Enough influence to get exciting and challenging assignments.
2. "Inner circle" membership in important decisions.
3. The ability to influence events and policies in support of personal values and philosophies.
4. A balance among work progress, relationships (family life, friendships), and self-development activities.
5. The ability to maintain an equilibrium between one's personal and professional lives.

The study went on to assess where the executives stood with regard to five different career success orientations: getting ahead (upward mobility); getting secure (company loyalty and sense of belonging); getting free (autonomy); getting high (excitement of the work itself); and getting balanced (finding an equilibrium between personal and professional life). The entire sample had a getting-balanced orientation—perhaps because they all had been away from home for several weeks when they completed the survey. There were also cross-national differences in career orientations. The British and Swedes were significantly more getting-ahead oriented than the French, who had a higher getting-balanced orientation than the other groups. The researchers were surprised by the Swedish data, where they expected a more getting-balanced orientation. But interviews revealed that the respondents in the sample were from a small group of self-selected Swedish executives who were pursuing high-potential career tracks. In Sweden, it is difficult to find persons willing to go this route because it usually means geographic relocation and upsetting the spouse's career.

in the attainment of chosen career goals. Plans often should or must change as unforeseen opportunities or constraints arise. Thus, career planning and implementation should be considered a dynamic process.

CAREER PROGRESSIONS

There are several well-established models of the stages of career progress. Two widely accepted approaches are relevant here. The first, Hall and Nougaim's (1968) analysis of stages in management careers, identifies the general phases managers go through from the first year of employment through retirement. The second, Schein's (1971) model of career movement through an organization, highlights the important organizational dimensions and boundaries that characterize movements from one job to another.

Hall and Nougaim's Stages of Management Careers

Hall and Nougaim (1968) identified career stages from a study of relatively young AT&T managers in the first five years of their careers. The investigators discovered that the managers' needs and concerns changed significantly over time. This led to their proposal about the shifting stages in managerial careers.

The first stage is the *establishment* stage. It occurs in the first years of employment, and is a period of gaining recognition and getting established in the organization. This was supported by the finding that young managers in their first year needed achievement, esteem, and safety; by the fifth year, the need for safety dropped off dramatically.

The most successful managers were those with the lowest needs for safety in that first year. This, together with an earlier finding (Berlew & Hall, 1966) that tolerance of uncertainty correlates with managerial success, suggests that those young managers who can cope with insecurity and uncertainty will progress the furthest. This result was demonstrated for job attainment five and even ten years down the road.

The second stage is *advancement*. Here, concern for promotion and achievement dominates. The individual is no longer so concerned with fitting in: he or she wants to move up. In the AT&T study, achievement and esteem needs were significantly higher in this stage than they were during the first year.

A *maintenance* stage follows the advancement stage. Hall and Nougaim did not have data covering these years, so their impressions are speculative. However, their observations are consistent with other models (Miller & Form, 1951; Super, 1957). During this stage, people realize that they are nearing the end of their promotional opportunities and gratification must begin to come from sources other than achievement on the job. Some managers who have reached this terminal plateau become concerned with helping younger protégés. In this way, they can contribute to the organization differently than before and leave a lasting imprint. Other managers, bitter and frustrated over their career stalemate, turn to less constructive, even destructive, coping mechanisms. Such responses as alcoholism, midlife crisis, vindictive attempts to block the careers of others, and psychological withdrawal (becoming "deadwood") are legendary.

Self-initiated plateauing, in which people who are happy where they are refuse promotions, is risky (Hymowitz, 1987) but becoming more common (Hall, 1986). Careers often level off earlier than in the past for reasons beyond the person's control, including the trend toward fewer organizational levels and the number of baby-boomers in middle-level positions (Hall, 1986). Given the ramifications of undesired plateaus, it is clearly important for the organization to sensitively manage people who are in this career stage. Table 15–2 summarizes the various conditions and types of career plateaus, and offers appropriate suggestions for how these plateaus can be managed.

TABLE 15-2
Career Plateaus in Organizations

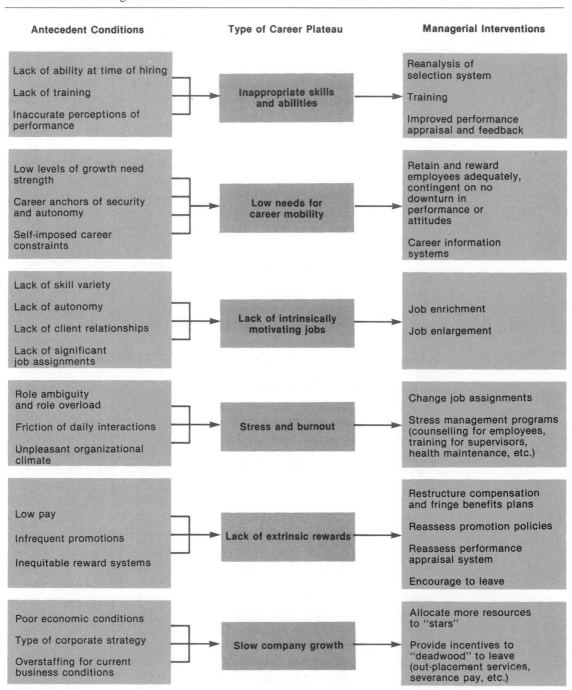

Antecedent Conditions	Type of Career Plateau	Managerial Interventions
Lack of ability at time of hiring / Lack of training / Inaccurate perceptions of performance	Inappropriate skills and abilities	Reanalysis of selection system / Training / Improved performance appraisal and feedback
Low levels of growth need strength / Career anchors of security and autonomy / Self-imposed career constraints	Low needs for career mobility	Retain and reward employees adequately, contingent on no downturn in performance or attitudes / Career information systems
Lack of skill variety / Lack of autonomy / Lack of client relationships / Lack of significant job assignments	Lack of intrinsically motivating jobs	Job enrichment / Job enlargement
Role ambiguity and role overload / Friction of daily interactions / Unpleasant organizational climate	Stress and burnout	Change job assignments / Stress management programs (counselling for employees, training for supervisors, health maintenance, etc.)
Low pay / Infrequent promotions / Inequitable reward systems	Lack of extrinsic rewards	Restructure compensation and fringe benefits plans / Reassess promotion policies / Reassess performance appraisal system / Encourage to leave
Poor economic conditions / Type of corporate strategy / Overstaffing for current business conditions	Slow company growth	Allocate more resources to "stars" / Provide incentives to "deadwood" to leave (out-placement services, severance pay, etc.)

SOURCE: Daniel C. Feldman, Managing Careers in Organizations (Glenview, Ill.: Scott, Foresman, 1988).

Retirement is the final stage of management careers. As recently as 100 years ago, people worked until prevented by illness or death. Now, retirement is common, and some people are forced to take early retirement. As a consequence, the retirement phase is rapidly becoming a major concern to organizations and social activists.

Retirement has been rather badly under-researched. However, certain key variables do seem predictive of successful retirement. Satisfaction in retirement is more likely when: the individual makes the decision about whether or not to retire; the retiree has worked in an occupation that helped him or her develop interpersonal skills; the retiree has retired peer groups or a spouse; retirement income is adequate; health is good; leisure activities are pursued; and the retiree has planned adequately for the retirement (Howard & Marshall, 1983). Moreover, more people are turning to options other than pure retirement. For example, retired executives can maintain their involvement by consulting with small business managers, or going overseas to help Third World managers make their companies more effective (Moran & Harris, 1982).

Schein's Model of Career Movement

Whereas Hall and Nougaim's model considers the changing needs and concerns of managers as their careers unfold, Schein (1971) focuses on the specific types of job movements that people make in organizations. In his view, organizations can best be depicted as three-dimensional spaces shaped like cones (see Figure 15–1). Movement to a different job within one of the dimensions, or crossing a boundary into a different dimension, defines the important characteristics of a job change.

According to Schein, most people move along a *hierarchical* dimension as their careers develop. Movement along this dimension involves promotions and raises as the individual rises to higher levels in the organization. Some people will rise to higher levels than others. Some organizations (and occupations) have many levels that people can move through, whereas others are relatively "flat," having few levels.

The *functional* dimension describes areas of special expertise, talents, or skills. Some individuals are highly specialized in such areas of expertise as law, accountancy, or chemical engineering, and have little movement along this dimension (from one functional area to another). Others, not so specialized, rotate through many functional areas, such as production, marketing, and personnel, perhaps eventually moving into general management while losing some of their original technical training and knowledge.

Schein's third dimension is more subtle. The *inclusion* dimension involves movement toward the inner core of the organization. In Figure 15–1, this would be depicted by movement from the periphery of the cone toward its center. Unlike the more clearly defined vertical and horizontal movements in the hierarchical and functional dimensions, greater inclusion is signaled by more subtle clues like greater trust from powerful

FIGURE 15–1

A Three-Dimensional Model of an Organization

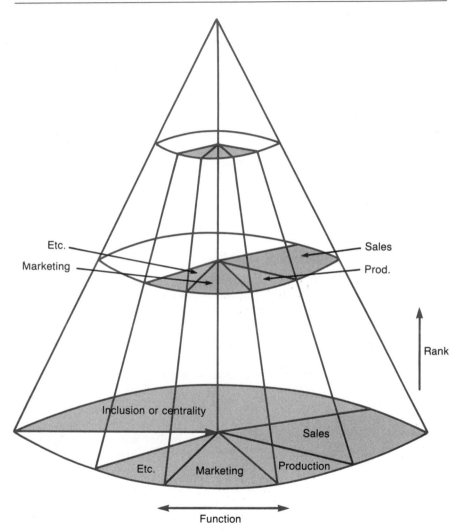

SOURCE: F. Schein, "The Individual, the Organization, and the Career: A Conceptual Scheme," *Journal of Applied Behavioral Science* 7 (1971), pp. 401–26.

members of the organization, more important responsibilities, or being privy to company secrets.

Movement up the hierarchy usually implies movement toward the central core, but it is also possible to become more central without getting a promotion. Further, being "kicked upstairs" suggests a promotion without much added (or even with reduced) responsibility and possible movement away from the central core.

The job changes described above can have both advantages and disadvantages. Transfers and promotions can offer new responsibilities, learning opportunities, and higher pay (Feldman & Brett, 1985), but adapting to new positions may be difficult (Brett, 1982). Job changes are stressful; compared to new hires, newly transferred and/or promoted employees receive relatively little training and are expected to contribute immediately in their new positions (Feldman, 1989). Moreover, the pace of job changes has increased — many corporations have created *fast-track programs* in which rapid promotions and transfers are given to identify and train future executives (Thompson, Kirkham, & Dixon, 1985). Organizations with fast-track programs should consider dysfunctional consequences like an emphasis on short-term work habits, strategies, and results (see Focus on the Future). Similarly, individuals should master their jobs before they move on to new ones, and consider their families before they grab at one job change after another (Feldman, 1989).

Alternate Career Forms

Hall and Nougaim's steady progression of establishment, advancement, and maintenance stages is a straightforward description of traditional careers. Schein's model, too, focuses on standard movement through a single organization. Such traditional careers, or *bureaucratic* careers, are defined by advancement through a sequence of positions in a hierarchy. But these stages are not as steady and predictable as they were when Hall and Nougaim did their research at AT&T. Now, "the tumultuous upheaval in corporate America has permanently altered these cycles for most executives. Gone is any sense of security as mass firings and company mergers shatter presumed career passages" (Hymowitz, 1987, p. 29). In today's world, two alternate career forms — professional and entrepreneurial — are increasingly important.

The *professional* career form is defined by craft or skill rather than by advancement (Kanter, 1989). The key determinant of occupational status is monopolization of socially valued knowledge. Professional reputation is the key resource for the individual. Instead of moving from job to job, people on professional career tracks may keep the same title and same job for a long time. Opportunity comes from taking on more challenging, important, or rewarding assignments that demand more skill, and upward mobility involves broadening and increasing one's reputation for greater skill. You can see these features in the careers of dentists, physicians, consultants, actors, tax accountants, and attorneys.

The *entrepreneurial* career form is one in which growth occurs through the creation of new value or new organizational capacity (Kanter, 1989). The key resource in an entrepreneurial career is not hierarchical position or knowledge and reputation, but the capacity to create valued outputs.

FOCUS ON THE FUTURE

The New Careerism

A generation ago, most managers and professionals expected to spend their entire careers in one organization; today, this assumption no longer holds. A "me-first" careerism, in which individuals try to get as much as they can out of their organizations and then move on, is now prevalent (Feldman, 1988).

The new attitude stems from a belief that organizations can no longer be depended on to take care of loyal employees, and that an uncertain future means employees have to fend for themselves. Positive consequences from this new outlook include more self-assertiveness, people seeking more frequent performance feedback, more critical self-analysis, better communication of career goals and aspirations, and attempts to buffer personal lives from work lives.

After 25 years of this new careerism, some unintended consequences also are becoming apparent (Feldman, 1985):

Anticipatory dissatisfaction. People may be dissatisfied with their jobs, not because of traditional factors like pay and working conditions, but because the job might not be a good launching pad for the next career move.

Lower job involvement and organizational commitment. Why make investments in the current company if the job is a short-term proposition?

Increased turnover. This is a result not only of higher dissatisfaction and lower commitment, but a belief that switching jobs shows ambition and looks good on résumés.

Inauthentic personal relationships. People spend less energy getting to know each other because they don't expect to work together for long. Relationships become more instrumental and shallow than sincere and long-lasting.

Concern with image management. People believe it is more important to *look* good than to *be* good. This leads to lower standards of individual and organizational performance.

Short-run orientation. Not only do people spend more time worrying about image and new job offers, but their home-run mentality dictates they try to make the big play, regardless of long-term consequences, and then move on.

Unethical behavior. Many of the above factors conspire to encourage self-absorbed, expedient behavior unconcerned with ethical distinctions.

How prevalent do you think the new careerism is today? What is your assessment of its consequences?

For business founders, growth in an entrepreneurial career derives from the increased power and responsibility that come from the growth of their organizations. But this career form is broader than the conception of entrepreneur as small business owner or someone who forms an independent business venture. The pattern can apply to everyone who stays in place in one company, but increases the territory for which he or she is responsible. Thus, instead of moving up, progress occurs when those in entrepreneurial careers see their territories grow below them — and they realize returns from the growth.

In large organizations like AT&T and Eastman Kodak, people have the opportunity to start businesses with the support of the parent company. Special venture participants are paid a base salary and asked to put part of their compensation at risk, with their percent ownership determined by how much they risk. They earn a return, sometimes based on a percentage of the profit from their venture, on the marketplace performance of their product or service (Kanter, 1989).

Entrepreneurial careers are riskier than bureaucratic and even professional careers. People in bureaucratic careers hope for predictability and security in return for lower income than they might receive from their own companies. Professionals have their skills and knowledge that command prices in the marketplace. But entrepreneurs — in their own independent companies or corporate-sponsored ventures — have only what they grow. There is risk and uncertainty, but they may gain autonomy and greater financial rewards if they succeed. When sponsored by their employers, entrepreneurs can enjoy lower costs and greater resources, while employers enjoy reduced risks because they do not have to pay unless they see results (Kanter, 1989).

SOCIALIZATION

As the new recruit enters the organization, a process of *socialization* takes place. Organizational socialization refers to the teaching of the organization's goals, norms, values, and preferred ways of doing things. Successful socialization results in dependable performance, innovation and cooperation, higher motivation and satisfaction, and lower turnover.

Three relatively distinct changes occur during the socialization process (Feldman, 1981). First, employees learn a set of appropriate role behaviors. They must define their jobs, establish priorities, and learn how to allocate their time and energies. They must learn how to deal with conflicts involving managers and employees outside their work groups. They must manage role conflicts between work and family lives.

Second, employees must develop new work skills and abilities. Some employees are hired based on skills already possessed, while others must acquire skills and knowledge through formal training or informal coaching. For example, when Peter Ueberroth was president of the Los Angeles Olympic Organizing Committee, he wanted all staff members to be thoroughly knowledgeable about the Olympic Games and the participating countries. Each new hire was randomly assigned a country. Ueberroth would call an employee into his office and ask the person to tell him everything he knew about Mozambique, or Uruguay, or whatever his assigned country was. He also personally administered tests about the history of the Olympic Games, current international news, and details about the LAOOC.

Unsuspecting employees were asked to recite the countries in Africa, o. the sports commissioners for 23 events of the 1984 Games. With Ueberroth's testing system, newcomers quickly learned about the organization and its environment (McDonald, 1988).

Third, socialization entails some degree of accepting group norms and values. Incumbent employees withhold essential information from new recruits until an adequate level of trust and friendship is established (Feldman, 1981). Such a relationship is developed through, and further encourages acceptance of, group norms and values.

The organization exposes employees to different kinds of behavior norms (Schein, 1971). Some norms are *pivotal,* in that people must adhere to them if they want to remain in the organization. An example might be to show a conscious effort to perform one's job dependably. Other organizational norms are *peripheral;* it is desirable but not essential for members to follow them. Examples might be espousing certain political views or wearing the right clothes. In one Mexican corporation, a manager's career is enhanced if subordinates carry his briefcase (Quezada & Boyce, 1988); in most organizations, this is not a pivotal norm.

Based on which sets of norms they adhere to, people adjust to these norms in three possible ways. Adherence to neither pivotal nor peripheral norms is called *active rebellion* and is likely to lead to the person quitting or being fired. Acceptance of both pivotal and peripheral norms is called *overconformity* and is likely to result in an organization man or bureaucrat. Acceptance of pivotal norms, but rejection of peripheral norms, is called *creative individualism.*

Schein's comments underscore the perennial dilemma of the individual versus the group or organization. On the one hand, the individual needs the support that a collective order can provide, and for such an order to endure, he or she must sacrifice some individual autonomy. On the other hand, an organization that enforces rigid uniformity and unthinking capitulation denies itself the full contribution of its members. The optimum resolution of this dilemma is to create conditions that make it possible for members to be creative individualists rather than conformists or rebels. Ultimately, organizations should not force people into the same mold, and individuals should not change completely just to fit in. Both parties should try to find a comfortable range of mutual acceptance and accommodation (Feldman, 1989).

Tasks and Problems of the Socialization Stage

As organizations face the task of inspiring creative individualism, the new member in an organization also faces problems. For those who are entering their first full-time job, the most general feature of socialization is *reality shock* (Hughes, 1958). This refers to the surprising gap between the new employee's expectations about the first job and what it actually turns out to be. You may recall from Chapter 13 that such unmet expectations explain why young employees have the lowest job satisfaction.

Schein (1978) and Webber (1976) have described the specific tasks newcomers face and the problems they must solve. Schein's tasks during organizational entry include accepting the reality of the human organization, dealing with resistance to change, learning how to do the job, and learning how to get ahead. Webber echoes some of these observations and adds other insights regarding personal passivity, tension between younger and older managers, and dilemmas surrounding definitions of loyalty and ethics.

Accepting the Reality of the Human Organization

Schein's first task involves dealing with the discovery that other people in the organization often are a roadblock to what the individual wants to get done. While the organizational reality is that most jobs are interdependent, many newcomers do not want to bother learning about dealing with other people. Their attitude commonly seems to be one of wishing other people would just go away and let them concentrate on their work. The unlearning of this attitude may be the key to becoming effective. Those who quickly accept the realities of the human organization soon learn to apply their intelligence and analytical abilities to performing their jobs within it. Managing these interdependencies is a focus of much of this textbook.

Dealing with Resistance to Change

A related shock, also due to human realities, is the discovery that technically good solutions to problems are not necessarily accepted by those who make decisions. The newcomer's ideas are undermined, sidetracked, sabotaged, or ignored by stubborn or illogical people, organizational procedures, or politics. Even a well-prepared technical analysis of a problem must be sold to others who may resist it for myriad reasons. Schein feels that differences in people's ability to cope with resistance to change may be an important determinant of their eventual careers in technical staff work, managerial work, or jobs outside the organization altogether. Dealing with resistance to change is discussed in depth in Chapter 21.

Learning How to Work

Organizational newcomers are often frustrated by not knowing what to do or how to contribute. The central task is to learn how to live with ambiguities on the job (recall the discussion of role ambiguity in Chapter 14 on stress). Unlike assignments during school, organizational problems are ill-defined, solution sets are more complex, and politics and inefficiencies interfere with rational pursuits. The important thing here, according to Schein, is to become a good judge of one's own performance. When valid feedback is not forthcoming, obtaining it either by asking others or collecting data on task performance helps eliminate ambiguities.

Learning How to Get Ahead

Learning how to get ahead in the organization involves deciphering the boss and the reward system. The immediate problem is determining how to get along with the boss. The very fact of having a boss is discomfiting to most new employees; beyond that, there remain questions of his or her competence, personal management style, and expectations for subordinates. There is a major psychological conflict between dependence on the boss—which is desirable and appropriate, given the differences in status and experience— and the need to demonstrate an ability to function independently as a competent contributor to the company.

The new employee's first boss is a critical career factor. The boss can assign work that is too difficult, leading to early failure, or too easy, leading to boredom and decreased motivation. If the boss holds low performance expectations, people aren't challenged and don't perform as well as they otherwise might (Berlew & Hall, 1966). If the boss is incompetent, the subordinate may be hindered politically by virtue of their association. An ideal first boss is one who gives challenging but manageable job assignments, holds high personal expectations as well as high expectations for subordinates, and is respected by other managers throughout the organization.

The new employee must also come to understand the prevailing reward system. He or she must determine what is really expected, what is really rewarded, how much trust can be placed in official organizational communications, and which observations in the informal grapevine are valid. This is a complex task, made more so by the existence of many different career paths, different possible routes to success or survival, conflicting information, and changing situations and personnel. Further compounding the problem is the need to have an appropriate, balanced concern for meeting the criteria for advancement. The new employee must not appear overly concerned with promotion, nor should he or she appear to lack long-term motivation.

Personal Passivity

Webber (1976) suggests that new managers are too passive—they inadequately probe the organizational world around them, assuming that their good intentions will ensure positive opinions of their worth. Managers should actively analyze, develop relationships, seek information, provide information, and initiate action rather than passively drift along and hope things will work out for the best.

Tension between Younger and Older Managers

Tension between managers of different age groups is common. Most probably attribute their differences to personality conflicts, but the tension is due more to differences in life and career stages. Young managers are armed with academic knowledge and vocabularies that are unfamiliar and threatening to older personnel. If the older manager is unreceptive to a new technique, the younger specialist or manager may infer that he or she is incompetent, behind the times, or over the hill. Such an inference, Webber suggests, can be a career crippling mistake, because contribution to the organization has little to do with technical skills. The disrespectful young person's future advancement can be blocked by an offended older executive.

Loyalty Dilemmas

People in authority value subordinates' loyalty. The dilemma for new recruits is that loyalty can be defined in so many ways. Different supervisors have different definitions, and they may be at odds with the newcomer's own version of what it means to be loyal. Loyalty can imply obedience ("Do what you're told"), effort ("Do your best, that's all I ask"), success ("Be successful whatever it takes"), protection ("Cover up for my mistakes; don't make me look bad"), or honesty ("Tell me the truth, including the bad news"). A given boss can believe in one version, any combination of versions, or even conflicting versions of loyalty. New subordinates can resolve the loyalty dilemma by deciphering and adhering to the boss's definition(s), selectively ignoring what can be gotten away with, attempting to change the superior's expectations, or leaving the work unit or organization.

Ethical Dilemmas

Most young people beginning their careers share a problem of determining what is ethical. Like loyalty, ethics are subjective and no single view is held by everyone. Some define ethics in terms of economic self-interest, as rationalized by references to what the market will bear, supply and demand, profit maximization, and shareholder wealth. Others might define ethics by whether the behavior in question violates the law, although Webber notes that such a stance is more concerned with prudence than ethics. Some define ethical standards according to religious beliefs. Others use common behavior ("Everyone else does it") or some personalized version of social responsibility (impact on other people) to define ethics.

No single ethical criterion is sufficient, and numerous ethical standards must be considered before one can personally judge what is right (Webber, 1976). Such judgments will be made throughout one's career, but during the early years, young managers often face the unexpected dilemmas that necessitate the search for standards of personal ethics that will guide future decisions.

Mutual Acceptance

As socialization progresses and new members learn to cope with problems and tasks, the stage of mutual acceptance should emerge. Mutual acceptance is a major transition during which the relationship between the new employee and the organization becomes more clearly defined (Schein, 1978). This transition is best conceptualized as the crossing of a major inclusion boundary, as illustrated in Figure 15–1. This movement toward the inner core symbolizes the organization's higher degree of acceptance of the employee. It is often accompanied by a promotional (hierarchical) or rotational (functional) move, but may also occur without such a formal job change.

At the same time, new employees come to accept the organization and the terms of the relationship. They may decide to remain in the organization, at least for some reasonable length of time. They may display a high level of motivation and commitment through long hours, enthusiasm, and a willingness to go above and beyond the call of duty. Similarly, they may accept undesirable work assignments or a low salary as a temporary sacrifice on the road to greater benefits in the future.

How does the employee know he or she has crossed an inclusion boundary toward greater acceptance by the organization? Schein discusses six symbolic events. Some are concrete and easily identifiable, while others are more subtle.

Positive Performance Appraisal   Positive performance feedback is one of the most common events symbolizing acceptance. The feedback can come from a formal appraisal system or on a more informal basis. The difficulty in interpreting informal signals is whether a comment from the boss such as "You're doing fine," is meant with sincere appreciation or as a perfunctory brush-off. Good managers will accurately communicate their appraisal; effective subordinates will learn to actively seek and interpret feedback about their own performance.

Salary Increase   A raise is certainly a concrete event that may connote acceptance. To be a truly meaningful indication of organizational acceptance, it must not be routine. Acceptance is best symbolized if the increase is significantly higher than average, given at a time other than the normal time for pay raises, or coupled with valid written or verbal positive performance feedback.

New Job Assignment   The most important event symbolizing acceptance may be when one's initial assignment is replaced by a second assignment that is more permanent, more challenging, or more obviously important to the organization. The *change* in status is the important signal, because it indicates that the person performed well on the initial assignment.

Sharing of Organizational Secrets   One of the most meaningful symbols of acceptance is the granting of privileged information. Only a person who has clearly accepted pivotal organizational norms and who can be trusted with important information would be privy to such secrets.

Schein places organizational secrets into several categories. Some secrets are *work-related information* that should not be revealed to competitors. Others involve *what others really think* of other employees, particularly those who have not progressed along the inclusion dimension. A third category concerns *how things really work* or *get done* in the organization. A final category includes the scoop on *what really happened* during important events. Exposure to such information can signal that one is well on the road to being accepted in the organization.

Initiation Rites   Some organizations hold ritual events — parties, formal initiations, special privileges like private offices or club memberships — to symbolize acceptance. They indicate some overt investment on the part of the organization, and demonstrate that the employee has moved further into the organization.

Promotion   Being promoted is the most obvious sign of acceptance. Nonetheless, certain types of symbolic promotions may involve no change, or even a decrease, in inclusion. People too often consider promotion the *only* tangible proof of acceptance. New assignments, the sharing of secrets, and the other symbolic events discussed above also constitute effective means of socializing new employees into the organization, as well as being personally gratifying indications of career progress.

CAREER MANAGEMENT BY THE ORGANIZATION

Responsibilities for career management lie both with the organization and with individual employees. In the final two sections of this chapter, we will summarize some of these key responsibilities, first addressing the important roles played by organizations, and then analyzing the roles employees should perform for themselves.

Organizations should carry out a wide range of important functions. These fall under the general categories of selection and entry, management of information, training and development, and other human resources (HR) policies. Proper attention to these activities can benefit both the organization and its members.

Selection and Entry

The first leverage point for career intervention is the selection of employees and the management of their entry into the organization (Hall, 1976). Universities, as well as employers, can help improve this process. Universities can provide students with more knowledge of the real work world to lessen the shock of the first job. Additionally, students tend to underestimate the importance of communication and other interpersonal skills, assuming that technical expertise is more important to success. These skills should be stressed in student training.

In addition, training in cross-cultural skills and the globalization of business is increasingly important. Graduate programs in the United States are adding more to their international curricula. Moreover, European business schools—like the Rotterdam School of Management at Erasmus University, the Netherlands; S.D.A. Bocconi, in Milan, Italy; the Instituto de Estudios Superiores de la Empresa with the University of Navarre in Barcelona, Spain; and the Insead Business School in Fontainebleau, France—are recruiting students in the United States (Fowler, 1989). Clearly, the more international exposure a student has, the more prepared he will be for the realities of a globalized business future.

Employers can also help lessen reality shock for new employees. Realistic job previews that give job candidates a true picture of the job, rather than just a sales pitch, will reduce turnover without initial loss of applicants or acceptances (Wanous, 1977). Employers should use better selection methods to identify those job candidates that will "fit in," or those with the highest potential for development. Many organizations rely too heavily on potentially misleading selection methods, like the interview, personality tests, or even handwriting analyses. More accurate selection methods, such as skill tests or assessment programs, are readily available or can be developed for particular organizations and jobs (Schneider, 1976).

Management of Information

The management of information is one of the major challenges in organizational career planning programs (London & Stumpf, 1982). The organization needs information about employees; employees need information about the organization.

Useful to *organizations* is information about the employee's job skills, work experience, performance ratings, career goals, and recommended future assignments. Newly acquired experiences can be added to the data base via computer technology, thereby providing accurate, up-to-date personnel information to management. Job descriptions and requirements can also be placed on file. Computers can then match personnel with job openings. Furthermore, analysis of demographic data—including current status and future trends of labor supply and demand—helps the organization cope with gluts or shortages of personnel in certain age groups and job classifications.

Useful to *employees* is information about career paths and opportunities, Equal Employment Opportunity (EEO) and affirmative action programs, procedures for filling vacancies and obtaining transfers, available training programs, retirement policies, and the company's economic condition. Such information can be provided initially in realistic job previews and orientation programs, and later by the employee's immediate supervisor, the human resources department, and other sources.

Training and Development

Organizations can offer a broad array of training and development activities to help employees' careers. Table 15–3 provides a set of guidelines for enhancing employee development, including specific activities for carrying

TABLE 15–3
Activities for Following Guidelines for Targeted Development

Guidelines	Activities
Ensure understanding of target job skills and abilities.	Prepare well-done, documented job descriptions. Supervisors clearly communicate job requirements.
Provide developmental activities.	Use learning contracts that specify a logical sequence of training experiences.
Set target jobs and time frames.	Discuss and establish as part of career planning.
Provide challenging job assignments.	Identify jobs and projects with components critical to the individual and the organization. Redesign jobs and projects along critical dimensions.
Assign effective role models.	Assign individuals to supervisors who are known to be good role models.
Provide feedback.	Train supervisors to give meaningful feedback.
Ensure a variety of experiences.	Vary assignments along such dimensions as line-staff, technical-nontechnical, working with others and alone. Take advantage of variation between jobs within departments for easy transfers.
Encourage commitment and involvement.	Involve supervisors and subordinates in designing and carrying out the program.
Allow evaluation and redirection.	Annual examination of career progress. Rewrite learning contract and reset targets.

SOURCE: M. London/S. Stumpf, *Managing Careers,* ©1982, by Addison-Wesley Publishing Co., Inc., Reading, Massachusetts. Table 6.1, page 167. Reprinted with permission of the publisher.

out these guidelines. Some of these guidelines and activities involve the management of information described above, while others highlight the critical roles of job assignments, feedback, and the supervisor.

Job Assignments   The job assignment is the most important variable in people's career development (Dalton, Thompson, & Price, 1977). Assignments can be used to expand employee skills, apply existing skills to new problems, broaden perspectives, provide stimulation from new colleagues, and help prevent technical obsolescence or overdependence on a single boss or mentor. Employees should be provided with challenge as early as possible, preferably in the first job assignment.

Career pathing is the process of formulating a planned sequence of job assignments. Job changes become more logical and systematic, and less random. Career counseling can help people plan their future moves with an eye toward long-term goals. Focus on Management describes how poor planning often characterizes job assignments, underscoring the importance of managing them effectively.

In some organizations, particularly engineering and R&D firms, professionals can choose between two types of career paths. In these dual-ladder systems, one's promotions can progress through either a managerial or a technical hierarchy.

Feedback   Employees need frequent feedback on their performance. The formal performance review process is supposed to inform employees about their boss's appraisal of them, reward employees for good performance, or make suggestions to correct poor performance. Unfortunately, formal reviews are not always conducted. Hall and Lawler (1969) refer to this situation as the "vanishing performance appraisal." Many managers avoid appraisal sessions because appraisals are often confrontational, and because managers lack time or the appropriate skills needed in potentially uncomfortable situations.

Moreover, the appraisals that do take place may be poorly executed. Inadequate feedback is provided, and emotions interfere with the constructive exchange of information. The employee may be left unsure of the outcome, or of ways to improve performance. And those who have proved to be good performers often don't get the rewards they deserve. Furthermore, performance reviews are often limited to discussions of past performance — rarely are longer-term career issues addressed. Performance and career planning should be discussed with employees, formally or informally, and exemplary performance must be rewarded.

Thousands of employers today operate employee assessment centers to further the career development of managers (Nichols & Hudson, 1981). *Assessment centers* are one- to three-day programs in which groups of managerial candidates participate in a series of structured exercises. Participants are evaluated on communication, decision making, leadership, and other interpersonal skills. Assessment centers aid in promotion decisions, and in providing feedback to participants for further training and personal development.

Supervisors   The boss plays a critical role in employees' career development. Managers can be trained to help subordinates with career planning and decision making, to analyze and redesign jobs, and to conduct effective performance reviews and informal feedback and counseling sessions. Although managers should be rewarded for developing subordinates, they rarely are, and often they are punished for such efforts (Hall, 1976). Their own training and development costs may come out of their department's budget, and they often lose to promotion or transfer their employees who benefit from their training. On the other hand, rewarding subordinate development efforts can provide potent reinforcement for the effective manager. Organizations should consider managers' efforts to develop their subordinates when it comes time for pay raises and promotions.

FOCUS ON MANAGEMENT

Expatriate Assignments: How Prepared are Americans?

Overseas assignments offer valuable experience to executives. Like other positions, training for such assignments is important for effective performance. How well-prepared are most American managers as they set out for overseas positions?

American expatriates have higher failure rates than expatriates from Europe and Japan (Tung, 1987)—failure defined as being fired or recalled home for inability to perform in the job. Exploring the reasons behind the higher failure rates for Americans, Tung uncovered a number of differences among American, European, and Japanese executives.

European expatriates were more successful in part because of their foreign language capabilities and a longer history of overseas operations (many of which were established during the height of European empire building). Moreover, they had a stronger international orientation and outlook. The spirit of internationalization derives from several factors: (1) the smaller size of domestic markets necessitates an export mentality (a British slogan is "export or die"); (2) geographic proximity among small countries makes exposure to foreigners and foreign ways much more common than in the United States; and (3) the military and economic strength of the United States had led Americans to be complacent about their own culture, leading to charges of arrogance and resentment from locals of other countries.

In Japan, the principal reasons for expatriate success are the selection process and the role of the family. The strong group orientation and after-hours socializing mean that supervisors know their subordinates much better than in the United States, including family backgrounds, preferences and values, and qualifications. Companies keep very detailed personal inventories. And because candidates for overseas assignments typically have been with the company for 10 years, mistakes in choosing people for overseas assignments are rare.

A primary reason for failure among U.S. managers is the inability of the spouse to adjust to a different physical or cultural environment. Conversely, the obedient Japanese woman, recognizing the cultural importance of saving face, cannot "fail" in her role as wife by succumbing to problems in her husband's assignment.

For Americans, the difficulties are not just in their overseas performance. In a recent *Wall Street Journal* survey of U.S. personnel managers (O'Boyle, 1989), 65 percent say their expatriates' foreign assignments are not integrated into their overall career planning; 56 percent say a foreign assignment is either detrimental or not helpful to one's career; and only 20 percent consider their repatriation policies adequate to meet the needs of their returning expatriates. Given all the problems of overseas assignments, what should U.S. multinationals do? They should sponsor rigorous training programs; provide support systems facilitating adaptation abroad (e.g., mentors or departments that oversee expatriate career paths); solve the problems of repatriation (e.g., losing opportunities for promotions while overseas); develop a longer-term orientation, including longer stints abroad and longer-term planning and performance assessment; and develop a more international orientation and outlook (Tung, 1987).

Other HRM Policies

Many other Human Resource Management (HRM) policies can improve employee career possibilities (Hall, 1976). Career specialists can be made available to employees on request. Managers with line responsibilities can be rotated through the human resources department to learn new skills and perspectives that will be useful when they return to a line department. Job rotation can become frequent in mid- and late-career, rather than just during early employee training.

Norms against downward hierarchical movement can be changed. Downward transfers enhance the organization's staffing flexibility and can even have developmental benefits to the employee. Companies including Heublein, Procter and Gamble, and Continental Can have used fallback positions, in which newly promoted individuals are guaranteed status and pay equal to their old jobs if the promotion doesn't work out to mutual satisfaction. Such policies can help eliminate the Peter Principle — employees getting promoted and then stuck in levels beyond their competencies.

Creative personnel practices can also be devised around tenure and retirement systems. Tenure, most commonly associated with businesses in Japan and universities in the United States, provides loyal and capable employees with job security. Retirement systems can range from the maintenance of special employment relationships beyond usual retirement age, to the provision of attractive incentives for early retirement.

Recently, more companies are providing career development opportunities for disabled and older workers entering the work force. For dual-career couples, companies are experimenting with flexible working hours, travel, job sharing, and tolerance for those who refuse transfers. (Focus on International OB describes similar changes just beginning in Japan.) These and other personnel practices provide rich opportunity for creative, progressive management. Most have a wide range of potential ramifications and must therefore be implemented with care. Proper planning, commitment, and execution can help assure that the resultant benefits will outweigh the costs.

CAREER MANAGEMENT BY THE INDIVIDUAL

The employing organization tends to have a disproportionate impact on careers; important decisions are made, whether well-planned or haphazard, by powerful higher-ups. As noted at the outset of this chapter, it is extremely important for individuals to manage their own careers.

Career analysts like Webber, Schein, and Hall offer practical advice for career self-management. Their ideas can be organized into these general strategies:

Develop Basic Career Competencies A person should practice self-appraisal and develop skills in goal setting, planning, and problem solving.

FOCUS ON INTERNATIONAL OB

The Changing Nature of the Work Force: Sex Roles and Careers in Japan

The U.S. work force has undergone dramatic changes in recent years, and will continue to diversify in the 1990s. Similar upheavals are just beginning in Japan. In fact, the Japanese are wrestling with cultural and labor force changes that U.S. firms began dealing with years ago, and with which they are still struggling. Specifically, Japanese women are staging a quiet revolution in the workplace (Lehner & Graven, 1989).

After decades of relentless effort to get Japan to the top of the world, some Japanese are questioning their all-consuming work ethic and the traditional roles of men and women. Women's opportunities at work have been blocked. Traditionally, a Japanese woman would work as an "office lady" serving tea, making photocopies, and cleaning ashtrays. Society (and her boss) expected her to marry and leave work by age 25, never to reenter the labor force. She was to wait at home for her husband, a workaholic who drank with colleagues and flirted with hostesses. When he finally arrived home, his wife drew his bath for him.

But now, more and more women are pursuing careers. They compete with men for the same jobs, and are protected by a 1986 law prohibiting sex discrimination. Moreover, five out of six new businesses in Japan are started by women.

Japanese men have always been able to work 15 hours a day, knowing their wives would clean house, raise the children, and manage family finances. "Most young men want the same things that their fathers wanted: Someone to take care of them," says one investment banker. And many conservative women resist the changes, as well. A government survey showed that 73 percent of Japanese parents expect their sons to complete university degrees, versus 28 percent for daughters. But there aren't enough men to fuel Japan's burgeoning industries. Young women students can now shun traditional majors like literature in favor of engineering and other majors with more career potential.

The top need for working women is day care for their children. Nahoko Hayashida, who works for Japan's national television network, NHK, is allowed to leave work a few minutes early to retrieve her son from day care. Her husband cannot do the same because he is expected to devote 24 hours a day to his job. "It's not his fault. That's how Japanese society works," she says. She also believes her bosses allow her to leave work early only in return for a certain tacit agreement from her not to compete with the men for certain top jobs.

These activities will provide a foundation for successful implementation of the remaining career strategies.

Collect Information and Assess Your Options before Making Choices   A person must find a good fit between self and work. This means not only conducting an honest self-assessment, but also gathering information on and evaluating all options. Such thorough assessment should be done when choosing occupations and organizations as well as during subsequent decisions about promotions, transfers, and changing jobs or careers.

Get a Challenging Initial Job   Your first job has a strong impact on your future career, and the challenge it offers should be weighed more heavily than more obvious, shorter-term considerations like salary and location. If you are already in a job that does not seem to offer adequate potential for career growth, you should try to acquire additional responsibilities.

Strive for High Performance   Although this is the cornerstone for success, it may not be sufficient. Good performance is not always recognized; performance may be hard to measure, or there may be other important criteria for advancement. Effective self-management requires identifying the key components of performance that are demanded and rewarded, and rigorously evaluating personal performance against those standards.

Recognize that Politics are Inevitable in Organizations   Establish alliances and fight necessary battles, but choose your allies and your fights carefully. Learn to interpret power structures, and to ascertain the alignments of various interest blocs. (These and related topics will be explored further in Chapter 18.)

Develop and Maintain Mobility   Eugene Jennings (1971) outlines the strategies of "executive chess," that is, the rules for attaining job and career mobility. The widest possible set of options should be maintained. This implies gaining experience in multiple areas (line as well as staff responsibilities, and administrative as well as technical assignments), and not becoming overspecialized or technically obsolete. Look for opportunities to increase your exposure and visibility, and be willing to nominate yourself for such opportunities if a sponsor doesn't step forward and nominate you.

The flip side of this advice is to avoid invisibility. American expatriates in overseas assignments, for example, sometimes feel forgotten during a prolonged absence from corporate headquarters. They fear they will miss out on chances for promotion within the corporate hierarchy. Expatriates should remain in frequent contact with a sponsor back home (Tung, 1987).

Options are very much dictated by your boss. A disrespected, immobile superior will block you by not challenging you. If you find yourself working under a boss who hasn't moved in several years, avoid becoming too important to that boss and take actions to get a transfer.

On the other hand, you *should* become important to your boss if he or she is well-respected and mobile. Such a superior is more likely to hold high expectations for your performance, give challenging job assignments, provide a good role model, and be a powerful sponsor. In addition, as your superior gets promoted, he or she may promote you as well, or at least provide you with additional exposure and important nominations.

Find a Mentor   Your boss isn't the only one in the organization who can aid your career. Any higher-level manager with a strong performance record can provide important mentoring functions: advice, information, a role model, a sounding board, and friendship. Close mentor-protégé relationships frequently arise outside the formal manager-subordinate relationship, and can be invaluable to younger people seeking professional competence and advancement. While some organizations create sponsorship programs in which protégés are assigned to mentors, such a formalized approach may not be necessary, or adequate; you should try to develop natural, informal relationships with people from whom you can learn most effectively (Lawson, 1985).

Recognize the Importance of Personal Ethics   No matter how moral you try to be, you will face ethical dilemmas. Don't commit an act you know to be wrong. From time to time, examine your personal values and question how much you are asked, and how much you are willing, to sacrifice for the organization.

Plan your Career with your Spouse   It is common for both husband and wife to have careers. Both careers may be of central importance to their lives, and both must be actively managed. Neither partner should assume that one career is more important than the other, or that the spouse will subordinate a career to the career that happens to have the best immediate opportunity. Mutual support, joint decision making, flexibility, and sometimes sacrifices are requirements of managing dual careers (Glickauf-Hughes, Hughes, & Wells, 1986).

Formulate Contingency Plans   Despite all your plans, unanticipated events will occur. You should consider alternative future scenarios and strategies for responding to different possibilities. Even successful managers who appear to be secure in their jobs should plan for disruptive occurrences. Recessions, changing supplies of labor, technological advances that lead to product obsolescence and organizational decline, and mergers, acquisitions, and divestitures can all lead to firings. These could leave even very capable people without jobs or with blocked careers. Nor should contingency plans be made only for negative events; they should also be formulated for recognizing, and being prepared to capitalize on, opportunities as they arise.

Continually Reassess   Career choices are made throughout your working life. Reassessment, of both self and options, should be done periodically. Perhaps career success implies a career that is developing satisfactorily — and has established a flexible set of options that allows adequate midcourse adjustment.

SUMMARY

Career success and failure hold a wide variety of meanings, depending on differences in individual preferences and perspectives. Responsibility for career management lies with both the individual and the employing organization. Individuals should realistically assess themselves and their options throughout the various stages in their careers—from choosing an occupation and a first job, through career progression, to retirement. Along the way, challenges, including becoming accepted, learning how to get ahead, and resolving ethical dilemmas, must be recognized and managed. Meanwhile, the organization should carefully select and place employees, lessen reality shock, and provide employees with useful information and developmental opportunities. The goal of career management should be to acquire and maintain an ability to respond flexibly to problems and opportunities as they arise.

CONCEPTS TO REMEMBER

Career anchors	Socialization	Symbols of acceptance
Career stages	Pivotal and peripheral norms	Realistic job previews
Career plateau	Creative individualism	Vanishing performance appraisal
Schein's career movement dimensions	Reality shock	praisal
Fast-track programs	Socialization tasks	Assessment centers

QUESTIONS FOR DISCUSSION

1. Develop a personal definition of career success. How do class members' definitions compare with one another? How might definitions differ as a function of peoples' career stage?

2. How might career success and personal success differ? How compatible are they—is it really possible to achieve both? Why or why not?

3. Do career goals and problems differ between men and women? If so, how?

4. Consider a full-time job in which you are interested after graduation, or one that you have already held. If the job is a future prospect, what are some key questions you should explore? If it is a previous job, are there any questions you wish you had investigated before accepting the position?

5. Discuss some of the problems of, and solutions to learning the ropes (becoming socialized) as a new student.

REFERENCES

Berlew, D., & Hall, D. (1966). The socialization of managers. *Administrative Science Quarterly* 11, 207–23.

Brett, J. (1982). Job transfer and well-being. *Journal of Applied Psychology* 67, 450–63.

Cummings, L. L. (1978). Toward organizational behavior. *Academy of Management Review* 3, 90–98.

Dalton, G., Thompson, P., & Price, R. (1977). Career stages: A model of professional careers in organizations. *Organizational Dynamics* 6, 19–42.

Derr, C. B., & Laurent, A. (1989). The internal and external career: A theoretical and cross-cultural perspective. In M. Arthur, D. Hall, & B. Lawrence (eds.), *Handbook of career theory*. Cambridge, England: Cambridge University Press.

Feldman, D. C. (1981). The multiple socialization of organization members. *Academy of Management Review* 6, 309–18.

Feldman, D. C. (1985). The new careerism: Origins, tenets, and consequences. *The Industrial Psychologist* 22, 39–44.

Feldman, D. C. (1988). *Managing careers in organizations*. Glenview, IL: Scott, Foresman.

Fowler, E. M. (1989). U.S. heavily recruited by foreign MBA schools. New York Times: *Chapel Hill Newspaper,* Nov. 12, p. D16.

Glickauf-Hughes, C., Hughes, G., & Wells, M. (1986). A developmental approach to treating dual-career couples. *The American Journal of Family Therapy* 14, Fall, 254–63.

Hall, D. T., & Associates (1986). *Career development in organizations*. San Francisco: Jossey-Bass.

Hall, D. T. (1976). *Careers in organizations*. Santa Monica, CA: Goodyear Publishing.

Hall, D., & Lawler, E. E. (1969). Unused potential in research and development organizations. *Research Management* 12, 339–54.

Hall, D., & Nougaim, K. (1968). An examination of Maslow's need hierarchy in an organizational setting. *Organizational Behavior and Human Performance* 3, 12–35.

Howard, J., & Marshall, M. (1983, Summer). Retirement adaptation – What research says about doing it successfully. *Business Quarterly,* pp. 29–39.

Hymowitz, C. (1987). Stable cycles of executive careers shattered by upheaval in business. *The Wall Street Journal,* May 26, p. 29.

Jennings, E. (1971). *Routes to the executive suite*. New York: McGraw-Hill.

Kanter, R. M. (1989). Careers and the wealth of nations: A macro-perspective on the structure and implications of career forms. In M. Arthur, D. Hall, & B. Lawrence (eds.), *Handbook of career theory,* pp. 506–21. New York: Cambridge University Press.

Lawson, J. G. (1985). Is mentoring necessary? *Training and Development Journal* 39, April, 36–39.

Lehner, U., & Graven, K. (1989). Japanese women rise in their workplaces, challenging tradition. *The Wall Street Journal,* September 6, pp. A1, A13.

London, M., & Stumpf, S. (1982). *Managing careers*. Reading, MA: Addison-Wesley Publishing.

McDonald, P. (1988). The Los Angeles Olympic Organizing Committee: Developing organizational culture in the short run. In M. Jones, M. Moore, & R. Snyder (eds.), *Inside organizations: Understanding the human dimension*. Beverly Hills: Sage.

Miller, D., & Form, W. (1951). *Industrial sociology*. New York: Harper & Row.

Moran, R., & Harris, P. (1982). *Managing cultural synergy*. Houston: Gulf Publishing Company.

Nichols, T. & Hudson O'Boyle, T. (1989). Little benefit to careers seen in foreign stints. *The Wall Street Journal,* December 11, p. B1.

Quezada, F., & Boyce, J. (1988). Latin America. In R. Nath, *Comparative management: A regional view,* pp. 245–70. Cambridge, MA: Ballinger.

Row, A., & Baruch, R. (1967). Occupational changes in the adult years. *Personnel Administration* 30, 26–32.

Schein, E. (1971). The individual, the organization, and the career: A conceptual scheme. *Journal of Applied Behavioral Science* 7, 401–26.

Schein, E. (1978). *Career dynamics: Matching individual and organizational needs*. Reading, MA: Addison-Wesley Publishing.

Schneider, B. (1976). *Staffing organizations*. Santa Monica, CA: Goodyear Publishing.

Super, D. E. (1957). *The psychology of careers*. New York: Harper & Row.

Thompson, Kirkham, & Dixon Tung, R. L. (1987). Expatriate assignments: Enhancing success and minimizing failure. *Academy of Management Executive* 1, 117–26.

Wanous, John, (1977). Organizational entry: The individual's viewpoint. In J. Hackman, E. Lawler, & L. Porter (eds.), *Perspectives on behavior in organizations*. New York: McGraw-Hill.

Webber, R. A. (1976). Career problems of young managers. *California Management Review* 18, 19–33.

Whyte, W. T. (1956). *The organization man*. New York: Simon & Schuster.

SECTION THREE

Cases

DEEP RIVER INSURANCE COMPANY*

Jim Anderson, the director of the Deep River office of a large insurance company, had for some time been concerned with problems of absenteeism, turnover, and generally poor morale. Job enrichment was suggested as a possible solution, and he decided to pursue this course of action.

The Program

Originally, Anderson proposed to conduct a program in the home office data input departments and possibly Deep River keypunch, but as of June 1972, he was actively promoting the possibilities of a much broader project encompassing all Deep River operations. While top management gave this proposal serious consideration, by the end of 1972 it was decided that a more limited program should be conducted in the Deep River office. To that end, an attitude survey was administered in the spring of 1973 to all Deep River clerical employees. The survey was designed to measure employees' attitudes toward 10 major aspects of their jobs: (1) advancement, (2) responsibility, (3) workload, (4) job content, (5) salary, (6) supervision, (7)

*Paul J. Champagne, "Deep River Insurance Company," in *People and Organizations,* ed. J. E. Dittrich and R. A. Zawacki (Plano, Tex.: Business Publications, 1981), pp. 307–15. Reprinted by permission of the author and publisher.

communication, (8) working conditions, (9) training, and (10) management. The results identified three problem areas: job content, responsibility, and communication. It was decided that a job enrichment program would effectively address itself to these issues.

The coding services department was chosen to participate in the program for several reasons. Attitude survey scores from this department were decidedly negative on all three problem areas. Moreover, in coding services no other major problems were identified through the survey, and there were enough task functions to make enrichment possible. After discussions with local area administrators and the superintendent of the department, a final "go" decision was made.

Early in May 1973, a four-day off-site workshop was conducted to provide a better understanding of the principles of job enrichment. Participants included all first-line supervisors and their assistants, Deep River management, organizational development personnel, and an outside, hired consultant. On the recommendation of the consultant, worker participation was rejected on the basis that (1) it was management's prerogative to restructure jobs, (2) it would be awkward for supervisors and subordinates to jointly plan changes in subordinates' jobs, and (3) the expectations of the subordinates might be unrealistic and the actual changes, therefore, disappointing. Workshop members began to apply the principles of Herzberg's motivation-hygiene theory, working out ways of translating responsibility, achievement, recognition, and growth into work-related items. During "greenlighting" or brainstorming sessions, supervisors contributed ideas for improvement of subordinates' jobs without criticism or comment. During "redlighting" sessions, priority items based on what had to be done first were listed, including possible barriers within management's control and possible steps to overcome them. Subgroups composed of pairs of supervisors and assistant supervisors then selected those items they wished to implement in their units.

At the conclusion of the redlighting and implementation sessions, five items were recommended: (1) coders would take turns handing out work; (2) individual coders would begin requisitioning materials directly from filing units; (3) coders were to become experts in their own areas of responsibility; (4) branch offices would be assigned to coders; and (5) coders would begin reviewing their own error sheets returned by the branch offices. Following the workshop, the supervisory teams met with internal and external consultants every two weeks through the early summer of 1973 to plan the implementation.

Early on, the problem of possible loss of earnings under the company's existing wage incentive plan was discussed by management. Under wage incentive, every job was studied, using time and motion techniques, to determine efficient work cycle times. When an employee produced at a rate equal to 70 percent of maximum possible efficiency, a bonus was added to the employee's base salary. For some this amounted to $40 or more per week.

The basic problem was that enrichment training time would not count toward the weekly bonus. Therefore, employees participating in a job enrichment program involving extensive retraining would be penalized. A number of possible solutions were suggested, including dropping the wage incentive and increasing base salary. It was finally decided to deal with the problem by (1) lengthening the overall training time to minimize time off measurement, and (2) giving participating employees a bonus equal to the amount lost under the wage incentive during training. Each trainee was compensated for the time off measurement with a single payment of $20 to $40. While this amount was small, it was sufficient to induce 55 percent of the coding services employees to participate in the program. Until this solution was proposed, only 28 percent of the eligible employees had volunteered for the program.

Once retraining was completed, jobs were retimed so that each participating employee's weekly wage incentive bonus would remain at about the same level as it had been prior to retraining. No attempt was made to reclassify the "larger" jobs (i.e., increase the weekly base pay) since management did not perceive the issue of money as a possible source of trouble.

Most job enrichment programs involve some anticipated changes in the job time cycle; not so here. Under enrichment, coders were expected to handle an entire unit of work, including correction of errors, but no change was made in the wage incentive time standards. For example, if an auto-liability coder performed all the 44 separate tasks required on one unit of work, the time standard for 100 percent efficiency was 33.42 minutes. During the enrichment program this did not change; 100 percent efficiency was still 33.42 minutes. The only difference was that participating coders were required to know and (if necessary) perform each and every task in a unit of work while nonparticipating coders were not. Participating coders were also accountable for errors made by the branch office or keypunch. If an error was detected in incoming work, the coders would contact the branch office by telephone, teletype, or memo. When an error was detected by the company computer, the coder was expected to pull the file, reconcile the error, and see that it was processed correctly by the keypunch operators. All of this took time and required that the coders work harder and faster than before in order to stay within the wage incentive time standards. Management did not seem to realize the negative effect of this on coders' attitudes toward enriched work.

On October 1, 1973, the program was officially launched using the training schedule devised during the workshop. Membership was strictly voluntary, but everyone was encouraged to participate. The program was presented by management as a method for increasing employee interest and job satisfaction. All those who participated in the program were female high school graduates (average age, 22).

Coding services were composed of three basic units: special multiperil (SMP); loss; and auto and liability coding (ALC), with each responsible for coding premium or loss evidence on all types of casualty insurance — i.e., marine, fire, auto, personal liability, etc. The coded information related to the billing, accounting, and statistical experience of the branch offices. This information was then forwarded to the keypunch department for input into the company's computer system.

Prior to job enrichment, work was distributed to individuals without regard to the branch office that initiated it. Under the program, task modules were established, providing complexity, completeness, discretion, and feedback for a unit of work. After employees had been retrained, all work forwarded from branch offices was assigned to specific individuals, requiring them to perform all tasks and functions necessary to process the work. This created continuing individual accountability for a whole unit of work, and clearly associated individual workers with particular branch offices.

At about the same time that job enrichment was getting under way, a number of other changes were being implemented which affected the entire Deep River staff. Late in 1973 and early in 1974 a number of steps were taken in an effort to deal with a variety of other problems identified by the 1973 attitude survey. For example, carpeting was installed, employees were given better explanations of the company bonus plan, job classifications in a number of departments were revised, improved vending machines were installed in the lunchrooms, rest room facilities were improved, open posting of jobs was begun, greater effort was made to open communication channels between supervisors and subordinates, and a modified flexi-time program was instituted. Since management was attempting to deal with several pervasive problems, no incongruity was seen between these changes and the ongoing job enrichment program.

By the early part of 1974, 41 out of 75 eligible employees were performing enriched jobs. In March 1974, a follow-up attitude survey was conducted focusing on the same issues as its predecessor. To management's surprise and dismay, there was little or no change in employee attitudes. Responsibility, job content, and communication were still reacted to negatively. The results were particularly disappointing in view of the ongoing job enrichment program. Management had expected that enrichment would improve employee attitudes and when it did not, faith began to wane in its ability to produce the desired outcomes.

The final evaluation at the end of one year's operation of the program indicated some reduction in turnover and absenteeism. The productivity figures were less conclusive, however. While the situation in coding services had improved, the rest of the Deep River staff showed even greater gains. Based on these findings, management labeled the program a failure and decided to discontinue all job enrichment activity. They felt that the results of the program were not sufficiently impressive to justify the expense of job enrichment.

Anderson and his staff decided not to expand the program to other units in the Deep River office. But even though future job enrichment programs

EXHIBIT 1

Employees Who Opted to Retain Enriched Jobs after Completion of the Trial Program

Unit	Number Eligible for Program	Number Opting for and Participating in Program	Number Opting to Remain in Program Three Months after End of Program	Number Opting to Remain in Program One Year and Three Months after End of Program	Percent Remaining in Program One Year and Three Months after End of Program
Auto-liability coding	31	23	9	3	13%
Loss coding	31	5	2	1	20
Special multi-peril coding*	13	13	13	13	100
Total	75	41	24	17†	41

*Special multiperil coders decided as a group to retain enriched jobs.

†The attrition from the program was not the result of turnover; two employees initially in the program quit the company in the spring of 1975; while two others quit in the spring of 1976. All had opted to retain the enriched jobs before quitting.

were shelved, branch coders were allowed to choose whether or not to retain their enriched jobs. Among the three units, SMP chose as a group to continue under the program; in ALC and loss, only 4 of the 28 participating employees chose to remain and were still in the program one year and three months later (see Exhibit 1).

The Results of Job Enrichment

Absenteeism   During the program absenteeism among participating employees showed marked improvement, as shown in Exhibit 2.

From October 1, 1974, average absenteeism in the enriched group dropped 2.2 days per year while among nonparticipating personnel it increased 2.9 days. During this same period the overall Deep River staff also experienced some improvement, but only 0.6 days.

According to the three unit supervisors in coding services, job enrichment had its most noticeable impact on absenteeism. When an enriched employee was absent for any period of time, the person's work was distributed to other members of the unit. This had an impact on the absent employee since errors made by someone else could interfere with the ongoing relationship established between the coder and the branch offices. Errors or delays, though made by someone else, were nevertheless the responsibility of the employee assigned to the branch. Rather than have to deal with problems created by others, employees apparently made a greater effort to be present.

Turnover   Turnover among participating employees was also reduced (see Exhibit 3). Turnover in the enriched group was reduced by 50 percent from the previous year. In addition, among employees on enriched tasks turnover was 10 percent less than among other personnel in coding services. However,

EXHIBIT 2

Annual Absenteeism*

Coding Services	October 1, 1972 through October 1, 1973 (before Enrichment)	October 1, 1973 through October 1, 1974 (during Enrichment)
Enriched job participants (n = 41)	5.6	3.4
Nonenriched job participants (n = 34)	7.0	9.9
Deep River clerical staff (exclusive of coding services) (n = 400)	7.8	7.2

*The average number of days absent per employee; the total number of absences in a year among the employees in a department divided by the average number of employees in that department.

EXHIBIT 3

Annual Turnover*

Coding Services	October 1, 1972 through October 1, 1973 (before Enrichment)	October 1, 1973 through October 1, 1974 (during Enrichment)
Enriched job participants (n = 41)	72.4%	32.6%
Nonenriched job participants (n = 34)	72.4	43.1
Deep River clerical staff (exclusive of coding services) (n = 400)	67.1	29.6

*The percentage of employee turnover per year; the total number of quits in a year divided by the total number of employees in the appropriate units.

this gain was overshadowed by the overall improvement in the Deep River office where turnover was 3 percent less than among the enriched group. To management it appeared that better results had been obtained without job enrichment.

Even though absenteeism had improved dramatically, turnover made a stronger impression on management. It was apparently viewed as much more important in terms of the company's operations.

Productivity   Management expected job enrichment to have a dramatic impact on productivity, but as Exhibit 4 indicates, the results of the program were inconclusive. Productivity through the third quarter of 1974 among enriched employees was 14.8 percent higher than the nonenriched group, but the overall trend in coding services was downward. From January 1, 1974,

EXHIBIT 4
Productive Efficiency in 1974 by Unit*

Unit		1st Quarter 1974	2nd Quarter 1974	3rd Quarter 1974	4th Quarter 1974
Loss coding	Enriched (n = 5)	94.8%	89.8%	94.0%	100.8%
	Nonenriched (n = 26 to 28)	98.8	90.0	92.5	89.0
Auto-liability coding	Enriched (n = 23 to 24)	97.7	97.0	91.7	94.0
	Nonenriched (n = 7 to 8)	95.8	86.8	69.7	73.6
Special multiperil coding	Enriched (n = 13 to 18)	99.4	95.5	100.1	97.8
	Nonenriched (n = 0)	—	—	—	—
Total coding services	Enriched (n = 41 to 48)	97.3	94.1	95.3	97.5
	Nonenriched (n = 33 to 34)	88.0	88.5	81.1	80.0
Total Deep River clerical staff (exclusive of coding services) (n = 400)		94.0	96.0	93.0	Unknown

*Productivity was measured by how effectively a unit of employees utilized its time: the unit's average efficiency (i.e., how much work it processed in a given period of time) multiplied by the average percentage of time on measurement (i.e., the amount of time the employees engaged in measured work. This excludes lunch breaks, rest breaks, training time, etc.).

† The utilization for the fourth quarter of 1974 was not computed for the total Deep River clerical staff by the company.

through October 1, 1974, productivity in the enriched group had dropped 2 percent (97.3 to 95.3). During the fourth quarter of 1974 this trend was reversed slightly. The enriched group increased to 97.5 percent by the end of 1974. During the first three quarters of 1974 productivity among the nonenriched employees declined from 88 percent to 81 percent, a drop of 7 percent, and the fourth quarter of 1974 showed a further decline to 80 percent.

Even though the overall experience of the enriched group was better than that of the nonenriched employees in coding services, the lack of a clear trend was disturbing to management. It was particularly so in comparison with the rest of the Deep River staff, where productivity through the third quarter of 1974 had been almost stable.

When third-quarter productivity for enriched employees was examined by unit only SMP showed any improvement. Loss was down slightly, as was ALC. Even though productivity among nonenriched employees in loss and ALC was also down, this offered management little solace. The productivity trends further reinforced management's growing skepticism about the utility of job enrichment.

EXHIBIT 5

Follow-up Interviews with Randomly Selected Participants
in the Enrichment Program*

Response	Percentage Agreeing (Total n = 28)
1. The job was more interesting and enjoyable	82
2. Should be paid more	79
a. Job classification should be raised	29
b. Bonus-making ability was a major problem	71
c. The job should be retimed	54

*Content analysis of interviews with 28 of the 59 participants in job enrichment.
SOURCE: Interviews conducted by home office organizational development personnel.

Exit Interviews   Shortly after the formal end of the program on October 1, 1974, company organizational development personnel conducted interviews with 28 employees, selected at random from among those involved in job enrichment. The results showed that 82 percent of those interviewed felt the enriched tasks to be more interesting, but a large majority (79 percent) also felt participants should be paid more. Bonus-making ability during enrichment was a major problem for 71 percent of these employees (see Exhibit 5).

While these data reveal the basic problem encountered by management, comments made by the employees interviewed indicated even more forcefully the primary reason for their continuing discontent. The one item of greatest concern to the coders performing enriched tasks was the problem of lost bonus money during the program.

Comments like the following were common:

> I like the idea of branch coding, but thank goodness I don't depend on the bonus money.

> I like branch coding, but because you get such a variety of work it is very hard to make your efficiency. I think the rates [basic job classification] should be raised.

> I don't like branch coding, because without my bonus money my base pay is nothing. I find myself becoming very disgusted and not even caring about my work. You work harder now and have nothing to show for it.

> I like branch coding because of the variety of work, but I find I have nowhere near the efficiency I used to. If someone offered me a job that paid about the same as my base pay right now, I'd take it. Before, I never would because of my great bonus money. But now, I'd jump at the chance.

I like branch coding because I like the variety of work . . . [but] I also think we do a lot of work for our pay—I mean I really work harder now than I did when I was a regular coder.

Within the individual units, employee reaction to job enrichment was much the same. For example, SMP branch coders felt the training was good, but the training payment was too low to adequately compensate for lost bonus earnings.

In response to the question "How do you feel about the changes?" all four people interviewed in SMP responded that they were generally more satisfied with the enriched job. They liked having responsibility for particular clients. Most (three of four) felt they had more control over the work. All mentioned the increased task variety of the enriched job as a favorable feature. Their major gripes centered around the loss of bonus money which accompanied job redesign. They felt they should be paid a higher base salary since it was definitely harder to earn the same bonus on the new job.

ALC branch coders felt that their training payments had been inadequate when compared to the bonus they could have made on the old job during the same time period. Four of the coders interviewed in this unit were making significantly less bonus money than they had on the old job. The problem was not due to the intrusion of extra jobs into their work by the supervisors, but rather was seen as the need for adequate retiming of work standards to allow for the numerous new tasks involved. As one of the employees put it, "They (management) didn't look at the whole picture before putting it in (job enrichment)." Or as another stated, "It's more mental work for less money."

The comments from the loss department were much the same. One coder, for example, said that her bonus had slipped from approximately $40 to $13 per week. This eventually caused her to drop out of the program, since, as she put it, "I'm working here for money."

Questions Do you share the apparent conclusion of Deep River management that the job enrichment program was a failure? How do you account for the results? What might management have done differently? What are the implications of the Deep River experience for *(a)* the theory supporting job redesign, *(b)* the practice of job redesign, *(c)* the empirical evaluation of such programs?

FRANK ROGERS*

Frank Rogers awakened with a start. The telephone at his bedside was ringing. It was the police department reporting that the back door of the Local Savings and Loan was unlocked and that he would have to come downtown to check the office and lock the door.

Frank was secretary-treasurer and assistant manager of Local Savings and Loan. He had started work at Local after being honorably discharged from the army some 12 years before. At that time, there were only two employees: the managing officer, Al Wilcox, and himself. (At the time this case was reported the organization had a staff of 18 persons.)

As he drove toward town, the midnight air cleared his head. He began to recall the events of the hectic day he had had at the office. It was the type of day that was becoming increasingly common. Such days left him exhausted — so much so that at home he inevitably got into arguments with his wife and scolded his three children over minor things that ordinarily left him unruffled.

Today it had all started early in the morning. The chairman of the board had come into his office and created a disturbance because he had not received the statistical data for the previous month for reviewing prior to the board of directors' meeting that afternoon. Frank had intended to get the information together, but in the little time he had had between customers he had made out the monthly report for the Federal Home Loan Bank because of a fast-approaching deadline.

After the chairman of the board departed, Frank went to tell Wilcox that he needed another stenographer to help him with his work. Wilcox said that the association was overstaffed at the present and more efficient use of the personnel on hand should solve such a problem. Frank agreed with him that the quantity of personnel was adequate, but that their efficiency was poor. Wilcox took this as a direct criticism of his three relatives in the office, and a fairly heated argument between the two men developed rapidly. Tempers soon cooled, and Frank returned to his office and proceeded with his work.

About three o'clock in the afternoon Frank had stepped out of his office and seen two customers waiting at the counter. Not a single teller was in evidence. His quick investigation disclosed three tellers downstairs having coffee. Another had gone out for cigarettes and the fifth was in the supply room getting some additional supplies. Frank called Wilcox out of his office and proceeded to point out the situation to him. Wilcox heatedly told him to take care of it, walked back into his office, and slammed the door. Frank hurried the tellers out of the lunchroom with

*Reprinted with permission from Edgar G. Williams, *People Problems* (Bloomington, Ind.: Bureau of Business Research, Indiana University Graduate School of Business, 1962).

a sharp reprimand and then went to see Roger Donaldson, who was supposed to supervise the tellers.

Donaldson was about 26 years old and had worked for the association for the past five years. At first he had not exhibited much ambition, but after he had got married and his wife had had a child, his interest picked up and he was now progressing quite rapidly.

Frank asked the supervisor for an explanation of the teller situation. Donaldson advised him that he had no real control over the employees. He said that he had asked Wilcox for help but got none and, on occasions when he had attempted to discipline some of them, Wilcox had called him into his office and had reprimanded him for his actions. By this time, Frank was sorely frustrated, but he managed to keep himself under control.

At almost five o'clock, Frank's stenographer had brought him the letters to sign that he had dictated earlier that day. While signing them, he noted that there were so many errors on two of them that he stayed late and retyped them himself.

As he drove up to the office parking lot Frank thought to himself, "I wonder why the door is open? This has never happened before. The last thing that Al does is to check both doors before he leaves the building. Could I myself have forgotten?"

Questions   What are the tell-tale symptoms that Frank is operating under a considerable degree of job-related stress? What are the origins of this stress? To what extent, and in what manner, might Frank himself be contributing to the stress level? If you were a friend of Frank's, what suggestions might you offer for handling the stress of his job?

TERRY FURNISS*

When I first met Terry as a second-year graduate student in 1961, he struck me as a handsome, articulate, somewhat diffident but confident young man. Large and imposing in manner and bearing, he spoke in a relaxed and comfortable manner during the interview, communicating maturity and integrity in the extreme.

Terry is the oldest son in an Irish immigrant family that settled in the Boston area in the 1920s. His father worked in a variety of semiskilled jobs, and his mother was a domestic in the home of a department store president. He has three sisters and two brothers. After attending public elementary

*E. H. Schein, *Career Dynamics: Matching Individual and Organizational Needs* (Reading, Mass.: Addison-Wesley Publishing, 1978), pp. 131–34.

school, Terry went to Junior Seminary in a nearby city, thinking that he would like to be a priest.

During his high school years this aspiration waned, because he realized that he was just not cut out for the life of routine and strict discipline the priesthood would entail. He transferred to Boston College High School with the help of a friend and began to do excellent academic work in physics and the classics because of some tough, challenging teachers. His good senior year earned him a scholarship to Boston College, where he majored in physics. After two years there he realized that he wanted to get into a managerial position sometime and that this would require some graduate work — either a Ph.D. or graduate management school. Terry applied for and won a General Electric summer scholarship at Rensselaer Polytechnic Institute following his junior year at college. During this summer he spent a substantial amount of time at the GE laboratories, which gave him an insight into how companies work and reinforced his desire for a graduate management degree.

Terry applied to several schools and was admitted to MIT's Sloan School in 1956. After one term he received an offer from a local R&D company to work as a field engineer. He accepted the offer because the draft was hot on his heels, and the job carried a draft deferment with it. He worked in this organization for three years and then returned to graduate school.

Based on the 1961 interview (during Terry's last semester at MIT), we drew several conclusions about his values and aspirations. He put a very high value on *task accomplishment, getting a job done, and doing it right.* Beyond that central value he wanted some challenge and adventure in his life, expressed particularly in terms of some ideas of starting up a business venture in Ireland, but he also put a great deal of emphasis on having a career which would not be so demanding that it would interfere with family life. He did not, for example, envision himself in a large corporation and being moved every few years, because this would be bad for his children (he expressed these views at a time when he was still single). Terry also put emphasis on being fair and honest in one's dealing with people.

In talking of his career in 1961, Terry was almost apologetic about his inability to be specific about his goals. He interviewed over 20 companies — some in relation to an overseas job, some in relation to data processing, which he had become interested in after his summer work for GE, and some in relation to the plan to go to Ireland. In the end he settled for the R&D company that had employed him prior to graduate school and worked in R&D administration. The job ended up being a kind of "odds and ends" situation involving the writing of technical proposals, setting up management systems for various R&D projects, and contributing to contract sales efforts.

Terry stayed with this company for two and a half years, first in administration, which he found "too vague," and eventually in marketing, which he "grew to dislike very much."

It involved finding money for people to conduct research, and I knew that I was never good enough to do the research for which I was out ringing the doorbells [various government agencies]. . . . I was never good enough to do the research myself, yet I was always forced to go out and dig up the money for somebody else to conduct the research. . . .

I grew to dislike it very much, and I thought for six to eight months before I finally decided what I wanted to do, so I wrote 20 letters blind to 20 different companies, and Acme Electronics was one of the few that I got any response from at all. [Acme is a very large electronics firm doing consumer and government contract work.]

The work in Acme was as a "simulation analyst" in a small staff group which was developing some new concepts about how to use computer simulations. Terry knew that this was a risky area and that if the work ran out, he would be the first to be laid off. One day about two years later, the leader of the group told Terry that he was thinking of starting a new consulting company and invited Terry and another member of the same work group to go into it with him. The group leader, John, asked Terry if he would be able to invest some money in the new concern and offered Terry a position on the board if he could raise more than $5,000. Terry convinced several of his friends to invest in the new venture and put up some of his own money to help launch it. John and the other man started the company while Terry continued at Acme for another six months, finishing off projects. He worked in the new company some nights and weekends, writing proposals, debugging programs, and otherwise helping in any way he could.

The new company became successful quickly through its contract research for government agencies. Terry joined with the title of Senior Analyst and put his main energies into helping the data-processing effort, using computer applications. In a questionnaire sent out some years after he joined the consulting company, he said:

I have gradually reached the point where I can clearly define what I need in a job to make it interesting and challenging to me. In the years ahead these needs may vary slightly, but I am zeroing in on them. Briefly, what I need in a job is a specific goal, for example, a computer system or program to solve some problem, or a production schedule to be met which involves producing a concrete product, within fixed dollars and time limits — using people and machines in an efficient fashion.

Right now I enjoy projects involving substantial intellectual challenge (e.g., systems analysis/programming), but I may eventually prefer production-oriented work where the major challenge is not intellectual. In any case, I am convinced that I would never enjoy a position in sales — regardless of product or level in the organization. I much prefer to do the job — design the system, produce the car, etc. — than to sell it.

What is striking about this statement is not only the rejection of sales, but also the absence of any reference to management per se. In the new consulting firm, though he is a part owner and on the board by virtue of his investment in the company, he has continued in a technical function, writing proposals and directing projects concerned with technical assistance, conducting research and evaluation on social science areas ranging from manpower and health to housing and criminal justice. Almost all of these projects are federally funded, with contracts awarded on the basis of competitive procurements. The projects extend from six months to several years, with budgets ranging from $100,000 to over a million dollars, and employ 2 to 10 staff members. Terry's specialty, as he sees it, is "project management."

Terry was married in 1968, now has three children, and is very family oriented. He lives on a large lot in a rural area, where he spends a lot of time with his children and on gardening. He is an adventurous person, as his original intentions to go to Ireland had indicated, and engages in sports such as canoeing, mountain climbing, and tennis, though he admits that in recent years he has had less time for these things because of the demands of his family.

Questions How would you describe the "career anchor" of Terry Furniss? In what terms do you think he would define "career success"? What factors would he—or should he—weigh in making a decision concerning any new job offers?

DICK SPENCER*

After the usual banter when old friends meet for cocktails, the conversation between a couple of university professors and Dick Spencer, a former student who was now a successful businessman, turned to Dick's life as a vice president of a large manufacturing firm.

"I've made a lot of mistakes, most of which I could live with, but this one series of incidents was so frustrating that I could have cried at the time," Dick said in response to a question. "I really have to laugh at how ridiculous it is now, but at the time I blew my cork."

Spencer was plant manager of Modrow Company, a Canadian branch of the Tri-American Corporation. Tri-American was a major producer of primary aluminum with integrated operations ranging from the mining of bauxite through the processing to fabrication of aluminum into a variety of

*This case was developed and prepared by Professor Margaret E. Fenn, Graduate School of Business Administration, University of Washington. Reprinted by permission.

products. The company also made and sold refractories and industrial chemicals. The parent company had wholly owned subsidiaries in five separate United States locations and had foreign affiliates in 15 different countries.

Tri-American mined bauxite in the Jamaican West Indies and shipped the raw material by commercial vessels to two plants in Louisiana where it was processed into alumina. The alumina was then shipped to reduction plants in one of three locations for conversion into primary aluminum. Most of the primary aluminum was then moved to the companies' fabricating plants for further processing. Fabricated aluminum items included sheet, flat, coil, and corrugated products: siding; and roofing.

Tri-American employed approximately 22,000 employees in the total organization. The company was governed by a board of directors which included the chairman, vice chairman, president, and 12 vice presidents. However, each of the subsidiaries and branches functioned as independent units. The board set general policy, which was then interpreted and applied by the various plant managers. In a sense, the various plants competed with one another as though they were independent companies. This decentralization in organizational structure increased the freedom and authority of the plant managers, but increased the pressure for profitability.

The Modrow branch was located in a border town in Canada. The total work force in Modrow was 1,000. This Canadian subsidiary was primarily a fabricating unit. Its main products were foil and building products such as roofing and siding. Aluminum products were gaining in importance in architectural plans, and increased sales were predicted for this branch. Its location and its stable work force were the most important advantages it possessed.

In anticipation of estimated increases in building product sales, Modrow had recently completed a modernization and expansion project. At the same time, their research and art departments combined talents in developing a series of twelve new patterns of siding which were being introduced to the market. Modernization and pattern development had been costly undertakings, but the expected return on investment made the project feasible. However, the plant manager, who was a Tri-American vice president, had instituted a campaign to cut expenses wherever possible. In his introductory notice of the campaign, he emphasized that cost reduction would be the personal aim of every employee at Modrow.

Salesman   The plant manager of Modrow, Dick Spencer, was an American who had been transferred to this Canadian branch two years previously, after the start of the modernization plan. Dick had been with the Tri-American Company for 14 years, and his progress within the organization was considered spectacular by those who knew him well. Dick had received a

Master's degree in Business Administration from a well-known university at the age of 22. On graduation he had accepted a job as salesman for Tri-American. During his first year as a salesman, he succeeded in landing a single, large contract which put him near the top of the sales-volume leaders. In discussing his phenomenal rise in the sales volume, several of his fellow salesmen concluded that his looks, charm, and ability on the golf course contributed as much to his success as his knowledge of the business or his ability to sell the products.

The second year of his sales career, he continued to set a fast pace. Although his record set difficult goals for the other salesmen, he was considered a "regular guy" by them, and both he and they seemed to enjoy the few occasions when they socialized. However, by the end of the second year of constant traveling and selling, Dick began to experience some doubt about his future.

His constant involvement in business affairs disrupted his marital life, and his wife divorced him during the second year with Tri-American. Dick resented her action at first, but gradually seemed to recognize that his career at present depended on his freedom to travel unencumbered. During that second year, he ranged far and wide in his sales territory, and successfully closed several large contracts. None of them was as large as his first year's major sale, but in total volume he again was well up near the top of salesmen for the year. Dick's name became well known in the corporate headquarters, and he was spoken of as "the boy to watch."

Dick had met the president of Tri-American during his first year as a salesman at a company conference. After three days of golfing and socializing they developed a relaxed camaraderie considered unusual by those who observed the developing friendship. Although their contacts were infrequent after the conference, their easy relationship seemed to blossom the few times they did meet. Dick's friends kidded him about his ability to make use of his new friendship to promote himself in the company, but Dick brushed aside their jibes and insisted he'd make it on his own abilities, not someone's coattail.

By the time he was 25, Dick began to suspect that he did not look forward to a life as a salesman for the rest of his career. He talked about his unrest with his friends, and they suggested that he groom himself for sales manager. "You won't make the kind of money you're making from commissions," he was told, "but you will have a foot in the door from an administrative standpoint, and you won't have to travel quite as much as you do now." Dick took their suggestions lightly, and continued to sell the product, but was aware that he felt dissatisfied and did not seem to get the satisfaction out of his job that he had once enjoyed.

By the end of his third year with the company Dick was convinced that he wanted a change in direction. As usual, he and the president spent quite a bit of time on the golf course during the annual company sales conference. After their match one day, the president kidded Dick about his game. The conversation drifted back to business, and the president, who seemed to be in a jovial mood, started to kid Dick about his sales ability. In a joking way, he implied that anyone could sell a product as good as Tri-American's, but that it took real "guts and know-how" to make the products. The conversation drifted to other things, but this remark stuck with Dick.

Sometime later, Dick approached the president formally with a request for a transfer out of the sales division. The president was surprised and hesitant about this change in career direction for Dick. He recognized the superior sales ability that Dick seemed to possess, but was unsure that Dick was willing or able to assume responsibilities in any other division of the organization. Dick sensed the hesitancy, but continued to push his request. He later remarked that it seemed that the initial hesitancy of the president convinced Dick that he needed an opportunity to prove himself in a field other than sales.

Troubleshooter   Dick was finally transferred back to the home office of the organization and indoctrinated into productive and administrative roles in the company as a special assistant to the senior vice president of production. As a special assistant, Dick was assigned several troubleshooting jobs. He acquitted himself well in this role, but in the process succeeded in gaining a reputation as a ruthless head hunter among the branches where he had performed a series of amputations. His reputation as an amiable, genial, easygoing guy from the sales department was the antithesis of the reputation of a cold, calculating head hunter which he earned in his troubleshooting role. The vice president, who was Dick's boss, was aware of the reputation which Dick had earned, but was pleased with the results that were obtained. The faltering departments that Dick had worked in seemed to bloom with new life and energy after Dick's recommended amputations. As a result, the vice president began to sing Dick's praises, and the president began to accept Dick in his new role in the company.

Management Responsibility   About three years after Dick's switch from sales, he was given an assignment as assistant plant manager of an English branch of the company. Dick, who had remarried, moved his wife and family to London, and they attempted to adapt to their new routine. The plant manager was English, as were most of the other employees. Dick and his family were accepted with reservations into the community life as well as into the plant life. The difference between British and American philosophy and performance within the plant was marked for Dick who was imbued with modern managerial concepts and methods. Dick's directives from head-quarters were to update and upgrade performance in this branch. However, his power and authority were less than those of his superior, so he constantly found himself in the position of having to soft pedal or withhold suggestions that he would have liked to make, or innovations that he would have liked to introduce. After a frustrating year and a half, Dick was suddenly made plant manager of an old British company which had just been purchased by Tri-American. He left his first English assignment with mixed feelings and moved from London to Birmingham.

As the new plant manager, Dick operated much as he had in his troubleshooting job for the first couple of years of his change from sales to administration. Training and reeducation programs were instituted for all supervisors and managers who survived the initial purge. Methods were studied and simplified or redesigned whenever possible, and new attention was directed toward production which better met the needs of the sales organization. A strong controller helped to straighten out the profit picture through stringent cost control: and, by the end of the third year, the company showed a small profit for the first time in many years. Because he felt that this battle was won, Dick requested transfer back to the United States. This request was partially granted when nine months later he was awarded a junior vice president title, and was made manager of a subsidiary Canadian plant, Modrow.

Modrow Manager   Prior to Dick's appointment as plant manager at Modrow, extensive plans for plant expansion and improvement had been approved and started. Although he had not been in on the original discussions and plans, he inherited all the problems that accompany large-scale changes in any organization. Construction was slower in completion than originally planned, equipment arrived before the building was finished, employees were upset about the extent of change expected in their work routines with the installation of additional machinery, and, in general, morale was at a low ebb.

Various versions of Dick's former activities had preceded him, and on his arrival he was viewed with dubious eyes. The first few months after his arrival were spent in a frenzy of catching up. This entailed constant conferences and meetings, volumes of reading of past reports, becoming acquainted with the civic leaders of the area, and a plethora of dispatches to and from the home office. Costs continued to climb unabated.

By the end of his first year at Modrow, the building program had been completed, although behind schedule, the new equipment had been installed, and some revamping of cost procedures had been incorporated. The financial picture at this time showed a substantial loss, but since it had been budgeted as a loss, this was not surprising. All managers of the various divisions had worked closely with their supervisors and accountants in planning the budget for the following year, and Dick began to emphasize his personal interest in cost reduction.

As he worked through his first year as plant manager, Dick developed the habit of strolling around the organization. He was apt to leave his office and appear anywhere on the plant floor, in the design offices, at the desk of a purchasing agent or accountant, in the plant cafeteria rather than the executive dining room, or wherever there was activity concerned with

Modrow. During his strolls he looked, listened, and became acquainted. If he observed activities that he wanted to talk about, or heard remarks that gave him clues to future action, he did not reveal these at the time. Rather he had a nod, a wave, a smile, for the people near him, but a mental note to talk to his supervisors, managers, and foremen in the future. At first his presence disturbed those who noted him coming and going, but after several exposures to him without any noticeable effect, the workers came to accept his presence and continue their usual activities. Supervisors, managers, and foremen, however, did not feel as comfortable when they saw him in the area.

Their feelings were aptly expressed by the manager of the siding department one day when he was talking to one of his foremen: "I wish to hell he'd stay up in the front office where he belongs. Whoever heard of a plant manager who had time to wander around the plant all the time? Why doesn't he tend to his paper work and let us tend to our business?"

"Don't let him get you down," joked the foreman. "Nothing ever comes of his visits. Maybe he's just lonesome and looking for a friend. You know how these Americans are."

"Well, you may feel that nothing ever comes of his visits, but I don't. I've been called into his office three separate times within the last two months. The heat must really be on from the head office. You know these conferences we have every month where he reviews our financial progress, our building progress, our design progress, etc.? Well, we're not really progressing as fast as we should be. If you ask me we're in for continuing trouble."

In recalling his first year at Modrow, Dick had felt constantly pressured and badgered. He always sensed that the Canadians he worked with resented his presence since he was brought in over the heads of the operating staff. At the same time he felt this subtle resistance from his Canadian work force, he believed that the president and his friends in the home office were constantly on the alert, waiting for Dick to prove himself or fall flat on his face. Because of the constant pressures and demands of the work, he had literally dumped his family into a new community and had withdrawn into the plant. In the process, he built up a wall of resistance toward the demands of his wife and children who, in turn, felt as though he was abandoning them.

During the course of the conversation with his university friends, he began to recall a series of incidents that probably had resulted from the conflicting pressures. When describing some of these incidents, he continued to emphasize the fact that his attempt to be relaxed and casual had backfired. Laughingly, Dick said, "As you know, both human relations and accounting were my weakest subjects during the master's program, and yet they are two fields I felt I needed the most at Modrow at this time." He described some of the cost procedures that he would have liked to incorporate. However, without the support and knowledge furnished by his former controller, he busied himself with details that were unnecessary. One day, as he describes it, he overheard a conversation between two of the accounting staff members with whom he had been working very closely. One of them commented to the other, "For a guy who's a vice president, he sure spends a lot of time breathing down our necks. Why doesn't he simply tell us the kind of systems he would like to try, and let us do the experimenting and work out the budget?" Without commenting on the conversation he overheard, Dick then described himself as attempting to spend less time and be less directive in the accounting department.

Another incident he described which apparently had real meaning for him was one in which he had called a staff conference with his top-level managers. They had been going "hammer and tongs" for better than an hour in his private office, and in the process of heated conversation had loosened ties, taken off coats, and really rolled up their sleeves. Dick himself had slipped out of his shoes. In the midst of this, his secretary reminded him of an appointment with public officials. Dick had rapidly finished up his conference with his managers, straightened his tie, donned his coat, and had wandered out into the main office in his stocking feet.

Dick fully described several incidents when he had disappointed, frustrated, or confused his wife and family by forgetting birthdays, appointments, dinner engagements, etc. He seemed to be describing a pattern of behavior which resulted from continuing pressure and frustration. He was setting the scene to describe his baffling and humiliating position in the siding department. In looking back and recalling his activities during this first year, Dick commented on the fact that his frequent wanderings throughout the plant had resulted in a nodding acquaintance with the workers, but probably had also resulted in foremen and supervisors spending more time getting ready for his visits and reading meaning into them afterwards than attending to their specific duties. His attempts to know in detail the accounting procedures being used required long hours of concentration and detailed conversations with the accounting staff, which were time-consuming and very frustrating for him, as well as for them. His lack of attention to his family life resulted in continued pressure from both wife and family.

The Siding Department Incident   Siding was the product which had been budgeted as a large profit item of Modrow. Aluminum siding was gaining in popularity among both architects and builders because of its possibilities in both decorative and practical uses. Panel sheets of siding were shipped in standard sizes on order; large sheets of the coated siding were cut to specifications in the trim department, packed, and shipped. The trim shop was located near the loading platforms, and Dick often cut through the trim shop on his wanderings through the plant. On one of his frequent trips through the area, he suddenly became aware of the fact that several workers responsible for the disposal function were spending countless hours at high-speed saws cutting scraps into specified lengths to fit into scrap barrels.

The narrow bands of scrap which resulted from the trim process varied in length from 7 to 27 feet and had to be reduced in size to fit into disposal barrels. Dick, in his concentration on cost reduction, picked up one of the thin strips, bent it several times, and fitted it into the barrel. He tried this with another piece and it bent very easily. After assuring himself that bending was possible, he walked over to a worker at the saw and asked why he was using the saw when material could easily be bent and fitted into the barrels, resulting in saving time and equipment. The worker's response was, "We've never done it that way, sir. We've always cut it."

Following his plan of not commenting or discussing matters on the floor, but distressed by the reply, Dick returned to his office and asked the manager of the siding department if he could speak to the foreman of the scrap division. The manager said, "Of course, I'll send him up to you in just a minute."

After a short time, the foreman, very agitated at being called to the plant manager's office, appeared. Dick began questioning him about the scrap disposal process and received the standard answer: "We've always done it that way." Dick then proceeded to review cost-cutting objectives. He talked about the pliability of the strips of scrap. He called for a few pieces of scrap to demonstrate the ease with which it could be bent, and ended what he thought was a satisfactory conversation by requesting the foreman to order heavy duty gloves for his workers and use the bending process for a trial period of two weeks to check the cost saving possible.

The foreman listened throughout most of this hour's conference, offered several reasons why it wouldn't work, raised some questions about the record-keeping process for cost purposes, and finally left the office with the forced agreement to try the suggested new method of bending, rather than cutting, for disposal. Although he was immersed in many other problems, his request was forcibly brought home one day as he cut through the scrap area. The workers were using power saws to cut scraps. He called the manager of the siding department and questioned him about the process. The manager explained that each foreman was responsible for his own process, and since Dick had already talked to the foreman, perhaps he had better talk to him again. When the foreman arrived, Dick began to question him. He received a series of excuses, and some explanations of the kinds of problems they were meeting by attempting to bend the scrap material. "I don't care what the problems are," Dick nearly shouted, "when I request a cost-reduction program instituted, I want to see it carried through."

Dick was furious. When the foreman left, he phoned the maintenance department and ordered the removal of the power saws from the scrap area immediately. A short time later the foreman of the scrap department knocked on Dick's door reporting his astonishment at having maintenance men step into his area and physically remove the saws. Dick reminded the foreman of his request for a trial at cost reduction to no avail, and ended the conversation by saying that the power saws were gone and would not be returned, and the foreman had damned well better learn to get along without them. After a stormy exit by the foreman, Dick congratulated himself on having solved a problem and turned his attention to other matters.

A few days later Dick cut through the trim department and literally stopped to stare. As he described it, he was completely nonplussed to discover gloved workmen using hand shears to cut each piece of scrap.

Questions   How does the trimming incident illustrate *(a)* Spencer's managerial strengths and weaknesses and *(b)* the stressors to which he is most vulnerable? What would you recommend *(a)* for dealing with the immediate problem and *(b)* for Spencer's long-term future career?

Groups and Their Leadership

16 Group Function and Process

What are the types and functions of groups in organizations?

How do cohesiveness, norms, and roles affect group functioning?

How can these group properties be managed?

How are individual attitudes, behavior, and performance levels influenced by the work group?

The primary focus of previous chapters was the individual within the organization. In this and the next chapter, we will examine groups in organizations. Our discussion will illustrate the significance of work groups' impact on the organization, as well as group influences on individual attitudes, behavior, and job performance.

WHY STUDY GROUPS?

The assignment of group projects at the beginning of a term is often bad news for students. Many will remember past assignments that were ruined by uncooperative, argumentative, lazy, or untalented teammates.

Despite the negative reactions, important reasons underlie such assignments. A group task creates a situation in which each student is dependent *on* others and accountable *to* others. Aspiring managers must learn to cope with both of these circumstances. Members of a work group are dependent on their boss for information, budget, and other job-related and personal needs. The manager is likewise dependent on the subordinate group. The group's productivity may be a major part of the manager's performance evaluation. To echo a recent commercial slogan, "If they don't look good, you don't look good."

Groups are the building blocks of organizations. Operative level employees work in assembly groups, specialists are assigned to project teams, and office secretaries interact with one another on an ongoing basis. Executive committees make, and management teams implement, important policy decisions. Informal cliques develop at all organizational levels, and boards of directors monitor corporate performance.

While many managers wish fervently for more time alone, group activities are an inescapable fact of managerial careers. Up to 80 percent of a manager's time is wrapped up in group interactions.

Positive and Negative Effects of Groups

Understanding groups is essential because group processes have a direct impact on problem solving, decision making, and productivity. The outcomes are important, but the processes leading to them are often subtle, and many managers are frustrated in their attempts to ascertain what makes groups tick.

Groups have both positive and negative impacts in organizational settings:

In *The Soul of a New Machine,* Tracy Kidder (1981) described a team of talented computer scientists at Data General that seemed to push themselves beyond the limits of endurance and ability, often working 80 to 100 hours per week. Their combined creative energies and enormous dedication helped the team develop a 32-bit supermini-computer in a seemingly impossible period of time.

In the famous Hawthorne studies at the Western Electric Company (Roethlisberger & Dickson, 1939), various changes were made in the working conditions of a group of five women. Regardless of the change introduced (increased lighting, change in work hours, break times, even decreased lighting), productivity increased. This was true even after the 14th change, which eliminated all the benefits introduced previously and restored the original conditions. The investigators concluded that productivity improved because they had sought the women's advice at each stage. Communication among the women increased, and the women were able to coalesce as a group. Thus, group development in this instance had a positive impact on employee performance.

In a later phase of the same study, investigators observed that a group had established and maintained a very steady, but less than maximum, rate of productivity. Any group member who worked at rates beyond the normal level was chastised for being a "rate buster"—one who made the others look bad and increased the chance that management would start demanding more productivity out of everyone.

These messages escalated in severity, including initial "talking-to's," sterner talking-to's, social isolation, the "silent treatment," "binging," or punching an offender in the bicep, and at least one instance of a co-worker hitting a stubborn ratebuster in the head with a piece of two-by-four lumber! This was a blatant case of a group operating effectively to decrease, rather than increase, employee performance.

Irving Janis (1982) has analyzed some of the potential negative repercussions of group decisions, including groupthink. *Groupthink* includes overconfidence, underestimating the competition, and a suspension of critical thinking. This results in decisions that are overly risky, poorly thought out, and ultimately disastrous. Two examples of groupthink are the Bay of Pigs invasion of Cuba, ordered by President Kennedy, and decisions to continue escalating the Vietnam War by President Johnson and his advisors. The same process doubtless goes on in boardroom meetings at private sector corporations.

When will groups work the right way, and when the wrong way? In this and the following chapter, we will introduce concepts that will aid in understanding how groups operate, and offer suggestions for making them work effectively.

A Little History

The study of groups has a rich historical tradition dating back to 1897, when Triplett studied the enhancing effects of the presence of other people on an individual's performance. The rise of dictatorships, international aggression,

TABLE 16–1
The Evolution of Worker Participation in the United States

	Problem-Solving Teams	**Special-Purpose Teams**	**Self-Managing Teams**
Structure and function	Consist of 5 to 12 volunteers, hourly and salaried, drawn from different areas of a department. Meet one to two hours a week to discuss ways of improving quality, efficiency, and work environment. No power to implement ideas.	Duties may include designing and introducing work reforms and new technology, meeting with suppliers and customers, linking separate functions. In union shops, labor and management collaborate on operational decisions at all levels.	Usually 5 to 15 employees who produce an entire product instead of subunits. Members learn all tasks and rotate from job to job. Teams take over managerial duties, including work and vacation scheduling, ordering materials, etc.
Results	Can reduce costs and improve product quality. But do not organize work more efficiently or force managers to adopt a participatory style. Tend to fade away after a few years.	Involve workers and union representatives in decisions at ever-higher levels, creating atmosphere for quality and productivity improvements. Create a foundation for self-managing work teams.	Can increase productivity 30 percent or more and substantially raise quality. Fundamentally change how work is organized, giving employees control over their jobs. Create flatter organization by eliminating supervisors.
When introduced	Small-scale efforts in 1920s and 1930s. Widespread adoption in late 1970s based on Japanese Quality Circles.	Early-to-middle 1980s, growing out of problem-solving approach. Still spreading, especially in union sectors.	Used by a few companies in 1960s and 1970s. Began rapid spread in mid-to-late 1980s, and appear to be wave of future.

SOURCE: J. Hoerr, "The Payoff from Teamwork," reprinted from *Business Week*, July 10, 1989, p. 57, by special permission, copyright © 1989 by McGraw Hill, Inc.

and worldwide economic depression prior to World War II generated a wave of postwar group studies designed to improve the effectiveness of democratic organizations (Zander, 1979). The war itself was a huge group effort, spawning a number of group research studies. For example, Kurt Lewin was asked to find ways to motivate housewives to serve liver and brains at the dinner table, because those meats were not in short supply. Lewin found that women who participated in group discussions about how to persuade others to serve the meats were 10 times more likely to serve them to their own families than women who had only heard a stirring patriotic lecture (Aron & Aron, 1989).

Studies of group participation in decision making, leadership, and group productivity, as well as democratic processes in general, proliferated during this period. "Group dynamics" became a buzzword and a popular topic of study in the 1950s and 1960s. The faddishness of sensitivity training and other "groupy" topics eventually waned, but important topics like social power and influence, cooperation and competition, group problem solving, quality circles, and self-managed work teams still attract attention. Table 16–1 describes how team concepts have evolved in U.S. industry during recent years (Hoerr, 1989).

TYPES OF GROUPS

A group is a set of people who are interdependent, who are psychologically aware of one another and perceive themselves as a group, and who share some common goal. In organizations, members of formal groups focus on the common goal of a new product, service, a marketing plan, or a policy decision (Ancona, 1987). Work organizations have formal groups — the groups to which a member is officially assigned as a part of the job — and also informal groups, friendship groups that develop naturally on the basis of mutual attraction. A manager must understand both types, since both influence organizational behavior.

Formal Groups

Formal groups are based on the principle of division of labor. The Close-Up gives an example of one type of formal group. Virtually all formal work groups have some specialized task. Group task specialization can be based on hierarchy, function, product/service, and role (Gowler & Legge, 1981).

Different tasks are required at different *hierarchical levels.* Groups at higher levels are more likely to specialize in long-term decisions with potentially far-reaching effects, while middle-management groups are more likely to plan the implementation of senior management's policies. Junior-management groups often make the more routine, short-term decisions about implementation, and nonmanagerial employees at the lower levels of the hierarchy follow well-defined procedures for carrying out particular tasks.

Members of a particular business *function,* such as production, human resources, accounting, or marketing, will be differentiated by hierarchical level, but their shared skills, knowledge, and language will also separate them from other functions. The group will share a common perspective that will differ from other groups in the organization. This provides different points of view and expertise that can contribute to effective organizational decision making. (It can also form the basis for intergroup conflict. More will be said about this in the next chapter.)

Specialization also may be based on the *product* or *service* for which a group is responsible. A project manager, for example, heads a group responsible for planning a specific project and carrying it through to successful completion. Team members may include individuals from different levels in the organization's hierarchy, and commonly represent a number of different functional areas.

A *role* reflects a set of expectations about how one should behave or perform in a social interaction. Committees, negotiating teams, and problem-solving groups are examples of groups that specialize in roles defined by particular social relationships, unconstrained by the other bases of task specialization.

CLOSE-UP

Formal Groups in the Cockpit

The popular image of a pilot is that of a fearless, macho, maverick Top Gun making instantaneous life-or-death decisions. While this type of hero may epitomize "the right stuff," he would not be the most effective pilot in a commercial aircraft. Captains must manage crews, and it is team performance, not individual derring-do, that is crucial to a successful flight (Stark, 1989).

Team performance is necessitated by the sheer amount of information flight crews must process. Captains should have more than "stick and rudder" skills; they need an effective management style that includes delegating responsibility, taking advice from subordinates, and ultimately achieving great team coordination. Unfortunately, mistakes are made; the Federal Aviation Administration (FAA) estimates that between 60 and 80 percent of all accidents are due to communications breakdowns, lack of crew coordination, and other human factors in the cockpit.

A common problem occurs when a junior crewmember knows about a problem but doesn't mention it or is ignored by the captain. When one copilot reminded a captain that they were breaking a speed limit, the captain responded, "I'll do what I want." When advised again, the captain ordered him to "just look out the damn window." In one major crash, a ground controller who knew the plane was descending, timidly asked, "How are things comin' along out there?"

Part of the blame for mismanagement lies with the fact that flight crews often don't know each other; some meet just one hour before takeoff. Many in the airline industry believe that crews should be trained so they can coalesce into an effective team. The goal of special training, which uses flight simulations, is to enhance safety through the development of effective management skills and team performance. At least 16 airlines now offer such training, and even branches of the military are adopting it.

Hard data on training effectiveness are not yet available, but reports are favorable. It appears that pilots will soon be evaluated not only on the basis of technical skills, but also on their ability to lead an effective team.

Informal Groups

Formal groups are created to serve the organization, but beyond formal assignments, people belong to various informal groups. The importance of informal groups can be seen in Roy's (1961) studies of the culture and interaction patterns of work groups. In one study, Roy described a small group of men engaged in operating a punch press, a simple task that could be learned in about 15 minutes. While working in this small group, he noticed that several of the men had formed an informal group in order to reduce the boredom of the task. The men engaged in bantering and kidding, which Roy described as follows:

> What I saw at first, before I began to observe, was occasional flurries of horseplay so simple and unvarying in pattern and so childish in quality that they made no strong bid for attention. For example, Ike would regularly switch off the power at Sammy's machine whenever Sammy made a trip to the lavatory or the drinking

fountain. Sammy invariably fell victim to the plot by making an attempt to operate his clicking hammer after returning to the shop. And, as the simple pattern went, this blind stumbling into the trap was always followed by indignation and reproach from Sammy, smirking satisfaction from Ike, and mild paternal scolding from George. My interest in this procedure was at first confined to wondering when Ike would weary of his tedious joke or when Sammy would learn to check his power switch before trying the hammer.

But, as I began to pay closer attention, as I began to develop familiarity with the communication system, the disconnected became connected, the nonsense made sense, the obscure became clear, the silly actually funny. And as the content of the interaction took on more and more meaning, the interaction began to reveal structure (p. 61).

Note the phrases, "Before I began to observe," and later, "But, as I began to pay closer attention." The manager who observes his or her work group will often be rewarded with useful insights and revelations about the structure and functioning of the group. These informal interaction patterns are pertinent to more than just the shenanigans Roy observed on the shop floor. They affect the workings of groups throughout the organization, including executive ranks.

ATTRACTION TO GROUPS

Why do people join groups? People are attracted to groups because both formal and informal groups can serve vital functions for their members. Groups can provide rewards, or personal need satisfaction, to their members. Several types of rewards can motivate people to join groups (Shaw, 1981):

Interpersonal Attraction An individual may simply like or get along well with group members. This can be a powerful aspect of group functioning.

Activities Campus groups such as sports clubs, science fiction societies, political groups, or computer clubs, and community groups such as bridge clubs, country clubs, or track clubs exist in large part because members share interests in common activities. As discussed above, work groups often are formally organized (not to mention informally developed) on the basis of similar activities dictated by similar functions, products, and services.

Goals Joining a charity group, labor organization, school board, or coalition of executives in favor of some major policy change often occurs because espoused goals of the group are seen as worthy. Joining a group may also help individuals attain personal goals. Associating with certain executives on the golf course or tennis courts may not be appealing, but it may be seen as crucial toward promotion.

Power in Numbers From labor unions to executive coalitions, it may be difficult for separate individuals to accomplish their shared goals unless they band together, and this provides another reason for people to join groups.

How do people evaluate and choose *specific* groups? Two general concepts—comparison level and comparison level of alternatives—subsume the various specific rewards outlined above and help us understand and predict attraction to groups. The extent of attraction is manifested in such behaviors as joining, remaining, or leaving one group to join another (Thibaut & Kelly, 1978).

An individual's *comparison level* (CL) is the personal standard by which an interpersonal relationship—current or prospective—is evaluated. The CL represents a level of outcomes (rewards minus costs) that the person has become accustomed to in past relationships. If a person's outcomes (O) in a relationship are greater than CL, that person is likely to be satisfied with the relationship. Dissatisfaction results when outcomes are less than CL.

Consider two individuals who have recently joined the same sales team. Their rewards and costs, in objective terms, are about the same: same boss, same co-workers, same starting salary, same organizational performance. Person A has come from a third-rate organization with a lousy boss, low salaries, and a sagging performance record, whereas Person B has come from a real "winner." Person B will have a higher CL than Person A. It is not hard to predict who will be more satisfied with the new situation.

A comparison of CL with O helps to predict a person's attitude toward a relationship. But what about the person's behavior, specifically, the likelihood of joining or leaving a group? Here a second concept, *comparison level of alternatives,* becomes useful. A person's CL_{alt} is the standard established by the outcomes obtainable through membership in the best available alternative relationship. If $O > CL_{alt}$, the person is likely to remain in his or her current relationship, because the best available alternative is not as attractive as what he or she currently has; if $CL_{alt} > O$, leaving the current relationship and entering the new one would be predicted. Salesperson B, while less than happy with the situation because $O < CL$, will leave only if $O < CL_{alt}$; he will stay if $O > O_{alt}$. By comparing current outcomes with alternatives, people attempt to maximize their outcomes as described by expectancy and SEU theories discussed in Chapters 4 and 9.

SOCIAL INTERACTION

One aspect of our definition of groups involved the interaction of members. The nature of these interactions has a major impact on the characteristics the group develops and ultimately on group functioning.

Proximity: The Beginnings of Interaction

A group cannot form, or a friendship develop, without an opportunity to interact. An important basis for communication in an organization is proximity, that is, an opportunity to interact or experience some degree of closeness to one another (Farris, 1981). *Physical proximity* is important. We are more apt to strike up a conversation with someone who shares our office than someone on another floor, and less likely still to interact frequently with someone in another building or another city. To increase contact with others, some people like to have offices close to high-traffic areas of the building such as coffee rooms, busy halls, or restrooms. Similarly, the importance of physical proximity is not overlooked by those who jockey for an office positioned close to powerful individuals they want to get to know better.

Proximity also exists with respect to *profession* and *task*. Scientists are more likely to interact with other scientists, professional athletes with professional athletes, nurses with nurses, and custodians with custodians. People working on the same project, account, or committee are more likely to communicate with one another (on both work and nonwork issues) than people who do not have such task proximity. Computers can also provide proximity, as people can overcome geographical and organizational barriers to exchange information, explore common interests, or work on projects (Kiesler, 1986). When a group of students at a small college asked the college president if a heavy investment in computers would make it impossible to build a new student union, he replied, "With a computer network, the whole campus will be your student union" (Kiesler, 1986, p. 58).

Dyadic Interaction

For the time being, let us restrict our discussion to the interactions of just two members within a group. The groundwork for the relationship has been laid via some proximity that facilitates the meeting of two individuals. Now the interaction between the two people—a dyad—begins to unfold.

These two people interact in a process of social exchange. Just as in the economic exchange of goods and services between two parties in a business transaction, our two group members can be considered parties in a social exchange of interpersonal goods and services.

Consider yourself in interaction with a friend, co-worker, boss, family member, or mortal enemy. The two of you can exchange positive (or neutral) things like conversation, jokes, compliments, favors, help, advice, and gifts. You can share concerns, information, gossip, and opinions. You can trade invitations, rides to work, and baseball cards. You can also exchange more negative things like silence, insults, glares, and obstacles to each other's job performance. The list of possible exchanges is endless.

Rewards and costs are associated with any social relationship, and over time, the rewards and costs that flow from each individual to the other tend roughly to balance one another. A lack of balance, in which one person is receiving more from the relationship than the other, may cause ultimate problems between the parties.

Social Exchange Concepts

Numerous concepts point to the idea of balance in a relationship. The *norm of reciprocity,* which appears to apply in all cultures, states that when a person does something for you, you are obligated to return the favor in some way (Gouldner, 1960). The rule of *distributive justice* also governs social exchange (Homans, 1961). According to this rule, a person expects profits or outcomes in the exchange relation with another person to be proportionate to the investments made.

A person who feels interpersonal outcomes have been justly distributed will be comfortable with the relationship; if both parties to the exchange feel this way (and the outcomes are positive!), the relationship will be healthy and harmonious. On the other hand, a person who feels he or she receives less than distributive justice is likely to demonstrate emotional behavior, take aggressive action to restore justice by getting even, or leave the relationship. Thus, distributive justice may also be achieved through negative ways, such as getting back at someone who has wronged us.

There are many other examples of the same basic principle. The Golden Rule admonishes, "Do unto others as you would have them do unto you." Many experienced managers can testify to the prevalence of the "you scratch my back and I'll scratch yours" philosophy. The Beatles closed their *Abbey Road* album with, "And in the end, the love you take is equal to the love you make." Finally, Adams's (1965) theory of equity, described in Chapter 3, has added precision and greater analytical utility to social exchange concepts.

Unspecified Obligations

Social exchange entails unspecified obligations. When one person does a good turn for another, the first person expects some future return, but its nature is not stipulated in advance (Blau, 1964). There is some ambiguity concerning the nature, value, and timing of the reciprocal obligations incurred in social exchange.

This ambiguity raises an important issue. The parties to the exchange may differ in their subjective perceptions of the nature and degree of the obligations incurred. Suppose another manager does you a favor, such as backing you on a decision you hope to get approved. He may feel you "owe him one," that you are obligated to repay your social debt by backing him up next time he's in favor of something. You may not feel that way. First, you may feel that the exchange has simply been evened up, because you have gone out of your way to help him many times in the past. Second, you might view his support as neutral, because he probably would have agreed with it anyway, or because he stands to gain personally from it, or because you could have passed it through just as easily without his support. For many reasons, you may feel no obligation to him.

Now suppose that at some later time you stand by your own convictions about a new policy issue and disagree with him. Now he feels inequitably treated, responds with anger and resentment, and tries somehow to get even with you. You, in turn, feel inequitably treated and desire to get back at him. This vicious cycle toward the restoration of equity or distributive justice — in a negative rather than positive direction — usually ends only when one party stoically endures what he or she might regard as inequity in order to restart the social exchange process on a more auspicious footing.

INTERPERSONAL ATTRACTION

Much of what goes on in organizations depends on friendship allegiances. Many would not disagree with the observation that "it's who you know more than what you know" that counts in business. The immense popularity of Dale Carnegie's *How to Win Friends and Influence People* (1936) testifies to the importance many people place on their relationships with others and their desire to learn the techniques that will bring them interpersonal and ultimately business success.

How do two people in an exchange relationship develop their attitudes toward one another? What determines whether they will become friends, or merely acquaintances? The dynamics of the exchange relationship determine the extent to which the members of a group will come to like one another.

Psychologists have argued that attraction to another person is generally derived from experiencing reinforcement associated with that person (Byrne & Clore, 1960; Lott & Lott, 1960). The reinforcement model further proposed that we like those who may only be *associated* with reinforcing stimuli. No doubt you can think of persons toward whom you have especially warm feelings because they were present when you had a lot of fun or received some great news. The other person may not have administered or directly caused the reinforcement, but the affective response elicited by the reinforcement generalized to the surrounding stimuli. If you are rewarded in the presence of others, you will develop more positive attitudes toward them (Byrne, 1971).

People also can provide us *directly* with various forms of reinforcement, such as compliments, favors, or shared attitudes or interests (Aronson, 1988). Most people can testify to the good feelings that can result from receiving praise or a personal favor from another person. We not only feel good about the compliment; we also tend to feel more kindly disposed toward the person who gave it. Compliments that are more indirect — asking someone for advice, laughing at a person's jokes, or even remembering a family name (techniques well-used by many salespeople) — convey some degree of interest or liking that will leave a positive impact.

The expression of similar attitudes is also a positive influence on interpersonal attraction. Imagine that you meet a new manager from another department at a local gathering place. You strike up a conversation. You discover that you agree on the president's economic policies, the role of business in American society, the development of a new product, and the recent decision to promote a mutual acquaintance to vice president of marketing. As the conversation becomes more informal, you learn that you like the same music, movies, and football team.

Most likely, you will take an instant liking to one another. The more similar peoples' attitudes are, the greater the affective bond between them. If you and your conversation partner had disagreed on most of the topics discussed, you would be less likely to pursue a friendship.

None of these processes automatically increases interpersonal attraction. Praise and attitude agreement must be sincere, nonmanipulative, and credible. Favors should not be granted condescendingly, or in such a way that the receiver feels inferior, guilty, or indebted. Like so many other behavioral processes, there are conditions that may limit or even reverse their effects. But when sincere and natural, these interpersonal rewards increase the positive attraction between people.

PROPERTIES OF GROUPS

Every group, from the shop floor to boards of directors (see Focus on Management), comes to develop a unique personality. This is due not only to the uniqueness of individual members of the group, but also to group characteristics. Through the course of interaction among the group members, differences will begin to emerge. Some persons exert more influence than others. Some have more knowledge, others have more social skills, more prestige, or leadership qualities. Some groups are more tightly knit than others. And, of course, some groups are better than others at getting the job done.

Thus, numerous properties affect group functioning and distinguish one group from another. Perhaps the most significant properties for group functioning are cohesiveness, norms, and roles.

COHESIVENESS

The cohesiveness of a group is the degree to which its members are attracted to the group, are motivated to remain in the group, and mutually influence one another. Cohesiveness is related to a number of important aspects of group interaction.

Many of the effects of group cohesiveness are beneficial to the group. Although it may be intuitively apparent that a manager would be better off heading a group that gets along together, not all effects of cohesiveness are positive. And even the aspects of cohesiveness that are favorable to the group do not necessarily operate on behalf of the organization. Cohesiveness is a powerful factor in the operation of groups, and managers can benefit greatly by understanding its consequences and its causes.

FOCUS ON MANAGEMENT

The Invisible Director on Corporate Boards

Group dynamics affect team performance at every organizational level, including boards of directors (Alderfer, 1986). Even though most directors believe that their relationship with the chief executive officer (CEO) is more important than their relationships with other directors, no individual director can escape group forces.

Consider some of the effects of group properties like cohesiveness, norms, and roles. One behavioral norm widely shared by directors is that new members should not speak out until they become thoroughly knowledgeable about the company and the board. In fact, new members' naive questions can be valuable in prodding members to consider their assumptions and biases. Another norm is to speak euphemistically. "Frank has a problem with Tom" may actually mean "the CEO should fire his chief financial officer." Different norms are established by one CEO who stated: "The job of the board should be to support management," and another who said, "The job of management should be to create an atmosphere in which directors feel free to ask management thoughtful and penetrating questions."

The CEO's leadership style sets the tone for meetings by the issues they elect to bring to the board, the quality and timeliness of information they share, their responses to members' questions, and the nature of their presentations. Furthermore, the CEO—even though initially selected by the board—plays a key role in choosing new directors. New directors feel obligated to the CEO, and over time the CEO can formulate a cooperative, passive board.

As in other groups, subgroups form in boards of directors. Inside and outside directors form natural subgroups. Outside chief executives also may form a subgroup because they have faced similar problems. But a large group of CEOs is unlikely to offer an adequately diverse set of perspectives, and as boards become large, more and more work is done in committee.

Effective boards have many characteristics, but two group process factors are particularly important. First, directors and executives should cooperate in an effort to improve group effectiveness, rather than collude to establish a rubber-stamp board or undermine management's capacity to lead the corporation. Second, the board should establish a mechanism to review its own structure and process. For example, the last few minutes of each meeting can be used to critique the session. Such self-reflection can keep members more involved and committed, increase mutual influence, and enhance team performance (Alderfer, 1986).

Consequences of Cohesiveness

A wide array of consequences of cohesiveness has been documented. The cohesiveness of a group has an impact on numerous attitudes, perceptions, and behaviors.

Members of cohesive groups are generally more satisfied with the group than members of less cohesive groups. Many jobs are made more (or less) tolerable by the quality of the interpersonal relationships that develop between co-workers. Cohesiveness is thus an important source of *employee satisfaction*.

Members of cohesive groups exhibit more *responsible activity* on behalf of the group. They are more energetic in group activities, participate more in meetings, are less likely to be absent from group meetings, and are happy when the group succeeds and sad when it fails (Shaw, 1971). Members of noncohesive groups are less concerned and involved with the group's activities.

These tendencies clearly represent potential advantages to cohesiveness. However, this very concern for the group may be dysfunctional for the larger organization. Highly cohesive groups identify more strongly and immediately with their own product or function than with the larger goal or purpose of their organization. This creates a tendency toward *suboptimization:* the attempt to optimize at a lower level of a social system. Thus, a highly cohesive product-development group might care more about their success in designing and promoting their product—regardless of costs—than about the profit the product generates for the firm. Similarly, a close-knit group in the credit department may take such pride in its ability to minimize uncollectible receivables that it closes the door to risky (but potentially profitable) accounts.

Cohesive groups have greater levels of interaction between members than noncohesive groups. This higher level of *communication* is a potential benefit for task performance. There is also more communication directed toward straightening out deviant group members, which makes members of highly cohesive groups more likely to conform to group pressures. Thus, communications are not necessarily task-related, and the resulting uniformity of opinions and behavior may or may not enhance group effectiveness.

The more cohesive a group, the greater the extent to which its members will differentiate insiders from outsiders (Dion, 1973). In other words, cohesiveness generates a collective feeling of "we-ness," often in opposition to "them." The group develops a positive *bias in perceptions* of itself, and negative or derogatory biases toward others that may create hostility and conflict.

Both biases combine to increase the likelihood that outsider groups are perceived as inferior or as threats. Even nonconspiratorial actions by the outside group can be interpreted in negative ways. Thus, seemingly unimportant management decisions can become vested with profound symbolism and regarded as threats, disparagements, or inequities. The cohesive group's unified response may trigger a succession of moves and countermoves that escalate into psychological combat.

In similar fashion, cohesive work groups are more likely to *resist changes* that affect the structure, activities, or members of the group. Well-intentioned attempts by management to improve worker motivation and satisfaction by redesigning jobs have backfired because job redesign often breaks up the group. Hence, even if an active hostility is not engendered, cohesiveness provides a strong conservative force in favor of preserving the status quo.

Finally, what are the effects of cohesiveness on the *task performance* of the group? Logically, a group that meshes well should be capable of performing more effectively than one that is not so cohesive. But numerous investigations into this question have yielded mixed results — some found a positive relationship between cohesiveness and productivity, others found a negative relationship, and still others found no relationship at all.

Resolution of these mixed findings comes from the fact that the relationship depends on the goals and motivation of the group (Greene, 1989). All else being equal, cohesive groups with high production goals will perform at higher levels than noncohesive groups. Conversely, high cohesiveness in a work group will be associated with low productivity if the goals of the group are contrary to organizational or managerial goals (Roy, 1961).

In short, cohesive groups are generally better at achieving their goals than noncohesive groups. The question with respect to actual task performance is, "What *are* the group's goals?" Performance is determined by whether goals reflect high or low performance standards.

The group's goals can be even more detrimental to management if they represent active hostility rather than merely low productivity. For example, if a group developed a goal of sabotaging the company, a cohesive group would foul up company operations better than a less cohesive group.

The overall impact of high cohesiveness on group behavior can be very positive or very negative, depending on whether members feel that management is supportive or threatening to them (Seashore, 1954). The best management situation is having a cohesive work group with goals consistent with management's. Great difficulties can arise when one's group is cohesive but against management. Given the many important consequences of cohesiveness, summarized in Table 16–2, a manager is well advised to consider the cohesiveness in a work group before making important decisions. Furthermore, the manager should understand the factors — also summarized in Table 16–2 — that can cause cohesiveness.

TABLE 16–2
Consequences and Causes of Group Cohesiveness

Consequences of Cohesiveness	**Causes of Cohesiveness**
Satisfaction	Member similarity
Responsible activity	Group size
Suboptimization	Entrance standards
Communication	Isolation
Feeling of "we-ness"	External threat
Resistance to change	Participation
Performance	Dependence patterns
	Reward systems

Causes of Cohesiveness

What can a manager do to build cohesiveness and management-oriented goals in a work group? Numerous factors influence levels of group cohesiveness; the following factors are useful if a leader is in charge of creating a new group:

Member Similarity   Similarity in attitudes contributes to individuals liking each other. Other dimensions of similarity are also important to interpersonal attraction and group cohesiveness. Commonly held values, which are more broadly based than attitudes toward specific objects or issues, represent a critical factor.

For example, ethnicity traditionally has served as a basis for work group cohesion. Workers conscious of their Italian, Polish, Jewish, or transplanted Appalachian heritage coalesce around shared values concerning religion, the family, the meaning of work, and tradition. In this era of work force diversity, as non-English speaking immigrants contribute to labor-force growth, people from the same countries form subgroups and speak together in their native tongues (Solomon, 1989). Shared values, ideologies, and world views promote agreement on criteria for behavior in the group and purposes of group activities. Homogeneity of characteristics such as sex, age, or educational attainments does not seem to be as critical for group cohesion (Seashore, 1954).

Group Size   Smaller groups are more likely than large groups to develop a cohesive structure. Small size provides ease of interaction among all group members and helps even the least assertive members contribute to and feel a part of the group. Larger groups provide more opportunity for the development of internal cliques and factions.

High Entrance Standards   Being one of the select few to get accepted into Harvard, become a Marine, make it through IBM's management training program, or survive the difficult initiation rites of a prestigious fraternity increases the value of membership in the group. It also engenders positive attitudes toward the group, through the cognitive dissonance process, as covered in Chapter 7. Cohesiveness increases accordingly.

Several other factors can be used to build cohesiveness in existing groups as well as newly formed groups.

Isolation   Physical distance increases the sheer cost of interacting with outsiders, so that communicative activities become directed internally. Also, physical isolation promotes the psychological sense of distinction between the group and outsiders. Group members can more easily distort and stereotype outsiders as "different from us." The cohesion of mining crews is legendary, in large part due to their chronic isolation from others.

External Threat A big game against a hated rival unites a school and a team just as a despised boss brings a work group together against him. A threat, while increasing cohesiveness, can operate to create goals either desired or undesired by management. If the immediate supervisor, higher management, or some specific policy change is viewed as threatening, the goals that develop will be counterproductive from the standpoint of management. On the other hand, if the threat is in the form of an impending deadline, or competition against another organization, it may command a cooperative pattern of teamwork built around productive work goals.

Prestige Honors and recognition, higher visibility in the organization, or heightened feelings of the importance of their work will bring about positive changes in the group.

Shared Success Success becomes a psychological lens that filters members' interpersonal perceptions of one another. By the same token, the experience of defeat or failure often damages relations among the group members. Dissension and scapegoating, particularly when extended over significant periods of poor group performance, will strip away any positive features of cohesiveness that had existed previously.

Participative Decision Practices Participation in work-related decisions can enhance cohesiveness and may help align group goals with management's goals. Participation enhances communication among the group members and creates or highlights interdependencies. It also generates more commitment to joint decisions, as opposed to decisions that are handed down unilaterally from above.

It must be recognized, though, that a group characterized by interpersonal hostilities — as opposed to mere lack of cohesiveness — and/or goals contrary to those held by management may not respond as desired to increased participation in decision making. Getting the group together may create an opportunity for more infighting, or for arriving at decisions that are dysfunctional to the organization. More will be said about the pros and cons of participative decision making in the next chapter.

One thing is very clear: a manager is well advised to consider the cohesion of a group before making important decisions that affect it. If the group is strongly cohesive, it is imperative that the manager try to anticipate the group's interpretation of, and response to, the contemplated action. Some degree of participation on the part of the group — ranging from consultation with informal group leaders to full discussion with the assembled group — may be advisable. To paraphrase Congreve, hell hath no fury like that of a scorned cohesive work group.

Rewards The importance of reward systems in influencing individual motivation and behavior was covered in earlier chapters. The reward system is particularly important in groups — it has a major impact on cohesiveness and it influences the extent to which the group's goals are congruent with management's goals for the group.

As with *individual* goals and performance, rewards that are contingent on the performance of the *group* will motivate higher group performance and constructive (in management's eyes) cohesion. Rewards or positive benefits tied to group performance will increase the desirability of group success. Similarly, punishments tied to poor group performance would increase the desire to avoid group failure. Individualized rewards, lack of group rewards, or rewards not contingent on group performance will interfere with group cohesiveness, group goals and motivation, and group performance.

GROUP NORMS

Group norms are "shared ways of looking at the world." Norms prescribe the attitudes, values, and rules for member behavior.

Some degree of uniformity of action is necessary if the group is to survive and move toward its goal. Once a standard or norm is established, there is pressure to adhere to it. Control and coordination of norms regulating the conduct of members promotes the group's continuity and success.

Success of the group does not inherently imply benefit to the organization. Group norms may prove dysfunctional to the larger organization. Table 16–3 provides numerous examples of issues around which group norms may develop. It is clear that norms may arise that are detrimental to the organization, even if those norms have been consciously derived and are perceived by group members as promotive of their own goals.

Moreover, norms can become dysfunctional even for the group's goals. Norms can become ends in themselves because of tradition and their symbolic nature. Norms may endure long after the conditions that made them useful have changed, and eventually they become counterproductive.

For example, a work group may protect itself from a hostile supervisor by insisting that members refrain from casual socializing during breaks or lunch hour with any "suits" or "white-collar people." This dictum may continue when a new, more supportive boss succeeds the old one. The new supervisor may become alienated and prevented from demonstrating the support and consideration she might otherwise offer.

Even when group members wonder about the usefulness of a long-standing norm, they may be afraid to take the chance of violating it. Usually it is up to the leader to adjust the group's norms to new conditions.

ROLES, LEADERS, AND STATUS

As a group develops, it becomes apparent that some members can contribute more than others to group goals, and that members have different *comparative advantages* (relative strengths and abilities) in carrying out different functions for the group. As this occurs, roles develop. A *role* is a

TABLE 16–3

Categories of Organizational Norms with Positive and Negative Examples

| | Examples | |
Categories	Positive Norms	Negative Norms
Organization and personal pride	Members speak up for the company when it is criticized unfairly	Members don't care about company problems
Performance/excellence	Members try to improve, even if they are doing well	Members are satisfied with the minimum level of performance necessary
Teamwork/ communication	Members listen and are receptive to the ideas and opinions of others	Members gossip behind the backs of others rather than deal with issues openly and constructively
Leadership/supervision	Members ask for help when they need it	Members hide their problems and avoid their supervisors
Colleague/associate relations	Members refuse to take advantage of fellow workers	Members don't care about the well-being of fellow workers
Customer/consumer relations	Members show concern about serving the customers	Members are indifferent and, when possible, hostile to customers
Honesty and security	Members are concerned about dishonesty and pilferage	Members are expected to steal a little and be honest only when necessary
Training and development	Members really show they care about training and development	There is much talk about training and development but no one takes it seriously
Innovation and change	Members are usually looking for better ways of doing their jobs	Members stick to the old ways of doing their jobs

SOURCE: D. Hellriegel and J. Slocum, *Organizational Behavior,* 2nd ed. (St. Paul, Minn.: West Publishing, 1979), p. 295. Adapted by permission of the publisher from *Organizational Dynamics*, Spring 1973. Copyright © 1973 by Amacom, a division of American Management Association.

set of norms for the behavior of one or more but not all persons in the group. Roles consist of the norms that define different expectations for different members.

Task Specialist

In most groups, the first role to emerge is that of the task specialist or task leader (Bales, 1950). Whether the group is an intramural basketball team, a case study group, or a work group, it soon becomes clear that one person has the edge over the others in some skill or trait most relevant to the group's objective. That person is looked to for advice, instructions, and decision making. Whether or not this selection is formalized by a title (such as captain or chairperson), the task leader is expected to behave differently from the others.

Furthermore, the leader is accorded an elevated status in the group because of his or her contributions. He or she will be accorded a deference not shown toward others and will rightfully expect to receive a disproportionate share of the outcomes (honor, prestige, perquisites) realized by the group.

Maintenance Specialist

Sooner or later, the task specialist—despite the higher status—will wear down the morale of group members by continually exerting task pressure on people. Members may chafe at the restrictions and chores, especially if the rewards for group activity are seen only dimly in the distant future. In the meantime, the task leader imposes only costs to the members. At this point, a different kind of leader (and role), the human relations or maintenance specialist, emerges (Bales, 1950). The maintenance specialist bolsters morale—smooths over ruffled feathers, injects a note of humor, and takes a personal interest in members' feelings.

These roles vary in importance across cultures. Task considerations prevail in North America and Latin America, and Japan has a stronger maintenance orientation (Nath & Sadhu, 1988). Generally, the task and maintenance specialist roles do not coincide in the same person, since serving either role tends to conflict with the other. It is very difficult to play disciplinarian and humorist simultaneously. Those who have served as residence hall counselors are familiar with this dilemma. They are expected to serve as confidante and counselor to troubled undergraduates. Yet they also are counted on to impose law and order in the residence hall.

Other Roles

Task and maintenance specialists are not the only kinds of roles performed in effective groups. Leadership roles must be filled, and group members must perform other vital functions. Unless the group's task is simple and redundant, groups of similar people performing similar roles will not have the diversity to function effectively over time or as new challenges arise.

Some important roles, like task and maintenance leaders, focus on internal group functioning, and others concentrate on the group's relationships with outside groups. In high technology companies, project groups develop specialized roles of sentry, guard, scout, and ambassador (Gladstein & Caldwell, 1985). Sentries and guards protect their teams by buffering them from political pressure and attempts to control or take group resources. Scouts scan the environment and bring information to their groups. Ambassadors represent their groups to outsiders and negotiate for more resources. Thus, sentry and guard roles allow the group to focus on internal innovation, and scout and ambassador roles deal with external relations (Ancona, 1987).

Status

The status of a group member is determined, in part, by the importance of the role performed and his or her effectiveness in performing it. Also contributing to status in the group is the extent to which a person's behavior lives up to the general norms and values of the group. Even a "regular," who plays no special role, may earn the status of member in good standing by carefully observing the rules set by the group and serving in good spirit.

At the bottom of the status hierarchy are two types: those who lack the ability or resources to contribute in any significant way, and those who continually violate group norms. The latter frequently are marginal members of the group; they might prefer to belong to a different group, from which they are for some reason excluded, and they look to this other reference group as a guide for beliefs and behavior.

We will say more about the influence of status differences in the next section, as we address more explicitly the effects of groups on the attitudes and behavior of their individual members.

GROUP INFLUENCE ON INDIVIDUALS

The emphasis of this chapter has been on the whole group as it develops a structure, a pattern of relationships, cohesiveness, norms, and role and status differentiation. In concluding this chapter, and to reinforce some of the ideas presented thus far, let us consider the ways in which the work group affects an individual's attitudes, behavior, and task performance.

Attitudes

Several general statements can be made about the effects of groups on the attitudes of individual members. First, the work group is a potentially strong influence on an employee's job satisfaction or dissatisfaction. As discussed in Chapter 13, co-workers constitute a major part of the work environment and therefore affect satisfaction. Co-workers' competencies and interpersonal compatibilities, cohesiveness, and other aspects of group structure contribute directly to the pleasure, or pain, of work life.

Second, group members tend to develop congruent attitudes. Studies consistently demonstrate that people acquire new attitudes, or change existing ones, when they are exposed to the expressed attitudes of others. This can happen consciously or subtly and over significant periods of time, without full realization by the individual.

This *social information processing* is important in organizations (Salancik & Pfeffer, 1978). Employees evaluate their jobs based partly on the social cues provided by others. If a person's co-workers make positive statements about their jobs, the positive aspects of the job will become more salient and perceptions of the work situation will then become more positive. Similarly, frequent complaints from co-workers will negatively affect one's attitudes.

Third, an important attitude called organizational commitment is similar to some of the aspects of group processes discussed in this chapter. *Organizational commitment* is a psychological construct that refers to an employee's loyalty to, desire to remain a member of, and willingness to exert effort on behalf of the organization. This represents an important employee attitude, as it has been consistently found to be related to such behaviors as turnover, absenteeism, quality of work, and sometimes productivity (Steers, Mowday & Porter, 1982). Organizational commitment is a single, combined reconceptualization of cohesiveness, desire for group success, and conformity to group standards (Zander, 1979).

Behavior

As with attitudes, behavior within groups tends to be more uniform than behavior exhibited by individuals who are in different groups. The effects of group norms on individual group members depend on two properties of norms: the amount of a given behavior that is exhibited by a group member, and the degree to which other group members approve or disapprove of that behavior (Nadler, Hackman, & Lawler, 1979). Figure 16–1 shows how any norm can be depicted graphically based on these two properties. The

FIGURE 16–1

An Illustrative Norm for Leadership Acts

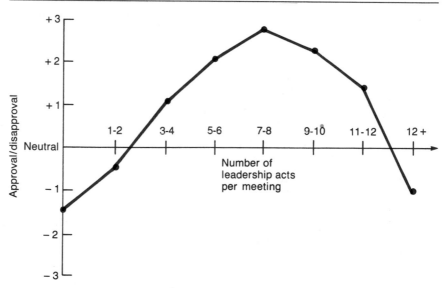

From MANAGING ORGANIZATIONAL BEHAVIOR by David A. Nadler, J. Richard Hackman, and Edward E. Lawler III. Copyright © 1979 by David A. Nadler, J. Richard Hackman, and Edward E. Lawler III. Reprinted by permission of HarperCollins Publishers.

FIGURE 16–2

a. A High-Intensity Norm about Productivity

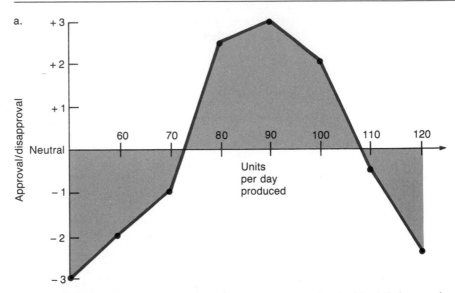

behavior analyzed here is the initiation of "leadership attempts" in group meetings. The amount of approval or disapproval shown by the group can range from strongly positive ($+3$), through neutral (0), to strongly negative (-3), as shown on the vertical axis of the graph. The amount of the behavior under analysis is shown on the horizontal axis. The resulting curve is called a *return potential curve,* since it shows the return or social payoff to the individual (by the responses of other group members) for various amounts of the behavior (Jackson, 1965).

The peak of the return potential curve reveals the point of maximum return, and the range of tolerable behavior is indicated by the portion of the curve falling in the approval range. Leadership initiatives at the rate of seven to eight per meeting will receive the most approval from the group, although a fairly wide range of behavior is tolerated or approved.

Disapproval comes from too much deviation in either direction from the norm, that is, too little or too much leadership initiative. This represents a fairly common pattern of social reinforcement and punishment for individual behavior with respect to some norm of behavior.

Figure 16–2 illustrates another property of a group norm—intensity. Both graphs analyze group norms surrounding productivity. In both groups, the point of maximum return (90 units) and the range of tolerable behavior (about 72 units to about 108 units) are equal. Nonetheless, the enforcement

FIGURE 16–2 *(concluded)*

b. A Low-Intensity Norm about Productivity

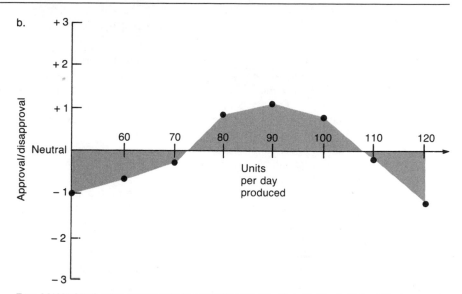

From MANAGING ORGANIZATIONAL BEHAVIOR by David A. Nadler, J. Richard Hackman, and Edward E. Lawler III. Copyright © 1979 by David A. Nadler, J. Richard Hackman, and Edward E. Lawler III. Reprinted by permission of HarperCollins Publishers.

of the two norms is quite different between the two groups. In the first group, the norm is much more intensely held than in the second group, as evidenced by different amounts of social approval and disapproval accruing from adherence to and deviance from the norm.

Individual Task Performance

One of the first studies in psychology (Triplett, 1897) investigated the manner in which an individual's performance is enhanced by the presence of others. *Social facilitation* deals with how an individual's task performance is affected by working in the presence of other individuals, but independently of them. Allport (1924) called this a co-acting group situation and predicted that the presence of others has an energizing effect on the individual, causing him or her to work with greater intensity but to lose accuracy. The conclusion was that the presence of other people increases motivation, but reduces the quality of performance (see Close-Up).

Zajonc (1965), a psychologist at the University of Michigan, explained social facilitation effects by suggesting that the presence of other people facilitates the performance of previously learned behaviors, but impairs the learning of new responses. The presence of other people has drive-producing

CLOSE-UP

Racers, Rats, and Roaches

Interest in social facilitation is not new, nor limited to social motivation at work. The original study, published in 1897, examined the effects of pacing on bicycle racers. The attention has not focused purely on human subjects (Zajonc, 1965). Chickens that had eaten until they were fully satisfied ate two thirds again as much grain when joined by a hungry companion chicken. Eating alone also has been shown in rats and in puppies to lead to less consumption than eating with others. Ants excavated more soil in nest building when working in the presence of other ants.

But these behaviors are already well learned; when new learning is required, performance is inhibited by the presence of others. Learning inhibition has been demonstrated in finches trying to discriminate between palatable and unpalatable foods, and in rats trying to avoid electric shock. Perhaps most intriguingly, cockroaches took longer to learn mazes when other cockroaches were present! Reputedly, the same effect has been demonstrated in the presence of *crushed* cockroaches *under* the maze. Apparently, the aroma of other roaches provided the social interference.

properties that raise our awareness, arousal, or activation level. In a well-learned task this energizing effect enhances performance, but in a poorly learned task, the individual is "overenergized." The new task also has drive-producing properties. Thus, one tends to be "overaroused," and performance quality is therefore impaired. A recent review of social facilitation research concluded that the presence of other people leads to slightly lower performance on complex tasks, and faster (but not more accurate) performance on simple tasks (Bond & Titus, 1983).

Social Loafing and Free Riding

When group members work together to accomplish a task, the effect on individual productivity may be negative rather than positive. The output of several individuals in a group often is significantly lower than the total output produced by the same individuals working alone (Harkins, Latané, & Williams, 1980). The tendency for individuals to produce at less than their maximum capability when working as a member of an interacting group has been labeled, appropriately enough, *social loafing.* When a loafer slacks off more than other group members, yet receives the full benefits of group membership, the member has become a *free rider.*

The extent of social loafing and free riding varies across cultures. Social loafing has been observed among managers in the United States, where individualistic beliefs are a cultural norm. Social loafing does not occur among Chinese managers, who hold more collectivistic beliefs. In fact, Chinese managers work harder, rather than less, in a group than when alone. In contrast with American managers, Chinese managers appear to place group goals and collective interests ahead of self-interest (Earley, 1989).

One explanation for social loafing and free riding considers the effect of group size on individual productivity (Steiner, 1972). Free riding is more prevalent in large groups than in smaller groups, for three reasons: noticeability, perceptibility, and individual share in the public good (Albanese & Van Fleet, 1985). First, in small groups, members and their contributions to the group are more noticeable; in large groups, a person is more likely to get away with loafing or free riding. Second, in small groups, members feel that their efforts matter; in large groups they may conclude that their efforts will make no real difference. Third, the smaller the group, the greater the share of rewards each group member receives. You may recognize the components of expectancy theory in this analysis, as group members' efforts are a function of perceived probabilities and magnitudes of positive and negative outcomes.

Other Influences

Finally, as with other work behaviors, task performance of individual members is influenced by the group's goals, norms, and cohesiveness. These factors will influence the extent to which the group monitors and reinforces performance.

Figure 16–3 demonstrates some possible distributions of individual performance levels within a group. Group A represents a relatively noncohesive group, with poorly defined goals and norms. Variance in individual performance levels will be high, assuming no severe performance constraints, like assembly-line technology. Performance will be influenced by individual differences in skills, motivation, and understanding of the job requirements, and the group will not make great efforts to monitor and change the performance of its members.

Group B and C, conversely, are highly cohesive groups. Cohesiveness and fairly well-defined norms of performance are suggested by the low variance in performance. Cohesive groups, of course, monitor member adherence to norms. What variance does exist in performance may be accounted for by individual differences in skills.

Groups B and C differ from one another, however, in the nature of their goals and norms. Group B apparently has goals consistent with management's goals, due to the reward structure or other factors, and has a norm of high performance standards. Group C has goals generally counter to management's goals, resulting in an enforced norm of low performance.

Individual Differences in Compliance

Characteristics of the individual group member will help predict the extent of his or her compliance with group norms. Individuals differ on the general importance they attach to social approval (recall McCleland's need for

FIGURE 16–3
Distributions of Individual Performance

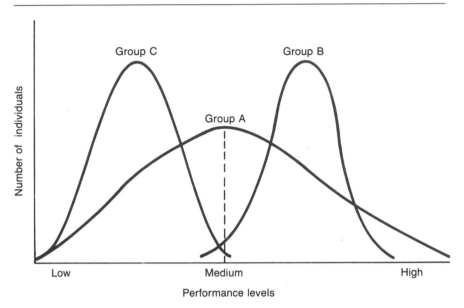

affiliation or Maslow's social needs). Thus, the same social approval may result in one person rebelling, another conforming, and a third exhibiting the creative individualism response (recall Chapter 15).

Differing roles and status levels within the group often determine the levels of disapproval resulting from deviance. In other words, a return potential curve may hold one general shape for all group members, but ranges of tolerable behavior and the intensities of approval and disapproval may vary somewhat from person to person.

Sociologists have found that the middle classes of a large society hold most tenaciously to accepted conventions of social behavior. This is also the case in small groups. "Regulars" have more to lose from deviance, and more to gain from compliance. On the other hand, high-status members—including the accepted leaders—may have *idiosyncracy credits* (Hollander, 1964). Their contributions to the group and "credits" for generally conforming to important group norms give them the latitude to occasionally depart from group norms, especially if they do so in a fashion that may benefit the group. They have the "political capital" for taking the risks of controversial actions.

SUMMARY

Organizations, of necessity, create groups of interacting individuals. Groups, in turn, serve multiple functions for employees as well as for the organization. Interaction among members is initiated by some form of proximity; it then proceeds in the context of a social exchange process, governed by norms of reciprocity, distributive justice, and equity.

Groups come to vary in cohesiveness, or the extent to which members identify with the group and exert mutual influence on each other. Cohesion has many important consequences, including conflict with outsiders, resistance to change, identification with group rather than organizational goals, and higher employee satisfaction. The effects of cohesion on productivity depends on whether the group supports organizational and management goals. Variables that influence cohesion include interpersonal attraction, size, extent of isolation, external threat, prestige of the group, participation in decision making, and reward structures.

Groups develop performance goals and norms, and roles evolve for individual group members. Status is determined in part by the importance of members' roles. Group norms in particular were used in this chapter to illustrate the effects of the group on the behavior of individual members. Goals and cohesiveness were then added to the analysis to explain the patterns of individual job performance within work groups.

CONCEPTS TO REMEMBER

Group	Types of proximity	Maintenance specialist
Formal versus informal groups	Social exchange concepts	Social information processing
Bases of group task specialization	Cohesiveness	Organizational commitment
Attraction to groups	Suboptimization	Return potential curves
Functions of groups	Causes of cohesiveness	Social facilitation
Comparison level	Group norms	Social loafing
Comparison level of alternatives	Comparative advantage	Free riding
	Task specialist	Idiosyncracy credits

QUESTIONS FOR DISCUSSION

1. What advantages do cohesive groups present to the employing organization? Disadvantages?
2. What can a manager do to make a group more cohesive?

3. Given what was discussed in the chapter, what predictions would you make about the relative cohesion of: basketball versus football teams; coal miners versus auto-assembly workers; textile workers in a small town versus home-office insurance workers in a metropolitan area; a submarine crew versus a naval shipyard maintenance unit?

4. Explain the following situation by rank ordering the magnitudes of outcomes (rewards minus costs), comparison levels, and comparison levels of alternatives: *(a)* being happy with a romantic relationship and remaining in it; *(b)* being unhappy with a career and leaving it; *(c)* being happy with a job, but leaving it; and *(d)* being unhappy with a graduate school, but remaining in it.

5. Consider a group with which you are familiar. Identify some key norms in the group. Analyze the norms in terms of their impact on group effectiveness, how they are enforced, and how individual group members are influenced.

REFERENCES

Adams, J. S. (1965). Inequity in social exchange. In L. Berkowitz (ed.), *Advances in experimental social psychology*, vol. 2. New York: Academic Press.

Alderfer, C. P. (1986). The invisible director on corporate boards. *Harvard Business Review,* November-December, 38–52.

Ancona, D. G. (1987). Groups in organizations: Extending laboratory models. In C. Hendrick (ed.), *Perspectives on social psychology.* Beverly Hills: Sage Publications.

Albanese, R., & Van Fleet, D. (1985). Rational behavior in groups: The free riding tendency. *Academy of Management Review* 10, 244–55.

Allport, F. H. (1924). *Social psychology.* Boston: Houghton Mifflin.

Aron, A., & Aron, E. (1989). *The heart of social psychology,* 2nd ed. Lexington, MA: Lexington Books.

Aronson, E. (1988). *The social animal.* New York: W. H. Freeman.

Bales, R. F. (1950). *Interaction process analysis: A method for the study of small groups.* Reading, MA: Addison-Wesley Publishing.

Blau, P. (1964). *Exchange and power in social life.* New York: John Wiley & Sons.

Bond, C., Jr., & Titus, L. (1983). Social facilitation: A meta-analysis of 241 studies. *Psychological Bulletin* 94, 265–92.

Byrne, D. (1971). *The attraction paradigm.* New York: Academic Press.

Byrne, D., & Clore, G. L. (1970). A reinforcement model of evaluative responses. *Personality: An International Journal* 1, 103–28.

Carnegie, D. (1936). *How to win friends and influence people.* New York: Simon & Schuster.

Dion, K. L. (1973). Cohesiveness as a determinant of ingroup-outgroup bias. *Journal of Personality and Social Psychology* 28, 163–71.

Earley, P. C. (1989). Social loafing and collectivism: A comparison of the U.S. and the People's Republic of China. *Administrative Science Quarterly* 34, 565–81.

Farris, G. (1981). Groups and the informal organization. In R. Payne & C. Cooper (eds.), *Groups at work.* New York: John Wiley & Sons.

Gladstein, D., & Caldwell, D. (1985). Boundary management in new product teams. *Academy of Management Proceedings,* 161–65.

Gouldner, A. (1960). The norm of reciprocity. *American Sociological Review* 25, 161–78.

Gowler, D. & Legge, K. (1981). Groups that provide specialist services. In R. Payne & C. Cooper (eds.), *Groups at work.* New York: John Wiley & Sons.

Greene, C. N. (1989). Cohesion and productivity in work groups. *Small Group Behavior* 20, 70–86.

Harkins, S., Latané, B., & Williams, K. (1980). Social loafing: Allocating effort or "taking it easy." *Journal of Experimental Social Psychology* 16, 457–65.

Hellriegel, D., & Slocum, J. (1979). *Organizational behavior,* 2nd ed. St. Paul, MN: West Publishing.

Hoerr, J. (1989). The payoff from teamwork. *Business Week,* July 10, 56–62.

Hollander, E. P. (1964). *Leaders, groups, and influence.* New York: Oxford University Press.

Homans, G. C. (1961). *Social behavior: Its elementary forms.* New York: Harcourt Brace Jovanovich.

Jackson, J. (1965). Structural characteristics of norms. In I. D. Steiner & M. Fishbein (eds.), *Current studies in social psychology.* New York: Holt, Rinehard & Winston.

Janis, I. L. (1982). *Victims of groupthink.* Boston: Houghton Mifflin.

Kelley, H., & Thibaut, J. (1978). *Intergroup relations: A theory of interdependence.* New York: John Wiley & Sons.

Kiesler, S. (1986). The hidden messages in computer networks. *Harvard Business Review,* January-February, pp. 46–58.

Kidder, Tracy (1981). *The soul of a new machine.* Boston: Little, Brown.

Lott, B. E. & Lott, A. J. (1960). The formation of positive attitudes toward group members. *Journal of Abnormal and Social Psychology* 61, 297–300.

Nadler, D., Hackman, J., & Lawler, E. (1979). *Managing organizational behavior.* Boston: Little, Brown.

Nath, R., & Sadhu, K. (1988). Comparative analysis, conclusions, and future directions. In R. Nath (ed.), *Comparative management: A regional view,* pp. 271–96. Cambridge, MA: Ballinger.

Roethlisberger, F., & Dickson, W. (1939). *Management and the worker.* Cambridge, MA: Harvard University Press.

Roy, D. (1961). Efficiency and "the fix": Informal intergroup relations in a piecework machine shop. In S. M. Lipset & N. J. Smelser (eds.), *The progress of a decade.* Englewood Cliffs, NJ: Prentice Hall.

Salancik, G., & Pfeffer, J. (1978). A social information processing approach to job attitudes and task design. *Administrative Science Quarterly* 23, 224–53.

Seashore, S. E. (1954). *Group cohesiveness in the industrial work group.* Ann Arbor: University of Michigan Press.

Shaw, M. E. (1971). *Group dynamics.* New York: McGraw-Hill.

Shaw, M. (1981). *Group dynamics: The psychology of small group behavior.* New York: McGraw-Hill.

Solomon, J. (1989). Firms grapple with language barriers. *The Wall Street Journal,* November 7, p. B1.

Stark, F. (1989). Wild blue yonders. *Psychology Today,* October, pp. 30–32.

Steers, R., Mowday, R., & Porter, L. (1982). *Employee-organization linkages: The psychology of commitment, absenteeism, and turnover.* New York: Academic Press.

Steiner, Ivan (1972). *Group process and productivity.* New York: Academic Press.

Thibaut, J., & Kelly, H. (1978). *The social psychology of groups,* 2nd ed. New York: John Wiley & Sons.

Triplett, N. (1897). The dynamogenic factors in pacemaking and competition. *American Journal of Psychology* 9, 507–37.

Zajonc, R. B. (1965). Social facilitation, *Science* 149, 269–74.

Zander, A. (1979). The psychology of group processes. In M. Rosensweig & L. Porter (eds.), *Annual Review of Psychology* 30, 417–52.

Zander, A. (1982). *Making groups effective.* San Francisco: Jossey-Bass.

17

Group Performance and Intergroup Relations

What makes a work group effective?

How do groups make decisions?

How should meetings be managed?

What are the special problems of managing relations between groups?

Now it was done. The Eclipse Group and the many others who had worked on the machine — including, especially, Software and Diagnostics — had created 4,096 lines of microcode, which fit into a volume about eight inches thick; diagnostic programs amounting to thousands of lines of code; over 200,000 lines of system software; several hundred pages of flowcharts; about 240 pages of schematics; hundreds and hundreds of engineering changes from the debugging; 20 hours of videotape to describe the new machine; and now a couple of functioning computers in blue-and-white cases, plus orders for many more on the way. Already, you could see that the engineers who had participated fully would be looking back on this experience a long time hence. It would be something unforgettable in their working lives. (Kidder, 1981, p. 276).

The Eclipse Group was thus described by Tracy Kidder in his Pulitzer Prize-winning nonfiction book, *The Soul of a New Machine.* The group worked overtime for a year and a half to create a 32-bit supermini-computer, code named Eagle, that would herald the next generation of minicomputers. The team sacrificed their personal lives and responded with enthusiasm and creativity, against long odds, to produce a new machine in a remarkably short period of time. They surpassed all expectations for what they could produce for the benefit of their employer, Data General. The project director, Tom West, ultimately received credit for forging and leading the team to a major success that startled the computer industry.

Work groups are the building blocks of organizations. Enhancing group performance is a key contributor to both managerial and organizational effectiveness. In this chapter, we will expand on Kidder's description of the factors that contributed to the productivity of the Eclipse group, and provide a general model of group effectiveness. We then will discuss the functioning and management of decision-making groups in particular. Finally, we will discuss how to understand and manage relations between different groups.

A MODEL OF WORK GROUP PRODUCTIVITY

A useful general model of work group effectiveness would capture the essence of the Eclipse example at Data General as well as characteristics of work groups engaged in other kinds of performance tasks. To be sure, the Eclipse Group was unique in many ways. Nonetheless, it illustrates the major factors that contribute to the effective functioning of virtually any work group.

Figure 17–1 presents a general model of work group effectiveness. The model is summarized in three variables, culminating with group effectiveness. These variables — task demands, resources, and group processes — contribute to the ultimate effectiveness of the group.

FIGURE 17–1

A General Model of Work Group Effectiveness

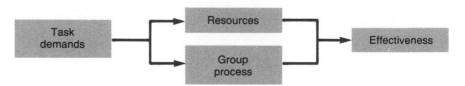

Group Effectiveness

Group effectiveness may be defined along three dimensions. First, and most obvious, is the group's level of *productive output.* In the Eclipse example, this would refer to the creation of the new machine and the time frame within which the machine was developed. It includes such specifics as the number of pages of programming and other products listed in the first paragraph of the chapter. Measures of productivity of other groups might include automobiles built, paperwork processed, patients treated and released, ideas generated, or trees planted. The number of units produced, whatever form those units might take, is the most tangible and salient feature of a group's effectiveness.

Two other dimensions of group effectiveness relate to effects on the group's members. *Member satisfaction* is a less tangible measure of effectiveness than productivity levels, but is important for many reasons, as outlined in Chapter 13. Truly effective groups are also characterized by a high degree of *member commitment to future involvement* in the group. Some groups are high on one or perhaps two of these dimensions but low on the other(s); but truly effective groups, over time, achieve optimal levels of productivity, member satisfaction, and future commitment to the group.

Group effectiveness is a function of three things: task demands, the resources available to the group, and the process through which these resources are transformed into final group products (Steiner, 1972). The demands of the task determine what resources are needed by the group to perform its task. The resources possessed by the group determine its potential productivity. Finally, the processes by which the group employs its resources determine the degree to which the group's performance potential is realized.

At Data General, the task demands were clearly delineated. Tom West, the project director, and Carl Alsing, one of his key lieutenants, created or provided the resources necessary (including human resources) to meet those demands. They also encouraged group processes that facilitated a fast, effective transformation of those resources into a final group product.

Task Demands

Task demands are the technological and other requirements imposed on the group by the job itself or the rules that govern it (Steiner, 1972). These demands determine what resources (knowledge, abilities, skills, or tools) are needed and how they should be combined for optimal performance. **Work groups operate under the demands created by task characteristics, other technological factors, interdependencies with other groups, time pressures, product features, competitive pressures, formal policies and rules, and other aspects of their working environment.** These task demands determine the nature of the group's task requirements and also facilitate or constrain the group's ability to meet those requirements. The Focus on Management gives an example of the interrelationships between task demands and group functioning.

At Data General, West clearly stated the task demands:

> West established the rules for the design of Eagle and he made them stick. The team should use as little silicon as possible, a mere few thousand dollars' worth of chips. The CPU should fit on far fewer than VAX's [an existing machine] 27 boards, and each major element of the CPU should fit on a single board. If they could fulfill those requirements, Eagle would be cheaper to build than VAX. On the other hand, it had better run faster than VAX, by certain widely accepted standards. It should be capable of handling a host of terminals. A CPU is not a functioning computer system; Eagle also had to be compatible with existing lines of Data General peripherals as well as with Eclipse software . . . make it an inexpensive but powerful machine and don't worry what it'll look like to the technology bigots when they peek inside . . . give 'em guidelines so that if they follow them, they're gonna be a success . . . no bells and whistles . . . tell a guy to do this and fit it all on one board, and I don't want to hear from him until he knows how to do it. (Kidder, 1981, p. 119)

Task requirements having been established, other demands arose from the group's organizational environment. Most notably, the Eclipse Group was in competition with a higher-status group that had moved to North Carolina to work on a more important project. Thus, the Eclipse Group was competing not only for financial resources and the active cooperation of support groups throughout Data General, but also for time. Time was critical to Data General, and it was crucial to the Eclipse Group for beating North Carolina to a finished product. West promised seemingly impossible deadlines to higher management, imposed them on his group, and worked feverishly to carry through on those promises.

Resources

As task demands dictate resource requirements for a group, the group must then gather those needed resources. Resources include members' knowledge, abilities, and skills; raw materials; information; tools; and whatever else is necessary to get the job done.

Explicit consideration of a group's resource needs for meeting task demands will indicate management interventions for improving productivity. The effective group leader will identify the resource needs of the group and then take the actions necessary to ensure that those resources are available to the group.

FOCUS ON MANAGEMENT

Tasks and Teamwork at AT&T

The use of teams to perform what previously were considered separate, individualized tasks is spreading rapidly in U.S. industry. In 1989, the United Auto Workers voted overwhelmingly in favor of employee involvement in self-managing work teams. The team concept appears to be the wave of the future, as exemplified by such companies as Boeing, Digital Equipment, Ford, Procter & Gamble, and Tektronix.

AT&T Credit Corp. (ATTCC) provides a case in point from the financial services sector (Hoerr, 1989). ATTCC provides financing for customers who lease equipment from AT&T and other companies. ATTCC had retained a bank to process lease applications, but the bank couldn't keep up with the high volume of new business.

ATTCC President Thomas C. Wajnert saw the problem and solved it. His solution involved changing the task and adopting the team concept. The bank had divided labor into narrow tasks (recall the discussion of job enrichment in Chapter 11) and organized work by function—one department handled applications and checked customer credit standing, a second department drew up contracts, and a third collected payments. Wajnert changed the operations so customer calls were not shunted from one department to another. Eleven teams were formed, and each team handled all three major lease-processing functions. Teams were given regional responsibility, so that the same teams always worked with the same sales staff. The teams established personal relationships with sales staff and customers. Moreover, they took full responsibility for managing customers' problems. The new slogan: "Whoever gets the call owns the problem."

By and large, the teams manage themselves. Team members make their own decisions about work scheduling, assignments, dealing with customers, and interviewing prospective new employees. Supervisors are regional managers who serve as resources to the team, giving advice rather than orders. The results? Decisions that used to take several days now take 24 to 48 hours, and productivity is up from 400 to 800 lease applications a day. ATTCC is now growing at a 40 to 50 percent annual rate.

A first step for West and Alsing was to recruit team members—the human resources of the Eclipse Group. "To make it work they'd have to find the very best new engineers they could find, ones who would know more about the state of the art in computers than they did" (p. 59). They also wanted "engineers who took an interest in the entire computer, not just in the parts that they had designed" (p. 150). Knowing there would be risks, but figuring the potential gains were worth it, they decided to select most of their engineers right out of college. They felt that one advantage to hiring engineers fresh out of school is that they don't know what's impossible.

Tom West worked hard at employee selection to attract the human resources he knew he needed. In other situations, training the work force in the skills necessary for a new work technology can accomplish the same end. Management information system (MIS) can be upgraded to meet the information needs of groups whose effectiveness can be improved through the provision of more timely information. Similarly, controlling inventory, planning, and actively managing the interfaces with other groups located earlier in the production process, can help assure reliable availability of the materials needed to perform.

The Eclipse Group also needed time, financial support, and other resources to perform at peak effectiveness. One of the group's greatest time wasters was debugging (correcting programming errors). After much agonizing and disagreement, Alsing decided to assign two team members (working independently) to create a program, called a simulator, to perform the debugging operations. Despite the beliefs of some that there was no time to build a simulator, it was accomplished within six weeks. In retrospect, "the team would have been nowhere without it; everyone said so" (p. 169). The amount of time saved by creating this resource was enormous.

Resources were also critical in the forms of materials and other types of support from outside groups. West spent constructive time working on public relations for his group, within the company,

> to get the various arms of the company increasingly interested in helping out . . . Before a designer finished specifying the architecture, West had the team designing the boards that would implement the architecture; before the engineer cleaned up their designs, West was ordering wire-wrapped, prototype boards; before the wire-wraps could possibly be made right, he was arranging for the making of printed-circuit boards; and long before anyone could know whether Eagle would become a functioning computer, West had the designers stand in front of a TV camera and describe their parts of the machine. This last . . . was . . . a tool for spreading the news of Eagle all around Data General headquarters. (p. 118)

This quote implies that groups must work to attract resources from outside groups. One vital resource is information. Groups that have inadequate communication with outside sources are isolated from new ideas and feedback, and ultimately perform poorly (Katz, 1982). Information can be not only imported but exported, in order to shape the beliefs and images of outsiders and proactively manage the demands and constraints they might impose. Tom West presented his computer as insurance to top management—the company would have it in case the other one didn't work—which enabled him to set up his team to compete with the North Carolina project team. He also presented his computer to engineers as a technical challenge, in order to attract the best people. To protect his group and his company, no information was presented to external competitors (Ancona, 1987).

Group Process

Available resources must be transformed into a group product. Group process, or the actual behaviors of the individuals within the group, determines how this transformation occurs.

Task demands and the group's resources determine the maximum attainable level of productivity (Steiner, 1972). If a group (or individual, for that matter) has all the necessary resources, it has the capacity to effectively perform the task. However, actual productivity often does not live up to this potential productivity.

Actual productivity is defined by potential productivity minus losses due to faulty group process. Faulty process generally refers to a failure to effectively utilize group resources. This can easily occur through mismanagement of many of the group concepts described in the last chapter, including inappropriate group goals and norms, low member motivation, low or dysfunctional cohesiveness, and inefficient allocation of roles.

Motivation was very high in the Eclipse Group. A major source of motivation to the engineers was the simple fact that it is generally considered a "sexy job" to be a builder of new computers. In school, engineers typically are trained to work on big projects, but early career assignments often are routine and tedious. The immediate, intrinsic rewards offered by work on the Eagle project would be followed later by other good assignments, stock options, salary increases, and promotions. However, most seemed to feel that they would have responded to the challenge even without the promise of extrinsic rewards down the line.

Other aspects of the group process, at least some of which developed from tangible management actions, facilitated the group's effectiveness.

> The work was divided, but it was not cut to ribbons. Everyone got responsibility for some important part of the machine, many got to choose their piece, and each portion required more than routine labor . . . many of those who made it through declared that they had been given as much freedom as they could have wished for. (p. 274)

Freedom—to design, innovate, exchange ideas, critique, ask questions, take on voluntary and mutual responsibilities—was a part of a work culture that was commensurate with, and that reinforced, the strong norms of professionalism that existed among the group members.

Managing group process is a question of considering and implementing many of the ideas outlined in the previous chapter. Building cohesiveness, establishing group goals that are consistent with management's goals, developing appropriate role differentiation, and other interventions aimed at improving the internal processes of the group will help ensure that task demands are met by transforming group resources into productive group output.

DECISION-MAKING GROUPS

The task demands on a group do not always require the production of a tangible, physical product, such as a working computer or an automobile off the assembly line. Many groups are convened for the purpose of solving a problem or making a decision. Often, group tasks in management ranks, and meetings between supervisors and their work groups, require making or implementing decisions as final products. This section of the chapter will focus on the performance of decision-making groups.

In keeping with the group effectiveness model introduced in Figure 17–1, performance on group decision-making tasks depends on the resources available to the group and the process through which the group transforms those resources into output.

Group Resources for Decision Making

The members of the group are key resources in group decision making. Merely by convening as a group, there is potentially more and better input into the decision than if only one person were making the decision.

Is it really true that two heads are better than one? An enormous amount of research has addressed the question of whether interacting groups make better decisions, are more creative, or solve problems better than an equivalent number of individuals working alone. The comparison has been made using various tasks that require logic, factual data, subjective judgments, and novel insights. The closest thing to a general conclusion is that groups as a whole usually perform better than the average of the individuals working alone, but seldom as well as the best individual effort of those working privately. Even this conclusion has to allow for a number of exceptions, and its validity depends somewhat on the nature of the task.

The performance of a group on a decision task depends on the nature of the resources brought to bear on the issue and the ways in which resources are utilized (Bottger & Yetton, 1988). Maier (1967) argues that groups present both assets and liabilities in problem solving. The liabilities are predominantly process issues. The assets, on the other hand, primarily refer to the added resources that are provided by having more than one person contribute to the decision task.

Group Members as Resources   Human resources provide the most important assets for group decision making. First, group members provide a potentially *greater pool of information.* Furthermore, additional members working on a decision are capable of bringing a *greater number of approaches* to an issue. This is especially valuable when the task is unstructured or ill-defined. Individuals working alone often get in a rut, working through the same sterile approach over and over again.

A key consideration in enlisting the help of a group in making a decision is whether the individual decision maker has all the pertinent information and insights for making an appropriate decision. If not, there is an advantage to soliciting the input of others. The composition of the group also is crucial. When a group is heterogeneous in terms of opinions, abilities, and perspectives, the group is more likely to possess the characteristics necessary for efficient group performance (Shaw, 1981).

These conclusions about the advantages of a heterogeneous group have direct relevance for managers. In the selection process, particular attention should be paid to the ability of the new member to complement the existing knowledge and perspectives of others in the decision-making body. Unfortunately, we often tend to prefer people who are like ourselves over those who are unlike us. This tendency can be detrimental to the overall success of the group. At the very least, such a tendency will minimize the advantage of using a group by marshalling essentially redundant resources.

So, maximizing the quality of the human resources used in a deliberating group means selecting members based on their ability to provide additional input useful toward making a quality decision. However, there are other considerations in choosing group members. These potential assets pertain less to the quality of the final decision than to the subsequent implementation of the decision (Maier, 1967). When the people who are affected by the decision, and those who must implement it, are involved in the actual making of the decision, they *better understand* the decision and are *more committed* to carrying it out effectively. Because they understand the tradeoffs made and why certain approaches had to be rejected, they are less likely to regard the decision as arbitrary or wrong.

Thus, critical human resources in the decision process include those who are most involved or affected after a decision is made. These are just the people who often are left out of the decision proceedings, as the key decision makers hammer out their decision and then hand it down to those who are supposed to implement it. The implementing group can provide important group assets—knowledge and perspectives—that make for the highest-quality decision in the first place.

Other Resources   Besides people, other resources help the group function effectively. For example, optimal decisions cannot be made without *information,* as discussed in Chapter 9 on decision making. Useful information is valid, pertinent, and timely, although invariably it will be imperfect due to being incomplete, open to interpretation, or suspect in its validity. Available information may be outdated and often must be used as a basis for predicting an uncertain future.

There are still other needed resources. *Time* is often of the essence. Reasonable time demands can energize a group and increase its efficiency, but if time constraints are too severe, high-quality decisions become less likely. Lack of time may make it impossible to mobilize the group, making a quick individual decision the only option. Time also affects another resource need: an *opportunity to communicate.* This implies a mutually agreeable time for getting together, a place in which to convene, or appropriate communication technologies.

GROUP PROCESS IN DECISION MAKING

As with any other group task, decision-making performance requires more than the marshalling of needed resources. These resources must be transformed into a final group product, in this case a decision. The previous section highlighted some of the potential assets of using a group rather than an individual to make decisions. Unfortunately, not all of these assets may be realized, because aspects of the group process often act as liabilities.

Process Liabilities

A number of problems can arise in the course of group discussion (Maier, 1972). One or a few members may *monopolize the discussion* so that potential contributions of other members are not shared. This is less a problem if the dominant member happens to be the one with the most useful input (although this would suggest that the presence of the others is unnecessary). However, monopoly of the conversation may as easily come from a dominant, aggressive, or high-status person as from more valid contributors. Other members who have much to contribute may experience evaluation apprehension in a group setting; afraid of possible criticism or ridicule, they do not voice their ideas.

Conflict, or a *win-lose psychology,* may develop as members or subgroups become ego-involved with a particular alternative. A form of *goal displacement* thus arises, as individuals care more about saving face, winning the argument, or pushing their pet projects than arriving at a good solution. Finally, a group setting presents a chance that purely *social motives* will take precedence over a hardheaded task orientation. Too much time may be spent in activities irrelevant to the task.

Groupthink

Social motives may do more harm than just taking time away from task involvement. Cohesiveness, while often a desirable attribute of groups, can contribute to disastrous results when groups make decisions under pressure (Janis, 1982). If a decision-making group has developed a close-knit, clubby feeling of "we-ness," the group may become so preoccupied with seeking consensus on a course of action that critical thinking is suppressed. This constitutes a malady that Janis labeled "groupthink," which includes the following symptoms:

> **The Illusion of Invulnerability** — Members overemphasize the strengths of the group (and the organization to which it belongs) and gloss over possible weaknesses. Any admission of weakness or liability is taboo because it would puncture the cozy consensus sought by the group. This bias leads the group to approve of risky actions about which each member acting alone might have had serious reservations.

Stereotypes—The group distorts and oversimplifies its conceptions of competing or opposing groups, viewing them as weak, unprincipled, or ridiculous. The group disregards the stated aims of outside groups or possible reactions of outsiders to the group's decision.

Assumption of Morality—The group assumes that its own ends and purposes are of such unquestioned morality that any means adopted to pursue those ends is justified. Thus, members feel no need to debate ethical issues.

Rationalization—Any previous decision or information that does not square neatly with the group's emerging consensus is explained away by group members. Unlike the rationalization employed by individuals in private thought as a defense mechanism to reduce dissonance, this shared and collectively structured form of rationalization inhibits the group's objectivity.

Self-censorship—To maintain the group's cohesiveness and provide its members with psychological support, each person suppresses any doubts or disagreements with the enveloping consensus.

Illusion of Unanimity—Because each member censors any privately held misgivings, each person mistakenly thinks he or she is the only one with doubts. Thus, no one wants to challenge what is erroneously believed to be a unanimous agreement.

Mindguarding—Much like a bodyguard that physically protects a leader, some members take it on themselves to prevent negative feedback (bad news) from reaching the influential members of the group.

Direct Pressure—Should a member timidly inject a note of caution into the deliberations, the other members quickly pressure the deviant to step into line with the group's thinking.

Several consequences of groupthink interfere with effective decision making. The group conducts inadequate searches for pertinent information, fails to examine the full set of alternatives available, and fails to examine adequately the risks associated with the preferred course of action. It does not make use of expert knowledge that might be contributed by outsiders, does not formulate contingency or backup plans, and fails to reappraise potentially viable options that were rejected early in the decision process. In general, it is selectively biased in its processing of the available information. In short, the group generally suspends critical, hardheaded thinking and fails to engage in vigilant decision making (recall Chapter 9). The decision reached may be disastrous.

Janis has studied a number of decisions made by government policy groups that resulted in colossal blunders—for example, Neville Chamberlain's inner circle that repeatedly ignored warnings and events indicating that appeasing Hitler in 1938 would be a disastrous policy; President Lyndon

B. Johnson's "Tuesday luncheon group" whose members supported the decision to escalate the war in Vietnam, despite intelligence reports and other information pointing to deleterious consequences; and the failure of Admiral Kimmel's group of naval commanders to respond to warnings of a possible attack on Pearl Harbor by Japanese planes. In every instance, Janis found an elaborate, documented pattern of groupthink leading up to such decision failures. For example, before the Bay of Pigs' invasion, President Kennedy assembled his cabinet and members of his White House staff to plan a strategy for dealing with Cuba. White House adviser Schlesinger noted:

> Had one senior advisor opposed the adventure [the invasion of Cuba], I believe Kennedy would have canceled it. No one spoke against it . . . Our meetings took place in a curious atmosphere of assumed consensus . . . .
>
> In the months after the Bay of Pigs I bitterly reproached myself for having kept so silent during those crucial discussions in the Cabinet Room, though my feelings of guilt were tempered by the knowledge that a course of objection would have accomplished very little save to gain me a name as a nuisance. I can only explain my failure to do no more than raise a few timid questions by reporting that one's impulse to blow the whistle on this nonsense was simply undone by the circumstances of the discussion. (Janis, 1972, pp. 39–40)

Groupthink undoubtedly occurs in the private sector as well. The Buffalo Mining Company in West Virginia continued heaping slag to dam up Buffalo Creek, despite repeated warnings that their dam could burst at any time; the dam broke, 125 people were killed and thousands made homeless, and the company was made to pay $26 million to survivors (Janis, 1989). At Lehman Brothers Kuhn Loeb, the Wall Street investment firm, the co-chief executives proposed an ill-conceived organization plan. Seven of the eight board members passively acquiesced without questioning its potential adverse consequences; the lone dissenter was unable to mobilize a constructive discussion. Misgivings went unstated and the board rubber-stamped the proposal. A few months later, the firm was on the verge of bankruptcy and was bought out by Shearson/American Express (Auletta, 1986; Janis, 1989).

Group Polarization

Imagine that you are a member of a five-person committee that meets on a monthly basis to decide expenditures on product development. One of the decisions to be reached at the next meeting concerns whether to invest $500,000 to bring a radically new product to market. The product is so different in design and concept from existing products (either yours or competitors') that it is almost certain to be either a fantastic success — paying back its investment in under three years and achieving at least a 30 percent return on invested funds — or a total flop, resulting in a waste of the money. Alternatively, the money can be spent on minor improvements of the existing product line, with a virtually certain return on investment of at least 5 percent, but no more than a 10 percent return. What probability of success for the new product would you require before allocating the funds to that option?

Group discussions will lead to a significant shift in the positions of the group members toward a more extreme position in the direction toward which they were leaning before discussion (Myers & Lamm, 1976). This shift is called *group polarization*. Suppose the group as a whole leans slightly to the risky side of the neutral point, prepared to invest in the new product if the chances of success are between .4 and .5. After discussion, the group probably will accept greater risk with the new product than the prediscussion average would suggest; it might be willing to accept a probability of between .3 and .4.

Why does this occur? One answer could be that group decision making produces a diffusion of responsibility. No single person can be held accountable. Blame can be shared with others; it may even be plausible to shift the blame entirely from oneself to the others. Collective decision making diminishes the individuals' sense of accountability for negative outcomes (Mynatt & Sherman, 1975).

But if diffusion of responsibility were the entire explanation, groups would invariably make riskier decisions than individuals. But this is not the case. If, as happens in a minority of instances, the initial attitudes of the group members tilt toward caution, discussion leads to the group's becoming more cautious.

Figure 17–2 shows that, in general, group discussion produces a shift toward greater extremity in the direction in which the members already lean. If the initial tilt is toward risk (Group A), group discussion results in a shift toward even greater risk; if the initial tendencies favor conservatism (Group B), a less common but occasional occurrence, discussion leads to a conservative shift.

Group polarization occurs because of the following processes (Myers & Lamm, 1976). First, the prediscussion leaning of individual members creates a bias toward the kinds of information and arguments that will be generated in the discussion. If the tendency is toward risk, then most arguments voiced will be in support of risk. Since not all of these arguments will have been initially considered by all the members, each person who leaned toward risk will hear new reasons in support of risk.

Second, in the group discussion, social comparison processes are at work. If risk is a general cultural value in the context of the issue discussed, those who thought that they stood favorably on this cultural value realize that others stand even more favorably—that is, are even more in favor of risk. The motivation to present oneself favorably in comparison to others induces a shift in opinion and attitude by those who were less extreme in the attitude.

Finally, the process of publicly verbalizing one's arguments on an attitudinal issue has a dissonance-producing effect. The more one finds

FIGURE 17–2

Group Polarization: Risky and Cautious Shifts

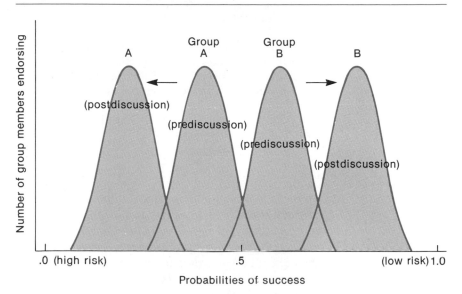

oneself verbally supporting a position, the more one must believe that is one's true, strongly held position. The more people talk, the more they believe what they say.

MANAGING DECISION GROUPS: CAPITALIZING ON GROUP ASSETS AND MINIMIZING PROCESS LOSSES

Effective performance in decision-making groups means taking full advantage of the group's resource assets while minimizing liabilities and process losses. We will now describe a number of suggestions for effectively accomplishing these goals, with the ultimate goal of enhancing group performance. First we will discuss two differing types of group process: problem solving and persuasion. We then will describe the roles of the leader and other group members, and we will conclude with some structural approaches to introducing formalized conflict into the discussion and using alternatives to face-to-face interaction.

Two Differing Processes: Problem Solving versus Persuasion

It is easy to distinguish between constructive group processes that indicate cooperative problem-solving activity and dysfunctional processes indicative of persuasion or selling approaches (Maier, 1967):

Problem-solving activity includes searching, trying out ideas on one another, listening to understand rather than to refute, making relatively short speeches, and reacting to differences in opinion as stimulating. The general pattern is one of rather complete participation, involvement. Persuasion activity includes the selling of opinions already formed, defending a position held, either not listening at all or listening in order to be able to refute, talking dominated by a few members, unfavorable reactions to disagreement, and a lack of involvement of some members. During problem solving . . . "It just developed," is a response often used to describe the solution reached. In contrast, groups characterized by selling or persuasive behavior do not function as integrated units but as separate individuals, each with an agenda. (p. 244)

Obviously, the problem-solving approach is preferable; the group leader and members should be sensitive to these indicators and modify their behavior accordingly.

The Role of the Leader

Maier (1967) compared the functioning of an effective leader with the nerve ring of a starfish. In a healthy starfish, the function of the individual arms is coordinated by the nerve ring. The nerve ring itself does not do the behaving; rather, it receives and processes the data relayed to it by the separate arms. This central organization integrates the responses of the arms into a larger pattern so that together they constitute a coordinated group response rather than a group of individual responses. Similarly, a decision group's leader facilitates communications between individuals and integrates the incoming responses so that a unified response occurs.

Other writers have offered suggestions regarding useful leader behaviors in this context. For example, Bales (1950) identified two important leadership roles—task and maintenance—described in Chapter 16. Janis (1972) provided recommendations for the prevention of groupthink. To minimize groupthink, the leader should assign the role of critical evaluator to each member, encouraging the group to air objections, doubts, and contrary opinions. Furthermore, several independent decision groups could be set up to work on the same question, under different leaders. Similarly, a single policy group could periodically split into two or more subgroups to work independently before reconvening to work out their differences. One or more qualified colleagues or outside experts who are not members of the group could be invited to each meeting to provide information and different viewpoints on the deliberations. If the issue involves relations with a rival organization, a sizable block of time should be spent surveying warning signals from the rivals and constructing alternative scenarios of the rivals' intentions. Finally, after reaching consensus, the group might hold a "second chance" meeting at which members are expected to express any residual doubts and rethink the entire issue before making a final commitment.

Other techniques are useful in managing group polarization (Myers & Lamm, 1976; Cecil, Cummings, & Chertkoff, 1973). Several tactics encourage a shift. If group leaders call for an original vote preceding any discussion, arrange for certain people to speak before others, or express initial positions themselves, a shift in the initially voiced directions might occur. Group leaders wishing to guard against a shift might suppress early mention of preferences, require group members to write down in advance both pro and con considerations on the issue and share these relevant arguments, and encourage detailed consideration of minority viewpoints.

Group shift is not inherently either a desirable or an undesirable occurrence. However, the prescriptions for guarding against it are useful for other reasons as well: they generate more thorough exploration of issues, maximize the contributions of members, and help avoid other negative aspects of the process, such as early entrenchment and goal displacement (a focus on winning the argument). On the other hand, leaders with vested interests in a particular solution can stack the deck in their favor by encouraging the things that lead to a shift. It is very common, for example, for leaders to elicit the opinions of powerful members who are sympathetic to their preferred decision, thereby setting the tone for the ensuing discussion. A controlling leader can also select team members on the basis of their personal leanings. The composition of the group should affect the occurrence and direction of a shift. Groups composed of individuals with high-risk propensities may become even riskier, while the reverse would be true for groups made up of individuals known to be conservative.

The Role of Group Members

The most useful ways for group members to contribute to effective group process are implicit in the discussion above. Members should critically evaluate ideas (and the group process itself) and not be reluctant to air their concerns. If the leader fails to suggest some useful technique for improving the quality of the decisions, members might offer the idea to the leader, perhaps in private to avoid embarrassment or aggravation. Members can also help encourage and facilitate the participation of less vocal group members, and indicate a willingness to entertain new or minority viewpoints. Finally, members of policy-making groups should discuss periodically the group's deliberations with trusted associates in their own unit of the organization, and report back the implications of their reactions (Janis, 1972).

Alfred P. Sloan, the first great chief executive of General Motors, performed his leadership role effectively in part by recognizing the important role of group members. According to Peter Drucker, Sloan called a conference to consider an important technical change he was known to favor. When he asked for opinions, one person after another came down in favor of the innovation. After all group members had spoken, Sloan said, "Gentlemen, let's think about it some more tonight and meet again tomorrow. If no one has arguments against this, we're not in a position yet to decide" (Ewing, 1983).

Introducing Constructive Conflict

Sloan's approach indicates a useful strategy for enhancing quality decision making: the introduction of conflict into the group. This idea guards against groupthink, when the group's desire for consensus generates pressures to conform and a lack of expression of alternative viewpoints. Two common techniques for generating constructive conflict are devil's advocacy and dialectical inquiry.

Groups can appoint one or more members to play the role of *devil's advocate* (Janis, 1972) to ensure that someone criticizes the assumptions and proposals of other members of the group. By being assigned the role of devil's advocate, inhibitions about disagreeing with others should be lessened because it is now the person's "job" to criticize. Because pressures to conform are replaced by an obligation to fulfill an assigned responsibility, alternative perspectives are more likely to surface.

Devil's advocates point out what is wrong with ideas. An alternative approach, dialectical inquiry, goes one step further. *Dialectical inquiry* introduces formal debate between advocates of one plan and others who propose a counterplan (Mason, 1969). This debate can lead to the formulation of a final plan that reflects some synthesis of the original conflicting ideas.

The dialectical approach has been criticized because it is more expensive than devil's advocacy and could lead to compromises, which frequently are suboptimal decisions (Cosier, 1981). Others (Mitroff & Mason, 1981) argue for the advantages of the dialectic. The controversy over their relative effectiveness, and associated costs, will likely continue. Nonetheless, they both represent structural approaches to formalizing conflict that hold the potential advantages of encouraging necessary disagreement, lessening the emotionality engendered by more personalized conflict, and ensuring exploration of alternative solutions.

Alternatives to Interacting Groups

Groups can make decisions without verbal interaction. Sometimes, group members interact via computer networks (as discussed in the Focus on the Future). Or, decision-making bodies can purposely use techniques that avoid direct discussion. Two useful techniques capture the assets of groups and minimize their liabilities by limiting verbal interaction. The *nominal group technique* is a structured format for decision making among individuals seated around a table. This technique proceeds as follows:

1. Individual members first silently and independently generate their ideas on a problem in writing.
2. This period of silent writing is followed by a recorded round-robin procedure in which each group member (one at a time, in turn, around the table) presents one idea to the group without discussion.

FOCUS ON THE FUTURE

Group Processes on the Computer

As you know, national and local computer networks are proliferating. Decision making via computer, rather than face to face, will become more common. Computer-mediated communication presumably can lead to better-informed participants and higher-quality decisions. But the impact may be more complex than that, as evidenced by an experiment contrasting face-to-face with computer-mediated group decisions (Siegel, Dubrovsky, Kiesler, & McGuire, 1986).

Compared with groups seated at a table, groups separated physically and communicating with keyboards and CRTs made fewer statements to one another about the problem. They participated more equally in discussions, and were more uninhibited in their communications. Without social cues like status differences or dominating personalities, participation rates were more equal. Lack of inhibition was indicated by stronger and more inflammatory remarks (sometimes

known as "flaming"): swear words, name-calling, and insults (for example, "you jerk" and "you fool"). The computer also affected final group decisions—there was a greater degree of choice shift when compared with the face-to-face groups.

The researchers concluded that these social psychological effects of computer-mediated communication occur for three reasons. First, there is not yet a well-established etiquette for communicating via computer, and the distinctive computing subculture rejects conventionality and social restrictions. Second, the computer focuses attention on verbal messages rather than the social context, reducing concern about how one's behavior relates to social norms and how others will react. Third, the technology may induce feelings of loss of identity and uninhibited behavior. The experimental results support these explanations, and indicate how computers can affect both process and outcome in group decision making.

The ideas are summarized and written on a blackboard or a sheet of paper on the wall.

3. After all the individuals have presented their ideas, the recorded ideas are discussed for the purposes of clarification and evaluation.

4. The meeting concludes with a silent, independent vote on priorities through a rank ordering or rating procedure. The group decision is the pooled outcome of individual votes.

Participants in the *delphi technique* are physically dispersed and do not meet face-to-face. Although numerous options exist for the administration of the delphi process, the basic approach uses two iterations of questionnaires and feedback reports. First, a questionnaire designed to obtain information on a topic or problem is distributed by mail to a group of respondents who are anonymous to one another. The respondents independently generate their ideas in answering the questionnaire, which is then returned. The responses are summarized into a feedback report and sent back to the respondent group along with a second questionnaire that is designed to probe more deeply into the ideas generated by the first questionnaire. After receiving the feedback report, the respondents independently evaluate it and answer the second set of questions. Typically, respondents are requested to vote independently on ideas included in the feedback report and to return their second replies, again by mail. Generally, a final summary and feedback report are then developed and mailed to the respondent group.

The Japanese use a procedure called *ringi* (Zander, 1982). A written document is circulated from member to member for sequential editing with no person-to-person interaction. Each new draft of the document is sent around to participants until no more changes are needed and each participant has put his seal on a final version. Sometimes, groups assign separate parts of a problem to each of several subgroups, who prepare draft-answers for their parts. These smaller reports are then circulated before discussion begins in the larger body (Rohlen, 1975).

The comparisons between interacting groups, nominal groups, and the delphi method are shown in Table 17–1.

Managing a Meeting

Table 17–2 summarizes the resources and processes affecting the performance of decision-making groups. We now conclude with additional suggestions for the effective management of group meetings, including considerations that should be taken into account before the meeting and at the conclusion of the meeting.

Before the Meeting   Thoughtful planning and preparation for a meeting are crucial (Seibold, 1979). The chairperson or leader should first undertake to determine whether a meeting is necessary. Perhaps some other means of communication, such as memos, phone calls, or meetings with individual members, would suffice. Second, the purpose and goals of the meeting should be identified. Why is the meeting being called, and what are the desirable outcomes?

Third, the leader must decide on the composition of the group. Whose input is needed? Is it an established group? Will outsiders be invited? How will the participants differ in status, power, ability and desire to contribute, and interpersonal relations? Consider how appropriate group roles, such as group recorder, expert adviser, devil's advocate, and others might be defined and assigned to group members.

Between four and seven participants is an ideal number (Jay, 1976). Ten people is tolerable, and 12 is the outside limit. The chairperson should keep numbers down as much as possible, consistent with the need to invite everyone who can provide an important contribution.

TABLE 17–1

Comparison of Qualitative Differences between Three Decision Processes Based on Evaluations of Leaders and Group Participants

Dimension	Interacting Groups	Nominal Groups	Delphi Technique
Overall methodology	Unstructured face-to-face group meeting High flexibility High variability in behavior of groups	Structured face-to-face group meeting Low flexibility Low variability in behavior of groups	Structured series of questionnaires and feedback reports Low-variability respondent behavior
Role orientation of groups	Socioemotional Group maintenance focus	Balance focus on social maintenance and task role	Task-instrumental focus
Relative quantity of ideas	Low; focused "rut" effect	Higher; independent writing and hitchhiking round robin	High; isolated writing of ideas
Search behavior	Reactive search Short problem focus Task-avoidance tendency New social knowledge	Proactive search Extended problem focus High task centeredness New social and task knowledge	Proactive search Controlled problem focus High task centeredness New task knowledge
Normative behavior	Conformity pressures inherent in face-to-face discussions	Tolerance for non-conformity through independent search and choice activity	Freedom not to conform through isolated anonymity
Equality of participation	Member dominance in search, evaluation, and choice phases	Member equality in search and choice phases	Respondent equality in pooling of independent judgments
Method of problem solving	Person centered Smoothing over and withdrawal	Problem centered Confrontation and problem solving	Problem centered Majority rule of pooled independent judgments
Closure decision process	High lack of closure Low felt accomplishment	Low lack of closure High felt accomplishment	Low lack of closure Medium felt accomplishment
Resources utilized	Low administrative time and cost High participant time and cost	Medium administrative time, cost, preparation High participant time and cost	High administrative time, cost, preparation
Time to obtain group ideas	1½ hours	1½ hours	Five calendar months

SOURCE: From A. H. Van de Ven and A. L. Delbecq, "The Effectiveness of Nominal and Delphi Techniques in Interacting Group Decision Making Processes," *Academy of Management Journal* 17 (1974), p. 618.

Fourth, the leader should decide the logistics of the meeting. When and where should the group meet? How long should the meeting take? Important written materials should be considered, planned, prepared, and distributed in advance of the meeting.

The Agenda   The agenda is "by far the most important piece of paper" (Jay, 1976, p. 49). Agendas are usually too brief; the leader should not be afraid of a fairly long agenda. Each item should be defined, the reason for its inclusion discussed, and labeled with headings like "for information,"

TABLE 17-2

Influences on the Effectiveness of Decision-Making Groups

Resources	Group Process
Group members:	Monopolized discussion
Information	Goal displacement
Approaches to problem	Groupthink
Understanding of solution	Group shifts
Commitment to solution	Problem solving versus persuasion
Other resources:	Leader roles
Additional information	Member roles
Time	Conflict
Opportunity to communicate	Noninteractive techniques

"for discussion," and "for decision" so members know what they are supposed to accomplish with each item. Other suggestions include circulating the agenda about two or three days in advance (any longer, and people will lose it; any shorter, and some won't have time to prepare), and specifying time deadlines for the meeting as well as for specific items on the agenda.

The order of items is also important—items requiring creativity and mental energy should be high on the agenda so they will be considered early; a "star" item of great interest and concern might be saved until later, when it can carry the meeting through the inevitable attention lag that begins to appear after 15 or 20 minutes; and the meeting should, if possible, be closed with some kind of good news, an upbeat item, or a major agreement or note of achievement.

After a Decision   Too often, group decisions stop after the decision is made (Schein, 1968). The crucial next step—implementation of the decision—is ignored. Once a group has identified a solution to a problem or reached some consensus decision about what needs to be done, a procedure like PERT (Program Evaluation Review Technique) can be used to plan the details of implementation (Seibold, 1979). PERT may be carried out in a small group meeting to:

1. Determine the final step, that is, the form the solution should take when it is fully operational.
2. Enumerate the events that must take place before the final step is realized.
3. Order these steps chronologically.
4. Develop a flow diagram of the steps in the process (if necessary).
5. Generate a list of all resources and activities needed to accomplish each step.
6. Estimate the time needed to take each step, and then the total time needed for implementation of the entire plan.

7. Compare the total time estimate with deadlines or expectations, and correct as necessary.

8. Determine which members should be responsible for each step.

Adjournment   Once the agenda is completed, or difficulties indicate that no further movement is possible in the meeting, it is time to adjourn. The time and place of the next meeting can be confirmed or arranged (members should have their appointment diaries). Finally, the minutes of the meeting should be prepared and distributed (Jay, 1976). Minutes can be brief, but should include:

1. The time and date of the meeting, where it was held, and who chaired it.

2. Names of all present and apologies for absence.

3. All agenda (and other) items discussed and all decisions reached. If action was agreed on, record the name of the person responsible for the assignment.

4. The time at which the meeting ended. This is important because it may be useful later to know whether the discussion lasted a few cursory minutes or was an all-day marathon.

5. The date, time, and place of the next meeting.

MANAGING RELATIONSHIPS BETWEEN GROUPS

No group exists in a vacuum; all are interdependent with numerous other groups. Thus, a key activity of any group is to effectively manage the interfaces between units (Ancona, 1987). The previous sections of this chapter focused on managing a single work group; the following sections describe the special problems of, and suggestions for managing, relationships between different groups.

Conflict between Groups

In an earlier section we discussed techniques for creating conflict within decision-making groups. This undoubtedly strikes a lot of people as paradoxical. Conflict is something most organizations have more than enough of already—why should we purposely create more? The need for some conflict within deliberating bodies should have become apparent with the description of groupthink and other maladies that hinder the effectiveness of the group process. Nonetheless, many organizations are plagued by too much conflict, particularly between different units.

In fact, conflict is the most important issue surrounding the interface between work groups (Brett and Rognes, 1986). We now turn to a discussion of the factors that give rise to intergroup conflict and general approaches for handling conflict. Subsequent sections will deal with more specific strategies and tactics for dealing with "the opposition."

Causes of Conflict   Three major factors contribute to intergroup conflict in organizations (March & Simon, 1958). First, a *need for joint decision making* creates potential for conflict. This refers to the interdependence between groups dictated by the systems nature of organizations. At least two factors are particularly crucial in generating this need for joint decision making. The greater the mutual dependence on a limited resource, the greater the need for joint decision making with respect to that resource. Budget allocations are a prime example of mutual dependence and conflict over a limited resource. In addition, interdependence of timing of activities creates a need for joint decision making with respect to scheduling. If two groups are interdependent with respect to scarce resources or scheduling, an action by one manager will affect the other group. This creates pressure toward joint decision making and the potential for conflict between the two groups.

A second major factor giving rise to conflict, especially under conditions of interdependence, is a *difference in goals*. In one sense, all members of the same organization should share common goals like the good of the organization, or something more specific like profit or sales maximization. In reality, however, multiple goals exist within the same organization. Different individuals, and different groups, develop different goals by virtue of internally inconsistent reward systems, competition for scarce resources, or organizational goals that are so subjective they are open to differing interpretations. These complications help give rise to a third factor contributing to conflict, *differences in perceptions,* which are also exacerbated by departmentalization and different flows of information to different organizational subunits.

To help make these abstract ideas more concrete, Table 17–3 provides an example of one department's potential conflicts with other departments in the organization. The multitude of issues is readily apparent. It is clear that marketing's goals are discrepant with those of other departments. This summary hardly represents an exhaustive list of marketing's conflicts; furthermore, it focuses solely on marketing as just one example of departmental interdependencies. Considering the iterations generated by all interdependencies throughout an entire organization, including labor-management relations (see Focus on Management), it is not surprising that conflict is endemic to organizational life.

Responses to Conflict   Organizations respond to conflict with four basic processes (March and Simon, 1958). The first is *problem solving*. Problem solving assumes that objectives are shared. The problem is to identify a solution that will meet the criteria on which all participants agree. In the problem-solving process, problems are solved when search behavior is increased, information gathered, and alternatives generated and evaluated in a constructive, nonhostile manner.

TABLE 17–3

Differentiation between Marketing and Other Departments.

Department	Their Emphasis	Marketing's Emphasis
R&D	Basic research	Applied research
	Intrinsic quality	Perceived quality
	Functional features	Sales features
Engineering	Long design lead time	Short design lead time
	Few models	Many models
	Standard components	Custom components
Purchasing	Narrow product line	Broad product line
	Standard parts	Nonstandard parts
	Price of material	Quality of material
	Economical lot sizes	Large lot sizes to avoid stock-outs
	Purchasing at infrequent intervals	Immediate purchasing for customer needs
Manufacturing	Long production lead time	Short production lead time
	Long runs with few models	Short runs with many models
	No model changes	Frequent model changes
	Standard orders	Custom orders
	Ease of fabrication	Aesthetic appearance
	Average quality control	Tight quality control
Finance	Strict rationales for spending	Intuitive arguments for spending
	Hard-and-fast budgets	Flexible budgets to meet changing needs
	Pricing to cover costs	Pricing to further market development
Accounting	Standard transactions	Special terms and discounts
	Few reports	Many reports
Credit	Full financial disclosures by customers	Minimum credit examination of customers
	Low credit risks	Medium credit risks
	Tough credit terms	Easy credit terms
	Tough collection procedures	Easy collection procedures

SOURCE: Philip Kotler, *Marketing Management: Analysis, Planning, Implementation, & Control,* 6/e, © 1988, p. 717. Reprinted by permission of Prentice Hall, Inc., Englewood Cliffs, New Jersey.

Unlike problem solving, *persuasion* assumes that individual or group goals may differ. It further assumes that ultimately objectives are shared at some level. Participants who disagree probe to discover some superordinate goal that all would like to attain. This process has fewer benefits than the true problem-solving approach because there is less reliance on information gathering and other useful behaviors and more emphasis on talking one another into a preferred alternative. Nonetheless, the persuasion process is constructive in the sense that it attempts to secure true agreement among participants.

Two other processes seek to secure only a tacit resolution of the conflict, settling for public acceptance of terms without private agreement. *Bargaining* takes disagreement over goals as given and unalterable, and involves power plays, threats and promises, entrenchment, concessions, and often compromise. *Politics* goes one step further in that, like bargaining, there is intergroup conflict of interest, but the bargaining arena is expanded.

FOCUS ON MANAGEMENT

The Trust Gap

Managers and subordinates are interdependent, need to make joint decisions, and often have different goals. They certainly have different perceptions. Today, the trust gap between the top executives and lower organizational levels (see Chapter 7) is wider than it has been in years (Farnham, 1989).

Chief executive officers in the United States sometimes make 100 times the pay of their average workers; in Europe and Japan, the ratio is rarely higher than 15 to one. (Peter Drucker favors 20-to-1; Socrates recommended 5-to-1.) Hourly workers, supervisors, and middle-level managers resent senior management's pay and perks and doubt their intentions and competence. And, management often says one thing but does another — as when it proclaims that people are the company's most important asset, but then cuts benefits and orders major layoffs. The results are a psychological wall between top management and the rest of the organization, poor communications, lack of cooperation, and even sabotage.

Breaking down the barriers and resolving the conflicts requires egalitarianism and cooperative problem solving. Egalitarianism diminishes the rift between top management and employees, and is accomplished in part through symbolic actions. President Ken Iverson of Nucor, a steel company in North Carolina, took a 60 percent cut when the company went through tough times rather than make the workers shoulder the entire financial sacrifice. Union Carbide, when it moved headquarters from Park Avenue to Danbury, Connecticut, used an egalitarian approach: 2,300 private offices, all the same size, and no executive parking or executive dining room. Herb Kelleher of Southwest Airlines cut his bonus by 20 percent and his officers 10 percent, to send the message that management and workers faced its problems together.

Preston Trucking of Maryland, and Alabama Gas, were two companies experiencing poor relations between labor and management. At Alabama Gas, CEO Mike Warren got a 20-foot papier-mâché dinosaur, plunged a stake through its heart, and wheeled the corpse around from department to department. Of course, the symbolism has to be followed up with concrete action. Warren surveyed employees, solicited suggestions, ate dinner regularly with union leaders, and visited workers in the ditches. Two years later, the steel workers' union sent Warren a brontosaurus statuette inscribed, "Dinosaur Killer of the Year."

Last year at a Preston dock in New Jersey, after years of efforts like those described above to reduce the labor-management gap, management wanted to save money by closing down the dock on the Friday before Christmas. Since the Teamsters' contract didn't recognize Friday as a holiday, the company would have to pay the 35 drivers even if the dock were closed. The shop steward, Carl Conoscenti, offered to help the manager. He told the drivers that they were due the money, that no one would raise an eyebrow if they took it, and that no one would even *know* if they took it. None took their money. "These are *Teamsters*," said Chuck Dunlap, the manager, in disbelief. This is *New Jersey*" (Farnham, 1989, p. 74). Clearly, the company had moved from a culture of conflict to one of cooperative problem solving.

Participants form coalitions; that is, they bring in allies in support of their position. Coalitions are a perpetual, changing, fickle aspect of the organizational decision process, and they provide an important technique for dealing with conflict. Power and politics will be discussed in more detail in the next chapter.

Tactics of Conflict Relationships

How does one cope with conflict relationships with other units in the organization? What tactics do people use when others cause problems? George Strauss (1962–1963) conducted a classic study of the techniques used by purchasing agents to manage their conflicts with engineering and production scheduling.

Purchasing's relationships with other departments were analyzed in terms of work flow. The work flow began when the sales department received an order. On this basis, the engineering department prepared a blueprint. Next, the production scheduling department initiated a work order for manufacturing and a requisition for purchasing. Finally (for the present purpose), the purchasing department bought the needed parts.

Conflicts arose when engineers wrote specifications for the products that were too tight or that called for one brand only. When this happened, agents had no freedom to choose among suppliers, rendering them powerless. Yet engineers found it much easier to write down a known brand name than to draw up lengthy specifications. Other disagreements arose because engineers demanded quality and reliability, whereas agents also had to look for low cost and quick delivery.

Additional conflicts arose with production scheduling. Production scheduling typically determined the size of the order and the date of delivery. Delivery dates often were requested on excessively short notice. This was due to real need, sloppy planning, or "crying wolf" by claiming that orders were needed earlier than truly necessary. Purchasing agents were forced to pay premium prices and ask favors of salespeople (creating obligations that later would have to be repaid). When schedulers were accused of short lead times, they turned around and blamed departments up the line in the work flow, such as engineering (which delayed its blueprints) and sales (which accepted rush orders). Purchasing agents also were in conflict with schedulers over order sizes — schedulers were accused of ignoring inventory costs or savings from quantity discounts and ordering uneconomic lot sizes.

Purchasing agents used a number of techniques to deal with these and other problems. *Rule-oriented tactics* included appealing to the boss, referring to company rules, requiring written explanations, documenting acceptance of responsibility for difficult or unreasonable requests, and charging other departments for additional costs incurred. For example, if an agent received a request for a rush delivery, the agent might ask the department whether they were willing to authorize overtime or air freight. This was charged against the department's budget, and too many extra charges got the attention of the auditor. If the department was willing to go along with the extra charges, the agent knew the rush delivery was really needed.

Rule-evading tactics included feigning compliance while knowing the request was impossible, or exceeding authority by unilaterally changing the terms of requisition. One agent described an engineer who had been lavishly entertained by a salesman and had then placed a requisition for that company's products. The agent wrote a memo explaining why this was a poor choice, presented it in a way that he knew would be rejected by the engineer, and then placed the order as requested. As the agent had expected, the products arrived late and proved to be inappropriate. The result was twofold: the engineer was transferred and demoted, and the other engineers gained greater respect for the agent's advice.

Personal-political tactics included relying on friendship contacts, interdepartmental politics, and the exchange of favors following the principle of "reward your friends, punish your enemies." Cooperative engineers were rewarded by the purchasing agent recommending that a salesman take the engineer to lunch, or extra help was given in an emergency to production schedulers who typically gave plenty of lead time. On the other hand, salesmen who operated behind agents' backs by dealing directly with engineers were very unlikely to receive future orders from the agent.

Educational tactics included direct persuasion — the frank attempt to sell a point of view — and indirect persuasion, more subtle forms of manipulation also aimed at convincing others to adopt the agent's viewpoint. For example, some successful agents encouraged engineers, foremen, or production schedulers to sit in on or even help out in the negotiation process so they would come to know the agent's constraints and goals.

Finally, *organizational-interactional tactics* included arranging for a convenient office location to facilitate informal daily contacts with other departments, and seeking a formal organization change such as placing inventory control and production scheduling within the same department as purchasing. Agents seeking to expand their power also worked to induce other departments to look to purchasing for advice on problems, preferably at the earliest possible stages of the work flow.

Additional techniques aimed at expanding power domains will be described in the next chapter, where power and politics are explored more fully. For now, it is important to note not only the specific types of tactics employed, but also the fact that there is a wide range of tactics available to the agent. As one agent put it, "You have to choose your weapons. I vary them on purpose . . . I ask myself, who has the final decision? How does the chief engineer operate? What does he delegate? What does he keep for himself? It all involves psychological warfare. Who are the people to be sold? Who will have the final say?" (Strauss, 1962, p. 183).

Patterns of Work Group Relationships

> From the point of view of subordinates, managers who are respected—and followed—are those who can anticipate problems "in the system," get them the things they need, and protect them from unreasonable demands. To be effective at "representation" and "buffering" for subordinates, managers must comprehend correctly and be able to "work" the interfaces of their jobs. (Sayles, 1989, p. 110)

Some relationships between work groups involve subtle give-and-take, others require a good deal of deference, and still others give real power. The nature of these relationships typically is specified only vaguely, and often is not apparent to role incumbents. Learning to distinguish these relationship types can greatly enhance your ability to "work the interfaces."

According to Sayles, there are six basic types of lateral relationships:

1. *Work-flow relationships* arise from the sequential processing of ideas, papers, or materials through different departments. A manager's department is in a work-flow relationship with departments coming before it and after it in the work process. The department usually receives unfinished work from other departments, and then passes along its finished work to subsequent departments for further processing or use. Sooner or later, a department ends up with too much demand or too little supply of goods, or work that is considered unsuitable, giving rise to interdepartmental coordination problems and conflict.

2. *Service relationships* are created by the existence of some centralized activity to which other organizational units must gain access. Essentially a monopoly is created, like centralized computational facilities. Pressures on managers (and employees) of service units arise from conflicting demands from various users. Priorities must be worked through in such a way that customers believe they are being treated fairly and that their needs will be cared for.

3. *Advisory relationships* exist when centralized sources of expert knowledge are called on by troubled departments that have problems requiring more knowledge and experience than they themselves possess. One frustration of this advisory position is the expectation that experts should limit their advice to problems for which they are called, and should wait to be called rather than proactively seek and point out problems.

4. *Audit relationships* occur when managers use their technical expertise to evaluate existing methods and identify where improvements can be made. Top management establishes financial, technical, legal, personnel, and other standards and then relies on auditors to uncover and communicate defective performance.

5. *Stabilization relationships* refer essentially to auditing before the fact. Managers sometimes must justify their actions and obtain permission before beginning or continuing an activity.

6. *Liaison relationships* involve bridging the gap between two or more different groups or organizations. The need to mediate between two interdependent, sometimes conflicting groups requires the ability to understand both sides and to communicate the goals, expectations, and needs of one group to another.

Sayles suggests that all managers need to assess their jobs in terms of these relationship patterns. By breaking down their management activities into these components, they can better understand what they are expected to do, with whom, and how they should accomplish these requirements. The analytical procedure involves asking two questions with regard to each of the six types of relationships.

1. For work-flow relationships: "From whom do I receive?" and "To whom do I send?"
2. For service relationships: "To whom am I a service?" and "Of whom do I make service demands?"
3. For advisory relationships: "To whom do I go for aid with problems?" and "Who calls on me for specific types of technical assistance?"
4. For audit relationships: "What other units do I audit for specific criteria?" and "What other managers audit me?"
5. For stabilization relationships: "What permissions, sign-offs, and authorizations do I control, and for whom?" and "To whom must I go for authorizations?"
6. For liaison relationships: "Whom do I 'connect', that is, act as an intermediary or broker for maintaining communications and relationships?" and "Who acts as an intermediary between me and others?"

Incidentally, these questions also might be asked in the future tense in anticipation of changing relationships.

The coordination of managerial work across units is much more difficult than coordination of work within a single unit. This is because of the many types of interdependencies with a variety of other departments having different goals and perceptions. As Sayles concludes,

> What appears to the untutored eye as either stubbornness or a free-for-all is actually an orchestrated work process designed to pull together a large number of legitimate viewpoints and concerns. Management thus becomes in large part a process of working interfaces.
>
> Lack of understanding in this area leads, at the least, to frustration, more likely to failure or needless additional complexity; for example, neglecting to give information to another manager in the work flow or to check with a manager having stabilization functions or being unresponsive in service roles. All such actions begin a series of countermoves that require many more interventions than would have been required had the process been done properly the first time. (Sayles, 1989, p. 107-108)

In anticipation of the next chapter about power and politics, the reader might think about (1) which of the six patterns of lateral relationships are most, and least, powerful; and (2) how a manager might go about changing these relationships to gain personal and departmental power.

SUMMARY

Group effectiveness is a function of task demands, the resources available to the group, and the process through which these resources are transformed into final group products. In decision making, group members are important resources, providing information, different approaches, and understanding of and commitment to solutions. But groups do not always capitalize fully on these resources; monopolized discussion and goal displacement can interfere with effective group decision making. When the liabilities outweigh the assets, the result can be groupthink, or undesired shifts in decisions, especially with respect to risk. Formalized conflict, and nominal group and delphi techniques, can be used as procedures for capitalizing on group assets while minimizing liabilities.

Managing groups pertains not only to group productivity, team decisions, and committee meetings, but also to managing relationships between groups. Common causes of organizational conflict—the need for joint decision making, goal differences, and perceptual differences—give rise to general responses including problem solving, persuasion, bargaining, and politicking. More specific managerial tactics of conflict handling are rule-oriented, rule-evading, personal-political, educational, and organizational-interactional tactics.

Specific patterns of interactions between groups also influence the tactics used to manage conflictual intergroup relations. Lateral relationships can be characterized as work-flow, service, advisory, audit, stabilization, and liaison. Managers can better understand and handle interfaces with other groups by identifying the types of lateral relationships, anticipating future changes, and forging different patterns of relationships.

CONCEPTS TO REMEMBER

Group effectiveness	Starfish analogy	Ringi
Work group effectiveness model	Devil's advocacy	Causes of intergroup conflict
Assets and liabilities in group problem solving	Dialectical inquiry	Responses to conflict
Groupthink and its symptoms	Nominal group technique	Tactics of conflict relationships
Group polarization	Delphi technique	Types of lateral relationships

QUESTIONS FOR DISCUSSION

1. You have been asked to chair a task force charged with solving some organizational problem—say, high levels of employee turnover. Devise a comprehensive strategy for managing the task force.

2. Assume that your first meeting of the above-mentioned task force is soon to take place. Prepare an agenda for the meeting and a strategy for managing group process in the meeting.

3. A few corporations in this country have experimented with the concept of "Office of the President," in which two or three persons share the role of chief executive officer. What do you anticipate would be the advantages and disadvantages of such a system?

4. Groups in organizations are of essentially two kinds: ongoing work groups and decision-making groups (such as committees and management teams). Discuss the implications of this distinction for *(a)* desired levels of cohesion, *(b)* the handling of conflict within the group, and *(c)* the role of the leader.

5. Choose any work group with which you are familiar and use the effectiveness model to generate suggestions for improving the group's performance.

REFERENCES

Ancona, D. G. (1987). Groups in organizations: Extending laboratory models. In C. Hendrick (ed.), *Group processes and intergroup relations,* pp. 207-31. Beverly Hills, CA: Sage Publications.

Auletta, K. (1986). *Greed and glory on Wall Street: The fall of the House of Lehman.* New York: Random House.

Bales, R. F. (1950). *Interaction process analysis: A method for the study of small groups.* Reading, MA: Addison-Wesley Publishing.

Bottger, P., & Yetton, P. (1988). An integration of process and decision scheme explanations of group problem solving performance. *Organizational Behavior and Human Decision Processes* 42, 234-49.

Brett, J., & Rognes, J. (1986). Intergroup relations in organizations: A negotiations perspective. In P. Goodman (ed.), *Designing effective work groups,* pp. 202-36. San Francisco: Jossey-Bass.

Cecil, E., Cummings, L., & Chertkoff, J. (1973). Group composition and choice shifts: Implications for administration. *Academy of Management Journal* 16, 412-22.

Cosier, R. (1981). Dialectical inquiry in strategic planning: A case of premature acceptance? *Academy of Management Review* 6, 643-48.

Ewing, D. (1983). *Do it my way or you're fired!* New York: John Wiley.

Farnham, A. (1989). The trust gap. *Fortune,* December 4, pp. 56-78.

Hoerr, J. (1989). The payoff from teamwork. *Business Week,* July 10, pp. 56-62.

Janis, I. L. (1972). Victims of groupthink. Boston: Houghton Mifflin. Copyright © 1972. Used with permission.

Janis, I. L. (1989). *Crucial decisions.* New York: The Free Press.

Jay, A. (1976). How to run a meeting. *Harvard Business Review* 54, 43-57.

Katz, R. (1982). The effects of group longevity on project communication and performance. *Administrative Science Quarterly* 27, 81-104.

Kearns, D. (1976). *Lyndon Johnson and the American dream.* New York: Signet.

Kidder, T. (1981). *The soul of a new machine.* Boston: Little Brown.

Kotler, P. (1988). *Marketing management,* 6th ed. Englewood Cliffs, NJ: Prentice Hall.

Maier, N.R.F. (1967). Assets and liabilities in group problem solving: The need for an integrative function. *Psychological Review* 74, 239-49.

Maier, N.R.F. (1972). *Psychology in industrial organizations,* 4th ed. Boston: Houghton Mifflin.

March, J., & Simon, H. (1958). *Organizations.* New York: John Wiley & Sons.

Mason, R. O. (1969). A dialectical approach to strategic planning. *Management Science* 15, B403-B414.

McGrath, J. E. (1984). *Groups: Interaction and performance.* Englewood Cliffs, NJ: Prentice Hall.

Mirtroff, I., & Mason, R. (1981). The metaphysics of policy and planning: A reply to Cosier. *Academy of Management Review* 6, 649-51.

Myers, D. G., & Lamm, H. (1976). The group polarization phenomenon. *Psychological Bulletin* 83, 602-27.

Mynatt, C., & Sherman, S. J. (1975). Responsibility attribution in groups and individuals: A direct test of the diffusion of responsibility hypothesis. *Journal of Personality and Social Psychology* 32, 1111-18.

Rohlen, T. P. (1975). The company work group. In E. Vogel (ed.), *Modern Japanese organization and decision making.* Tokyo: Tuttle.

Sayles, L. (1989). *Leadership: Managing in real organizations.* New York: McGraw-Hill.

Schein, E. (1968). *Process consultation.* Englewood Cliffs, NJ: Prentice Hall.

Seibold, D. R. (1979). Making meetings more successful. *Journal of Business Communication,* Summer.

Shaw, M. (1981). *Group dynamics: The psychology of small group behavior.* New York: McGraw-Hill.

Siegel, J., Dubrovsky, V., Kiesler, S., & McGuire, T. (1986). Group processes in computer-mediated communication. *Organizational Behavior and Human Decision Processes* 37, 157-87.

Steiner, I. (1972). *Group process and productivity.* New York: Academic Press.

Strauss, G. (1962-1963). Tactics of lateral relationships: The purchasing agent. *Administrative Science Quarterly* 7, 161-86.

Van de Ven, A. H., & Delbecq, A. L. (1974). The effectiveness of nominal and delphi techniques in interacting group decision making processes. *Academy of Management Journal* 17, 605-21.

Zander, A. (1982). *Making groups effective.* San Francisco: Jossey-Bass.

18 Power and Politics in Organizations

What are the common misconceptions about control and influence in organizations?

What are the different means of influence in organizations?

How does authority operate in organizations?

How can power be assessed, acquired, and used?

How and why do political processes operate in organizations?

Recently, employees in one organization voted by a wide margin to cut their own pay by 20 percent, across the board. They hoped to avoid layoffs, in which they or their colleagues would lose their jobs. At the same time, their proposal would cut costs and help meet shareholders' profit requirements. What do you think was top management's response? If you were CEO, how would you respond to the employees' recommendation?

The CEO, collaborating with a small group of top- and middle-management supporters, fired 20 percent of the workforce. The CEO stated, "It was very important that management's prerogative to manage as it saw fit not be compromised by sentimental human considerations" (Harvey, 1989, p. 275).

The employees in this case were offering a solution to an organizational problem. Management apparently saw the suggestion as a threat to their own power. The CEO responded by reasserting his authority and attempting to "regain" control of the situation and the workforce. But did he really increase his power?

MISCONCEPTIONS ABOUT CONTROL IN ORGANIZATIONS

It is probably impossible for two or more people to interact without having each person influence, and be influenced by, the others. Influence — the process by which one person affects the behavior of another — is not unique to formal organizations. Nor is power, which we define as the ability to influence. What sets organizations apart from informal interaction seems to be a higher degree of control — influencing the behavior of others by limiting it to a predetermined range of responses. The exercise of control serves to restrict behavior. This process, exercised properly, can enhance organizational effectiveness and increase personal power. If the application of control is unbridled or exercised inappropriately, both personal power and organizational effectiveness suffer.

Although everyone recognizes the need for control in organizations, many people — including the CEO in the opening paragraphs — cling to oversimplified assumptions about the nature of control (and about the related concepts influence and power). We will discuss three such assumptions: the presumed physical concentration, fixed amount, and one-way nature of power and control.

Physical Location   Many people seem to believe that power and control are concentrated in some physical location. Student activists in the 1960s thought they could capture control by seizing some office or university official as though power and control were "located" or "hidden" somewhere. Even their more law-abiding comrades, who petitioned college presidents and deans, held the notion that control was personalized. The activists may have had a flair for the dramatic and certainly received their share of publicity, but they did not find the control they were looking for, because control actually was diffused throughout the university. Control in any organization is diffused because of the complex web of interdependence among parts of the system.

What about business corporations? Surely these efficient engines of enterprise must be tightly controlled by a handful of tough-minded titans at the top. Here again, we are misled by such symbols as organization charts, titles, and written descriptions of formal authority. Control is broadly distributed throughout the middle layers of the business organization in what Galbraith (1967) called the technostructure. This is the phalanx of engineers, scientists, accountants, and other professionals whose combined efforts shape the activity of the firm.

Fixed Amount   A second widespread misconception is that, for any organization, there is a fixed amount of control. What follows is the belief that, if some groups exert increased control, there must be a corresponding decrease in the control exerted by other groups. Thus, if workers or staff gain control, then managers sacrifice it. This erroneous belief has given rise to pointless arguments about the proper way to divide up the "influence pie."

In fact, the total amount of influence in an organization can increase. What differentiates effective from ineffective plants, unions, and voluntary organizations is not the distribution of the influence pie, but the total amount of control exerted by all groups — officers and members alike (Tannenbaum, 1962). The correlation between the control exerted by rank-and-file groups and the control exerted at the management level is not negative, but positive: when lower-ranking groups exert more influence, the management and administrative echelons also exert more influence. (The Tannenbaum studies were correlational in nature. Thus, the effectiveness of the organization may have led to greater total and mutual influence, rather than the other way around.)

Therefore, effective managers *empower* others — they share power. They do this by allowing subordinates to participate in decision making, delegating decision responsibility, encouraging self-management in individuals and work teams, and developing leadership in others through mentoring and role modeling (Hollander & Offermann, 1990).

One-Way Nature   Finally, there is the mistaken idea that influence and control are one-way processes. The implicit assumption is that managers attempt to influence in only one direction. In reality, managers don't initiate actions for subordinates and end their exchanges once they issue their directives; relationships are reciprocal, mutual, and ongoing rather than unilateral (Campbell, Dunnette, Lawler, & Weick, 1970).

The manager's actions and words are indeed stimuli to which others respond. When an administrator makes a request, issues a directive, specifies a procedure, or clarifies a situation, subordinates typically respond. But that does not end the influence episode. The responses made by subordinates are also stimuli — stimuli that the manager cannot ignore. If the subordinates comply in good spirit, they reinforce the behavior of the manager. Furthermore, they earn credits with the manager, credits that they may draw on if they later seek favors, privileges, or special consideration. If regular compliance generates expected credits that are later "presented for payment," the manager will react by amending the directive or seeking modification of procedures from his or her own superiors. The point is that the manager cannot exert influence without displaying a willingness to be influenced in turn.

These considerations give rise to an important paradox surrounding power: the excessive use of power actually diminishes a manager's influence and therefore is self-defeating (Whetten & Cameron, 1986). Leaders who believe that there exists only a fixed pie of power in their organization, that the power resides in themselves, at the top of the hierarchy, and that power is a one-way street (downward, as they exercise control over those at lower levels), will exaggerate their own importance, denigrate others, and attempt to overcontrol. This leads to others' resistance and stronger attempts at countercontrol. In contrast, those who recognize the diffusion of power, its two-way nature, and the importance of sharing power and empowering others, ultimately find themselves even more influential.

AUTHORITY IN ORGANIZATIONS

The most fundamental type of power in organizations is the exercise of authority. Authority is power that is vested in a particular person or position, and that is recognized and accepted as legitimate and appropriate (Katz & Kahn, 1978). In other words, authority is the ability to influence specified others in accordance with the definition of formal organizational role relationships. Authority inheres in the office occupied by an individual; all persons holding a given office possess the same degree of authority. Some may be more influential than others due to their ability to draw on other bases of influence (such as expertise or friendships).

The social exchange character of influence by authority is represented by an "informal contract" entered into by the individual and the organization. The individual, in exchange for material benefits or for the attainment of some valued goal, endorses the authority structure of the organization — implicitly agreeing to comply with any request by a superior that the authority structure legitimates. Failure to comply with such requests constitutes grounds for disciplinary measures or expulsion. Discipline and expulsion, however, are unusual, because people are socialized to respect and defer to authority figures.

Functions of Authority   What functions does authority serve? First of all, it is a force toward the *reduction of human variability* (Katz & Kahn, 1978). The natural variability inherent in human action must be constrained if

FOCUS ON MANAGEMENT

Executive Views on Power Sharing

In a recent survey by *Fortune* magazine, virtually all the chief executives polled said that they *share* power more than they did five years ago (Stewart, 1989). States USX's Charles Corry: "My predecessor was more imperial, and I tend to be more collegial." Reuben Mark, CEO of Colgate-Palmolive, says, "The more you have, the less you should use. You consolidate and build power by empowering others." Peter Drucker predicts that, in today's knowledge-based companies, old-fashioned pyramids and traditional hierarchies of command-and-control will be replaced by a structure more like a symphony orchestra, with up to hundreds of specialists reporting to the CEO (conductor). CEOs must set a strategic direction, get people committed, and then empower them to do their jobs by giving them money and authority and leaving them alone. CEO Ralph Stayer of Johnsonville Foods maintains, "Real power comes from giving it up to others who are in a better position to do things than you are. Control is an illusion. The only control you can possibly have comes when people are controlling themselves."

Chairman Anthony J. F. O'Reilly of Heinz noted that the point is not to simply diffuse power. He gave as an example, "a local planning commission, where many people can say no but it's unclear who can say yes." Giving people greater responsibility won't work without also giving them authority and holding them accountable for results. Empowering people in this way gives them a clearer sense of what they must accomplish. Power is thus pinpointed as well as shared.

organizations are to survive; individuals must operate reliably within their roles. Since most organizational roles are defined imperfectly by formal job definitions—which can never completely anticipate the changing environment and operational problems—authority enables managers to define subordinate role requirements and control behavior.

Second, authority helps in *coping with the time lag* between subordinates' efforts and their rewards. It would be awkward if subordinates had to be tangibly reinforced for every appropriate behavior. Organizational participants must often endure prolonged periods of deprivations and impositions en route to the attainment of goals. Authority helps overcome the extinction in task behavior that would otherwise occur during periods when rewards are not at hand.

Third, authority—since it is an organizational creation—*outlives individuals who use it.* This guarantees that new managers will possess some minimum degree of power by which to influence subordinates. Lacking authority, they would require an inordinate amount of time to establish other bases of influence.

Finally, authority gives the administrator *bargaining chips* (Gouldner, 1954). The manager often has the power to enforce a great many rules (no smoking, no early breaks, no extended breaks, no early punch-out, and no gambling on the premises). If he or she chooses to enforce these rules to the letter, subordinates may defer to authority, but perform only at the absolute minimum. On the other hand, the boss may wink if members of the crew match coins to see who buys the Cokes, or take a few minutes extra at lunch during the World Series, in exchange for which the crew may do some things (say, work extra hard to clear up a production bottleneck) that the boss could not demand by authority alone. Ironically, then—as discussed earlier—the boss may gain power by occasionally giving up some power and not exercising authority to the hilt.

Limitations of Authority　　Authority would hardly suffice as the sole basis of influence in organizations. Authority is feasible only under certain conditions and because it has certain side effects.

Since authority, like the law, must apply equally to all subordinates, it must therefore be *geared toward the lowest common denominator.* Overemphasis on authority as a means of influence "tends in practice to mean that the minimal acceptable standard for quantity and quality of performance becomes the maximal standard" (Katz & Kahn, 1978). Once a person has complied with the minimum standard, authority alone can hardly influence the worker to do more. Otherwise, authority would become so subjective in varying demands from one person to another that the consensus that legitimates authority eventually would break down.

Authority is also limited in that the official authority inherent in an organizational position *applies only to subordinates* who report directly to the occupant of that office. Most responsible organizational officials, however, must also exercise lateral (and sometimes upward) influence. A production line supervisor depends on people outside the unit for materials maintenance, information, and various other services. The purchasing officer depends on parties totally outside the organization—vendors or suppliers. The sales or marketing manager must influence the people in the plant to schedule production. In these situations, a manager must influence people who, by definition, are not under the jurisdiction of his authority. At these times, the manager has to operate with other bases of influence, such as friendship or exchanges of favors. The manager who becomes so accustomed to influencing subordinates by authority that he makes requests in lateral job contacts in an authoritative tone will find himself dealing with uncooperative colleagues. The latter will be only too quick to remind him, in words or in manner, that "I don't work for you" or "You're not my boss!"

A third limitation to the exclusive use of authority is that it generates *unwelcome side effects.* Most people have ambivalent feelings toward authority figures. On the one hand, they respect authority. On the other hand, they tend to avoid authority figures. Differences in authority imply such differences as superior/inferior, more valuable/less valuable, and more mature/less mature. People generally do not like to be confronted in such a way that they are on the short end of these dimensions. Because authority figures are associated with the threat of punishment, people prefer not to be around such persons. Kids on the playground at recess time become uneasy when the principal is nearby, even though they are behaving themselves; drivers start to squirm when they see a police car close behind in the rearview mirror, even when they are law-abiding. This generalized avoidance tendency works at cross-purposes with the superior's aims to coach, teach, and nurture. The point here is not that authority per se is undesirable, but rather that influence based solely on authority has costs associated with it.

SOURCES OF POWER

What gives power to an individual or organizational subunit? We will describe five general bases of power in organizations: legitimacy, control over resources, expertise, social relationships, and personal characteristics (see Figure 18–1). Each of these power sources is potentially available in one form or another to persons occupying virtually any organizational role.

Legitimacy

Often when people think about power and influence in organizations, they focus on who has the right to issue orders, make decisions, and do as they please. This line of reason emphasizes the legitimacy of actions taken. And legitimacy implies authority; without doubt, formal authority confers legitimacy and power in organizations.

But there are forms of legitimacy that afford power to even the lowest employees, including those who have no authority at all. Sometimes workers can defend their actions, or inaction, on the basis of formal rules within the organization. Similarly, national and state laws—such as those addressing

FIGURE 18–1

Sources of Power in Organizations

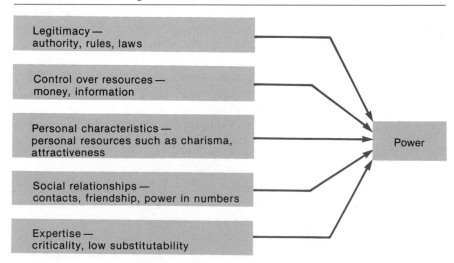

discrimination and unfair treatment of employees—must be obeyed. Thus, employees may have legitimate shelters against illegitimate demands by their employers.

Control Over Resources

Power accrues to those who have control over organizational resources, particularly those resources that are scarce and important. Resource control can include any reward or sanction, but the most obvious example is money (such as controlling budget allocations, or pay raises).

Moreover, one does not need the authority to allocate resources to have the kinds of resource control that confer power. The salesperson who brings in the highest revenues, the professor who attracts the biggest research grants, the manager who accumulates useful information about market trends, and the vendor who monopolizes the supply of raw materials to the company, all are providing critical resources to the organization. Their personal power increases accordingly.

Personal Characteristics

Just as control over organizational resources confers power, some people are powerful because they have what Kipnis (1974) calls personal resources. That is, they have an appeal, charm, or charisma that commands attention and respect. Lee Iacocca, Ronald Reagan, and John Madden are visible examples.

Of course, stature in the organization—via legitimacy, resource control, or expertise—may add to this attractiveness. However, charismatic attributes can contribute significantly to the power of an individual who has not yet established his or her other power bases. They seem also to account for differences in influence among those who would seem equal in power when assessed by more "objective" means.

Social Relationships

Power can also come from social relationships. Contacts with others, particularly those with power, can help to get things done. A strong network of social contacts includes subordinates and persons outside the organization as well as peers and superiors. Power accrues to those who have easy access to numerous networks (Brass, 1985), because those persons will typically help form coalitions between these cliques. By plugging into several intersecting grapevines, these persons will be sensitive to areas of mutual concern and interest to various groups. Thus, a manager—in order to "bring home the bacon" for the group—must cultivate entrance into networks outside the department and be more sensitive to external power than to internal formal authority.

Social relationships also provide power because there is power in numbers. Executives form coalitions when they realize that they alone cannot champion their ideas. Similarly, labor unions exist in large part because of the historical powerlessness of individual laborers. Even today, labor leaders know that their powers wax and wane with fluctuations in the size of their memberships.

Social contacts may operate primarily on a formal, professional basis, but can also evolve into friendships. Friendship is a very powerful basis for social influence. When two persons enjoy mutually rewarding interactions, reciprocated esteem, and interpersonal attraction, they generally wish to continue and reinforce their association. Each wants to continue to be well thought of by the other. Therefore, when one makes a request of the other, the latter must either grant the request or else strain the relationship. To the degree that such a strain threatens the rewards from the association, the friend will comply with the request. The basis of the social exchange, then, is compliance in return for continuation of a personal relationship.

The recognized force of friendship power has led some to suggest that a manager should go easy on exercising authority and try instead to build personal relationships with subordinates. The assumption is that they will then carry out their roles conscientiously because they want to (that is, because they like the boss) rather than because they have to, and that they will be willing to do a number of things that they could not legitimately be ordered to do. This argument, however, should not overlook some subtle aspects of influence based on friendship.

Friendship must be genuine if it is to endure. A façade built on contrived attempts at ingratiation (Jones, 1964; Liden & Mitchell, 1988) soon wears out and may even backfire. A superior who is friendly for ulterior motives will be put to the test when subordinates come back with personal requests of their own. If favors run on a one-way street, even the most obtuse underlings will see the relationship for what it is—a manipulative ingratiation. Of course, once someone acquires the reputation of being manipulative, others are less likely to befriend him or her.

Expertise

Physicians, attorneys, and tax accountants have no formal authority over their clients, yet they often exert great influence. They influence others because they have a degree of expert power (French & Raven, 1959) and others need their expertise to solve a problem or get something done. Likewise, in business organizations, eloquent staff advisers with MBAs may influence important strategic and operational decisions. In today's large corporations, expertise is a vital personal resource conferring great influence on those who have it and use it effectively.

What Kind of Expertise?   Expertise alone is not sufficient for acquiring power. The expertise must also be *critical* to the success of the organization. The role of criticality is shown by an apparent anomaly in a French factory (Crozier, 1964). The maintenance engineers, although characterized by modest formal rank and authority, exerted considerable influence in the organization.

Analysis revealed that the only critical area of uncertainty and unpredictability facing plant personnel was the periodic breakdown of machinery. The maintenance engineers were the only members who could cope with this uncertainty; consequently they possessed power vastly disproportionate to their hierarchical station.

Thus, power accrues to those groups who have the ability or expertise to cope with *strategic contingencies* that pose uncertainty (Hickson, Hinings, Lee, Schneck, & Pennings, 1971). For example, if the volume of business of a contracting firm depends heavily on government orders, those in the firm who have important contacts with officials in the relevant government departments will have considerable power. If an organization is highly vulnerable to lawsuits, legal officers' opinions will carry weight. The most critical expertise is associated with those functions "the organization finds currently problematic: sales and marketing people when markets are competitive; production experts when materials are scarce and demand is high; personnel or labor relations specialists when labor is scarce; lawyers, lobbyists, and external relations specialists when government regulations impinge; finance and accounting types when business is bad and money tight" (Kanter, 1977; cited in Mintzberg, 1983, pp. 170–71).

Groups that can reduce uncertainty for others become natural candidates for alliances. Dominant coalitions are those that have the expertise to handle the pressing problems of the day. Members of units that are highly visible, in the mainstream of strategic operations, will be better able to wield influence. On the other hand, groups that handle only routine operations or that work outside critical areas will have much less influence on major policies and decisions.

Finally, a key component of power conferred by critical expertise is one's degree of *substitutability*. To the extent that other persons or departments, or even persons outside the organization, are able to provide the same expertise, power is less stable. Being irreplaceable means being powerful, and there is frequent maneuvering to maintain at least the appearance of irreplaceability. At the same time, people try to reduce others' power by seeking the same kinds of knowledge or critical expertise.

Using and Maintaining Expert Power   What conditions must exist for you to influence another person by means of expert power? First, someone else must admit ignorance on a subject and become aware of a need for another's expertise. A financial analyst can influence a client's investments only to the extent that the client realizes he or she lacks the expertise to select stocks and bonds.

Second, the other person must recognize that *you* have the requisite information, expertise, or judgment. This condition may be fulfilled by your official credentials, the testimonials of others, or by your assertions about your knowledge. It is most likely to be guaranteed, however, by your demonstrated ability to solve problems. Furthermore, you can preserve your credibility by not making prescriptions about things in which you have no expertise and by being open-minded on topics that aren't an exact science — showing that you know the limits to your knowledge.

Third, you must be careful not to punish — however unintentionally — the other person's admission of ignorance and request for help. Otherwise, he or she will not soon ask for help again, and you will be prevented from influencing the person further. If a student asks in class, "What is a correlation?" and the teacher responds, "Didn't you study the assignment?" or "Just where did you go to school?", such inquisitiveness will be extinguished. Along the same lines, the manager should reinforce (or in any case, not punish) admissions of ignorance.

Fourth, people find it easier to seek knowledge from others if they can also occasionally give knowledge to those same others. Repeated requests for information, no matter how genuine or urgent, do something to the status of requesters by making them feel obligated and in a sense inferior. Such obligations are easier to bear if requesters can count on repaying the obligation by sharing some of their own expertise. A superior, therefore, should feel no hesitancy about seeking the expertise of subordinates, for that makes it easier for the subordinates to approach the superior with questions.

Thus, expertise works best as a two-way street of influence. Unfortunately, some managers are afraid that they will lose respect if they admit ignorance; if they then try to bluff it, they probably do lose respect. Most of us are more inclined to respect the superior who is mature enough to admit to ignorance.

Of course, a superior may draw on expertise in the exercise of authority. The boss's engineering knowledge may be the basis for ordering a subordinate to use certain procedures. But the dynamics of the social exchange process are different — giving advice and issuing orders have opposite consequences (Blau, 1964). Giving helpful advice to others creates obligations and is a credit to you; ordering people to do something uses up obligations, and is a credit to their account but a debit to yours.

ASSESSING POWER

Power and politics are important in organizations, and it is useful to be able to identify the organization's most and least influential people. The ability to discern power differences can affect one's ability to progress, or even survive, in an organization.

Who are the powerful people in organizations? Which jobs confer more power than others? Some individuals are proud and confident of their skill in "intuiting" the powerful organization members. Others are uncertain about how to analyze what is often an ambiguous, changing political scene. They are not even aware of people's job titles, let alone who wields the most clout among a group of managers at the same organizational level.

Fortunately, one can identify, gather, and analyze information that can help even inexperienced employees draw useful conclusions about the power structure of the organization. Power can be identified by assessing (1) status symbols; (2) symbols of actual influence; (3) consequences of power; (4) representational indicators of power; and (5) behavioral symptoms of powerlessness.

Status Symbols

Status symbols are a readily available source of concrete information. People use these visible manifestations of status in the formal hierarchy to convey their own positions of power, and conversely, to infer the power of others. Formal job titles, and special parking, dining, and washroom facilities are common examples. Offices and their furnishings also provide strong clues; the number of windows, type of carpeting, value of furniture and decorations, office size and location are visible status symbols.

A routine perusal of status symbols can provide a quick and useful assessment of organizational status to even the most naive observer. Nonetheless, such visible indicators are imperfect. Titles, for example, can be misleading because they often are artificially inflated rewards for long service, devoid of real meaning. Moreover, people with the same status symbols may differ dramatically in their actual influence in the organization.

Symbols of Actual Influence

Status symbols are tangible indicators of position and power in the organization. Since they hardly tell the whole story, symbols of actual influence also must be identified. Managers' organizational power can be evaluated by evidence of their influence over others, above and outside the group over whom they have direct authority.

Kanter (1979) provides examples of some common symbols of a manager's upward and outward influence. Some managers are particularly adept at landing favors for their more deserving subordinates—above-average pay raises, desirable job placements and responsibilities, protection against hostile higher-ups, and exemption from restrictive policies. Powerful managers also show more signs of involvement in decision making: they can get items placed on policy-meeting agendas, have frequent access to top decision makers, and are quick to learn about important decisions and policy shifts. These symbols of influence often translate into some of the more tangible consequences of power discussed below.

Consequences of Power

Powerful individuals influence, and consequently benefit from, important decisions made in the organization. Particularly if decisions are contested, it stands to reason that those who benefit most "won," and those who benefit least "lost." Thus, analyzing the consequences of decisions can provide an important indicator of power (Pfeffer, 1981).

Pfeffer offers some examples of the decisions that indicate power: favorable budget distributions, allocation of positions, and benefits of controversial strategy decisions. The extent to which you can use these and other decisions to assess power depends on the availability of their results, your skills in uncovering such information, and your ability to draw accurate inferences in the absence of concrete data.

Representational Indicators

Representational indicators of power identify the occupants of critical organizational roles like membership on influential boards and committees or occupancy of key administrative posts (Pfeffer, 1981). Membership on important committees derives from being powerful in the first place and then increases power via access to resources, information, and decision making. The power of organizational subunits, as well as individuals, can be assessed in this way. For example, historically, finance has dominated at General Motors, as evidenced by its disproportionate representation in the backgrounds of GM chairmen (Pfeffer, 1981).

Behavioral Symptoms of Powerlessness

Lack of power can be determined simply by noticing that some people act powerless. Employees in jobs that are inherently powerless, because they are dependent on others for resources and information, may use an *acquiescence* strategy to cope with powerlessness. That is, they resign themselves to the power imbalance, decide that not much can be done, and act passive, helpless, and dependent (Mainiero, 1986). Or, they may exhibit evidence of frustration, including alienation, loss of job involvement and organizational identification, and disruptive behaviors (Ashforth, 1989).

Paradoxically, among managers, powerlessness can engender bossiness rather than true leadership (Kanter, 1979). Particularly in large organizations, powerlessness breeds petty, dictatorial, rules-minded management. Since they cannot make things happen easily, the powerless turn to their ultimate weapon—oppressive power. This manifestation of presumed power (more accurately, powerlessness) is characterized by use of threat and punishment, close supervision, restrictive control, turf-mindedness, and resistance to change.

ORGANIZATIONAL POLITICS: THE PURSUIT AND USE OF POWER

Traditionally, the word *politics* has had an unsavory connotation among managers. We are prone to request that certain issues be "above politics," and "political appointments" implicitly refer to promotions of those who are undeserving.

Yet politics is virtually inevitable in organizations, which serve a plurality of interests that are almost never totally consonant with each other

FOCUS ON MANAGEMENT

Powerlessness at the Top

Many people assume that chief executives hold great power by virtue of their positions at the tops of organizations. In fact, top executives often experience feelings of powerlessness, of being buffeted by forces beyond their control. Changes in the external environment come so rapidly, and sometimes so dramatically, that the capacity of leaders to lead becomes severely limited (Kanter, 1979).

In his recent book, *Why Leaders Can't Lead* (1989), a prominent leadership scholar, Warren Bennis, reflects on his years as president of the University of Cincinnati. Toward the end of his first year in the job, he found himself muttering at 4:00 A.M., "Either I can't manage this place, or it's unmanageable." He faced 150 letters in the day's mail that required a response. About 50 of them were angry letters about the dean of the School of Education, who had been pictured in his office with his baby in a bassinet. The dean, who believed in equality of sex roles, took the baby to work two days a week. Letters from an outraged public urged his arrest for child abuse or at least his immediate dismissal.

A professor complained that his classroom temperature was down to 65 degrees. A student wanted course credit for acting as assistant to a city council member. Another student couldn't get into the student health center. A parent was upset about four-letter words in a Philip Roth book used in an English class. Alumni wanted better football seats and wanted the coach fired. One person complained that the squash courts closed too early.

A problem at the teaching hospital took up perhaps a fifth of Bennis's time that year. Some terminal-cancer patients consented to whole-body radiation, and the Pentagon, wanting to use the data to learn about protecting civilian populations in nuclear warfare, provided funds for the research. When the story broke, it called up comparisons with Nazi experiments on human guinea pigs. Separating facts from fantasy and distortion took endless hours, while Bennis was accused by some of interfering with academic freedom.

Forces in the external environment frustrated this top executive. Internally, employees called on the person at the top to exercise his authority to handle trivial issues. Bennis spent his time fighting fires, but felt powerless to change the status quo and lead his organization as he saw fit (Bennis, 1989).

(Yuchtman & Seashore, 1967). The abstract, publicly espoused goals of organizations seldom provide a clear basis for making operational decisions. A university may be said to exist in order to "disseminate knowledge, train tomorrow's leaders, and search for truth," but these laudable aims do not tell us whether to emphasize the humanities or professional schools or where the new student union building should be located. A private firm supposedly strives to maximize return on investment, but no one can say which of an array of options for uses of funds would really accomplish that end.

The major function of organizational politics is to fill the void of vague, inoperable goals with specific goals that can be translated into decisions and commitments. The greater the disagreement as to preferences and interests, the greater the need for the political process to effect a working agreement of commitments to action.

The extent of politics also will be determined by the degree of concentration of authority in the organization (Pfeffer, 1977). If one person or a very small group can dictate a course of action regardless of the sentiments of others, there is no point in politics. On the other hand, the greater the interdependence of various interest groups — that is, the greater the extent to which different groups can limit each other's actions — the greater the role of organizational politics in decision making.

Organizational Politics and the Individual

We have described how politics serves the organization, but we should also note the importance of the political process to individuals.

The fundamental motive for individuals to participate in organizational politics is to manage dependency relationships (Kotter, 1977). We have already discussed how groups in organizations are dependent on each other; individuals, likewise, can accomplish little without the help of others. To some extent, one can rely on well-established working rules and procedures for ensuring this support. But as one goes beyond the most routine and trivial operations, one inevitably needs cooperative actions of a kind or degree not mandated by established policies. The only recourse is to informal bases of influence that arise from negotiation, implicit appeal to reciprocity for past favors, or a tacit acknowledgment of how each part stands to gain from a cooperative relationship — in short, politics.

The political process influences personal outcomes like performance appraisals and pay raises. Even among CEOs, financial rewards may be more a function of politics than of the firm's financial performance (Ungson & Steers, 1984). The following Close-Up describes how politics operate in the important domain of performance appraisal, in which bosses assess and communicate their opinions of subordinates.

Individuals also need a political base for self-defense. Decisions in organizations never affect everyone equally. Some benefit very much while others suffer diminished resources, lower status, onerous constraints, more difficult work, or even loss of their job. People with little or no clout will be sacrificed when it is necessary to make a cut. Those with power and political skills have a better chance of defending themselves.

Finally, the political process offers an intrinsic appeal to some. The ability to exert influence on the social environment can offer a sense of competence. Those who eventually gravitate toward managerial roles are those who discover that they actually enjoy the wheeling and dealing, the compromising, the horsetrading, the bluffing and calling of bluffs, and the coalition building that are required to be effective in such roles (Schein, 1978). The leaders of corporations in high-technology,

CLOSE-UP

The Politics of Performance Appraisal

A team of academic researchers set out to determine the cognitive processes executives use to appraise subordinates (Longenecker, Gioia, & Sims, 1987). They were surprised to find that conducting accurate appraisals is not their primary objective. Instead, appraisals are conducted behind a mask of objectivity and rationality, and are manipulated intentionally to the executives' advantage. In short, performance appraisals are political, and used to enhance and protect executives' self-interest.

The executives in the study admitted that they almost always consider politics in the evaluation process. They take into account the interpersonal dynamics between them and their subordinates. They deliberately misstate performance levels if they think it would improve future performance. Although raters sometimes bias their ratings in a negative direction to teach a subordinate a lesson or remind him who the boss is, they do this rarely because of the problems this tactic could cause. More commonly, they inflate appraisals in the subordinate's favor to avoid confrontation, if they don't want to look like a bad guy, if they feel sorry for the subordinate, or to get an "up and out" promotion for someone they don't want in their department.

A few quotes enrich the study's findings (Longenecker et al.):

"Call it being politically minded . . . but in the end I've got to live with him, and I'm not going to rate a guy without thinking about the fallout."

"There is no doubt that a lot of us manipulate ratings at times to deal with the money [pay raise] issue."

"If the boss plays games with the review, it seems like the subordinate [manager] is more likely to do so."

"The higher you rise in this organization the more weird things get with regard to how they evaluate you . . . As the stakes get higher, things get more and more political."

"A lot of people inflate ratings of people they can't stand, or who think they are God's gift to the department, just to get rid of them. Amen."

dynamic industries are individuals who are, at heart, "gamesmen," motivated by the desire to win the game defined by the political process (Maccoby, 1976).

The Political Process

How does the political process unfold? Organizations are networks of individuals who interact with one another regularly (Tushman & Nadler, 1980). A *network* may evolve simply because the flow of work requires a distinct patterning of interaction, or because of shared values, interests, attitudes, or mutual attraction. An individual may belong to any number of networks, but individuals differ in the number of networks in which they are involved. Furthermore, within any one network, individuals vary in terms of the frequency with which others initiate interaction with them — some people are "stars" frequently sought by the others. Tushman and Nadler call these overlapping networks *cliques* and consider them the "basic building blocks of political organizations, much as the formal work group or subunit is seen as the major building block of formal organizations" (p. 182).

A clique, by itself, is usually too small to exert much control over major issues concerning the organization. Instead, cliques come together in *coalitions* to influence the outcome of major decisions. Coalitions are not as stable as cliques; they develop around specific issues. Once the issue has been decided, the coalition may dissolve; the cliques may realign themselves in a different fashion when a different issue comes to the fore. However, some cliques constitute an *axis* because they recurrently form coalitions of the same individuals who pursue a cooperative strategy and determine organizational policy to their own advantage.

POLITICAL TACTICS

The pursuit of power takes many forms. We will organize our discussion of the tactics used by political actors around four categories of attempted influence: (1) tactics of control, or downward influence; (2) tactics of upward influence; (3) tactics of lateral influence; and (4) the general types of political "games."

Tactics of Downward Control

Tactics of downward control arise from a superior's attempts to establish or maintain power over subordinates. The use of rewards and punishments to influence behavior, described in earlier chapters, fits roughly into this category. Other means of directly controlling the behavior of subordinates include giving direct orders, setting decision premises, reviewing decisions, and allocating resources (Mintzberg, 1983).

A boss can give a direct order to a subordinate, in effect making decisions and compelling the subordinate to execute them. Without a direct order, the manager can still exercise control by establishing constraints or guidelines, such as with purchases and other financial decisions, within which the subordinate makes the final choice. Or, the manager might delegate the decision-making authority to the subordinate, but retain the right to review the decision and veto it, approve it, or modify it before it is implemented. Finally, a manager can delegate all decision-making authority while still retaining the right to set resource constraints within which all the subordinate's decisions must fall. An example of the latter would be when a budget allocation is made, determining a subordinate's latitude in decision making.

Managers can also establish more formal systems of planning and controlling work content and performance output. By using these techniques — direct supervision and order giving, setting decision premises, and establishing bureaucratized control systems — and coupling them with the appropriate application of rewards and punishments, the controlling manager is dictating both the constraints on, and the outcomes of, their subordinates' behavior. Hence, the manager establishes and reinforces his authority over subordinates.

Tactics of Upward Influence

Many influence attempts are in an upward direction. That is, individuals often try to influence others who are higher, not lower, in the formal hierarchy (Gabarro & Kotter, 1980).

Tactics of upward influence can be used for two general purposes: to promote self-interests, usually attempted proactively, and to protect those interests, usually in a reactive manner (Allen, Madison, Porter, Renwick, & Mayes, 1979). The former usually is initiated by the subordinate, and attempts to improve the subordinate's position; the latter is usually a response to a superior's initiation, and attempts to protect the subordinate (Porter, Allen, & Angle, 1981).

There are two major categories of upward political influence methods— sanctions and informational methods (Porter et al., 1981). Sanctions involve the use of rewards and punishments, while informational methods involve the open, discrete, or manipulative use of information to influence higher-ups.

Sanctions are frequent downward control tactics, but probably are used less commonly than information in upward influence attempts. However, both positive and negative upward sanctions may be used, sometimes quite effectively. A subordinate may be unable to reward his or her boss in a formal sense, but exhibiting exemplary performance, doing favors, and solving work problems are rewards in the sense that they make a superior's job easier. Employees can also punish their superiors by withholding effort, spreading vicious stories, filing grievances, or sabotaging the product, the "system," or the boss's pet project. A common example is the secretary to several bosses who gives preference to (rewards) her favorite and gives slower or low-quality service to (punishes) another.

Informational tactics include open persuasion, manipulative persuasion, and true manipulation. Open persuasion often is aboveboard and nonpolitical, but its intent may be to enhance or to protect self-interests. Persuasion becomes manipulative when the influence attempt is open, but the objective is hidden. For example, an executive may argue for a policy change on the basis of organizational interests, when in fact it is he who stands to gain the most. Finally, real manipulation occurs when both the intent and the fact that an influence attempt is taking place are kept hidden. Examples would be the conscious withholding or distorting of information. The tightrope here is akin to the "ingratiator's dilemma" of buttering up the boss or trying to create a positive impression while keeping the true intent, and even the effort, concealed.

Tactics of Lateral Influence

Not all power maneuvers flow in the vertical (downward and upward) directions. Many political influence tactics are attempted between managers and departments that are not in a direct authority relationship with one another. You can increase your power by horizontally expanding your activities and responsibilities (Whetten & Cameron, 1986). "If the average middle-level manager spent as much time figuring out ways to increase his or her power through horizontal expansion as scheming how to increase his or her power through promotion, he or she probably would be much more successful" (Whetten & Cameron, 1986, p. 253).

In the last chapter, we highlighted a number of tactics used by purchasing agents in their conflicts with engineers. We also noted that interunit relationships can be categorized by the nature of the work roles that are performed by the units: for example, service, audit, and stabilization. Concluding the chapter, we suggested that the reader contemplate the differences in power among these roles, and how one might attempt to change from less to more powerful roles. Such considerations provide a useful means of viewing the "power moves" that transcend authority relationships and cut across departmental boundaries.

Power Roles Service, advisory, and liaison roles are of relatively low status and power; the more powerful roles are work flow, audit, and stabilization. Furthermore, those late in the work flow are dependent on (and therefore relatively powerless in comparison to) those placed earlier in the flow. Attempts to increase power often are intended to create movement toward roles that control the work of others, and away from roles that must defer to the needs of others.

Thus, common patterns of attempted power ploys (Sayles, 1989) include an advisory role becoming an audit role ("I tell you what is wrong so you'll take my advice") and a service role becoming a stabilization role ("I tell you what you require or will be permitted to have instead of responding to your requests"). Work flow can be conveniently ignored ("Rather than keeping you informed of changes or responding to your requests, I pretend we have no relationship"). Routine service work may also be unloaded onto others, and attempts may be made to shift the department to an earlier stage of the work flow.

Changing Roles: An Example Sayles offers a useful example of a packaging design department that initially recommended (in an advisory role) package designs and product materials. Over time, the manager noticed that he was either not consulted or consulted too late to be effective. Consequently, he made efforts to change his department's role, thereby enhancing its power and effectiveness. For example, he changed the work flow sequence: he started participating in early discussions about new product designs, so that packaging needs could be considered along with other requirements. In addition, he decreased service work by having certain kinds of packaging requests originate only in cost-reduction committees rather than in the production department.

He also added roles to his department. By evaluating existing product designs, shipment sizes, and other policies for their impact on packaging costs, he added an auditing role. By requiring that all engineering managers get his department's approval before changing product shape, he created a stabilization role. He even added a desirable advisory role by being available to assist cost-reduction committees. Throughout these efforts to increase his power and effectiveness, the manager justified the changes in terms of lowered costs and improved departmental and organizational effectiveness.

Political Games

Our discussion thus far has implied that political tactics have a tidy, unidirectional flow (down, up, or sideways). Of course, real political arenas are much messier (see Figure 18–2). Mintzberg (1983) calls organizational politics a "collection of goings on, a set of 'games' taking place . . . a kind of multiple-ring circus" (p. 187). He describes four predominant categories of games: those that (1) resist authority or counter the resistance to authority, (2) build power bases, (3) defeat rivals, and (4) effect organizational change.

Authority Games   Games to resist authority, and to counter resistance to authority are, respectively, insurgency games and counterinsurgency games. *Insurgency games* range from mild resistance or forgetting to carry out an order to outright mutiny, and may be played by individuals, small groups, or large, organized groups of workers. *Counterinsurgency games* occur when

FIGURE 18–2
A Simplified Political Arena

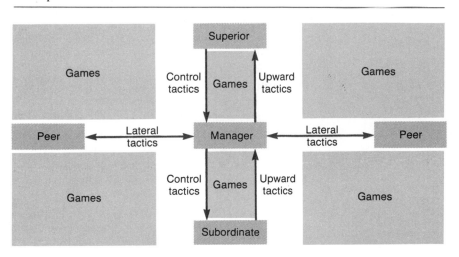

those in authority fight back. The typical, knee-jerk response is to invoke stricter authority and control—but tactics like persuasion and bargaining often emerge, especially when tighter controls prove ineffectual.

Power Base Games   Many types of games build power bases. The *sponsorship game* is played when an individual professes loyalty to a powerful, typically senior manager in return for advice and information, political favors, organizational resources, and reflected glory. *Alliance games* are similar in that implicit contracts of mutual support are negotiated. However, these games are more commonly found among groups of peers than between two individuals of unequal status.

Other games to build power bases include expertise games and empire building. *Expertise games* involve either the flaunting or the feigning of expertise. *Empire building* is the attempt of managers to collect subordinates and subunits—to enlarge their "territory." This is among the riskiest and most highly politicized of all the games, largely because salaries and resource allocations often are based on numbers of controlled positions. An important subset of empire building is the *budgeting game,* in which the object is to get more—more positions, space, equipment, and especially money.

Rivalry Games   Examples of games to defeat rivals are the line versus staff game and the rival camps game. *Line versus staff* conflict arises between managers with formal authority and staff advisers with specialized expertise but no authority. This represents a classic, and seemingly universal, power conflict over who achieves the greater influence over decisions. The *rival camps game* is essentially a two-person, zero-sum game in which someone loses. The opponents may be rival personalities, conflicting units, or two informal factions. Because one side will ultimately lose, these games inspire the most bitter and divisive organizational infighting.

Change Games   Finally, there are several types of games to effect organizational change. The *whistle-blowing game* is played when an organization member, often secretively, tells a powerful outsider of some organizational wrongdoing. If the right people or agencies are informed, they will investigate and perhaps force the organization to change its ways.

In the *strategic candidates game,* important battles take place during organizational decision making, as political actors promote their own pet projects. This game features elements of all the other games: managers champion strategic changes to build personal empires; insurgencies and counterinsurgencies arise; alliances emerge; expertise is feigned and flaunted; and so on. This complex game is vitally important. Since, as Mintzberg notes, a strategic decision typically results in a great many actions, those likely to be affected are far wiser to try to influence the decision while it is being made, rather than trying to resist the many actions that result.

The last of Mintzberg's games, the *young Turks game,* is the one played for the highest stakes. Far-reaching changes—a complete strategy reorientation, or an overthrow of existing leadership—are secretly, but vigorously, attempted by an enclave of charismatic rebels. This is insurgency in its extreme. It is also the ultimate zero-sum game because, in Mintzberg's (1983) words, "the intensity of the challenge is such that the organization can never be the same again" (p. 212).

PERPETUATING POWER

Power in most organizations is characterized by stability, not change. For three primary reasons, the powerful tend to stay powerful (Pfeffer, 1981).

First, *commitment to past decisions and strategies* causes persistence in behavior and, consequently, stable power distributions. If problems occur, they tend to be seen as shortcomings in implementation rather than as faulty initial decisions—a little more time, money, or effort is "all it will take" to turn things around. When more resources, staff, and information are therefore provided to those in charge of implementing programs, their power is increased even further.

Second, *patterns of authority go unchallenged.* Over time, rules, decisions, and power distributions become defined as part of the organization's culture; they are accepted without question by organizational members because "that's the way it's always been."

Third, *those in power can take actions* that help them perpetuate their own power. The greater the power of a unit or an individual, the more able they are to acquire additional positions, budget, and staff; their power increases accordingly. For example, a department that is powerful by virtue of its low substitutability and its ability to cope with critical contingencies can attract more resources than other departments. These resources further increase their ability to cope with uncertainty. At the same time, the department with power can eliminate competing units or consolidate them into their own unit. This lowers the department's substitutability and ensures its monopoly over critical problem-solving capacities. Thus, "power begets power"—not only via the naturally evolving respect and deference of others, but through willfull and skillful actions by the powerful.

Nonetheless, power structures sometimes change. When major external challenges—an economic downturn, regulatory pressures, or increased competition—create or forewarn of declines in organizational effectiveness, opportunities to supplant the Old Guard arise. We will have more to say about the signals that precipitate major organizational changes in Chapter 21.

CONCLUSION

Managers who are successful at acquiring and effectively using power share a number of common characteristics (Kotter, 1977). First, they understand the various types of power and influence tactics, and are capable of applying all the various methods flexibly, as they become appropriate. Second, they establish career goals and seek out positions that enable them to develop and use power. Third, they use power to further develop and perpetuate their power.

Effective managers also temper their power-related behaviors with maturity and self-control. This includes the avoidance of impulse and the reluctance to use risky tactics. Finally, effective managers are comfortable using power—they recognize that influencing other people's behavior and lives is a legitimate part of performance in their managerial roles.

SUMMARY

Organizational control is the exercise of power, influence, and authority toward specific ends. Misconceptions about the nature of control in organizations include the belief that it is localized, the assumption that the total amount of control is fixed, and the notion that control is a one-way process.

Authority is perhaps the most fundamental source of power in organizations, but it has a number of limitations to go with its functions. Its functions include reducing variability in employee behavior, coping with the time lag between subordinates' efforts and their rewards, providing an initial base of power to newcomers in the position, and providing bargaining chips to the administrator. Its limits are that it is geared to the lowest common denominator, it can be used with subordinates but not with peers, bosses, and others outside the company, and it has a variety of negative side effects.

Other sources of power, besides authority and legitimacy, are personal resources, social relationships, and critical expertise. While resulting power structures usually are rather ambiguously defined, information can be gathered that enables a reasonably valid assessment of power differences.

Organizational politics inevitably arise from the conditions of inoperable goals, lack of consensus, uncertainty, and interdependence. The political process is founded on overlapping networks or cliques of recurrently interacting persons. These cliques form coalitions in order to determine the outcomes of significant issues. Other political tactics can be categorized according to their emphasis on downward, upward, or lateral influence. Despite shifting power patterns in organizations, in the end there is some tendency toward stability because power is often self-perpetuating.

CONCEPTS TO REMEMBER

Functions of authority	Ingratiation	Coalitions
Limitations of authority	Assessing power	Axis
Empowerment	Representational indicators	Tactics of downward control
Strategic contingencies	Powerlessness syndrome	Upward influence tactics
Critical expertise	Acquiescence	Lateral influence tactics
Substitutability	Political games	Perpetuating power
	Cliques	

QUESTIONS FOR DISCUSSION

1. Lyndon Johnson once defined politics as "the art of the possible." Explain.

2. Organizational decisions are often political. Explain. What are the pros and cons of reaching decisions in such a manner?

3. Some observers believe that authority is becoming less and less viable as a basis for influencing people in organizations. In his book *Nice Guys Finish Last,* Leo Durocher wrote a chapter entitled "Whatever Happened to Sit Down, Shut Up, and Listen?" What developments do you suppose account for this observation? Does it still pertain today?

4. How important to furthering a career are *(a)* an understanding of, and *(b)* involvement in, office politics?

5. Discuss the ethics of politicking in organizations.

REFERENCES

Allen, R., Madison, D., Porter, L., Renwick, P., & Mayes, B. (1979). Organizational politics: Tactics and characteristics of its actors. *California Management Review* 22, 77-83.

Ashforth, B. E. (1989). The experience of powerlessness in organizations. *Organizational Behavior and Human Decision Processes* 43, 207-42.

Bennis, W. (1989). *Why leaders can't lead.* San Francisco: Jossey-Bass.

Blau, P. (1964). *Exchange and power in social life.* New York: John Wiley & Sons.

Brass, D. J. (1985). Men's and women's networks: A study of interaction patterns and influence in an organization. *Academy of Management Journal* 28, 327-43.

Campbell, J. P., Dunnette, M. D., Lawler, E. E., III, & Weick, K. E., Jr. (1970). *Managerial behavior, performance, and effectiveness.* New York: McGraw-Hill.

Crozier, M. (1964). *The bureaucratic phenomenon.* Chicago: University of Chicago Press.

French, J.R.P., Jr., & Raven, B. (1959). The bases of social power. In D. Cartwright (ed.), *Studies in social power.* Ann Arbor: Institute for Social Research, University of Michigan.

Gabarro, J., & Kotter, J. (1980). Managing your boss. *Harvard Business Review* 58, 92-100.

Galbraith, J. K. (1967). *The new industrial state.* Boston: Houghton Mifflin.

Gouldner, A. (1954). *Patterns of industrial bureaucracy.* New York: Free Press.

Harvey, J. B. (1989). Some thoughts about organizational backstabbing. *Academy of Management Executive* 3, 271-77.

Hickson, D. J., Hinings, C. R., Lee, C. A., Schneck, R. E., & Pennings, J. M. (1971). A strategic contingencies theory of intraorganizational power. *Administrative Science Quarterly* 19, 22-44.

Hollander, E., & Offermann, L. (1990). Power and leadership in organizations. *American Psychologist* 45, 179-89.

Jones, E. E. (1964). *Ingratiation.* New York: John Wiley & Sons.

Kanter, R. M. (1977). *Men and women of the corporation.* New York: Basic Books.

Kanter, R. M. (1979). Power failure in management circuits. *Harvard Business Review* 57, 65-75.

Katz, D., & Kahn, R. L. (1978). *The social psychology of organizations.* New York: John Wiley & Sons.

Kipnis, D. (1974). The powerholder. In J. T. Tedeschi (ed.), *Perspectives on social power.* Hawthorne, NY: Aldine Publishing.

Kotter, J. (1977). Power, dependence, and effective management. *Harvard Business Review* 55, 125-36.

Liden, R., & Mitchell, T. (1988). Ingratiatory behaviors in organizational settings. *Academy of Management Review* 13, 572-87.

Longenecker, C., Gioia, D. & Sims, H. (1987). Behind the mask: The politics of employee appraisal. *Academy of Management Executive,* 1, 183-93.

Maccoby, M. (1976). *The gamesman.* New York: Simon & Schuster.

Mainiero, L. A. (1986). Coping with powerlessness: The relationship of gender and job dependency to empowerment-strategy usage. *Administrative Science Quarterly* 31, 633-53.

Mintzberg, H. (1983). *Power in and around organizations.* Englewood Cliffs, NJ: Prentice Hall.

Pfeffer, J. (1977). Power and resource allocation in organizations. In B. M. Staw & G. R. Salancik (eds.), *New directions in organizational behavior.* Chicago: St. Clair Press.

Pfeffer, J. (1981). *Power in organizations.* Marshfield, MA: Pitman.

Porter, L., Allen, R., & Angle, H. (1981). The politics of upward influence in organizations. In L. L. Cummings & B. M. Staw (eds.), *Research in organizational behavior,* 3, 109-50.

Sayles, L. (1989). *Leadership: Managing in real organizations.* New York: McGraw-Hill.

Schein, E. (1978). *Career dynamics: Matching individual and organizational needs.* Reading, MA: Addison-Wesley Publishing.

Stewart, T. A. (1989). New ways to exercise power. *Fortune,* November 6, pp. 52-64.

Tannenbaum, A. S. (1962). Control in organizations: Individual adjustment and organizational performance. *Administrative Science Quarterly* 7, 236-57.

Tushman, M. L., & Nadler, D. A. (1980). Implications of political models of organization. In R. H. Miles, (ed.), *Resourcebook in macro organizational behavior.* Santa Monica, CA: Goodyear Publishing.

Ungson, G., & Steers, R. (1984). Motivation and politics in executive compensation. *Academy of Management Review* 9, 313-23.

Whetten, D., & Cameron, K. (1986). *Developing Management Skills.* Glenview, IL: Scott, Foresman.

Yuchtman, E., & Seashore, S. E. (1967). A system resource approach to organizational effectiveness. *American Sociological Review* 32, 891-903.

19 Leadership

Is leadership different from management?

How important are a leader's personal traits?

What are the dimensions of leader behavior?

How does leader behavior affect subordinate satisfaction and performance?

Is leadership a myth?

In the preceding chapters we examined the structural and environmental determinants of group cohesion and performance. We noted the dynamics of group interaction that can help or hinder the attainment of task goals. There is no question that groups are powerful forces in organizational affairs. But whatever the group's talents, its ultimate contributions will be largely determined by its leadership. Leaders must orchestrate the distinctive personalities, motives, and abilities of the individuals. Leadership fine-tunes group structure and transforms the potential energy of a cohesive group into the kinetic energy of a dynamic, constructive force.

This leadership may emerge in one or more informal leaders. However, in organizations, much of the leadership responsibility is vested in a formally designated leader role.

LEADERSHIP VERSUS MANAGEMENT

Is formal leadership simply another word for manager? Finespun arguments have been woven in response to this question.

Baron and Greenberg (1990) define leadership as "the process whereby one individual influences other group members toward the attainment of defined group or organizational goals" (p. 374). Few would argue with this definition, yet it would also seem to fit much of what we call management.

Gardner (1990) suggests that the "utterly first-class managers . . . turn out to have quite a lot of the leader in them" (p. 4). In his view, leader/managers distinguish themselves from "the general run of managers" in several respects: They think longer term (beyond the crises of the moment or the quarterly report); they grasp the relationship between their own organization and larger realities; they reach and influence constituents beyond their own jurisdiction; they heavily emphasize the intangibles of vision, values, and the nonrational; and they think in terms of renewal, always seeking revisions of process and structure to adapt to external forces.

Kotter (1990) sees the fundamental qualitative distinction between leadership and management in terms of the degree of *constructive or adaptive change* that is effected. Management contributes to *order* and *stability* by planning, budgeting, organizing, staffing, monitoring processes to spot deviations from the plan, and taking actions to correct the deviations. Leadership, on the other hand, establishes direction by developing a vision of the future—what *can be* rather than what *is*; articulating this vision to others in compelling ways and aligning people into the coalitions that make the vision achievable; and providing the motivation and inspiration that keep people working to overcome obstacles to attain that vision. In short, management stabilizes the status quo while leadership transforms. Kotter contends that both management and leadership are necessary; good management without leadership results in

FOCUS ON MANAGEMENT

Leadership as Nudging

Andrew S. Grove, president of Intel Corporation, believes that a manager/leader's most valuable resource is time, and thus the manager has to engage in activities that have "high leverage"—that is, maximum amount of impact per unit of time.

Grove reports that much of his day is spent acquiring information. The information he finds most useful to him comes from quick, casual bits of conversation; because such information is so timely, it is also valuable. Written reports are useful for validating information obtained otherwise and providing an archive. Scouting expeditions into specific areas of company operations—simply walking through, occasionally stopping to ask a question or just to observe, but not breaking the momentum with the formality of entering someone's office—also constitute an efficient means of getting information. As Grove sees it, the base of information governs the quality of everything else a leader does.

Another high-leverage leader activity is what Grove calls "nudging." "For every decision we make, we probably nudge things a dozen times." A nudge is to be distinguished from an order or an outright decision. Yet the nudge is more than the mere conveyance of information. It may be a short memo, a phone call, or a brief comment in a meeting. It indicates how you see a problem or the type of criterion to be emphasized. It has just enough force to nudge people in a given direction, but it can be resisted without loss of face if there are good reasons for such resistance.

Finally, "Nothing leads as well as example." Leaders are role models. Their behavior sets the standard for others.

Grove spends, by his own estimate, two thirds of his time in meetings. "Before you are horrified at how much time I spend in meetings answer one question: Which of the activities—information gathering, information giving, decision making, nudging, and being a role model—could I have performed outside a meeting? The answer is practically none."

stagnation, while forceful leadership without the stabilizing touch of good management can result in chaos.

Kotter suggests that good management alone was sufficient for many North American businesses from 1950 to 1970, since this period was characterized by emphasis on the domestic marketplace, little competition from abroad, and stable technologies and products protected by patents and government regulation. Good management ensured efficient operation. The 1980s changed all of that, ushering in for most firms an era of vulnerability to a turbulent economic environment. Thus we have recently seen an outpouring of books and articles on the need for leadership, not just management.

The leadership/management distinction is a particularly pressing conceptual question for several reasons. First, many would argue that much of the research supposedly addressed to leadership actually had more to do with management. Second, critics of present-day graduate programs of business argue that such programs may excel at providing technical skills for managers, but they do little or nothing to prepare students for leadership. Finally, there are those who doubt if leadership can ever be taught — or even learned — past some early, critical stage of life.

THE PARADIGM OF LEADERSHIP THEORY AND RESEARCH

Traditionally, leadership studies have taken as their *independent variable* (that is, the cause or antecedent) either an attribute of the leader (such as a skill or a personality trait) or a dimension of leader behavior (such as the style of supervision or interaction with subordinates). *Dependent variables* (effects of the independent variables) have been satisfaction of subordinates and performance (such as productivity, efficiency, or effectiveness). Some theories have gone further and speculated about *intervening variables,* those that link or transmit the independent leader variables to ultimate dependent variables. Examples of intervening variables include the motivations, attitudes, or expectancies of subordinates. Finally, more recent models of leadership have introduced *moderator variables,* factors that determine when a specific leader variable has one effect or another on the dependent variables.

LEADER ATTRIBUTES

The oldest tradition in leadership theory and research, and one most familiar to the public, is that leadership is a stable quality possessed by some but not others. This notion is seen in three somewhat related assumptions: (1) leadership is stable across situations; that is, the persons who lead in some contexts are, to some extent, the same persons who lead in other settings; (2) some trait or cluster of traits can predict which persons, in a given setting, are most likely to lead; and (3) certain traits are either necessary or sufficient for a person to be an effective leader.

Is Leadership Transferable? Does the person who emerges as leader in one situation have a better-than-even chance of retaining that status in a different situation? Carter (1953) and Gibb (1949) concluded from their studies that leadership is at the very least not entirely situation specific. Instead, it seems to be somewhat general over some range of tasks. Kenny and Zaccaro (1983), in an analysis of an earlier study by Barnlund (1962) in which both tasks and member composition of groups were systematically varied, reached a somewhat stronger conclusion. They estimated that over half of the variation of the leader role was attributable to some stable individual characteristic. We cannot carry this logic to its extreme; the leader in a group of prison inmates will not necessarily achieve that status in a flower and garden club. But the available evidence does suggest that whatever leadership is, it can be predicted from one setting to others with better than chance success.

Are Specific Traits Related to Leader Status? In an article that stands as a benchmark in the leadership literature, Stogdill (1948) reviewed 124 empirical studies—conducted between 1904 and 1946—that sought to identify the traits associated with leadership status. In a later volume (Stogdill, 1974), he updated this record, and House and Baetz (1979) reviewed and reassessed his findings. Most of these studies sought to determine if certain personal characteristics predict *who will have the opportunity, formally or informally, to exert leadership over others.*

The cumulative evidence suggests that leaders tend to be taller than average, or at least taller than the particular group's average height. Leaders are usually more physically attractive than the average. Presumably, height and physical attraction operate as halo factors (Chapter 6); others are more likely to attribute positive qualities to tall, attractive people, and thus are more likely to admit them into leadership roles.

Copyright King Features Syndicate Inc., 1976

Leaders tend to be more intelligent than the group average (provided there is some reasonable range of variation in intelligence within the group). Verbal fluency and conceptual skills are especially predictive of leader status. This is not to say that a person with a genius-level IQ would invariably command deference, but in a reasonably heterogeneous group, the most influential person will usually have a higher intelligence than the general population mean.

In the studies reviewed by Stogdill and by House and Baetz, there is a slight tendency for the leader to be an extrovert, but the tendency is not consistent. Of the studies examined by Stogdill, five found extroverted leaders, two found introverts, and four found no differences in this respect between leaders and others. The relationship between leader status and emotional stability showed a similar trend: 11 studies found leaders to be more stable, but five found them to be less stable, and three found no relationship.

The personality trait that appears to correlate most consistently with leader status is variously labeled "dominance" or "ascendance." This trait underlies a need to influence others. It also suggests assertiveness: Dominant persons make their presence known. Dominance, however, must usually be coupled with intelligence or task-specific ability, and there must be a group expectation that someone will emerge as leader. Otherwise this trait has less predictive power with respect to leader status.

Leaders have a high energy or activity level. Different studies provided different names for this characteristic, but it seems clear that people who demonstrate initiative, persistence, and both physical and emotional stamina have an advantage in gaining leader roles. To elaborate, leaders are not "lost in thought," wistfully and seclusively gazing down on the human scene. Rather, they are embroiled in the thick of things. They do more and they do it more intensively. We noted before (Chapter 6) that our perceptual focus is biased toward movement; we notice things that move relative to a stable background. It is not surprising, then, that those we think of as leaders command our attention with their high level of activity.

Finally, the literature suggests that leaders are a relatively self-confident breed. Intelligence and physical attraction undoubtedly bolster self-confidence, just as self-confidence predisposes a person to be active and to attempt to influence others.

A few caveats are in order as we interpret these findings. First of all, most of these studies are correlational; they don't demonstrate cause and effect. While it is plausible that dominance, energy level, and self-confidence predispose persons to leadership, it is equally plausible that experience as a leader could cause a person to become more dominant, confident, and active. Second, it is not clear which of these traits are most important, or primary, and which are secondary to attaining leader roles. For example, it may be that intelligence is most important for leadership, and it simply happens that intelligence is generally accompanied by self-confidence and dominance. Third, some of these traits probably are moderated by others in their tie to leadership. Dominance and self-confidence are less likely to predict leadership when accompanied by below-average intelligence.

Correlates of Leader Effectiveness A separate question is whether the same traits that help individuals become leaders also help them to be effective in that role. This has proved a much tougher issue to address. To begin with, defining an "effective" leader is a problem. One can seldom get group members or observers to agree whether a given leader is effective. Abraham Lincoln is revered as the definitive national leader, but in his time many observers (including his own cabinet members) regarded him as a disaster. Pick almost any college basketball coach or corporation president, and regardless of their objective records, some observers will say that they were remarkable leaders, while others will say that a really good leader could have accomplished much more.

Nonetheless, a number of studies — some using objective indicators, others using expert opinion or aggregated ratings of many observers — have yielded evidence concerning the predictors of effective leadership, particularly in the managerial role. Ghiselli (1971), for example, found that the traits of intelligence, self-confidence, and initiative not only differentiated managers from nonmanagers, but were also correlated with ratings of effectiveness in the managerial role. Goodstein and Schrader (1963) reached similar conclusions. Undoubtedly the most consistent correlate with effectiveness in the managerial role is verbal intelligence (Campbell, Dunnette, Lawler, & Weick, 1970), although the correlations are modest.

Thus, an overlap occurs between the characteristics of those most likely to attain leader roles and those most likely to perform well once they are leaders. Height and physical attraction help some people become leaders, but thereafter do not seem to confer special benefits. Dominance helps one attain the leader role, and probably helps one enact the role, but most likely its effect is attenuated once leader status is secure. Verbal skills, confidence, and stamina help one to acquire leadership and appear to aid in successful performance as a leader.

Kenny and Zaccaro (1983) reach a somewhat different conclusion. They argue that "persons who are consistently cast in the leadership role possess the ability to perceive and predict variations in group situations and pattern their own approaches accordingly. Such leaders ;may be highly competent in reading the needs of their constituencies and altering their behaviors to more effectively respond to these needs" (p. 683). In other words, the key attribute of leaders is not any simple trait but a combination of (1) the ability to discern in a given situation what behaviors are needed to command deference; and (2) the capacity to adapt their own behavior to these needs. On a gross level, this is consistent with what we have reviewed above, in that some form of intelligence is certainly implied here. But it also argues that leaders are not so much controlled by their particular traits as much as they choose which traits to accentuate in a given setting. This suggests that leadership is associated with a certain makeup, but is not likely to be reflected in a single stereotyped behavior pattern.

If effective leaders are noted mainly by their choice of behavior, then we are prompted to ask what kinds of behavior are important in leadership.

LEADER BEHAVIOR

Since 1950, the study of leadership has looked more closely at what the leader does as opposed to the leader's traits. Paving the way were the pioneering *Ohio State leadership studies,* carried out in the late 1940s and early 1950s under the direction of Ralph Stogdill, Edwin A. Fleishman, and others.

These studies identified two relatively independent dimensions of behavior along which leaders differ. One of these, *consideration,* involves the extent to which the leader establishes mutual trust, rapport, and communication with subordinates. A high consideration score indicates psychological closeness between leader and subordinate; a low consideration score indicates a more psychologically distant and impersonal leader.

The second factor, *initiating structure,* pertains to leader acts of organizing, defining relationships, setting goals, emphasizing deadlines, giving directions — in short, concern for the task or getting the work done.

Studies suggest that these dimensions are independent (that is, not necessarily correlated or conflicting) dimensions of leader behavior. A leader could be high on both consideration and initiating structure, low on both, or high on one and low on the other. Leadership style, then, could be defined by the combination of relative standings on these two dimensions of behavior.

A comprehensive review of empirical studies investigating the relationships between consideration and initiating structure, on the one hand, and various criteria of leader effectiveness, on the other, would be inappropriate here. However, reviews by Korman (1966) and Fleishman (1973) provide some perspective on the cumulative evidence. Leader consideration appears to be a consistent, reliable predictor of subordinate satisfaction and the behavioral consequences of job satisfaction (such as turnover, absenteeism, and grievances). This effect varies from weak positive to strong positive, suggesting that the importance of consideration for morale depends on the situation.

The extent to which a leader's initiating structure affects the level of satisfaction varies from one extreme to the other, from strong positive to strong negative. Nor is there any consistency in the relationship between either consideration or initiating structure and various measures of performance. The extent to which these leader behaviors affect subordinate performance is either negligible or very dependent on the situation (a statement which, in itself, tells us little). Korman called for more explicit categorization of situations in order to determine when consideration and initiating structure become important determinants of group functioning.

Intuitively, one would regard the high consideration-high structure combination as optimal. After all, both task effectiveness and human relations (or participant satisfaction) are desirable end products of group activities. Presumably, initiating structure facilitates task accomplishment, and consideration promotes group maintenance and involvement by affecting participant attitudes.

These assumptions formed the basis of the Managerial Grid, a management development program that Robert Blake and Jane Mouton (1968) have used in numerous corporations (see Figure 19–1). Blake and Mouton think of "concern for production" and "concern for people" as two independent but essential factors for managerial effectiveness. Concern for

FIGURE 19–1
The Managerial Grid®

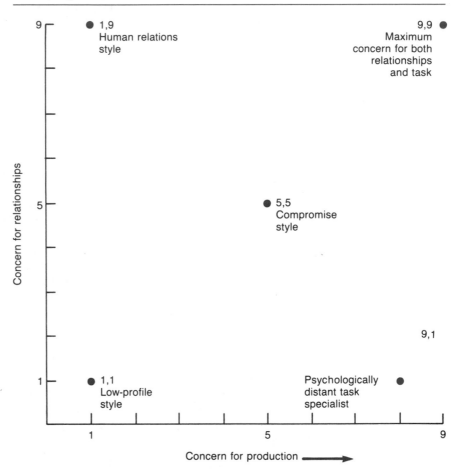

SOURCE: R. R. Blake and J. S. Mouton, *Corporate Excellence through Grid Organizational Development* (Houston: Gulf Publishing, 1968).

each factor can be represented as varying from 1 (very low) to 9 (very high). A 9,1 manager places high emphasis on production and little on people; a 1,9 leader invests energy in attending to the feelings and satisfactions of subordinates. A 5,5 leader compromises by placing moderate emphasis on both production and people. All three of these combinations apparently reflect an individual's assumption that concern for production and concern for people conflict with each other. The Managerial Grid program uses diagnostic tools to help the manager realize his or her current blend of these concerns and then embarks on a training regimen to bring each manager to a 9,9 philosophy—maximal emphasis on both task and relationships, without making a trade-off between the two.

Unfortunately, the findings from North American leadership studies do not seem to support the underlying premise of the Managerial Grid, since those findings show nothing even resembling a consistent pattern of high consideration and high initiating structure linked to effectiveness.

The Japanese Studies   More supportive of the Managerial Grid assumptions are the results of a 35-year research program conducted by Japanese scholar Jyuji Misumi (1985), whose work has only recently come to the attention of American students of leadership. Studying Japanese leaders in a broad array of contexts in both field and laboratory investigation, Misumi has found that leaders vary in performance orientation (P) and maintenance (i.e., relationships) orientation (M). Almost invariably he has found that the most effective leaders, in terms of both group morale and performance, are the PM type: balanced, but with strong emphasis on both performance and maintenance orientations. Somewhat less effective than the PM are both the P (strong emphasis on performance, slight emphasis on maintenance) and M (strong emphasis on maintenance, slight emphasis on performance) type leaders, neither of which consistently excels over the other. Least effective of all are the pm types, who show weak orientations toward either performance or maintenance.

Misumi argues that a performance orientation is essential to effective leadership. However, in the absence of a strong maintenance orientation, performance-oriented behaviors are experienced by the group as pressure and control imposed by the leader. In contrast, when M is present, the same P behavior seems more like helpful planning and teaching.

Why do Misumi's results show a consistency not evident in North American studies of consideration and initiating structure? House (1987) suggests some possible explanations. Perhaps Misumi's studies, carried out as part of an integrated, cumulative program, have featured more consistency in measurement and methods, while North American studies—carried out by many independent researchers—achieved less standardization in those respects. Conceivably Misumi's findings reflect the cultural homogeneity of the Japanese and the more generalized expectation that the leader, as a surrogate father, should emphasize both task and relationships.

In a reanalysis of some of Misumi's published data, House finds reason to think that the PM leader, while above average in both P and M, is neither so high in rated P behaviors as the pure P type, nor rated as high by the group in M behaviors as the pure M leader. In other words, in Managerial Grid terms, perhaps the PM leader Misumi found so consistently effective is something like a 7,7, rather than a 9,9.

Leader's Initiating Structure and Subordinate Response

SOURCE: G. B. Trudeau, *The President Is a Lot Smarter Than You Think* (New York: Popular Library, 1973).

THE PARTICIPATION CONTROVERSY

Should leaders exercise influence in an autocratic or a democratic fashion? This emotionally charged issue continues to reverberate in the leadership literature as well as in informal discussions about managerial behavior. Unfortunately, the labels *autocratic* and *democratic* contain obvious value connotations that make it difficult to investigate this issue objectively. The labels suggest analogies with dictatorial versus democratic regimes, and such analogies are not necessarily appropriate when viewing leader behavior in the context of groups striving to achieve task goals. More recent discussion of this issue has used the term *participation,* which is not as value laden.

We can define participation in terms of the following leader behavior: the degree to which the leader unilaterally makes decisions (especially the important ones); the extent of consultation by the leader with subordinates; the amount of communication between leader and subordinates in comparison to that which takes place among subordinates; and the degree of input by subordinates in setting goals. A highly participative leader consults frequently with subordinates concerning group affairs and encourages subordinates to work out problems among themselves. The directive, more nonparticipative leader makes decisions based on his or her own convictions and expertise, and closely watches group members' activities. He or she uses the formal authority of the role as the dominant mode of influence, whereas the participative counterpart prefers collaborative, reciprocity-based forms of influence. Of course, the directive-participative dimension is a continuum, and as Tannenbaum and Schmidt (1958) suggest, a variety of styles exist between the extremes.

Does participation equal consideration, and nonparticipation equal initiating structure? Intuitively, we might expect a leader who emphasizes consideration to be participative and a leader high in initiating structure to be directive. However, these are separate issues. Consideration and initiating structure emerged as independent (not polar opposite) dimensions of leader behavior, whereas the participation continuum represents a single dimension anchored by opposite styles. Furthermore, one could imagine a highly directive, nonparticipative manager who nevertheless exhibits considerable concern over the welfare and feelings of subordinates (the "benevolent autocrat"). Similarly, a manager might view a highly participative style as mandated solely by task considerations, and use participation as a means of exerting pressure for task performance.

The argument for directive leadership rests implicitly on assumptions about human nature and about the manager's job: most people need security and clarity in what is expected of them; people hold more respect for the leader who acts decisively; groups find it vexing to try to achieve consensus; and the "buck stops" with the manager.

The case for participative leadership follows from two separate sets of premises, first noticed by Miles (1965). One rationale, which he dubs the *human relations argument,* says that if subordinates can contribute to group goals and strategies, they satisfy needs for self-esteem and achievement. This need satisfaction leaves them more amenable to organizational influence and more committed to group goals. In other words, participation leads to greater satisfaction, which in turn leads to greater effort and less resistance to the manager's influence. Miles suggests that managers use this rationale when justifying a participative style toward subordinates, but that they often "fudge" by simply going through the ritual of participation in order to sell their own decisions.

The *human resources* rationale for participative management assumes that knowledge and expertise are widely distributed throughout work groups and that decisions are best made by those closest to, or most conversant with, the particular problem addressed. Participation, then, because it represents decentralized decision making, leads to higher-quality and more informed decisions, which lead to better group performance, which may result in greater satisfaction. This, Miles conjectures, is the argument managers pursue to urge a participative style on their own superiors.

So much for the argument. What does the empirical research literature say? We will look briefly at some of the more celebrated studies.

Beginning in the late 1930s, Lippitt and White (1958) carried out a series of experimental studies regarding the effects of adult supervisory styles on the behavior of 11-year-old boys. The adults had been trained to supervise the recreational activities of these boys in either a democratic, autocratic, or laissez-faire fashion. When the leader was present, the groups under autocratic leaders spent more time at work than did the groups under democratic leaders, but the reverse was true when the leader left the room. No overall objective measures of productivity were reported, so the studies failed to provide an answer to the question of which leadership style leads to greater productivity. The investigators did find that the autocratic groups expressed more hostility to the leader and to each other, and that they seemed to exhibit less spontaneous interest in work activities than did the democratic groups. Moreover, unlike the autocratic groups, the democratic groups experienced no dropouts.

Coch and French (1948), in a classic field experiment, studied the effects of participation on worker resistance to changes in methods of production. The Harwood Company, where the study took place, had historically encountered stiff resistance by the work force whenever it had introduced new work processes. Such resistance took the form of higher turnover, hostility toward management, grievances, and output restriction. Coch and French seized on the occasion of a work-methods change to compare the subsequent behavior of groups allowed to participate in the change versus those not allowed to participate. One group, the no-participation group, was simply called together and told about the changes that would be effected. A second group was allowed to elect representatives, who discussed with management and the engineering staff the best ways to implement the change. Two other groups were given a "total participation" treatment — all members of those groups participated in planning the job modifications. In the no-participation group, 17 percent of the workers quit in the first 40 days after the change, and a number of those who stayed processed grievances about the new production standards. Furthermore, production dropped and remained low long after the passage of the time needed to master the changes. No turnover occurred in either the representative-participation or the total participation groups, and productivity in both of these groups climbed to record highs after a temporary drop. The total participating groups experienced the highest rates of productivity increases.

In an 18-month study conducted in four divisions of the offices of a large insurance company, Morse and Reimer (1956) varied the level of decision making for 500 clerical workers, the majority of whom were women under age 25. Decision making was made more centralized in two divisions and more decentralized in the other two. Both groups showed increases in productivity over the one-and-a-half-year span, with the centralized (autocratic) divisions registering a slightly greater increase than the decentralized divisions. Morse and Reimer suggest that this difference in productivity increases was attributable to the fact that the centralized groups experienced greater turnover, leaving fewer workers to accomplish a roughly constant flow of work and therefore yielding higher production per individual employee. With regard to job attitudes, the centralized groups showed a statistically significant drop in job satisfaction and the decentralized groups a statistically significant increase. The actual changes, however, were quite small.

Vroom (1960) investigated the extent to which differences in personality might determine people's responses to autocratic versus participative management. His study, which focused on supervisors in a delivery service company, found that supervisors who scored high in need for independence or low in authoritarianism preferred a participative boss. Those low in need for independence or high in authoritarianism were indifferent to the degree of participation they were allowed. Tosi (1970) found a positive relationship between participation and satisfaction, but—unlike Vroom—did not find need for independence or authoritarianism to affect this relationship.

Numerous other studies, varying in methodology and the types of populations used, have addressed the participation issue, but those cited above suffice to illustrate the mixed nature of the empirical results accumulated. Generally speaking, we find that participative leadership is associated with greater subordinate satisfaction. At worst, participation does not seem to lower satisfaction. It is not as easy to summarize the findings with respect to productivity. Some studies find participative groups more productive; some find nonparticipative groups more effective; quite a few show no appreciable differences in productivity between autocratically versus democratically managed work groups. Either participation has no appreciable effect on performance or its effect depends on one or more important situational variables.

CONTINGENCY THEORIES OF LEADER BEHAVIOR

Leadership theory and research in the last two decades has taken a contingency approach. This line of inquiry identifies moderator variables (Chapter 2) that govern the relationships between leader behavior and such criteria as subordinate satisfaction and performance. The assumption—well supported by studies long since on record, with the significant exception of the work recently reported by Misumi—is that no invariant relationship exists between, for example, a leader's initiating structure and subordinate satisfaction, but that the magnitude and direction of this relationship depends on other variables. Contingency theories seek to identify these other variables and their moderating effects.

FOCUS ON INTERNATIONAL OB

The Cultural Legitimacy of Participative Leadership

Recall from Chapter 2 that according to the empirical work by Hofstede (1984), one of the four major dimensions of culture affecting organization is *power distance,* or the extent to which subordinates (as well as leaders) endorse inequality, hierarchy, and status distinctions. Perhaps the reason for inconsistent evidence on the effects of participative forms of leadership in the United States is that this country scores just about at the middle of the distribution of this dimension.

Hofstede contends that leaders cannot choose their styles at will, because what is feasible depends on the cultural conditioning of a leader's subordinates. In countries marked by strong emphasis on power distance (such as France, India, Mexico, and Yugoslavia), a participative leadership style would often cause confusion and tension for subordinates. Hofstede notes that the

Western ex-colonial power with the highest Power Distance norm — France — seems to have been most appreciated by its former colonies and to have maintained the most cordial post-colonial relations with them. "This suggests that subordinates in a large Power Distance culture feel even more comfortable with superiors who are real autocrats than with those whose assumed autocratic stance is out of national character" (p. 124).

On the other hand, those societies (as in Denmark, Austria, Israel, Sweden) with low power-distance values show considerable sympathy for participative approaches, as well as for institutional forms of industrial democracy.

SOURCE: G. Hofstede (1984). *Culture's consequences.* Beverly Hills, CA: Sage Publications.

Fiedler's Contingency Model

Fiedler's (1964) work on leadership actually began over 35 years ago when he found that psychotherapists with reputations of clinical effectiveness tended to see their clients as more similar to themselves than did therapists not regarded as effective. This suggested that counselors or helping agents who see similarities between themselves and others tend to feel psychologically closer to them and to be more supportive and less judgmental. The analogy between a counselor and a group leader immediately suggested itself, since a leader's responsibilities include — but are not limited to — the nurturance, coaching, and developmental growth of subordinates.

To extend this inquiry to the study of leadership in applied settings, Fiedler developed an instrument that purports to measure the leader's Esteem for Least Preferred Co-Worker (LPC). Fiedler asks the leader to think about the person he least prefers to work with, and to rate that person in terms of a number of adjectives that imply personal evaluation (pleasant-unpleasant, friendly-unfriendly, and so forth). The higher the LPC score, the more the leader can distinguish between the person as a worker (not wanted) and the person as an individual (who may have a number of good qualities, despite his or her deficiencies as a co-worker). The lower the LPC score, the more the leader rejects the least-preferred co-worker out of hand—not only as a worker, but as a person. Fiedler assumed that the leader who scores high on the LPC measure tends to operate in a nondirective, relationships-oriented manner toward group members, whereas the leader with a low LPC score acts in a more controlling, task-oriented, even punitive manner.

Impressed by the results he had obtained in the psychotherapy study, Fiedler anticipated that high-LPC leaders would generally show greater group effectiveness than their low-LPC counterparts. However, his early leadership studies—carried out with high school basketball teams and student surveying parties—suggested just the opposite. Contrary to expectation, leader LPC score correlated negatively with group performance. These results argued against the idea of the leader as one who must play primarily the role of therapist, and raised the possibility that in task-oriented groups, the leader must be able to reject poor performers. Presumably, a psychologically distant leader does this best.

Further studies with other types of work groups muddied the waters even more, for sometimes the low-LPC leaders proved more effective and at other times the high-LPC leaders were associated with better team performance. After a decade of seemingly inconsistent, erratic findings, Fiedler attempted to sort out the crucial situational factors that determined which leadership style would predict effectiveness. Fiedler (1964) identified three situational factors which, in combination, helped account for the inconsistent findings: *leader-group relations, task structure, and position power*.

The leader-group relations factor refers to the tone of the personal relationships between the formal leader and his or her subordinates, especially key subordinates. The more positive and pleasant the tone of these relationships, the more the leader feels accepted by the group.

Task structure concerns the clarity or ambiguity of the task confronting the group. Tasks can vary from the highly programmed (such as assembling an appliance or planting pine seedlings) to the vague and amorphous (developing a policy for corporate social responsibility or formulating a program to decrease employee absenteeism). Task structure is defined by the degree to which the final decision can be verified as correct or incorrect, the ease with which procedures for accomplishing the task can be specified, the number of ways to approach the problem, and the number of solutions that are equally correct or good.

Position power is defined by the formal authority in the leader's organizational role and the leverage over the rewards and punishments meted out to group members.

Leader-member relations, task structure, and position power—in that order of importance—interact, according to Fiedler, to determine the *ease*

FIGURE 19–2

Fiedler's Analysis of Situations in which the High- or the Low-LPC Leader Is Most Effective

Leader-member relations	Good				Poor			
Task structure	Structured		Unstructured		Structured		Unstructured	
Leader position power	High	Low	High	Low	High	Low	High	Low
	1	2	3	4	5	6	7	8

Favorable for leader ——————————————————→ Unfavorable for leader

Type of leader most effective in the solution	Low LPC	Low LPC	Low LPC	High LPC	High LPC	High LPC	High LPC	Low LPC

or difficulty with which the leader can influence group members. Put another way, these factors make the situation more or less favorable for the leader, as shown in Figure 19–2. The extreme left combination—good leader-member relations, highly structured task, and high position power—represents a very favorable situation for the leader, one in which it should be easy to influence subordinates. The opposite extreme (relatively poor relationships with subordinates, unstructured task, low power) is a leader's nightmare.

Fiedler found that psychologically distant (low-LPC) leaders were more effective—in terms of objective performance criteria—than psychologically close leaders when the situation was either very favorable or very unfavorable for the leader, whereas high-LPC leaders were more effective in situations of intermediate favorableness.

> In very favorable conditions, where the leader has power, informal backing, and a relatively well-structured task, the group is ready to be directed on how to go about its task. Under a very unfavorable condition, however, the group will fall apart unless the leader's active intervention and control can keep the members on the job. In moderately favorable conditions . . . a relationship-oriented, nondirective, permissive attitude may reduce member anxiety or intra-group conflict, and this enables the group to operate more effectively. [Fiedler, 1964, p. 165]

Fiedler has assumed that the LPC measure taps a dimension of the leader's personality that predisposes the leader toward a certain interpersonal style vis-à-vis subordinates. He therefore argues that leaders cannot easily change their behavioral styles since, in the mature adult, personality does not change easily within reasonably short periods. To maximize leadership effectiveness, we must try to make the situation fit the leader's style — or, as Fiedler puts it, "engineer the job to fit the manager." We can do this by altering the position power of the leader, changing the task structure, or improving the interpersonal climate between the leader and subordinates.

Fiedler's model, which once promised a major breakthrough in the situational approach to leadership, has been the focus of considerable controversy in the past few years. Critics of the model contend that the LPC measure remains something of a mystery. Little evidence exists that it accurately reflects a person's predisposition toward any particular leadership style, either in terms of participativeness or of initiating structure and consideration levels. Critics charge that Fiedler used inappropriate statistical analysis to support his propositions and that laboratory studies designed to test the theory provide little or no support for the validity of the model. Fiedler's critics have also raised the question of whether the Esteem for Least Preferred Co-Worker model is independent of the three major situational dimensions proposed by Fiedler, especially relations between the leader and the group members.

Fiedler readily concedes that the personality factor tapped by the LPC instrument needs clarification. Recently, he suggested that it reflects a leader's behavioral inclinations only under stress. Low-LPC leaders may display a relationships-oriented style in a climate of security, but when threatened by the possibility of group failure on a task, they change to a task orientation and maintain psychological distance from subordinates. Fiedler dismisses the evidence from laboratory studies of ad hoc groups as irrelevant to his model, which he regards as an attempt to understand and predict leader effectiveness in organizations.

Although the status of Fiedler's model remains in doubt, his theory shares with other contemporary approaches a concern for task dimensions that moderate the effects of leader behavior on group effectiveness. While a considerable amount of effort has gone into analyzing task characteristics, there is still no consensus on what comprises the most important aspects of the task. Nor are there reliable or valid measures of task dimensions. Indeed, a workable theory of task requirements appears to be the bottleneck we must work through before we can add significantly to our knowledge of leadership.

Path-Goal Theory

House and Baetz (1979) describe the path-goal theory of leadership as a "situational theory that is deliberately phrased so that additional variables . . . can be added as the effects of these variables become known" (p. 385). The immediate inspiration for this theory seems to be the challenge to reconcile the contradictory findings from field studies concerning the effects of leader initiating structure. The theory has expanded to include several classes of leader behavior and a number of moderator variables.

The path-goal theory rests, at bottom, on two plausible assertions: (1) that leader behavior is satisfying to the extent that it meets the immediate wants or needs of subordinates or is seen as a means to attain future satisfaction; and (2) that leader behavior is motivational to the extent that it makes subordinate satisfaction contingent on effective behavior. Thus, the criteria of concern to the theory are subordinate satisfaction and motivation.

In its present version, the major classes of leader behavior are: (1) instrumental leader behavior, which is roughly synonymous with initiating structure, but lacking any suggestion of punitive leader behavior; (2) supportive leader behavior, which is much the same as the earlier concept of leader consideration; (3) participative leader behavior; and (4) achievement-oriented leader behavior.

The predicted effects of these forms of leader behavior derive from a general expectancy theory of motivation. Evans (1970) originally sketched out a link between supervisory behavior and subordinates' views of the work behaviors that provided the means to their own goals. Earlier, Georgopoulos, Mahoney, and Jones (1957) had introduced the concept of path-goal to explain why employee productivity is only loosely related to satisfaction. They argued that higher productivity may not represent a "path" to the goals that bring satisfaction. House (1971) penned the mature and elaborate version of path-goal theory by making the precise links between leader behavior and the constructs of expectancy theory of motivation. He noted from expectancy theory that the motivation to perform is determined by extrinsic rewards based on performance, the intrinsic rewards derived from task performance, and the intrinsic rewards inherent in task effort. Furthermore, motivation ultimately depends on the subordinate's belief that present effort will lead to high performance and that high performance will bring increased extrinsic rewards.

Thus, expectancy theory underscores the importance of various types of rewards and group member conceptions of how behavior leads to those rewards. House argues that leader behavior is potentially relevant to all of these rewards and to subordinate conceptions about how to attain them. For example, leader structuring may be essential to provide the task information needed to do the job—thus increasing a worker's confidence that a high level of effort will accomplish something rather than result in a waste of energy and time. Leader participation might help subordinates derive more intrinsic satisfaction from work effort.

Whether and how a given class of leader behavior affects subordinate satisfaction and motivation depends, however, on moderator variables. The path-goal theory emphasizes the moderating effects of the task. When the task is already highly structured, instrumental leader behavior is negatively related to worker satisfaction. If the task is aversive, instrumental leader behavior again reduces satisfaction, though it may be essential to offset the subordinate's natural tendency to avoid the task. On the other hand, instrumental leader behavior is hypothesized to be positively related to employee satisfaction when the job is shrouded in ambiguity. This condition may exist if the job is new, the employee is untrained, or organizational rules and procedures are unclear or confusing.

Leader consideration (or supportive leader behavior) almost "never hurts," and we would expect it to positively affect satisfaction. However, previous studies have shown that this positive effect ranged from near-trivial to substantial. In path-goal theory, again, we see the effect of consideration as moderated by the task. The more routine the task, the greater the effect of supportive leader behavior on job morale. The more aversive the task, once again the greater the importance of leader consideration—especially since it may help offset the otherwise negative effect of leader structuring on morale. On ambiguous jobs, consideration has much less effect on satisfaction, since the more urgent need of the group is to clarify the path from effort to performance, and consideration offers little assistance. When the job is intrinsically rewarding, task effort is the path to subordinate satisfaction, and leader consideration only slightly boosts group morale.

Leader participative behavior may provide subordinates with (1) an immediate means of increasing the rewards of task effort, (2) the intrinsic rewards of job performance (because of greater ego-involvement in task goals due to their role in establishing such goals), and (3) a means by which subordinates can clarify what constitutes effective behavior. Again, though, these effects are contingent on the task. Participation is hypothesized to be motivating primarily when the task itself is ego-involving. If the task is routine or otherwise not ego-involving, effects of participating are moderated by the subordinate's characteristics. Even on relatively mundane jobs, participating in group decisions is presumed to be intrinsically satisfying to persons with a strong internal locus of control orientation, that is, those persons who believe their own behavior determines their outcomes in life. Other subordinate characteristics, such as level of self-perceived ability and competence, may moderate the effects of leader participative behavior. Thus, in addition to task characteristics, subordinate attributes are also important moderator variables in path-goal theory.

A third category of moderator variables pertains to the organizational environment. This category includes such elements as the degree of formalization or bureaucratization of the organization structure. Specifically, the more formalized the system, the less likely that a leader emphasis on structure will have positive effects and the more important the level of supportive behavior proffered by the manager. Conversely, in loosely structured organization environments, leader directives are more likely to be needed by subordinates. Group cohesion is another environmental moderator of the effects of leader behavior; the satisfactions that accrue from identifying with such a group may reduce the need for either leader structuring or consideration, while making participation a more viable mode of working with the group.

The final category of leader behavior—leader achievement-oriented behavior—is one on which House has not elaborated. This category emphasizes high standards and the setting of challenging goals. Achievement-oriented behavior is presumed to increase a subordinate's sense of efficacy and provide confidence that greater effort will produce a significant level of accomplishment. Once again, this effect is thought to require a nonroutine, skill-invoking task that is ego-involving. It would also seem to be moderated by a subordinate's own achievement orientation.

Assessment of the Path-Goal Theory   Over the last 15 years, the path-goal theory has stimulated numerous empirical field studies. Most of these have dealt with propositions about the moderators of the effects of leader structuring and consideration (e.g., Greene, 1975; and Sheridan, Downey, & Slocum, 1975). Some studies have tested the theory's predictions concerning the moderators of leader participativeness (e.g., Schuler, 1976). While many studies have produced evidence concerning the effects of leader behavior on satisfaction, relatively few have addressed subordinate motivation or performance. Considering all the evidence, with added weight to studies that provide for causal inferences (such as Greene, 1975), it appears that the path-goal theory scores well in predicting the situational factors that interact with leadership to determine satisfaction or morale. On the other hand, the theory has not shown an ability to account for individual or group performance. The theory does its best in predicting the task and environmental characteristics that moderate the effect of leader structuring on subordinate morale.

Empirical support aside, the attractive features of the theory are that (1) it builds on a well-established and widely accepted model of job motivation (expectancy theory), and (2) it provides a convenient way to organize and summarize data on a large number of relationships between variables. The weakness of the model is that it grasps for too many variables and it attempts to explain too much. As more variables are brought in, it becomes more difficult to keep them internally consistent with each other.

The Vroom-Yetton Model

Consider this situation confronting a manager:

> Sharply decreasing profits for the firm has resulted in a directive from top management that makes it impossible to take on any new personnel even to replace those who leave. Shortly after this directive is issued, one of your five subordinates resigns to take a job with another firm. Your problem is how to rearrange the work assignments among the remaining four subordinates without reducing the total productivity of the group. [Vroom & Yetton, 1973, p. 14]

A manager could address this problem in a number of ways, depending on how much participation the manager solicits from subordinates. Vroom and Yetton (1973) have developed a model that avoids endorsing directive or participative approaches as ends in themselves, but that provides a logical framework for deciding on the proper degree of participation. The model first discriminates between five different levels of participation by subordinates. Second, it identifies the criteria that may be most relevant to the decision. Third, it describes attributes of decision problems that determine which levels of subordinate participation are feasible. Finally, it offers the manager rules for making the final choice from among the array of feasible options.

The levels of participation range from AI, in which the manager personally makes the decision based on the available information, to GII, in which the manager relinquishes the problem to the assembled group of subordinates for discussion and resolution, with the manager at most acting as a referee. But Vroom and Yetton correctly note that there are other possibilities between these extremes. They label as AII an approach in which the superior solicits from one or more subordinates some specific information before rendering a judgment. A considerably more participative process is the CI, in which the manager not only hunts for information, but actually discusses the larger problem with one or more group members individually. With reference to the hypothetical problem above, AII might entail asking individual subordinates which tasks they find hardest to perform or which projects are ahead of schedule. With CI, the leader explains the whole problem to one or more subordinates and asks for suggested solutions or reactions to certain solutions. Moving further along the continuum of participation, the manager could use CII: the manager consults with the assembled group to hear opposing points of view and to discuss the merits of various arrangements, but makes it clear that he or she will make the final decision, even if it does not represent group consensus (see Table 19–1).

Vroom and Yetton (1973) have shown that managers quite readily understand and recognize the distinctions between these five approaches, and most agree where these approaches lie along the continuum of participation. The general perception of AII is that it is only marginally less autocratic than AI — the significance of the margin, however, is considerable in certain instances. People seem to view CI as roughly a midpoint between the extremes. CII is regarded as almost as participative as GII, and both are seen as considerably more participative than CI.

The manager's choice between these five options should be guided by the *quality requirement* in the situation and by the *need for subordinate acceptance* of the decision. Is it necessary that the solution be a high-quality one? Instinctively, one might say that all solutions should be high quality. But, realistically, you would have to agree that in many situations there are few clear-cut alternatives, none is inherently superior, and the most urgent consideration is not which particular solution to choose so much as the need

TABLE 19–1

Vroom-Yetton Typology of Management Decision Rules

AI	You solve the problem or make the decision yourself, using information available to you at that time.
AII	You obtain the necessary information from your subordinate(s), then decide on the solution to the problem yourself. You may or may not tell your subordinates what the problem is in getting the information from them. The role played by your subordinates in making the decision is clearly one of providing the necessary information to you, rather than generating or evaluating alternative solutions.
CI	You share the problem with relevant subordinates individually, getting their ideas and suggestions without bringing them together as a group. Then *you* make the decision that may or may not reflect your subordinates' influence.
CII	You share the problem with your subordinates as a group, collectively obtaining their ideas and suggestions. Then *you* make the decision that may or may not reflect your subordinates' influence.
GII	You share a problem with your subordinates as a group. Together you generate and evaluate alternatives and attempt to reach agreement (consensus) on a solution. Your role is much like that of chairman. You do not try to influence the group to adopt "your" solution and you are willing to accept and implement any solution that has the support of the entire group.

SOURCE: V. H. Vroom and P. W. Yetton, *Leadership and Decision Making.* (Pittsburgh: University of Pittsburgh Press, 1973).

TABLE 19–2

Problem Attributes in the Vroom-Yetton Model

Problem Attributes	Diagnostic Questions
A. The importance of the *quality* of the decision.	Is there a quality requirement such that one solution is likely to be more rational than another?
B. The extent to which the leader possesses sufficient information/expertise to make a high-quality decision by himself or herself.	Do I have sufficient information to make a high-quality decision?
C. The extent to which the problem is structured.	Is the problem structured?
D. The extent to which *acceptance or commitment on the part of subordinates is critical* to the effective implementation of the decision.	Is acceptance of the decision by subordinates critical to effective implementation?
E. The prior probability that the leader's autocratic decision will receive acceptance by subordinates.	If I were to make the decision by myself, is it reasonably certain that it would be accepted by my subordinates?
F. The extent to which subordinates are motivated to attain the organizational goals as represented in the objectives explicit in the statement of the problem.	Do subordinates share the organizational goals to be obtained in solving the problem?
G. The extent to which subordinates are likely to be in conflict over preferred solutions.	Is conflict among subordinates likely in preferred solutions?

SOURCE: V. H. Vroom and P. W. Yetton, *Leadership and Decision Making.* (Pittsburgh: University of Pittsburgh Press, 1973).

to choose something. In such situations, the real issue is not quality, but arriving at a choice people can live with.

With respect to subordinate acceptance, Vroom and Yetton clearly intend something more than grudging, forced compliance. They imply an internalized, active sense of commitment by group members to the solution, to do their reasonable best to make it work even if they may not agree with it (see Table 19–2).

FIGURE 19–3

Problem Types Identified in Vroom-Yetton Model

A. If decision were accepted, would it make a difference which course of action were adopted?
B. Do I have sufficient info to make a high quality decision?
C. Do subordinates have sufficient additional info to result in high quality decision?
D. Do I know exactly what info is needed, who possesses it, and how to collect it?
E. Is acceptance of decision by subordinates critical to effective implementation?
F. If I were to make the decision by myself, is it certain that it would be accepted by my subordinates?
G. Can subordinates be trusted to base solutions on organizational considerations?
H. Is conflict among subordinates likely in preferred solutions?

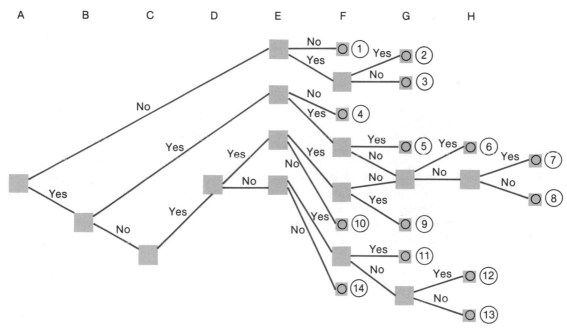

SOURCE: V. H. Vroom and P. W. Yetton, *Leadership and Decision Making*. (Pittsburgh: University of Pittsburgh Press, 1973).

Vroom and Yetton have shown that their model can be represented as a decision tree unfolding from considerations of the respective quality and acceptance requirements involved in the decision problem (see Figure 19–3). If quality is important, and the leader lacks information needed to make a quality decision, then AI is not in the feasible set (the array of workable options). If the problem is unstructured—that is, the manager does not really know what information is important in defining the problem—then AI and AII are both ruled out, since they are inadequate to confront an unstructured problem. Finally, if the leader cannot trust subordinates to base their decision on organizational requirements, then GII would also be ruled out, leaving only CI and CII in the feasible set.

TABLE 19–3

Problem Types and the Feasible Set of Decision Methods in the Vroom-Yetton Model

Problem Type	Acceptable Methods
1	AI, AII, CI, CII, GII
2	AI, AII, CI, CII, GII
3	GII
4	AI, AII, CI, CII, GII*
5	AI, AII, CI, CII, GII*
6	GII
7	CII
8	CI, CII
9	AII, CI, CII, GII*
10	AII, CI, CII, GII*
11	CII, GII*
12	GII
13	CII
14	CII, GII*

SOURCE: V. H. Vroom and P. W. Yetton, *Leadership and Decision Making*. (Pittsburgh: University of Pittsburgh Press, 1973).

* Within the feasible set only when the answer to question *G* is yes

Suppose that subordinate acceptance is just as essential as solution quality. That in itself does not mandate subordinate involvement, since subordinates might readily accept whatever the manager decides anyway. This might be the case if the group deeply respected the leader because of his or her expertise or character. Otherwise, AI and generally AII would be excluded from the feasible set (see Table 19–3).

Assume that quality is not important, but acceptance is; assume also that subordinates would disagree among themselves over the alternative solutions and would not automatically accept the boss's decree. The *Fairness* rule, one of several that Vroom and Yetton propose, would suggest that GII is likely to be the only feasible approach. One is reminded that quality aside, group decisions often have the stamp of legitimacy.

When quality and acceptance requirements have been weighed, more than one approach—sometimes all five—may be feasible (see Table 19–3). How does the manager decide on the level of participation by subordinates? Vroom and Yetton offer two secondary criteria: time and subordinate development. The less participative modes in the feasible set will be more efficient if time is short. On the other hand, if there is no time urgency, the manager may choose the more participative method because it could benefit development of subordinate knowledge, experience, and judgment.

Note that the Vroom-Yetton model, in a sense, endorses both the human relations and human resources philosophies of participation. Drawing on earlier work by Maier (1963), they see subordinate involvement in decision making as potentially advantageous both for arriving at better-quality decisions and for promoting acceptance of the decision once it is reached. However, their model does not unconditionally promote the greatest possible use of participation. Instead, the appropriate level of subordinate involvement varies with the situation.

Research conducted by Vroom and others (Vroom & Yetton, 1973; Vroom & Jago, 1978) to test the model indicates that managers, when asked to recall instances of successful and unsuccessful resolution of decision problems, generally report actions consistent with what the model predicts. When their action was in the model's feasible set, their outcome was successful, whereas unsuccessful episodes resulted from actions not in the feasible set. Interestingly, Vroom and Yetton find that managers do not vary their level of participation across situations as much as they should. Also, when managers deviate from what the model prescribes, it is more apt to be due to lack of considering the acceptance requirement rather than insensitivity to the quality issue.

Recent evidence (Heilman, Hornstein, Cage, & Herschlag, 1984) suggests that subordinates often prefer a more participative approach than those considered feasible by the model in certain situations. Of course, previous research had indicated rather consistently the positive effect of participation on subordinate satisfaction, but the model does not purport to maximize satisfaction per se. Crouch & Yetton (1987) found that, in decision situations characterized by conflict among subordinates, the effectiveness of the leader's use of participative methods hinged on the leader's tolerance for, and ability to handle, conflict.

House and Baetz (1979) have argued that the model is too complex to be useful for managers. In its full-blown decision-tree format, which generates 23 different types of problems and varying mixes of participation, the model is indeed intimidating. But this criticism is perhaps unfair, since it is the logical thrust of the model that is important. The logic is fairly easily communicated and permits the decision maker to generate ad hoc the relevant "branch" of the decision tree. Once the reader puts the five possible levels of participation (AI, AII, CI, CII, GII) in juxtaposition with the quality and/or acceptance requirements, the important rules of the model follow in a straightforward fashion.

Another criticism of the model is that it does not consider subordinates' predisposition toward engaging in the participative decision process. House and Baetz's review of the relevant literature suggests that such a disposition moderates the relationship between participation and leader effectiveness. However, one could also argue that this disposition is not fixed in absolute terms; more likely it is a function of the characteristics of the decision problem. Those problems in which group acceptance is vital and in which acceptance of the leader's unilateral decision is not guaranteed are probably those on which the group has a predisposition toward engaging in participation. If the Vroom-Yetton model is to be faulted, perhaps it should be on the grounds that it does not provide a priori a means of predicting when the leader's decision would be accepted as a matter of course. The model leaves it up to the manager to ascertain this.

Substitutes for Leadership

It can be argued that two things are needed for a group to perform effectively. First, the people must know what they are supposed to do and how to do it. Second, they must have a reason for doing it—they must, in some sense, imagine themselves better off for doing the task. Much of leader behavior, then, is a mixture of defining the task and providing instructions or role assignments, on the one hand, and on the other hand giving people a stake in the results of work—directly or indirectly, by positive incentives or by threat. Thus, leaders initiate structure to clarify roles and expectations, and sometimes to punish unacceptable job behavior. Leaders may use consideration in various forms to reinforce desired behavior, or withhold consideration when performance is below par.

Kerr and Jermier (1978) have argued, however, that certain attributes of the subordinate, of the task, and of the organization may serve as substitutes for leadership in providing the functions otherwise served by leader-initiated structure or of consideration. For example, substitutes for the leader's initiating structure, in clarifying the "what" and "how" of task activities, may include the professional training of the subordinates, a highly mechanized and unvarying task design, or detailed rules and procedures specified by the organization. Substitutes for leader consideration could include any intrinsic appeal of the task itself, a supportive and very cohesive work group, or the esteem of professional colleagues (see Table 19–4).

The more substitutes for leadership that exist in the work setting, the less influence leader behavior will have on subordinate attitudes and performance. Alternatively, one may conclude that appropriate leader behavior is that which complements existing sources of structure and performance-related rewards. For example, a work setting may contain such abundant sources of structure that virtually any degree of additional structure provided by the leader is redundant; but the same work setting may not offer alternative sources of reinforcement. In that case, supervision that emphasized supportiveness would be appropriate. Thus, the concept of "substitutes for leadership" leads toward many of the same predictions as does the path-goal theory concerning the situational importance of directive and supportive leader behavior.

Kerr and Jermier (1978) also note the significance of "neutralizers" that simply blunt or negate the influence of leader behavior. For example, if subordinates have strong needs for independence, are indifferent to the rewards the leader can provide, or work at considerable spatial distance from the superior, the leader's behavior is essentially nullified insofar as its psychological impact on subordinates is concerned. Unlike substitutes, neutralizers do not in themselves provide any function otherwise contributed by leadership; they simply suppress the effect of leadership. To the extent that several strong neutralizing variables exist in the work situation, no leadership orientation is likely to be much better than any other, because none will have enough impact to be very good or very bad.

TABLE 19–4
Substitutes for Leadership

Characteristic	Will Tend To Neutralize	
	Relationship-Oriented, Supportive, People-Centered Leadership; Consideration, Support, and Interaction Facilitation	Task-Oriented Instrumental, Job-Centered Leadership; Initiating Structure, Goal Emphasis, and Work Facilitation
Of the subordinate		
1. Ability, experience, training, knowledge		X
2. Need for independence	X	X
3. "Professional" orientation	X	X
4. Indifference toward organizational rewards	X	X
Of the task		
5. Unambiguous and routine		X
6. Methodologically invariant		X
7. Provides its own feedback concerning accomplishment		X
8. Intrinsically satisfying	X	
Of the organization		
9. Formalization (explicit plans, goals, and areas of responsibility)		X
10. Inflexibility (rigid, unbending rules and procedures)		X
11. Highly specified and active advisory and staff functions		X
12. Closely knit, cohesive work groups	X	X
13. Organizational rewards not within the leader's control	X	X
14. Spatial distance between superior and subordinates	X	X

SOURCE: From S. Kerr and J. M. Jermier, "Substitutes for Leadership," *Organizational Behavior and Human Performance* 22, 1978, p. 378.

As Kerr and Jermier note, "Few organizations would be expected to have leadership substitutes so strong as to totally overwhelm the leader" (p. 400). In most organizations, leader roles are necessary. The point is that, while structure and rewards are needed, leadership seldom carries the entire burden of providing them. The varying degree to which other sources provide structure and incentives, combined with the varying degree to which factors neutralize leader behavior, rule out any universally valid prescriptions about a single best leader style.

A Functional Analysis of Leader Behavior

Scott and Podsakoff (1982) have presented a strong case for the explanatory power of operant concepts in the analysis of leader behavior. Taking as their premise the definition of leadership as "behavior which makes a difference in the behavior of others" (Bowers & Seashore, 1966), they have grounded their functional analysis of leader behavior in the constructs of antecedent (or discriminative) stimuli, reinforcing stimuli, and contingencies of reinforcement. Other contributions toward a functional analysis of leadership include those of Sims (1977) and Mawhinney and Ford (1977). While a functional analysis of leadership is not explicitly cast as a contingency theory, its implications clearly suggest the importance of situational variables.

The antecedent stimuli that evoke leader behavior include the formal rules and policy statements of the organization, the presence of subordinates, the behavior of subordinates, and the effects (desirable and otherwise) of subordinate behavior. Reinforcers of leader behavior include constructive subordinate behavior, the positive effects of such behavior, and contrived reinforcers provided either by the group, the formal organization, or the leader's own direct superior.

A functional analysis of leadership defines effective leadership largely in terms of (1) the leader's role in providing the discriminative stimuli that evoke desired subordinate behavior, and (2) the reinforcing stimuli that sustain and enhance such behavior. An important type of discriminative stimulus is the tact, or verbal description of a contingency that operates in nature and whose consequences the leader does not directly control. A tact, then, is roughly the same as advice. The leader is an important potential source of knowledge about the task, formal organization rewards, informal political contingencies, and contingencies that are outside the organization. The effective leader keeps abreast of prevailing contingencies and describes these in terms that are useful to group members.

An especially interesting aspect of Scott and Podsakoff's treatment has to do with their focus on the leader's problem-solving behavior. A problem, in terms of a functional analysis, is a situation in which an otherwise strong response cannot be executed because of the absence of the appropriate antecedent or evoking stimuli. An important class of leader behaviors is the set of verbal operants the leader emits, operants that provide the missing cues that evoke constructive subordinate responses. By consulting with others, scanning the environment, or rearranging the immediate stimulus context, the leader generates a new stimulus that becomes the occasion for an effective response chain.

For example, a sales representative has difficulty locating high-potential customers. The response of demonstrating his or her product is strong, but cannot be performed because of the absence of the appropriate stimulus (presence of a particular type of person). The leader (e.g., district sales manager) is effective to the extent that he or she can generate verbal or nonverbal cues that trigger a response sequence resulting in finding the type of person sought. That is, the district manager searches his or her own experience, consults archival material (such as specialized directories), telephones someone with a particular expertise or background, introduces the sales rep to a valuable associate, or perhaps engages in a long discussion with the rep, reviewing and commenting on the approaches heretofore found unavailing.

It is also important that the leader provide differential rewards for differential contributions by subordinates. Ideally, the organization enables the leader to do this, perhaps by granting some control over compensation or over the distribution of other extrinsic rewards. When the leader helps determine and distribute rewards, the generalized reinforcing effect of the leader's presence increases. The leader otherwise will have to rely on the reinforcing effect of social rewards such as praise, recognition, and verbal feedback.

Of course, it is not always necessary that the leader be the direct source of reinforcement. By means of task design, or by proper placement of specific persons on specific tasks, the leader may be able to arrange conditions such that subordinates will experience intrinsic rewards for constructive behaviors. Intrinsic rewards include the naturally occurring effects that a subordinate's responses have on the physical environment, on task materials, or on the social environment (such as the smile of a satisfied customer).

A functional analysis of leadership leads to propositions consistent with previous empirical studies. For example, verbal skills, which have been found to be consistently related to leader effectiveness, would be crucial in the process of describing prevailing reinforcement contingencies. Activity level would also be important, since an active leader is more likely to be abreast of prevailing contingencies and is more apt to generate stimuli that would include useful cues to problem solutions.

Functional analysis highlights some of the more frequent causes of ineffective leadership. Perhaps the most general cause is that leaders do not reinforce frequently enough, especially when the task itself provides little or infrequent reinforcement. "A rather crude but useful guideline is to look for instances of functional operant behavior (or results) on each occasion the leader has other reasons for being present or for a total of at least one hour a day, and to deliver social-evaluative reinforcers when functional behavior is occurring or has obviously occurred" (Scott & Podsakoff, 1982, p. 62). Of course, the sooner such reinforcers are provided after the behavior has occurred, the better; but even delayed reinforcers can be effective if the leader explains what prompted the supportive action. As an example, the leader might explain, "Susan, you handled that irate customer yesterday with incredible tact and patience, and I sure will put in a good word about that in my next report to home office."

A second frequent problem is that leaders, if not careful, will misuse the limited and precious store of extrinsic reinforcers available. That is, they may fail to discriminate between behavior that is merely pleasing (or displeasing) to them personally and behavior that actually has significance for group performance. Leaders must understand this distinction and develop rules for their own behavior so that they focus on the contingencies for constructive member behavior.

A third problem area concerns the formal organization reward contingencies for the leader's own performance. The organization may reward the leader for doing what is counterproductive to group effectiveness. For example, senior officials may favor those leaders who conserve resources. This may cause the leader to ration extrinsic reinforcers too sparingly to maintain effective member behavior. When the leader recognizes this, he or she should try to change such faulty contingencies.

Contrary to what some critics of operant concepts would argue, a functional analysis of leadership does not exclude any of the various forms of "participation." Instead, a functional analysis views participation as a special case of the leader's role in promoting subordinate self-control. Self-control here is not construed as "inner will" or "internalized discipline," but as subordinate behavior reinforced by its own effects on subsequent behavior. When group members help design the contingencies under which they work, they are more apt to specify behavior within their own repertoire and to specify consequences more powerfully reinforcing to their own behavior. Furthermore, given the chance and the requisite training and experience, subordinates may be able to articulate subtle contingencies operating in the environment that the formal leader would overlook.

The functional approach also leads to some propositions about the situational factors that render various leader actions more or less important. For example, if subordinates' work is routine and uninspiring, the leader's encouragement, praise, and expressions of consideration are important—of course, such supportive behavior must be contingent on good work and effort by the subordinate. When the task is unclear and rules and policies are incoherent, the leader must actively help formulate, discover, and articulate the contingencies—a notion very close to what the path-goal theory labels as initiating structure. As House and Baetz (1979) note, "leader behavior that functions as discriminative stimuli can also be considered path-clarifying behavior" (p. 406). House and Baetz also note that the major differences between path-goal theory and a functional analysis have to do less with the prescriptions they ultimately yield than with the question of whether cognitive variables—such as intentions, role perceptions, and expectancies—provide additional explanatory or predictive power by their presence in the path-goal model.

OTHER DEVELOPMENTS IN LEADERSHIP THEORY

The Reciprocal Causality Question

Studies about leadership style or leader behavior have usually assumed that leader behavior affects subordinate behavior. Particularly in correlational field studies, any correlation between leader behavior and subordinate performance has been interpreted as measuring the impact of the leader's actions on group responses.

Lowin and Craig (1968) raised the question of whether correlations between leader style and subordinate behavior might not also be reflecting a reverse causal sequence: the effect of subordinate behavior on what the leader does. To answer this question, they conducted a study in which they had a stooge typist named Charlie deliberately play the role either of conscientious-competent worker or of unconscientious-incompetent subordinate. The subjects, who were actually applicants for a temporary supervisory job, were exposed to one of these two subordinate work styles enacted by Charlie. The results showed quite clearly that when Charlie performed competently, the supervisor displayed more consideration, initiated less structure, and allowed Charlie to participate more in decision making.

Greene (1975) conducted a field study of reciprocal causality between leader and subordinate behavior. His study took place in ongoing organizations, but his method of research was a departure from the usual field studies of leadership. He obtained measures of subordinate performance and satisfaction, along with descriptions of supervisors' leadership styles (in terms of consideration and initiating structure) at three one-month intervals. His analysis took the form of cross-lagged correlations. If, for example, leader consideration exerts a positive effect on subordinate performance, then we would expect to find a reasonably high positive correlation between leader consideration in Time 1 and subordinate performance at Time 2. On the other hand, if leader consideration is a result of (or response to) subordinate performance, then we would expect the correlation between subordinate performance at Time 1 and leader consideration at Time 2 to emerge as high and positive.

In support of previous thinking, Greene did find that leader consideration directly affected subordinate job satisfaction. However, his evidence suggested that the causal relationship between leader style and subordinate performance ran in the reverse direction. When subordinates' performance was unsatisfactory, supervisors responded by increasing the emphasis on task and structure; when subordinates' performance was satisfactory or better, supervisors reacted by decreasing the emphasis on structure and increasing the emphasis on consideration toward subordinates. In other words, whether knowingly or unconsciously, supervisors appeared to be using consideration as a contingent reinforcer for performance, and initiating structure as a punisher for unacceptable work.

The Vertical Dyad Linkage Model

If leader behavior toward a subordinate is at least partly a function of the subordinate's performance, and if subordinates vary considerably in the quantity and quality of their performance, then leaders will probably experience different types of relationships with different subordinates. Dansereau, Graen, and Haga (1975) have taken this conclusion as the starting point of their Vertical Dyad Linkage (VDL) model. They argue that it is misleading to think of a leader's style, in a general or average sense, with respect to the group as a whole — unless the group is rather homogeneous in terms of work attitudes, skills, and performance. Subordinates usually vary widely on such dimensions, and it is more fruitful to look at the dyad — the relationship between the leader and a particular subordinate — rather than at the relationship between the leader and the group.

Some members of the group will have neither the ability nor the inclination to exceed the minimum performance required of them by the formal job definition. Such persons will accept the leader's authority insofar as that authority is legitimated by the implicit contract between the member and the organization. They will do what they have to do and little beyond that. In return, the leader will provide the support, consideration, and assistance likewise mandated by his or her own role duties, but will not go beyond such limits. In effect, the leader is practicing a contractual exchange with such members (Kim & Organ, 1982). Dansereau et al. refer to these members as "hired hands," who are being influenced by supervision rather than leadership.

But quite often the leader's responsibilities are such that they cannot be carried out merely by holding subordinates to minimal role obligations. The leader's own time and energy may be insufficient to attend to all of the critical functions performed by the group.

> Fortunately, a subset of his members usually can perform the majority of the critical functions of the unit. Therefore, the superior invests a disproportionate amount of his time and energy in developing a select subset of his members. Once these members shoulder their share of the burden of the unit, the superior maintains his disproportionate attention to these members and their critical tasks. [Dansereau et al., 1975, p. 72]

In short, the leader will come to count on contributions by some members beyond their contractual obligations. However, to obtain such contributions, the leader must allow those members some latitude in their roles — in effect, the leader and key subordinates negotiate (perhaps renegotiate) the latter's responsibilities in a noncontractual exchange relationship.

> The superior for his part can offer the outcomes of job latitude, influence in decision making, open and honest communications, support of the member's actions, and confidence in the consideration for the member, among others. The member can reciprocate with greater than required expenditures of time and

energy, the assumption of greater responsibility, and commitment to the success of the entire unit or organization, among others. The larger the extent of this vertical exchange, the more the superior must be ready to negotiate. [Dansereau et al., 1975, pp. 49–50]

Those with whom the leader negotiates become "cadres," or "ins" (as contrasted to the "outs," who are merely supervised according to contractual obligations).

The VDL approach suggests that effectiveness in a leadership role is a function of (1) the ability to identify those subordinates who can provide critical contributions beyond their formal role obligations and (2) the ability to obtain and maintain these contributions by offering inducements beyond those guaranteed by the contractual relationship. The latter may, in turn, depend on the external power of the leader — the ability to obtain resources from superiors, other work units, or parties external to the organization.

Transactional versus Transformational Leadership

Bass (1985) has argued that some of the confusion and inconsistency in the empirical study of leadership might arise from our failure to distinguish between two fundamentally different forms of leadership. The methods and measures researchers have used pertain to what Bass terms *transactional leadership*. Transactional leadership operates within the framework of an existing organizational culture; it identifies present subordinate wants and needs, exchanging ("transacting") the means to satisfy those needs in return for subordinate exertion toward a goal or outcome desired by the leader. The transacting leader — or perhaps we should say transacting leadership — uses degrees of *initiating structure* and *consideration* and the formal reward system as needed to provide negative feedback and reinforce desired behavior.

Transformational leadership seeks to alter (transform) the culture rather than accept its constraints, and to change the make-up of the group's needs and wants. Transformational leadership is characterized by a vision of what can be and articulates that vision to others; it inspires confidence in others that the vision can be achieved; it arouses *different* needs in subordinates; it awakens something more than self-interest, even eliciting self-sacrifice for some greater good. Transformational leadership provides intellectual stimulation to followers, using a rich supply of metaphors to communicate values, but avoiding the oversimplifications of propaganda.

Trying to measure leader behavior by frequency of consideration, initiating structure, and various forms of participation would not, according to Bass, capture the quality of transformational leadership; those devices would only tell us about transacting. Bass reports that when measures appropriate to both forms of leadership are used, factors inherent in transformational leadership — such as charisma and intellectual stimulation — predict the highest levels of subordinate satisfaction and effort.

The thrust of Bass's argument calls to mind the distinction between management and leadership discussed earlier in this chapter. Perhaps management or transactional leadership is important in a context of stability and makes use of skills that can be learned, while transformational leadership comes to the fore in times of crisis or challenge and presupposes certain personality and aptitude traits that a person can have, but not learn. Perhaps, as Kotter would seem to think, some combination of both is important, or that truly outstanding leaders intuitively know when and how to vary their emphasis on one or the other.

IS LEADERSHIP A MYTH?

Is leadership, in fact, causally related to organizational performance? Either as an article of faith or as a self-evident truism, we instinctively respond, "Obviously it is." But Pfeffer (1978) has presented some arguments, supported by empirical findings, that appear to challenge this assumption.

Pfeffer offers three reasons why we are unlikely to find unambiguous evidence showing significant effects of leaders on organizational outcomes. First, organizations usually limit the range of attributes or behavioral styles permitted in leadership roles. We have already noted the apparent existence of a broadly accepted "lay theory" of leadership holding that only persons with certain characteristics are likely to have an opportunity to demonstrate leadership. Beyond this conception of what leaders should be like, specific organizations impose their own norms and traditions concerning what is acceptable or ideal in a leader. For example, according to Wright, 1979, General Motors traditionally has not sought a flashy, individualistic executive for its top management positions. The result is that, in a given organization, one can observe little variation among those who succeed each other as leaders. Therefore, any variation over time in an organization's functioning cannot logically be explained by variation in leadership.

Second, the leader is constrained by the expectations of others in the organization. Even should a maverick slip through the gate, his or her behavior will be restricted by prevailing norms and role pressures exerted by others — such as peers, subordinates, and the general climate or personality of the larger organization.

Finally — and, for Pfeffer, the most important consideration — the organization's success is predominantly determined by external forces over which the leader has no control:

> Consider, for example, the executive in a construction firm. Costs are largely determined by the operation of commodities and labor markets over which the executive has little, if any, control. Demand is largely affected by interest rates and the availability of mortgage money. These, in turn, are affected by governmental policies over which the executive has little influence. . . .
>
> School superintendents have little influence on birth rates and community economic development, both of which profoundly affect school system budgets. . . .

FOCUS ON THE FUTURE

The 1990s: The Decade of Women in Leadership

Until recently, we have thought of leadership—especially at the highest levels of organization in business—as the province of the male. According to Naisbitt and Aburdene (1990), that has already begun to change and at a rate that will accelerate in the 1990s.

The average age of senior executives is about 50. Women who were 25 years old in 1975—when large numbers of women started earning MBAs—will be 50 by the year 2000.

In the professions, the ranks of women have increased from 10 percent in 1970 to a critical mass of 30–50 percent in fields such as banking, accounting, and computers. Women hold 40 percent of the nearly 15 million executive, administrative, and management jobs. And women are starting new businesses twice as fast as men.

Most of the influx of women into the labor force in the last two decades has occurred in the information-processing sector of the economy. And, according to Naisbitt and Aburdene, "Women and the information society—which celebrates brain over brawn—are a partnership made in heaven." They believe that the forms of leadership most effective in the prototypic organizations of the 1990s will eschew coercive

influence and use instead the power that derives from commitment and collegial relationships. And Naisbitt and Aburdene see that women are as well-adapted as men to this type of leadership.

The signs of this emerging trend appear even in Japan, where the number of women in administrative positions has doubled in 10 years and where a woman (Takao Doi) heads the major opposition political power. The examples of Corazon Aquino in the Philippines, Benazir Bhutto in Pakistan, Margaret Thatcher in Great Britain, and prime minister Gro Harlem Bruntland in Norway provide ready examples of the ability of women to break through the so-called glass ceiling, the invisible barrier that has kept women from major leadership roles. Naisbitt and Aburdene predict that in the early years of the next century, we will look back on the 1970s and "remark on how quaint were the days when women were excluded from the top echelons of business and political leadership, much as we today recall when women could not vote."

SOURCE: J. Naisbitt & P. Aburdene (1990) *Megatrends 2000: Ten New Directions for the 1990s.* New York: William Morrow and Company, Inc.

Organizations have capacities—strengths and weaknesses that are relatively enduring. [Pfeffer, 1978, p. 21]

Pfeffer concludes that the importance we attach to leadership stems from a profound need to believe that we can control our fate. To think that we are totally at the mercy of distant, vague, uncontrollable, and inexorable forces is frightening and therefore to be repressed. If we believe that leaders cause success or failure, however, we can retain a sense of self-control, since we can select and remove leaders. Thus, we attribute organizational outcomes to leader characteristics, leader strategies, leader behavior. A widely shared consensus maintains the legend of leadership. We have, then something like a "romance" of leadership (Meindl & Erlich, 1987):

> A faith . . . that leadership is the premier force in the scheme of organizational events . . . an intellectually compelling and emotionally satisfying comprehension of the causes, nature, and consequences of organizational activities . . . it reduces and translates these complexities into simple human terms that they can understand, live with, and communicate easily to others. [Meindl & Ehrlich, p. 92]

Furthermore, since some leaders have enough insight to anticipate a turn in fortunes, they may take calculated steps that will lead observers to associate the leaders personally with success and to disassociate them from failure. Indeed, Meindl and Ehrlich found that any given level of organizational performance was rated more favorably if it were attributed to leadership rather than technology or economic climate.

Pfeffer's point is not literally that leaders make no difference whatever. Rather, he suggests that we have vastly exaggerated the difference they do make. This sobering analysis need not suggest a moratorium on leadership theory and research, but it should temper our expectations as to what we hope to find.

SUMMARY

Traditionally, the study of leadership has taken as its independent variables the leader's attributes, dimensions of leader behavior, and leadership style. Dependent variables have been subordinate satisfaction and performance. Stogdill (1948, 1974) found certain personal characteristics to be related to attainment of leader status and, to a lesser extent, some traits correlated with measures of leader effectiveness. The Ohio State leadership studies identified initiating structure and consideration as two important dimensions of variation in leader behavior. Correlations between these dimensions and dependent variables have varied from study to study in magnitude and direction. Participative leadership has also varied in its relationship to important outcomes.

House's path-goal theory, the substitutes for leadership approach, Fiedler's contingency model, and the Vroom-Yetton model have sought to account for, predict, and explain the situational effects of different dimensions of leader behavior. These theories emphasize the role of moderator variables, such as task type or group characteristics, that determine the effect of different leader behaviors. Recent evidence suggests that leader behavior is as much an effect of subordinate behavior as it is a cause of subordinate behavior. The functional analysis of leadership, using operant concepts of leader behavior, and the Vertical Dyad Linkage (VDL) model take due account of this reciprocal causality in leader-subordinate relationships.

Recently we have noticed labored distinctions between management and leadership, a distinction similar to that drawn by Bass between transactional and transformational leadership. Perhaps continued clarification of these distinctions will resolve some of the inconsistencies in previous leadership research. Conceivably Misumi's studies of Japanese leadership, which have found rather consistent evidence for a generally effective blend of leader behaviors, will lead us to reassess the need for, and value of, complicated situational theories of leadership. Increased understanding of the romance of leadership — of leadership as attribution — might mitigate our expectations for what any theory of leadership will generally explain in terms of group performance and organizational outcomes.

CONCEPTS TO REMEMBER

Ohio State leadership studies
Consideration
Initiating structure
Managerial Grid
Contingency-type theories
Moderator variables
Path-goal theory of leadership
Substitutes for leadership
Participation controversy

Human relations/Human resources rationales for participation
Contingency model of leadership effectiveness
Esteem for Least Preferred Co-Worker (LPC) scale
Vroom-Yetton model

Reciprocal causality
Vertical Dyad Linkage (VDL) model
Functional analysis of leader behavior
P, M, PM, pm leader styles
Transactional versus Transformational leadership

QUESTIONS FOR DISCUSSION

1. How do you explain Fleishman's finding that leaders high in consideration could also generate high levels of initiating structure without increasing turnover and grievances?

2. Under what job conditions, or in what types of work environments, would a leader profile high in both consideration and initiating structure probably not be appropriate?

3. What are the risks inherent in holding a "human relations" rationale for participative supervision?

4. What background, motivational, or personality factors do you think would make a leader high LPC or low LPC?

5. Why have leadership theorists and researchers only recently addressed the reciprocal causality question?

6. Suppose that we are eventually forced to conclude from accumulated empirical research findings that differences in leader behavior or leader style have a negligible effect on group or unit productivity. Should we discontinue the study of leadership? Why or why not?

REFERENCES

Barnlund, D. C. (1962). Consistency of emergent leadership in groups with changing tasks and members. *Speech Monographs* 29, 45–52.

Baron, R. A., & Greenberg, J. (1990). *Behavior in organizations*. Needham Heights, MA: Allyn and Bacon.

Bass, B. M. (1985). *Leadership and performance beyond expectations*. New York: Macmillan.

Blake, R. R., & Mouton, J. S. (1968). *Corporate excellence through grid organizational development*. Houston: Gulf Publishing.

Bowers, D. G., & Seashore, S. E. (1966). Predicting organizational effectiveness with a four-factor theory of leadership. *Administrative Science Quarterly* 11, 238–63.

Campbell, J. P., Dunnettee, M. D., Lawler, E. E. III, & Weick, K. E., Jr. (1970). *Managerial behavior, performance, and effectiveness*. New York: McGraw-Hill.

Carter, L. F. (1953). Leadership and small group behavior. In M. Sherif & M. O. Wilson, *Group relations at the crossroads*. New York: Harper & Row.

Coch, L., & French, J. P. (1948). Overcoming resistance to change. *Human Relations* 1, 512–32.

Crouch, A., & Yetton, P. (1987). Manager behavior, leadership style, and subordinate performance: An empirical extension of the Vroom-Yetton conflict rule. *Organizational Behavior and Human Decision Processes* 39, 384–96.

Dansereau, F. D., Jr., Graen, G., & Haga, W. J. (1975). A vertical dyad linkage approach to leadership within formal organizations: A longitudinal investigation of the rolemaking process. *Organizational Behavior and Human Performance* 13, 46–78.

Evans, M. G. (1970). The effects of supervisory behavior on the path-goal relationship. *Organizational Behavior and Human Performance* 5, 277–98.

Fiedler, F. E. (1964). A contingency model of leadership effectiveness. In L. Berkowitz (ed.), *Advances in experimental social psychology,* vol. 1. New York: Academic Press.

Fleishman, E. A. (1973). Twenty years of consideration and structure. In E. A. Fleishman & J. C. Hunt (eds.), *Current developments in the study of leadership*. Carbondale: Southern Illinois University Press.

Gardner, J. W. (1990). *On leadership*. New York: Free Press.

Georgopoulos, B. S., Mahoney, G. M., & Jones, N. W. (1957). A path-goal approach to productivity. *Journal of Applied Psychology* 41, 345–53.

Ghiselli, E. E. (1971). *Explorations in managerial talent*. Santa Monica, CA: Goodyear Publishing.

Gibb, C. A. (1949). The emergence of leadership in small temporary groups of men. Unpublished doctoral dissertation. University of Illinois, 1949. Cited in Gibb, C. A. (1954). Leadership. In G. Lindzey (ed.), *Handbook of social psychology,* vol. 2. Reading, MA: Addison-Wesley Publishing.

Goodstein, L. D., & Shrader, W. J. (1963). An empirically derived key for the California Psychology Inventory. *Journal of Applied Psychology* 47, 42–45.

Greene, C. N. (1975). The reciprocal nature of influence between leader and subordinate. *Journal of Applied Psychology* 60, 187–93.

Grove, A. S. (1983). Manager's Journal. *The Wall Street Journal,* September 12.

Heilman, M. E., Hornstein, H. A., Cage, J. H., & Herschlag, J. K. (1984). Reactions to prescribed leader behavior as a function of role perspective: The case of the Vroom-Yetton model. *Journal of Applied Psychology* 69, 50–60.

Hersey, P., & Blanchard, K. H. (1972). *Management of organizational behavior,* 2nd ed. Englewood Cliffs, NJ: Prentice Hall.

Hofstede, G. (1984). *Culture's consequences*. Beverly Hills, CA: Sage Publications.

House, R. J. (1971). A path-goal theory of leader effectiveness. *Administrative Science Quarterly* 16, 321–38.

House, R. J., & Baetz, M. L. (1979). Leadership: Some empirical generalizations and new research directions. In B. M. Staw (ed.), *Research in organizational behavior,* vol. 1, Greenwich, CT: JAI Press, 341–423.

House, R. J. (1987). The "all things in moderation" leader. *Academy of Management Review* 12, 164–69.

Kenny, D. A., & Zaccaro, S. J. (1983). An estimate of variance due to traits in leadership. *Journal of Applied Psychology* 68, 678–85.

Kerr, S., & Jermier, J. M. (1978). Substitutes for leadership: Their meaning and measurement. *Organizational Behavior and Human Performance* 22, 375–403.

Kim, K., & Organ, D. (1982). Determinants of leader-subordinate exchange relationships. *Group and Organizational Studies* 7, 77–90.

Korman, A. K. (1966). Consideration, initiating structure, and organizational criteria – a review. *Personnel Psychology* 19, 349–61.

Kotter, J. P. (1990). *A force for change.* New York: Free Press.

Lippitt, R., & White, R. K. (1958). An experimental study of leadership and group life. In E. E. Maccoby, T. M., Newcomb, & E. L. Hartley (eds.), *Readings in social psychology,* 3rd ed. New York: Holt, Rinehart & Winston.

Lowin, A., & Craig, J. R. (1968). The influence of level of performance on managerial style: An experimental object-lesson in the ambiguity of correlational data. *Organizational Behavior and Human Performance* 3, 440–58.

Maier, N. R. F. (1963). *Problem-solving discussions and conferences: Leadership methods and skills.* New York: McGraw-Hill.

Mawhinney, T. C., & Ford, J. D. (1977). The path goal theory of leader effectiveness: An operant interpretation. *Academy of Management Review* 2, 398–411.

Meindl, J. R., & Ehrlich, S. B. (1987). The romance of leadership and the evaluation of organizational performance. *Academy of Management Journal* 30, 91–109.

Miles, R. E. (1965, July-August). Human relations or human resources? *Harvard Business Review,* pp. 148–63.

Misumi, J. (1985). *The behavioral science of leadership: An interdisciplinary Japanese research program.* Ann Arbor, MI: University of Michigan Press.

Morse, N., & Reimer, E. (1956). The ambiguity of leadership. In M. W. McCall, Jr., & M. M. Lombardo (eds.), *Leadership: Where else can we go?* Durham, NC: Duke University Press.

Naisbitt, J., & Aburdene, P. (1990). *Megatrends 2000: Ten new directions for the 1990s.* New York: William Morrow and Company, Inc.

Schuler, R. S. (1976). Participation with supervisor and subordinate authoritarianism: A path-goal theory reconciliation. *Administrative Science Quarterly* 21, 320-25.

Scott, W. E., Jr., & Podsakoff, P. M. (1982). Leadership supervision, and behavioral control: Perspectives from an experimental analysis. In L. W. Frederiksen (ed.), *Handbook of organizational behavior management.* New York: John Wiley & Sons.

Sheridan, J. E., Downey, H. K., & Slocum, J. W., Jr. (1975). Testing causal relationships of House's path-goal theory of leadership effectiveness. In J. G. Hunt & L. L. Larson (eds.), *Leadership frontiers.* Kent, OH: Kent State University Press.

Sims, H. P., Jr. (1977). The leader as a manager of reinforcement contingencies: An empirical example and a model. In J. G. Hunt & L. L. Larson (eds.), *Leadership: The cutting edge.* Carbondale: Southern Illinois University Press.

Stogdill, R. M. (1948). Personal factors associated with leadership: A survey of the literature. *Journal of Psychology* 25, 35–71.

Stogdill, R. M. (1974). *Handbook of leadership: A survey of theory and research*. New York: The Free Press.

Tannenbaum, R., & Schmidt, W. H. (1958, March-April). How to choose a leadership pattern. *Harvard Business Review,* pp. 95-102.

Tosi, H. A. (1970). A reexamination of personality as a determinant of the effect of participation. *Personnel Psychology* 23, 91–99.

Trudeau, G. B. (1973). *The president is a lot smarter than you think*. New York: Popular Library.

Vroom, V. (1960). *Some personality determinants of the effects of participation*. Englewood Cliffs, NJ: Prentice Hall.

Vroom, V. H., & Jago, A. G. (1978). On the validity of the Vroom-Yetton model. *Journal of Applied Psychology* 63, 151–62.

Vroom, V. H. & Yetton, P. W. (1973). *Leadership and decision-making*. Pittsburg, University of Pittsburgh Press.

Wright, J. P. (1979). *On a clear day you can see General Motors*. New York: Avon Books.

Yukl, G. (1971). Toward a behavioral theory of leadership. *Organizational Behavior and Human Performance* 6, 414–40.

Cases

PERFECT PIZZERIA*

Perfect Pizzeria in Southville, in deep southern Illinois, is the second largest franchise of the chain in the United States. The headquarters is located in Phoenix, Arizona. Although the business is prospering, it has employee and managerial problems.

Each operation has one manager, an assistant manager, and from two to five night managers. The managers of each pizzeria work under an area supervisor. There are no systematic criteria for being a manager or becoming a manager trainee. The franchise has no formalized training period for the manager. No college education is required. The managers for whom the case observer worked during a four-year period were relatively young (ages 24 to 27) and only one had completed college. They came from the ranks of night managers or assistant managers, or both. The night managers were chosen for their ability to perform the duties of the regular employees. The assistant managers worked a two-hour shift during the luncheon period five days a week to gain knowledge about bookkeeping and management. Those

*Adapted from a course assignment prepared by Lee Neely for Professor J. G. Hunt, Southern Illinois University—Carbondale. Reprinted with permission from John E. Dittrich and Robert A. Zawacki, eds., *People and Organizations* (Plano, Tex.: Business Publications, 1981), pp. 126-28.

583

becoming managers remained at that level unless they expressed interest in investing in the business.

The employees were mostly college students, with a few high school students performing the less challenging jobs. Since Perfect Pizzeria was located in an area with few job opportunities, it had a relatively easy task of filling its employee quotas. All the employees, with the exception of the manager, were employed part time. Consequently, they worked for less than the minimum wage.

The Perfect Pizzeria system is devised so that food and beverage costs and profits are set up according to a percentage. If the percentage of food unsold or damaged in any way is very low, the manager gets a bonus. If the percentage is high, the manager does not receive a bonus; rather, he or she receives only his or her normal salary.

There are many ways in which the percentage can fluctuate. Since the manager cannot be in the store 24 hours a day, some employees make up for their paychecks by helping themselves to the food. When a friend comes in to order a pizza, extra ingredients are put on the friend's pizza. Occasional nibbles by 18 to 20 employees throughout the day at the meal table also raise the percentage figure. An occasional bucket of sauce may be spilled or a pizza accidentally burned. Sometimes the wrong size of pizza may be made.

In the event of an employee mistake or a burned pizza by the oven man, the expense is supposed to come from the individual. Because of peer pressure, the night manager seldom writes up a bill for the erring employee. Instead, the establishment takes the loss and the error goes unnoticed until the end of the month when the inventory is taken. That's when the manager finds out that the percentage is high and that there will be no bonus.

In the present instance, the manager took retaliatory measures. Previously, each employee was entitled to a free pizza, salad, and all the soft drinks he or she could drink for every six hours of work. The manager raised this figure from 6 to 12 hours of work. However, the employees had received these six-hour benefits for a long time. Therefore, they simply took advantage of the situation whenever the manager or the assistant was not in the building. Though the night manager theoretically had complete control of the operation in the evenings, he did not command the respect that the manager or assistant manager did. That was because he received the same pay as the regular employees; he could not reprimand other employees; and he was basically the same age or sometimes even younger than the other employees.

Thus, apathy grew within the pizzeria. There seemed to be a further separation between the manager and his workers, who started out to be a closely knit group. The manager made no attempt to alleviate the problem, because he felt it would iron itself out. Either the employees that were dissatisfied would quit or they would be content to put up with the new regulations. As it turned out, there was a rash of employee dismissals. The manager had no problem in filling the vacancies with new workers, but the loss of key personnel was costly to the business.

With the large turnover, the manager found he had to spend more time in the building, supervising and sometimes taking the place of inexperienced workers. This was in direct violation of the franchise regulation, which stated that a manager would act as a supervisor and at no time take part in the actual food preparation. Employees were not placed under strict supervision with the manager working alongside them. The operation no longer worked smoothly because of differences between the remaining experienced workers and the manager concerning the way in which a particular function should be performed.

Within a two-month period, the manager was again free to go back to his office and leave his subordinates in charge of the entire operation. During this two-month period, the percentage had returned to the previous low level and the manager received a bonus each month. The manager felt that his problems had been resolved and that conditions would remain the same, since the new personnel had been properly trained.

It didn't take long for the new employees to become influenced by the other employees. Immediately after the manager had returned to his supervisory role, the percentage began to rise. This time the manager took a bolder step. He cut out any benefits that the employees had—no free pizzas, salads, or drinks. With the job market at an even lower ebb than usual, most employees were forced to stay. The appointment of a new area supervisor made it impossible for the manager to "work behind the counter," since the supervisor was centrally located in Southville.

The manager tried still another approach to alleviate the rising percentage problem and maintain his bonus. He placed a notice on the bulletin board, stating that if the percentage remained at a high level, a lie detector test would be given to all employees. All those found guilty of taking or purposefully wasting food or drinks would be immediately terminated. This did not have the desired effect on the employees, because they knew if they were all subjected to the test, all would be found guilty and the manager would have to dismiss all of them. This would leave him in a worse situation than ever.

Even before the following month's percentage was calculated, the manager knew it would be high. He had evidently received information from one of the night managers about the employees' feelings toward the notice. What he did not expect was that the percentage would reach an all-time high. That is the state of affairs at the present time.

Questions   How do you account for these developments? What would you recommend to the manager?

DECISION BY THE GROUP*

John Stevens, plant manager of the Fairlee Plant of Lockstead Corporation, attended the advanced management seminar conducted at a large midwestern university. The seminar, of four weeks' duration, was largely devoted to the topic of executive decision making.

Professor Mennon, of the university staff, particularly impressed John Stevens with his lectures on group discussion and group decision making. On the basis of research and experience, Professor Mennon was convinced that employees, if given the opportunity, could meet together, intelligently consider, and then formulate quality decisions that would be enthusiastically accepted.

Returning to his plant at the conclusion of the seminar, Mr. Stevens decided to practice some of the principles he had learned. He called together the 25 employees of Department B and told them that production standards established several years previously were now too low in view of the recent installation of automated equipment. He gave the workers the opportunity to discuss the mitigating circumstances and to decide among themselves, as a group, what their standards should be. Mr. Stevens, on leaving the room, believed that the workers would doubtlessly establish much higher standards than he himself would have dared propose.

After an hour of discussion the group summoned Mr. Stevens and notified him that, contrary to his opinion, their group decision was that the standards were already too high, and since they had been given the authority to establish their own standards, they were making a reduction of 10 percent. These standards, Mr. Stevens knew, were far too low to provide a fair profit on the owner's investment. Yet it was clear that his refusal to accept the group decision would be disastrous. Before taking a course of action, Mr. Stevens called Professor Mennon at the university for his opinion.

Questions   Was Stevens's procedure well advised? What might he have done differently?

---

*Reprinted with permission from John M. Champion and John H. James, eds., *Critical Incidents in Management*, 4th ed. (Homewood, Ill.: Richard D. Irwin, 1980), pp. 62-63.

FALLS CITY SAVINGS AND LOAN*

Shortly before 1960, the assets of the Falls City Savings and Loan Association were acquired by a small group of investors headed by Taylor Rapp, a local construction magnate. The rapidly increasing economic prosperity of the community coupled with Rapp's initiative and drive caused the association to expand rapidly. He was both brilliant and energetic; but, he ran a "one-man show" — as he always had in his many successful enterprises. Delegating authority to someone else did not come easily for him.

As the association grew, it became necessary to increase the appraisal staff to handle the increased flow of work. Rapp brought in his nephew, Eldon Brant, to be trained as an appraiser. Brant was in his late 40s, had little formal education, and had no previous savings and loan or real estate experience.

His age and inexperience tended to work against him. He had trouble adjusting to the demands of the appraisal work, but eventually he learned to do a creditable job and then his uncle permitted him to make real estate and construction appraisals on his own.

Rapp believed that normal inflation or appreciation would cure most of the mistakes an inexperienced appraiser might make. Then, too, the association confined itself to making conservative loans on residential properties. Because of these facts, Rapp was not overly concerned with the inadequacies of his nephew although he certainly was aware of them.

Brant worked as an appraiser for three years and finally was able to do an adequate and satisfactory job — at least according to his uncle's standards.

Rapp, ever alert to new business opportunities and perhaps a little bored, decided to form a mortgage company. He installed Dick Fisher, who had been chief appraiser for the Falls City Savings and Loan Association, as the manager. Brant was promoted to chief appraiser even though it was the consensus among his associates that he was the least well qualified of the four appraisers on the staff. At no time did he make an effort to improve his knowledge through outside study. Even at this time he possessed only a rudimentary understanding of the fundamentals of appraising. He did work hard, however, and was completely loyal to Rapp and the association. It was much to his credit that he had acquired fairly good judgment of real estate values in the area.

While there was some resentment from the other appraisers, it wasn't too overt or serious. As individuals, they were, for the most part, competent; but none was very anxious to assume additional authority and responsibility.

Surprisingly, Brant did not encounter a lot of difficulty in his new

---

*Reprinted with permission from Edgar G. Williams, *People Problems* (Bloomington: Bureau of Business Research, Indiana University Graduate School of Business, 1962).

position. His staff was competent and good loans were easy to arrange. Before long his uncle had him appointed to the loan committee and named to a vice presidency.

Two years after Brant was made chief appraiser, Bill Davis was hired as an appraiser. He was very capable and ambitious for advancement. The tough assignments soon gravitated toward him and he handled them with ease. No one was surprised when after a year he became Brant's chief assistant.

A short time later Rapp sold his interest in the association. He did not want to continue as the managing officer, but he did consent to remain on the board of directors. A. J. Hockwalt, a very capable man, was brought in as his replacement.

It didn't take Hockwalt very long to learn about Brant's weaknesses as chief appraiser. He knew that the increased lending volume of the association made it absolutely necessary that its chief appraiser be well qualified administratively as well as technically. He was certain that Brant was weak in both of these areas. He knew, too, that Davis, who was well qualified to assume the duties of the chief appraiser, would not be satisfied to remain indefinitely as Brant's assistant. Davis was aware, as were all of the other employees, that Brant was the obstacle that stood between him and another immediate promotion—that of chief appraiser.

Hockwalt decided on a solution to the problem, but carrying it out was an entirely different matter. Rapp was still a power on the board of directors with whom to reckon, and he was not an easy man to reason with. The manager was certain that Rapp would not take kindly to the demotion or dismissal of Brant. In addition he needed the former owner's support on the board in order to carry out some of his plans for the future expansion of the association.

Questions   What are the influence bases of *(a)* Rapp, *(b)* Brant, and *(c)* Hockwalt? Suggest an approach by which Hockwalt might manage the dilemma he faces.

WHICH STYLE IS BEST?*

The ABC Company is a medium-sized corporation which manufactures automotive parts. Recently, the company president attended a leadership seminar and came away deeply impressed with the effect various leadership styles could have on the output and morale of the organization.

---

*W. D. Heier, "Which Style is Best?" Reprinted from J. E. Dittrich and R. A. Zawacki, eds., *People and Organizations* (Plano, Tex.: Business Publications, 1981). ©1981 by Business Publications, Inc.

In mulling over how he might proceed, the president decided to utilize the services of Paul Patterson, a management consultant, who was currently reviewing the goals and objectives of the company. The president told Paul about the leadership seminar and how impressed he had been and that a leadership survey of the company was desired.

It was determined that the division headed by Donald Drake should be the test case and that Paul would report to the president on completion of that survey. Some of the notes made by Paul in his interviews with the key managers in Drake's division follow.

Ancil Able

Ancil is very proud of the output of his section. He has always stressed the necessity for good control procedures and efficiency and is very insistent that project instructions be fully understood by his subordinates and that follow-up communications be rapid, complete, and accurate. Ancil serves as the clearinghouse for all incoming and outgoing work. He gives small problems to one individual to complete, but if the problem is large he calls in several key people. Usually, his employees are briefed on what the policy is to be, what part of the report each subordinate is to complete, and the completion date. Ancil considers this as the only way to get full coordination without lost motion or an overlap of work.

Ancil considers it best for a boss to remain aloof from his subordinates, and believes that being "buddy-buddy" tends to hamper discipline. He does his "chewing out" in private and his praising, too. He believes that people in his section really know where they stand.

According to Ancil, the biggest problem in business today is that subordinates just will not accept responsibility. He states that his people have lots of opportunities to show what they can do, but not many really try too hard.

One comment Ancil made was that he does not understand how his subordinates got along with the previous section head who ran a very "loose shop." Ancil stated his boss is quite happy with the way things go in his section.

Bob Black

Bob believes that every employee has a right to be treated as an individual and espouses the theory that it is a boss's responsibility and duty to cater to the employee's needs. He noted that he is constantly doing little things for his subordinates and gave as an example his presentation of two tickets to an art show to be held at the City Gallery next month. He stated that the tickets cost $5 each, but that it will be both educational and enjoyable for the employee and his wife. This was done to express his appreciation for a good job the man had done a few months back.

Bob says he always makes a point of walking through his section area at least once each day, stopping to speak to at least 25 percent of the employees on each trip.

Bob does not like to "knock" anyone, but he noted that Ancil Able ran one of those "taut ships" you hear about. He stated that Ancil's employees are probably not too happy, but there isn't much they can do but wait for Ancil to move.

Bob said he had noticed a little bit of bypassing going on in the company but that most of it is just due to the press of business. His idea is to run a friendly, low-keyed operation with a happy group of subordinates. Although he confesses that they might not be as efficient in terms of speedy outputs as other units, he considers he has far greater subordinate loyalty and higher morale and that his subordinates work well as an expression of their appreciation of his (Bob's) enlightened leadership.

Charles Carr

Charlie says his principal problem is the shifting of responsibilities between his section and others in the division. He considers his section the "fire drill" area that gets all the rush, hot items, whether or not they belong in his section. He seems to think this is caused by his immediate superior not being too sure who should handle what jobs in the division.

Charlie admits he hasn't tried to stop this practice. He stated (with a grin) that it makes the other section heads jealous but they are afraid to complain. They seem to think Charlie is a personal friend of the division manager, but Charlie says this is not true.

Charlie said he used to be embarrassed in meetings when it was obvious he was doing jobs out of his area, but he has gotten used to it by now, and apparently the other section heads have also.

Charlie's approach to discipline is just keep everybody busy and "you won't have those kinds of problems." He stated that a good boss doesn't have time to hold anybody's hand, like Bob Black does, and tell the guy what a great job he's doing. Charlie believes that if you promise people you will keep an eye on their work for raises and promotion purposes, most of the problems take care of themselves.

Charlie stated that he believes in giving a guy a job to do and then letting him do it without too much checking on his work. He believes most of his subordinates know the score and do their jobs reasonably well without too much griping.

If he has a problem, it is probably the fact that the role and scope of his section has become a little blurred by current practices. Charlie did state that he thinks he should resist a recent tendency for "company people above my division manager's level" to call him up to their offices to hear his ideas on certain programs. However, Charlie is not too sure that this can be stopped without creating a ruckus of some kind. He says he is studying the problem.

Donald Drake

As division manager, Don thinks things are going pretty well since he has not had any real complaints from his superiors in the company, beyond the "small problem" type of thing. He thinks his division is at about the same level of efficiency as the other divisions in the organization.

His management philosophy is to let the section managers find their own level, organizational niche, and form of operation and then check to see if the total output of the division is satisfactory. He stated that he has done this with his present section heads. This was the policy being used when he (Don) was a section head and it has worked fine for him.

Don considers his function as that of a clearinghouse for division inputs and outputs, and sees his job basically as a coordinating one, coupled with the requirement for him to "front" for the division. He believes that you should let a man expand his job activities as much as he is able to do so. Don noted that Charlie Carr had expanded greatly as a manager since he (Don) had arrived. Says he frequently takes Charlie with him to high-level meetings in the company, since Charlie knows more about the division's operations than anyone else in it.

Don noted that both Ancil and Bob seem to do a creditable job in their sections. He has very little contact with Ancil's employees, but occasionally has to see one of Bob Black's boys about something the employee has fouled up. This results from the fact that Bob considers such a face-to-face confrontation between the division manager and a lower-level section employee a good lesson to impress on the subordinate that he has let down his boss. Don Drake said he is not too keen on this procedure but that Bob considers it a most valuable training device to teach the employee to do a good job every time, so Don goes along with it.

Questions How is the Vertical Dyad Linkage model illustrated in this case? How can both Ancil and Bob "seem to do a creditable job in their sections" with such contrasting approaches?

Organizations
The Bigger Picture

20 Organization Design

Considerations of Structure

What are the dimensions of organizational structure?

How does size affect structure?

How does technology affect structure?

How does external environment affect structure?

How does strategy dictate structure?

How important is structure in determining organizational performance?

We noted in Chapter One that an important difference between behavior in organizations and behavior in other contexts involves the degree of explicit external constraints on behavior. Chapter 19 noted that these constraints reduce the freedom of action even for leaders. This chapter will give an account of these constraints, their origins, and how they are interrelated, providing a glimpse of the bigger picture — the "macro" framework that circumscribes the behavior of individuals and groups.

As Pfeffer (1982) has commented, organization theorists differ in their opinion as to what level of analysis provides the best explanation for organizational phenomena. Some theorists feel that any proper explanation of an organization's success or failure must ultimately be couched in terms of the behavior of individuals. This view essentially conceives organizational phenomena as aggregations of individual actions and the forces that motivate them. The opposite view argues that the important forces determining organizational outcomes arises from organizational *context* — the larger internal *structure* of the organization, its *technology*, and the *external environment*.

These contrasting viewpoints comprise what Pfeffer (1982) called the *individualist-structuralist controversy*. We suspect that managers as well as theorists differ in the position they would take in this controversy. Some managers would see the most important issues as those involving the motives, perceptions, attitudes, skills, and personalities of individuals. Others would place priority over the structure within which these individuals are constrained, arguing that the larger framework will dictate much of what follows.

We have given the preponderance of our attention to the "micro" level of analysis — the analysis of individual and group behavior. This does not represent our own bias in the individualist-structuralist controversy, but instead our training and intellectual interests. No matter what position is taken in that controversy, one must appreciate the inevitable linkages between the two different levels of analysis. Without some understanding of the larger context of organizations, students are ill-equipped to reckon with the forces that can determine relationships, frustrate the attainment of personal goals, and shape careers.

ORGANIZATION STRUCTURE

One dictionary defines structure as the "arrangement or interrelation of all the parts of a whole." Organization structure is the formal, systematic arrangement of the operations and activities that constitute an organization and the interrelationships of these operations to one another. Miles (1980) captures this essential notion and makes it more precise by characterizing structure as the systematic patterns of *differentiation* and *integration* of organized activities. Differentiation refers to the process of breaking down the total system into parts that perform different, specialized functions. Integration consists of the processes that coordinate the different parts to each other. To design a structure is, first of all, to divide the organization into various parts according to some criterion. Second, to design a structure is to provide some means of coordinating the functions of these parts, to link them in a coherent fashion so that various functions complement and support each other.

Differentiation: Horizontal

Patterns of differentiation occur along both *horizontal* and *vertical* lines. Horizontal differentiation is defined by the *division of labor* and the method of grouping such divisions, or *departmentalization*.

Division of labor refers to the manner and extent to which the total work is divided into smaller jobs for individuals to perform. If you hired several teenagers to work on a part-time basis to staff a car wash, you would have to decide how to divide the work among them. You could assign different persons to different groups of cars, each individual could wash and wax a certain portion of each car (the grille, the roof, the doors), or each person could handle a part of the process (e.g., hosing down) for each car.

When breaking up work into individual tasks, the question can arise as to how specialized the division of labor should be. The more specialized it is, the narrower the range of any individual's activities and the more efficiently each person can perform his or her own task. Furthermore, it is easier to find people capable of doing or learning a specialized task. But there are limits to the feasible extent of labor specialization. The great economist Adam Smith noted, "Specialization is limited by the extent of the market." The market determines the volume of work to be performed by the organization. If there is a small volume of work, it cannot be spread around a large number of people who perform highly specialized tasks. Also, the efficiency of work simplification might be offset at some point by loss of intrinsic task motivation. Finally, the more narrow the specialization of individual tasks, the greater will be the eventual challenge of integrating the diverse specialties.

Departmentalization   Once specialization of labor has reached some level, especially with large numbers of people, no one person could conceivably oversee the various activities associated with it. The organization designer must therefore identify a basis for grouping activities into larger blocks of structure (see Figure 20–1).

The *functional* basis of departmentation groups works activities into manageable units according to similarity in function or process. Hospitals often departmentalize in this fashion, with separate units for radiology, pathology, anesthesiology, food service, and record keeping. In manufacturing firms, the major functional groupings pertain to such critical operations as production and sales. At lower levels of departmentation, production is further divided into units based on the subfunctions of fabrication and assembly.

FIGURE 20–1

Functional and Product Bases of Organization Structure: A Manufacturing Example

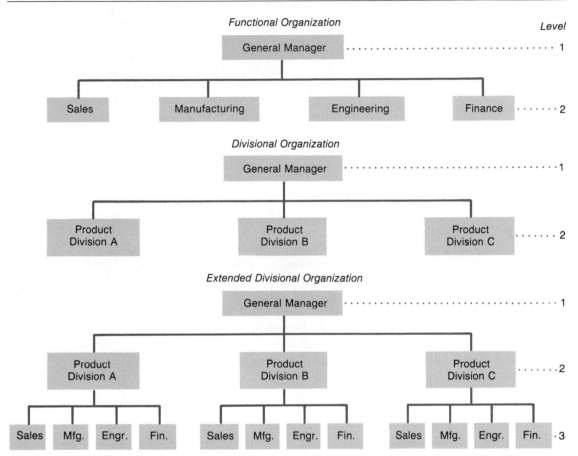

SOURCE: Adapted from R.H. Miles, *Macro Organizational Behavior* (Santa Monica, Calif.: Goodyear Publishing, 1980), p. 29.

Students of organization design generally regard the functional mode of departmentation as most consistent with a high degree of skill specialization and efficient use of human and material resources. This method also presents the fewest problems of coordination and supervision *within* departments, because a narrower range of technical expertise is required of the supervisor, and different individuals can easily understand the nature of their work relationships with each other. However, this means of grouping activities fosters a parochial point of view — specialists surrounded by like-minded specialists tend to see the world in terms of their own specialty — and creates a burden on someone (or some device) for orchestrating the functional operations toward specific products or services.

An alternative method of departmentation is the *product structure,* which groups activities according to major products or product groups. Procter & Gamble, General Foods, and General Electric are corporations divisionalized around the numerous products they offer. Departmentation on this basis would house a variety of functional operations within each product or product group division. One advantage of this approach is that each division can be evaluated on the basis of its profitability (since the division generates revenues and incurs costs on its own), which enhances accountability and a "bottom line" mentality. The end result—the product—more naturally takes precedence over any one specialist or specialized function. The drawback is the likelihood of duplication of investment in human resources and capital equipment. Generally no single product or product group generates sufficient demand for a highly specialized machine or a certain type of technical professional. Thus, either the capacity of the specialized resources is not fully utilized within any single department (waste and inefficiency), or the department must make do with more general purpose, less-specialized resources (foregoing a high degree of technical excellence).

Departmentation can also occur on the basis of *customer* or customer group, as in banks that have different loan departments for consumer and business, or large clothing stores that feature different units for catering to men and women in varied age groups. The pros and cons for this method of grouping are much like those of the product structure: an orientation toward the market and overall outcomes rather than the excellence of any one function at the potential cost of duplication and underutilization of resources.

Geography is another basis for departmentation, and is used by multinational corporations. Daniels, Pitts, and Tretter (1984) found that firms initially characterized by functions or product structures restructured according to geography as a result of increased foreign sales. Such an arrangement provides for adaptation to local markets, legal and political constraints, and economic conditions. Within the United States—even within a single state—some firms find it advantageous to divisionalize on the basis of local areas, especially when the scale of investment in human and material resources in each different area is minor compared to the disadvantages of attempting to coordinate physically dispersed activities from a central location. Organizations that render labor-intensive services—such as income tax preparation, product repair, or hairstyling—find geography a logical basis for departmentation.

The larger the organization, the greater the likelihood that various forms of departmentation will exist. The major issue then becomes the relative priority of the various bases of departmentation. A multinational corporation might choose to departmentalize at the highest level according to geographic area, such as North America, Europe, and the Far East. Within each of those areas might reside major product groups, and within each product group of each area there may be lower level groupings around

FIGURE 20–2

Matrix Structure of Departmentation

(Circles denote offices with dual lines of responsibility.)

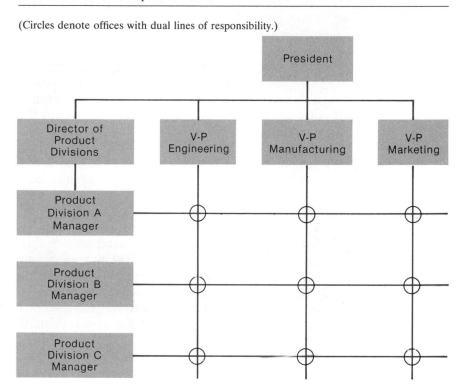

separate functions such as sales, production, and engineering. On the other hand, even a large firm with essentially one product type might divisionalize according to function, with each functional head responsible for coordinating that function across all territorial groupings.

A more recent answer to the question of departmentation comes in the form of the *matrix* structure (see Figure 20–2). The matrix hopes to combine the efficiency and technical specialization afforded by the functional form with the accountability and orientation to overall outcomes fostered by the product structure. Thus, both the functional and product structures exist simultaneously, at the (theoretically) same level of priority — intersecting at a point where some members (usually highly skilled specialists, often with some supervisory responsibilities of their own) report to both a functional superior and a product group superior. Some students of organization design see the matrix structure as virtually mandated by certain strategic and environmental considerations. Others regard it as a fragile form of structure that exacts a huge toll on participants in conflict, confusion, and time spent in meetings.

Differentiation: Vertical

Whatever the basis of departmentation and extent of specialization of labor, the responsibility for overseeing the varied activities gives rise to different levels within organizations—vertical differentiation. A simple structure with an owner-manager overseeing the activities of three mechanics, a receptionist, and a bookkeeper poses only two levels of organization. A larger structure with major product divisions, functional departments within each division, and further subdivisions of function might require seven or eight levels of organization from chief executive officer to the lowest operating level. The underlying basis of vertical differentiation is responsibility for outcomes. The first-level supervisor has responsibility for the outcomes of a certain group of operators, while a divisional vice president is accountable for the overall results of a much larger number of functions and activities.

One factor that determines the number of organization levels is the average *span of control*—the number of people supervised by any one person. Some theorists of organization structure and design (Massie, 1965) argued for a narrow span of control, suggesting an optimum between three and eight. The rationale for this argument was that the number of potential relationships within a group increases exponentially as group size increases arithmetically. However, the narrower the span of control, the greater the number of levels of organization that results (with the same total number of members).

Structures with narrow spans of control and greater extent of vertical differentiation are described as "steep"; those with broader spans of control and fewer layers of vertical differentiation are "flat." Without question, recent structuring trends have gone in the direction of flatter structures. Both General Motors and Ford Motor Co., for example, have experimented successfully with the elimination of several layers of plant management; the Dana Corporation structure had 15 layers in 1974, but its Chairman and CEO Gerry Mitchell successfully restructured the company down to five layers. Advocates for flatter structures argue that today's communications technology removes practical limits on the span of control; that flatter structures enable faster responses to customers; that self-managed work groups obviate the need for lower levels of supervision; and that more layers of responsibility tie up more resources in administrative overhead.

Integration

The means of integrating the differentiated parts of an organization—the varied activities performed by different individuals, the groupings that define the basis of departmentation, and the various levels of responsibility—provide the other major aspect of structure. In practice, almost all organizations rely on a mix of integrative devices. What sets one structure apart from others is the relative emphasis on any one device.

Some organizations integrate primarily on the basis of a set of written rules, policies, and standard operating procedures. Each department has rules for its own operations and also follows prescribed procedures for transactions with other departments. *Formalization* of structure describes the emphasis accorded to this device for integrating organized activity.

Organization structures also differ according to the degree that integration is accomplished by *centralization,* or the concentration of decision-making authority at higher levels of organization. Centralization and formalization can substitute for each other; the greater the proportion of activities that can be controlled by formal procedures, the less the need for centralized authority. This substitution assumes that enforcement of the rules is not problematic, and that few occasions arise either for changing the rules or dealing with exceptions not covered by the rules.

DETERMINANTS OF STRUCTURE

Size

According to archaeologist Olga Soffer (Pfeiffer, 1986), our Cro-Magnon forebears lived as small bands of egalitarian hunter-gatherers, with no formal leadership, until about 15,000 years ago. At that time (the Late Ice Age), bands strayed farther from their home base to search for game, crossing the paths of other bands and undertaking an increasing number of cooperative ventures with them. As people came together in larger groups for longer intervals, status distinctions emerged, as did taboos, rules, and regulations. Thus we have the earliest noted instance of increased size of organization spawning a variation in structure.

Early theorists of organization design directed their energies mainly to the need for a structure that would enable individuals to administer large organizations. Until the 19th century, organization occurred on a relatively small scale. The differentiation and integration of individual activities occurred largely in response to the direct personal orders of a single owner-manager. With the growth in markets, accelerated increases in population, and the expansion of the scale of industry made possible by new energy sources and production methods, the personal control exerted by the owner-manager could not guarantee efficient operation. Inefficient firms failed and were absorbed by larger concerns. Some survived by selling stock to the public. Ownership became more distant from the actual day-to-day running of the firm. A new managerial class evolved: one whose rewards depended on performance instead of family ties. By the end of the 19th century, large organizations had gradually developed some effective methods of formal structure. German sociologist Max Weber took note of the common features of what seemed to be the most effective structure and called it *bureaucracy*.

THE BUREAUCRACY

Weber described the defining characteristics of the bureaucratic structure as follows (Gerth & Mills, 1968):

1. The organization is founded on a system of authority that is legal in character. Authority inheres in an office, not in the person who holds the office. Participants consent to the influence of those whose power is legitimated by the formal rules defining the offices and their relationships to one another. (Legitimate formal authority, founded on rules, contrasted with traditional authority derived from past practice, and charismatic authority based on the characteristics of the person.)

2. Activities required for organizational purposes are distributed in a fixed way as official duties.

3. Authority is distributed in a stable way and "strictly delimited by rules concerning the coercive means, physical, sacerdotal, or otherwise, which may be placed at the disposal of officials" (Gerth & Mills, 1968, p. 196).

4. There is an explicit system by which each office is made subordinate to others in authority.

5. Selection and promotion of officials is based on training and objective criteria; entrance into an office means acceptance of specific obligations, rights, and compensation. Dismissal can result only from unwillingness or inability to carry out such obligations.

6. Management follows a set of written and publicly available rules, policies, and procedures.

7. Official duties are performed without regard to "personal, irrational, and emotional elements which escape calculation." (Gerth & Mills, 1968, p. 197)

Of course, no organization then or now would operate totally according to such guidelines. Weber was describing an ideal toward which emergent organizations seemed to be developing. The closer an organization's structure approximated such ideals, the more it constituted his notion of a rational bureaucracy. This, he contended, would increasingly dominate modern life because of its

> purely technical superiority over any other form of organization. The fully developed bureaucratic mechanism compares with other organizations exactly as does the machine with the nonmechanical modes of production.
>
> Precision, speed, unambiguity, knowledge of the files, continuity, discretion, unity, strict subordination, reduction of friction and of material and personal costs—these are raised to the optimum point in the strictly bureaucratic administration. [Gerth & Mills, 1968, p. 214]

PRINCIPLES OF BUREAUCRATIC STRUCTURE

The Scalar Principle   According to Massie (1965), "the heart of the classical organizational structure is the idea of hierarchy, which the classical theory calls the scalar principle" (p. 396). This principle states that authority should flow in an unbroken line from top to bottom of the organization. Starting from the bottom, every position is related by subordination to another position to which it is accountable – everyone has a boss.

Unity of Command   No member of an organization should be responsible to more than one superior. Violation of this principle would only result in conflicting orders, confusion, and hesitation. Some theorists recognized that perfect fidelity to this principle might be impossible and qualified it to state that no member of an organization should be accountable to more than one superior for any single function. Most of the early management writers felt that any qualifications whatsoever of this principle should be contemplated only with the greatest reluctance.

Span of Control   This principle stated that the number of subordinates responsible to any one superior should be limited to three to eight. A narrow span of control results in more levels in the hierarchy, while wider spans produce a flatter structure.

Distinction between Line and Staff   Classical theorists took account of the increasing role of highly specialized experts in such areas as engineering, logistics, and quality control. The impressive victories of the Prussian army in the late 19th century were attributed largely to the availability of a technical staff to the commanding generals. The example of the Prussian army also offered a solution to the problem of how to use such expertise without violating the principle of span of control. Classical writers carefully distinguished between the *line,* which performs the major functions of the organization, and *staff,* the offices that provide support, service, and advice to line officials. Formal authority follows the line; staff officials have an advisory role.

Departmentation by Function   The theorists who articulated the principles of bureaucratic structure recognized various criteria for departmentation. However, they preferred the functional basis for grouping activities because that method seemed consistent with the efficiencies of a high degree of labor specialization and refinement of technical skills, and more generally adapted to the basic principles of bureaucratic structure.

An Overview of Classical Principles of Bureaucratic Structure   As noted above, the bureaucratic structure arose in response to the challenge of administering large-scale organizations. The bureaucratic solution for efficient operation on a large scale represented a structure with high degrees of formalization, and division of labor, a steep hierarchy resulting from narrow spans of control, and typically a functional basis for departmentation. The implication was that sheer size forced an organization in this direction, especially if the overriding objective was the efficient production of goods and services.

TECHNOLOGY AND STRUCTURE

A technology is a set of human and mechanical activities that transforms information, materials, or people (such as clients or patients) from one state to another. Put another way, a technology is an interrelated set of operations for processing inputs into outputs. Organizations have characteristic technologies, mandated in part by the product or service they provide.

A study conducted by British sociologist Joan Woodward suggested that technology as well as size determines structure. Woodward's study (1965) included about 100 manufacturing firms in the South Essex region of England. She found no basis for predicting effectiveness from span of control, steepness of hierarchy, type of departmentation, or mix between line and staff. Only when the firms were sorted out according to the dominant form of technology employed did structure predict effectiveness.

Woodward identified three distinctive types of technology: unit (or small-batch) production, continuous process, and mass production. Unit or small-batch companies produced made-to-order products in small lot sizes to satisfy specific customers — for example, custom-tailored suits and special-purpose tools. Technologies in mass production manufactured standardized products in huge volume according to fixed specifications, typically in an assembly-line format. Finally, those firms that employed continuous-process technology were associated with homogeneous products — chemicals, pharmaceuticals, petroleum, or gases — that underwent intensive refinement, typically in highly automated processes.

Woodward found that structure varied according to the dominant technology employed. Furthermore, the more successful firms possessed a structure generally similar to the statistical average of those firms using a particular technology. Unit and small-batch production technologies were associated with a relatively low-pitched hierarchical structure (few levels of authority), a small proportion of staff officials, a relatively low degree of formalization, and a narrow span of supervisory control. Mass production technologies were associated with the widest span of supervisory control, the sharpest distinction between line and staff functions, and the most formalized control and sanction procedures. Continuous-process technologies were characterized by steep hierarchical structures, a narrow span of control for top-level managers, and a greater ratio of managerial personnel to total work force (see Figure 20–3).

FIGURE 20–3
Technology-structure Profiles Associated with Effectively Performing Firms in
Woodward's Study (1965)

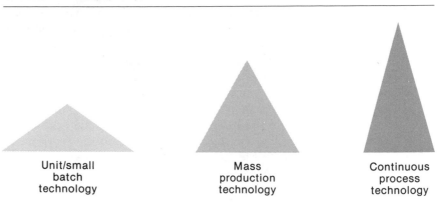

| Unit/small batch technology | Mass production technology | Continuous process technology |

Thus, Woodward's work seemed to "establish the idea of a contingency theory linking organizational effectiveness to an appropriate match between structure and technology" (Miles, 1980, p. 59). This idea has become known as the *technological imperative hypothesis*.

The firms in Woodward's studies were small to medium in terms of number of employees and scale of operations. Hickson, Pugh, and Pheysey (1969) later studied both small and large firms and found a correlation between technology and structure only for small firms in which the dominant production technology affected the majority of employees. Child and Mansfield (1972) found that larger firms, regardless of production technology, converged on common overall structures characterized by high degrees of formalization and specialization. Thus, the effect of technology on structure does not negate the effect of size. In larger organizations, the structural effects of technology appear to be limited to that portion of the organization "impinged" on by the dominant production technology—hence, *the technological impingement hypothesis*.

Thompson's Typology While Woodward's category scheme suggested that technology affects emergent organizational structure, it did not suggest the linkages by which technology has this effect. James D. Thompson (1967) offered a different taxonomy of technologies based on a linkage to structure.

Thompson based his categorization of technology on the type of *interdependence* inherent in the technology. Interdependence, in turn, determines the coordinative requirements posed by the technology and thus the structural devices that most effectively cope with such coordinative requirements.

Mediating technologies link constituencies who wish to be tied together. Retail stores, for example, link manufacturers and wholesalers with individual consumers. Banks mediate between sources of capital and borrowers of capital. Employment agencies mediate between employers who need personnel and individuals who seek jobs. Libraries, post offices, insurance companies, and brokerage houses are organizations in which the primary or core technology is the mediating type.

Mediating technology gives rise to *pooled interdependence,* the simplest kind of interdependence in terms of coordinative requirements. Each part of the system renders a discrete contribution to the total output. In the retail store, for example, each department contributes its share of available merchandise and handles its share of consumer services and purchases. Only to the most limited extent is any one department dependent on the other departments in providing its contribution. The contributions of the various parts are more or less aggregated in determining the store's total business.

Since pooled interdependence poses few coordinative requirements, these requirements can be efficiently addressed by standard rules and techniques for each type of transaction. The retail store usually adopts precise rules for processing customer orders, handling customer credit needs, and reordering stock. By dividing the store into categories of merchandise, special rules applicable to any one department (corresponding to the type of customer served or the type of merchandise handled) can be made operative within that particular area.

Long-linked technologies are defined by *sequential interdependence* among parties. This is the type of technology in which different operations must be performed in a rigidly defined sequence or order. Task A must precede task B, which in turn must precede C. The mass-production assembly line is the archtypical illustration of such technologies (see Table 20–1).

Sequential interdependence gives rise to more serious coordinative requirements than those posed by mediating technologies with their pooled interdependence. Therefore, long-linked technologies require more than standard rules and procedures. Planning becomes paramount to ensure smooth and predictable operations and considerable investments are made in a staff of experts to design and administer plans. Also, more demands are made on supervisory personnel to monitor performance and to ensure that plans are carried out.

Intensive technologies draw on a variety of techniques and areas of expertise to solve a problem, but the precise combination and ordering of operations cannot be determined in advance. Rather, the selection of techniques depends on feedback from the person or object that is being processed. Thompson uses the general hospital to illustrate this form of technology: for any given patient, some combination of laboratory, surgical, pharmaceutical, dietary, housekeeping, and financial services may be needed, but their exact nature or sequence would not be known until the

TABLE 20–1

Thompson's Classification of Organization by Task Interdependence

Technology Type	Dominant Form of Task Interdependence	Management and Design Requirements			Organizational Example
		Demands Placed on Decision Making and Communications	Extent of Organizational Complexity	Type of Coordination Required	
Mediating	Pooled O /|\ X Y Z	Low	Low	Standardization and categorization	Commercial bank
Long-linked	Sequential X → Y → Z	Medium	Medium	Plan	Assembly line
Intensive	Reciprocal X ⇄ Y ⇆ Z	High	High	Mutual adjustment	General hospital

SOURCE: R.H. Miles, *Macro Organizational Behavior* (Santa Monica, Calif:. Good-year Publishing, 1980), p. 68.

total treatment had been rendered. The basic notion underlying intensive technologies is that each case is unique, not standardized by any category system. Scientific research and development, advertising account agencies, building construction, criminal investigation, and many forms of custom-order manufacturing are intensive technologies.

Intensive technologies lead to *reciprocal task interdependence*. Each contributor, to be effective, depends on the availability and the effectiveness of the other contributors. Moreover, since the combination and ordering of operations cannot be specified a priori, neither standard rules nor planning can provide the coordinative devices required by this interdependence. Reciprocal interdependence is more complex and demanding than either pooled or sequential interdependence. Since it depends on spontaneous give-and-take between the contributors, a high volume of interaction and informal communication must flow between the operators. Coordination is, in large measure, achieved ad hoc in fashion that is effective, but may not always seem efficient.

A study by Mahoney and Frost (1974) empirically supports Thompson's propositions. The study, which sampled 297 formal organizational units, assessed the extent to which planning, cooperation, staff development, and supervisory control contributed to the effectiveness of these units (in the judgments of the officials who presided over the units). Planning was judged to be very important in units characterized by long-linked technology, moderate in importance to those units engaged in mediating technologies, and of little importance to groups working with intensive technologies. The same patterning of rated importance was seen with supervisory control. On the other hand, staff development and spontaneous cooperation were judged as vital to the success of units employing intensive technologies, and of limited value in units marked by long-linked technologies.

Large organizations often use all three technological forms delineated by Thompson. Thompson extends his model to predict how organization designers will configure a structure to accommodate mixes of technologies. He predicts that organizations will attempt to "place reciprocally interdependent positions tangent to one another, in a common group which is *(a)* local and *(b)* conditionally autonomous" (Thompson, 1967, p. 58). In other words, when the technology dictates a high level of spontaneous decision making and coordination by mutual adjustment, the needed positions are grouped into teams or crews. The idea is to keep reciprocal interdependence—the most vexing form, with the greatest coordinative costs—at the lowest possible level. Units reciprocally dependent on each other will be clustered together within the next level of the hierarchy. Once the lowest levels of the hierarchy have been structured to contain, first, reciprocal interdependence, and, second, sequential interdependence, organizations will seek to use higher levels of clustering to address pooled interdependence. For example, a firm structured according to product group divisions exhibits pooled interdependence at the highest level, since each division operates semi-independently of the others and contributes profits to the pool. Broad corporate policies would suffice to coordinate the linkages among the divisions.

Perrow: Task Uncertainty   With increased size, more organization units are differentiated and removed to some degree from the primary production process and its modal technology. Because of this, many units develop their own particular technologies, which may bear scant resemblance to the central production process. In an automobile plant, the long-linked technology of the assembly line calls for one type of structure, while ancillary units that perform record-keeping functions, shipping and receiving, sales, engineering, and research and development would use different technologies—dictated by different tasks—and might be better served by different internal structures.

Perrow (1967) suggested a scheme for classifying technology by the degree of uncertainty inherent in task type (see Figure 20–4). Two separate dimensions of tasks determine task uncertainty: *variety,* or the diversity of inputs (in the form of information or materials) comprising the task, and *analyzability,* or the degree to which task activities can be specified a priori for dealing with inputs. A task could combine a great variety of inputs with well-established principles for treating them. For example, engineering technologies would include not only engineering itself but also such tasks as auditing and accounting. The task could also deal with a narrow range of

FIGURE 20–4
Perrow's Classification Scheme for Task Technology

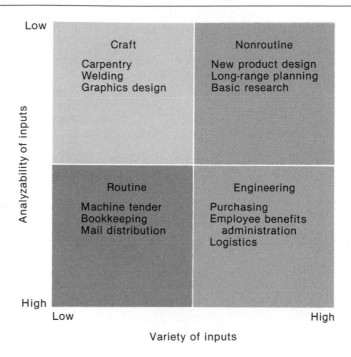

inputs which do not yield to fixed principles of treatment. Craft technologies—those that draw on intuitive skills or artistic talent—such as the work of a custom cabinet maker, graphics designer, or maybe even football coaching are examples of this narrow range of input. Routine technologies characterize tasks low in variety and highly analyzable; obvious examples would include many types of clerical work and repetitive tasks on production lines. Nonroutine technologies inhere in tasks with unpredictable variety of inputs for which there are few if any prescribed procedures for treating them. Much of the work in research and development, long-range planning, and professional treatment of individuals with either physical or psychological problems would fall into this category.

Because Perrow's system is based on task type rather than primary production process, organization design theorists have found his typology useful for analysis of structure at the departmental level. While measures of task variety and analyzability suggest that these two dimensions are empirically correlated, each dimension differentiates among task types when controlling for the other (Withey, Daft, & Cooper, 1983). Moreover, evidence supports the prediction that degree of routineness is associated with a number of aspects of departmental structure (Randolph, 1981;

Tushman, 1979). Centralized decision-making and a high degree of formalization accompany the most routine task types (low variety, high analyzability), while decentralized decision-making and low formalization arise in departments performing the most nonroutine tasks (high variety, low analyzability). The "craft" and "engineering" types of tasks — which are intermediate on the overall dimension of routineness — are associated with moderate levels of departmental formalization and a mixed pattern of centralization and decentralized decision-making.

THE ENVIRONMENT

A pervasive flavor of contemporary organization theory is the underlying concept of the organization as an *open system*. The open system notion emphasizes the dependence on a surrounding environment. The organization must, both in structure and process, effect compatibility with this environment — otherwise, like the hapless dinosaurs facing the Ice Age, the organization cannot survive.

Churchman (1968) defines the organization's environment as those forces that affect the organization's performance, but over which the organization has no direct control. This definition fails to specify the significant external forces that an organization must accommodate. Dill (1958) offers the concept of *task environment* and defines it in terms of four sectors:

1. *Sources of input* to the organization, which include suppliers of labor, raw material, capital, technology, and information.
2. *Receivers of outputs* from the organization, such as customers, users, distributors, clients, constituents.
3. *Competitors* for the organization's sources of inputs and for its relationships with output receivers. This category may be broadened to include the notion of *contenders* — those other organizations that seek to usurp, annex, or transgress the organization's domain or sphere of action.
4. *Regulatory groups* such as government agencies, community action organizations, trade associations, and unions. More broadly, one could define this category as those external groups with the means — through lobbying, public relations, or economic clout — to impose their criteria of legitimacy on the organization's purpose and activities.

Daft and Steers (1986) draw a distinction between the task environment, or those specific parts of the environment (usually other organizations) *directly* affecting the organization's functioning, and the *general environment*, which is the broader backdrop of values, trends, and events that indirectly impinge on the organization. The general environment includes population demographics, cultural traditions, consumer tastes and preferences, national and international economic trends, and technological and scientific developments. In the short run, those who govern organizations will direct their attention to the task environment, but the longer view will recognize the indirect influences emanating from the general environment. (See the Focus on International OB for examples of how the general environment influences structure.)

Dimensions of Organization Environments

Because the external environment significantly affects organizational functioning, organization theorists have attempted to develop conceptual frameworks to identify and analyze the critical dimensions of environment and their implications for structure. A recurrent theme in these frameworks is *environmental uncertainty* (Galbraith, 1974). The more uncertain the environment, the less organization decision-makers know about the immediate state of the environment, the greater the difficulty in predicting future states of the environment, and the greater the risk of failure for actions taken by the organization.

One determinant of environmental uncertainty is its *complexity*. Complexity refers to the number and heterogeneity of discrete elements in the task environment. A multinational, multi-product corporation would obviously face a rather complex environment, configured by many suppliers, competitors, distributors, government regulatory groups, and technology sources. A single-product firm with franchises concentrated in three adjacent states would almost certainly confront a much more simple environment. Environmental complexity threatens the capacity for rational decision-making because (1) more information must be processed, and (2) it becomes more difficult to take actions that are effective with respect to any one element in the environment without sacrificing effectiveness on some other front.

Uncertainty also depends on the *rate of change* in the task environment. *Stable* environments (or sectors of the environment) change only gradually and in an orderly, predictable manner. Firms that make footlockers and trunks, for example, have seen little change over the last quarter of a century in the basic patterns of market structure, competition, relationships with suppliers, distributors, technology, or government regulation. *Dynamic* environments exhibit abrupt shifts in the patterning of their elements. One of the effects of the trend toward deregulation in the 1980s was to render the environments of many financial and transportation firms more dynamic, with virtually overnight shifts in competitor tactics, supplier costs, and customer responses.

Like complexity, high rates of change in organization environments constitute a threat to rational decision making. A decision that is optimal with respect to external dependencies today is likely to be suboptimal tomorrow. Again, the effect is to increase the amount of information that

FOCUS ON INTERNATIONAL OB

Culture and Organization Structure

Recall from Chapter two that Hofstede's (1984) study based on over 100,000 respondents in 40 countries identified four significant dimensions of national culture. One of these, *power distance,* reflects the extent of endorsement of unequal power distribution within organizations and institutions. Another dimension, *uncertainty avoidance,* concerns the degree to which a society feels threatened by uncertain and ambiguous situations and thus seeks to establish prescribed codes for behavior and beliefs.

Exemplars of the combinations of high and low relative values on these two dimensions include the following:

Low Uncertainty Avoidance,
Low-Power Distance: Great Britain

High Uncertainty Avoidance,
Low Power Distance: West Germany

Low Uncertainty Avoidance,
High Power Distance: India

High Uncertainty Avoidance,
High Power Distance: France

Thus, the British prefer structures that give wide scope to discussion and direct interpersonal communication for resolving issues, while the French lean toward organization forms that signal clear distinctions in the authority to make a decision. The Germans (following the lead of their famous theorist of the bureaucracy, Max Weber) are attracted to highly formalized systems in which the rules protect the lower ranks from the abuse of power by superiors. The Indians model their organizations on the family — centralized power by dominant leaders, with personal relationships formalized, but low formalization of workflow processes.

Hofstede suggests that the French fondness for the concept of unity of command and the German insistence on organizational clarity explains why their managers have little attraction to the matrix type of organization structure. Hofstede also believes that the success of so many U.S.-based companies in different cultures is attributable to the fact that, culturally, we fall right in the center of the distribution of nations on these two dimensions.

SOURCE: G. Hofstede (1984). *Culture's consequences* (Beverly Hills, CA: SAGE Publications, Inc.).

must be processed per unit of time, while introducing a greater number of trade-offs between alternative courses of action.

Daft and Steers (1986) suggest a third dimension, *resource dependence,* that determines environmental uncertainty. Resource dependency arises from the disadvantageous power position held by an organization with respect to some element of its task environment. For example, a firm that depends on a single supplier for a critical raw material or a single customer for a large fraction of its sales inevitably faces a high degree of uncertainty if the firm has no control over the supplier or customer. Paradoxically, the firm might render its environment more certain by generating greater complexity—for example, cultivating relationships with a number of different suppliers or marketing its products through a heterogeneous set of distributors. The greater complexity could conceivably be more than offset by the lessened dependence on any one element, resulting in a more certain environment overall.

Environment and Structure

Galbraith (1974) argued that the greater the uncertainty of the environment, the greater the amount of information that organization decision-makers must process in order to attain any given level of effectiveness. Variations in structure represent variations in the ability to preplan, the flexibility to adapt to unforeseen contingencies, or decreased levels of performance required for continued viability.

An organization that operates in a simple, stable environment and has low dependence on outsiders for resources will have little need for information-processing capacity or adaptability. However, it will probably compete with other organizations that are similarly situated. Thus, the major imperative confronting such an organization will be efficiency in use of resources, and the logical structure for such a need would be one based on functional specialization. The prototype is one that Burns and Stalker (1961) called the *mechanistic* model, characterized by:

1. A highly specialized division of labor.
2. A centralized or hierarchical basis of authority and influence.
3. A preponderance of vertical, as opposed to lateral, communication.
4. Detailed policies, procedures, and rules for each participant, which are not to be deviated from.

On the other hand, an organization enmeshed in a complex, dynamic environment will have enormous difficulty processing the information necessary to preplan its contingencies. It will probably have to rely on quick response cycles to unanticipated developments, redeploying its human and material assets as needed. The kind of structure that permits such nimble response is one based on product or project groups rather than function and typifies the *organic* model. This model can be recognized by:

1. Continual revision of participants' role responsibilities and prerogatives, which change informally as a function of interaction with others.
2. Decentralized patterns of influence and authority, which inhere primarily in the expertise relevant to a problem rather than in office or rank.

3. A preponderance of lateral rather than vertical communication patterns, which convey expertise and advice as opposed to commands or decisions.

4. Reliance on judgments rather than detailed rules.

The organic structure would be judged inefficient by absolute standards, thus deliberately geared to a lower level of technical performance, but better suited to survive dramatic changes in undecipherable environments.

Suppose the organization faces a highly uncertain environment—thus ruling out the pure form of a mechanistic structure. But on the other hand, the organization must operate at a fairly high level of efficiency to stay competitive—therefore not permitting the "slack" and redundancy of the organic form. If the uncertainty is due to environmental complexity, one solution is to structure the core technology along mechanistic lines, buffering it from the environment with boundary substructures to absorb uncertainty from various segments of the task environment (Thompson, 1967). For example, the production process in many firms in consumer electronics industries is structured fairly rigidly in order to achieve high operating efficiency. This is made possible by boundary structures that are more loosely structured to adapt to changes in market forces, sources of raw materials, and technologies. Thus, the substructures for sales, purchasing, R&D, and engineering would take the forms best suited to their own particular subenvironments, and ideally they would resolve uncertainty to an extent preserving the stability of the technical core.

Sometimes the external environment is so turbulent that its shock waves penetrate to the technical core of the organization and mere "buffering" by boundary units does not suffice. Yet still the organization cannot tolerate inefficiencies beyond some level. In such cases, Galbraith (1974) argues that the firm will seek to retain a technical core based on functional lines, but increase its coordinative and information-processing abilities. By one means or another, the organization creates lateral relationships that cut across functional specialties. The devices for doing this include:

1. **Task forces**—When problems arise that involve several different line functions, a temporary task force of representatives from each function is created. Ideally, these groups resolve problems at lower operating levels without passing them on to higher levels.

2. **Teams**—Task forces may become permanent fixtures charged with resolving a large volume of nonroutine problems affecting several different departments.

3. **Integrating roles**—Leadership of the teams that coordinate the different functions is formalized in a new position, such as program or project manager. This person might initially manage interdepartmental coordination for a project through informal bases of power, such as expertise, contacts, and persuasion.

4.   **Managerial linking roles** — This device is much like the integrating role, albeit with formal authority to make coordinating decisions through budgetary means. However, the integrator does not exercise direct authority over any personnel in line functions.

5.   **Matrix organization** — The logical and ultimate end of the process of weaving lateral relationships across functional lines is to give the integrator direct authority over functional specialists — who nonetheless still report to a functional superior. At this point, a dual authority structure has evolved and certain professional and/or managerial personnel are accountable both to a functional or technical boss (such as marketing or electrical engineering). These personnel also report to a project or product manager charged with integrating across functions to meet the demands of a dynamic, unforgiving environment.

The matrix structure has aroused controversy since its inception. Supporters argue that no structural alternative better allows a firm to keep pace with technologically dynamic environments and still operate with requisite internal efficiency. Its detractors (e.g., Knight, 1976) contend that little hard evidence exists to support the touted advantages of the matrix form over straight-forward functional or product structures. Knight points to the problem inherent in the matrix structure, such as the stress (in the form of role conflict and overload) for those who work under dual authority structures. Also frequent disagreements and deadlocks between functional and project managers result in a steady stream of appealed decisions passed to top-level managers. A before/after study by Joyce (1986) of a company that adopted the matrix design found no effect on role conflict and an increase in the volume of communication across functional departments, but no improvement in the quality of communication and some evidence of lower job involvement by participants. Peters and Waterman (1982) suggested that matrix structures often become bogged down in paperwork and the minutiae of planning and analysis, aggravated by ambiguity concerning the real priorities for action. They noted that few of their "excellent" companies used the matrix, and those that did gave clear priority to one dimension (function, product, territory) or another. On the other hand, a survey by Larson and Gobeli (1987) of over 500 managers in firms emphasizing new product development showed a strong majority that had used the matrix design for product development projects, believed the matrix to be effective so long as the project leader had the requisite authority, and would continue to use the matrix.

Nonstructural Responses to the Environment   Daft and Steers (1986) note that organizations need not invariably use internal structure to deal with environmental uncertainty, particularly when uncertainty arises from resource dependence. Alternatives to structure redesign include the articulation of linkages to important segments of the task environment. For

FOCUS ON MANAGEMENT

The Matrix at Dow Corning

Dow Corning's version of the matrix structure has attracted widespread interest and emulation by corporate leaders. At Dow Corning, there are actually three dimensions of corporate responsibility: profit centers (the different businesses that the company operates); cost centers (functional activities, including marketing, manufacturing, technical service and development, research, and other supportive activities); and geographic areas (the United States, Asia, Europe, Australasia, and Interamerica).

The key element in this structure is the Business Board, of which there are 10 members—one for each of the company's businesses. The only full-time board member is the manager of the business. The business manager has responsibility for the profitability of the business, but does not have direct control over the resources needed to accomplish this. Instead, he enlists the aid of the other members of the board, which includes representatives from the marketing, research, manufacturing, and other functional areas. Each of these representatives reports directly to another boss, a vice president of a functional group, such as manufacturing or technical service and development. Each board member is evaluated by both the business manager and a functional manager. Thus, a manufacturing manager on a board must be concerned not only with technical excellence and cost controls, but also with a profit objective.

Area managers develop short- and long-term plans that are integrated into the plans for each business and function. Their objectives include sales, costs, and profit.

William C. Goggin, who as chairman of Dow Corning introduced this matrix structure in the late 1960s, recommends it for any company driven by new technology and operating in a competitive, global, and fast-changing market environment, especially if such a market cuts across diverse industries. Goggin concedes that the break-in period for this new system was three to four years, and that it entailed numerous costs, including the uprooting of many people from long-established jobs, and widespread uncertainty. He believes these costs were well worth the end results: more top-management time for long-range planning, a healthy balance of emphasis among products and functions, quick response to changing technological and market developments, and a faster pace of innovation.

SOURCE: W. C. Goggin (1974). How the multidimensional structure works at Dow Corning. *Harvard Business Review*, January-February.

example, a firm critically dependent on a supplier for a raw material can negotiate a long-term contract at a designated price. Some linkages use a patterned flow of personnel within clusters of interdependent organizations: defense contractors hire former military and government officials, universities include on their boards of trustees top managers of corporate benefactors, corporations develop ties to major customers indirectly through mutual connections to outside consulting firms, and managers of various organizations cultivate symbiotic personal relationships by means of working together in voluntary charitable enterprises.

A business can hedge its bets in the opening of a new market or development of a new product by means of a joint venture — an investment partnership with one or more other organizations that creates an entirely new company. When several firms cooperate in the formation of a new business, the new entity is called a *consortium*. In 1984 Congress amended the U.S. Antitrust Act to encourage joint research, and since then more than 100 cooperative research ventures have registered with the government. *The Wall Street Journal* (Chipello, 1989) reported that seven leading computer and semiconductor companies had formed a consortium, U.S. Memories, to produce memory chips; a government official described this venture (aimed not merely at research but also production) as "unprecedented." The trend toward more cooperative relations among would-be competitors is attributed to the increased cost, complexity, and risk of developing new technologies, as well as the globalization of markets.

Also, an organization can choose to be somewhat proactive vis-à-vis its environment rather than play a purely reactive role. Companies try to use political influence to determine the outcomes of legislation (Aplin & Hegarty, 1980) and varied forms of product and institutional advertising to shape the attitude of external groups.

STRATEGY

Bourgeois (1984) observes that the "organization theory literature is replete with deterministic contingency theories in which the role of human choice is relegated to a place quite secondary to . . . environmental turbulence . . . technological processes . . . size and ownership . . . information processing requirements" (p. 586). Bourgeois argues that such a perspective underestimates the freedom of action of managers. Organizations do not reflexively structure themselves in response to prescribed technologies or exogenously determined environments. Rather, organization leaders have some latitude for determining what the relevant environment is, as well as a range of options for choice of both technology and structure. Managerial decisions about overarching goals, environmental domains of action, technologies, and structure constitute what Child (1972) called "strategic choice."

Corporate strategy-making determines the overall purposes and objectives of an organization and the preferred paths for achieving them. A *strategic business unit* (SBU) is any part of the organization treated separately for strategy-making purposes. Each SBU (large corporations competing in a number of different industries or markets might contain a dozen or more SBUs) then has its own set of specific goals, external environment, technology, and internal structure.

One of the more popular typologies of business strategy is that of Porter (1980). A *differentiation* strategy aims at establishing a unique identity to its product or service because of the features, intrinsic quality, or esthetic appeal. For example, Leica cameras, BMW cars, and Nike shoes present distinctive images in their industries. Differentiation often revolves around the "upscale" continuum of product categories; if the strategy is successful, the product can command a premium price and lasting customer loyalty. A recent issue of a weekly news magazine speculated that a reunited Germany in the 1990s could become the world's economic leader by capitalizing on the success of West German companies in capturing the upscale market in a number of industries.

A *cost leadership* strategy tries to use cost-efficient operations to render a product or service at low price in order to capture large market share. Such a strategy can succeed even with a nondescript, generic product image if relentless cost controls provide sufficient price differentials vis-à-vis competitors.

A *focus* strategy concentrates on a niche in the market for which leaders of the firm believe they have a particular strategic advantage relative to competitors. The firm might have a favorable geographic location, an understanding of the peculiar needs of a special target customer, or the capability of custom tailoring a product to a narrow segment of the market. Some textbook publishing companies, for example, flourish by courting very specific user groups such as schools of engineering, medicine, and law. Nikon is the premier name among Japanese camera makers, not because of total sales (Canon holds first place), but because it caters to professional photographers in product repair services and special purpose accessories. The nichemanship strategy need not match the upscale quality of the differentiation nor the production efficiency of the cost leader, so long as it supplies a "value-added" dimension not easily emulated by competitors for a well-defined consumer group.

Managers might select a strategy to use, but effective pursuit of any particular strategy probably has definite implications for technology, structure, and other dimensions of management. Miles, Snow, Meyer, and Coleman (1978) have proposed a typology of strategy types somewhat analogous to those of Porter, but with elaboration on the mutually supporting mixes of structure, technology, and process that render any given strategy effective. The *Defender* strategy type competes by sealing off a portion of the market to create a stable domain, holding this ground with a limited product line and competitive pricing. To enact this strategy, the Defender must attain a high order of technological efficiency by investment in specialized plant and machinery and by centralized decision making in a formal structure departmentalized by function. Internal power will tilt to production and engineering managers, from whose ranks the top level officials are apt to come. Coordination is achieved at top levels because the firm's stable environment does not demand quick adjustments at the operating level. The Defender's low uncertainty makes it possible to invest huge sums in both forward integration (to control distribution) and backward integration (ownership of sources of supply). The Defender, however, is ill-equipped to respond to any unforeseen developments threatening its turf.

The *Prospector* strategy type frequently introduces new products and explores new markets for refinements of existing products. By "getting there firstest with the mostest" it can command high prices for its novel offerings. Since the Prospector must be able to move at the first signal of a new opportunity, its structure and technology must allow considerable flexibility. Thus, its internal design will feature loosely coupled product group divisions and the decentralized attributes of the organic structural model, and its technology will consist of multiple-purpose machinery. Marketing and R&D types, whose eyes and ears are more attuned to the external environment, will dominate administrative policy and decision-making. The Prospector, like the proverbial shark, must stay on the move, otherwise it dies. High profit margins on new products are needed to offset the internal inefficiencies, which pose the danger of pricing the Prospector right out of the market.

The *Analyzer* does not try to be first to the market, but hopes to follow the lead of the Prospector with more consistent quality in "second generation" versions of new products and with more competitive pricing. This strategy type seeks to exploit new product and market opportunities, yet hold onto a nucleus of well-established existing products and customer groups. The Analyzer must be able to respond quickly (though not as quickly as the Prospector), yet also achieve internal efficiency (though not to the degree required of the Defender). The Analyzer therefore turns to the matrix (or some approximation thereof) structure to effect an optimal balance between stability and efficiency in its technological core and flexibility and coordination of linkages across functions. The risk is that the Analyzer, in trying to achieve this balance, might veer too far in one direction or the other, finding itself neither sufficiently fleet of foot to adapt to fast-breaking developments seized by the Prospector, nor sufficiently cost-effective to prevent losing clientele to Defenders.

The *Reactor* is the fourth type, one that either lacks a consistent strategy or fails to achieve the appropriate mix of technology, structure, and process that supports this strategy. Presumably the Reactor does not survive unless it evolves in the direction of one of the other strategy types.

A study by Hambrick (1983) supports the Miles hypothesis of an empirical correlation between strategy, structure, technology, and process, at least to the extent of identifying well-defined firms as either Defender or Prospector. Contrary to the Miles positions that the two consistent strategy types would be equally effective, Hambrick found that Defenders consistently outperformed Prospectors in profitability and cash flow, regardless of industry environment. Prospectors excelled only in market share, and even there only in innovative industries.

FOCUS ON THE FUTURE

The Organization Form of the 1990s: The Dynamic Network

According to Miles and Snow (1986), rapid technological changes and intensified international competition have given birth to a new type of organization that will become increasingly evident. The new form of organization taking shape to meet the challenges of tomorrow is what Miles and Snow call the "dynamic network." They describe this evolving structure in terms of:

1. Vertical Disaggregation—Business functions such as product design, production, and distribution—traditionally carried out within one company—will in the future be conducted by independent organizations within a network.

2. Brokers—A broker will assemble the various organizations needed to form a network, subcontracting for needed services.

3. Market Mechanisms—Market forces rather than formal plans or controls will hold the major functions of the network together. Payment on delivery will substitute for progress reports and supervision.

4. Full-Disclosure Information Systems—Participants in the network will hook themselves together on a continuously updated information system so that each can monitor the contributions of the others.

The dynamic network—foreshadowed by such trends as the increased use of joint ventures, the contracting out of many business support services, the practice of leasing entire workforces (as seen in the construction industry) and new business ventures spinning off of existing firms—will permit individual companies to downsize and concentrate on what they do best. They can then adapt to new contingencies by redeploying assets in new networks or modifications of the old. Organization boundaries and membership will be flexible—some groups will be hard pressed even to say what organization they are "in," as they find their services contracted out to one network after another. Organizations will, in fact, intersect across a kaleidoscopic pattern of specialized functions and support services.

SOURCE: R. E. Miles & C. C. Snow (1986). Network organizations: New concepts for new forms. *California Management Review* 28, no. 3 (Summer), 62–73.

STRUCTURE: HOW IMPORTANT IS IT?

Ford and Hegarty (1984) presented to groups of graduate students and practicing managers a questionnaire that probed the respondents' beliefs concerning the causal relations among technology, structure, size, personnel competence, and effectiveness of the firm. The researchers used a method of analysis that enabled them to construct the implicit theoretical model that would be consistent with respondents' answers to a detailed set of questions. The data suggested some degree of consensus and correspondence to established theoretical models of the determinants of structure; for example, the subjects clearly thought in terms of increased size leading to a higher degree of specialization of labor and increased formalization. In certain respects, however, subjects failed to agree on how technology affects structure. For example, some believed that increased task variability would negate the usefulness of formal rules and procedures. Others thought that nonroutine tasks actually made formalization all the more important in order to provide control. More interesting was the observation that respondents showed strong consensus in attaching greater weight to *personnel competence* than to any of the other structural or task factors as a direct cause of organizational performance. Furthermore, professional competence itself was implicated as affecting structural dimensions of formalization and delegation. The findings imply that, at least in implicit "lay theories" of organizational performance, the caliber of participants is more important than structure by itself, perhaps more important than the "fit" between structure and technology. The prevalence of such intuitive causal models does not establish their validity; we have seen instances in previous chapters to challenge conventional thinking and the impressionistic data on which it rests. Nonetheless, considering the experience and varied backgrounds of the practicing managers among Ford and Hegarty's sample, the data command some respect.

Waterman, Peters, and Phillips (1980) conclude that "structure is not organization" and that perhaps both theorists and CEOs have accorded organization design a loftier status than it warrants. Waterman et al. argue that "in the face of complexity and multiple competing demands, organizations simply can't handle decision-making in a totally rational way . . . a single blunt instrument—like structure—is unlikely to provide the master tool that can change organizations with the best effect" (p. 16). Drawing from their extensive experience as professional management consultants, they find that perennial top performers among large corporations use a relatively simple underlying structure, supplementing it with a variety of temporary devices such as ad hoc discussion groups. Consistent with the findings of Ford and Hegarty (1984), Waterman et al. observe among the "excellent companies" a more focused emphasis on the quality of personnel—achieved through a combination of selection and massive investment in continual training and retraining—and a "strong culture" that coordinates and integrates via peer pressure, clearly articulated values, and role models.

In the next and concluding chapter, we will examine the process by which organizations proactively manage the process of change by altering their mixes of personnel, structure, technology, strategy, and culture.

SUMMARY

Organization structure consists of the patterns by which its component activities are differentiated from each other and integrated into a composite form. Patterns of horizontal differentiation include the degree of specialization of labor and the methods of departmentalizing or grouping activities (whether by function, product, customer, or geographic area, or—as in the matrix—by combinations of these at some level). Vertical differentiation refers to the number of levels of authority in the organization, which arise as a consequence of the average span of control of supervision. Structural integration is effected by the extent of formalization of procedures and the degree of centralization of decision-making authority.

Determinants of structure include size (number of activities and participants), technology, characteristics of the external environment, and corporate strategy. The overall effect of size is toward greater formalization, along the lines of the bureaucratic prototype as sketched out by Weber. However, with increased size and greater extent of internal differentiation, departments will show variations in structure according to technology type (because of such characteristics of technology as its routineness/ nonroutineness and the form of interdependence it generates). The creation of subunits to buffer the technical core of the organization from the environment also gives rise to differing departmental structures in order to cope with various sectors of the external environment.

From a different perspective, neither technology nor environment are constraints; they, along with an appropriate structure, follow from the choice of an internally consistent competitive strategy. Organizational actors can choose their environmental domain as well as modal technology, but must design a structure congruent with these other aspects of strategy—as noted in such strategy types as the Defender, Prospector, and Analyzer.

Finally, still another perspective considers the type of formal structure much less significant in determining performance than other aspects of organization, such as personnel competence and the intensity and coherence of the organization's informal culture.

CONCEPTS TO REMEMBER

Departmentation	Formalization	Reactor
Bureaucracy	Span of control	Centralization
Mediating technology	Long-linked	Unity of command
Routine/nonroutine	technology	Intensive technology
technologies	Technological imperative	Technological impingement
Matrix structure	hypothesis	hypothesis
Task environment	Mechanistic form	Organic form
Analyzer	Defender	Prospector

QUESTIONS FOR DISCUSSION

1. Max Weber, writing nearly a century ago, expressed undisguised admiration for the bureaucratic structure. Yet in our own times we often use the term *bureaucracy* with clearly negative connotations. Why?

2. In the chapter on leadership, we noted the functions that leadership performs and considered possible substitutes for leadership. Considering the purposes achieved by formal structure, what substitutes for structure can you identify? Under what conditions are these substitutes practical and viable?

3. Explain why organizations do not necessarily adapt to their environments.

4. One point of view contends that "the big picture"—the elements of formal structure, technology, external environment, corporate strategy—has causal priority over "lower level units of analysis" such as individual behavior, group dynamics, and leadership. Offer and defend a case for causality in the other direction: that lower level units of analysis exert some determination over the components of the bigger picture.

REFERENCES

Aplin, J. C., & Hegarty, W. H. (1980). Political influence: Strategies used by organizations to impact legislation in business and economic matters. *Academy of Management Journal* 23, 437-50.

Bourgeois, L. J., III (1984). Strategic management and determinism. *Academy of Managerial Review* 9, 586-96.

Burns, T., & Stalker, G. M. (1961). *The management of innovation*. London: Tavistock. Abridged and reproduced in part in H. L. Tosi & W. C. Hamner (eds.), *Organizational behavior and management: A contingency approach*. Chicago: St. Clair Press, 1974.

Child, J. (1972). Organization structure, environment and performance: The role of strategic choice. *Sociology* 6, 2-22.

Child, J., & Mansfield, R. (1972). Technology, size, and structure. *Sociology* 6, 369-93.

Chipello, C. J. (1989). More competitors turn to cooperation. *The Wall Street Journal,* June 23.

Churchman, C. W. (1968). *The systems approach*. New York: Dell Publishing.

Daft, R. L., & Steers, R. M. (1986). *Organizations: A Micro-macro approach*. Glenview, IL: Scott, Foresman and Co.

Daniels, J. D., Pitts, R. A., & Tretter, M. J. (1984). Strategy and structure of U.S. multinationals: An exploratory study. *Academy of Management Journal* 27, 292-307.

Dill, W. R. (1958). Environment as an influence on managerial autonomy. *Administrative Science Quarterly* 2, 409-43.

Ford, J. D., & Hegarty, W. H. (1984). Decision makers' beliefs about the causes and effects of structure: An exploratory study. *Academy of Management Journal* 27, 271-91.

Galbraith, J. R. (1974). Organizational design: An information processing view. *Interfaces* 4, 28-36.

Gerth, H. H., & Mills, C. W. (1968). *From Max Weber: Essays in sociology*. New York: Oxford University Press.

Goggin, W. C. (1974). How the multidimensional structure works at Dow Corning. *Harvard Business Review,* January-February.

Hambrick, D. C. (1983). Some tests of the effectiveness and functional attributes of Miles and Snow's strategic types. *Academy of Management Journal* 26, 5-26.

Hickson, D. J., Pugh, D. S., & Pheysey, D. C. (1969). Operations technology and organization structure: An empirical reappraisal. *Administrative Science Quarterly* 14, 378-97.

Hofstede, G. (1984). *Culture's consequences*. Beverly Hills, CA: SAGE Publications, Inc.

Joyce, W. F. (1986). Matrix organization: A social experiment. *Academy of Management Journal* 29, 536-61.

Katz, D., & Kahn, R. L. (1966). *The social psychology of organizations*. New York: John Wiley & Sons.

Knight, K. (1976). Matrix organizations: A review. *Journal of Management Studies* 13, 111-30.

Larson, E. W., & Gobeli, D. H. (1987). Matrix management: Contradictions and insights. *California Management Review* 3, 126-38.

Lawrence, P. R., & Lorsch, J. W. (1964). *Organization and environment*. Homewood, IL: Richard D. Irwin.

Lawrence, P. R., & Lorsch, J. W. (1969). *Developing organizations: Diagnosis and action*. Reading, MA: Addison-Wesley Publishing.

Mahoney, T. A. & Frost P. J. (1974). The role of technology in models of organizational effectiveness. *Organizational Behavior and Human Performance* 11, 122-38.

Massie, J. L. (1965). Management theory. In J. G. March (ed.), *Handbook of organizations*, Skokie, IL: Rand McNally.

Miles, R. E., & Snow, C. C. (1986). Network organizations: New concepts for new forms. *California Management Review* 28, 62-73.

Miles, R. E., Snow, C. C., Meyer, A. D., & Coleman, H. J., Jr. (1978). Organizational strategy, structure, and process. *Academy of Management Review* 3, 546-62.

Miles R. H. (1980). *Macro organizational behavior*. Santa Monica, CA: Goodyear Publishing.

Perrow, C. (1967). A framework for the comparative analysis of organizations. *American Sociological Review* 32, 194-208.

Peters, T. S., & Waterman, R. H., Jr. (1982). In search of excellence. New York: Harper & Row.

Pfeffer, J. (1982). *Organizations and organization theory*. Boston: Pitman Publishing Inc.

Pfeiffer, J. E. (1986). From the Cro-Magnons, a burst of technology. *Smithsonian*, October 1986, 74-84.

Porter, M. E. (1980). *Competitive strategy: Techniques for analyzing industries and competitors*. New York: Free Press.

Reif, W. E., Monczka, R. M., & Newstrom, J. W. (1973). Perceptions of the formal and informal organizations: Objective measurement through the semantic differential technique. *Academy of Management Journal* 16, 389-403.

Thompson, J. D. (1967). *Organizations in action*. New York: McGraw-Hill.

Waterman, R. H., Peters, T. J., & Phillips, J. R. (1980). Structure is not organization. *Business Horizons* 23, no. 3 (June), 14-26.

Withey, M., Daft, R. L., & Cooper, W. H. (1983). Measures of Perrow's work unit technology: An empirical assessment and a new scale. *Academy of Management Journal* 26, 45-63.

Woodward, J. (1965). *Industrial organization: Theory and practice*. London: Oxford University Press.

21 Organizational Change and Development

What is the difference between reactive and proactive organizational change?

What prompts organizations to undertake planned change?

What methods exist for changing behavior in organizations?

What are the essential elements of successful long-run change in organizational behavior?

How can managers assess the impact of change?

Inevitably, organizations change. They are born, grow, and decline, and many eventually die. They gain and lose customers, clients, leaders, personnel, and products. They respond to changes in markets, governments, competitors, creditors, communities, even the weather. They struggle with adversity and celebrate the good fortunes of prosperity.

No organization is the same today as it was five years ago. Organizations do not have to be taught to change; whether for good or ill, they do change. In fact, today, organizations are changing at incredible rates. Table 21–1 indicates some of the changes currently taking place in U.S. industry; these changes just scratch the surface, and do not include changes taking place in business functions like sales and service, MIS, and finance.

It is important whether change is passively unmanaged and reactive, or managed and proactive. Reactive change, like reflexive behavior, involves a limited part of the system; proactive change and instrumental behavior coordinate the parts of the system as a whole. For example, an individual will respond reflexively to a sudden intense light by eye blinking or pupillary

TABLE 21–1
Ongoing Organizational Change

Area	The Old	The New
People	Capital more important than people. Unions are a dragging force. People need tight controls, close supervision. Money is the only motivator.	Quality, service, and responsiveness through people more important than capital. Participation programs; people involvement in all plant activities.
International	Adjunct activity. "Global brands" managed by U.S. headquarters marketers.	Primary activity. Extensive off-shore product development, tailoring of all products.
Organization	Hierarchical, staff-centered. Officially "matrixed" to "solve" coordination needs. Span of control from 1 to 10 at lower levels.	Flat. Large span of control (1 to 100 at bottom; 1 to 20 at top). Pruning 80 percent of middle management and layers. Line dominated. Business team/task team/small group focused. Decentralized.
Leadership	Detached, analytic. Centralized strategy planning. Dominated by central corporate and group executive staffs.	Values set from the top, strategic development from below. Top executives in touch with customers and operations. Leader as tone setter and visionary.
Manufacturing	Volume, long runs. Automation more important than people. Volume, low cost, and efficiency more important than quality and responsiveness.	Short runs, flexibility (fast product changeover). People more important than capital—quality and responsiveness king.
Marketing	Mass markets, mass advertising, lengthy market tests, marketers in their offices.	Fragmented markets, new uses. Marketers in the field. Premium on speed.
Innovation	Central R&D, big projects as norm.	All areas hotbeds for innovation.

SOURCE: Adapted from T. Peters (1987). A world turned upside down. *Academy of Management Executive* 1, 231–241.

contraction. An instrumental response to the same stimulus would coordinate the central nervous system and psychomotor capacities, perhaps to shield or remove the light. Analogously, a firm's reactive change to lagging sales might take a knee-jerk form: simply putting more pressure on the sales force or increasing advertising. A proactive change would involve other parts of the organization (production, marketing, purchasing, human resources) in a coordinated response to the problem.

Reflexive behavior and reactive change respond to immediate symptoms, while instrumental behavior and proactive change respond to underlying forces producing the symptoms. In the example of declining sales, putting pressure on the sales force is a reactive response to the immediate symptom. The underlying problem may be much more complex. The problem may be due to inferior product quality because of high absenteeism and turnover in factory workers; changes in distribution channels through which consumers buy the product; an unfavorable public image of the firm; or excessive demands on the sales force to spend time on paperwork. In other words, the decline in sales merely represents the tip of the iceberg. Proactive change is a response to the underlying variables that led up to the visible problem.

This chapter primarily concerns proactive change: the deliberate attempt of organization officials to induce comprehensive, coordinated, purposeful change.

ANTECEDENTS OF CHANGE

Why do organizations embark on a concerted effort toward redirection and transformation? What prompts officials to break away from the status quo? Almost any issue of *The Wall Street Journal* or *Business Week* identifies one or more of the following as inspiration for planned change.

Barometers of Declining Effectiveness

Organizations change when they have to change—typically, when they uncover evidence of declining effectiveness. For example, an organization's financial resources may decrease at significant or even an alarming rate. Such a decline leads to changes like layoffs or pay cuts, other forms of cost cutting, and higher accountability and less autonomy for employees (Sutton & D'Aunno, 1989). At the national level, many argue that the United States has lost its competitive edge in the world economy (e.g., Mitroff & Mohrman, 1987). Companies are responding to this charge by changing their structure, redesigning work, introducing new technologies, and improving their products and services (Offermann & Gowing, 1990).

Organizations can "take their pulse" by looking at numerous indicators from their own information systems. A business firm monitors data on sales, absenteeism, turnover, scrap rates, manufacturing costs, and financial ratios.

Some firms conduct regular opinion surveys of their work force, which may reveal trends in employee morale, commitment, or motivation. Others have systematic methods for obtaining feedback from customers.

Proactive change does not respond in knee-jerk fashion. Rather, it interprets symptoms as "red flags": evidence of underlying problems requiring diagnosis, discussion, and a coordinated strategy for solving them.

Crisis

Often organizational change is caused by an unforeseen crisis that makes continuation of the status quo unthinkable. Major accidents—airline crashes, explosions at the workplace, consumers dying from a tainted product—stimulate investigations and procedural changes. The sudden death of a chief executive officer—especially after a long tenure during which that person had molded the organization—signals the end of the old regime and forces a reorientation of corporate posture. Similarly, the resignation of key managers, a strike by a critically important group of workers, loss of a major client or supplier, a drastic cutback in budget for a bureau or university, even spontaneous civil disturbances directed against an organization, may initiate a total revamping of policy, practice, and behavior. Crises are likely to become the stimulus for thorough self-assessment and reform.

Personal Goals

Not all organizational change is related to organizational effectiveness. Organizational goals reflect in part the preferences of those in influential positions; we will argue below that organizational change inevitably is shaped by political forces.

Leaders, interest groups, and coalitions have their own goals: to see the company become more aggressive, to shape the organization around some distinctive theme, to cast a particular corporate image, to further some ideology or philosophy. Seldom are these goals espoused in precisely those forms, at least for the record or for public consumption. More frequently they are clothed in rationalizations about their presumed effect on profits or service. Changes in informal power structures within organizations—such as Young Turks tilting the balance against the Old Guard, or a family losing control of a traditionally family-operated firm—frequently signal the onset of change.

Change in Corporate Strategy

An organization, like the one described in Focus on International OB, may undertake comprehensive change even when there is no indication of immediate problems. Trends, potential difficulties, or opportunities may prompt a decision to enter new markets, pursue a strategy of growth, become less dependent on certain suppliers, switch from a centralized to a

FOCUS ON INTERNATIONAL OB

Opportunity Meets Resistance

The United States restored diplomatic relations with China in 1979. The mainland offered large markets, low labor costs, and a strategic location for exporting to the rest of Asia and competing with the Japanese. Seizing the opportunity, American Motors Corp. (AMC) culminated a four-year, on-again/off-again negotiation with the Chinese government with an agreement to jointly produce jeeps in Beijing. The newly created Beijing Jeep Co. (BJC) was the largest manufacturing agreement to date between China and a foreign corporation (Mann, 1989). AMC's stock jumped 40 percent in two weeks, and the Detroit *Free Press* said the move "could turn out to be one of the shrewdest industrial strokes of the decade."

But AMC officials soon discovered that contract signings often mark the beginning, not the end, of a business negotiation. The Chinese sought new concessions, including salary increases for their top managers, changes in the nature of the new jeep, and how it would be made. The Americans wanted it just like other AMC jeeps; the Chinese wanted a military jeep for the People's Liberation Army. The Chinese relented on this last point—at least publicly. But other problems developed. The first Chinese Cherokee had to be pushed off the line; it couldn't be driven because workers hadn't tightened the clutch. China imposed severe foreign exchange restric-tions, greatly hampering Beijing Jeep Company. Moreover, when the first 200 Cherokees were sold to a Chinese government agency, the agency refused to pay for them.

The Americans had hoped to produce and sell 40,000 Cherokees annually by 1990. But the Chinese were less interested in the modern, technologically superior Cherokee—which represented huge potential profits for AMC—than in an old Chinese jeep, the BJ212. In 1986, of the 24,500 jeeps the venture produced, only 2,000 were Cherokees. The rest were the old Chinese jeeps, most of which were distributed through the central planning techniques established in the 1950s.

Still, sales were good enough to say that things were going well for BJC. Then on June 3, 1989, Chinese troops killed thousands of people in Tiananmen Square. The American executives left the country, and BJC resumed operations under Chinese management. Throughout the experi-ence, AMC was frustrated by the same cultural and bureaucratic obstacles faced by other private businesses and even by Christian missionaries trying a century ago to convert Chinese souls. "From the outside China has always seemed malleable. From the inside it seems deceptive, intractable, and endlessly capable of thwarting change" (Mann, 1989, p. 152).

decentralized structure, or adopt new technologies. All of these strategic decisions require changing the behavior of people in the organization. A "new order" is needed to put such strategies into effect.

Strategy responds to opportunities and challenges in the external environment and also to the stage of development of the organization. Organization theorists who have studied the histories of firms note that companies go through a characteristic sequence of growth stages. The type of strategy appropriate to the entrepreneurial stage — when the firm is small, battling the odds against survival, and seeking to grasp and maintain a toehold in some niche of the market — typically becomes obsolete when the firm undergoes rapid growth. At a later stage, still a different strategy mix becomes imperative when the firm tries to consolidate its position in periods of slower growth and stability. Effective transition from one stage to another requires a comprehensive program of organization change.

RESISTANCE TO CHANGE

AMC's experience in China illustrated a failure of stratetic change, due in part to unanticipated problems and external forces hindering its plans. The fact that the Chinese blocked AMC's intentions could be dismissed by some as the predictable result of a tradition-bound, unique, and unyielding culture. But the fact is, virtually all changes meet with more resistance than initiators bargain for — and the resistors are often inside the organization.

Many members of the organization respond with dogged resistance to altering the status quo. Since the Industrial Revolution began, workers have at times sought — sometimes violently — to block the introduction of new technology. As we dicovered in Chapter 11, supervisors and lower-level managers have balked at large-scale job redesign; even lower-level employees, the presumed beneficiaries of such changes, have fought them. Divisional managers have fought against realignment of corporate structure. In schools, even the proposal to adopt a different textbook can touch off a frenzy of resistance.

Early perspectives on resistance to change construed it either as an unhealthy trait of the particular persons demonstrating it or as a deep-rooted frailty of human nature in general. Not infrequently, those proposing change and confronting resistance viewed it as defensive, irrational, or pathological. The solution to overcoming resistance, it seemed, lay in "treating" the resistance by some therapeutic device.

We now realize that to view resistance to change as a form of irrationality is at best simplistic, if not self-serving on the part of those advocating change. The inescapable reality of organizational change is that it never redounds to the equal benefit of all parties affected, and usually — at least in the short run — some parties lose. It is therefore instructive to regard most forms of resistance to change as eminently rational behavior based in self-interest.

Reasons for Resistance

What do people lose as a consequence of change? They may lose job security, or at least have good reason to believe they will lose it. The Luddites who wrecked the new textile machines in the early days of the Industrial Revolution feared they would become expendable; more recently, companies installing robotics and other computer technologies have had to contend with labor strife for the same reason. Even when workers grudgingly admit that new technologies are crucial to remaining competitive, and resign themselves to cooperating, they have to "avoid thinking too hard about the loss of overtime pay, the diminished probability of jobs for their sons and daughters, the fears of seeming incompetent in a strange new milieu, or the possibility that the company might welsh on its promise not to lay off workers" (Zuboff, 1988, p. 4).

Changes in formal structure or work flow may drastically reduce the power and status of certain administrators; some offices may survive in little more than window-dressing form. The result for many people is an undesirable loss of autonomy because of new procedures, controls, and constraints; people resist any increase in dependence on others in their sphere of action.

The notion of "sunk cost" also is useful in accounting for resistance to change (Kerr & Kerr, 1972). People lose their investments in the status quo if long years of learning and mastering a set of operations have to be written off as a result of change. Anyone comfortable with an established routine will shrink from seeing this routine shattered and having to "gear up" all over again for the inevitable messy, inefficient relearning process. The "hassle factor" does not make a particularly eloquent argument, but it is not to be underestimated as a motive for resisting change.

The Politics of Change

To think of resistance to change as a rational response to the threat of losing security, status, autonomy, and investment in the status quo leads naturally to the consideration of organizational change as a political process. On one side are those who favor change: on the other side are the change resisters. What strategies and tactics will unfold?

Both sides will seek early on to appeal to those who are uncommitted, with no strong feelings for or against the change. Appeals to this group may take the forms of lobbying, distortion, propaganda, persuasion, cashing in credits from old favors, implied threats, appeals to loyalty and friendship, or mixtures of all of the above.

The issues central to the proposed changes cause a realignment of cliques (Chapter 18) — each of which is usually too small by itself to impose a resolution of the conflict — into larger, but more loosely held, coalitions. Both sides, in appealing to the uncommited, will attempt to invoke the name of some revered or prestigious individual (like the chief executive officer, the founder of the company, or an industry leader). Both sides will attempt (in public appeals) to show the implications for long-run profitability, service to the public, and other abstract goals.

The forces for change will usually find that winning over the uncommitted is a necessary but not sufficient condition for actually ushering in a change program. Frequently the resisters, even if a small minority, will include critically placed individuals or groups who, even if not able to block change, have the potential to sabotage it when put into operation. Successfully implementing change requires some means of co-opting these groups. This usually necessitates substantial modifications of the originally proposed program. Finalized change programs often contain patched-up arrangements and tack-ons that preserve the core concepts of the original, yet make the necessary concessions to resisters. The end result is somewhat less than total satisfaction by any particular interest group, but a workable arrangement for preserving goodwill.

Managing Resistance to Change

Because of the breadth and depth of employee resistance, managers often are frustrated in their attempts to create change. At the same time, managers underestimate their ability to positively influence others during a change. Several methods can be used to manage resistance.

One means of accommodating resisters is to invite their *participation* in the planning, design, and process of carrying out change programs. A classic field experiment by Coch and French in 1948 (this study was also reviewed in Chapter 18) demonstrated that workers allowed to help plan the installation of new production methods subsequently showed less resistance to learning and adopting the new methods. Since then, participation has been used effectively in introducing changes ranging from new technologies on the shop floor to redirection of corporate strategy. Controversial new programs, like employee drug testing, may go more smoothly if employees have a hand in shaping the program (Crant & Bateman, 1989).

One explanation for the effect of participation in dissolving resistance is ego-involvement (Miles, 1965). Providing a participative forum may give affected parties a sense of personal identification with the proposed change, thus leading to a commitment to see the change effectively implemented. But the effect of participation may also be explained in other ways. First, there is the straightforward explanation that real (as opposed to ceremonial) participation gives the affected parties an opportunity to veto, modify, or subvert those elements of the change program that they consider most threatening. Broad participation may reduce resistance, but it may be at the expense of watering down the most important features of the change, in which case participation may be a questionable strategy. More positively, participation may provide sufficient information about the nature and consequences of the change so that anxiety is reduced and distorted rumors are laid to rest.

There are many other techniques for overcoming resistance to change. One of the most common and easiest is to *educate* employees about the change. This involves communicating both the nature of the change and, ideally, the reasons behind the change. In the example of drug-testing programs, employees may be more receptive if they see a strong need for (and benefits from) such a program because of its potential impact on accident rates, insurance costs, absenteeism, and productivity. Employees who are not aware of the logic behind management decisions are not likely to support the new ideas. Also, employees should be informed about the change soon enough to give them ample time to prepare for any anticipated disruptions.

As difficult changes unfold, it becomes particularly important for managers to exhibit the kinds of leadership behaviors conveying *support* (referred to in Chapter 19 as considerate or supportive leadership). This includes listening to problems, expressing encouragement, and allaying concerns as employees become anxious about new expectations or conditions. With employee drug testing, support can take the form of rehabilitation via employee assistance programs, as opposed to punishment by dismissal.

Finally, resistance to change may be overcome through changes in the *reward structure*. In negotiated agreements, management might offer a union more representation in decision making in return for some work rule changes, or wage consessions for the union's support of a new productivity program. Similarly, an individual's support of a proposed change in corporate strategy can be "bought" through an immediate favor or with promise of support on some pet project.

Coercion can be used in similar ways. People can be threatened, implicitly or explicitly, with job loss, a low pay raise, and loss of promotion opportunities, if they fail to accept a change. This approach has its drawbacks, of course, but may be necessary if time is short, when it is clear that the change will be an unpopular one, and when other methods have failed.

Making Waves, or, Change from Below

The impetus for change does not always come from top management; the resistance to be overcome does not always come from below. Lower-level employees may make positive suggestions, or request or demand reform, and management may resist these initiatives.

According to O'Day (1974), management faced with subordinate dissent has two primary goals: to control reformers so they do not succeed, and to absolve themselves of any wrongdoing in the matter. Organizations adopt changes that accommodate dissidents only when intimidation rituals fail to silence reformers. The intimidation process begins with *nullification* — management assures subordinate reformers that their accusations are invalid, or offers to look into the matter without any intention of actually doing so. If the reformer persists, *isolation* is applied as the troublemaker is physically separated from peers and other potential sources of support. Continued agitation leads to *defamation,* as the organization impugns the reformer's character, challenges his motives, and questions his competence. If the reformer's credibility still is not eroded, the final step in the intimidation process is *expulsion,* or firing.

Despite the apparent power of the organization to squash internal dissent, things have changed dramatically in recent years. *Whistleblowing* — publicly accusing one's employing organization of wrongdoing — is on the rise. Furthermore, the balance of power is shifting more toward the individual. Employee rights have become a major legal issue, making it difficult for organizations to punish employees unjustly (Ewing, 1989). These forces are making dissent a more successful mechanism for change than in the past.

Even middle managers with innovative ideas valuable to the organization must anticipate and actively manage resistance by management. Creative proposals representing positive change can threaten higher-ups, or simply represent too big a hassle compared to the status quo of business-as-usual. Successful innovators are not just "idea people," but managers of the change process who set their ideas in motion (Kanter, 1982). They make presentations to higher-ups to communicate the advantages of their ideas; they marshall coalitions of supporters and accumulate money, information, and other resources to enhance their power; they bend rules, run interference, and otherwise make it as easy as possible for people to go along with the change; they involve bosses, peers, and subordinates in planning and decision making; they promise participants a share in the rewards from their successes. In these ways, innovators manage resistance and overcome organizational inertia.

THE PSYCHOLOGY OF CHANGE

In the most appealing and enduring metaphor yet conceived for understanding the requirements of successfully changing behavior, Lewin (1947) proposed a three-step model. The first step involves *unfreezing* the forces acting on an individual to maintain current behavior. Current behavior is supported by a web of interlocking variables that include the formal reward system, social reinforcement from the group, defense mechanisms used to protect against psychological threat, cues and "props" in the surrounding environment, and the individual's conception of what is proper role behavior. Successfully unfreezing the forces maintaining old behavior often requires shock treatment: disconfirming feedback about the efficacy of current behavior that is so direct and threatening that it pierces any perceptual defenses and overrides the effect of reinforcements for current behavior. To stimulate major organizational change, managers might develop dissatisfaction with the status quo among stakeholders by focusing on important business problems like lower profits, poor quality, or loss of market share (Beer & Walton, 1990).

The second stage is *moving*. Once the unfreezing process has occurred, and only then, the individual must be offered a very clear and attractive option representing new patterns of behavior and the rationale for this behavior. This may take the form of a new role model — a real person who can demonstrate the competence and efficacy of different patterns of behavior. Alternatively, the person may be given a cognitive map—a conceptual model, a theory, or a rationale—so that the person may devise and experiment with a new role conception. At the organizational level, leaders can communicate their vision of the structure, systems, and processes required in the future. This vision often can be developed by visiting "leading-edge" organizations to see how they operate (Beer & Walton, 1990).

Finally, the new patterns of behavior must undergo *refreezing*. The changed behavior must be supported by the formal and informal reward system if it is to endure. The refreezing stage is perhaps the most difficult of all, because the new behavior patterns are weak and often ineffective at first and cause a heightened, awkward sense of self-consciousness. Thorough reengineering of the work environment may be essential to reinforce the new behavior, to avoid punishing the new behavior, and to extinguish the residual components of old, undesired responses.

Unsuccessful efforts to induce significant and lasting change in organizational behavior generally can be traced to failure in one of the three stages described above. Either they fail to significantly alter the forces maintaining old behavior; they fail to offer a clear, satisfying alternative; or they fail to "stamp in" the new behavior. Any stimulus for change that does not change these variables either will be resisted or, at the most, the change will be only temporary or cosmetic.

CHANGING THE SITUATION VERSUS CHANGING THE PEOPLE

> During the period of severe electricity shortage, a university tried to help out in two ways: cards reading "Save a watt—turn off a switch" were placed everywhere, and janitors removed half the light bulbs from all fixtures. These are the two principal approaches to change: change the people or change the situation. [Webber, 1979, p. 498]

"Change the people" usually refers to attempts to change behavior by first changing attitudes, opinions, or value systems. This may take the form of promotional campaigns; providing new information via memos, conferences, or brochures; or special training programs. "Change the situation," by contrast, is a strategy of altering the technological environment or the formal structure (e.g., reward system, hierarchical arrangements, reporting relationships) in order to change behavior directly.

For example, suppose you (as company president or a human resources officer reporting to the president) seek to generate more innovation and creativity among your managers and professionals. Strategies of changing the people might include sending them to creativity workshops, persuading them that innovation is valued by the organization, and dismissing current people and attempting to recruit and hire creative innovators. But, this approach

TABLE 21–2

How to Stifle Innovation

1. Regard any new idea from below with suspicion – because it is new, and because it is from below.
2. Express your criticisms freely; let people know they can be fired at any time.
3. Treat identification of problems as signs of failure.
4. Control everything carefully.
5. Make sure that information is not freely given out to managers.
6. Assign to lower-level managers, in the name of delegation and participation, responsibility for figuring out how to cut back, lay off, move people around, or otherwise implement threatening decisions you have made, and get them to do it quickly.
7. Above all, never forget that you, the higher-ups, already know everything important about the business.

SOURCE: From R. M. Kanter; *The change masters* (New York: Simon & Schuster, 1983).

may be inadequate; as Table 21–2 indicates, obstacles to innovation often are situational (Kanter, 1983). Such environmental constraints need to be eradicated, while innovation is encouraged and actively reinforced.

In practice, the issue really is not so much which of the two strategies is more effective, but in what sequence they are used. Ultimately, either one alone is likely to be ineffective. A program aimed at changing attitudes may be successful to that extent (i.e., it may actually change attitudes), but – for reasons we noted in Chapter 7 – it cannot be assumed that attitudes will predict behavior very well. On the other hand, changing the situation as a direct means of inducing change in behavior without corresponding attitude change may generate frustrations that lead to displaced aggression, particularly if the change is perceived as coercive.

The optimal strategy would aim at changing both attitudes and the situation in alternating, overlapping phases. For example, structural change might be preceded by announcements that give the rationale for the change, a description of the change, and the expected consequences. After the early stages of implementation, attempts at persuasion can be more specific and aimed at helping people internalize the goals of subsequent structural change.

PROGRAMS FOR CHANGING BEHAVIOR IN ORGANIZATIONS

There are five common approaches to changing behavior in organizations: changing personnel, management development, survey feedback, employee involvement, and organization development.

Changing Personnel

The simplest and most popular method of changing organizations is to change their leaders. A school of business that seeks to start emphasizing scholarly research will recruit a new dean with a strong academic reputation, while a school that hopes to foster greater interaction with the business community will seek someone with status in a prestigious corporation. Business periodicals frequently report on companies that select particular candidates as CEOs in order to make the firm more aggressive in the marketplace, more cost conscious, or more socially responsive.

Change in leadership can be effective at the unfreezing stage because it forces members of the organization to wonder whether old behavior will continue to be appropriate and rewarded. In the early days of a new regime, people look (sometimes desperately) for clues as to who and what will now be rewarded, how existing cliques and coalitions might be realigned, and what projects will be assigned top priority.

Existing leadership can also attempt proactive organizational change through personnel choices at lower levels, including the rank and file. Many managers doubt the usefulness of trying to change the personalities, attitudes, and habits of people already in residence and question whether it is worth trying to "teach old dogs new tricks." They prefer, instead, to recruit new people with background, motives, and skills that are congruent with the contemplated new order.

Sometimes, in struggling organizations, boards hire turnaround specialists who clean house by firing the entire top management team or announcing massive layoffs. Alternatively, top executives fire managers more selectively, change the rank and file through attrition and retirement (as with IBM's 1989 announcement that it was trimming 10,000 jobs), or possibly through the selection of people added as the work force grows.

Managers must also be aware of major personnel changes currently taking place in a more reactive fashion. The work force of the year 2000 will be smaller, older, lacking in needed skills (including literacy), and much more diversified in terms of gender, race, and nationality (Offermann & Gowing, 1990). This is creating major challenges for companies who must compete for a smaller labor pool, make maximal use of each employee, provide skill training, balance the demands of work and family, and manage different groups of varied attitudes, values, and expectations. Companies that respond passively to these challenges will suffer from imposed, unmanaged change; others will take a leadership role, proactively manage these changes, and gain a competitive edge.

Management Development Programs

Many organizations invest heavily in educational programs for their managers as a means of promoting long-run organization development. Some companies send their most promising executive candidates to prestigious graduate programs. Many firms encourage officers to attend seminars conducted by business schools or professional consultants; others conduct their own in-house programs or subsidize self-directed study in correspondence courses. Some programs, at least the more ambitious ones, offer a combination of breadth and depth approximating a two-year MBA program, including all of the major functional areas (e.g., finance, marketing, operations management, human resources) of business administration.

Some companies send select groups of managers to Outward Bound-type programs: the managers learn a gut-level dimension of trust and cooperation as together they confront the rigors of rock climbing, whitewater rafting, ocean sailing, and living in the wilderness. Simulations, which involve participation in realistic business games or other representations of real-world organizational and managerial activities, often are used to teach problem-solving, leadership, and other skills (Thornton & Cleveland, 1990). Focus on Management describes a recent example of a cutting-edge management development program.

When the goal of these programs is training in specific knowledge areas (such as financial planning, use of the computer, implications of changes in government regulations), there is little reason to question their effectiveness in increasing participants' knowledge (a cognitive change). But when programs attempt to change attitudes and values as an indirect means to changing behavior (for example, ethics or leadership style), it is much less clear that such programs accomplish their objective. Such programs may succeed at the unfreezing stage of changing behavior, particularly if participants are removed from the office and exposed to fellow participants from diverse organizational cultures. The more formidable obstacle arises with the "refreezing" of new behavior patterns when participants return to the office. If the new behavior is not reinforced by the formal reward system or informally by co-workers, superiors, and subordinates, the new behavior tends to extinguish rapidly — even if the changes in attitudes persist for some time.

For example, a classic study reported the impact of a leadership training program for foremen from an agricultural equipment manufacturer (Fleishman, 1953). The program's goal was to improve skills in a relationships-oriented style of supervision (a previous study at the company had found that foremen lacking such skills had high levels of turnover and grievances among workers). At the program's conclusion, the foremen showed significant changes in their attitudes about the importance of warmth and supportiveness toward subordinates. But the foremen reported to higher-level supervisors who were much more oriented toward the "initiating structure" style of leadership — that is, planning, scheduling, pressure for production. Therefore, the higher-level bosses rewarded those behaviors among foremen and did not encourage any emphasis on human relations. Long-term changes in behavior were successful only among the few foremen who reported to bosses more inclined to the "consideration" aspect of supervision.

Survey Feedback

Many organizations use comprehensive audits of employee opinions as an approach to change. You may recall from Chapter 13 that opinion surveys initially evolved in industry from efforts to study the causes and effects of job attitudes. Subsequently, surveys became a standard tool for monitoring employee morale. They have evolved still further in many instances as an integral part of corporate information systems, going beyond measures of

FOCUS ON MANAGEMENT

The Global Leadership Program

A recent five-week executive development program aimed at training business leaders to be global managers (Main, 1989). Professor Noel Tichy of the University of Michigan's business school assembled 21 senior executives from major corporations. The group included eight Americans, 10 Japanese, and one executive each from Britain, India, and Brazil.

Days started at 7:00 or 8:00 A.M. and lasted until long after dinner. The global executives attended lectures and seminars and were constantly analyzed, videotaped, and asked to reflect on their actions. During a weekend on Hurricane Island off the Maine Coast, with Outward Bound, they rappelled down a cliff and competed in teams building and paddling rafts. After a day of briefings in Washington, they were met at the airport in Detroit by news reporters hired to simulate planeside interviews. The executives were bombarded with tough questions about the *Exxon Valdez* and the Japanese sex scandals, among other things. Two-week, fact-finding missions to Brazil, India, and China revealed the trials of doing business globally. Returning to Michigan, each team made final written, oral, and video reports.

Consider a few of the lessons participants drew from the training:

One Japanese learned about communications in different cultures: "We are a homogenous people, and we don't have to speak as much as you do here in the United States. When we say one word, we understand 10, but here you have to say 10 to understand one."

The Americans were astonished when a Japanese wrote a report about the China motorcycle market projecting volumes and market shares through the year 2040. "The Americans could barely see to 1995," said one.

One American visiting India decided there was no way to work there because of the amount of government control and bureaucracy. But his Brazilian teammate explained how Brazilian businessmen made money coping with extreme inflation and government interference. And, his Japanese teammates described how they used government agencies to their advantage. The American reconsidered his initial conclusion: "I saw there's more than one way a business can be successful" (Main, 1989, p. 78).

job satisfaction to reflect members' perceptions of the "state of the organization" and to enlist their opinions and suggestions concerning what should be changed. Sears, Roebuck & Co., for example, conducts an opinion survey in every one of its units at least every three years; the surveys probe attitudes not only about pay and supervision, but also about store esthetics, window displays, advertising, and the corporate image in the community.

In survey feedback, groups of managers and employees discuss survey findings. Once the survey data have been collected and statistically analyzed, a feedback process can begin at the top. For example, the president and the major divisional vice presidents meet and compare the results. Each vice president is able to see the summary data for his or her whole division and discuss the problems unique to this division, the implications of the findings, and any themes common to several divisions.

The next series of feedback discussions occurs as each vice president meets with subordinate department heads to discuss survey findings specific to each. The process continues until first-level supervisors discuss with operative-level employees the issues raised in each work group by the survey.

The survey feedback approach to change offers several advantages. First, it gives an objective and factual basis to problems that might otherwise be dismissed as groundless complaints by a disgruntled minority. Second, it includes the opinions of many participants who might otherwise feel inhibited from openly voicing criticisms of current policies and procedures. Third, the members of an organizational unit are able to see data about the issues with which they are most familiar and that are most relevant to them; the group discussion allows them to dig deeper into the analysis. Fourth, the group members become the immediate agents for putting into effect any major changes.

An important assumption underlying this method is that negative feedback can produce the desired "unfreezing." The method assumes that a manager who sees statistical evidence of, say, poor morale among subordinates will feel pressure toward change. In fact, the manager may react in a defensive fashion, disputing the validity of the data (citing any of the shortcomings we noted in Chapter 2 with respect to self-report research methods) and rejecting any interpretations of the data that might be seen as criticizing current practice. He or she might also discourage group discussion of the findings. Perhaps for this reason, some companies prefer to have outside consultants rather than the supervisor conduct group sessions to discuss survey results.

Quality Circles and Employee Involvement

Japan's incredible industrial success has led some American firms to adopt certain Japanese management techniques. One noteworthy example in the 1970s and 1980s was the widespread use of quality circles, or QCs. Like survey feedback, QCs were designed to stimulate an upward communications flow, from the rank and file to middle and higher management. But QCs also went an important step further, in that they regularly and actively solicit employee solutions to the problems they perceive. Now, in the 1990s, quality circles are just one form of employee involvement (EI) programs offering more worker participation in decisions and intended to increase labor-management cooperation, productivity, and U.S. industry competitiveness.

A QC is a group of employees, typically from similar jobs or the same work group, who meet periodically to identify and solve work-related problems. Each QC usually has an appointed group leader, and members are trained in techniques of problem solving and group process. Groups focus on departmental and organizational goals and submit proposals for change to higher-level managers. A steering committee typically reviews proposals, accepts or rejects them, and allocates resources for implementation.

Proponents of QCs say that properly implemented programs will yield many benefits, including increased productivity, higher product quality, cost savings, and higher levels of attendance and worker morale. As one example, *Industry Week* reported that at Nippon Kokon K.K., suggestions from thousands of employees involved in quality circles led to savings of $86 million in one year. Lockheed and other U.S. companies also have reported impressive results.

QCs can improve quality and cut costs, but are merely "off-line" discussion groups; they don't reorganize jobs or generate greater autonomy for workers (Hoerr, 1989). In Japan, most decisions still are made by management and engineers. Even at NUMMI (New United Motors Manufacturing Inc.), the prototypic joint venture between GM and Toyota in Fremont, California, Japanese-style teams work on conventional assembly line doing limited tasks under first-line supervision.

Newer, more participative forms of EI in the United States diverge from Japanese QC practices. With the American team concept, workers gain not only a direct voice in shop-floor operations, but they also take over managerial duties. They hire new team members, organize work, order materials, schedule work and vacations, and gain greater voice in higher-level decisions. In many plants, workers are now paid for their knowledge rather than hours or productivity; they can raise their salaries by completing technical, economic, and behavioral courses. There may be only a couple of job classifications, as workers are cross-trained to perform all tasks. This flexibility means workers can fill in for absent co-workers, and teams can respond quickly to production changes. At a General Electric plant in North Carolina, where product models are changed a dozen times a day, the team approach combined with flexible automation has increased productivity by 250 percent.

Partly due to results like these, states including Massachusetts, Indiana, Ohio, Pennsylvania, and New York promote EI and provide support to companies and unions. Some scholars are calling for the federal government to encourage EI through tax credits. They see worker participation as a vital necessity for a national competitiveness strategy in future years (Hoerr, 1989).

Organization Development

Organization development (OD) covers a broad array of strategies aimed at making organizations more effective (Beer & Walton, 1990). It includes not only the major approaches we have already described, but changes in technology, reporting relationships, marketing and product policies, and

TABLE 21–3

Thirteen Major Families of Organization Development (OD) Interventions

1. *Diagnostic Activities:* fact-finding activities designed to ascertain the state of the system, the status of a problem, the "way things are." Traditional data-collection methods—including interviews, questionnaires, and meetings—are commonly used.
2. *Team-Building Activities:* activities designed to enhance the effective operation of system teams.
3. *Intergroup Activities:* activities designed to improve effectiveness of interdependent groups. The focus is on joint activities.
4. *Survey Feedback Activities:* analyzing data produced by a survey and designing action plans based on these data. Survey feedback activities are a major component of the diagnostic activities category, but they are important enough to be considered a separate category as well.
5. *Education and Training Activities:* activities designed to improve skills, abilities, and knowledge of individuals. There is a wide range of possible approaches, from T-group and sensitivity training, to structured experiential exercises, to lecturing and concentrating on technical, interpersonal, or other competencies.
6. *Technostructural or Structural Activities:* activities designed to improve the effectiveness of the technical or structural inputs and constraints affecting individuals or groups. Examples would include job enrichment, matrix structures, management by objectives, and physical settings interventions.
7. *Process Consultation Activities:* activities on the part of the consultant that help managers understand and act on human processes in organizations. This includes teaching skills in diagnosing and managing communications, leadership, cooperation and conflict, and other aspects of interpersonal functioning.
8. *Grid Organization Development Activities:* activities developed by Robert Blake and Jane Mouton, constituting a six-phase change model involving the entire organization. The phases include upgrading individual managers' leadership abilities, team improvement activities, intergroup relations, corporate planning, development of implementation tactics, and evaluation of change and future directions.
9. *Third-Party Peacemaking Activities:* activities designed to manage conflict between two parties, and conducted by some third party, typically a skilled consultant.
10. *Coaching and Counseling Activities:* activities that entail working with individuals to better enable them to define learning goals, learn how others see their behavior, explore alternative behaviors, and learn new behaviors.
11. *Life- and Career-Planning Activities:* activities that help individuals identify life and career objectives, capabilities, areas of strength and deficiency, and strategies for achieving objectives.
12. *Planning and Goal-Setting Activities:* activities that include theory and experience in planning and goal setting. They may be conducted at the level of the individual, group, and total organization.
13. *Strategic Management Activities:* activities that help key policymakers identify their organization's basic mission and goals; ascertain environmental demands, threats, and opportunities; and engage in long-range action planning.

SOURCE: W. French and C. Bell, *Organization Development* 4/e, © 1990, pp. 117-119. Adapted by permission of Prentice Hall, Inc. Englewood Cliffs, New Jersey.

investments in new facilities. Table 21–3 conveys the richness and variety of approaches in a summary of 13 major "families" of OD interventions.

OD usually denotes a strategy aimed at changing the climate or culture of an organization. Its practitioners are usually consultants or corporate officials with advanced training in the behavioral sciences. The clientele are organizations seeking to foster an organizational culture based on trust, open and constructive handling of conflict, and receptivity to expertise and information as the ultimate basis of influence. Unlike forms of training and management development that emphasize cognitive changes among individual participants, OD views the work group as the elemental building block of the organization. It places strong emphasis on team development through collaborative problem solving, openness in expressing emotional as well as task needs, a tolerance for conflict, and periodic self-assessment.

The Roots of OD   OD traces its roots to the popularity of sensitivity training in the 1940s and 1950s as a form of management development. The goal of sensitivity training was to give the person insight into his or her own behavior and how that behavior affected others. It also sought to increase a person's skill in giving feedback to others about their behavior and to enable people to receive such feedback without the distortion caused by psychological defense mechanisms.

A standard procedure for sensitivity-training classes (or "T-groups") consisted of bringing together a group (usually strangers to each other) in an isolated retreat and, under the unobtrusive but watchful eye of a trainer, having them discuss their immediate reactions to each other. No other agenda or structure was provided. The intent was that participants generate their own behavioral data and study it. The trainer intervened only to prevent the group from straying away from the here-and-now focus of discussion, to make sure that participants based their feedback to each other on behavioral data, and to keep the level of psychological threat within acceptable bounds.

The consensus of expert opinion on sensitivity training was that it often reached its immediate goal, namely to make individual managers more interpersonally sensitive. On the other hand, there was scant evidence that this made them more effective at their jobs. The conclusion was that sensitivity training was an effective means of individual growth and development, but not necessarily effective for improving organizational performance (Campbell & Dunnette, 1968).

Most current OD efforts attempt to place the goals of sensitivity training—openness, trust, interpersonal awareness and sensitivity—into the task-oriented context of the organization. The focus of OD is only incidentally on individual enrichment; its orientation is toward the work group and relationships between groups. OD, as a rule, does not pull individual members of the organization out of their environment, but attempts to incorporate organizational relationships within the training sessions.

The Process of OD   OD is guided by a change agent, usually an external consultant or corporate officer trained in the concepts and methods of the applied behavioral sciences. The change agent typically begins with a thoroughgoing effort at diagnosis of the current organizational culture. This stage of OD may consist of interviews with individual managers, questionnaire administration and feedback, or exploratory discussions with work groups. The major goal of this phase of OD is to provide disconfirming feedback to participants attesting to the limitations of the existing culture, to unfreeze the members from complacency with the existing order, and to generate a sense of commitment from top to bottom to strive for more effective methods of working together.

The second stage of OD builds on the feedback provided from the first. Emphasis is usually placed on team development and constructive methods of handling conflict between groups. Participants may also experiment with structural changes. Subsequent stages of training aim at helping members systematically and critically evaluate the changes they have made. Assessments make use of "hard" performance criteria (such as profits, sales, scrap rates) as well as the "softer" data provided by opinion surveys and self-diagnosis. The more ambitious OD programs (which may run for several years) incorporate long-range planning and policymaking into the training exercises.

OD is not intended as a one-shot injection to cure a particular illness. Many OD specialists insist that their goal is not to cure a sick organizational patient. Rather, they aim to help essentially healthy organizations become more adept at continual self-renewal by means of a culture that reduces interpersonal threat, enhances collaborative problem solving, and legitimizes constructive conflict. The Close-Up provides such an example, of General Electric's ongoing OD effort.

The Effectiveness of OD   Any OD undertaking represents an uncontrolled field experiment, and it is impossible to attribute the outcomes to any one variable. Many organizations, such as Texas Instruments Incorporated and Donnelly Mirrors, have claimed a history of success with OD; others have been disappointed. Some programs have been aborted in the initial stages because of turnover at top executive levels, because politically powerful officials felt threatened by potential outcomes of the program, or because immediate financial crises overshadowed long-run development. In some instances, OD consultants themselves have terminated the program because they felt they did not have the full support of top management—which is a precondition for effective OD. Furthermore, the time scope of most OD programs is so great that it is nearly impossible to predict when the full benefits of OD will be reflected in unambiguous performance criteria. OD must rest its case on a hopeful but unclear set of evidence.

A current issue surrounds the effectiveness of different OD programs in different countries and cultures. For example, various conflict management and team building interventions that have been successful in the United States have failed in Italy, perhaps because the Italian culture is not as

CLOSE-UP

Workout at GEMS

GE Medical Systems (GEMS), the world leader in medical diagnostic imaging equipment, recently undertook a major effort to transform its human organization (Tichy & Charan, 1989). With the involvement of outside faculty members, its new "Work-Out" program proceeded through several initial stages. First, the consultants conducted in-depth interviews with managers at all levels of GEMS. The interviews revealed several areas of dissatisfaction, including pay and reward systems, career development systems, and an atmosphere characterized by blame and fear rather than trust and problem solving.

Second, Jack Welch, chairman and CEO of General Electric, visited GEMS headquarters for a half-day meeting with Work-Out participants. Middle managers offered constructive criticism and advice about senior management as well as about themselves. For example, they said senior management should listen better, stop pontificating, and respect others' opinions. As for themselves, they promised to make bolder decisions and not accept the status quo.

Next, 50 GEMS employees, including the senior vice president and informal leaders from finance, sales, service, marketing, manufacturing, and technology, met officials for a five-day Work-Out session. The objective was to build trust and more effective communication between senior staff and functional managers. Each functional group developed a vision of where its operations are headed, and cross-functional teams cooperated in solving business problems. The session ended with individuals and teams signing almost 100 contracts pledging to implement new ways of operating.

Since the five-day session, Work-Out has gained momentum. Managers from different areas conduct workshops aimed at implementing the new values and procedures. A Work-Out steering committee holds information meetings for field staff all over the world. And Jack Welch receives regular briefings on the progress of the Work-Out program (Tichy & Charan, 1989).

receptive to using a group context to deal with emotionally charged issues (Boss & Mariono, 1987). In Finland, an American managerial grid program led to visible, strong changes initially, but the impact was short-term with no deeper organizational impact (Tainio & Santalainen, 1984). The investigators concluded that even though American programs are frequently imported by other countries, resistance to them is growing, and that OD efforts must take into account cultural differences.

OD too often has been plagued by "evangelical hucksterism" (Strauss, 1973). No procedures for professional certification have evolved to separate competent, qualified OD consultants from the opportunistic amateurs who practice a simplistic set of gimmicks. Other detractors argue that OD glosses over the reality of organizational politics and is based on naive assumptions about the resolution of conflicts between people contending for power.

Nonetheless, OD goes well beyond previous forms of training in that it aims at something more than cognitive and attitudinal changes of individuals. OD can attain systematic behavior change, including greater information flow and collaboration, people taking responsibility, managers leading by vision and functioning strategically, effective problem solving, and experimentation and risk taking (Porras & Hoffer, 1986). OD seeks systematic change by treating the larger contexts of the work group, structural relationships between groups, and the task environment of the organization. Moreover, it is based on well-supported empirical findings about group dynamics. Perhaps more important, it has made considerable strides toward encouraging and developing the procedures needed to monitor its own effectiveness. While these methods do not permit unqualified conclusions about cause-and-effect relationships, the very insistence on a posture of databased self-assessment is noteworthy.

INSTITUTIONALIZING CHANGE

Earlier, we presented a model of change that involved three steps: unfreezing, moving, and refreezing. As GE appears to understand with its Work-Out program, only if the new behaviors are "refrozen" will the changes persist over a long period of time. What does it take to ensure that change will endure?

Changes become institutionalized when everyone understands the behavior, believes in it, performs it, and acknowledges that others have also deemed it appropriate and consistent with broader organizational values (Goodman & Dean, 1982). According to Goodman and his colleagues, five processes directly affect the degree to which a change becomes institutionalized: socialization, commitment, reward allocation, diffusion, and sensing and calibration.

Socialization was described in Chapter 15 as the process by which new organizational members are taught the organizational ropes. Here, the idea is expanded to include the process by which organizational changes are conveyed to existing employees. Information must be transmitted about the required new forms of work behavior. In addition, as discussed earlier in this chapter, employees should be educated about the reasons for change. Ultimately, as the new behaviors become more firmly entrenched among existing employees, new recruits will be socialized directly into the new ways of doing things.

Relatedly, one way to increase employees' *commitment* to the new ways is to have them take an active role in socializing new members. Training others, explaining the new system, or otherwise publicly implying agreement with the change may lead to more private agreement. Institutionalization also becomes more likely when commitment to the program is strong at higher levels of the organization, as well as when other groups throughout the organization are involved. Truer commitment also is generated when resistance to change is managed through processes like education, support, participation, and incentives, rather than through authority, manipulation, or coercion.

Reward allocation is crucial not just for overcoming initial resistance, but ultimately for institutionalizing the change as well. Goodman and Dean believe (and present evidence) that even job enrichment programs, with their newly created intrinsic rewards, are effective only in combination with extrinsic, contingent reinforcers. Learning new skills for performing different jobs, or jobs with added responsibility, may generate feelings of inequity if employees are not compensated for their greater worth to the organization. Generally, employees are much more likely to acquire and maintain new behaviors when their potential rewards outweigh the personal costs.

In a large organization, it is unlikely that a change within a single group will stabilize until there is some *diffusion* throughout the system. That is, a change in one group is more likely to become institutionalized if other groups, particularly those with which the focal group is interdependent, adopt the same patterns of change. As other groups make congruent changes, there are fewer pockets of resistance or antagonistic coalitions, and greater likelihood of mutual reinforcement and organizationwide commitment. If a change within a work group has repercussions for other groups, it must be accepted or reinforced—or at least not punished, resisted, or sabotaged—by the affected groups.

Finally, *sensing and recalibration* involve (1) determining whether the new work behaviors are performed adequately, and then (2) generating corrective actions. The role of sensing and recalibration is to activate the other processes (socialization, reward allocation, and so on) that are missing or poorly executed.

Often, there is a wide discrepancy between intended and actual work behaviors; moreover, organizations rarely have appropriate mechanisms for monitoring performance (Goodman & Dean, 1982). We now explicitly consider performance and its assessment during periods of organizational change.

ASSESSING ORGANIZATION CHANGE PROGRAMS

Successful organization-wide change often starts with innovations in outlying manufacturing plants or divisions. If the initial innovation is successful, the organization has a model for adoption by other subunits. The change then diffuses to other parts of the corporation, eventually changing the entire corporation culture (Beer & Walton, 1990).

To make valid decisions about whether an initial change *should* be disseminated throughout the organization, the effectiveness of the change must be assessed. Managers must determine whether a program is a success or a failure. However, like most managerial decisions, such determinations can be uncertain and complex. A program of organization change may succeed or fail in various ways and for any number of reasons. To adequately evaluate the effectiveness of organization change programs, criteria consistent with the goals of the program must be specified.

Effects of the Change Program

The desired effects of the change should be identified prior to program implementation. In fact, these desired outcomes should drive the selection of the program. For example, whether the problem is one of motivation, morale, or productivity should determine the relative usefulness of MBO, survey feedback, or EI programs.

The most common criteria involve measures of productivity like output volume or quality, or attitudinal and behavioral variables like job satisfaction, absenteeism, and turnover. These variables may be measured at the individual, work-group, departmental, or organizational levels.

The relevance of these variables may change over time. For example, job enrichment may have a short-term impact on employee satisfaction and attendance, a subsequent and intermediate effect on turnover, and an ultimate, longer-term impact on measures of organizational performance. Furthermore, the impact of a program on any single criterion may reveal different patterns of change over time.

Figure 21–1 portrays three common patterns of change. The dotted line shows immediate and dramatic improvement, only to decline rather quickly to prechange levels. This is the *Hawthorne effect,* in which workers immediately become more productive simply because they are flattered and excited that management is paying some attention to them and making minor improvements in their work environment. However, the changes are not significant enough to sustain high effort. Thus, performance increases are just a flash in the pan.

The darker solid line shows a pattern that declines immediately, but then steadily improves to high levels that are sustained over time. A new computer system in an office often has just such an effect. Productivity suffers due to unfamiliarity with procedures and lack of skills (not to mention high anxiety). As employees become comfortable with the system, however, its advantages become apparent.

Finally, the light solid line shows the ideal pattern of change. Here, the start-up is slow, but there is no short-term loss of productivity. The eventual benefits are large and enduring. The danger of this pattern is that it may portray change as managers *expect* it to occur; deviations from this ideal — say, in the form of short-term productivity drops — may cause frustrated managers or employees to give up too early on a program that

FIGURE 21–1
Three Patterns of Change in Results through Time

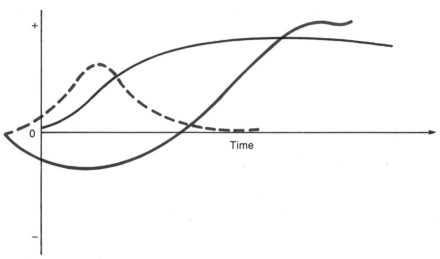

SOURCE: J. Gibson, J. Ivancevich, and J. Donnelly, Jr., *Organizations* (Homewood, Ill.: Business Publications/Irwin, 1985).

might have had long-term payoffs. For major changes, perhaps one should anticipate the pattern shown by the lighter line, and consider it merely a bonus if the immediate difficulties are not too severe.

Validity of the Change Program

Decision makers must determine (1) whether it was actually the change program, and not something else, that produced results; and (2) if the causal relationship between the program and its results can be generalized to other situations (Lawler, Nadler, & Mirvis, 1983). Three key considerations help in assessing these change program validities. First, criteria measurement must be done several times over a significant period of time. Measurements should be taken before, and several times during and after, the program. Referring back to Figure 21–1, you can see that in two of the three patterns of change, a single measurement taken shortly after the change is introduced would lead to erroneous conclusions.

Second, at least one comparison unit, or control group, should be used. By taking measurements in an otherwise comparable situation in which no change was introduced, it is easier to assess whether improvements (and problems) were in fact due to the change in question. Finally, appropriate statistical analysis will also help answer questions surrounding internal validity and generalizability. Chapter 2 offered more discussion of these important issues.

FIGURE 21–2

Framework for Assessing Costs and Benefits of Change Programs

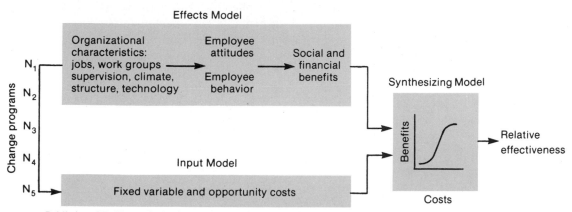

SOURCE: P. Mirvis and B. Macy, "Evaluating Program Costs and Benefits," in *Assessing Organizational Change*, ed. S. Seashore, E. Lawler, P. Mirvis, and G. Cammann (New York: John Wiley & Sons, 1983).

Valuation of the Change Program

The final aspect of assessment is the valuation of the results. The model in Figure 21–2 presents a framework for the financial assessment of change programs. The model depicts five change programs (X_1–X_5) and three distinct analytic components (Mirvis & Macy, 1983).

The first component is the *effects* model. It includes the measured effects of the change and the financial impact of these effects. For example, one can assess the monetary benefits associated with decreases in absenteeism, turnover, or accidents, or with increases in productivity or quality of service. Total savings, or savings on a per-employee basis, can be calculated. The value of higher morale or self-esteem in the work force and of improved life satisfaction or family relationships due to a more satisfying work situation are also important here.

The *input* model includes the costs of the change program. Fixed costs include overhead and salaries, wages, and benefits associated with employees' time diverted from normal work. Variable costs include direct program expenditures, such as fees paid to consultants and expenses associated with their activities. Opportunity costs are the value of foregone opportunities, or those in which the organization might have invested were it not for the resources allocated to the change program.

Finally, the *synthesizing* model compares program costs and benefits. The reader is referred to Mirvis and Macy (1983) for a useful discussion of cost-benefit, cost-effectiveness, and cost-utility criteria as well as a more complete introduction to human resource accounting and its use in assessing organizational change.

CONCLUSION

A critical task in coming decades will be to document the private benefits and public goods that result from planned organizational change (Mirvis & Macy, 1983). Through experimentation and assessment, both organizations and society can benefit from improved employee skills, satisfaction, teamwork, labor-management relations, and commitment to productive collaboration.

At this point, however, careful assessment coupled with a willingness to experiment has been the exception rather than the rule. Therefore, we have far to go in learning how organizational change programs can most improve organizational effectiveness and employee well-being. Careful attention to the ideas and issues raised in this chapter, and throughout the book, are requisite to future organizational and societal gains.

SUMMARY

Organizations change in either a reactive or a proactive fashion. Proactive change requires planning and the coordination of subsystems toward a well-defined target state. Reactive change, in contrast, occurs reflexively in response to problem symptoms. Inevitably, the process of change is influenced by the politics of coalition alignment and allegiance building. Because significant structural or policy changes usually redound to the comparative advantage of certain parties and to the detriment of others, proponents of change must be prepared to meet and manage resistance.

Resistance occurs because people fear loss of security, power, status, or autonomy. Moreover, investments in the status quo make it a hassle and a challenge to unlearn old methods and acquire new ones. Effectively managing resistance means inviting others' involvement in planning and implementing the change, communicating the reasons behind and benefits of the change, exhibiting supportive leadership, reinforcing the new behaviors, and sometimes using coercive measures.

Strategies of organizational change and development differ in the extent to which they emphasize changing the surrounding work environment versus changing personal attitudes and values. Successfully changing organizational behavior requires that the forces maintaining the status quo be "unfrozen" and that any changes be "refrozen" by reinforcement from the formal and informal reward systems.

Methods chosen by organizations to effect change include changing personnel, management development, survey feedback, employee involvement (EI) programs, and organization development (OD). OD uses concepts and methods from the behavioral sciences to transform the culture of an organization. OD emphasizes team development, collaborative modes of problem solving, constructive approaches to managing conflict, and interpersonal relationships built on trust and openness rather than threats and coercion.

Once change is introduced, it may or may not become institutionalized. Socialization, commitment, reward allocation, diffusion, and sensing and recalibration are vital processes in institutionalizing change. Given that there is often a wide discrepancy between intended and actual work behaviors, the costs and benefits of change programs should be carefully assessed using the effects, input, and synthesizing models.

CONCEPTS TO REMEMBER

Reactive change	Intimidation process	OD families
Proactive change	Whistleblowing	Sensitivity training
Antecedents of change	Unfreeze-move-refreeze model	Institutionalizing change
Reasons for resistance to change	Survey feedback	Valuation
	EI programs	Effects model
The politics of change	Quality circle	Input model
Methods of managing resistance to change	Organization development (OD)	Synthesizing model

---

QUESTIONS FOR DISCUSSION

1. What kinds of management development programs would probably be most effective at "unfreezing"? At "refreezing"?

2. Under what conditions might the undertaking of an OD program be ill-advised?

3. How would you define the "culture" of an organization? How is an organization's culture manifested? What effects might culture have on employees?

4. Why do you think careful assessment of change programs is a relative rarity?

5. Do executives today exhibit much willingness or ability to adapt to change and to experiment with new ideas? Why or why not?

6. Choose an organizational change you have experienced or read about extensively—the introduction of a new technology, a drug testing program, a tuition increase, whatever. Using concepts in this chapter, analyze: *(a)* people's reactions to the change; *(b)* how the change was managed; and (c) the effectiveness of the change.

REFERENCES

Beer, M., & Walton, E. (1990). Developing the competitive organization: Interventions and strategies. *American Psychologist* 45, 154-61.

Boss, R., & Mariono, M. (1987). Organization development in Italy. *Group & Organization Studies* 12, 245-56.

Campbell, J. P., & Dunnette, M. D. (1968). Effectiveness of T-group experiences in managerial training and development. *Psychological Bulletin* 70, 73-104.

Coch, L., & French, J. P. (1948). Overcoming resistance to change. *Human Relations* 1, 512-32.

Crant, J. M., & Bateman, T. (1989). Employee responses to drug testing programs. *Employee Rights and Responsibilities Journal*.

Ewing, D. W. (1989). *Justice on the job*. Cambridge, MA: Harvard Business School.

Fleishman, E. A. (1953). Leadership climate, human relations training, and supervisory behavior. *Personnel Psychology* 6, 205-22.

French, W., & Bell, C. (1990). *Organization development*. Englewood Cliffs, NJ: Prentice Hall.

Gibson, J., Ivancevich, J., & Donnelly, J. Jr. (1985). *Organizations*. Homewood, IL: Business Publications/Irwin.

Goodman, P., & Dean, J. (1982). Creating long-term organizational change. In Paul Goodman et al. (eds.), *Change in organizations*. San Francisco: Jossey-Bass.

Hoerr, J. (1989) The payoff from teamwork. *Business Week,* July 10, 56-62.

Kanter, R. M. (1982). The middle manager as innovator. *Harvard Business Review,* July-August, 95-105.

Kanter, Rosabeth Moss. (1983). *The change masters*. New York: Simon & Schuster.

Kerr, S., & Kerr, E. B. (1972). Why your employees resist perfectly "rational" changes. *Hospital Financial Management* 26, 4-6.

Lawler, E., Nadler, D., & Mirvis, P. (1983). Organizational change and the conduct of assessment research. In S. Seashore, E. Lawler, P. Mirvis, & C. Cammann (eds.), *Assessing organizational change*. New York: John Wiley & Sons.

Lewin, K. (1947). Frontiers in group dynamics. *Human Relations* 1, 5-41.

Mann, J. (1989). One company's China debacle. *Fortune,* November 6, 145-52.

Main, J. (1989). How 21 men got global in 35 days. *Fortune,* November 6, 71-9.

Miles, R. E. (1965). Human relations or human resources? *Harvard Business Review* 43(4), 148-63.

Mirvis, P., & Macy, B. (1983). Evaluating program costs and benefits. In S. Seashore, E. Lawler, P. Mirvis, & C. Cammann (eds.). *Assessing organizational change*. New York: John Wiley & Sons.

Mitroff, I., & Mohrman, S. (1987). The slack is gone: How the United States lost its competitive edge in the world economy. *Academy of Management Executive* 1, 65-70.

O'Day, R. (1974). Intimidation rituals: Reaction to reform. *Journal of Applied Behavioral Science* 10, 373-86.

Offermann, L., & Gowing, M. (1990). Organizations of the future: Changes and challenges. *American Psychologist* 45, 95-108.

Peters, T. (1987). A world turned upside down. *Academy of Management Executive* 1, 231-41.

Porras, J., & Hoffer, S. (1986). Common behavior changes in successful organization development efforts. *Journal of Applied Behavioral Science* 22, 477-94.

Strauss, G. (Winter 1973). Organizational development: Credits and debits. *Organizational Dynamics,* 2-18.

Sutton, R. & D'Aunno, T. (1989). Decreasing organizational size: Untangling the effects of money and people. *Academy of Management Review* 14, 194-212.

Tainio, R., & Santalainen, T. (1984). Some evidence for the cultural relativity of organizational development programs. *Journal of Applied Behavioral Science* 20, 93-111.

Thornton, G. C. III, & Cleveland, J. (1990). Developing managerial talent through simulation. *American Psychologist* 45, 190-99.

Tichy, N., & Charan, R. (1989). Speed, simplicity, self-confidence: An interview with Jack Welch. *Harvard Business Review,* September-October, 112-20.

Webber, R. A. (1979). *Management: Basic elements of managing organizations.* Homewood, IL: Richard D. Irwin.

Zuboff, S. (1988). *In the age of the smart machine.* New York: Basic Books.

Cases

THE PIEDMONT COMPANY*

The Piedmont Company, a large midwestern company with sales in excess of $2.5 billion, has experienced increasing difficulty in retaining highly qualified engineering and scientific personnel (technical and professional people) in its Technical Division. Many of those who have left expressed concern that the only way to get ahead in the company was to become a manager in the Technical Division or transfer to a nontechnical division such as marketing. They did not feel that adequate recognition was given to the individual contributor who preferred to develop his technical or professional expertise to the highest extent. Some of these technical and professional people who quit were managers who stated they were "forced" to accept managerial positions in order to advance their careers. As managers, however, they soon became dissatisfied and/or ineffective, with the net result that the company was losing good technical people and gaining poor managers.

The Piedmont Company is in a fairly competitive market which, although dominated by a few large firms, is most troubled by numerous small

---

*From R. S. Schuler, D. R. Dalton, and F. F. Huse, eds., *Case problems in management* (St. Paul, Minn.: West Publishing, 1983), pp. 87–90.

EXHIBIT 1
Organization Chart

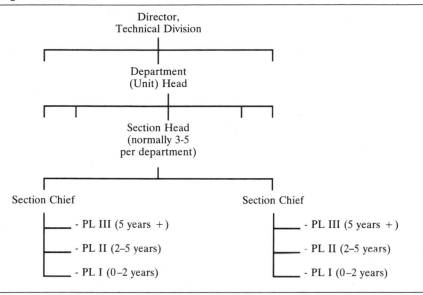

firms. These small firms have become more numerous and troublesome to Piedmont during the last 10 years because of the rapidly changing markets and technology in the manufacture of glass and foam containers. The small firms have been able to meet the changing consumer demand more readily than Piedmont because some of the recent technological breakthroughs have come from the labs of these small firms. Even more troublesome is that many of the technical and professional people at Piedmont have been leaving for these small firms.

The Technical Director, in reaction to this increasing problem, requested that the Organization Development (OD) Department explore the matter and make recommendations. Although the problem seemed rather urgent, the Technical Director did not impose any time restrictions on the OD Department.

The organization chart shown in Exhibit 1 represents a typical unit in the Technical Division, with three levels of supervision and three levels of individual contributors. Typically graduate engineers/scientists with limited or no experience were brought in at Piedmont at the entry level—Professional Level I; engineers/scientists with master's degrees came in at PL II; and those with Ph.D.s without experience started at PL III. The salaries at each level were extremely attractive. The fringe benefits were excellent. The highly competent technical and professional people also advanced rapidly. They tended to reach the maximum salary of the top individual contributor position — PL III — in approximately seven to eight years. However, merit increases were then-limited to cost of living adjustments. Further promotion required acceptance of a managerial position in the Technical Division or another division of Piedmont. This is where the problems began for many of the technical and professional people at Piedmont.

The cases of Bob Crawford and Jim Baldwin are similar to many professionals who left the company during the past three years. After graduating from college with BAs in electrical engineering, Crawford and Baldwin were hired at the PL I level and had progressed rapidly and reached the top nonmanagerial level (PL III) in four years. Both had developed corporate-wide reputations in their area of expertise and had filed for numerous patents. In addition to this rapid promotion path for both of these people they had received 10-12 percent annual merit increases since joining the company six years ago. However, at the end of their sixth year they were told they had reached the maximum of their salary range and would be limited to the 3-5 percent annual cost-of-living increases received by all employees. During the following three years they watched inflation (which during one year was 10 percent) erode their purchasing power. To add insult to injury, the salaries of average journeyman professions (PL I) approached their own.

Their Section Chief attempted to justify merit increases beyond the maximum of the salary range based on their significant contributions, but company policy was very strict on maintaining salaries within range. The company felt it would create too many inequities in the salary structure if it did not maintain a strict policy. The Section Chief had even attempted to rewrite their job descriptions but was told that he was basing the revised descriptions on individual performance rather than a change in basic duties, another violation of company policy.

Exit Crawford   After 10 years with the company, Crawford, whose family was now grown, decided to look elsewhere for increased salary potential and job recognition. He was soon hired by a research firm in the same city at a modest increase in salary, but with the promise that he could look forward to generous salary increases if things worked out.

Exit Baldwin   Baldwin, on the other hand, decided to remain with Piedmont Company and pursue opportunities at the supervisory level as a Section Chief. Although he preferred to remain as an individual contributor and did not have supervisory aspirations, he knew the next step up would mean a significant increase in salary plus participation in the management incentive plan. Thus, when the next Section Chief opening came up in his area, he applied and got the job. The next two years were frustrating ones as Baldwin found much of his time devoted to training new engineers and general administrative duties. After 13 years of service, Baldwin left the company "with a yearning to return to the 'the Bench' " and joined the same firm that hired Crawford.

The Recommendations

As part of the study by the Organization Development Department, it was found that many large industrial firms like Piedmont were experiencing similar problems in retaining high caliber engineers and scientists. However, the small research and development organizations, often competitors, did not seem to have the same turnover and morale problems. The small companies appeared to have more levels of individual contributor positions in their salary structure which rewarded the outstanding professionals.

After three months of research, the Organization Development Department proposed to the Technical Director and his staff the establishment of two additional levels of professional (and nonmanagerial) positions which would be roughly equivalent to Section Chief and Section Head positions in base salary.

Although the Technical Director's initial reaction was highly favorable, his department heads, section chiefs, and section heads—all of whom had MBAs in addition to their undergraduate technical degrees—did not feel individual contributors should be rewarded at the same compensation level as section supervisors. In fact, several threatened to leave if these two additional levels of professional positions were added. Interestingly enough, these section supervisors denied the importance of the turnover and morale problems. Their prime concern appeared to be that most top scientists and engineers might prefer to remain individual contributors if they knew the compensation potential was as great as that of a management position. This, they argued, would deny the company a natural source of future supervisors and managers.

The Section Heads also questioned whether the company should really be competing with the smaller research and development firms which might place more of a premium on pure research.

Although Piedmont's primary emphasis was on applied research, the Technical Director still felt strongly that the company should encourage highly inventive people since the creation of new products and processes was critical to the company's maintaining a competitive edge in the industry. However, because of the strong objections of his key managers, he was reluctant to accept the recommendations of two additional levels.

Questions To what extent is this problem one of structure? Of external environment? Of organizational change? What would you recommend?

SOUTHLAND SAVINGS ASSOCIATION*

The Southland Savings Association is one of the oldest financial institutions in its region. It is located in a trade area of approximately 200,000 population and has total deposits approaching $50 million. The association's management has always attempted to develop and maintain a progressive institution.

An outstanding feature of the association is that it seldom loses an employee to another financial institution. Checks made periodically with other institutions always indicate that its salary scale is one of the highest in the area. The association also has what the management considers to be a good program of fringe benefits, including hospitalization and life insurance, a retirement plan, paid vacations, sick leave, and lunchroom concessions. The entire cost of these benefits is borne by the association.

The association runs its operations on a decentralized basis. The top management has always maintained that decentralization is the best method of developing qualified managers and, in view of the organization's rapid growth during the last few years, the best way of solving the important problems of executive development.

The bookkeeping function has likewise been decentralized; each branch keeps its own books, and the auditor of the association periodically inspects them.

One day the auditor and the controller of the association decided that the current bookkeeping system needed to be revised. They had been giving attention to this area because the examiners had had trouble finding records. It had been suggested that the method of bookkeeping between the home office and the four branches could be improved.

With the above facts in mind, the two men held a conference with the officers of the association in an attempt to point out to them the action that needed to be taken.

After hearing the arguments posed by the auditor and the controller, the officers still felt that action was unnecessary. They said that the project would be too time-consuming and costly.

Two weeks later, however, the executive vice president of the association talked to the controller and admitted to him that the idea of revising the system was sound and that he and the rest of the officers were authorizing him to take control and to initiate the project.

---

*"Southland Savings Association," reprinted with permission from E. G. Williams, ed., *People Problems* (Bloomington: Indiana University Graduate School of Business Bureau of Business Research, 1962). While this case first appeared in the late 1950s, and the specifics of the case are dated, it illustrates the same phenomena that exist any time a major change is introduced in an organization. Thus, it is as relevant for the 1990s as it was for the 1950s.

The controller started on the task of centralizing the bookkeeping operations. For the first week he didn't know where to begin. He discovered that operational controls had been allowed to run down so long that now his problem appeared to be almost insurmountable.

When the executive vice president asked the controller about his progress, he was given a negative answer. The vice president was disturbed with this reaction and was determined to settle the problem once and for all. He called an executive meeting that included the controller and the auditor. At the meeting, the possibility of centralizing some of the operations of the branches in order to afford better administrative control was discussed. Someone suggested the possibility of buying some National Cash Register posting machines to help solve some of the operating difficulties.

After a lengthy discussion it was decided that these machines were the key to the elimination of many of the association's reporting problems. The controller admitted that they would make it easier to control operations, and the assistant vice president felt that their acquisition would add greatly to the customer service capacities of the association.

Three new machines were installed the following month. After closing hours each teller was instructed in the proper techniques of operating them. The management felt that they had made a sound investment, and their only worry was over the ability of the tellers to learn how to operate the new equipment. Most of the tellers were older women and seemed to be slow and reticent to learn the new process.

One month after the practice machines had been placed in the association, these shortcomings became so acute that immediate action had to be taken. The management realized that the morale of the teller staff was depressed and that the smoothness of operations at the home office had been completely disrupted. The personnel manager suggested that some type of formal training program should be developed and that the management should explain to the members of the work force their personal roles in the anticipated progress of the association.

The personnel manager has not found a method of eliminating the discontent, nor has he been able to give an adequate reason for it to the rest of the officers. Finally one officer stated in a committee meeting that he felt the work force had been "over human-relationed." He suggested that in many instances negative leadership was far superior to positive leadership. He stated in forceful language that he would inform those tellers who were complaining and failing to learn the process either to learn it quickly or be fired. Another officer felt that since some of them were employees who had been with the association for many years and whose work had always been satisfactory, some alternative must be found.

Questions   Why did the introduction of the new machines create problems? How might this change have been better managed?

ROBOT REPERCUSSION*

Victor Principal, vice president of industrial relations for General Manufacturing, Inc., sat in his office reviewing the list of benefits the company expected to realize from increasing its use of industrial robots. In a few minutes, he would walk down to the labor-management conference room for a meeting with Ralph McIntosh, president of the labor union local representing most of the company's industrial employees. The purpose of this meeting would be to informally exchange views and positions preliminary to the opening of formal contract negotiations later in the month, which would focus on the use of computer-integrated robotic systems and the resulting impact on employment, workers, and jobs.

Both Principal and McIntosh had access to similar information flows relevant to industrial robots, including the following: unlike single-task machines, installed in earlier stages of automation, robots can be programmed to do one job and then reprogrammed to do another one. The pioneering generation of robots is mainly programmed to load machines, weld, forge, spray paint, handle materials, and inspect auto bodies. The latest generation of robots includes vision-controlled robots, which enable the machines to approximate the human ability to recognize and size up objects, using laser-beam patterns recorded by television cameras and transmitted to "smart" computers. The computer software interprets and manipulates the images relayed by the camera in a "smart" or artifically intelligent way.

Experts concluded that the impact of robot installation on employment would be profound, although the extent of the worker replacement was not clear. Sources at Carnegie-Mellon University concluded that today's robots could replace a million workers by 1990 in the automotive, electrical equipment, machinery, and fabricated metals industries. Another prediction indicates that about 440,000 workers will be displaced by robots by 1990; but only 22,000 will actually be dismissed because of robotic automation. The conclusion was inescapable that robot usage has the capacity to increase manufacturing performance and to decrease manufacturing employment.

Principal walked down to the conference room. Finding McIntosh already there, and after exchanging appropriate greetings, Principal stated the company's position regarding installation of industrial robots. "The company needs the cooperation of the union and our workers. We don't wish

---

*From J. M. Champion and J. H. James, eds., *Critical incidents in management,* 5th ed. (Homewood, Ill.: Richard D. Irwin, 1985).

to be perceived as callously exchanging human workers for robots." Principal then listed the major advantages associated with robots: (1) improved quality of product due to the accuracy of robots; (2) reduced operating costs, as robots cost about $6 an hour to operate, a fraction of the $18-$20 per hour cost of wages and benefits paid to an average employee; (3) reliability improvements, as robots work tirelessly and don't require behavioral support; (4) greater manufacturing flexibility, since robots are readily reprogrammable for different jobs. Principal concluded that these robot advantages would make the company more competitive, which would allow the company to grow and increase its work force.

McIntosh's response was direct and strong. "We aren't Luddites racing around running machines. We know it's necessary to increase productivity and that robotic technology is here. But we can't give the company a blank check. We need safeguards and protection." McIntosh continued, "We intend to bargain for the following contract provisions: (1) establishment of labor-management committees to negotiate in advance about the labor impact of robotic technology and, of equal importance, to have a voice in deciding how and whether it should be used; (2) rights to advanced notice about installation of new technology; (3) retraining rights for workers displaced, to include retraining for new positions in the plant, the community, or other company plants; (4) spread the work among workers by use of a four-day week or other acceptable plan as an alternative to reducing the work force." McIntosh's final sentence summed up the union's position. "We in the union believe that the company is giving our jobs to robots in order to reduce the labor force."

Their meeting ended amiably, but Principal and McIntosh each know that much hard bargaining lay ahead. As Principal returned to his office, the two opposing positions were obvious. On his yellow tablet, Principal listed the requirements as he saw them. (1) A clearly stated overall policy was needed to guide negotiation decisions and actions. (2) It was critical to decide on a company position regarding each of the union's announced demands and concerns. (3) An implementation plan must be developed.

As Principal considered these challenges, he idly contemplated a robot possessing artificial intelligence and vision capability that could help him in this work. Immediately a danger alarm sounded in his mind. A robot so constructed might be more than helpful and might take over this and other important aspects of his job. Slightly chagrined, Principal returned to his task, needing help—but not from any "smart" robot.

Questions What considerations should enter into formulation of a company policy about robotics? How should the process of formulating such a policy be designed?

Name Index

A

Abraham, L. M., 352
Abramson, I. Y., 382
Aburdene, P., 577
Adams, J., 285
Adams, J. S., 73–75, 362, 461
Adler, N., 223, 350
Adler, S., 185, 201
Ajzen, I., 117, 157, 159
Albanese, R., 477
Alderfer, C. P., 65, 69, 464
Allen, R., 533
Allport, F. H., 475
Allport, Gordon, 155, 195, 205, 206
Alsing, Carl, 486, 488, 489
Ancona, D. G., 456, 471, 489, 505
Anderson, C., 203
Anderson, D. C., 117
Andrews, F. M., 384
Angle, H., 533
Antonoff, M., 280
Aplin, J. C., 617
Argyris, C., 66, 68
Aristotle, 73
Aron, A., 455
Aron, E., 455
Aronson, E., 164, 462
Arvey, R. D., 327, 330, 333, 352

B

Ashforth, B. E., 528
Atchison, 286
Atkinson, J. W., 72, 193
Auletta, K., 495
Austin, W., 363

Back, K. W., 396
Baetz, M. L., 546, 559, 567, 572
Baker, D., 298
Bales, R. F., 470, 471, 498
Bamforth, K. W., 265
Bandura, Albert, 109, 110–12, 324, 329
Barnard, Chester, 239
Barnlund, D. C., 545
Baron, R. A., 543
Barry, B., 221
Baruch, R., 401
Bass, B. M., 217, 225, 227, 229, 239, 575
Bateman, T., 221, 231, 362, 633
Battalia, O. William, 147
Beach, D. S., 327
Becker, W. S., 76, 104
Beer, M., 635, 636, 642, 648
Behrman, D., 204

Belcher, 286
Bell, C., 643
Bell, N. E., 352
Bem, D. J., 119
Bennis, Warren, 529
Benson, Herbert, 396
Berkowitz, L., 155
Berlew, D., 405, 414
Berscheid, E., 73
Beyer, J. M., 330
Bigoness, W., 204
Blake, Robert, 549, 550
Blanchard, K. H., 41
Blau, P., 362, 461, 526
Boal, K., 121
Bogdonoff, M., 396
Bohnert, Bill, 148
Boje, D. M., 157
Bond, C., Jr., 476
Borgida, E., 230
Boss, R., 646
Bottger, P., 491
Bouchard, T. J., Jr., 186, 352
Bourgeois, L. J., 617
Bowers, D. G., 570
Boyce, J., 412
Branden, N., 115
Brass, D., 523
Braustein, D., 219

Subject Index